AF333949

JANE DICKSON

IN

TIMES SQUARE

First published in the United States of America in 2018 by Anthology Editions, LLC

87 Guernsey Street
Brooklyn, NY 11222

anthologyeditions.com

Edited by Mark Iosifescu & Johan Kugelberg

Creative Director: Johan Kugelberg
Design: Bryan Cipolla
Design Assistants: Nicholas Law & Alexandra Tults

Image retouching: Bryan Cipolla & Justin Lubliner
Negative scanning: Amy Buckley

Proofreader: Grace Srinivasiah

Photography and artwork courtesy of Jane Dickson

Additional images courtesy of: Peter Bellamy (p. 12), Andrea Callard (p. 216 bottom),
Nan Goldin (pp. 9, 195, 196), Thierry Gourjon (pp. 230–235) Wolfgang Staehle (p. 211)

Cover photograph by Nan Goldin
Cover quote by Nan Goldin courtesy of University Galleries of Illinois State University

First Edition
ARC 050
Printed in China

ISBN: 978-1-944860-14-1
Library of Congress Control Number: 2018935196

JANE DICKSON IN TIMES SQUARE

Anthology Editions

New York

To Charlie, Joe, and Eve
for living this crazy life with me

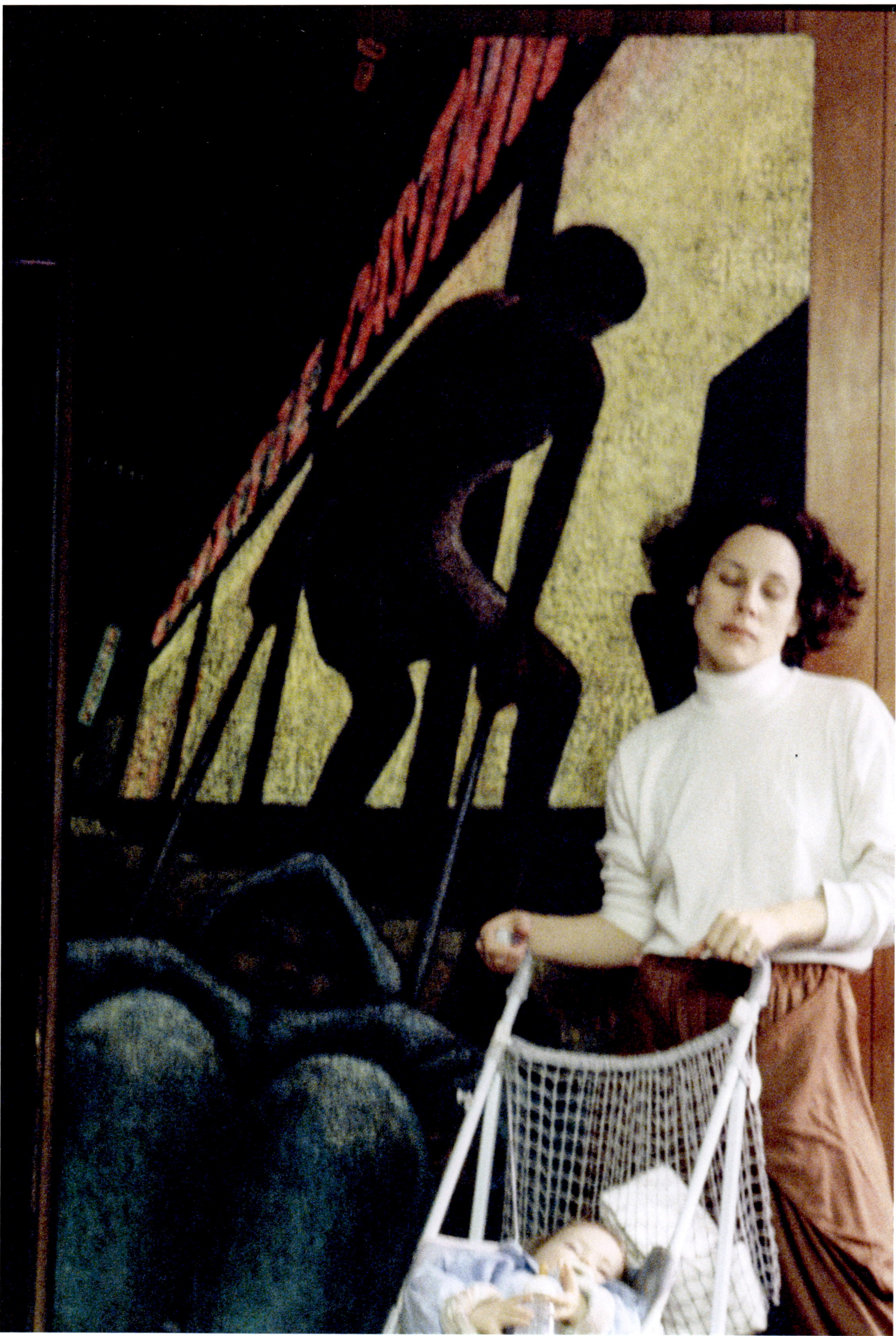

Chris Kraus

When I was younger, I was focused on individuals. The nuances of interpersonal drama were everything to me. As you get older, you realize there is a wider view. So I am thinking about things as part of a bigger pattern.

—Jane Dickson, interview with Jennifer Samet, 2013

In the photograph, Jane Dickson pushes a stroller as she walks past *Mother and Child* (1985), one of her mural-sized paintings. She's wearing a white turtleneck sweater and the same kind of loose pleated pants the women have on in a photo taken outside of Colab's famous Times Square Show. And the baby is small, so I'm guessing the photo was taken in the first half of the '80s. Or, wearing a long-sleeved gray T-shirt, Dickson looks out on a gray Times Square day through a large window of her loft. Then again, she's at home on the couch and the place is a mess. Or she's alert, in the street, her face bathed in red light, with heart-shaped clips on her ears.

This is the first time Dickson has placed her personal and research photographs alongside her finished work, and the effect is powerful. Unfiltered by personal memory, the images in *Jane Dickson in Times Square* show the texture of life within New York's geographically close but existentially loose artistic community at the end of the 20th century. The images show the extent to which Dickson and her husband, Charlie Ahearn, served as ambassadors from lower Manhattan to the South Bronx: not just posing for pictures at parties, but forging real friendships and doing more than symbolic collaborative work with artists like Joe Lewis and Fred Brathwaite (aka Fab 5 Freddy). The photographs also show just how *literally* Dickson transposed the colors, buildings, confrontations, exhaustions, and shapes of Times Square into her paintings; or, maybe more accurately, how she imagined the life around her as an ongoing series of painterly frames. In one photograph, three lemony lines of horizontal light—cornices of an old apartment building—seem to support a stocky white figure, leaning onto a pillow placed in the windowsill of her S.R.O. at the Times Square Motor Hotel. This already highly distilled photographic image will become the urtext for Dickson's chilling 1991 "Witness" series of paintings, in which she observes a world of voyeurs: neighborhood residents lounging in a thin slice of fresh air, or looking out of their windows at the streets below. In all of these street scenes, painted over the course of a decade, the police are never far off.

An early member of the artist group Colab, Dickson imported the group's sociographic ethos into a controlled and highly intentional formal realm. Over the years, Dickson has continued to paint strip malls, freeways, carnivals, demolition derbies, and slumbering suburbs, but as in the Times Square work, these investigations are marked by a fascination with how human beings navigate the soft coercion of highly constructed environments.

Jane Dickson famously arrived in Times Square in 1978, when she took a job programming the first Spectacolor billboard. She was two years out of college, and trying to figure out how she would paint. The billboard was a black sign with colored lights, and as she explained, "I would come home and want to paint my surfaces black with glowing lights emerging." Two years later, she and Ahearn moved into their loft overlooking Times Square, where she observed the neighborhood's 24/7 display of liquid neon and electric signage whenever she looked out the window or walked out the door. The compositional similarities between her photos and painting are also astonishing. The foregrounded car in an untitled photograph (p. 21) would appear in her 1981–83 paintings *El Dorado* and *Terminal Bar*. Featuring solitary, ambient figures against a deep and complexly lit urban backdrop, both the photograph and paintings evoke speed, chaos, and loneliness. Similarly, Dickson's "Witness" series was imagined first through her camera's lens. The forgotten world of Times Square lives on in these photos and paintings: the Times Square Hotel, the Hi-Hat Lounge, Show World Center, XXXtasy, and next door to Peepland, the same Tad's Steaks where 23-year-old Kathy Acker wrote in her notebooks between Fun City sex shows. The colors and grit of this world have been captured well in period films and David Simon's TV show *The Deuce*, but

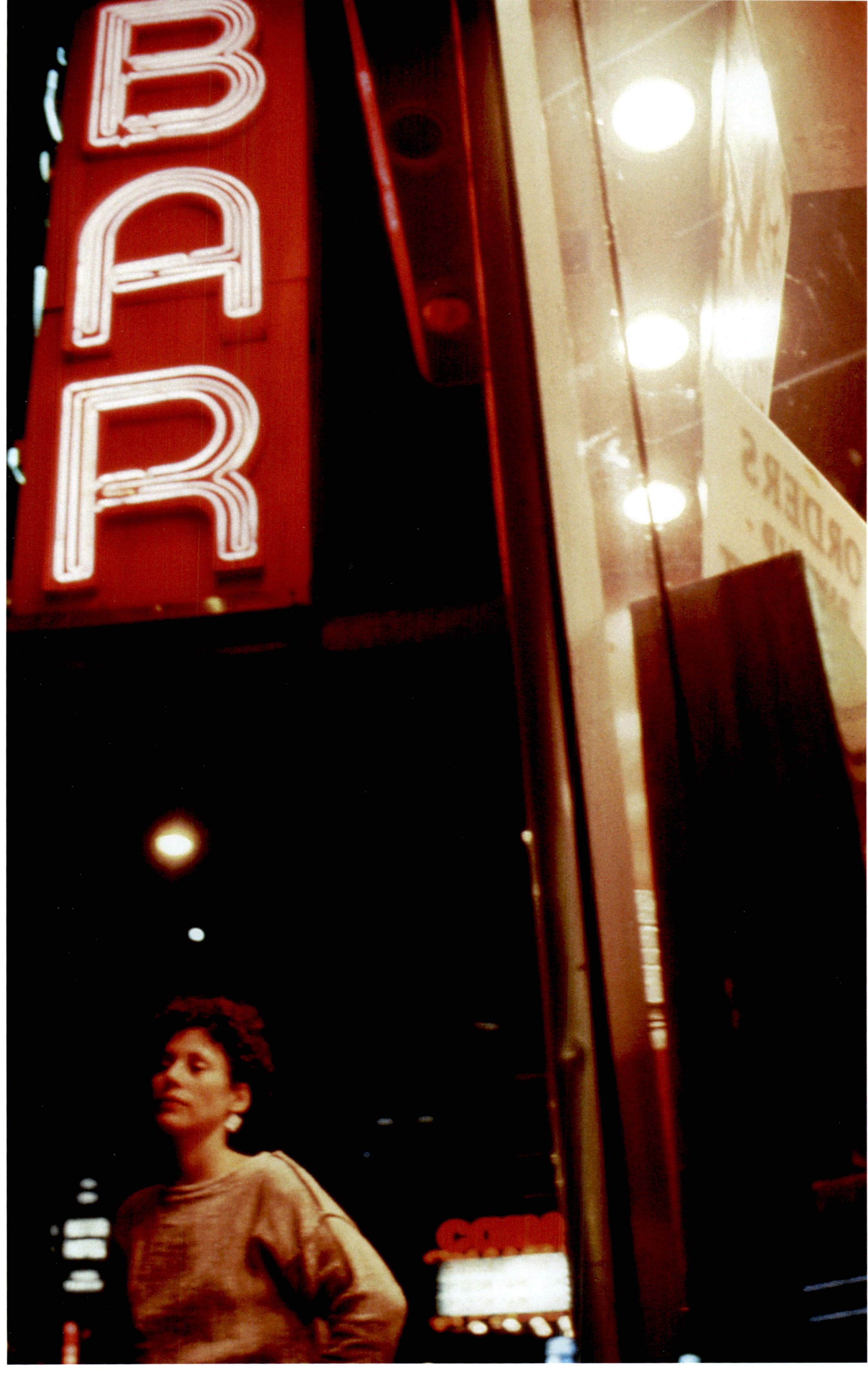

BAR

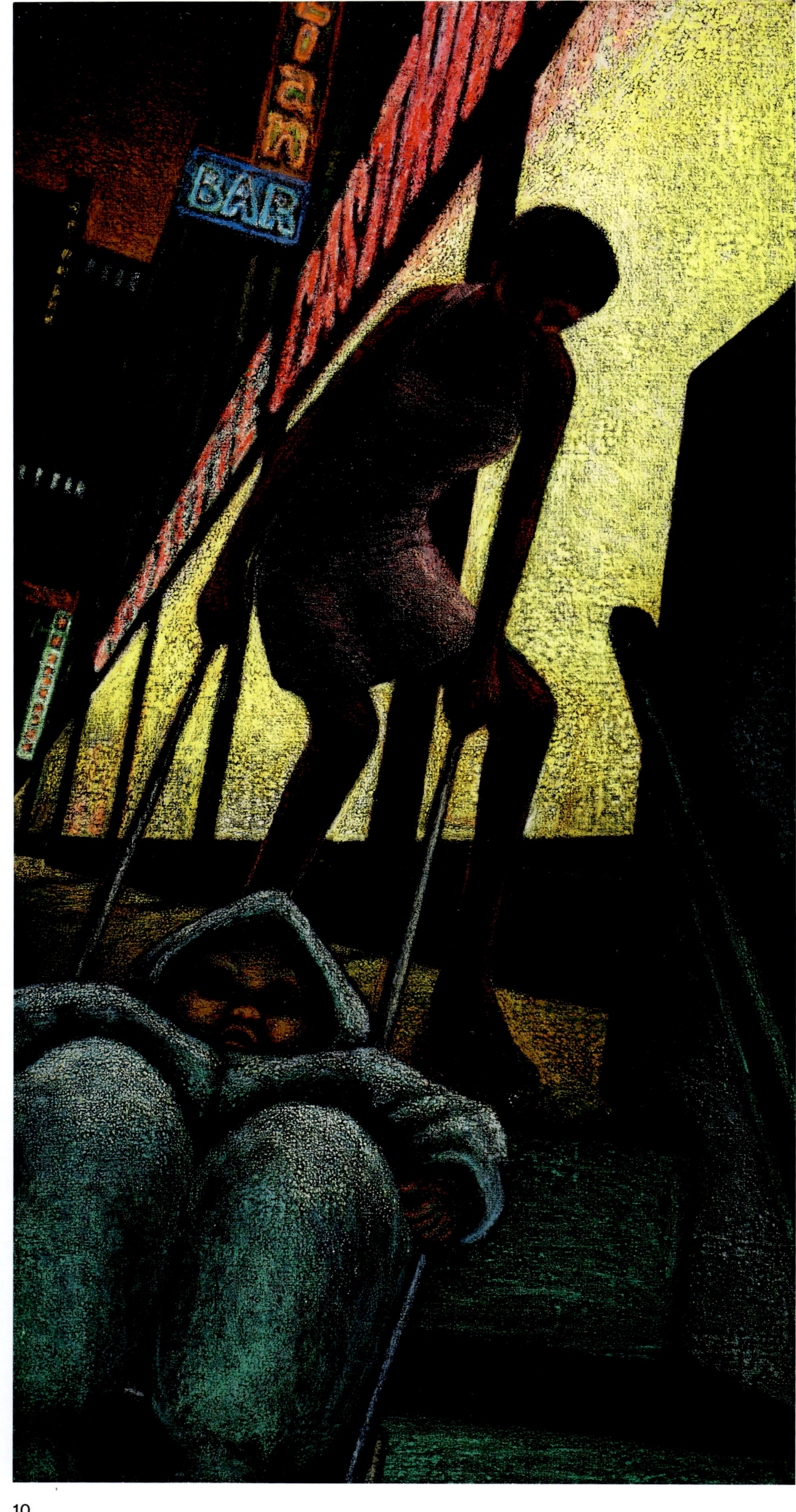

BAR

these iconic depictions don't come close to the muzzy realism of Dickson's "Peep" paintings. Featuring naked dancers kneeling on makeshift stages and grasping poles, the series also captures the gaseous rotation of boredom and mild danger that permeated that world.

In 2006, Dickson returned to Times Square with the triumphant series of mosaic murals "The Revelers," permanently installed in the tunnel that connects the Lexington and Broadway lines. By now, the "carny world" of 20th century Times Square is long gone, but Dickson examines the faces and drift of the visiting New Year's Eve crowd with beauty and real fascination. The old Times Square denizens have been replaced by reveling crowds, couples, children, and families: it's one of the few remaining public events that attracts visitors from, as they say, all walks of life.

This book represents the first site-specific grouping of images from Dickson's astonishingly rich body of work. Hopefully, there will be future books that curate her paintings of American suburbs, or freeways, or Las Vegas casinos. But Times Square is a good place to start.

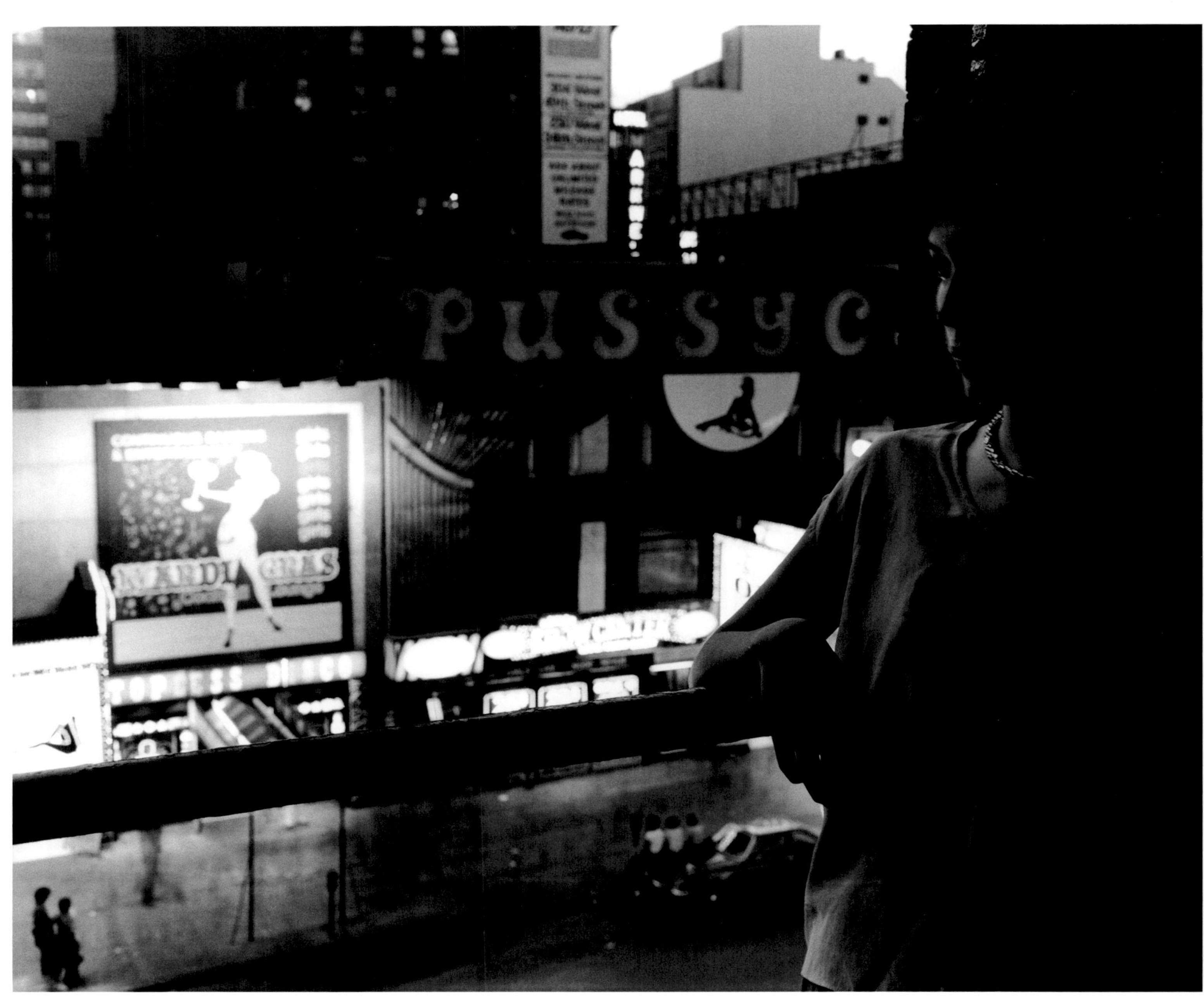

PUSSYC
MARDI GRAS
TOPLESS DISCO

I WAS INTERESTED IN FLEETING VIEWS OR DANGEROUS SITUATIONS THAT I COULDN'T REALLY STOP AND SKETCH, SO I BOUGHT A LITTLE HIGH-END CAMERA AND TOOK IT EVERYWHERE WITH ME. I WAS A FLÂNEUR, DOCUMENTING THIS CRAZY SCENE: A PAINTER, USING THE CAMERA TO TAKE NOTES, TRYING TO GET SOME GRIP ON WHAT THE HELL WAS GOING ON.

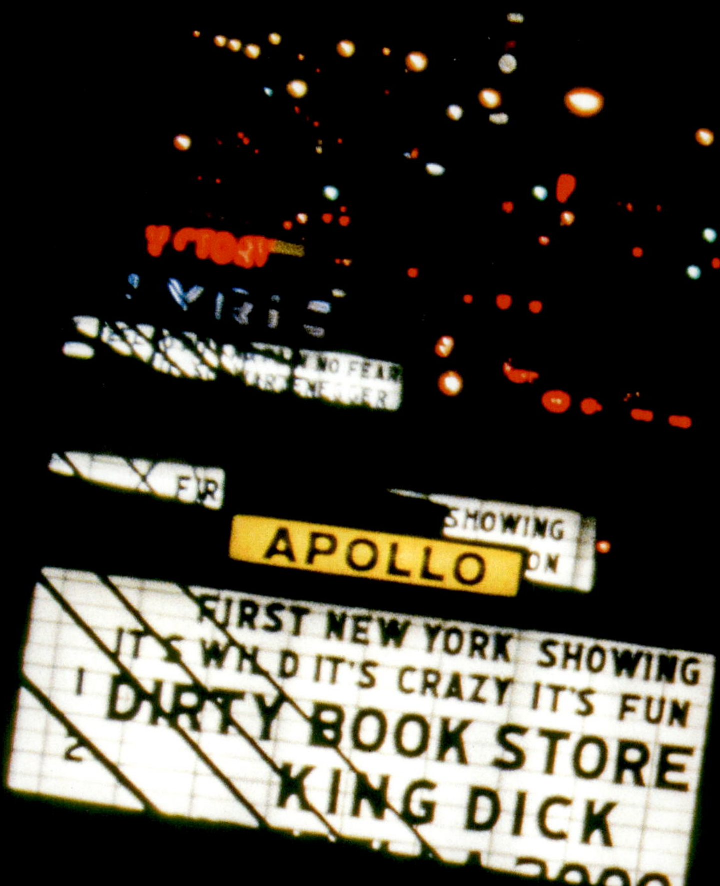

APOLLO
SHOWING
FIRST NEW YORK SHOWING
IT'S WILD IT'S CRAZY IT'S FUN
DIRTY BOOK STORE
KING DICK

TERROR IN THE AISLES
GRACE JONES WILT CHAMBERLAIN
CONAN THE DESTROYER

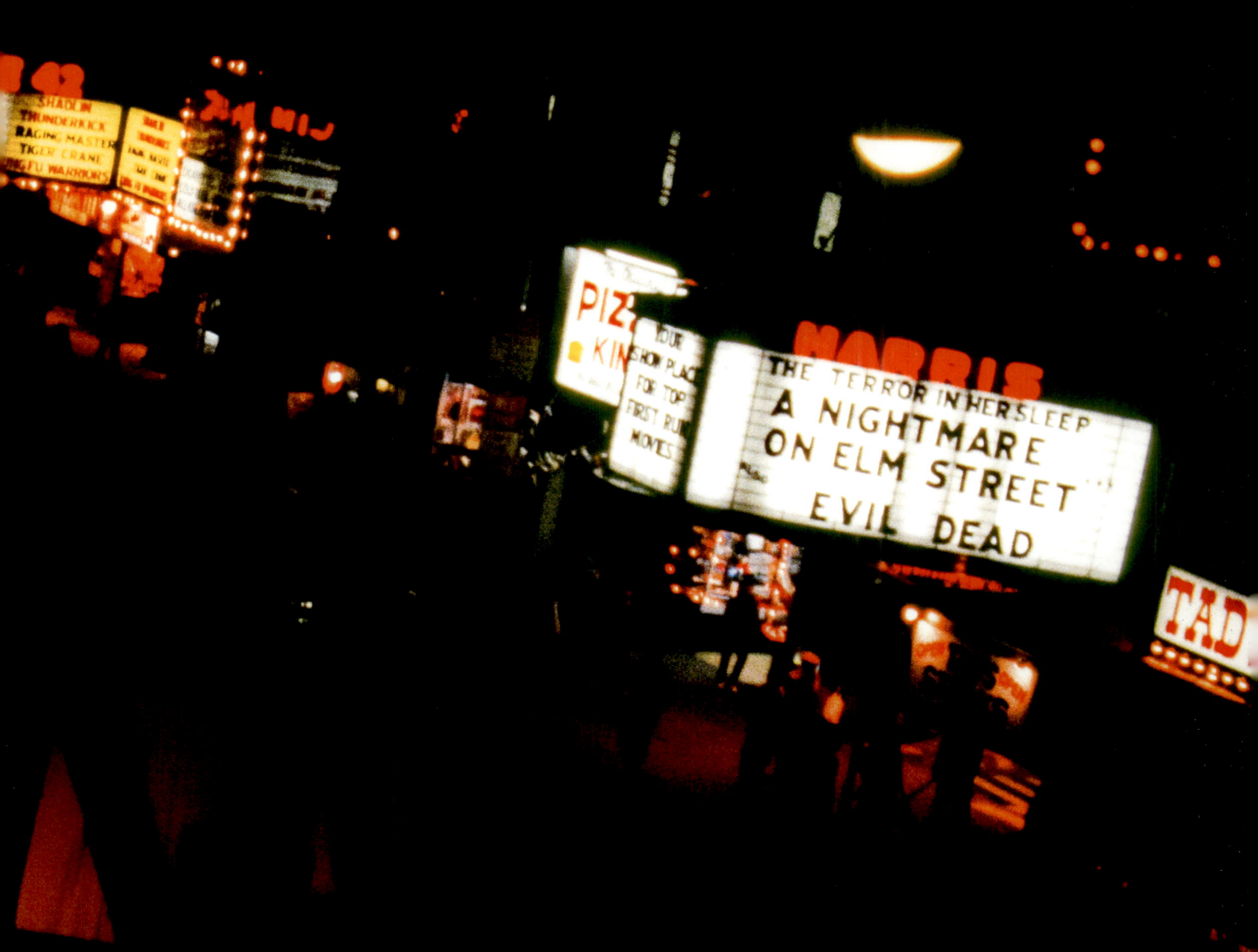

SHAOLIN
THUNDERKICK
RAGING MASTER
TIGER CRANE
KUNG FU WARRIORS
PIZ
KIN
YOUR
SHOW PLACE
FOR TOP
FIRST RUN
MOVIES
HARRIS
THE TERROR IN HER SLEEP
A NIGHTMARE
ON ELM STREET
EVIL DEAD
TAD

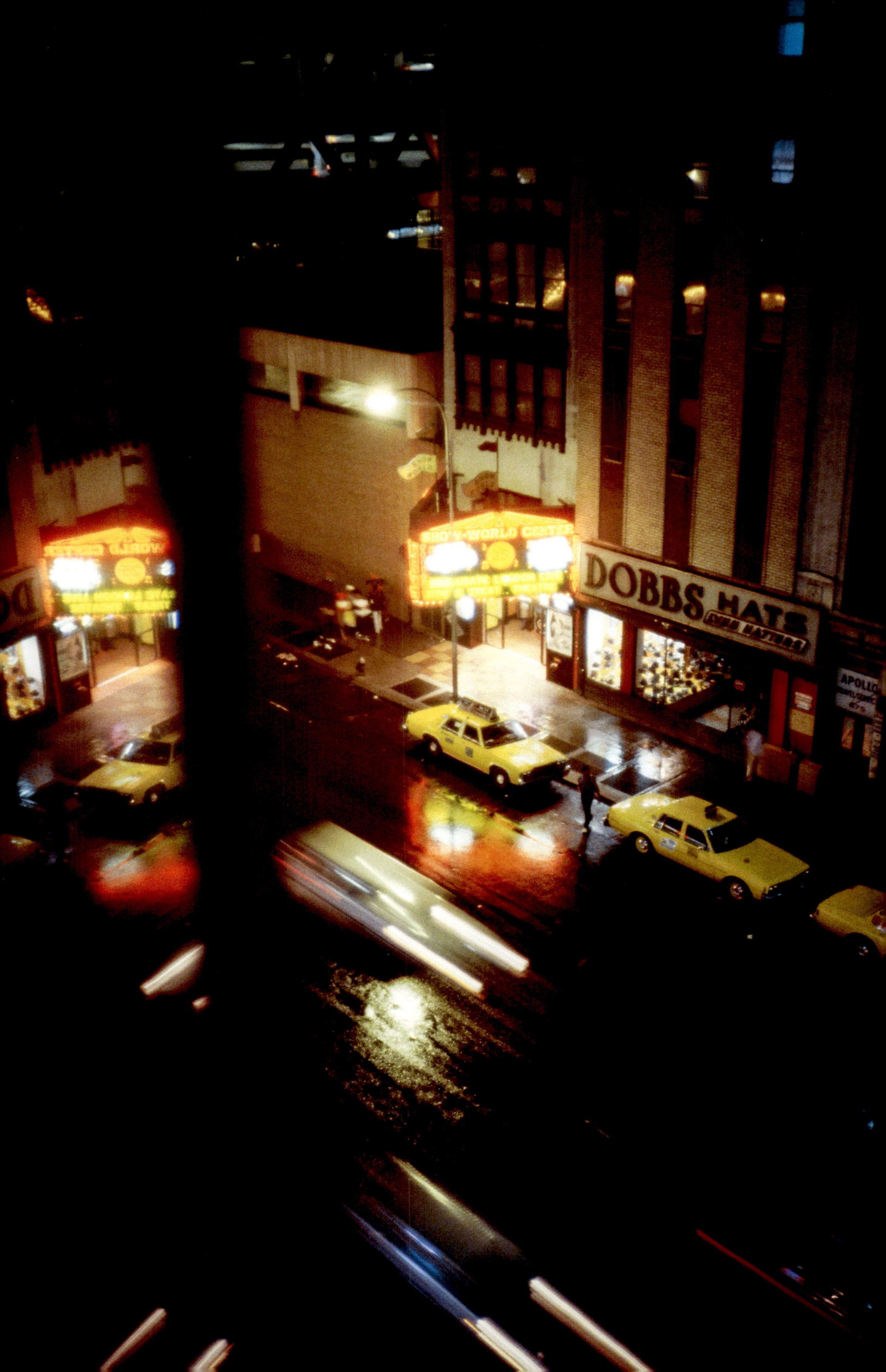

SHOW-WORLD CENTER
DOBBS HATS
APOLLO

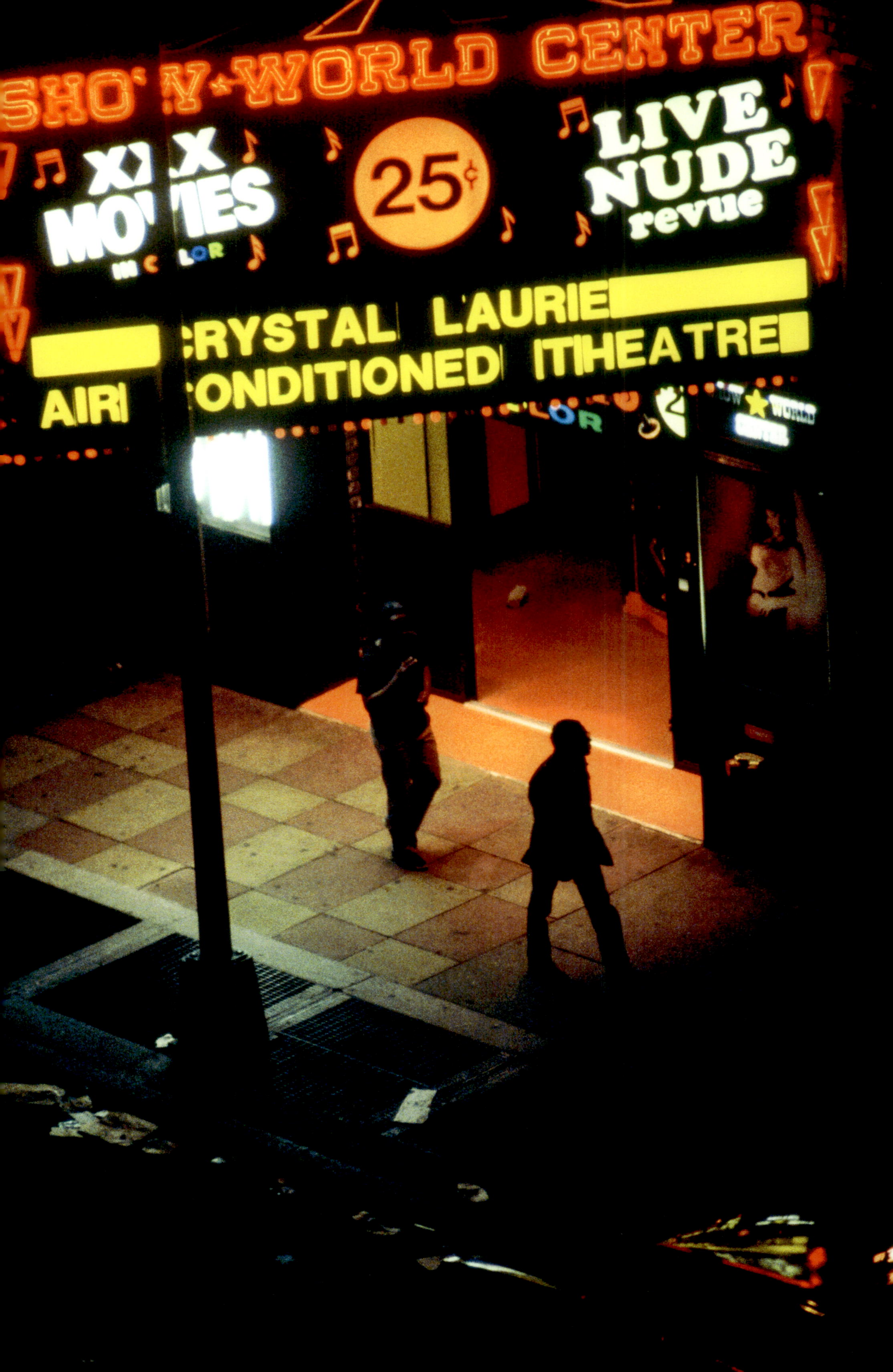

SHOW WORLD CENTER
XXX MOVIES
IN COLOR
25¢
LIVE NUDE revue
CRYSTAL L'AURIE
AIR CONDITIONED THEATRE

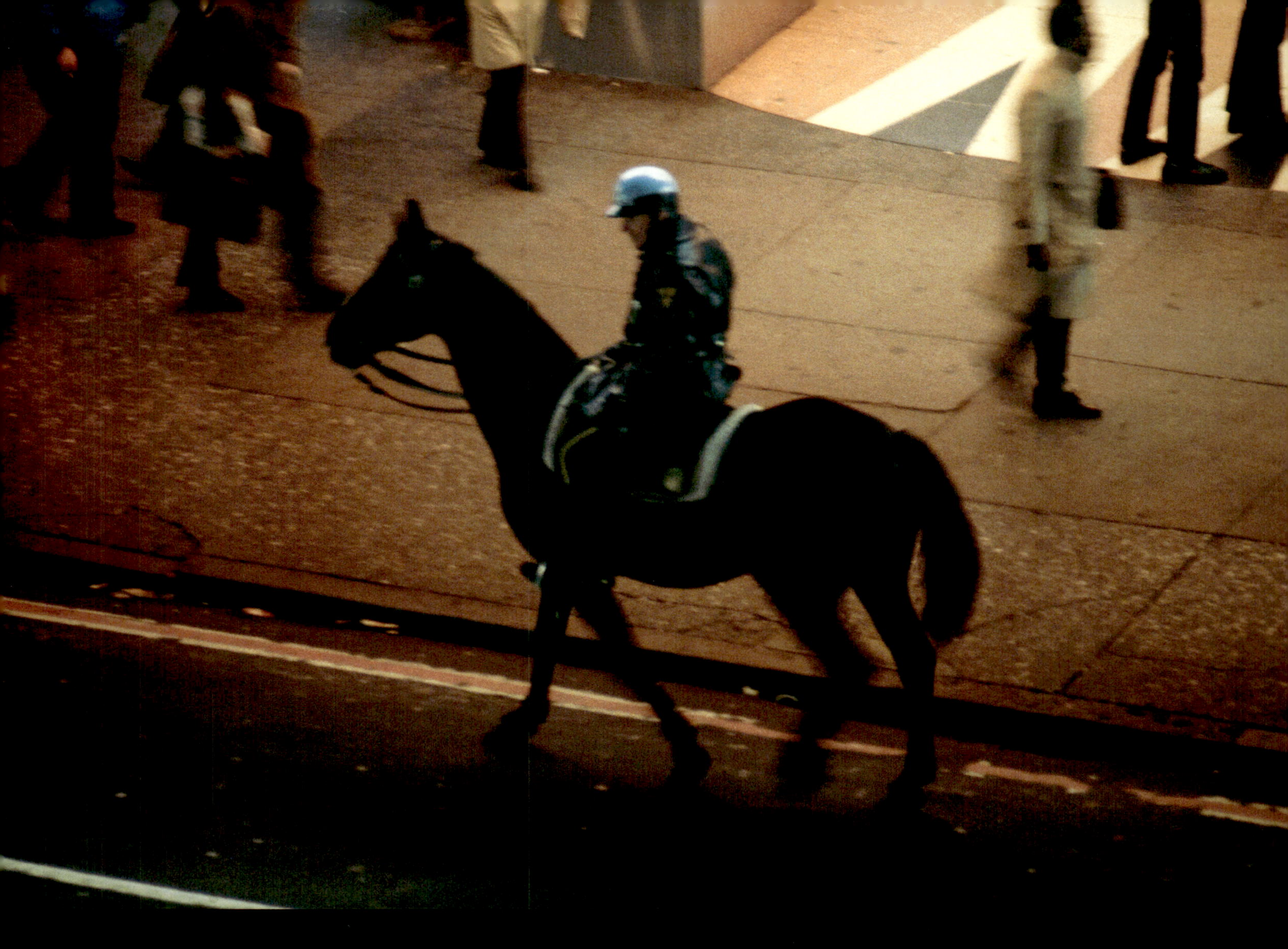

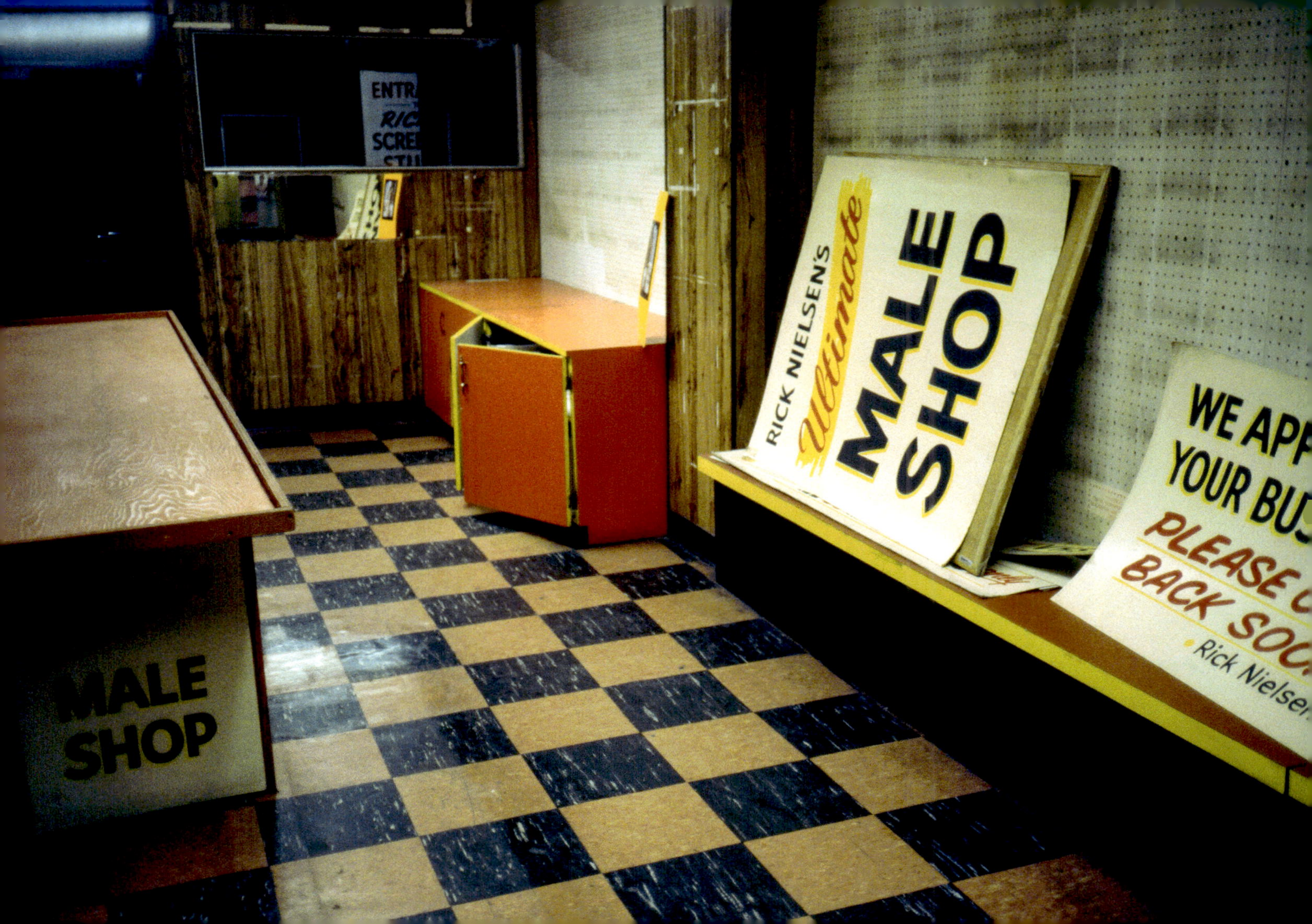
ENTRA
RIC
SCRE
STU
RICK NIELSEN'S Ultimate MALE SHOP
WE APP
YOUR BUS
PLEASE
BACK SO
Rick Nielsen
MALE SHOP

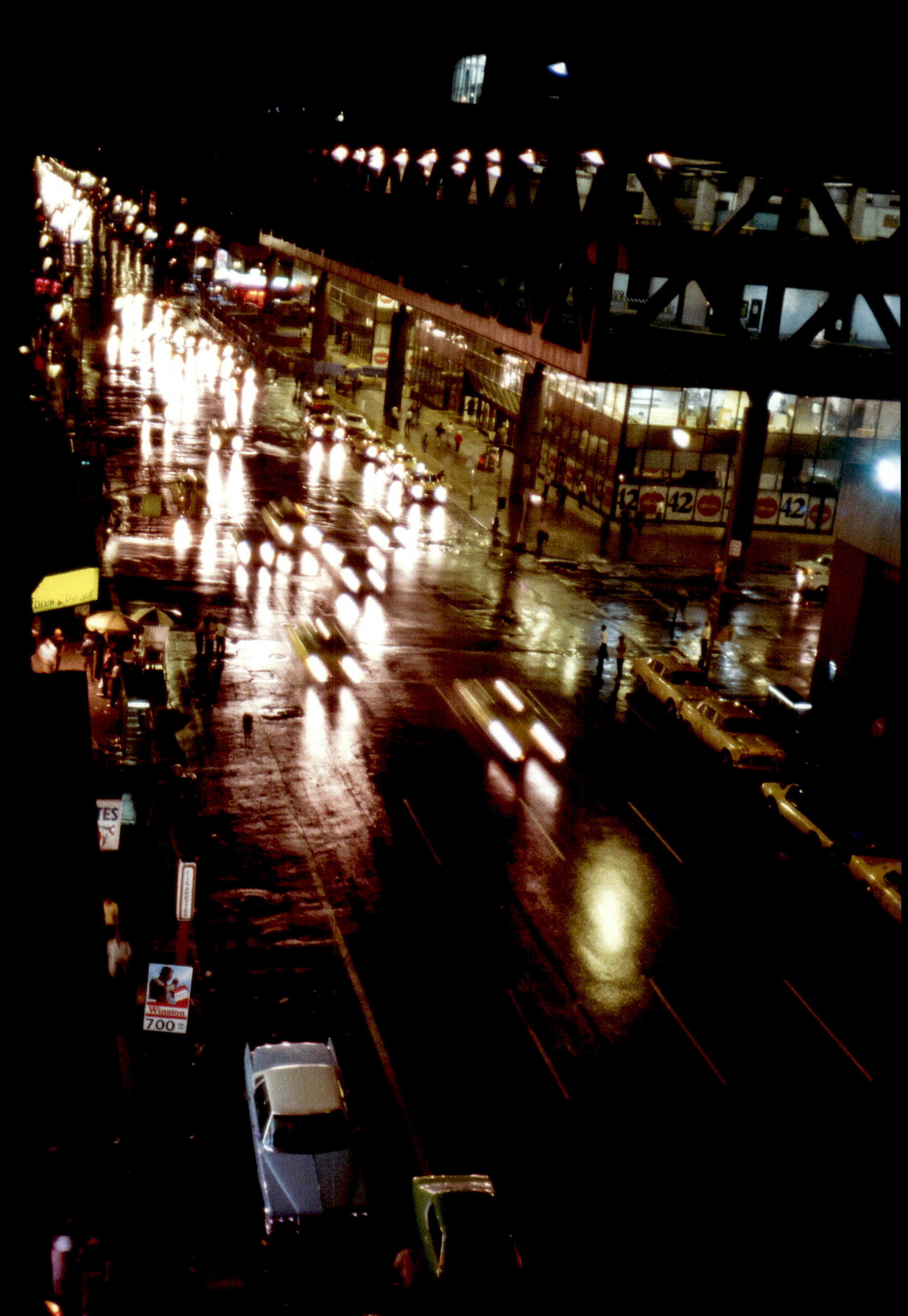

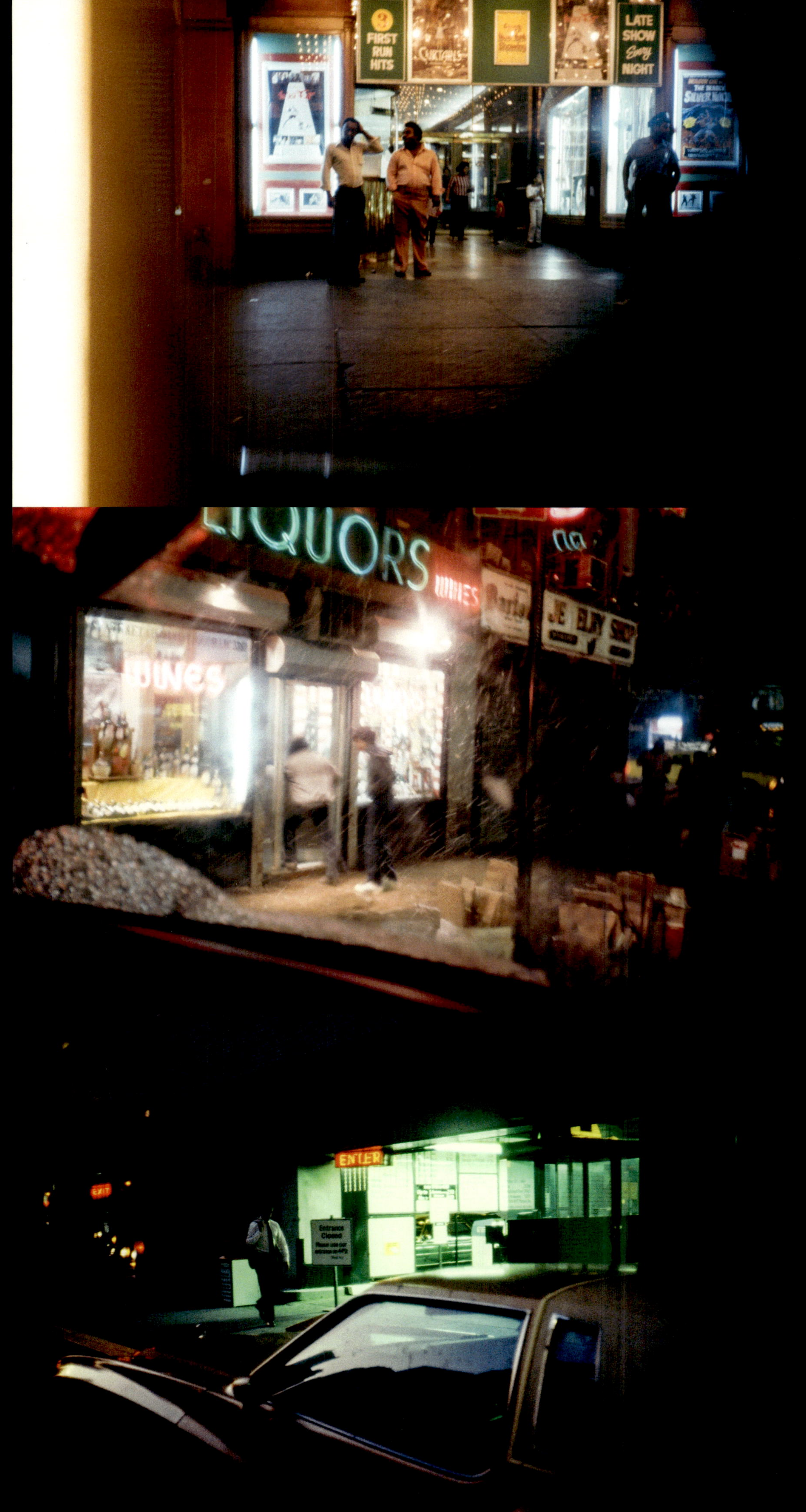
FIRST
RUN
HITS
LATE
SHOW
Every
NIGHT
LIQUORS
JEWELRY
ENTER
EXIT
Entrance
Closed

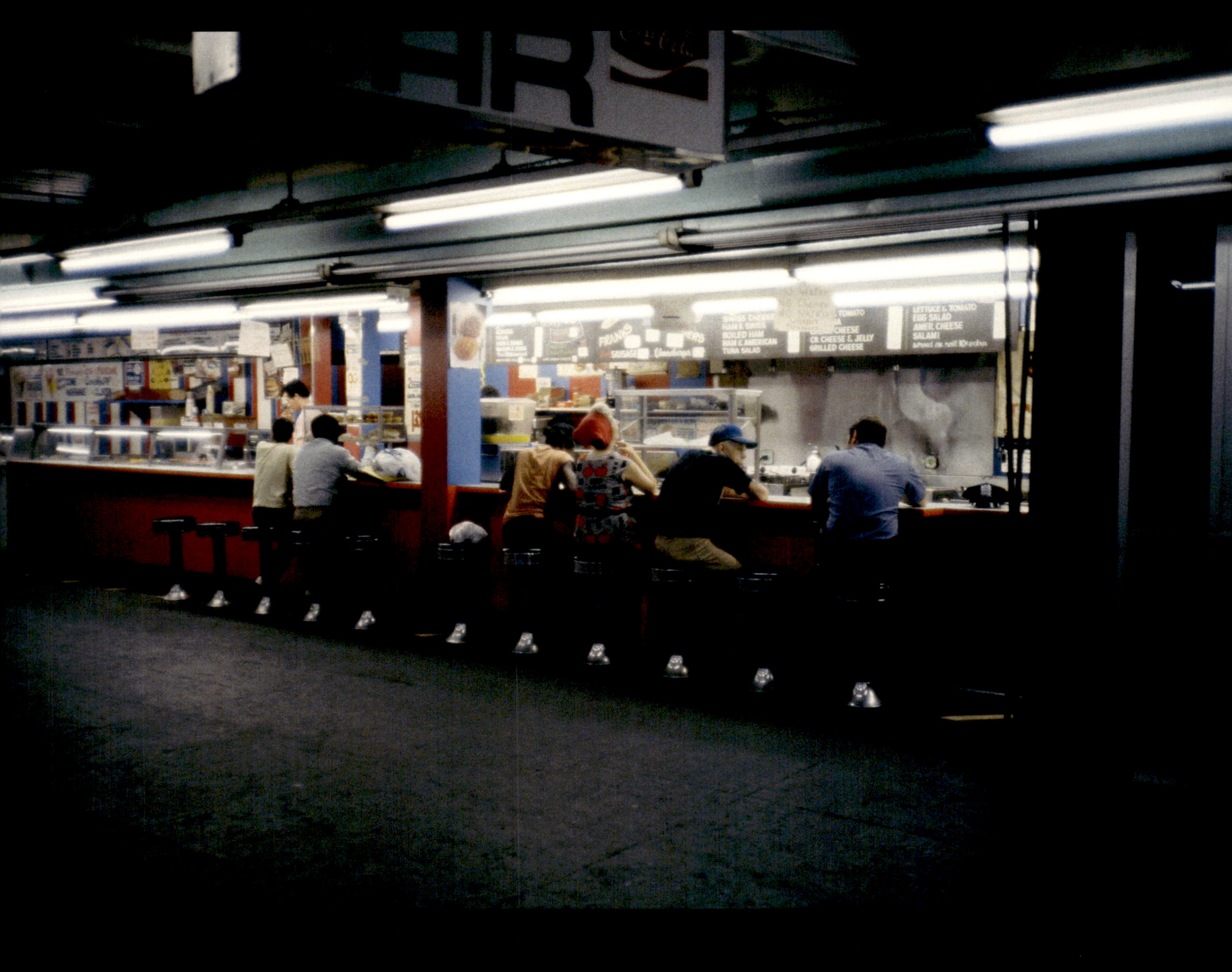

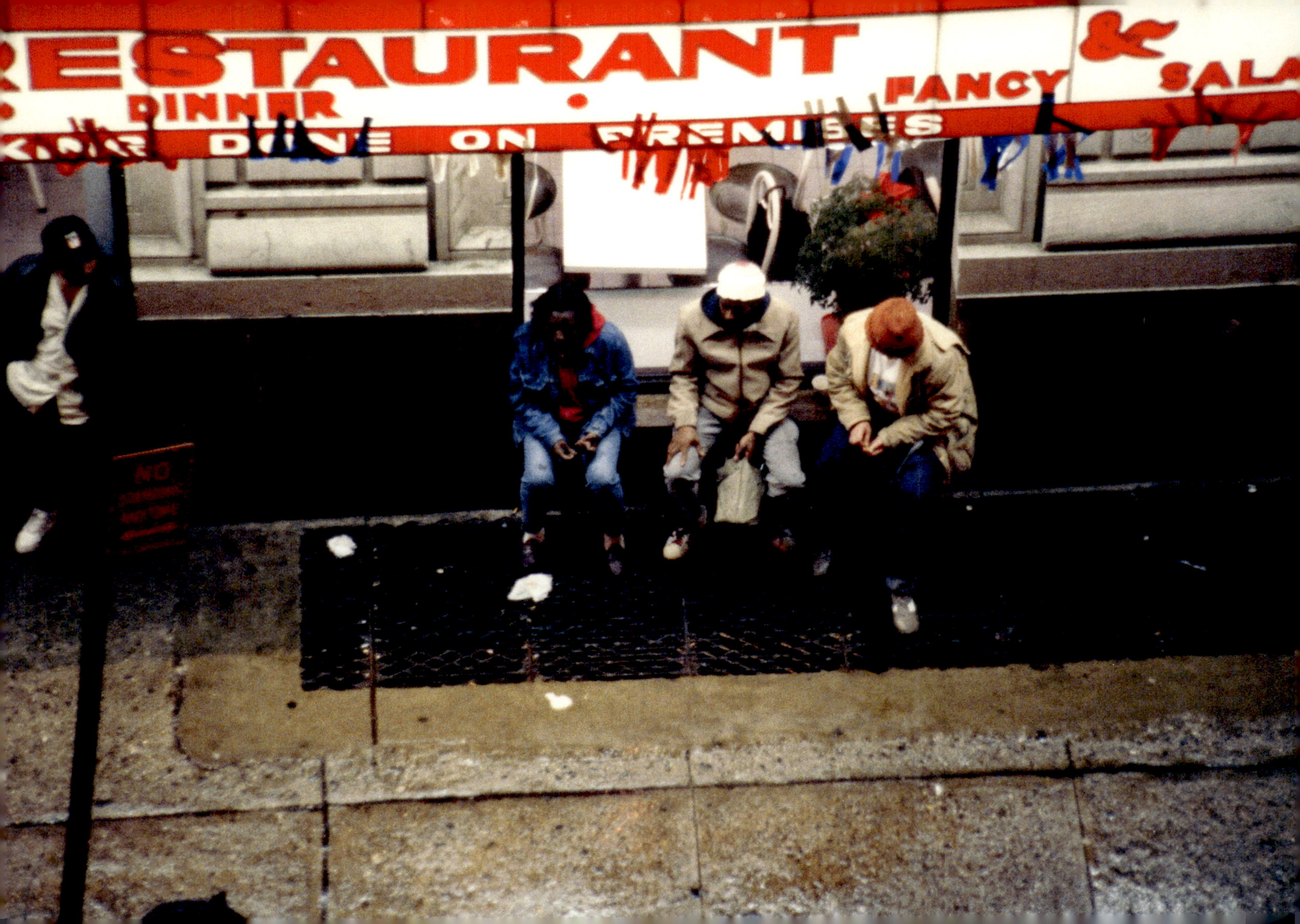

RESTAURANT
DINNER
FANCY
SALA
DINE ON PREMISES
NO

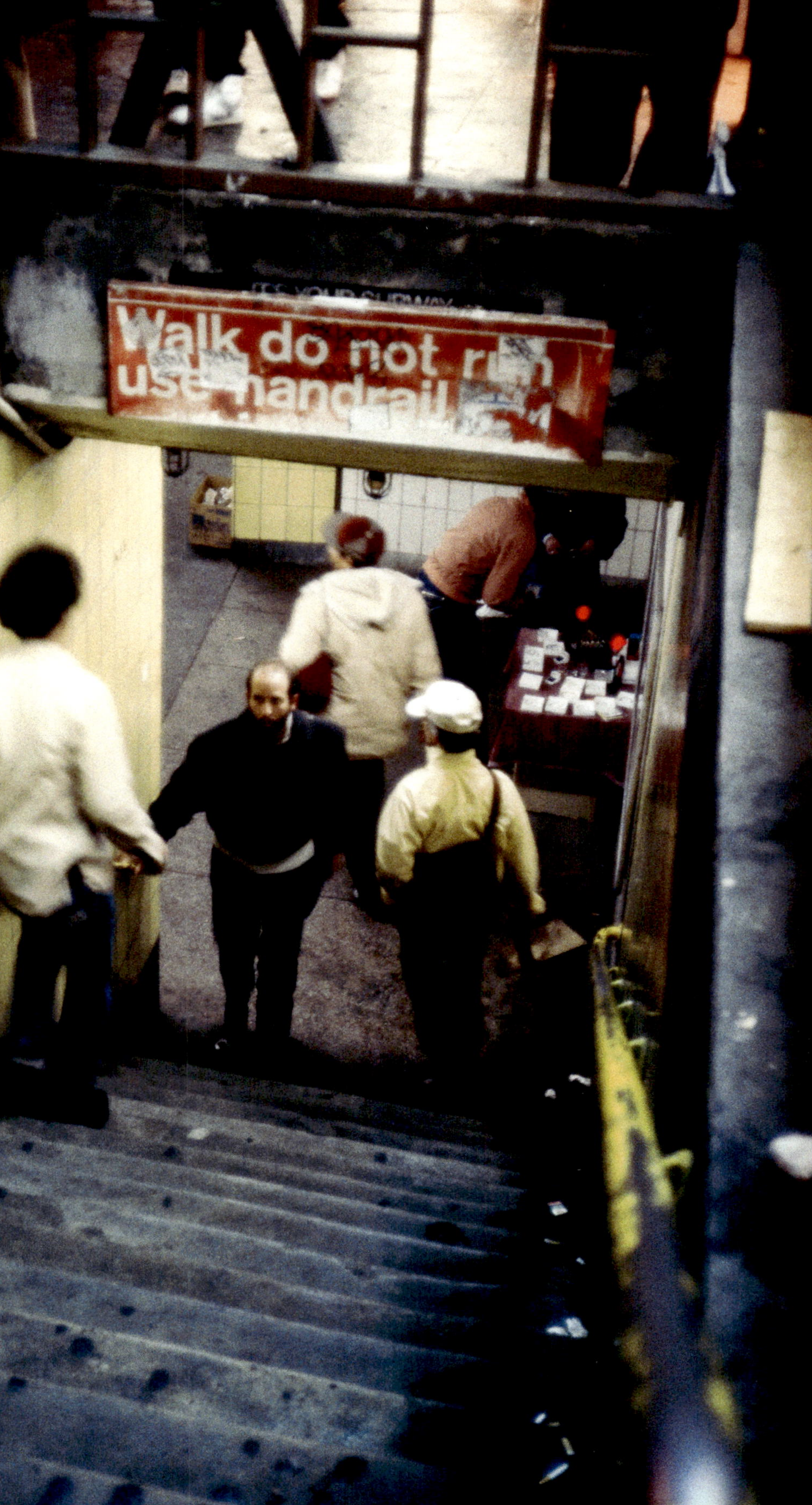
N Y C TRANSIT SYSTEM
SUBWAY BMT
BRONX · BROOKLYN · QUEENS
IT'S YOUR SUBWAY
Walk do not run
use handrail

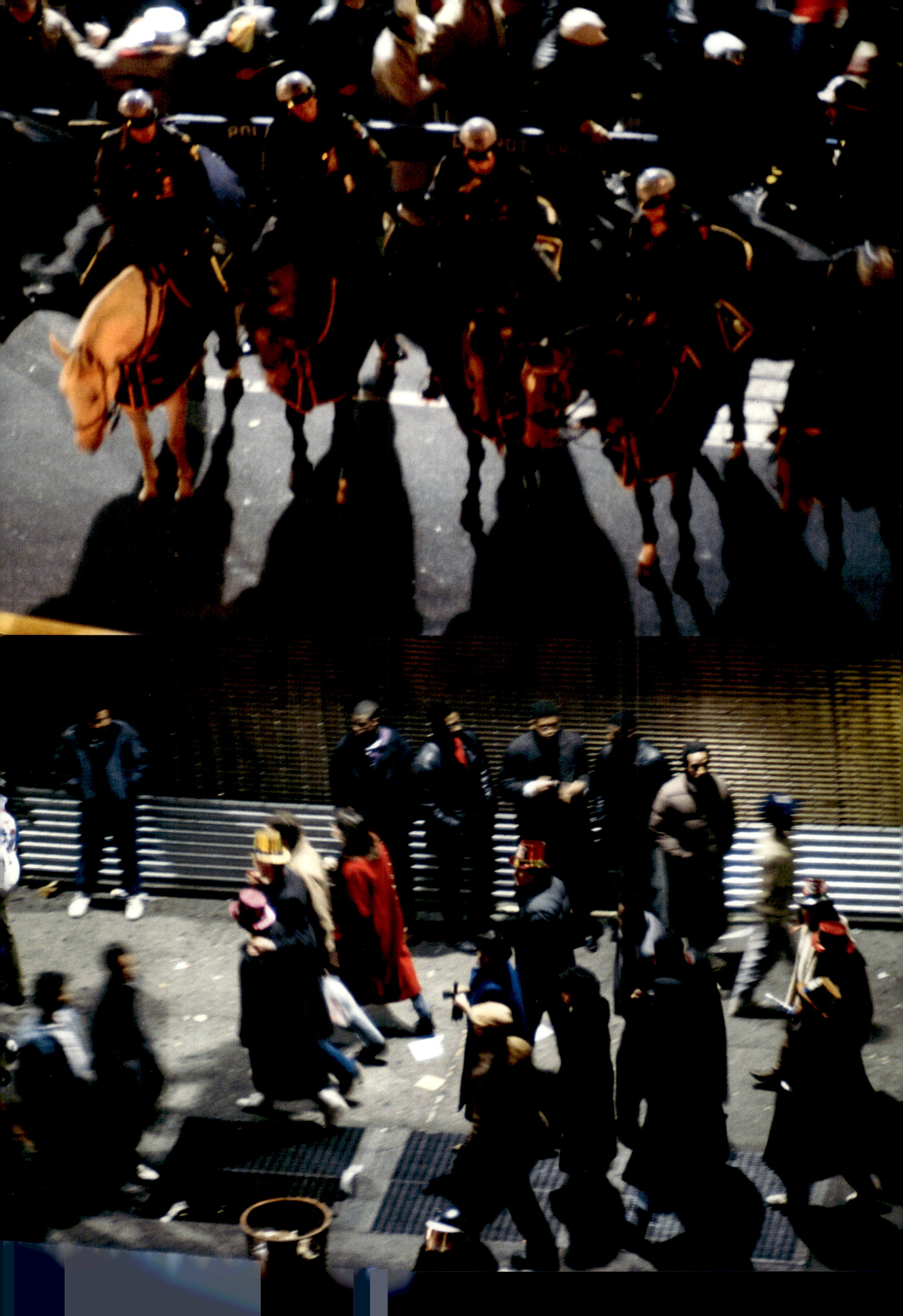

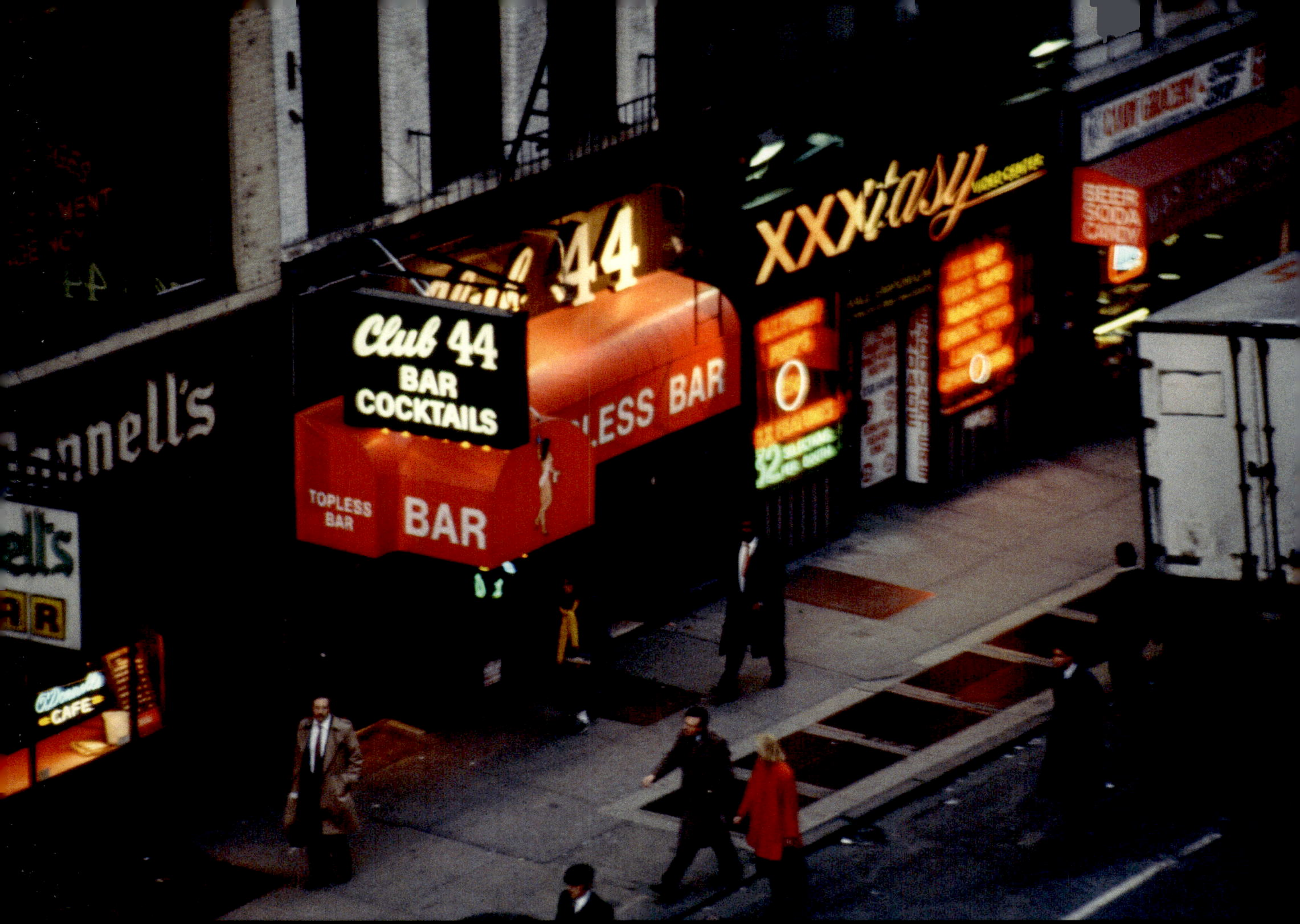

nnell's
CAFE
Club 44
BAR
COCKTAILS
TOPLESS
BAR
BAR
PLESS BAR
XXXtasy
BEER
SODA
CANDY
$2

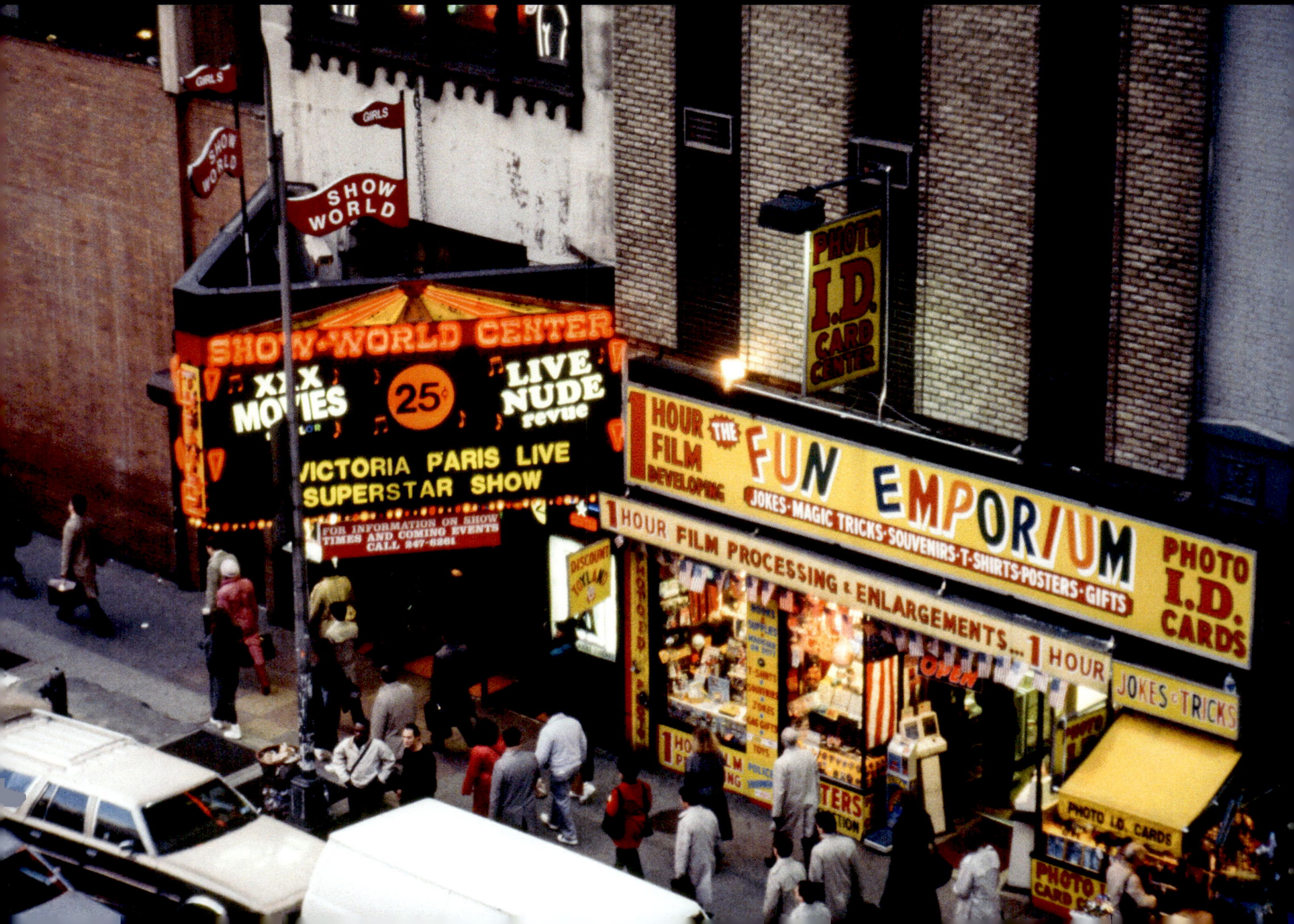

GIRLS
GIRLS
SHOW WORLD
SHOW WORLD
SHOW WORLD CENTER
XXX MOVIES
25¢
LIVE NUDE revue
VICTORIA PARIS LIVE SUPERSTAR SHOW
FOR INFORMATION ON SHOW TIMES AND COMING EVENTS CALL 247-6201
PHOTO I.D. CARD CENTER
1 HOUR FILM DEVELOPING
THE FUN EMPORIUM
JOKES · MAGIC TRICKS · SOUVENIRS · T-SHIRTS · POSTERS · GIFTS
1 HOUR FILM PROCESSING & ENLARGEMENTS ... 1 HOUR
PHOTO I.D. CARDS
JOKES · TRICKS
PHOTO I.D. CARDS

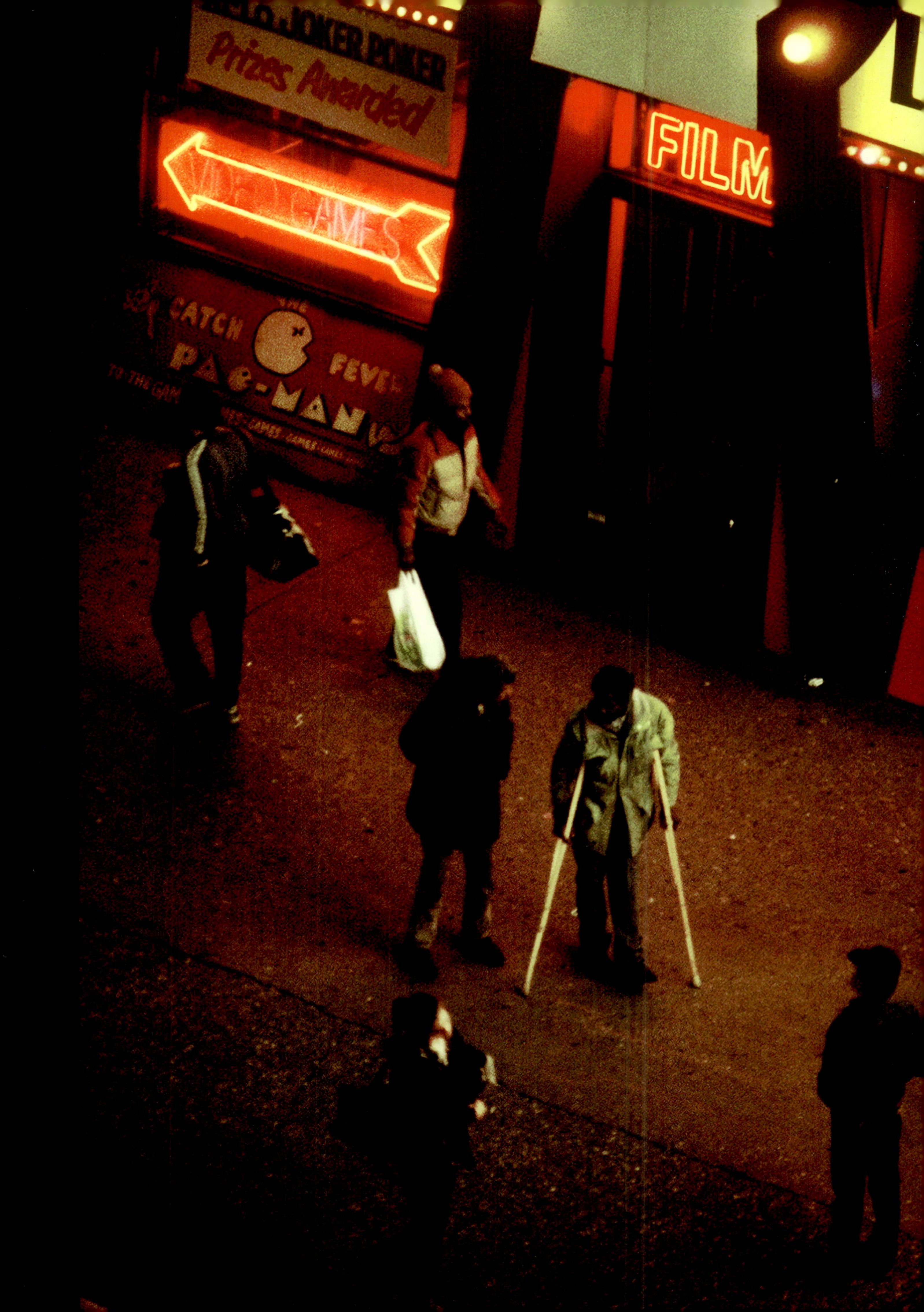
JOKER POKER
Prizes Awarded
VIDEO GAMES
CATCH THE FEVER
PAC-MAN
FILM

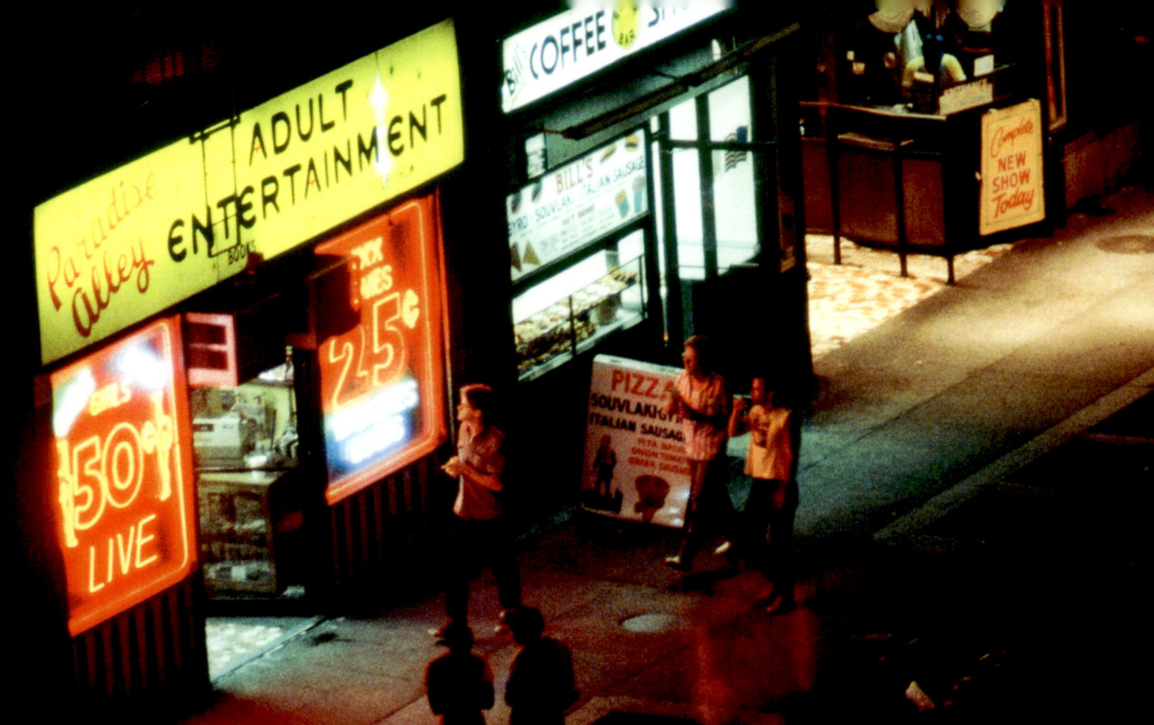

Paradise Alley
ADULT ENTERTAINMENT
BOOKS
50¢ LIVE
25¢
COFFEE SHOP
BILL'S
PIZZA
SOUVLAKI
ITALIAN SAUSAGE
Complete NEW SHOW Today

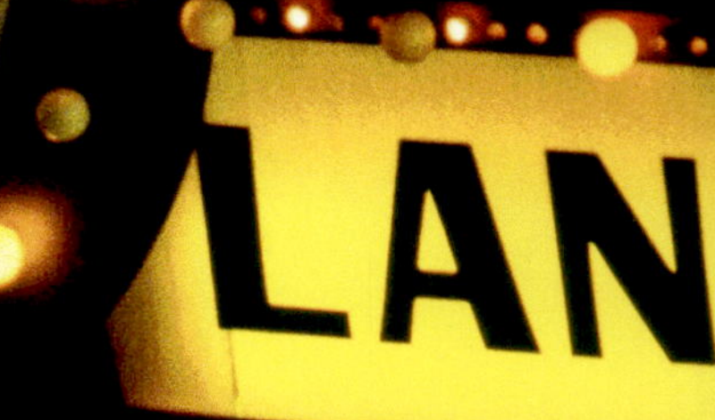

PEEP
GAME ROOM
LAN
FILM
25¢

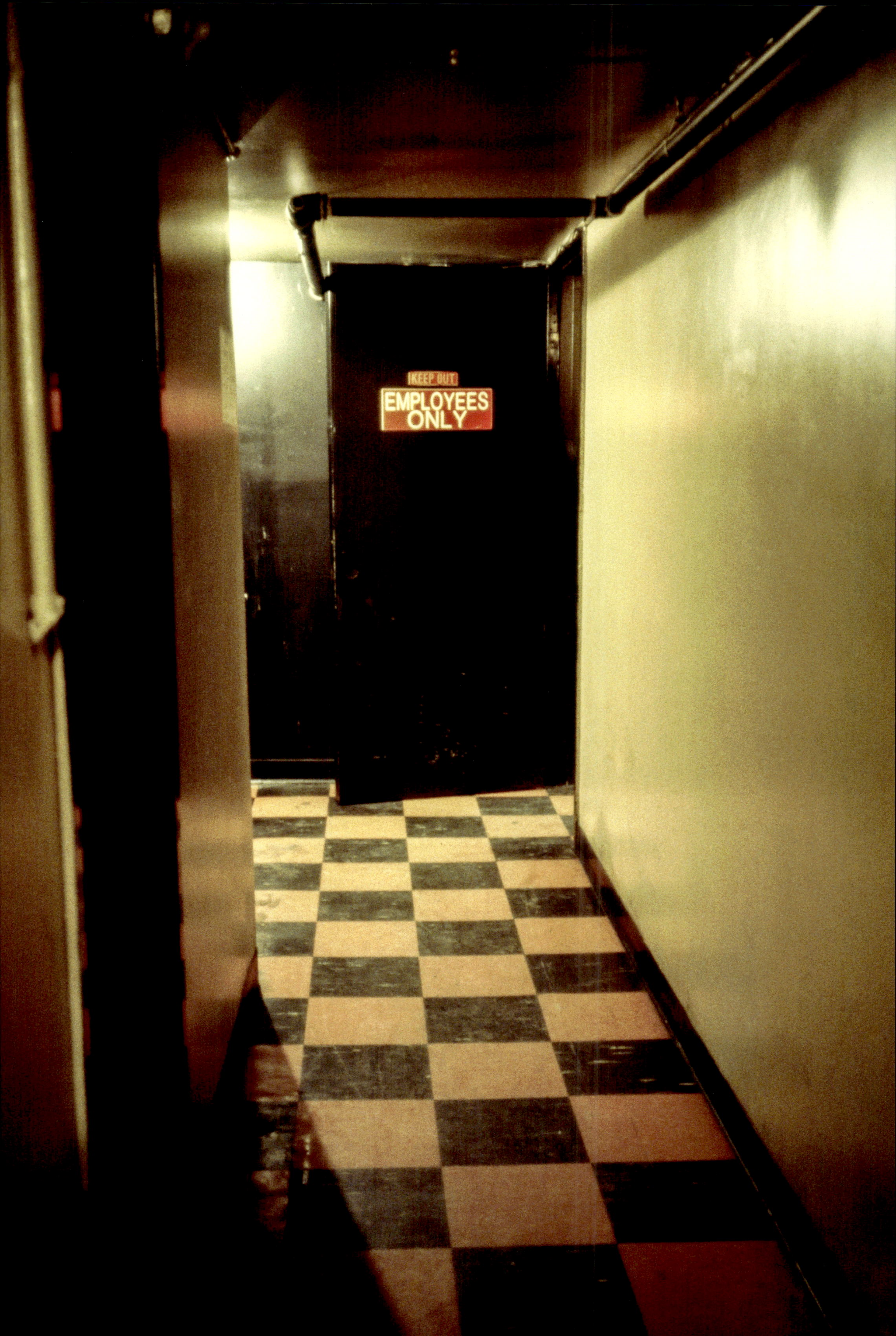
KEEP OUT
EMPLOYEES
ONLY

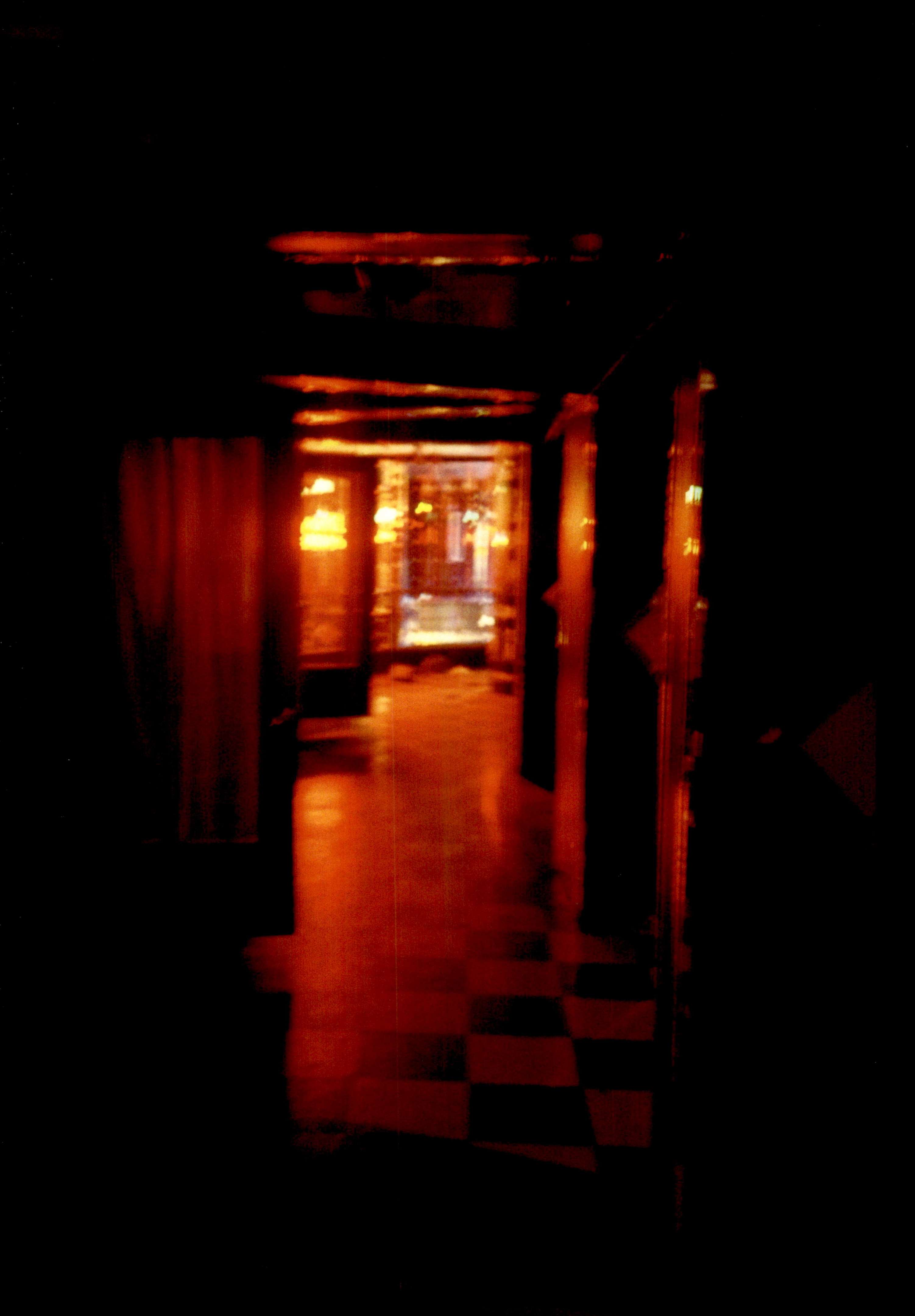

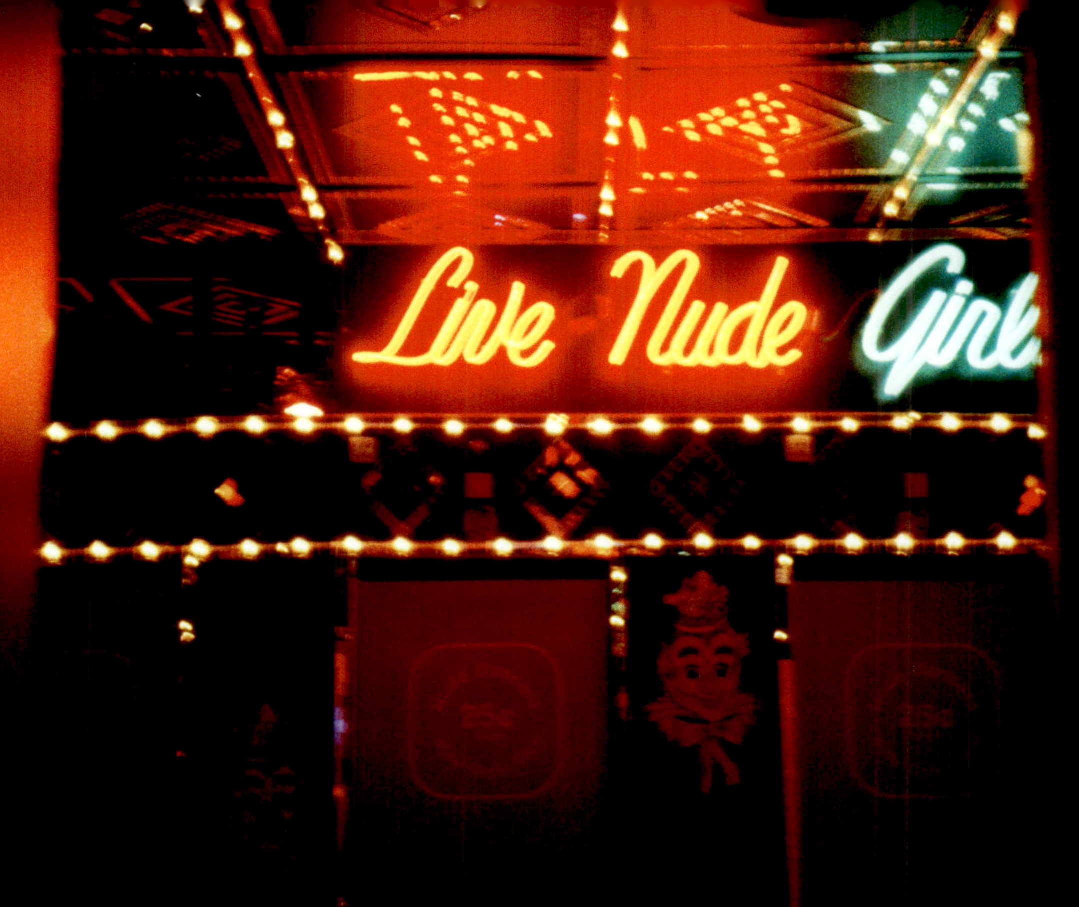
Live Nude Girls

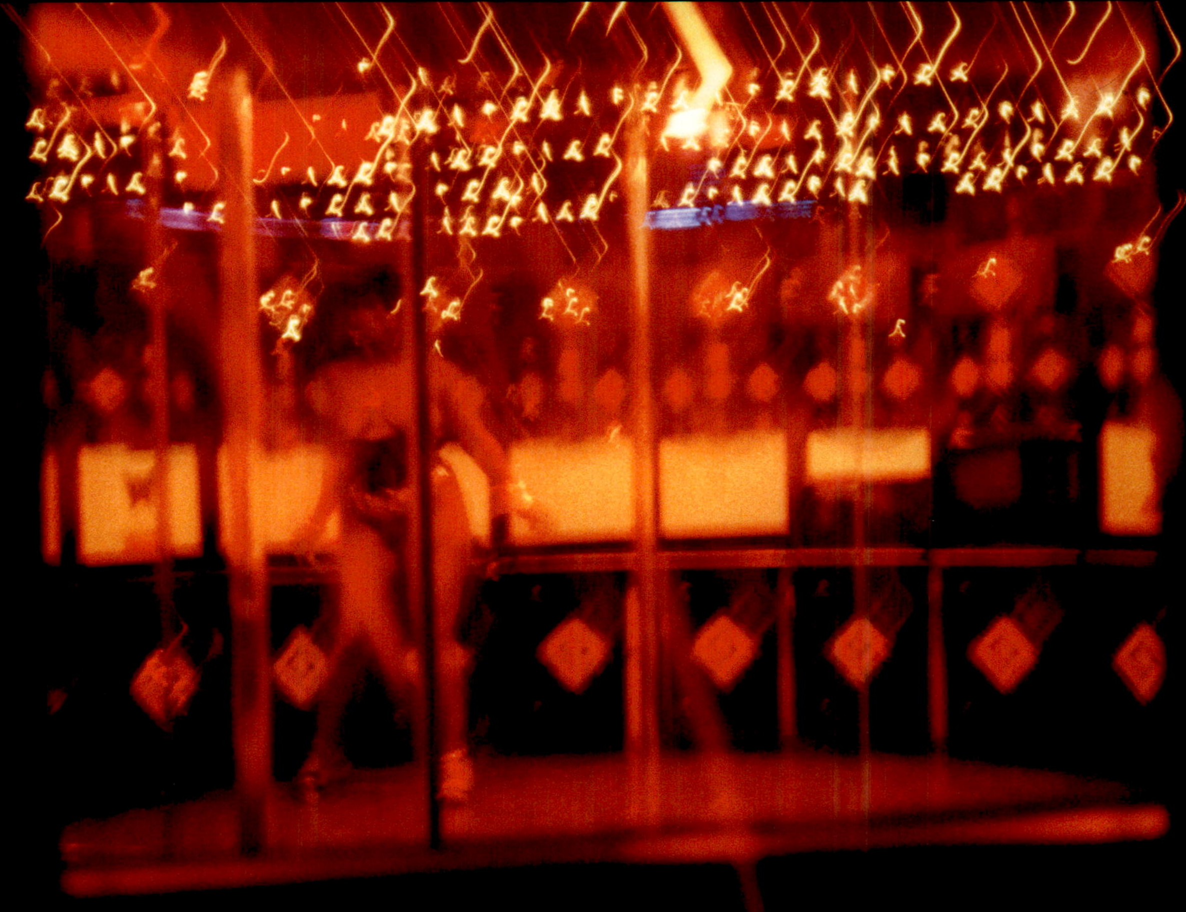

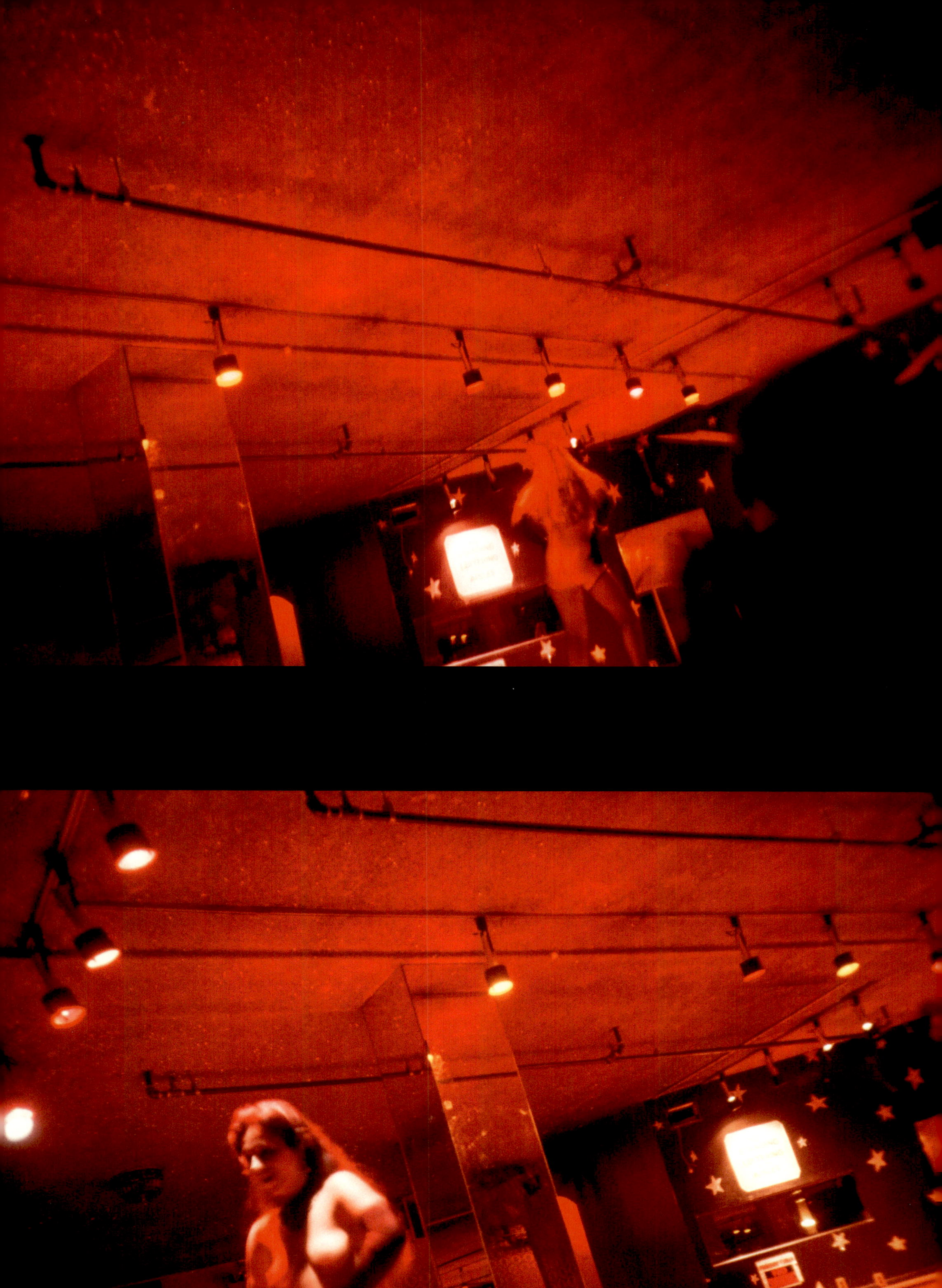

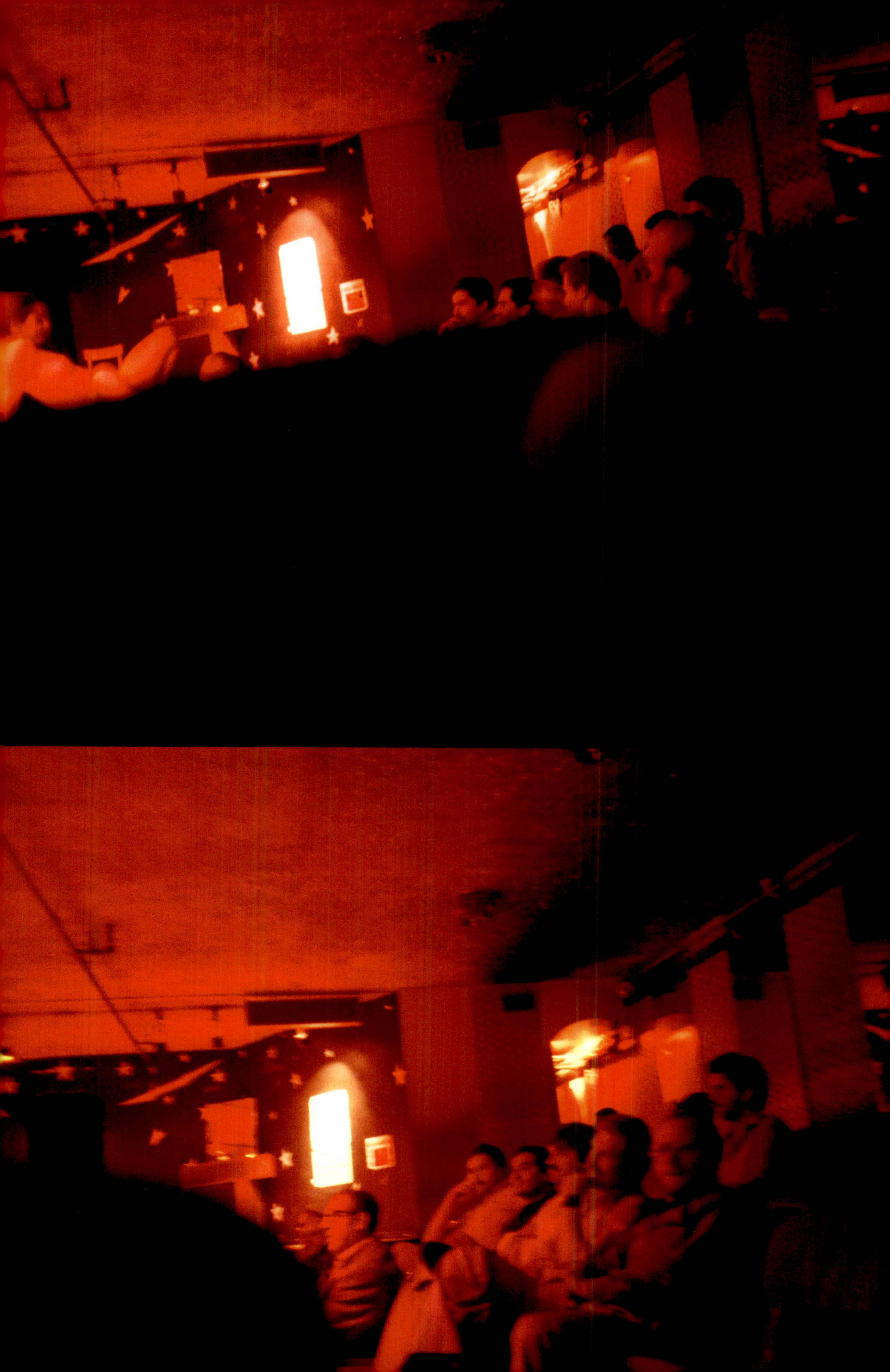

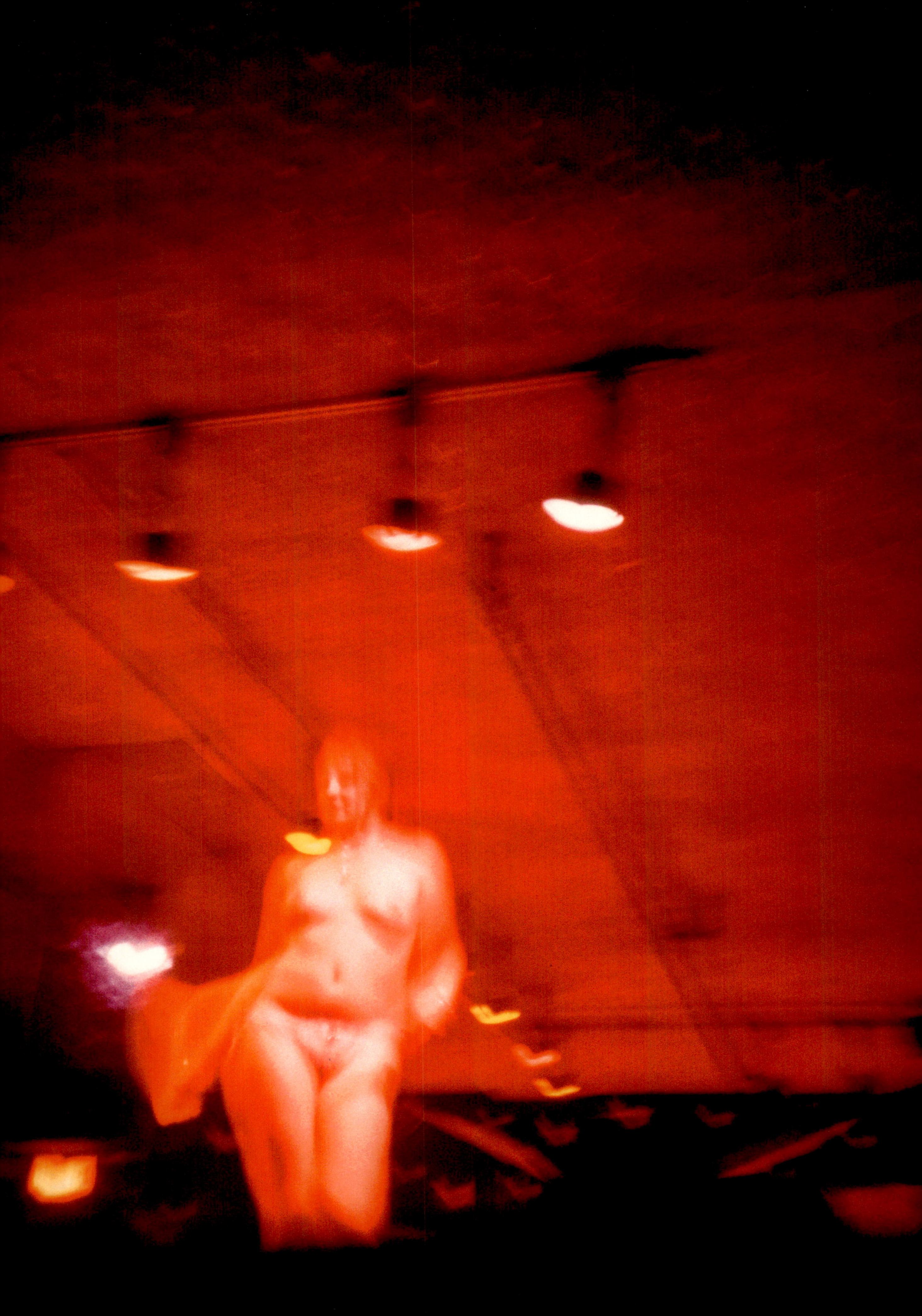

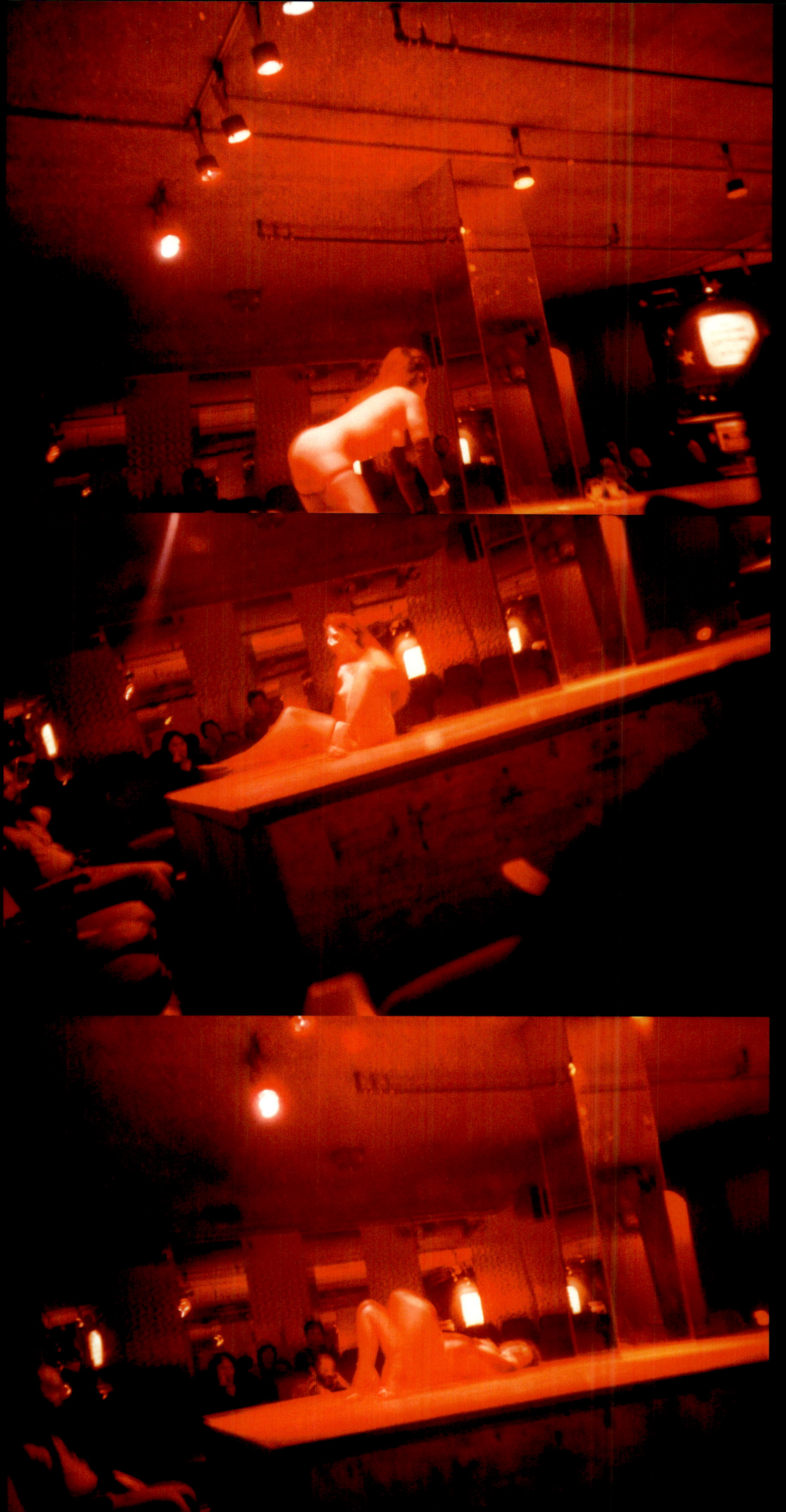

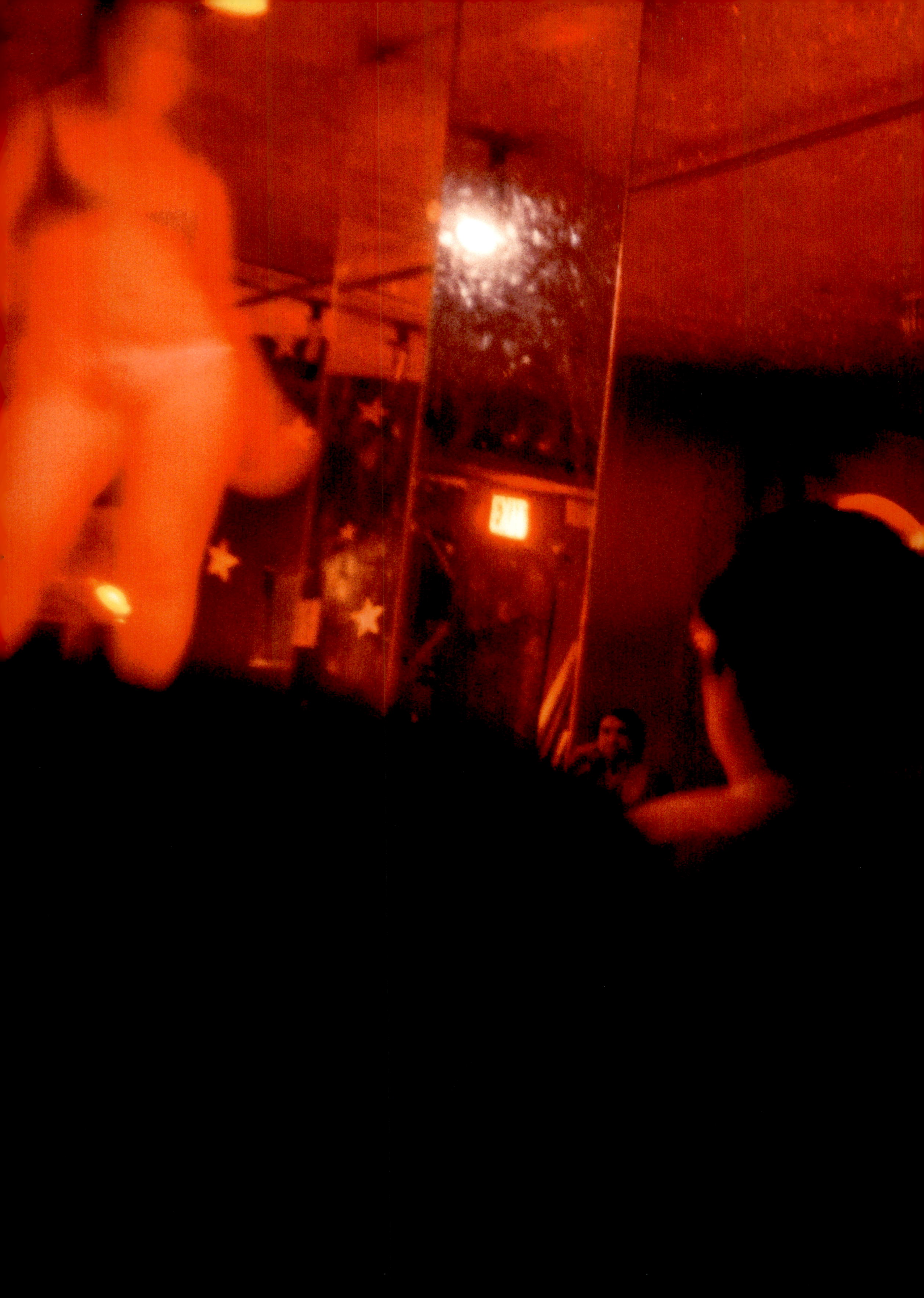

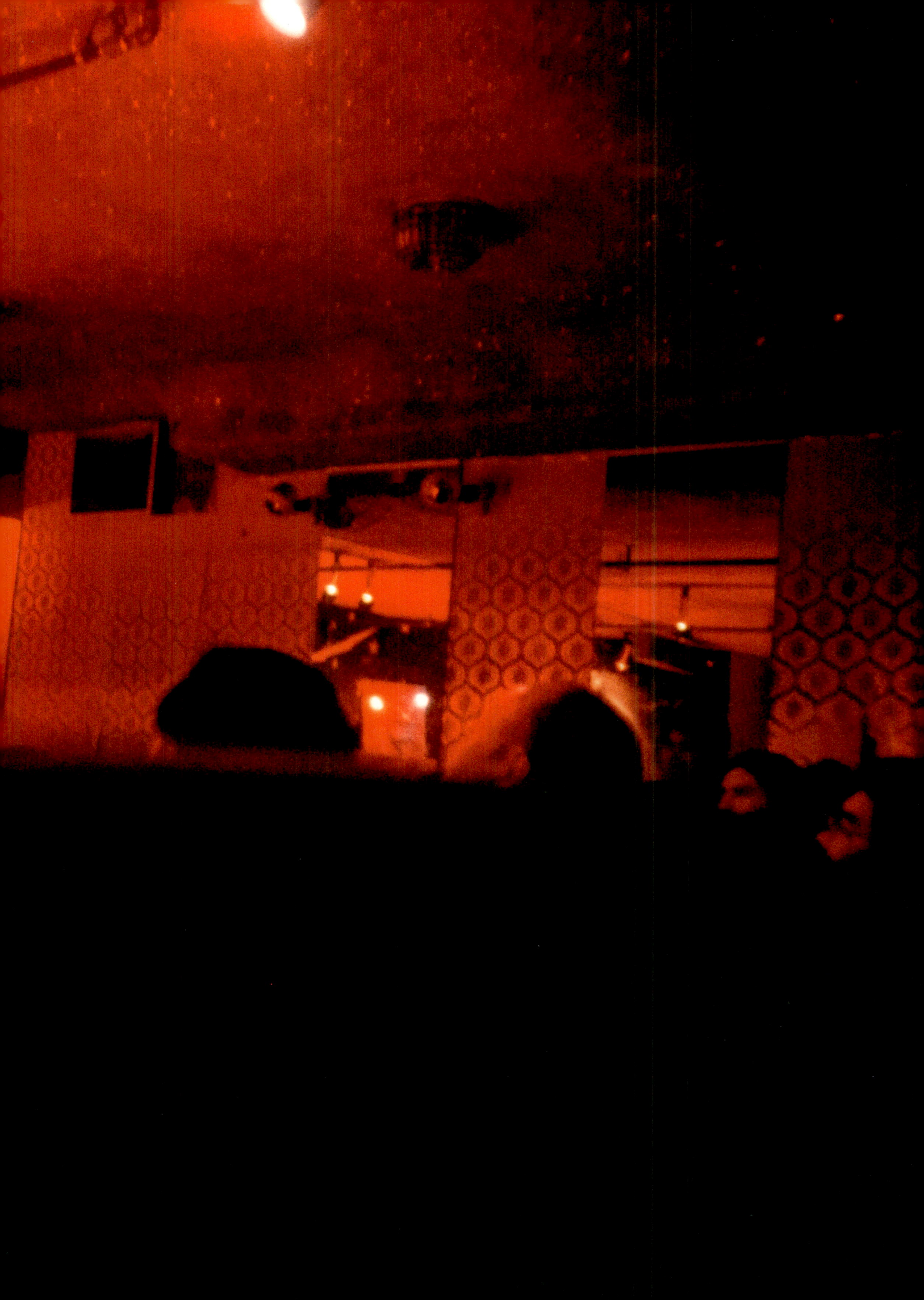

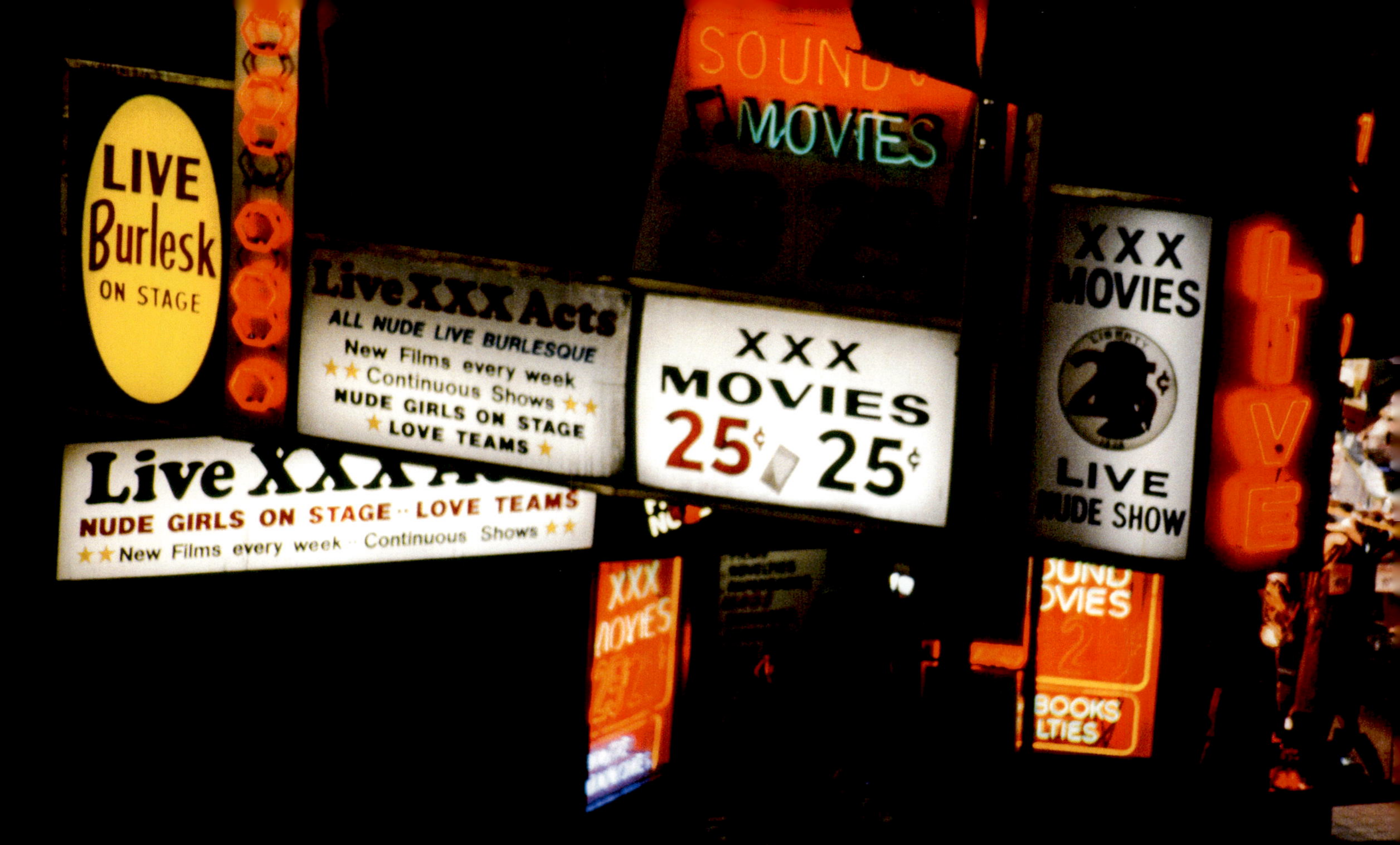

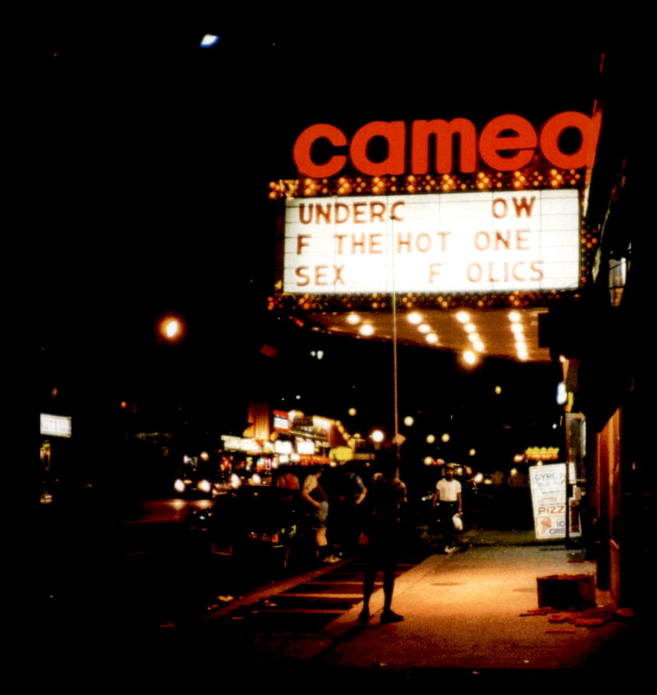

LIVE Burlesk ON STAGE
SOUND MOVIES
Live XXX Acts
ALL NUDE LIVE BURLESQUE
New Films every week
Continuous Shows
NUDE GIRLS ON STAGE
LOVE TEAMS
XXX MOVIES 25¢ 25¢
XXX MOVIES
LIVE NUDE SHOW
LIVE
Live XXX
NUDE GIRLS ON STAGE · LOVE TEAMS
New Films every week · Continuous Shows
XXX MOVIES
SOUND MOVIES
BOOKS LTIES
cameo
UNDERC OW
F THE HOT ONE
SEX F OLICS

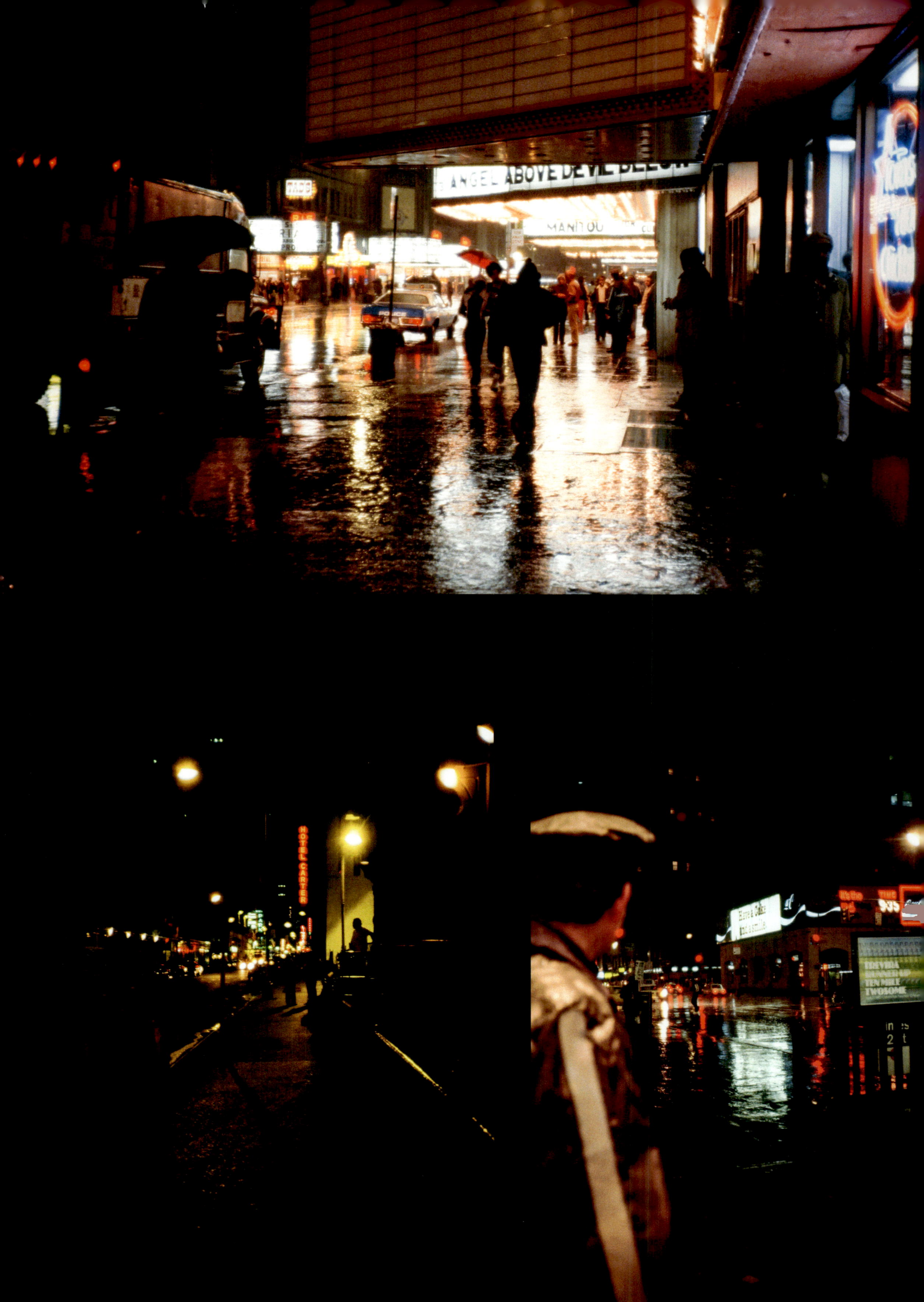
ANGEL ABOVE DEVIL BELOW
MANITOU
POLICE
HOTEL CARTER

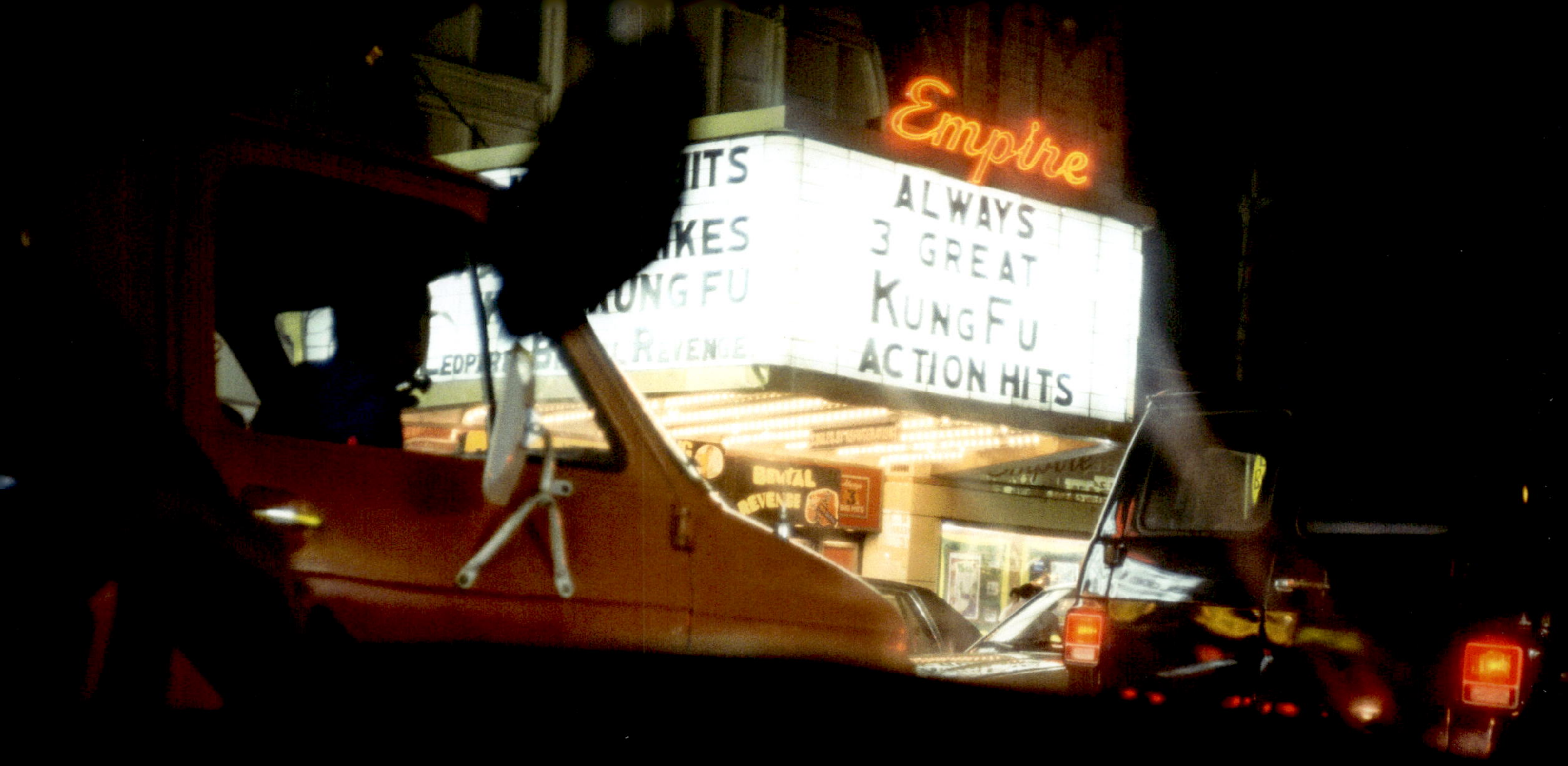

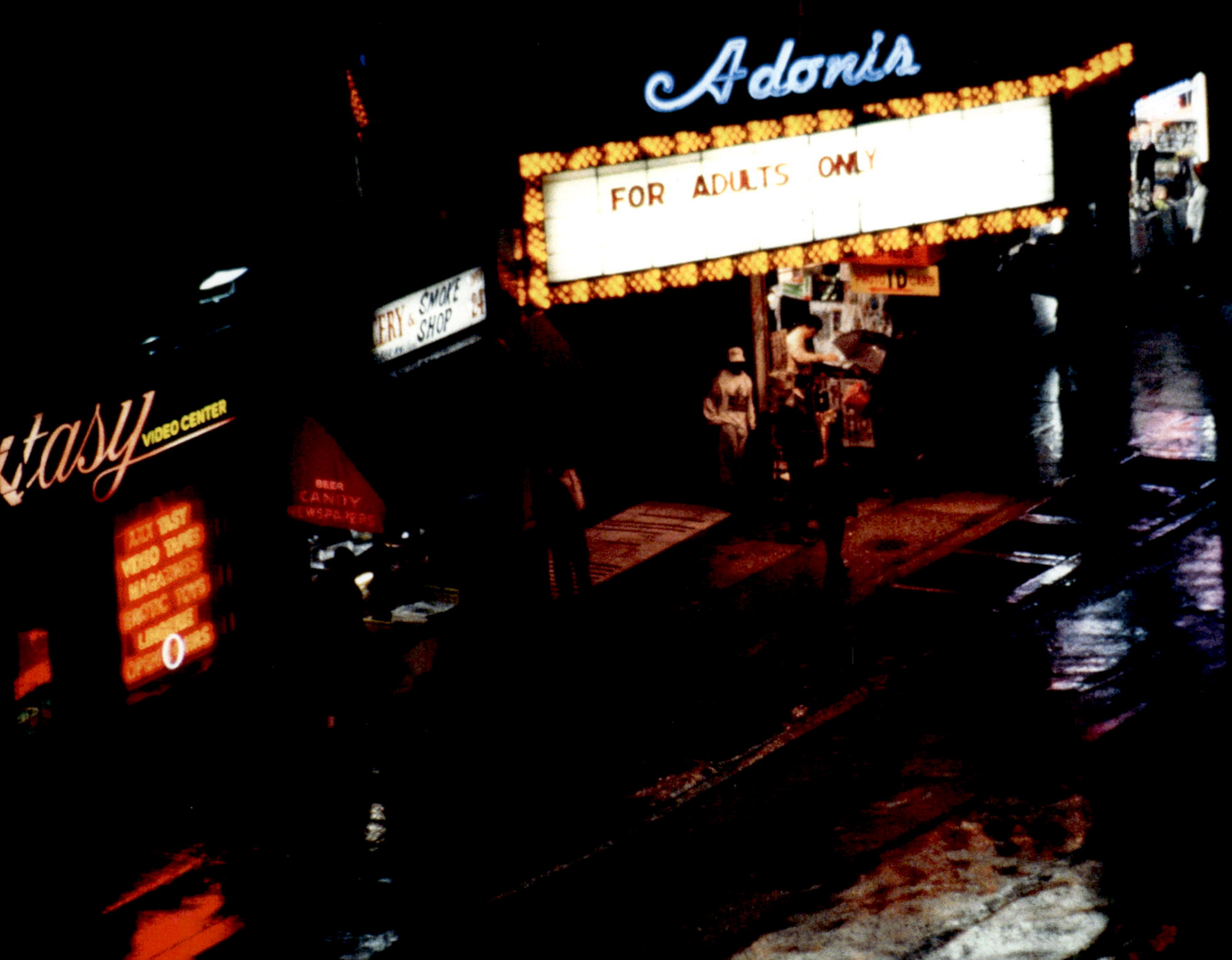
Empire
ALWAYS
3 GREAT
KungFu
ACTION HITS
HITS
KES
KUNG FU
BRUTAL REVENGE
Adonis
FOR ADULTS ONLY
tasy VIDEO CENTER
ERY & SMOKE SHOP
XXX BEST
VIDEO TAPES
MAGAZINES
EROTIC TOYS
LINGERIE
TOYS
BEER
CANDY
NEWSPAPERS

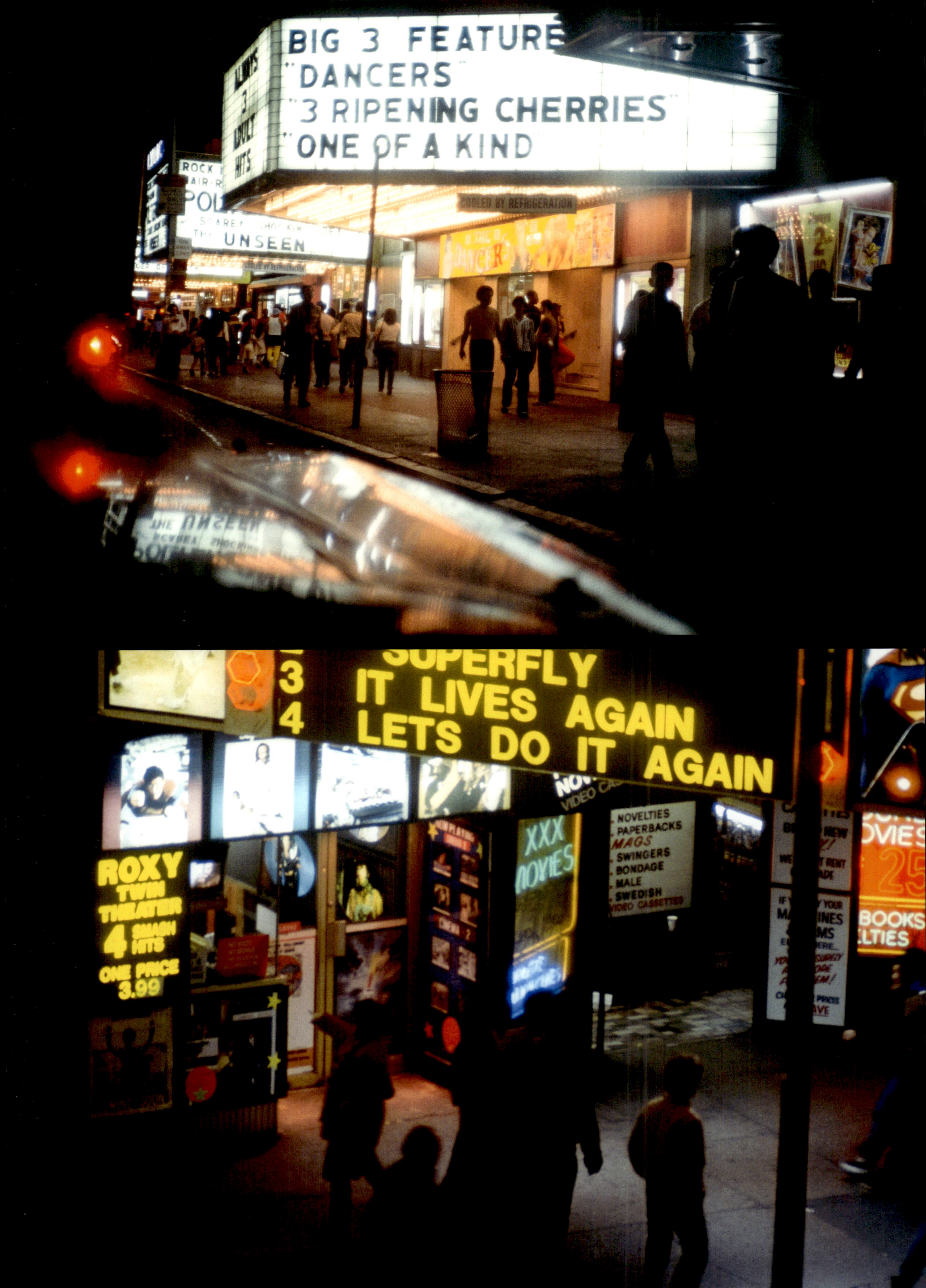
ALWAYS
3
ADULT
HITS
BIG 3 FEATURE
"DANCERS"
"3 RIPENING CHERRIES"
"ONE OF A KIND"
ROCK
AIR-R
POL
THE UNSEEN
COOLED BY REFRIGERATION
DANCER
SUPERFLY
3 IT LIVES AGAIN
4 LETS DO IT AGAIN
ROXY
TWIN
THEATER
4 SMASH HITS
ONE PRICE
3.99
XXX MOVIES
NOVELTIES
PAPERBACKS
MAGS
SWINGERS
BONDAGE
MALE
SWEDISH
VIDEO CASSETTES
VIDEO CASSE
BOOKS
MOVIES
25

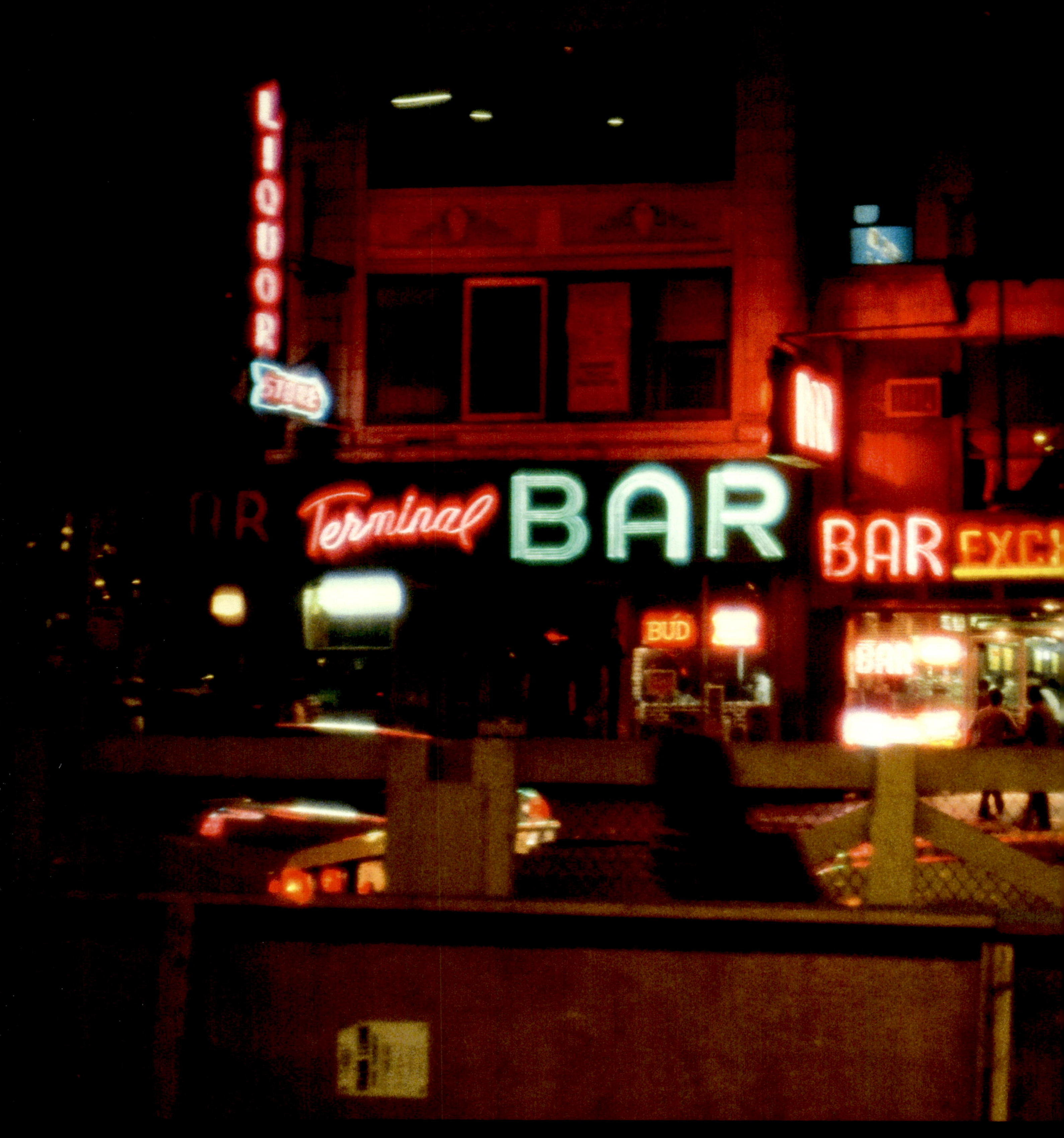

LIQUOR
STORE
AR
Terminal
BAR
BAR
BAR EXCH
BUD
BAR

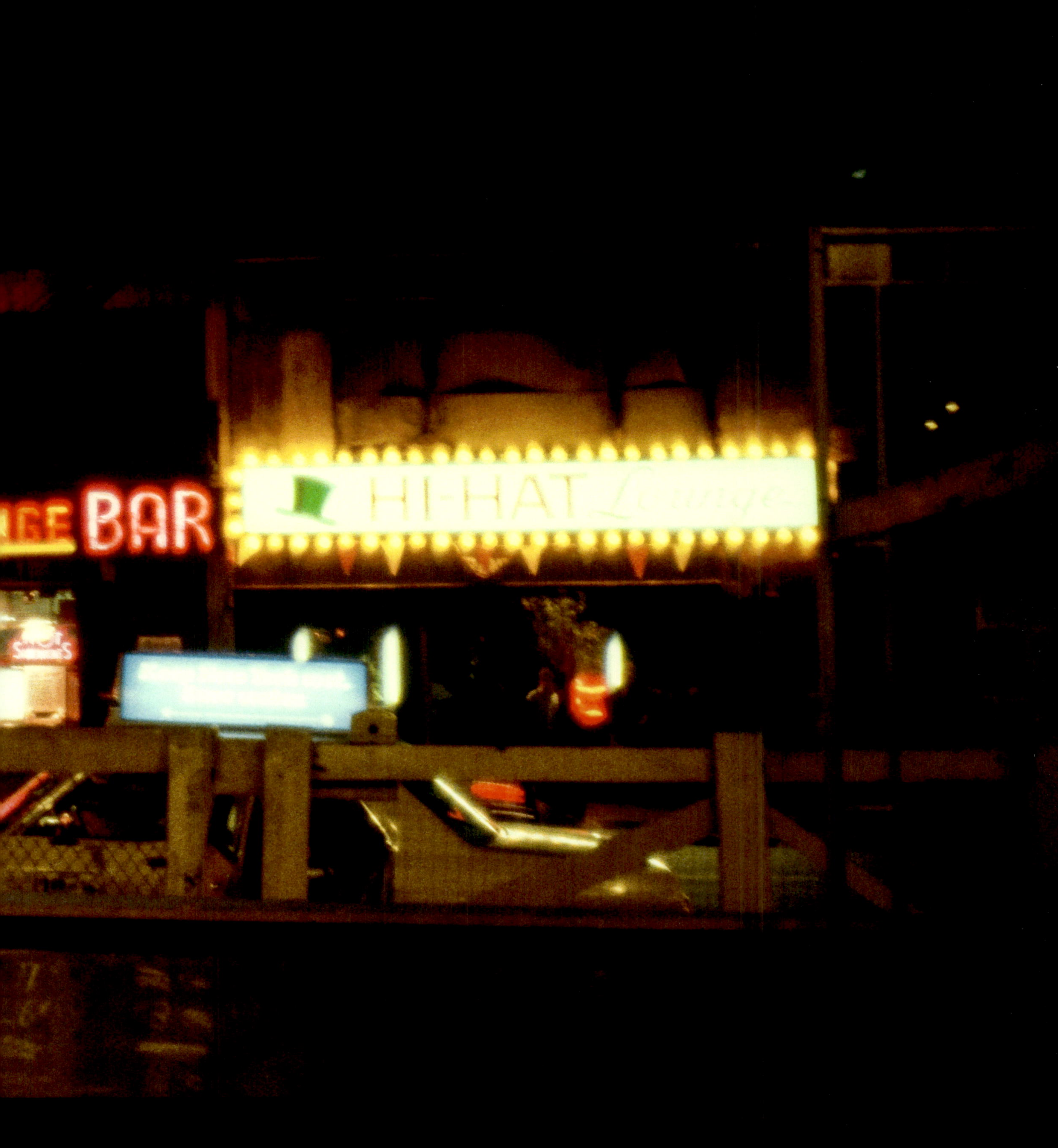
BAR
HI-HAT Lounge

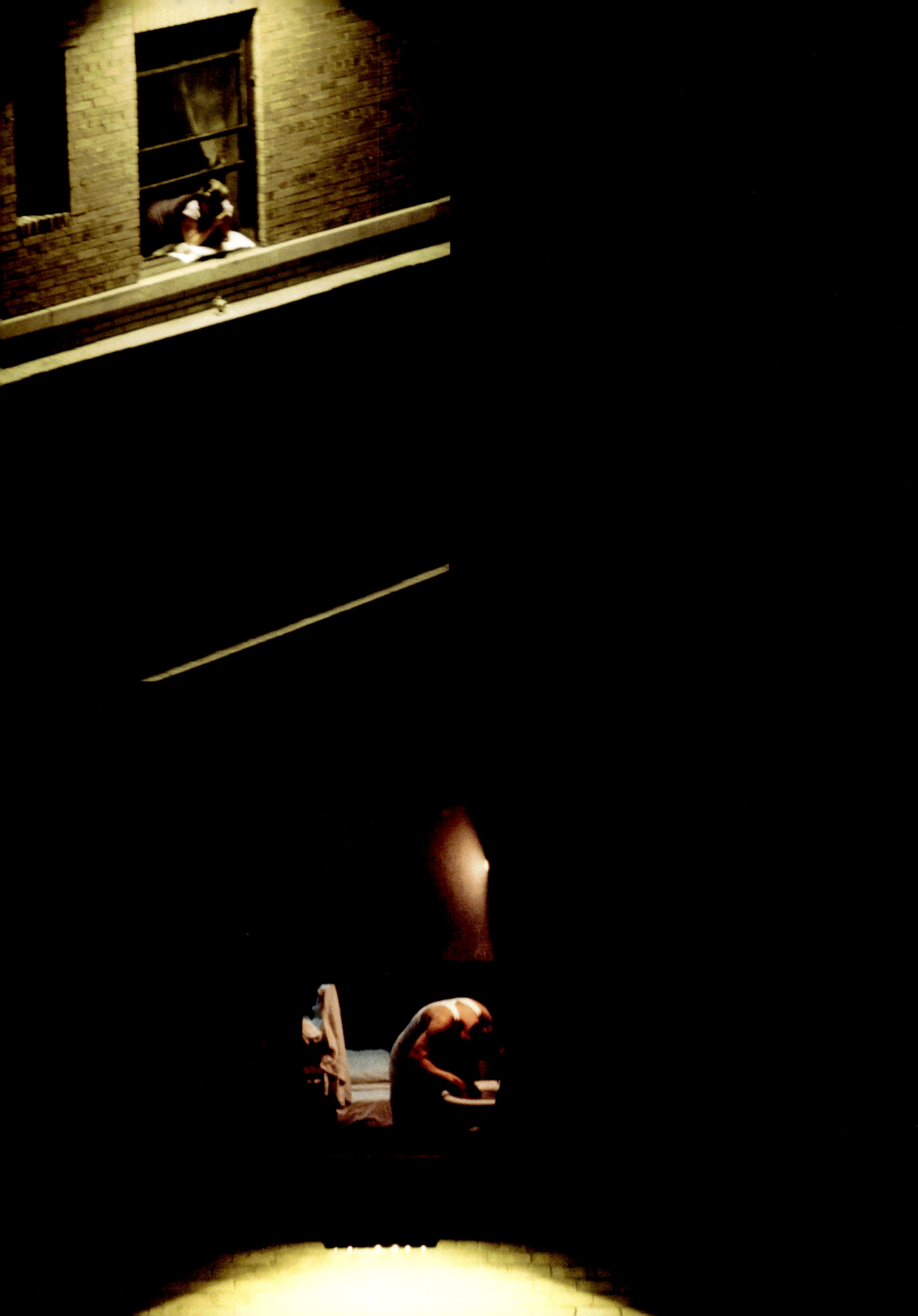

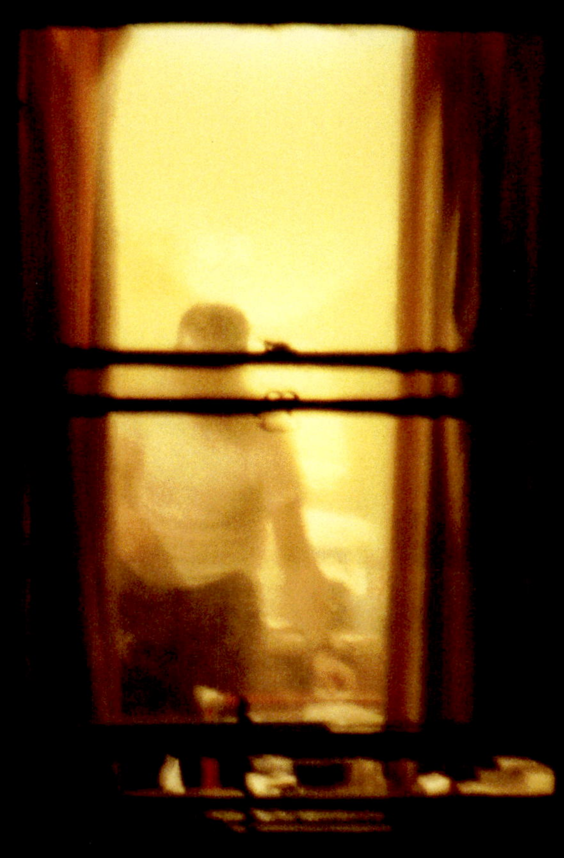

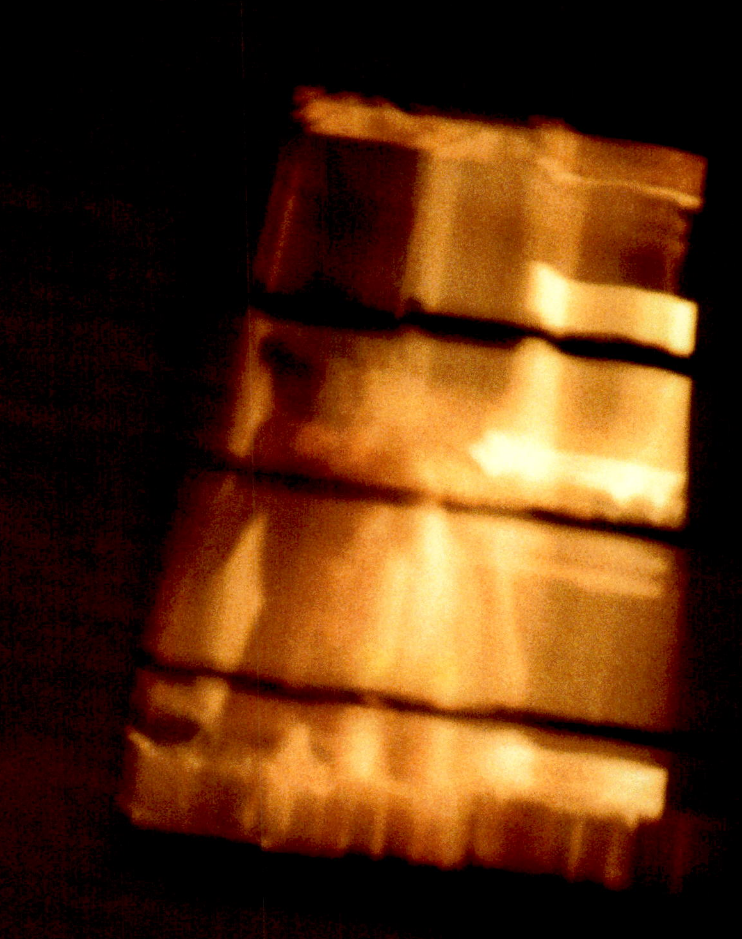

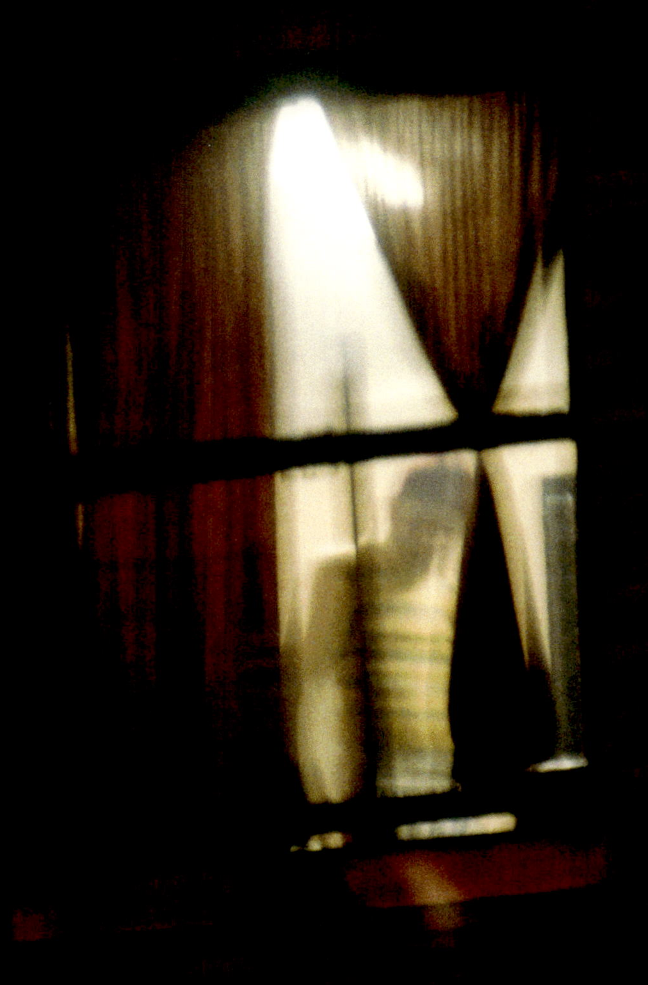

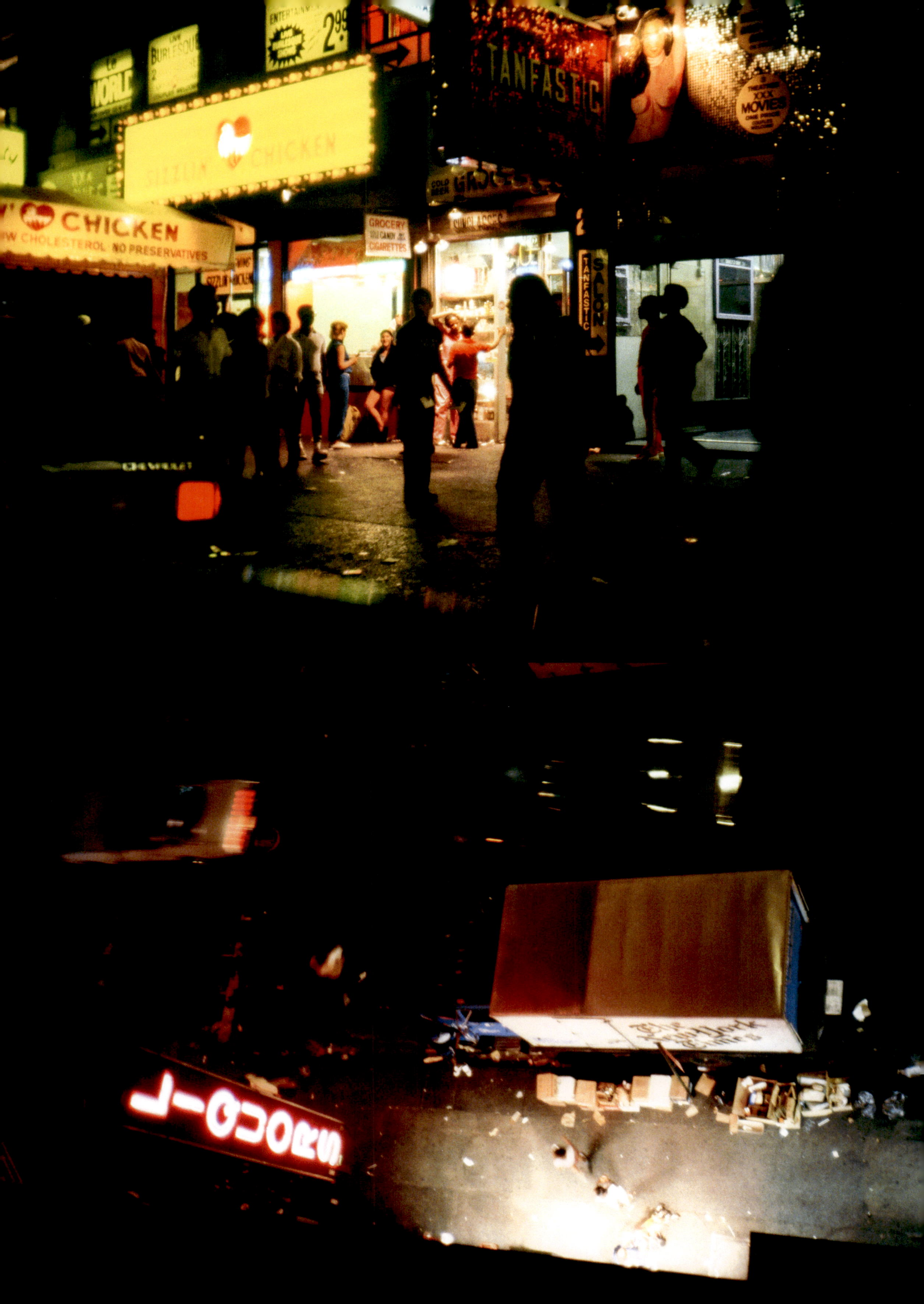

WORLD
LE
BURLESQUE
ENTERTAINMENT
2.99
CHICKEN
SIZZLIN' CHICKEN
CHICKEN
LOW CHOLESTEROL · NO PRESERVATIVES
TANFASTIC
MOVIES
XXX
GROCERY
CANDY
CIGARETTES
SUNGLASSES
COLD BEER GROCERY
TANFASTIC
SALON
CHEVROLET

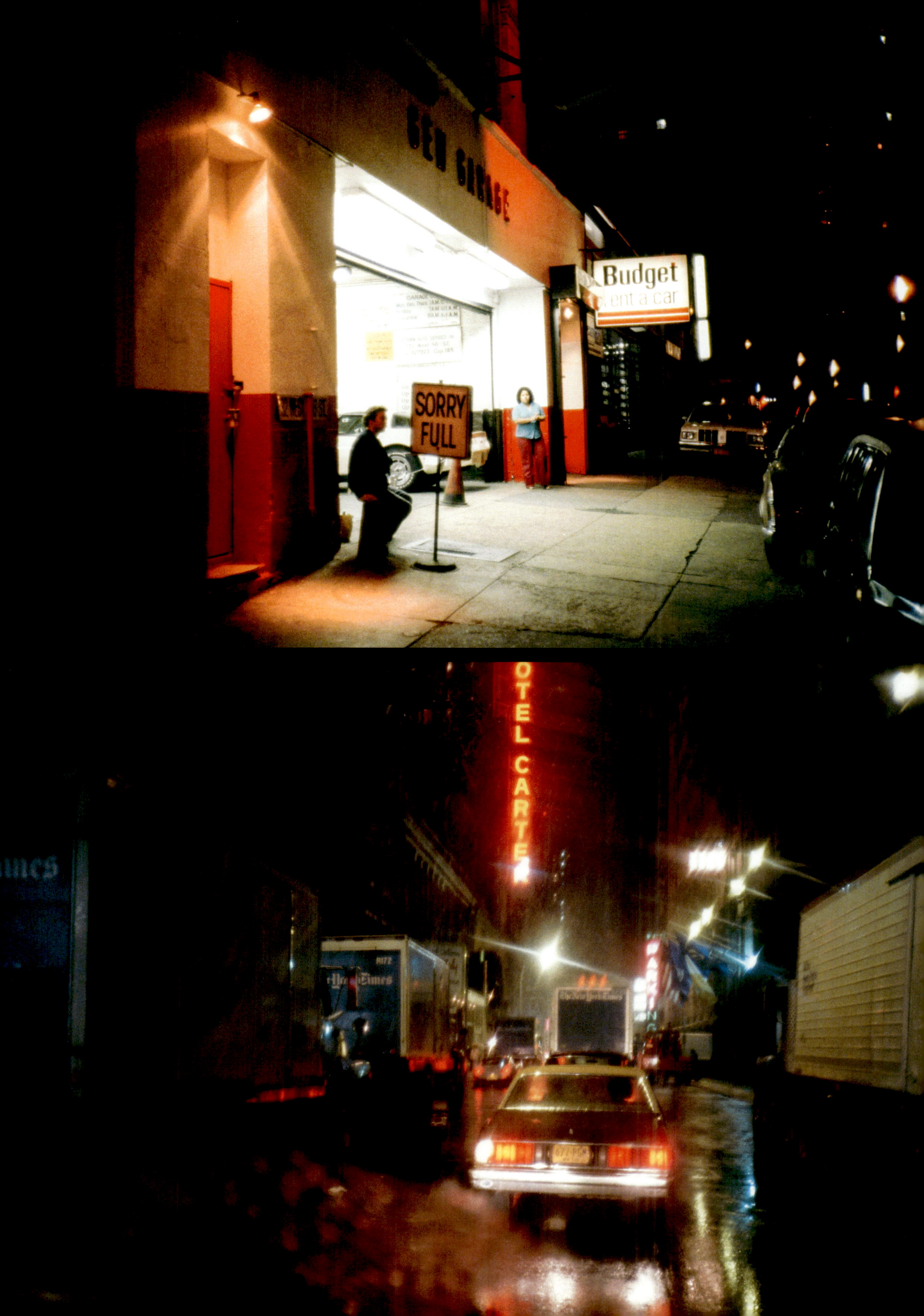
GEM GARAGE
Budget
rent a car
SORRY
FULL
HOTEL CARTE
The New York Times

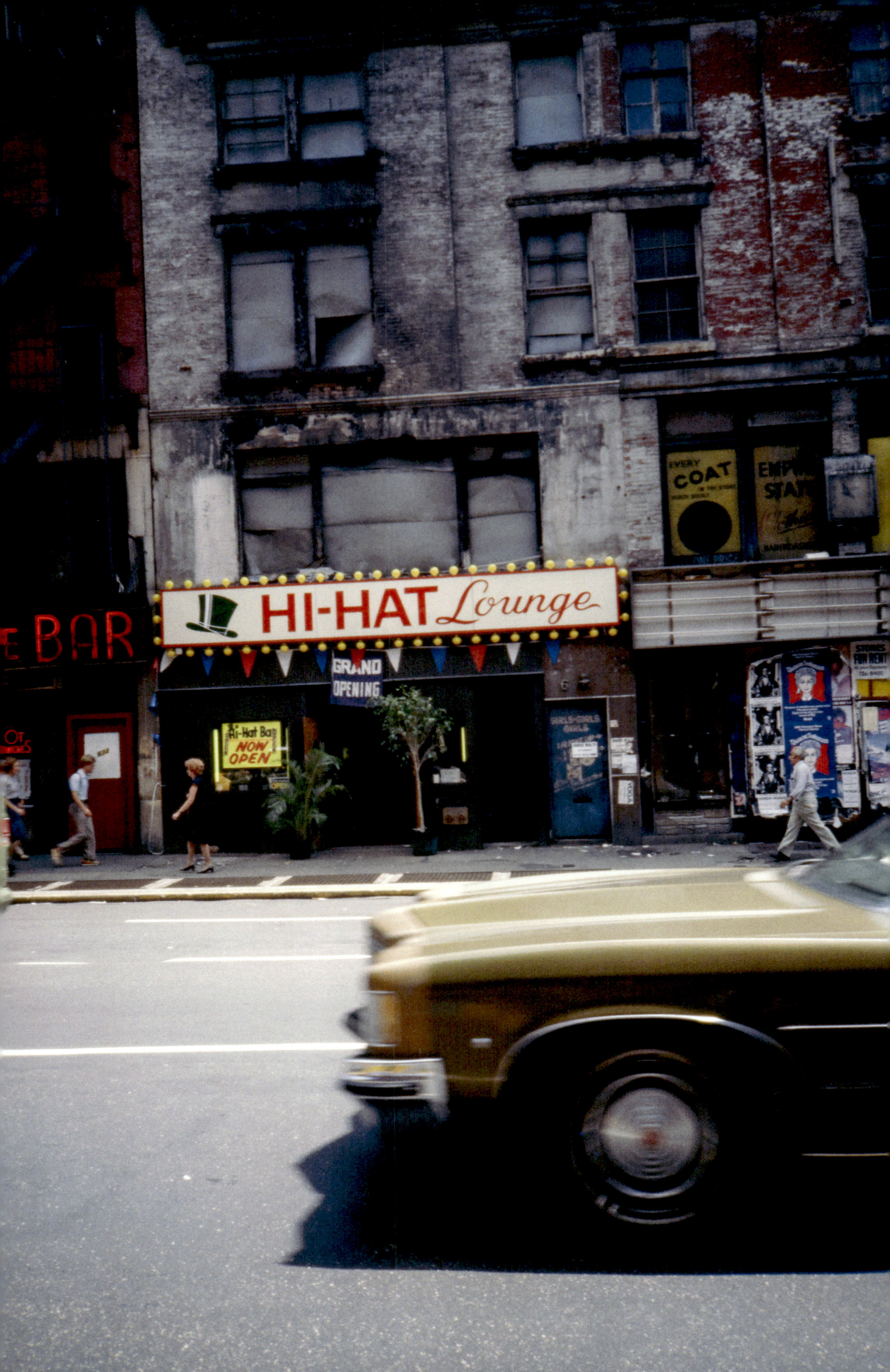

E BAR
HI-HAT Lounge
GRAND OPENING
Hi-Hat Bar
NOW OPEN
GIRLS·GIRLS·GIRLS
EVERY COAT IN THE STORE
EMP STAR
ONE PRICE
FOR RENT

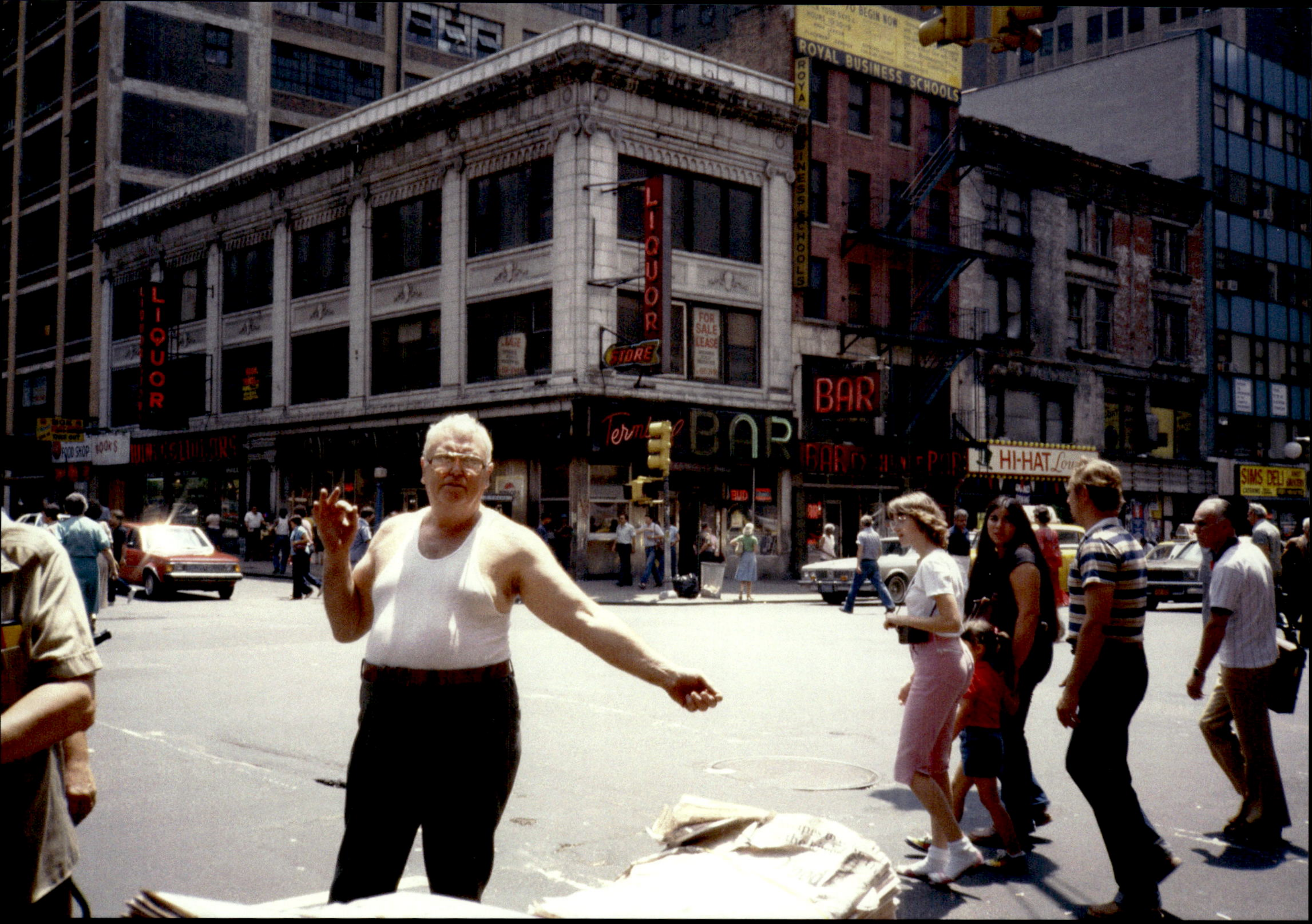
ROYAL BUSINESS SCHOOLS
LIQUOR
LIQUOR
STORE
FOR SALE LEASE
BAR
BAR
HI-HAT
SIMS DELI

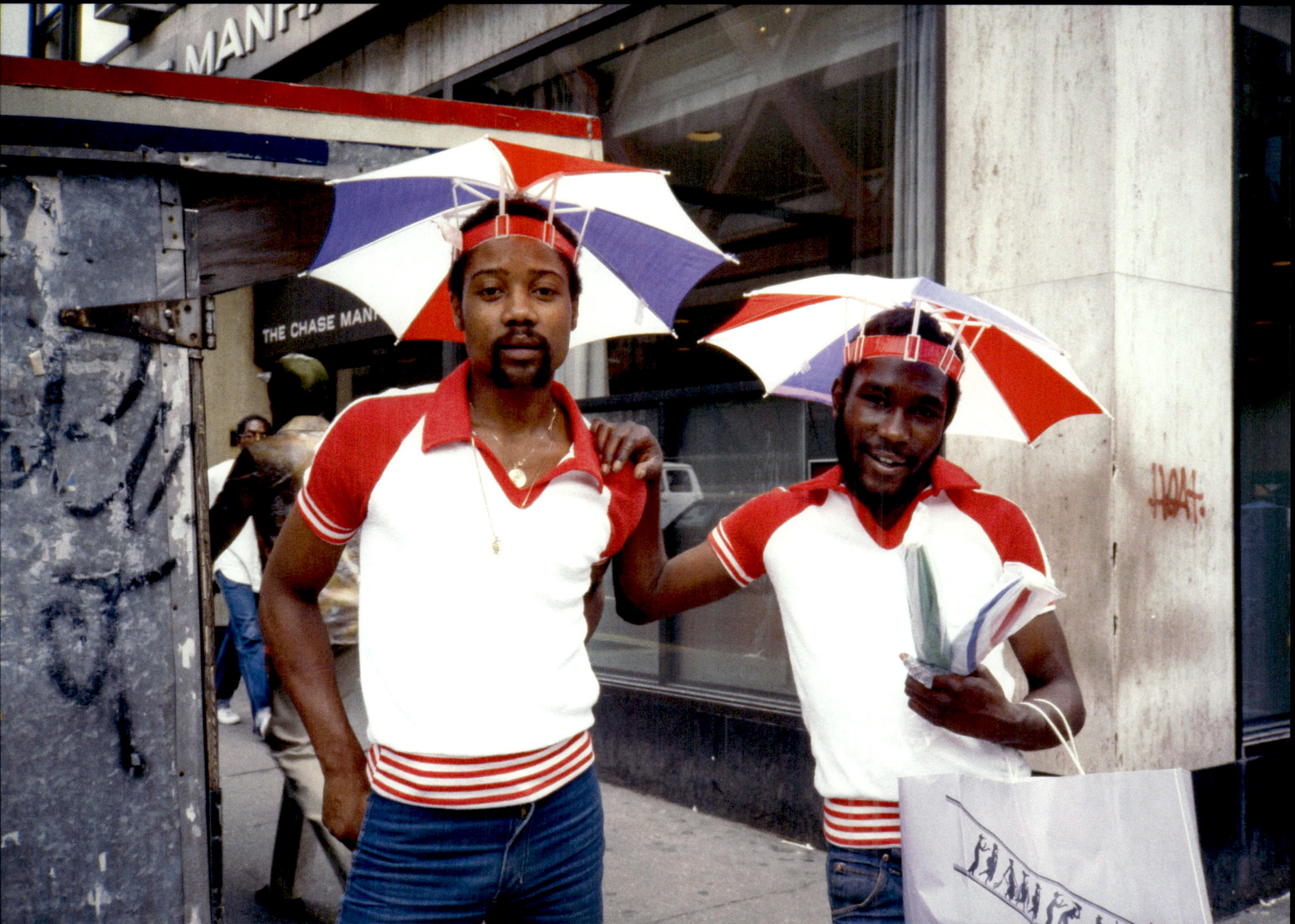

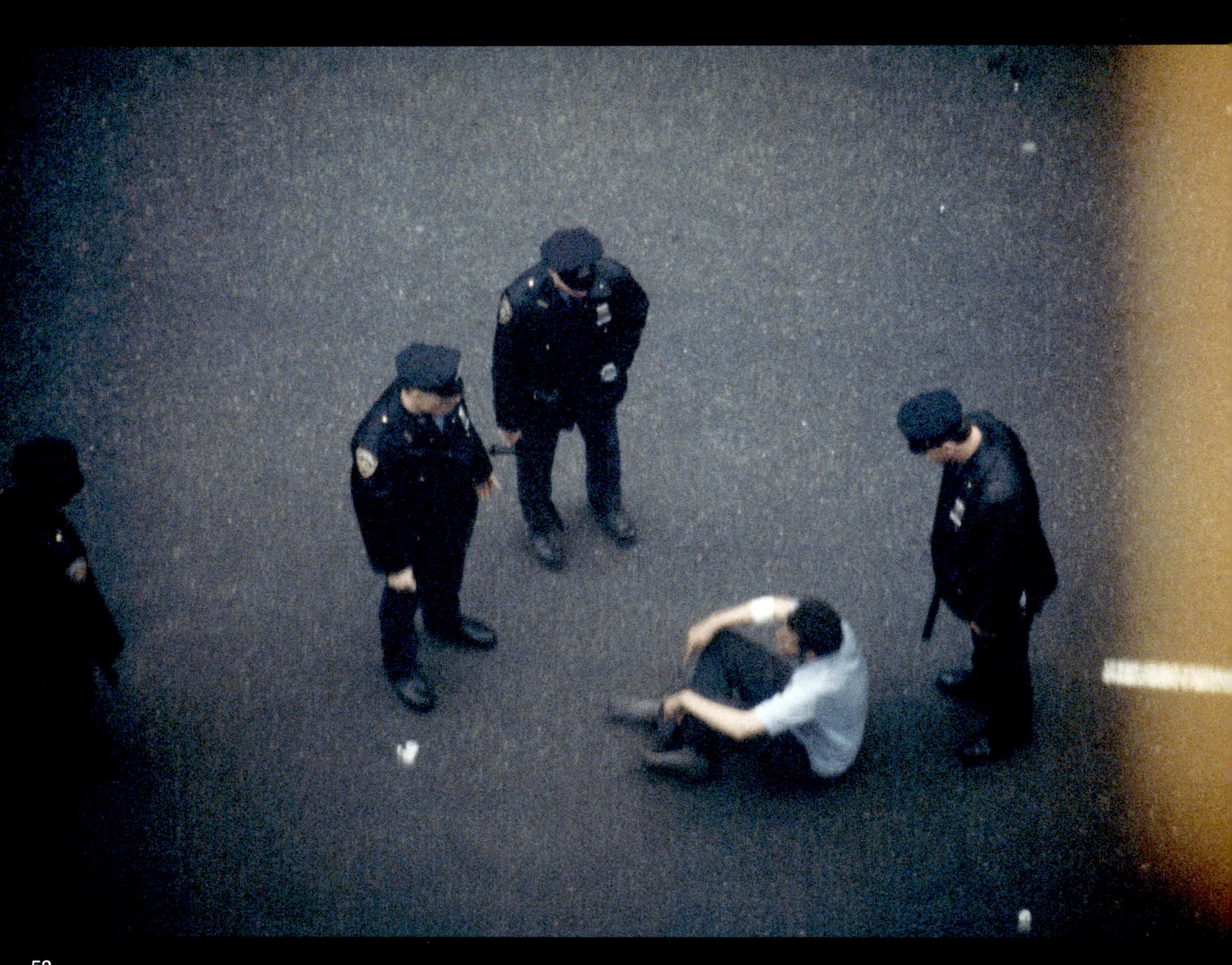

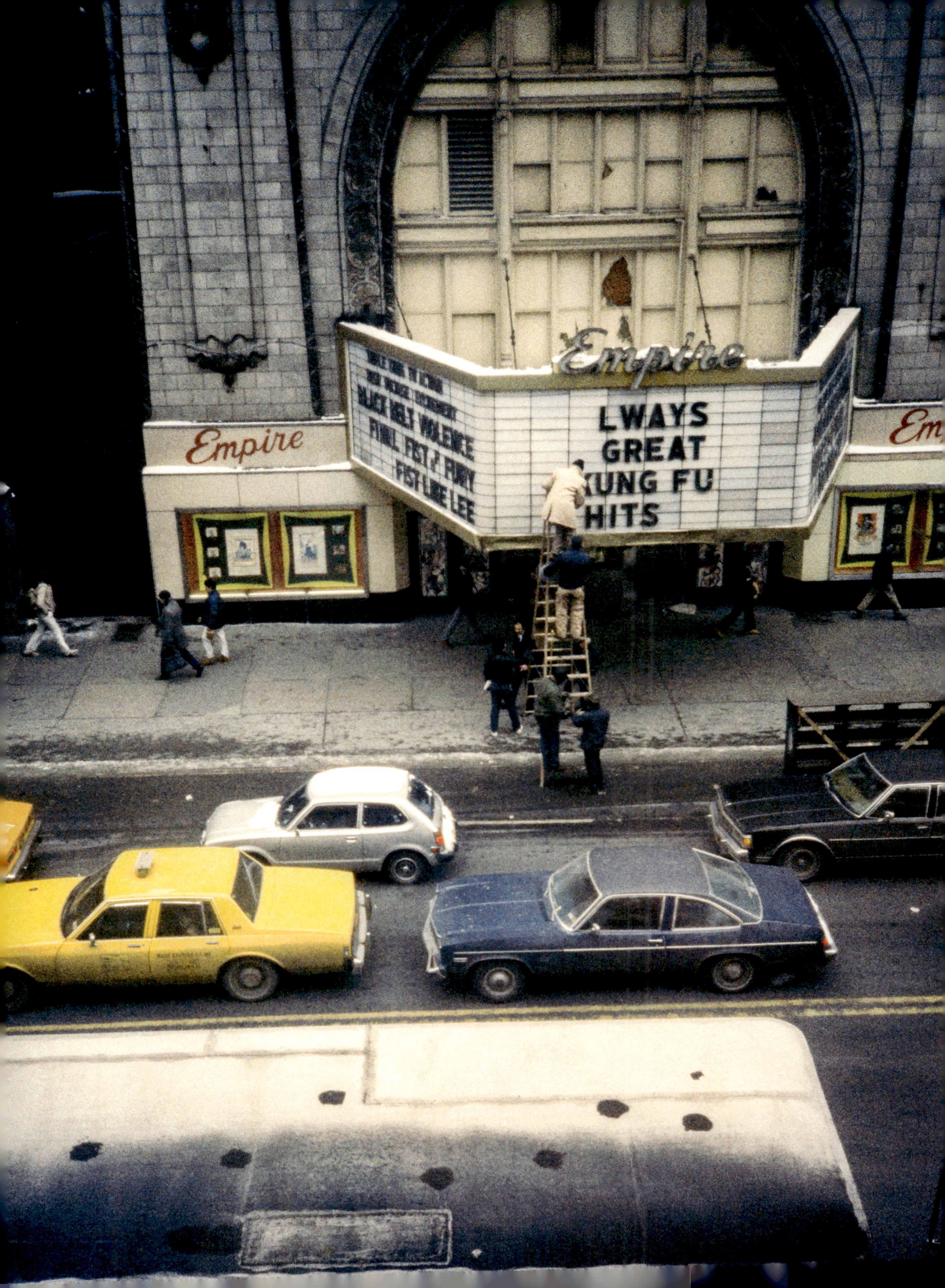
Empire
LWAYS
GREAT
KUNG FU
HITS
Empire
Empire
BLACK BELT VIOLENCE
FINAL FIST / FURY
FIST LIKE LEE

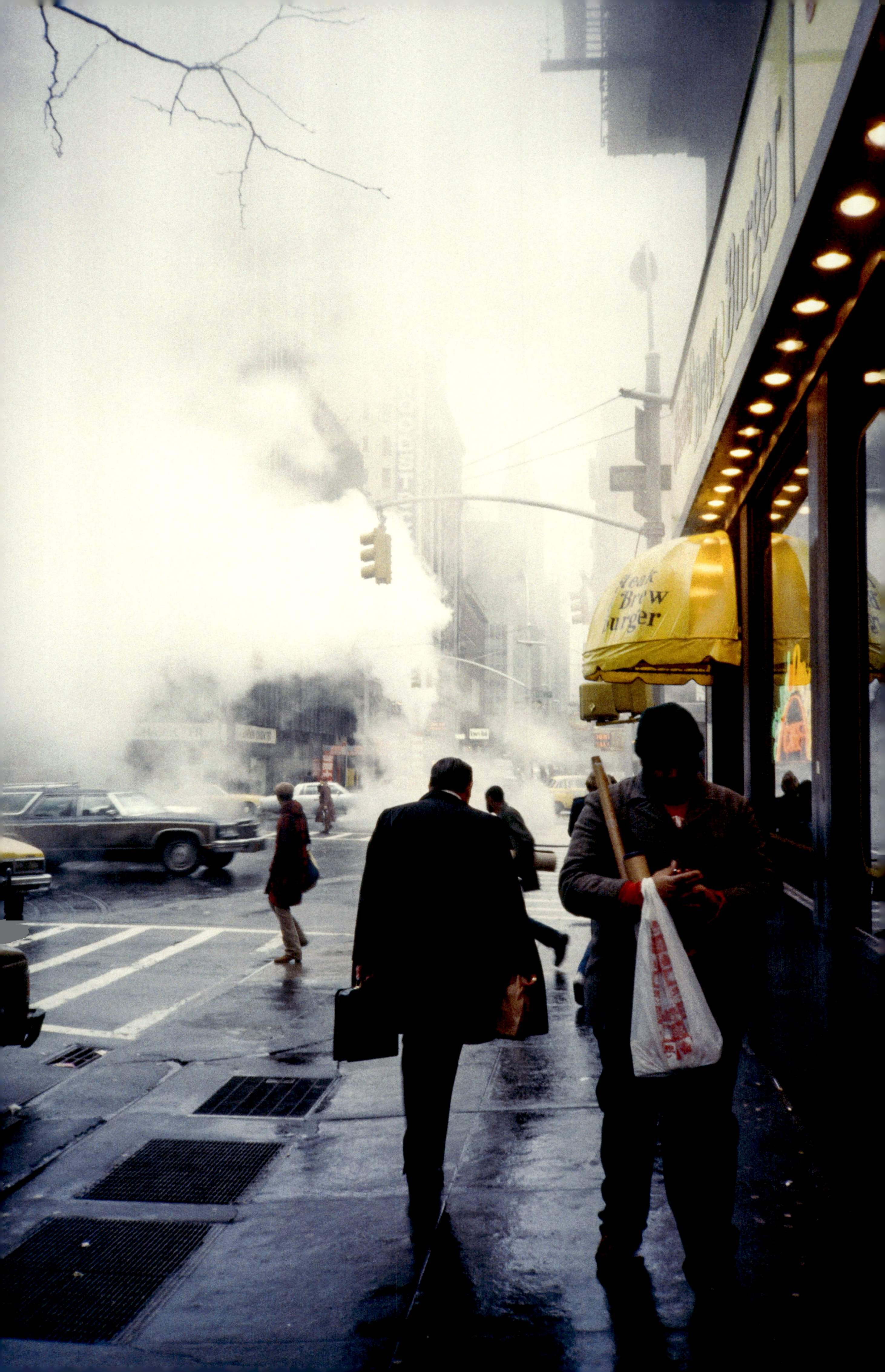
Steak
Brew
Burger

I'M NOT MAKING IMAGES THAT TELL YOU WHAT TO THINK. I SEE
PAINTING AS A SPACE WHERE YOU CAN SIFT THROUGH YOUR OWN
IDEAS: IS THIS PORNOGRAPHY? IS THAT BAD OR GOOD? SEXY OR
GROSS? FROM YOUR VIEWPOINT OR MINE?

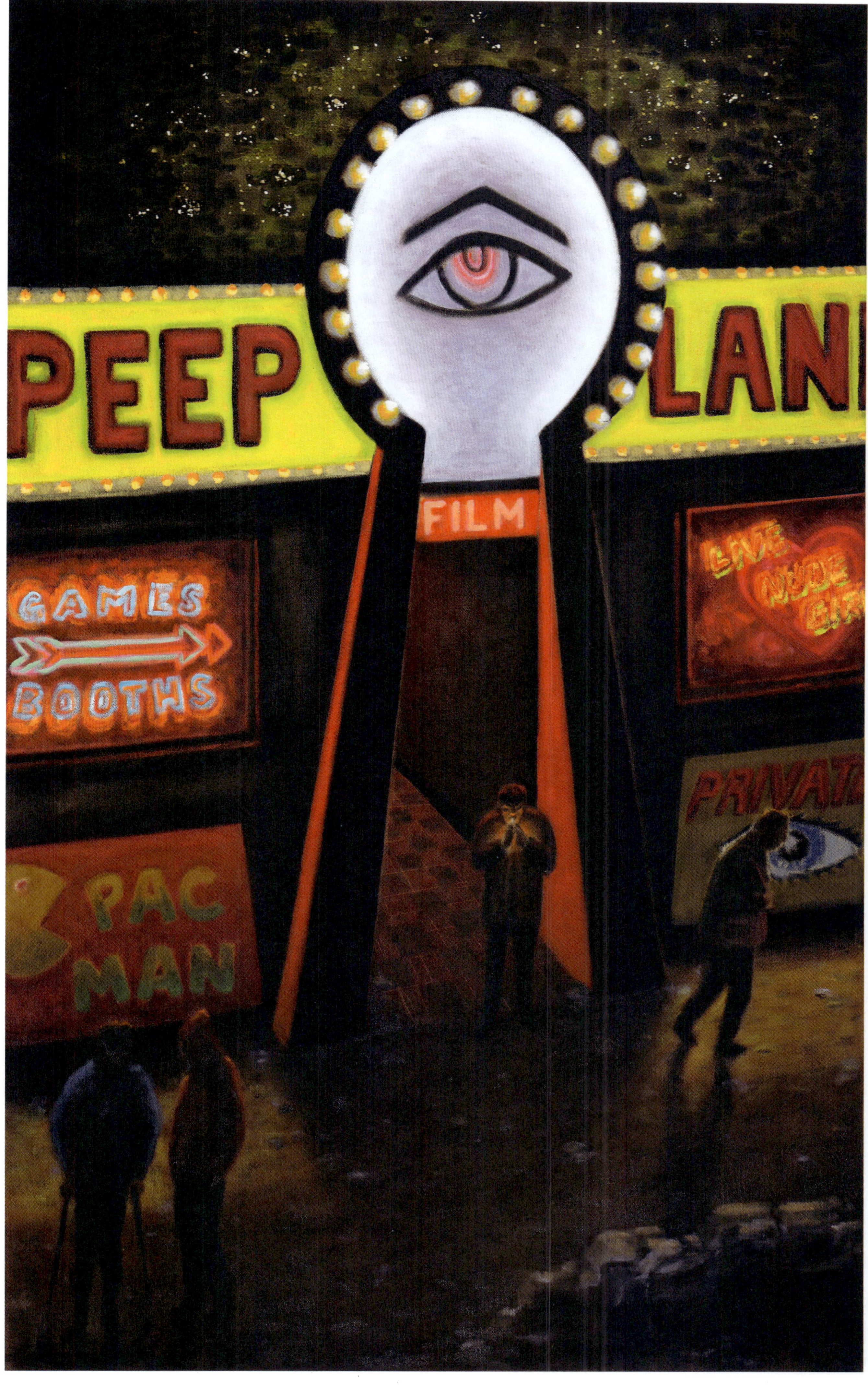

PEEP
LAN
FILM
GAMES
BOOTHS
PAC
MAN
LIVE
NUDE
GIR
PRIVAT

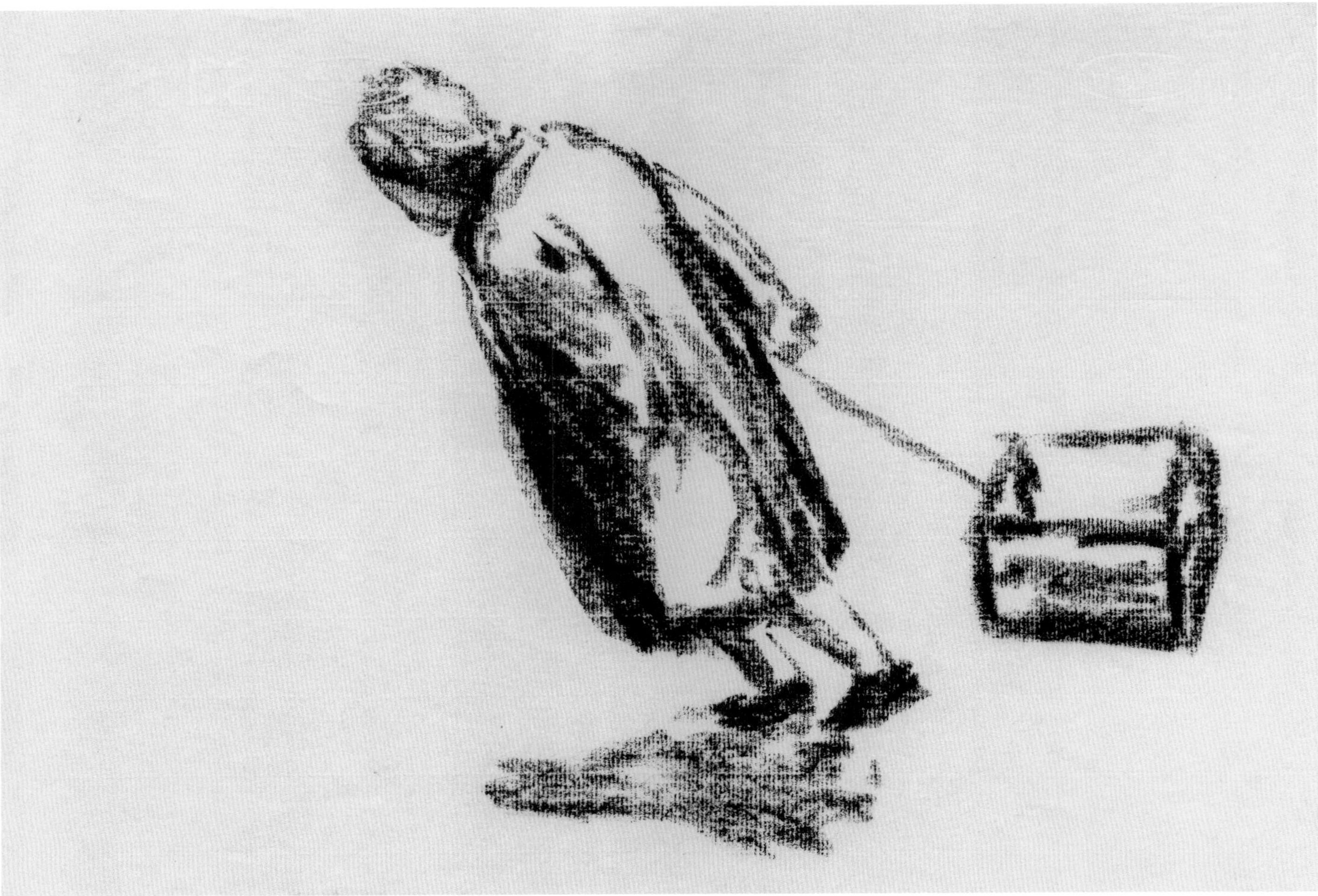

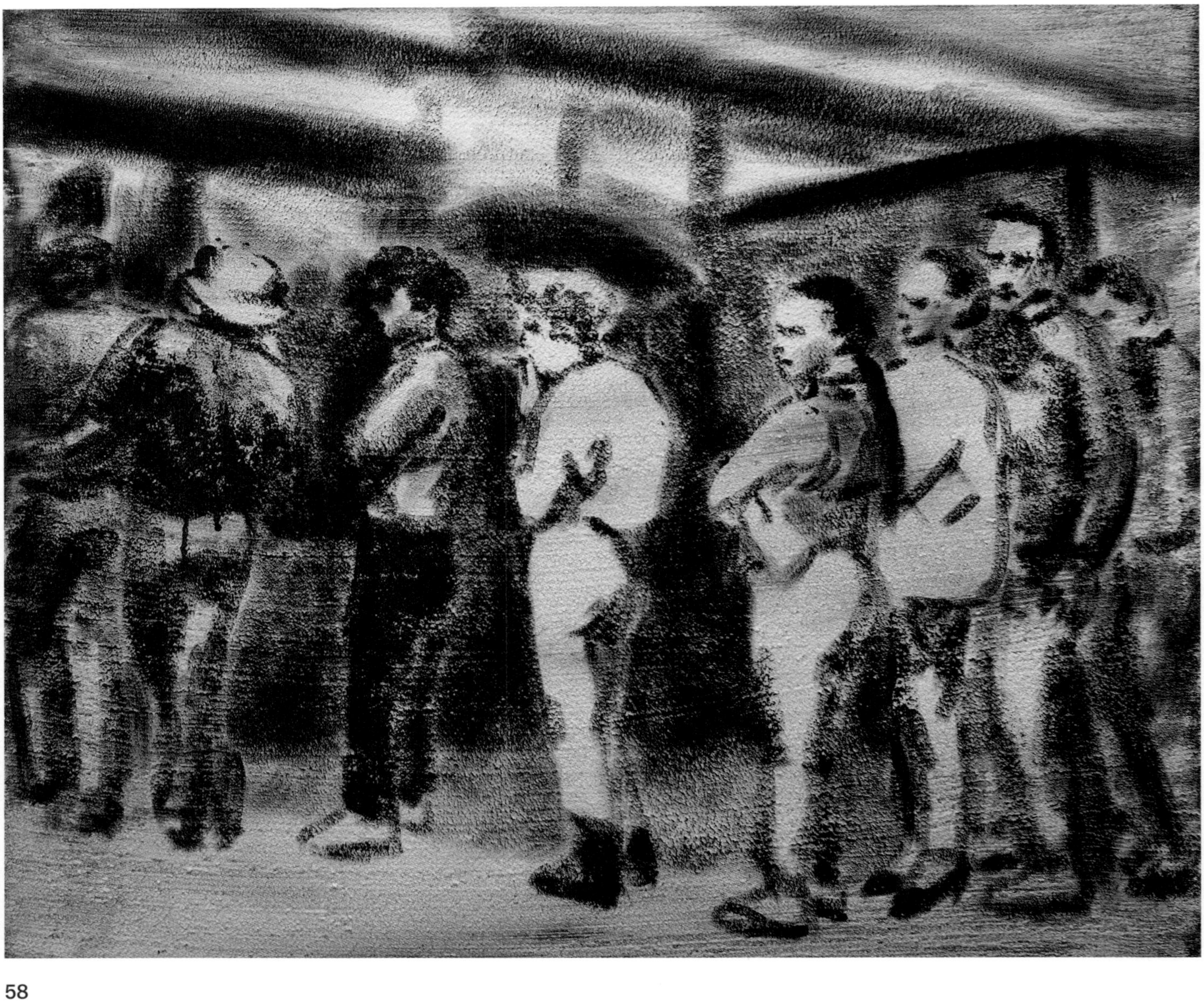

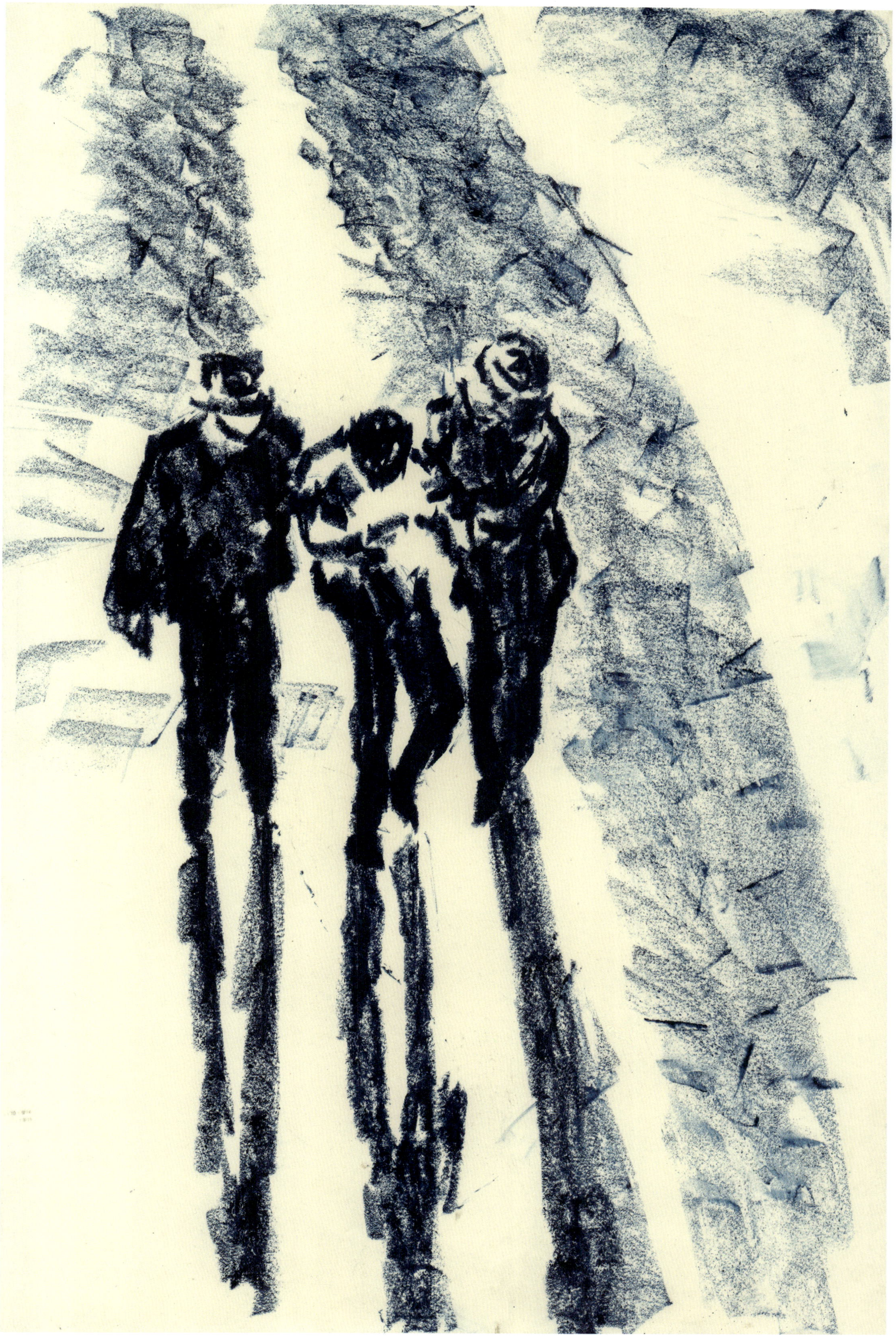

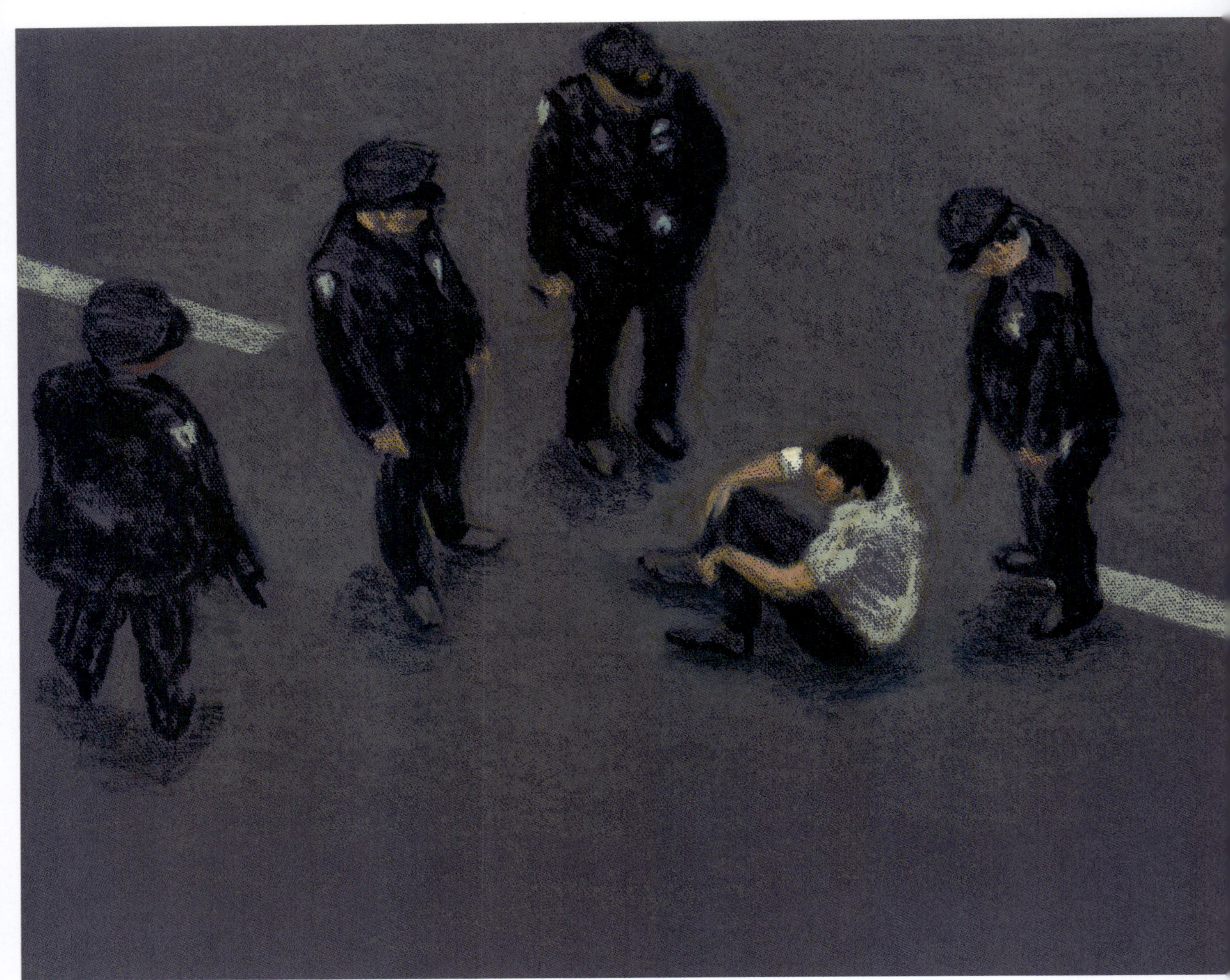

57   *Big Peepland*. Oil on linen, 70 x 44 in. 2016.

58   TOP: Study for *Woman with Crate*. Oil stick on paper, 12 x 18 in. 1984.
      BOTTOM: *Lotto Line*. Oil and Rolotex on canvas, 24 x 30 in. 1989.

59   *Cops & Perp & Headlights*. Oil stick on paper, 22 ¼ x 15 in. 1990.

60   *Sit Down Eighth Ave II*. Oil stick on blue paper, 23 x 30 in. 1990.

61   *Cops Man Down*. Oil stick on brown paper, 24 x 29 ½ in. 1990.

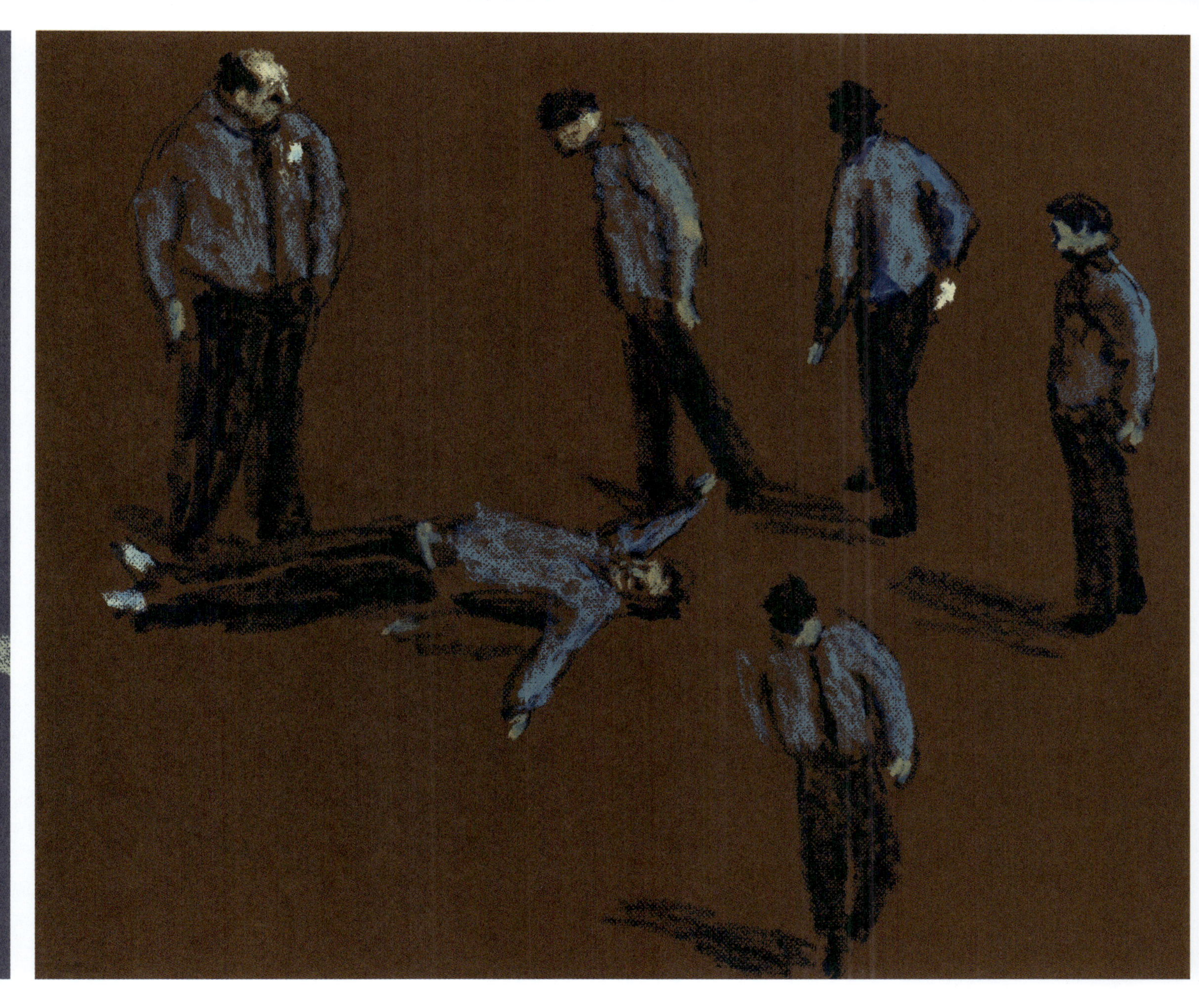

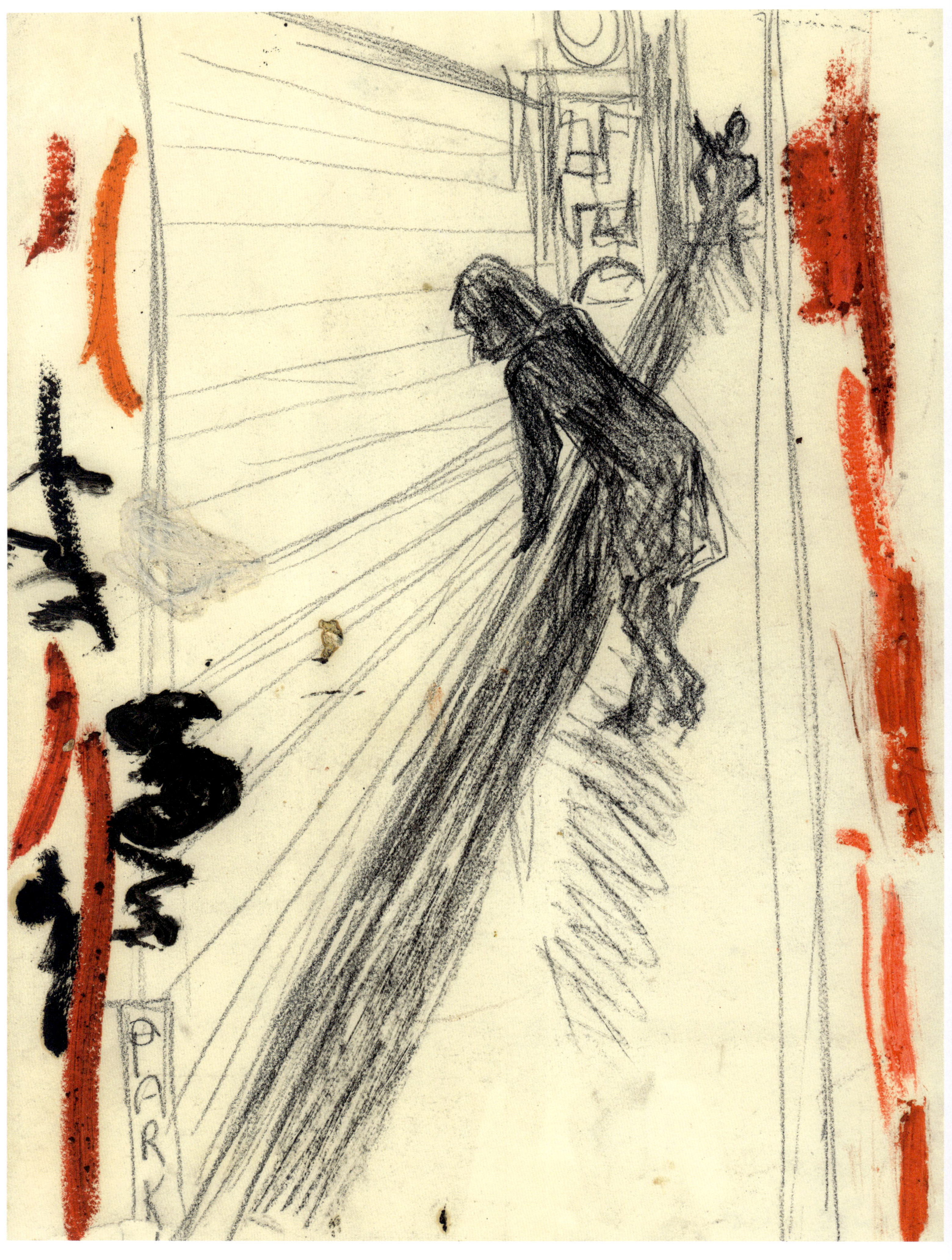

PARK

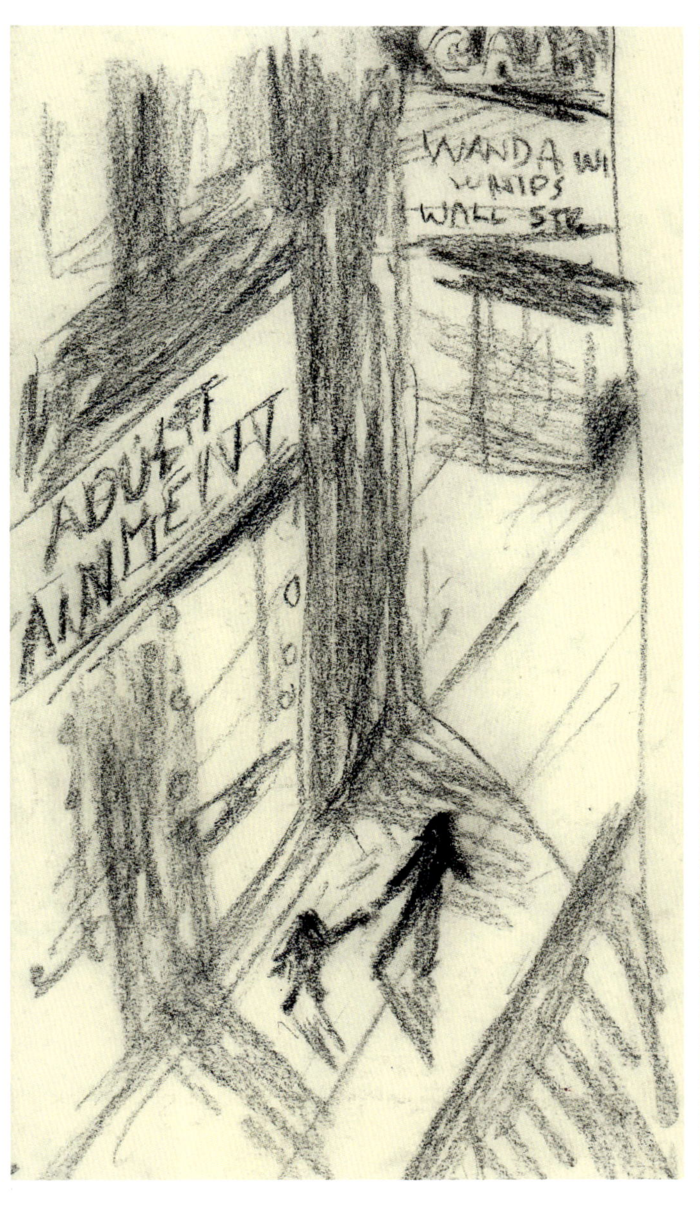
CAFE
WANDA WHIPS
WALL STR
ADULT
AINMENT

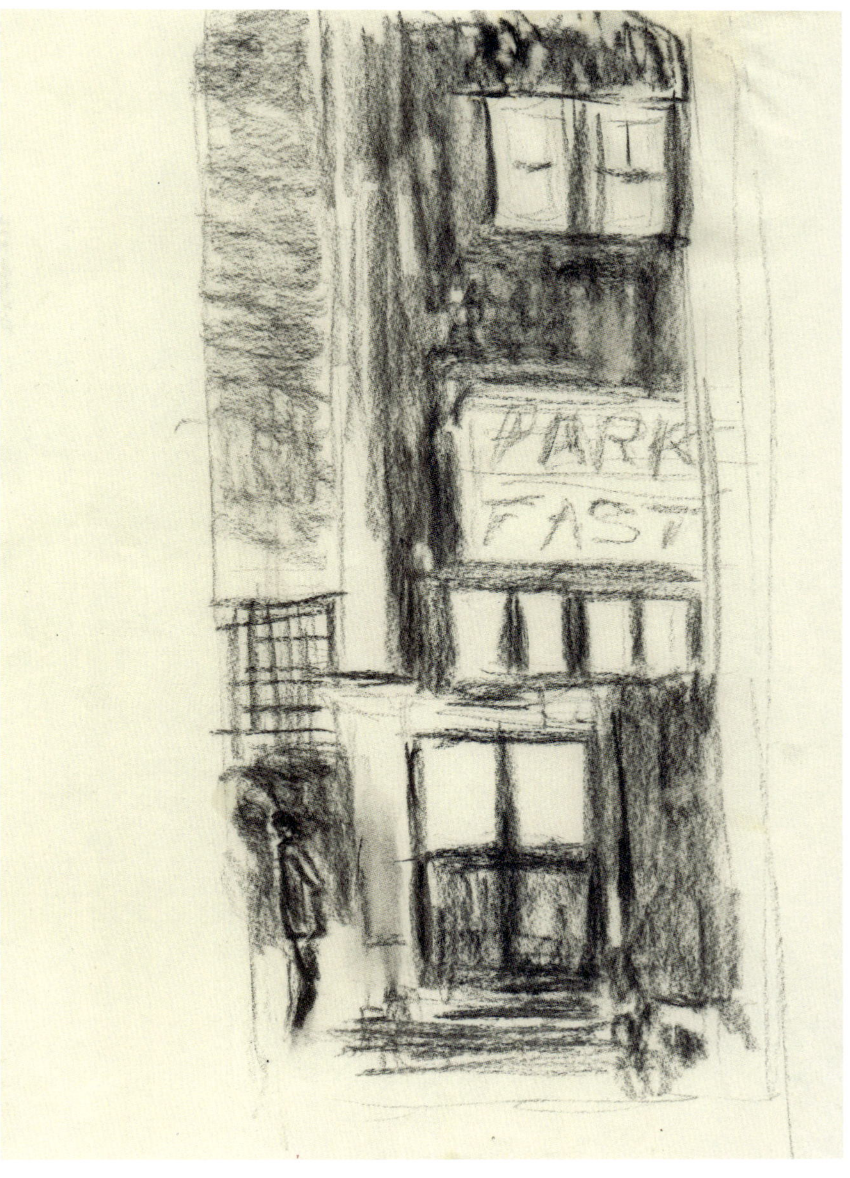
PARK
FAST

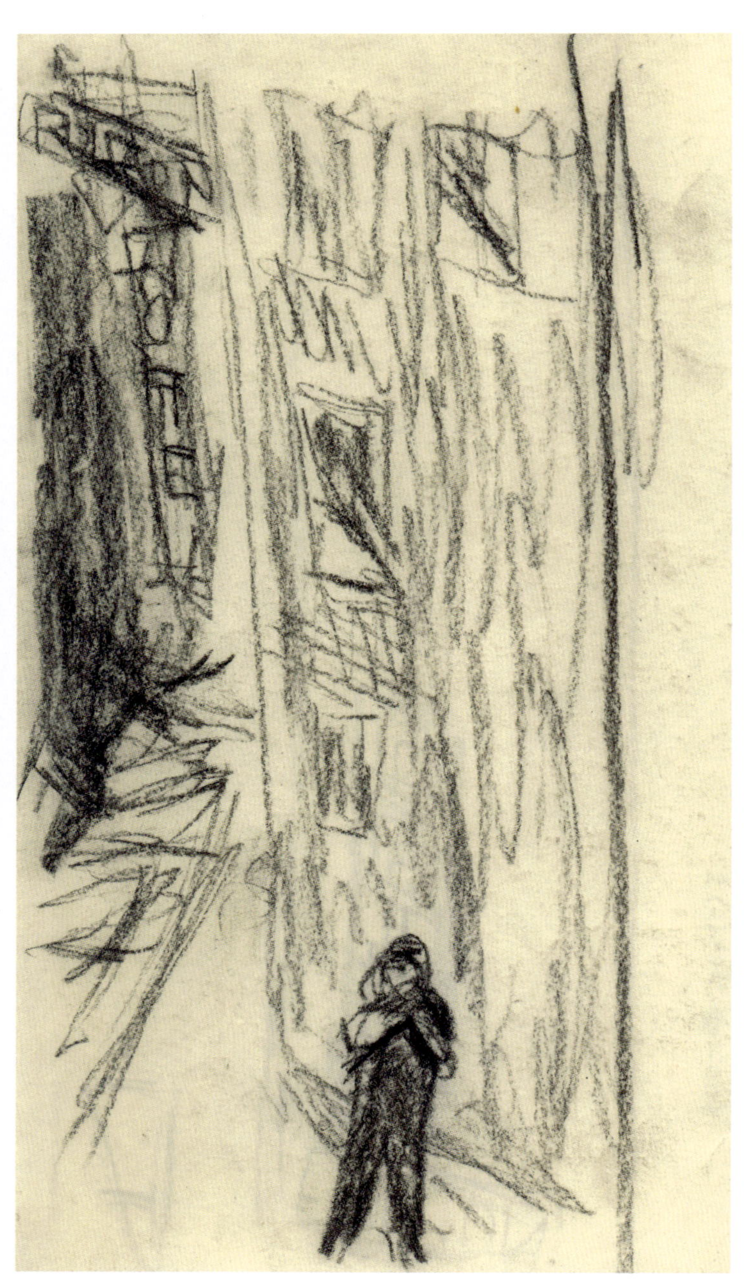
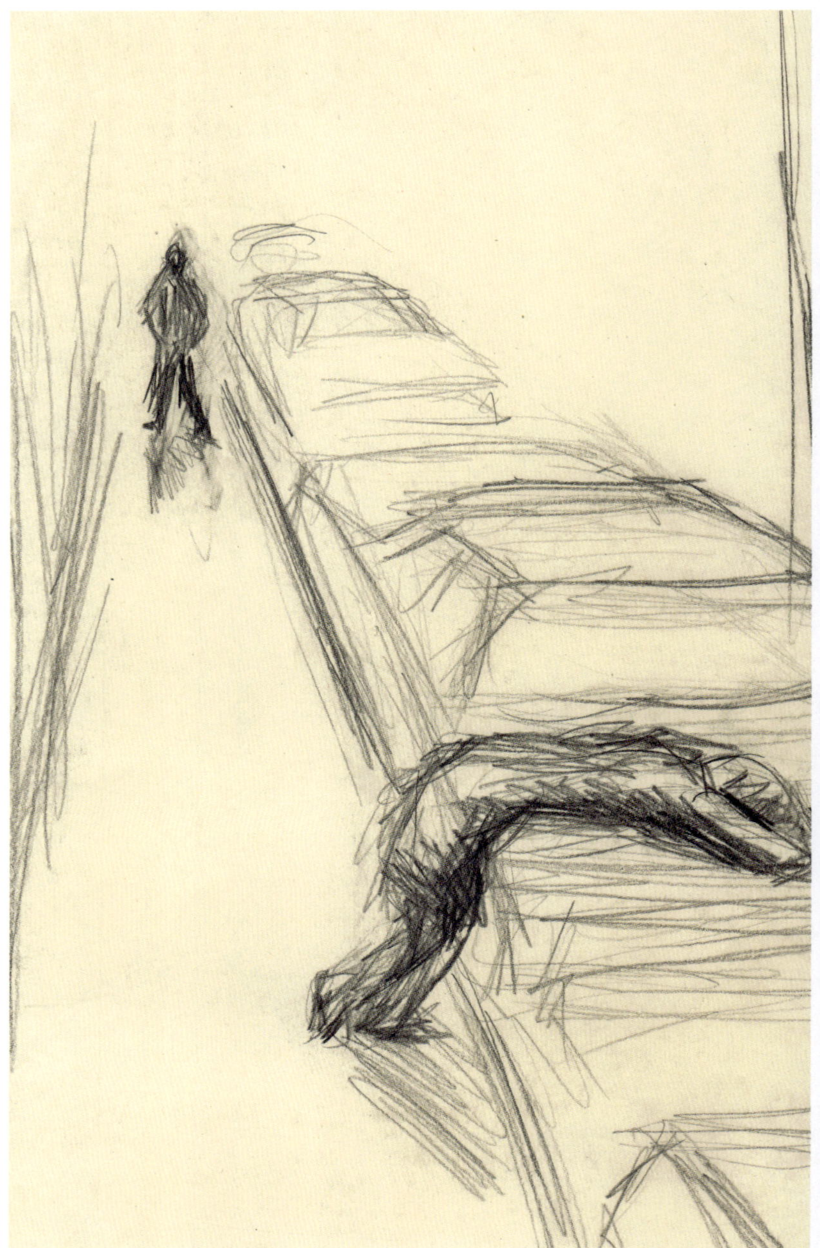

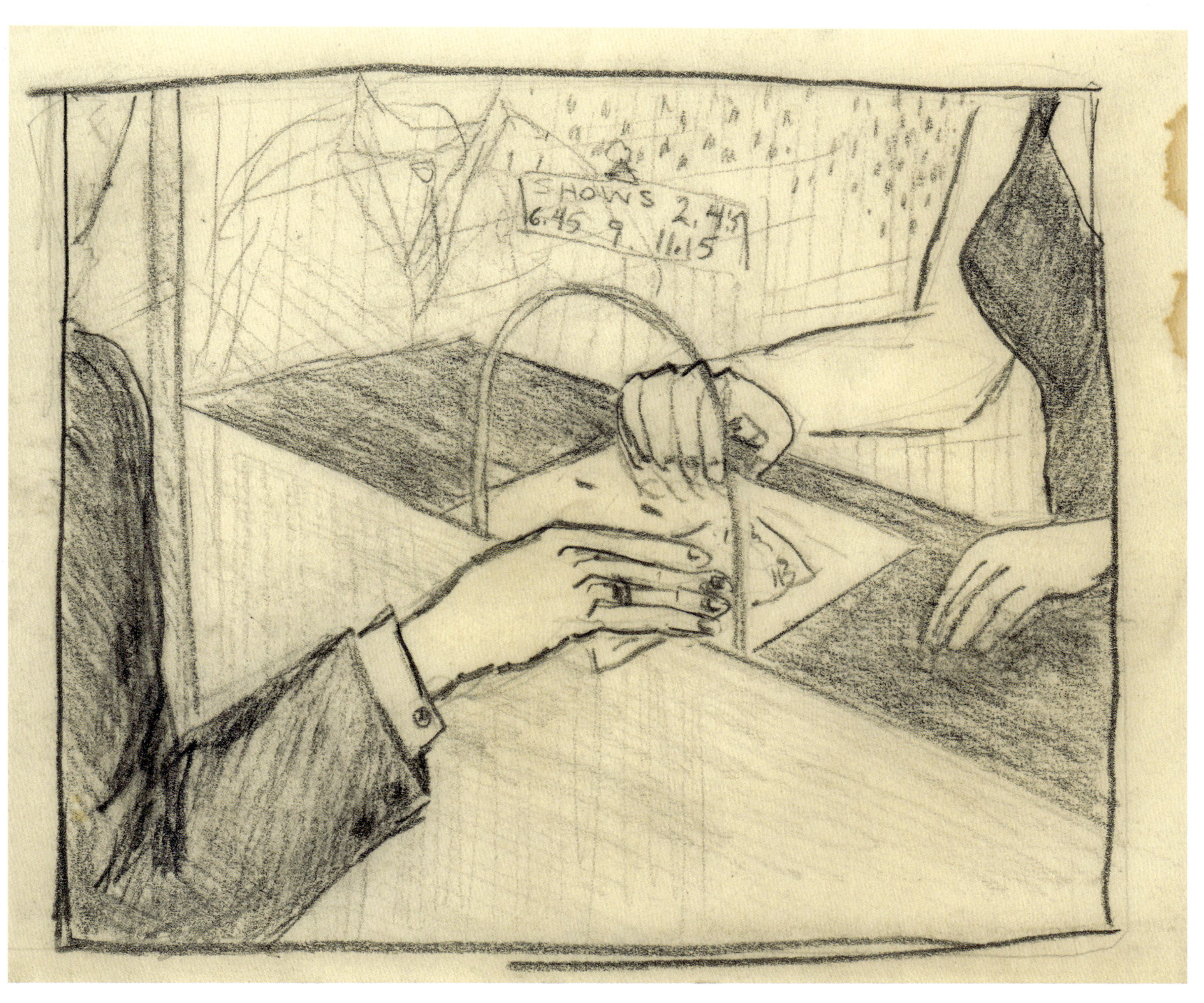

SHOWS 2, 4.5
6.45 9. 11.15

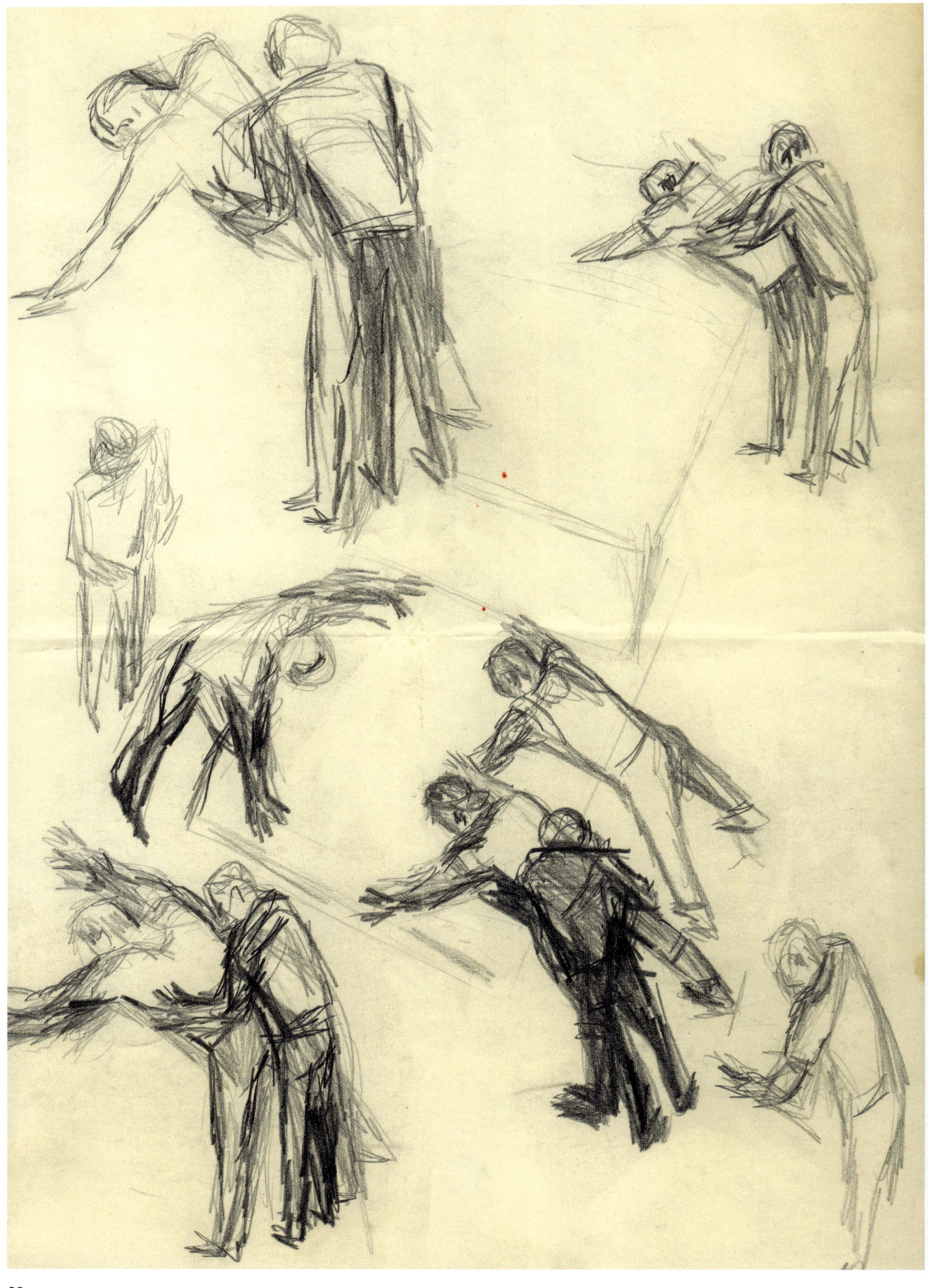

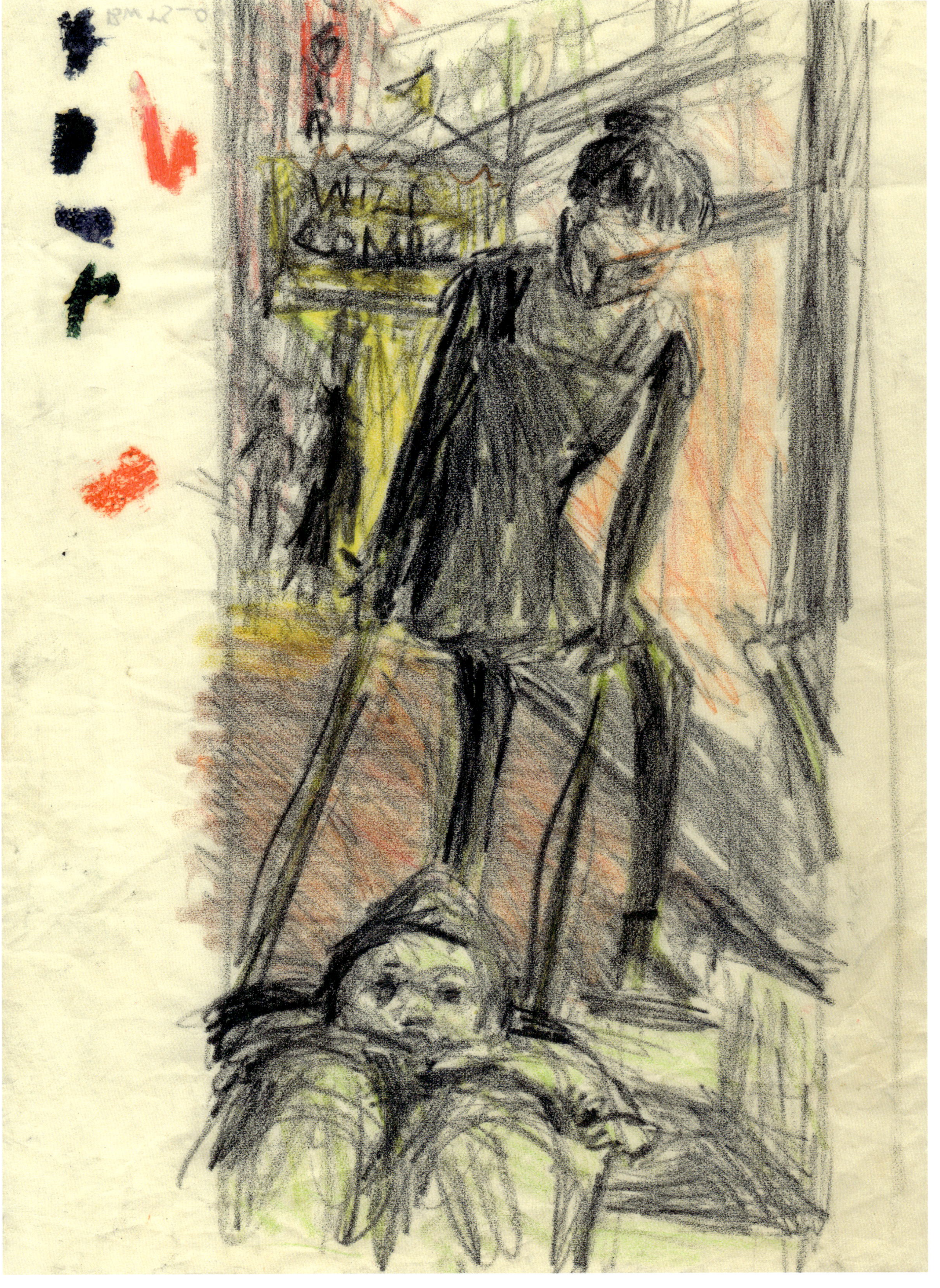
WEL
COME

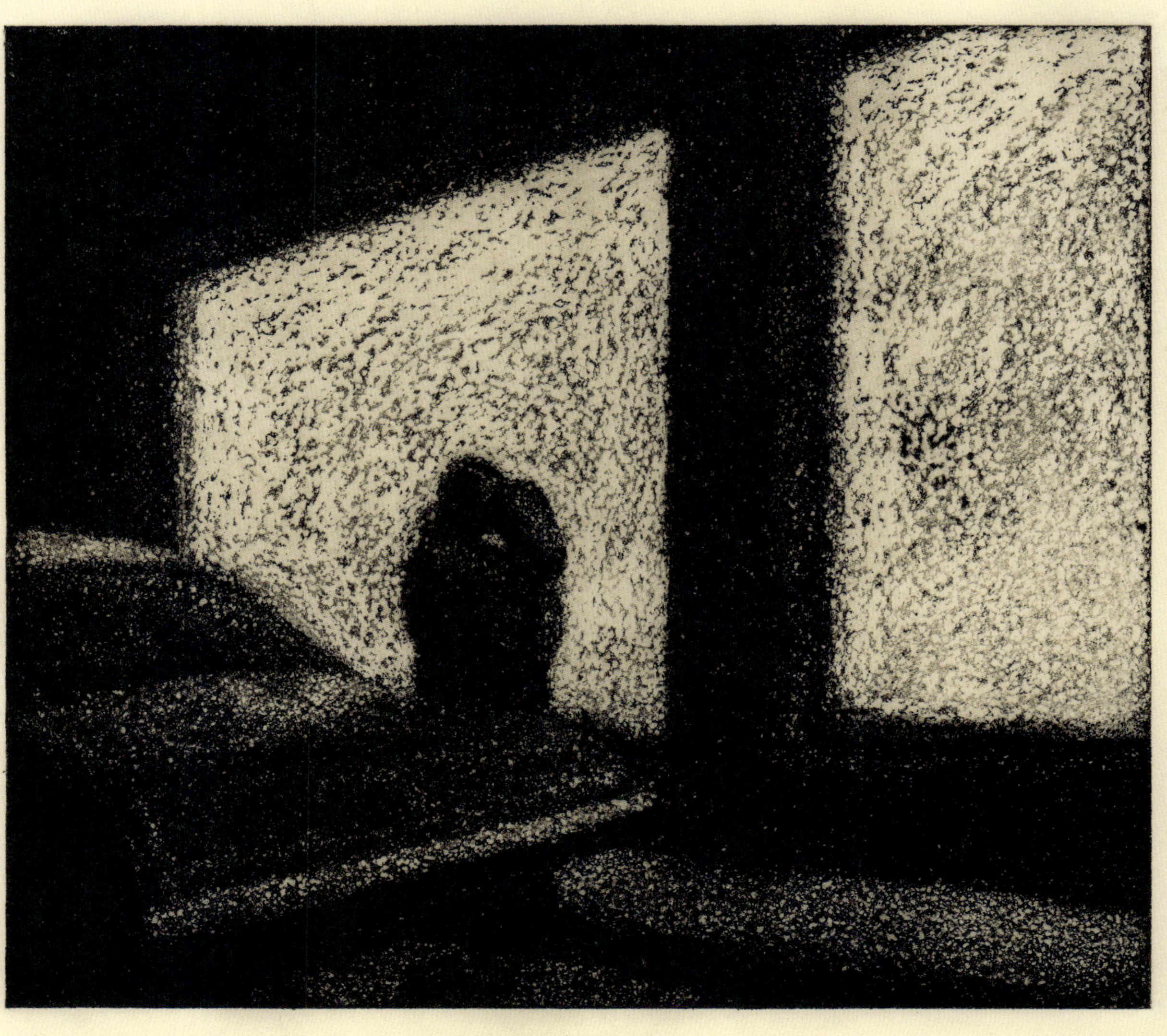

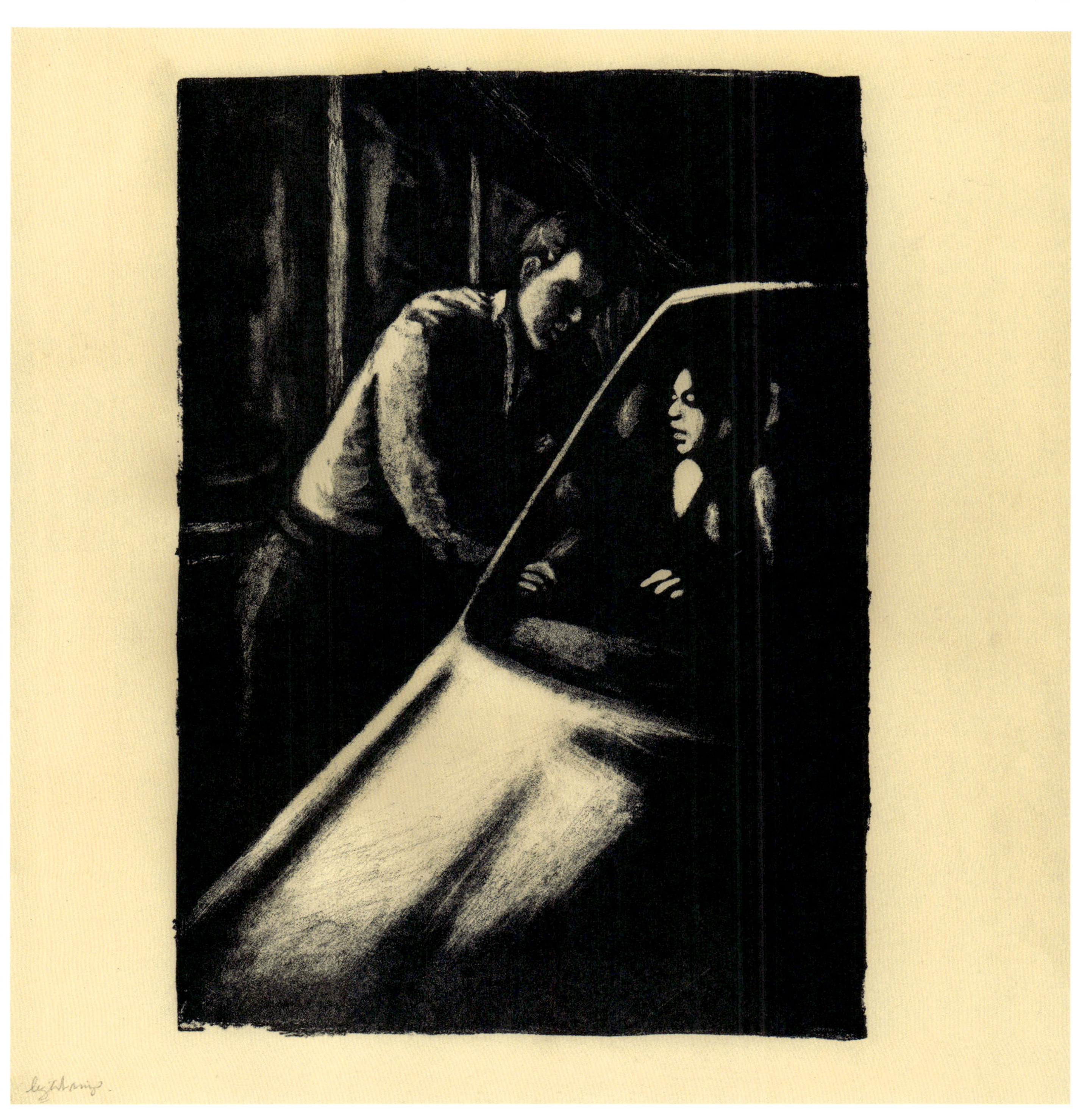

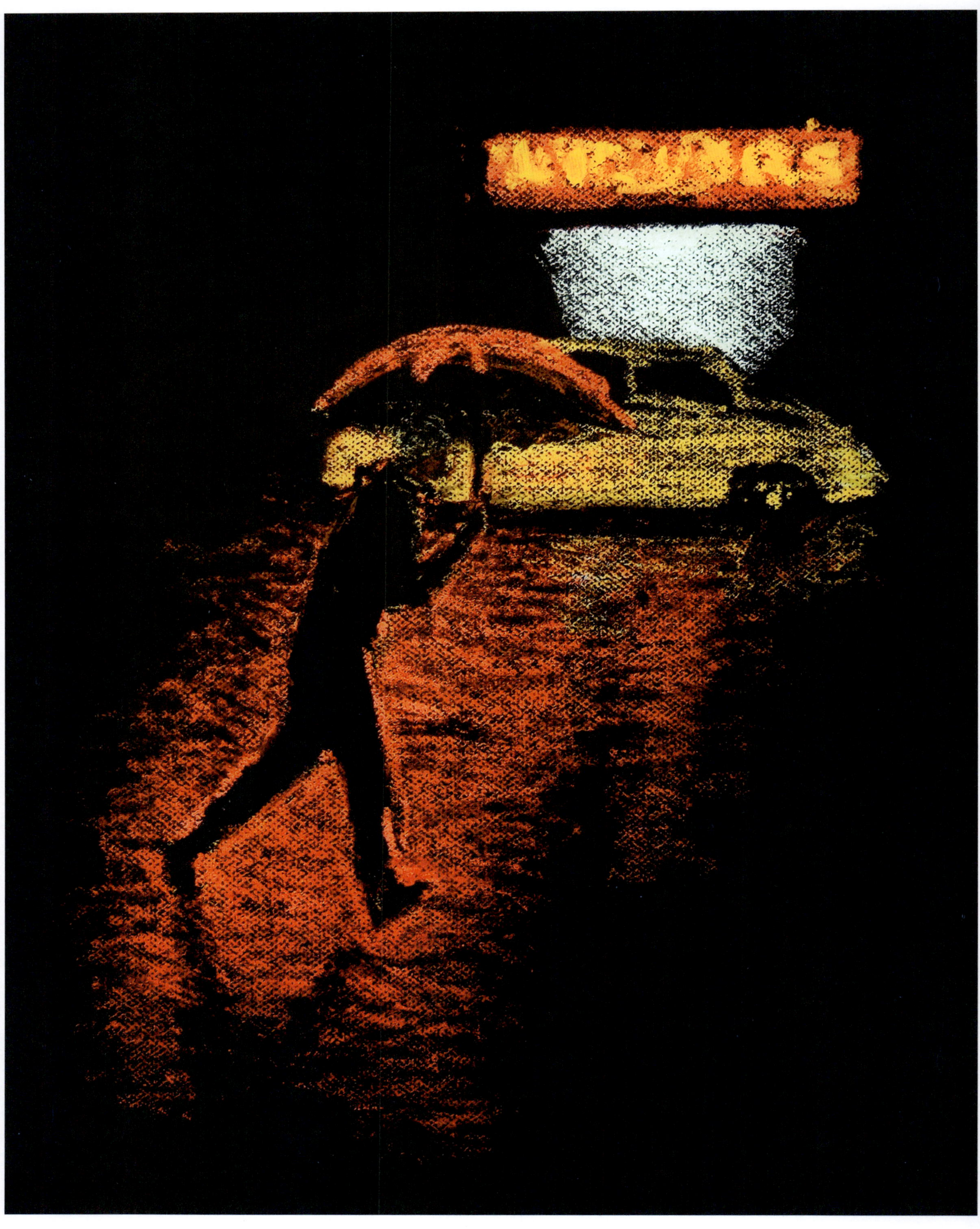

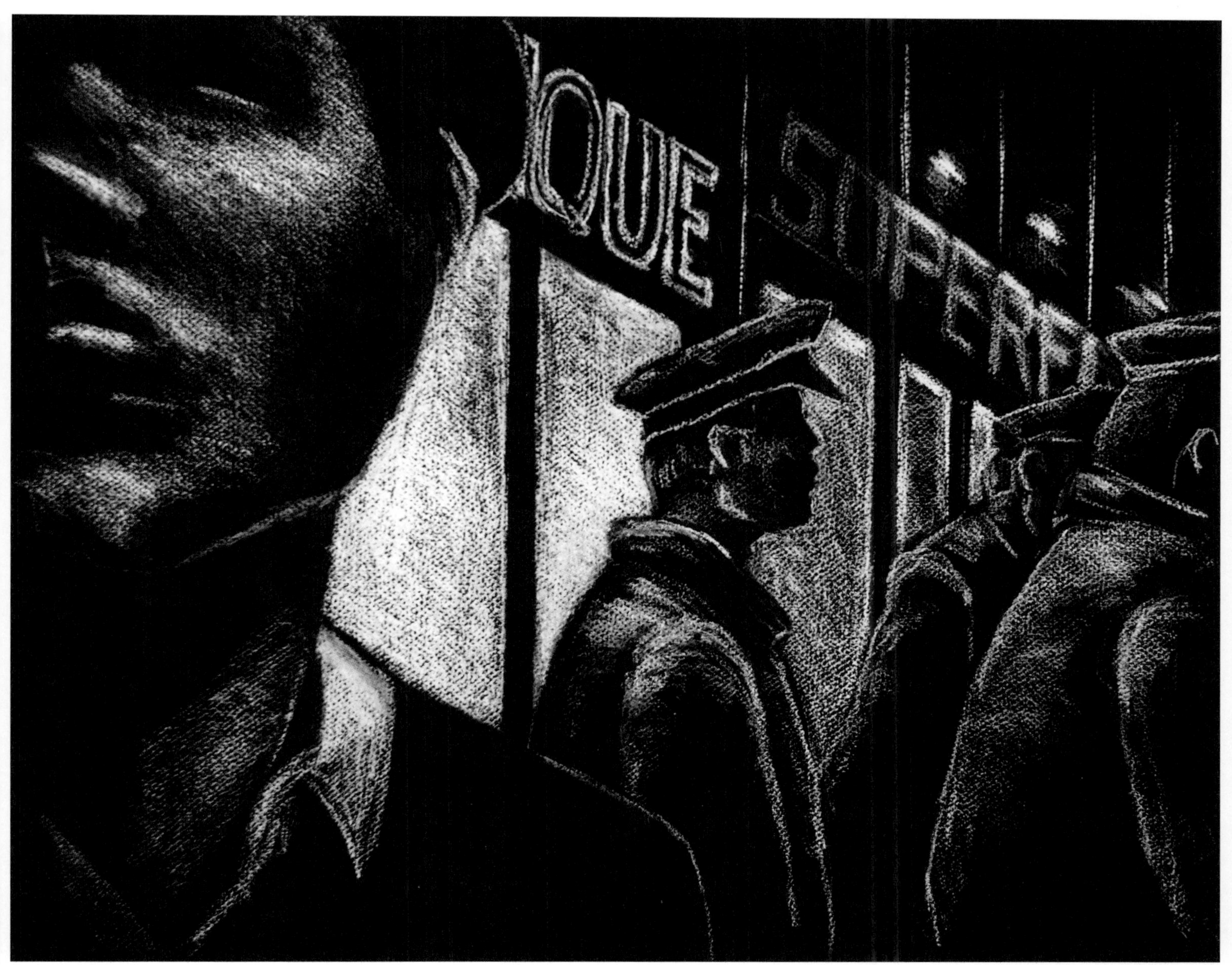

62   Study for *Hotel Girl*. Charcoal and oil stick on paper, 13 ½ x 10 ¼ in. 1982.
63   LEFT: Untitled. Charcoal on paper, 8 ½ x 5 in. 1981.
        RIGHT: Study for *Park Fast*. Charcoal on paper, 14 x 10 ¼ in. 1981.
64   LEFT: Untitled. Charcoal on paper, 8 ½ x 5 in. 1981.
        RIGHT: Untitled. Graphite on paper, 14 ½ x 9 ½ in.
65   Untitled. Graphite and charcoal on paper, 5 x 6 ½ in. 1979.
66   Studies for *Frisking*. Graphite and charcoal on paper, 14 x 10 in. 1982.
67   Study for *Mother & Child Subway Stairs*. Graphite, charcoal, and oil stick on paper, 12 x 9 ½ in. 1982.
68   *Kiss*. Aquatint etching, 15 x 18 in. 1984. Published by Maurice Payne, edition of 25.
69   *Pickup*. Lithograph, 16 x 16 in. 1991.
70   *Puddle Jumping 8th Ave*. Oil stick on black paper, 20 x 16 ½ in. 2004.
71   Untitled. Chalk on black paper, 15 x 19 ¼ in. 1979.

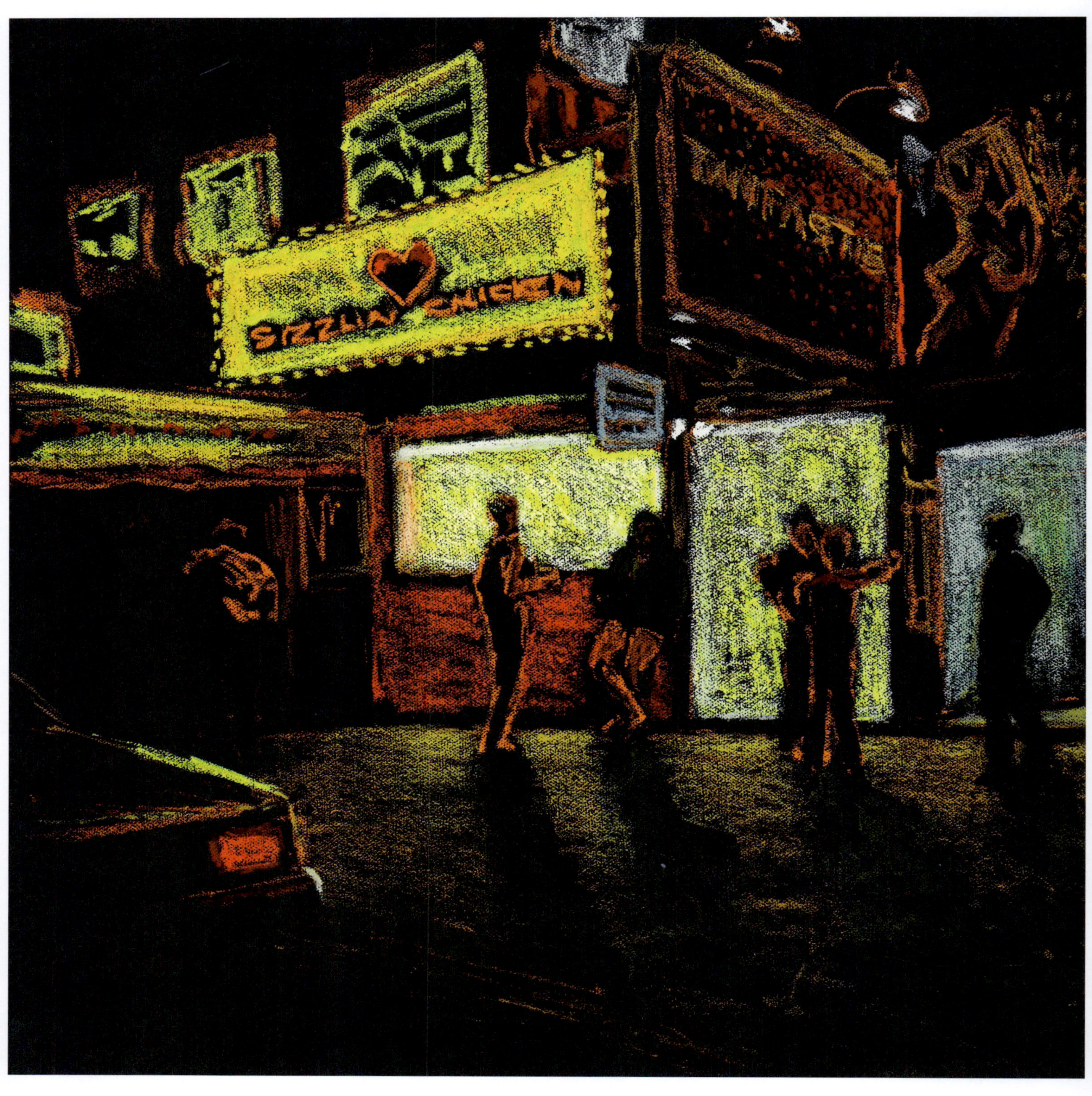

SIZZLIN' CHICKEN

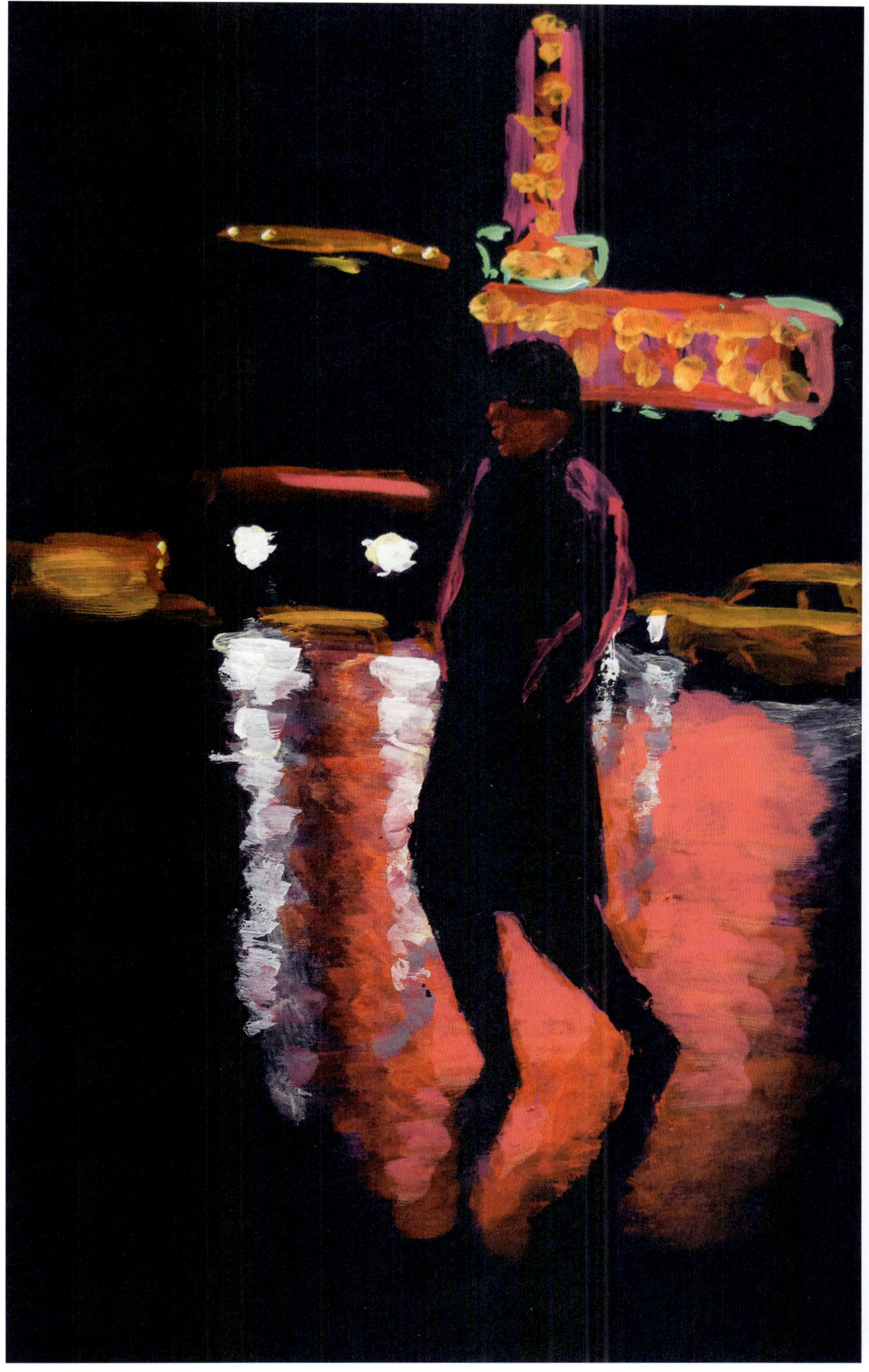

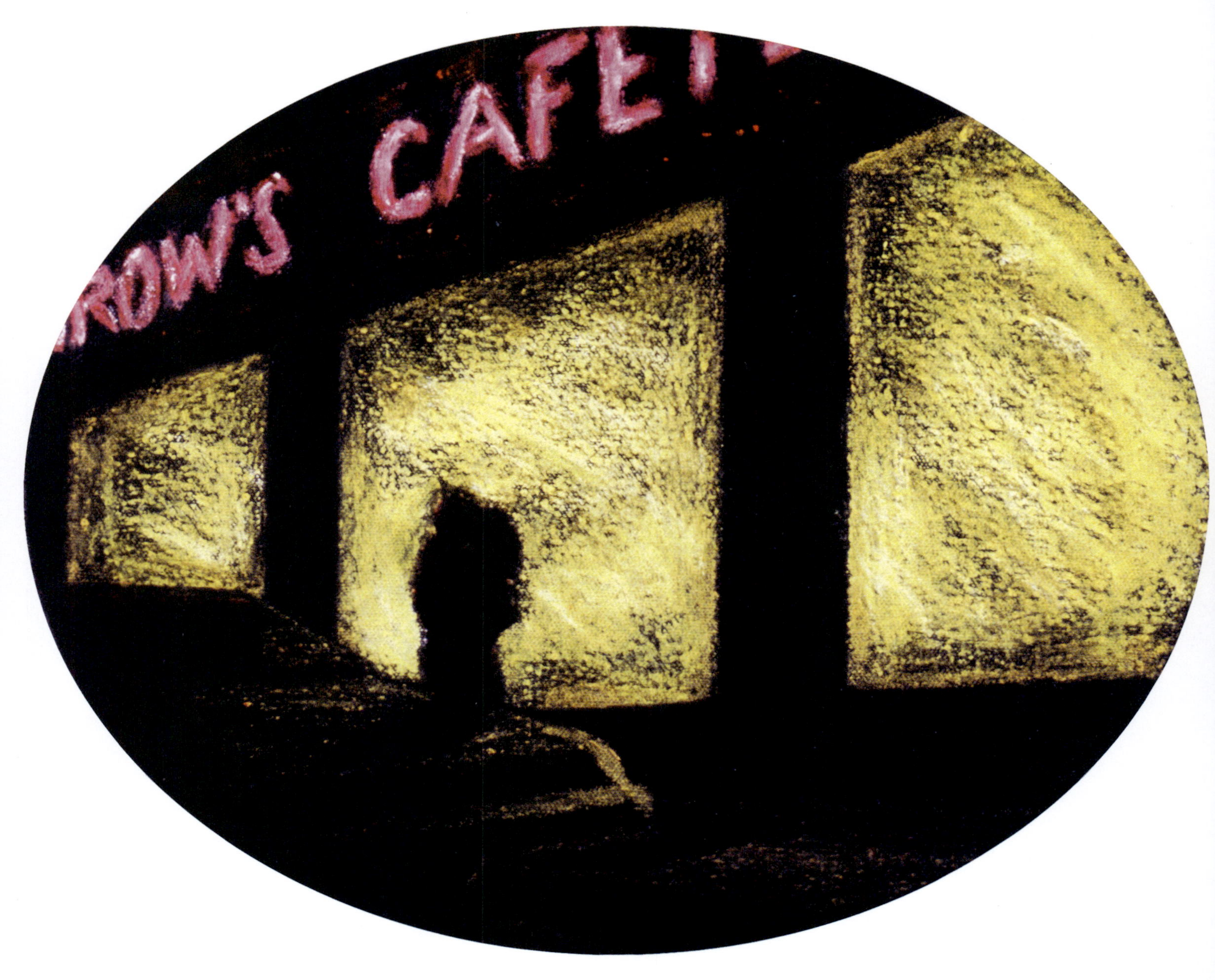

72   *Sizzlin Chicken*. Oil stick on black paper, 21 x 27 in. 1984.
73   *Rainy Neon Bus*. Acrylic on black plastic, 22 x 14 in. 2014.
74   *Dubrow's*. Oil on canvas, 11 x 17 in. 1983.
75   *Motor Hotel*. Oil stick on canvas, 42 x 18 in. 1983.

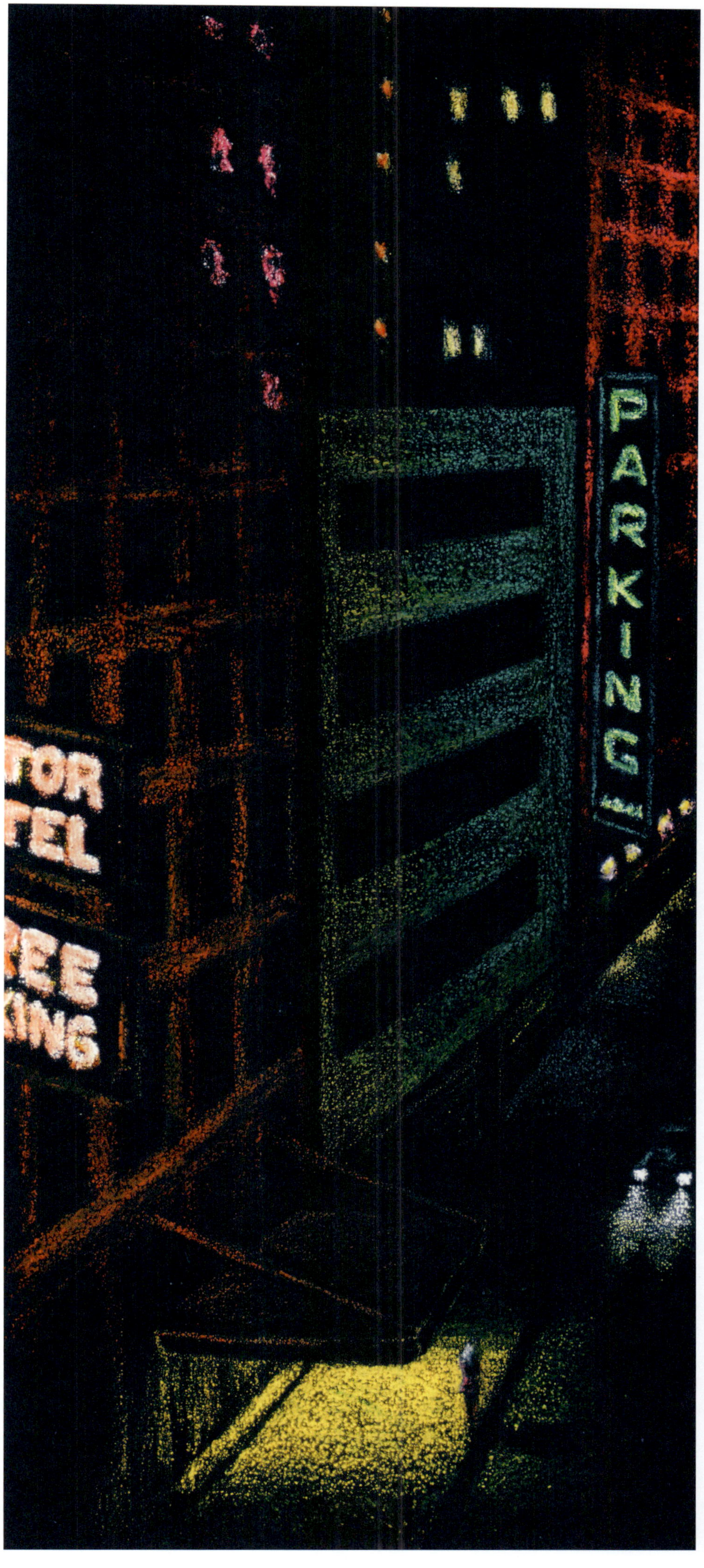

PARKING
TOR
TEL
EE
KING

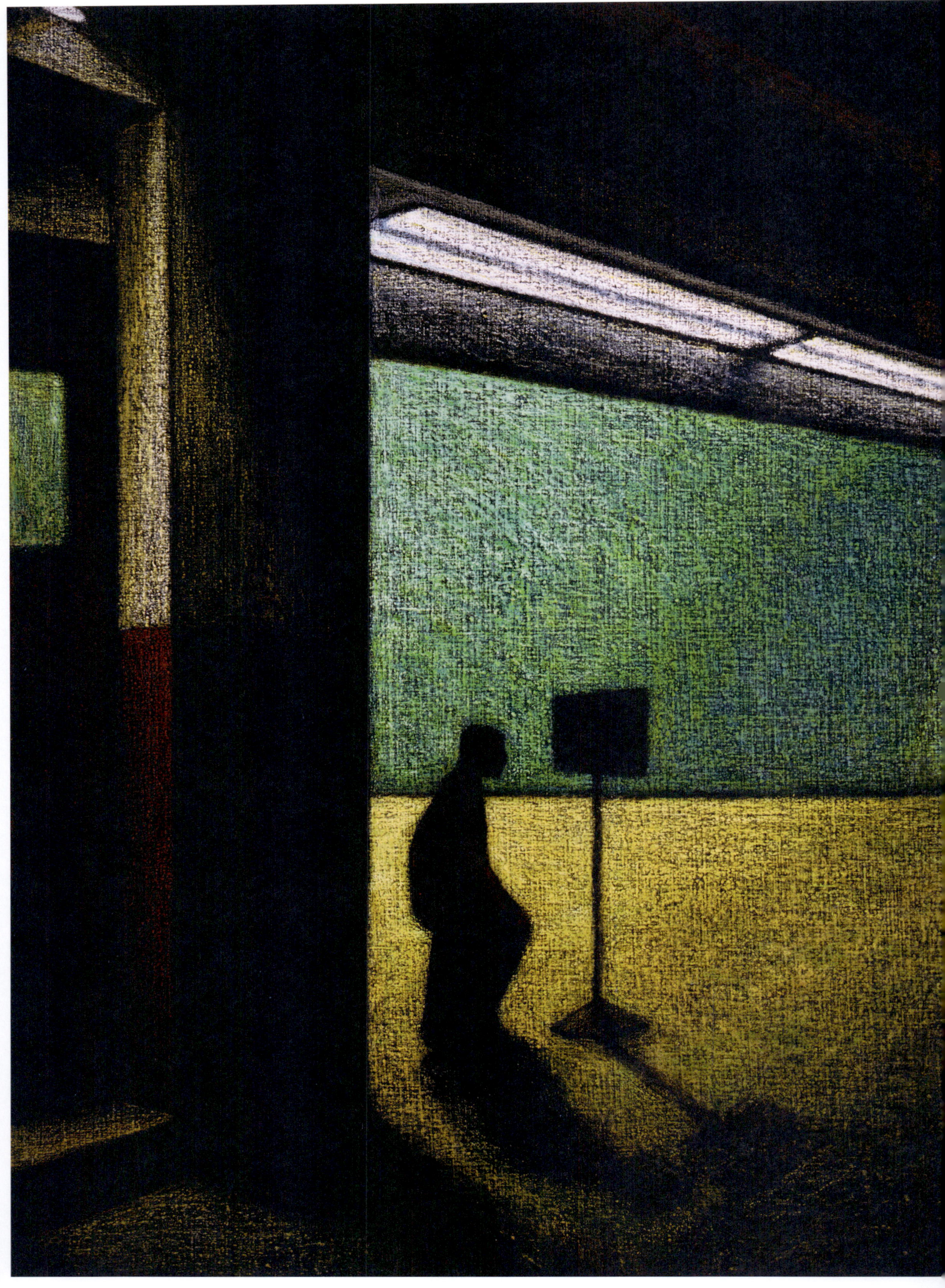

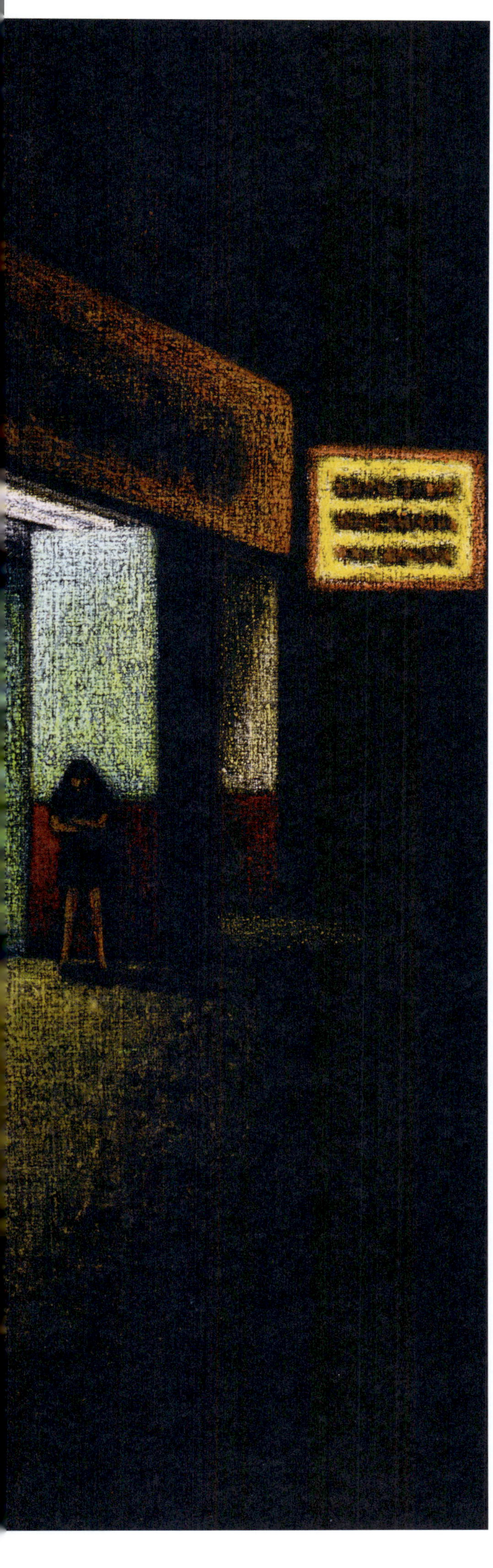

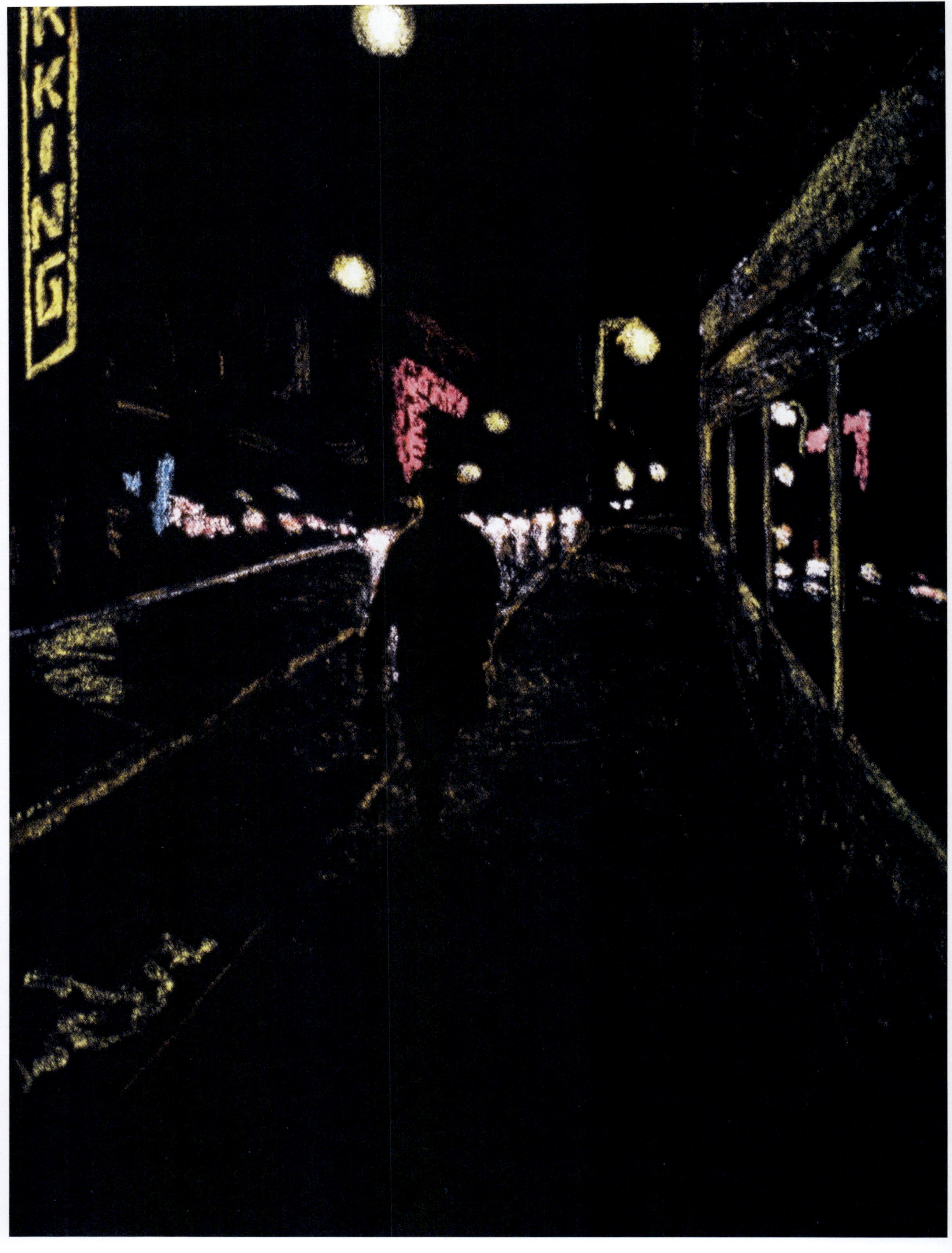
KING

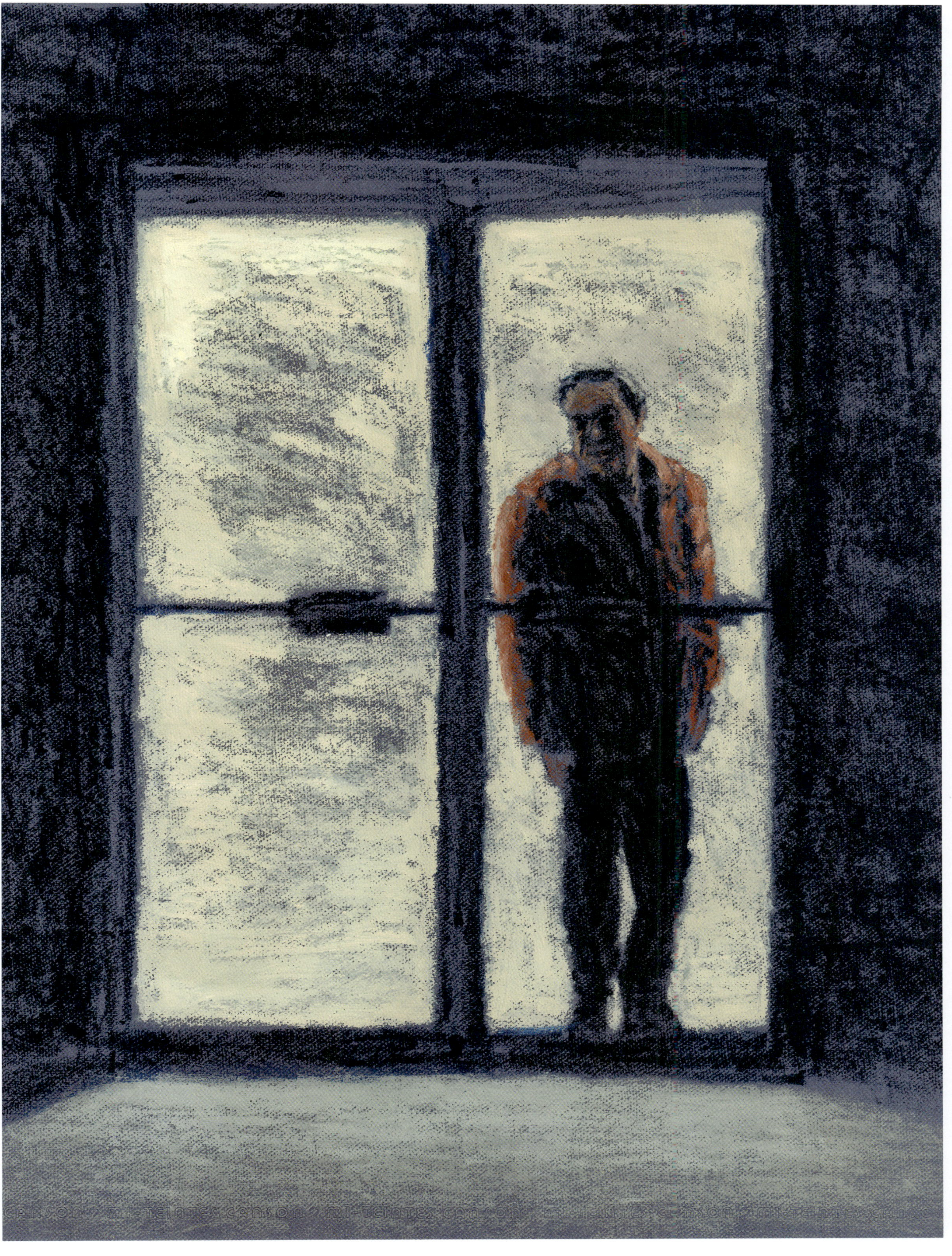

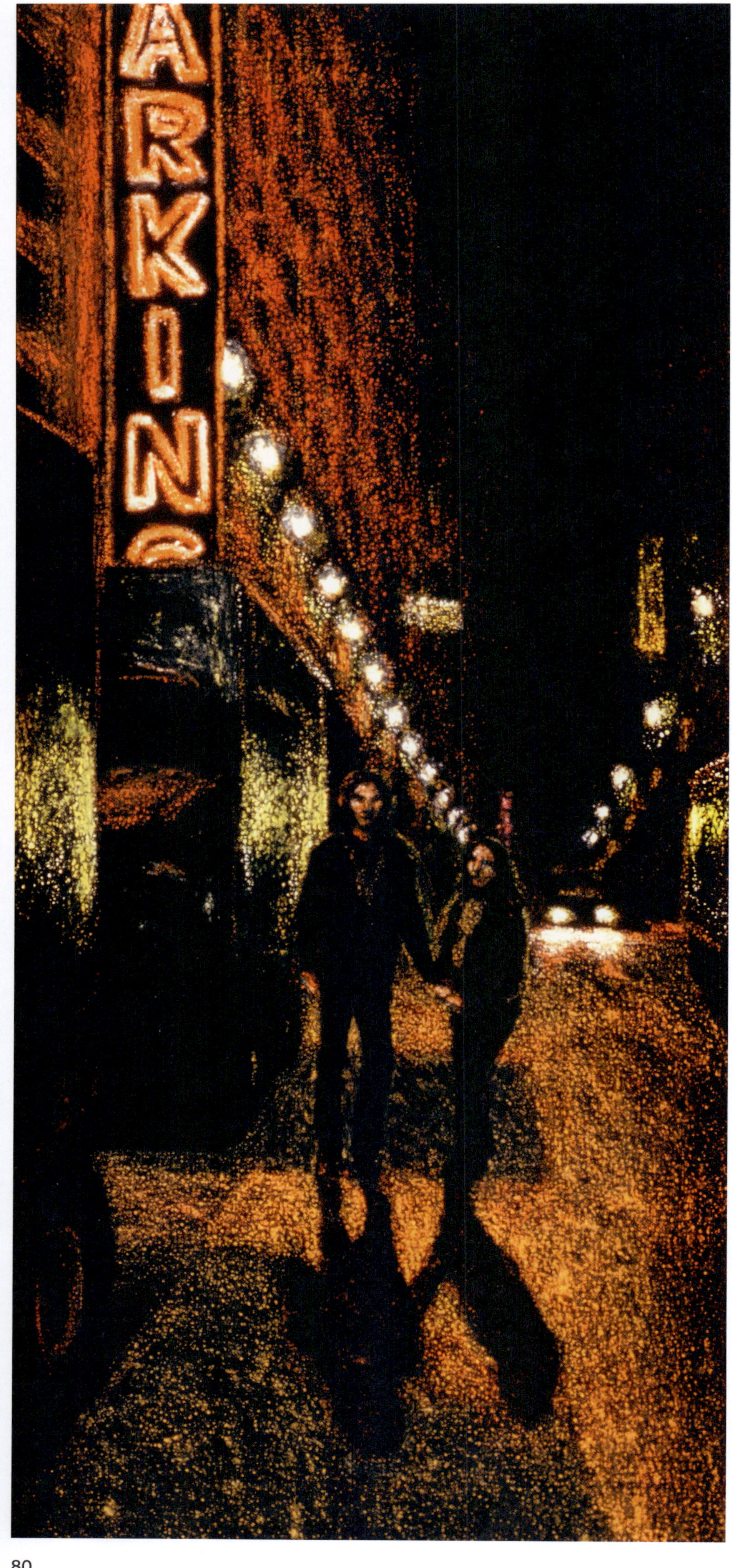
ARKING

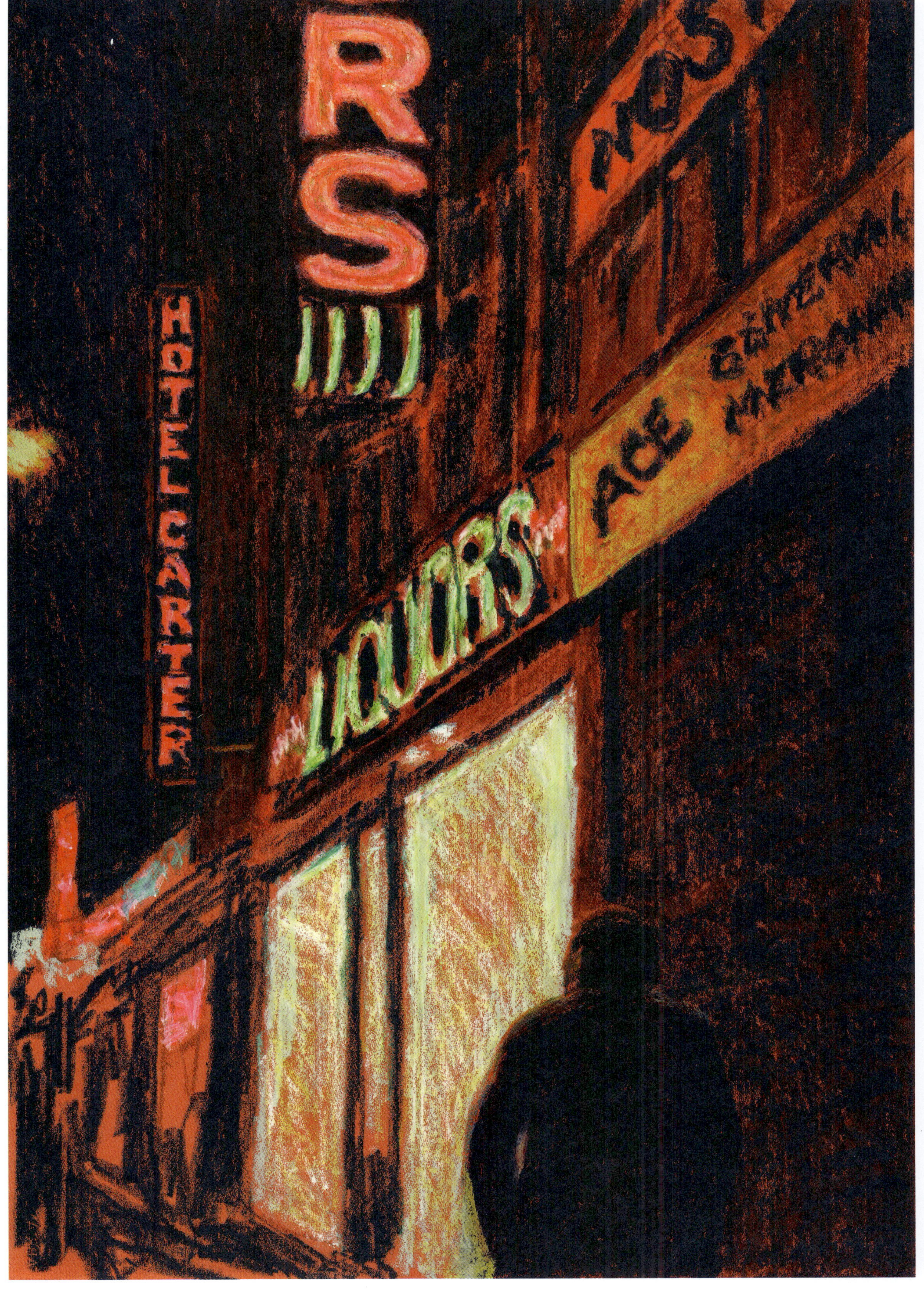
RS
HOTEL CARTER
LIQUORS
ACE
GENERAL
MERCHANDISE

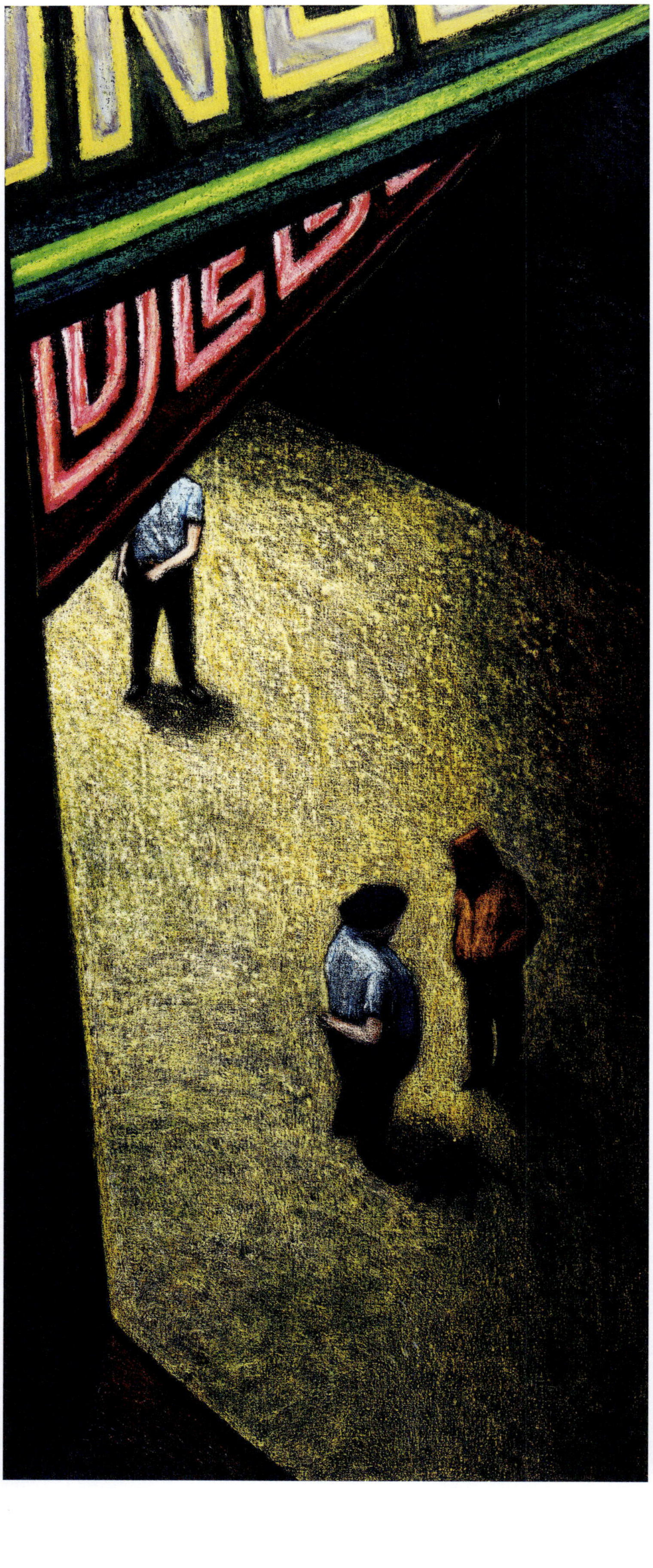

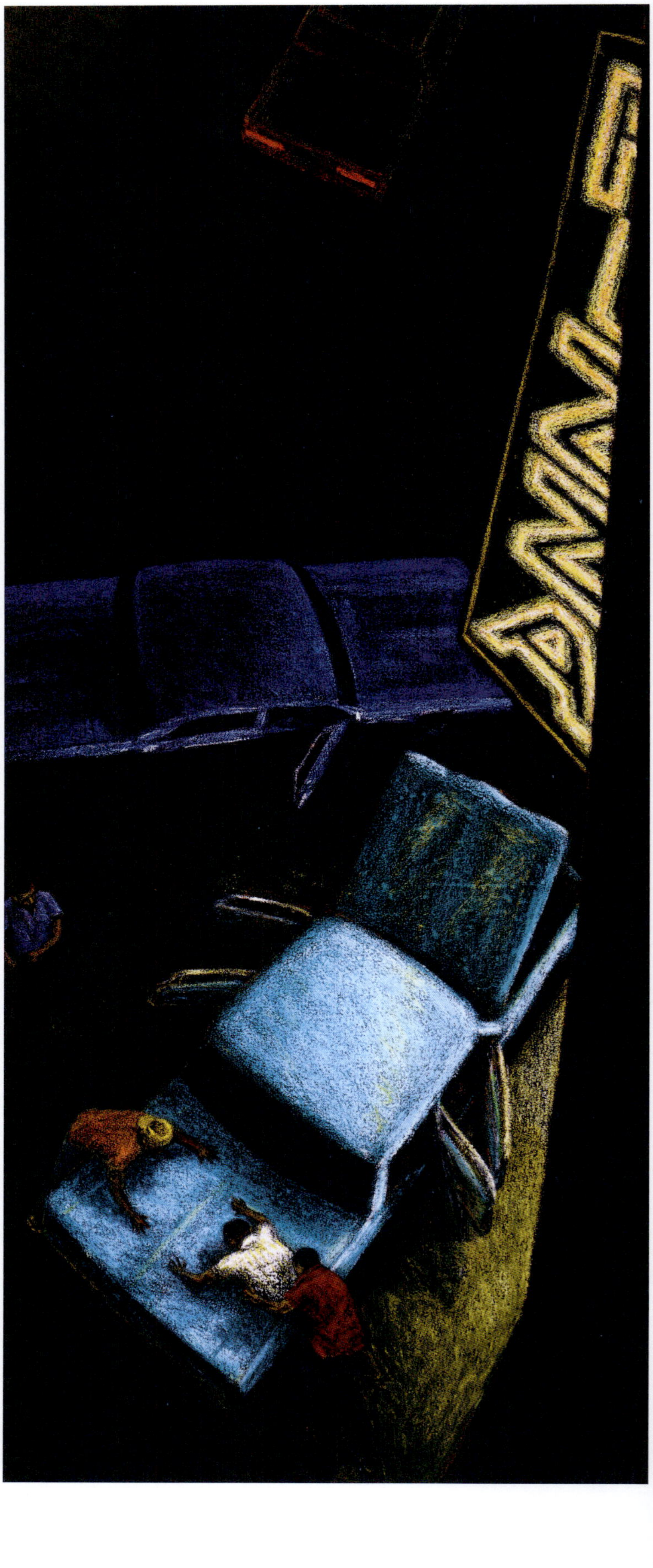

DINER
DISC
ANAL

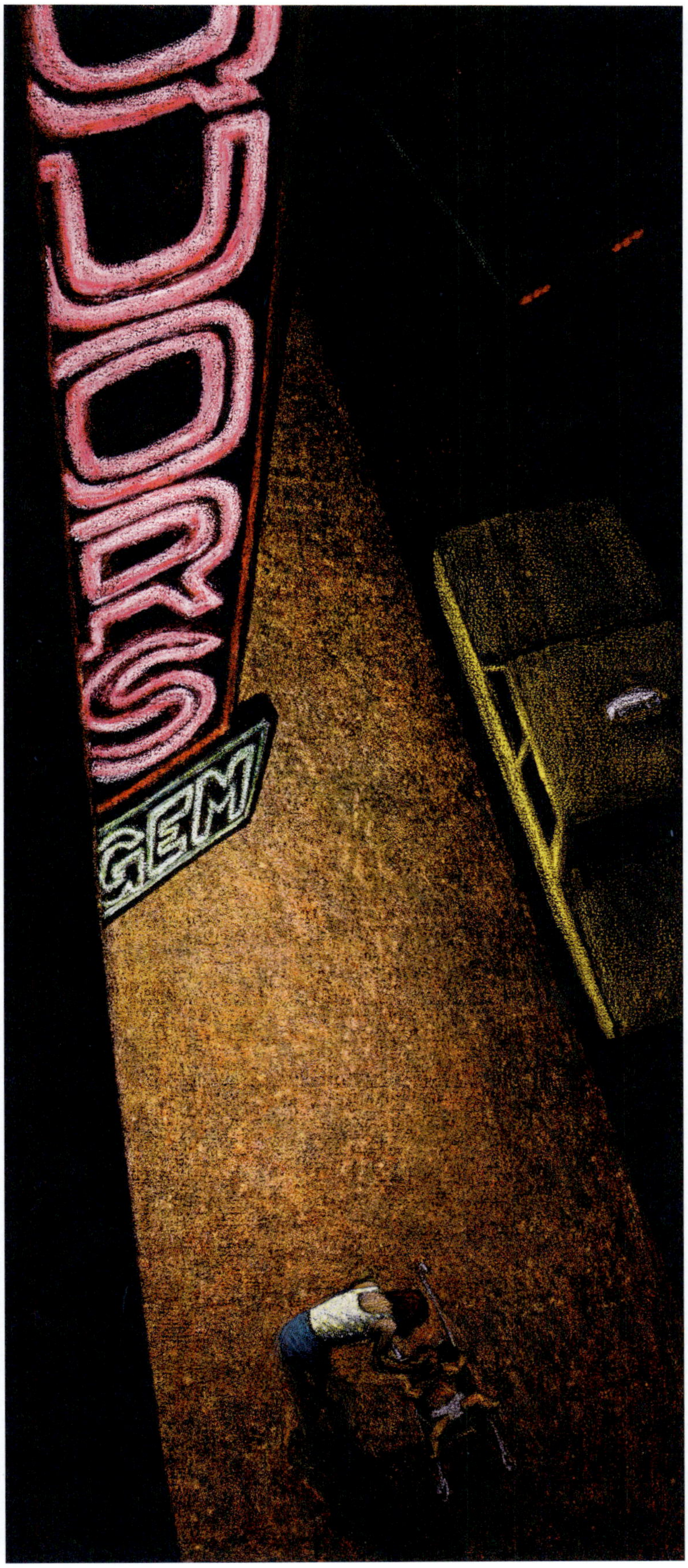

LIQUORS
GEM

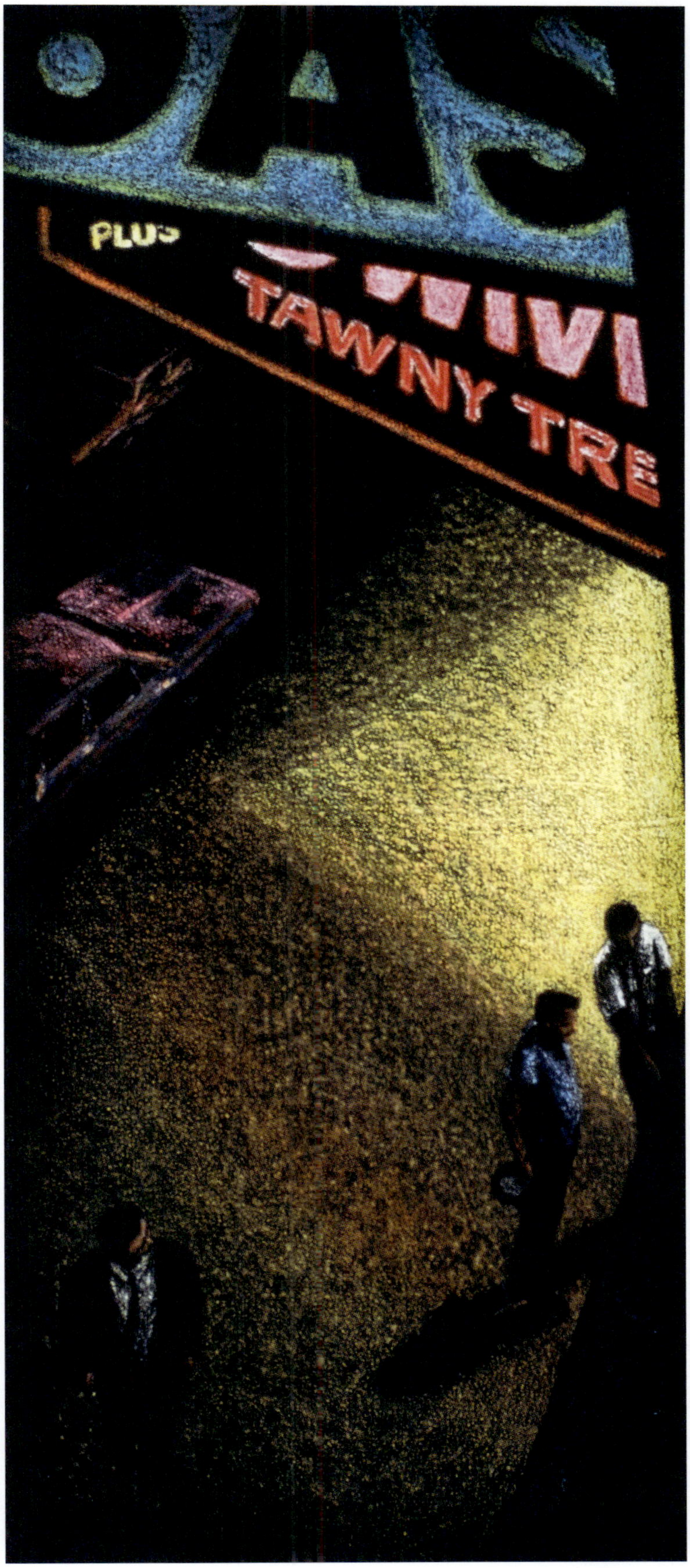

BAS
PLUS
VIVI
TAWNY TRE

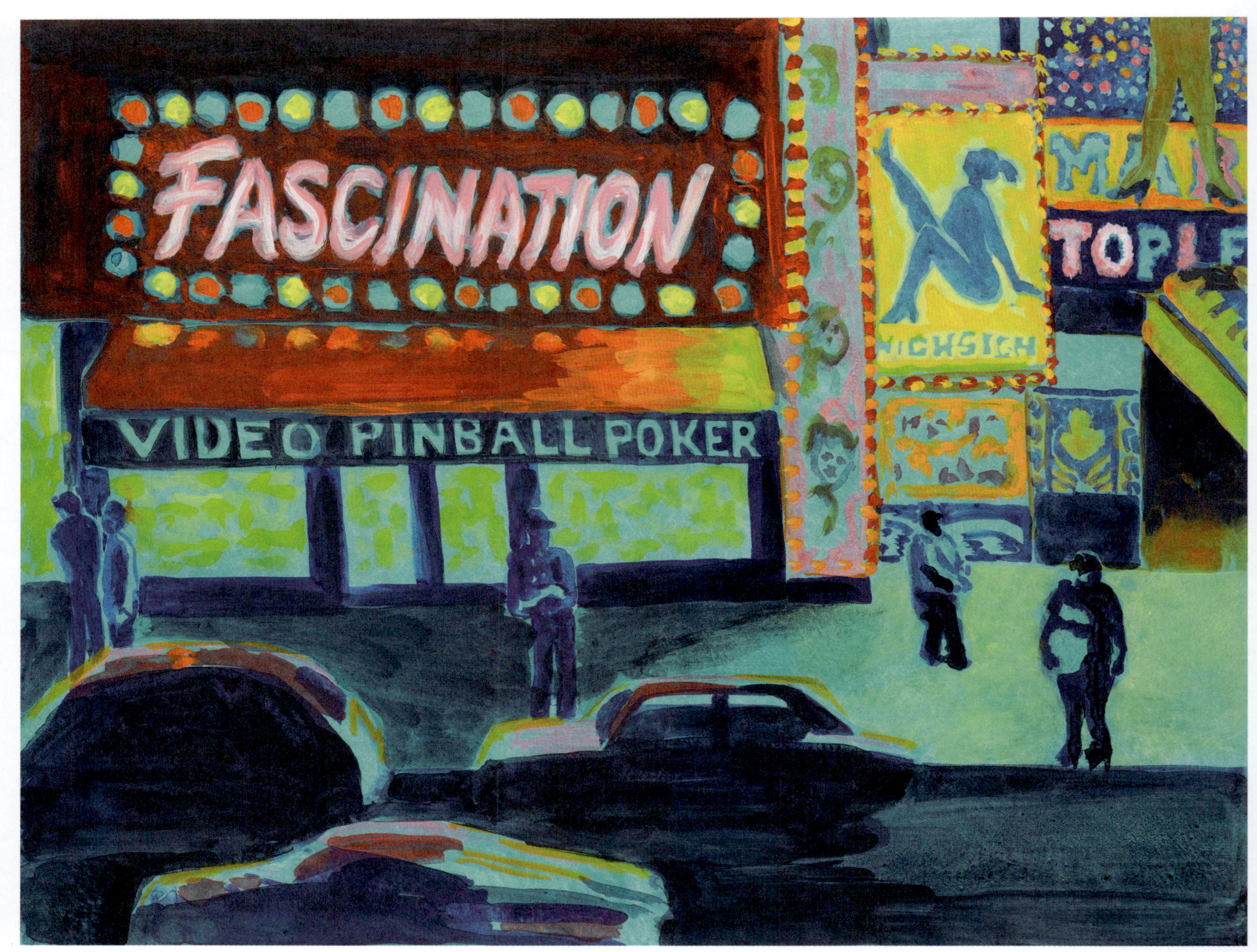

76   *Green Garage*. Oil stick on canvas, 66 x 74 in. 1983.
78   *Alone on the Street*. Oil stick on black paper, 30 x 20 in. 1984.
79   *Peepland Looking In*. Oil stick on blue paper, 28 ½ x 23 in. 1993.
80   *Runaways*. Oil stick on canvas, 42 x 19 in. 1983.
81   *Hotel Carter*. Oil stick on red paper, 39 ½ x 27 ½ in. 2016.
82   LEFT: *1600 Broadway*. Oil stick on canvas, 90 x 40 in. 1983.
      RIGHT: *Frisking*. Oil stick on canvas, 90 x 40 in. 1983.
83   LEFT: *Liquors*. Oil stick on canvas, 90 x 40 in. 1984.
      RIGHT: *Oasis Tawny Treat*. Oil stick on canvas, 90 x 40 in. 1983.
84   *Fascination 2*. Gouache on Tyvek, 18 x 24 in. 2017.
85   Study for *Hotel Girl*. Oil stick on blue paper, 25 x 15 ½ in. 2006.

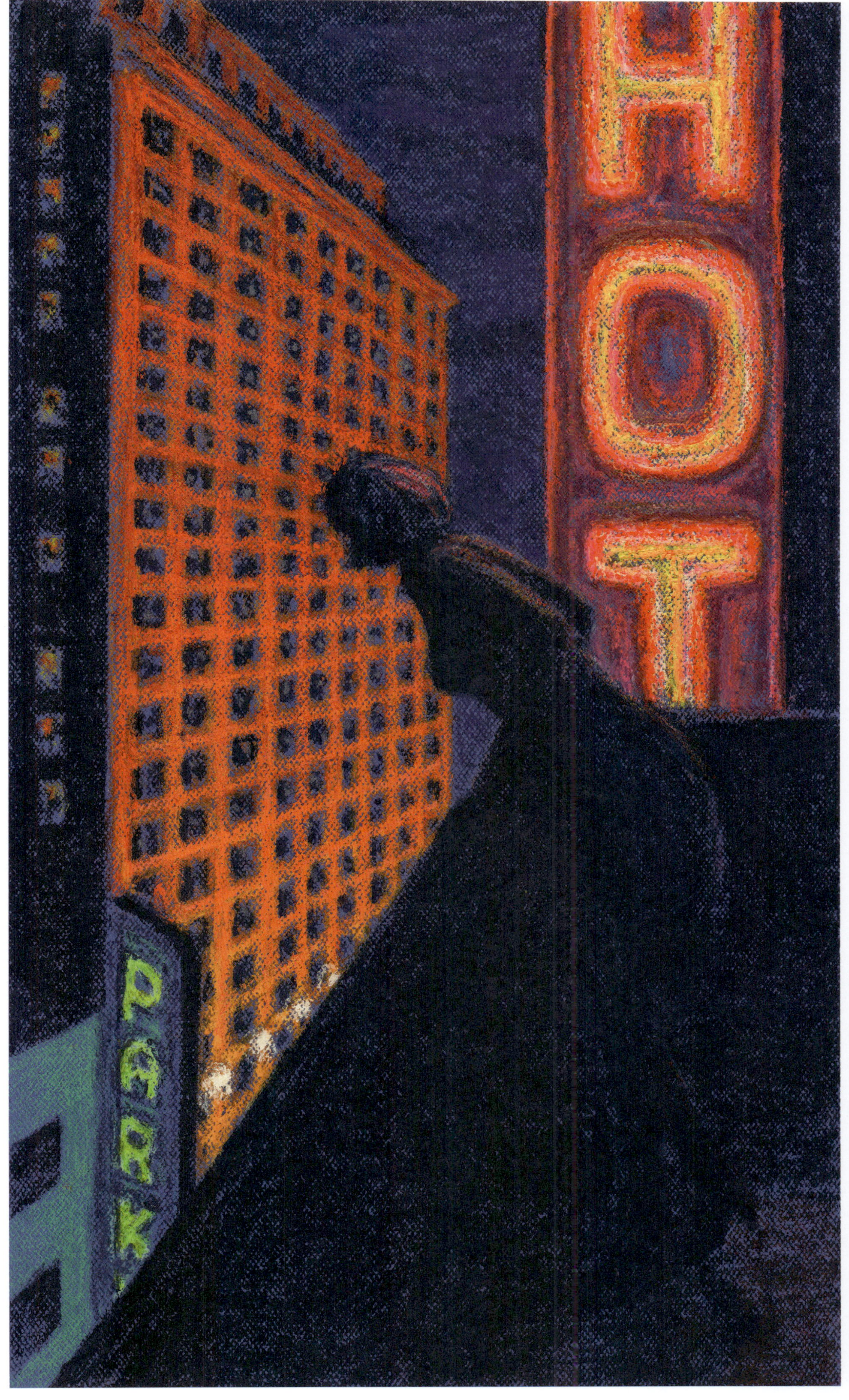
HOT
PARK

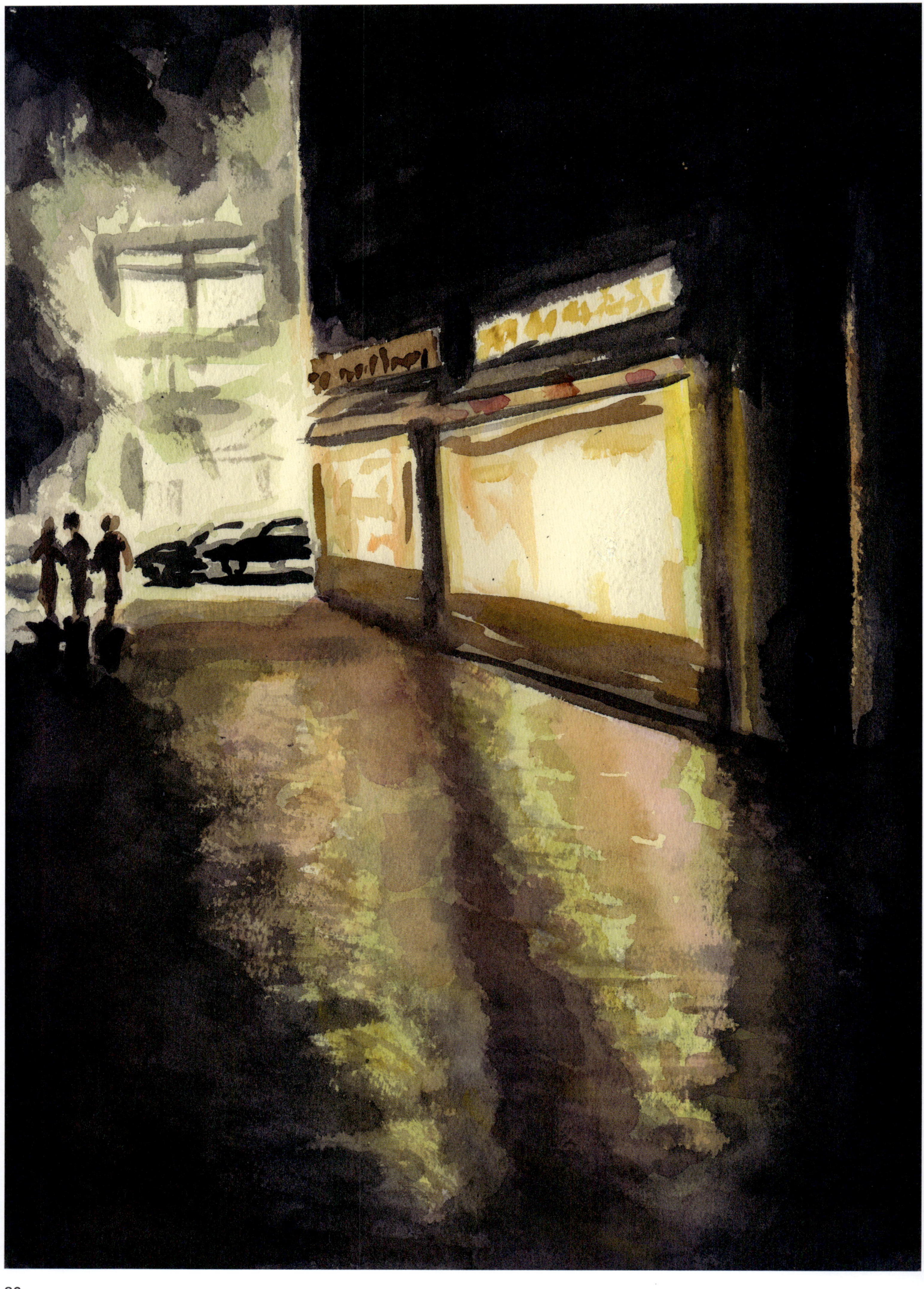

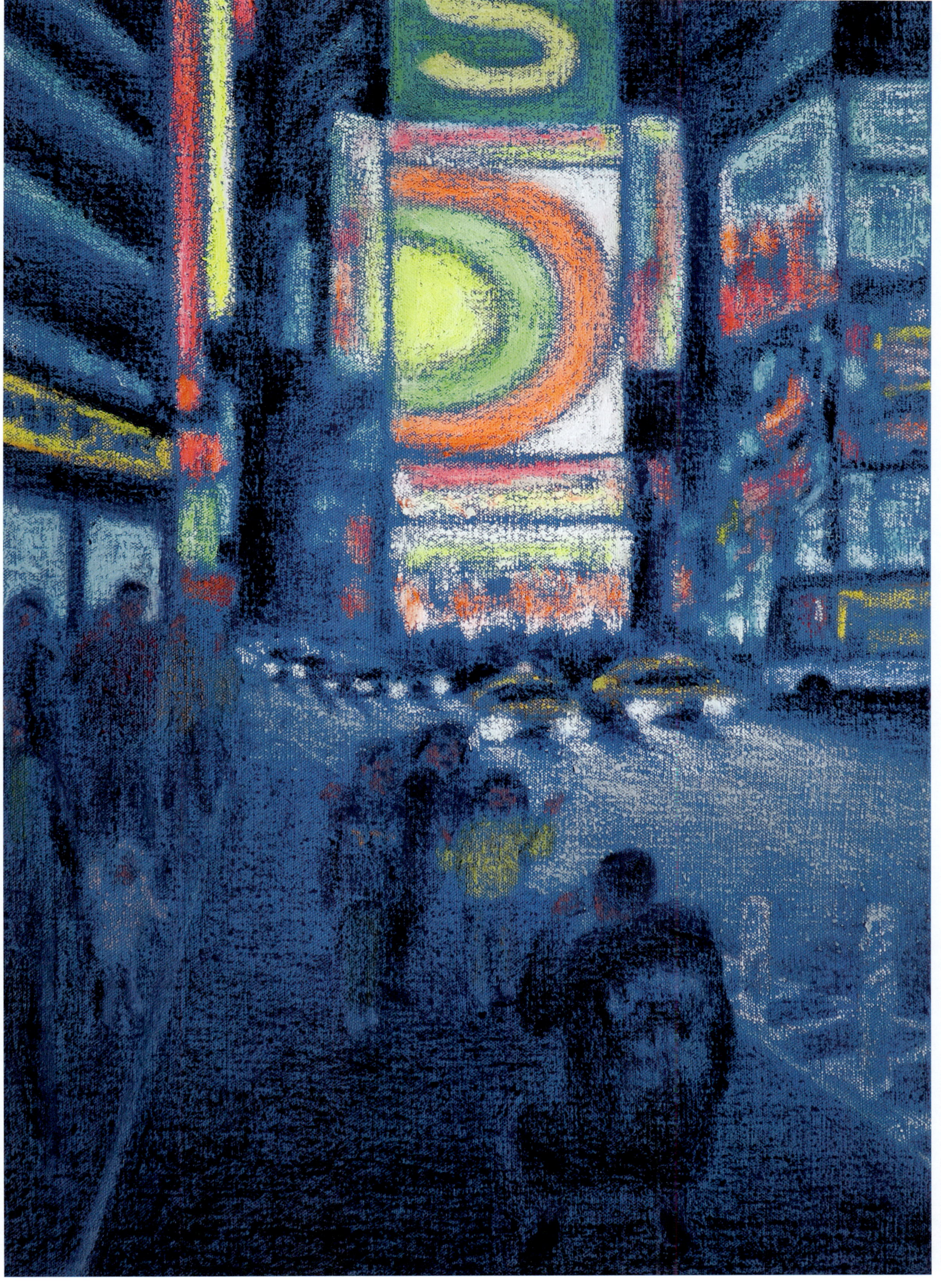

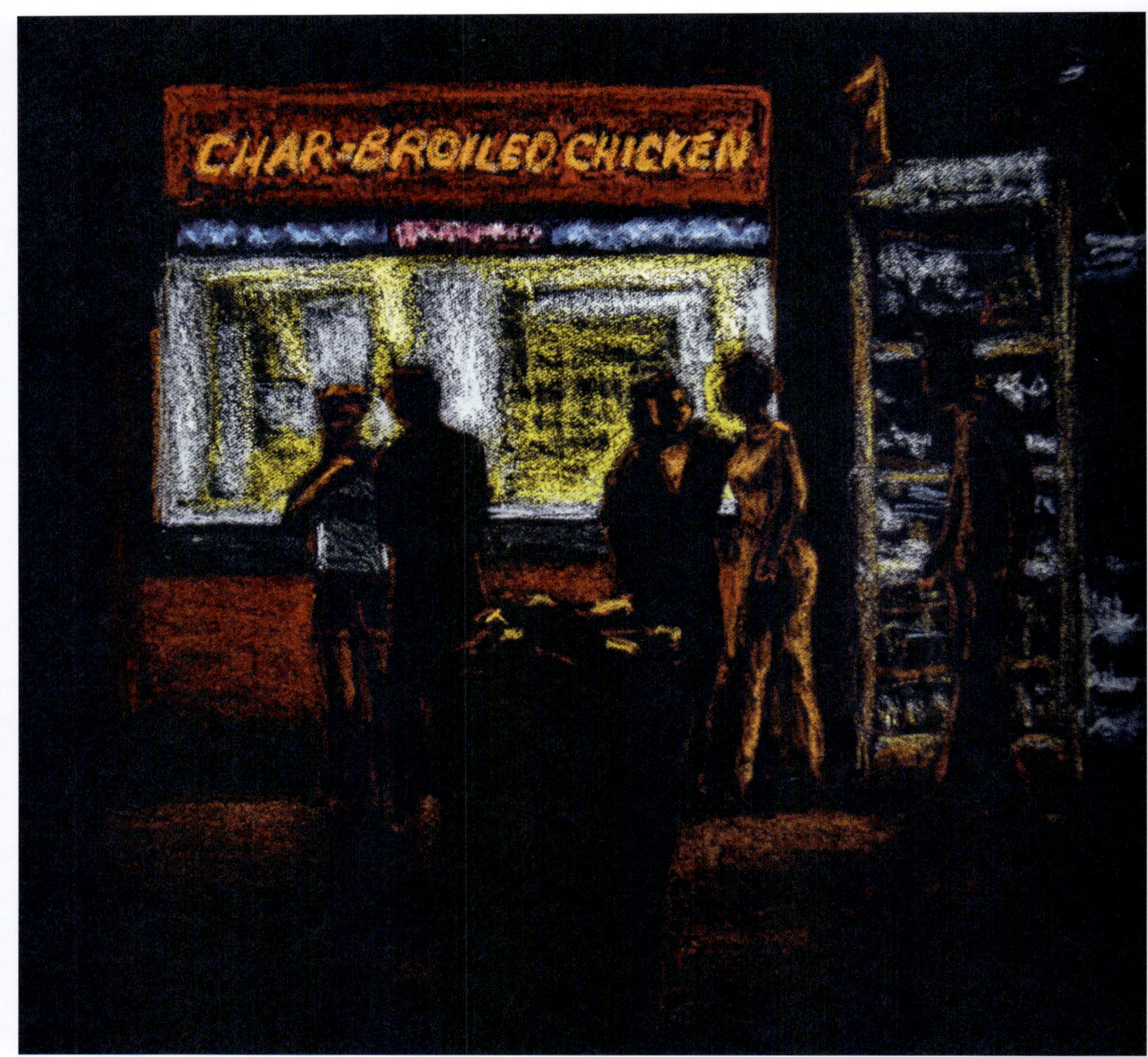

86   *54th St. Near 7th Ave.* Watercolor on paper, 15 x 11 in. 1992.
87   *Smile 1.* Oil stick on linen, 32 x 22 in. 2017.
88   *Char Broiled Chicken.* Oil stick on paper, 27 ¼ x 29 ½ in. 1985.
89   Study for *Peepland in Conversation.* Oil stick on black paper, 28 x 18 in. 1984.

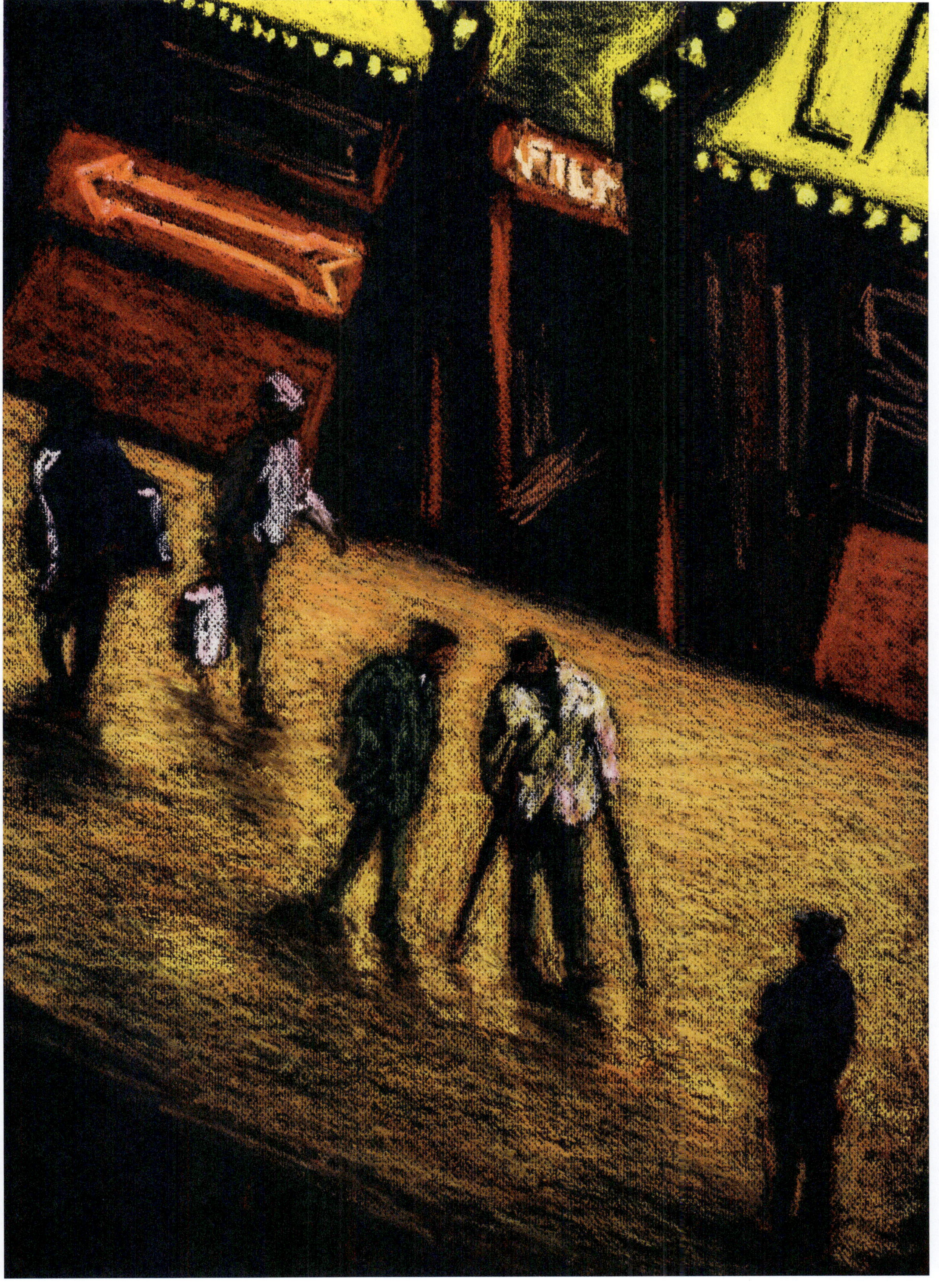

FILMS

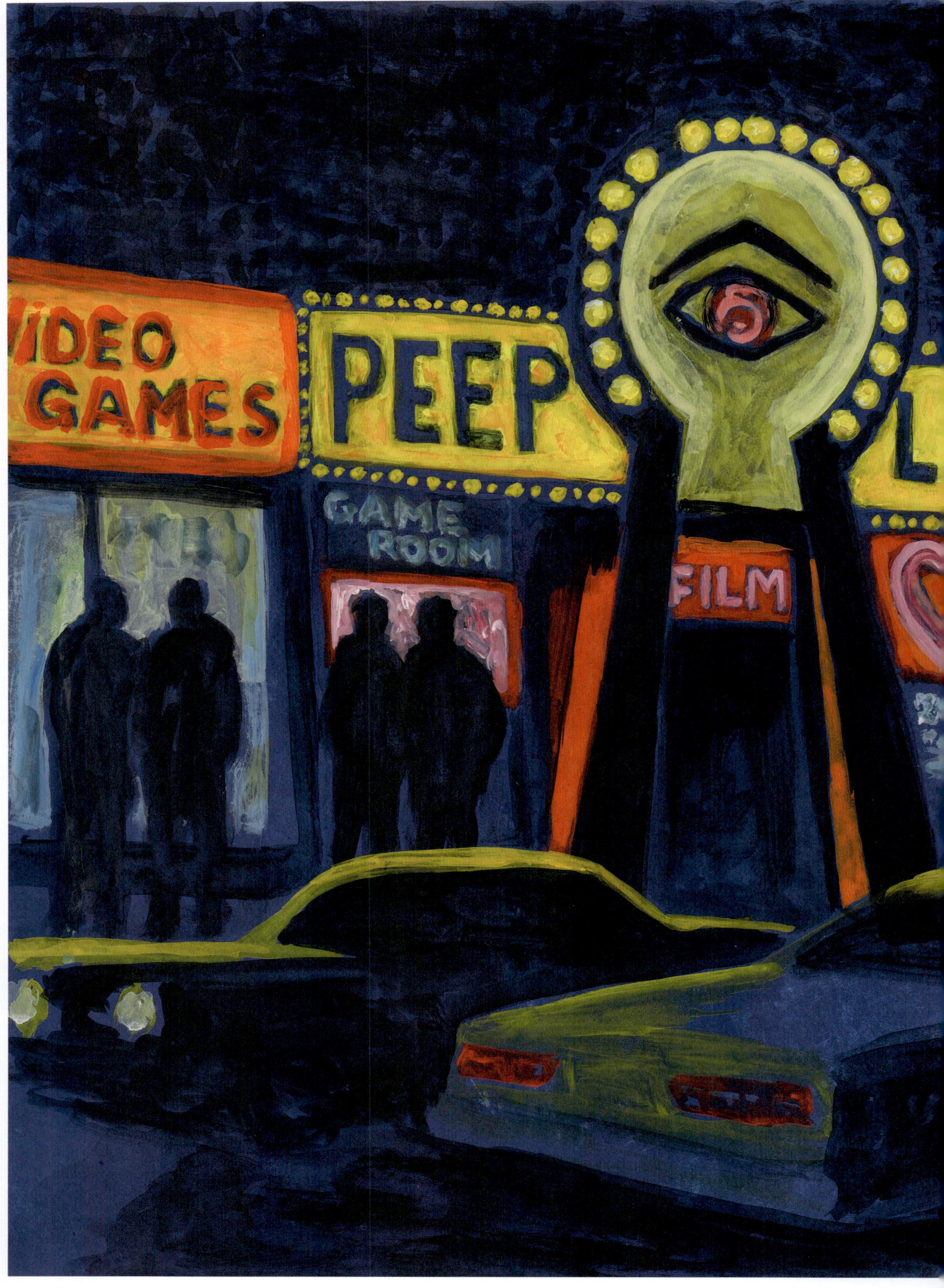
VIDEO GAMES
PEEP
GAME ROOM
FILM

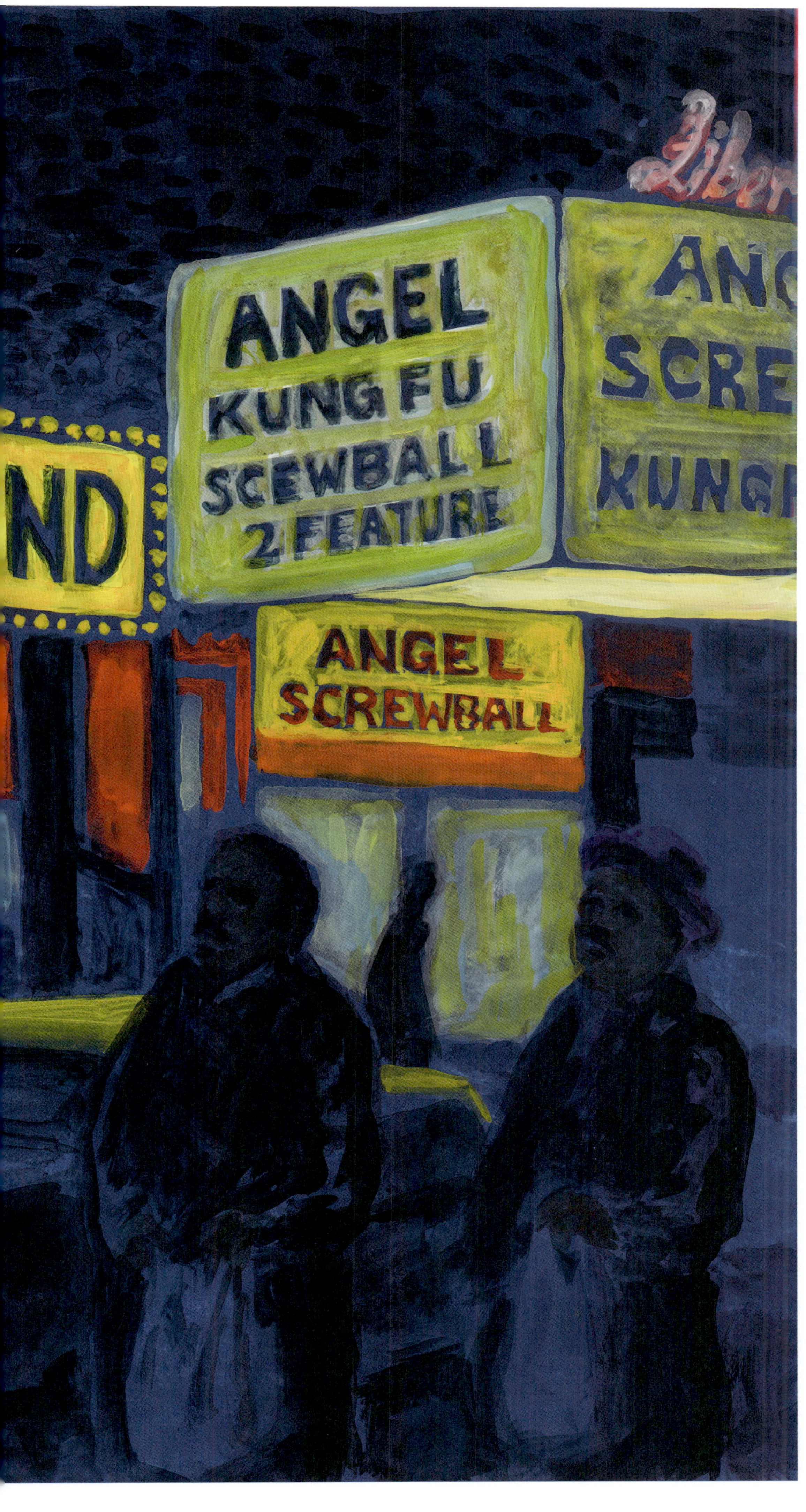
ANGEL
KUNG FU
SCEWBALL L
2 FEATURE
ND
ANGEL
SCREWBALL
Liber
AN
SCRE
KUNG

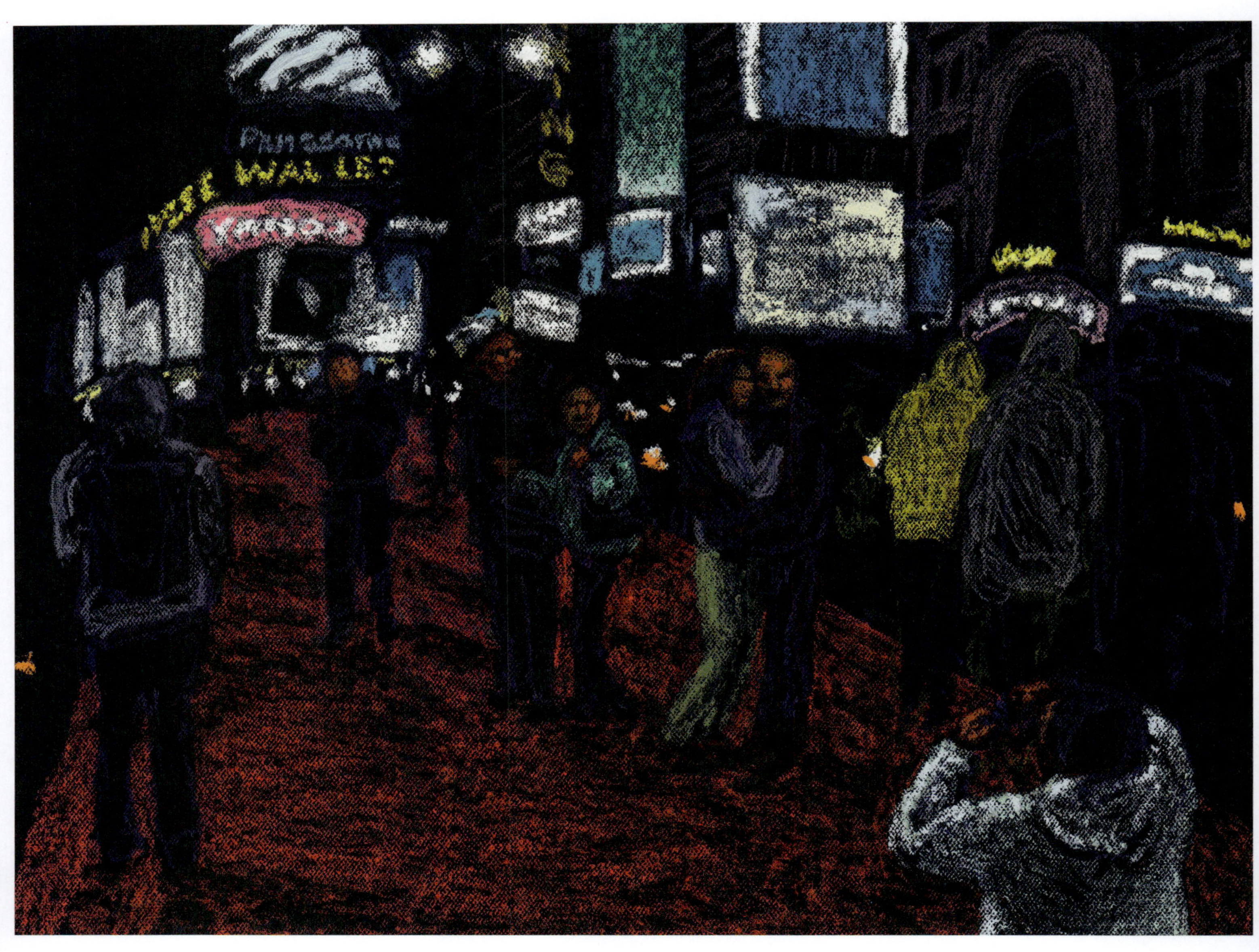

WAL LE?

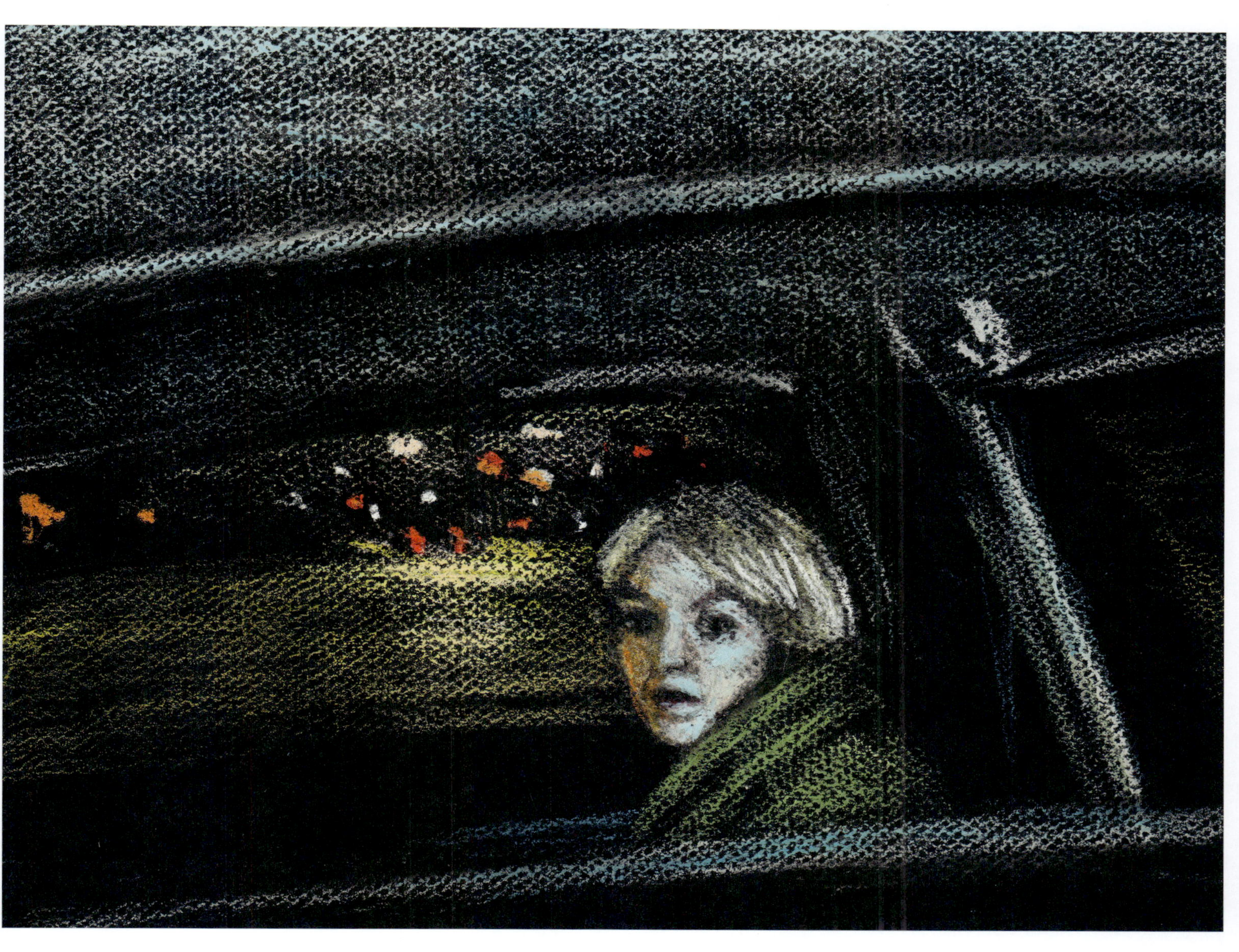

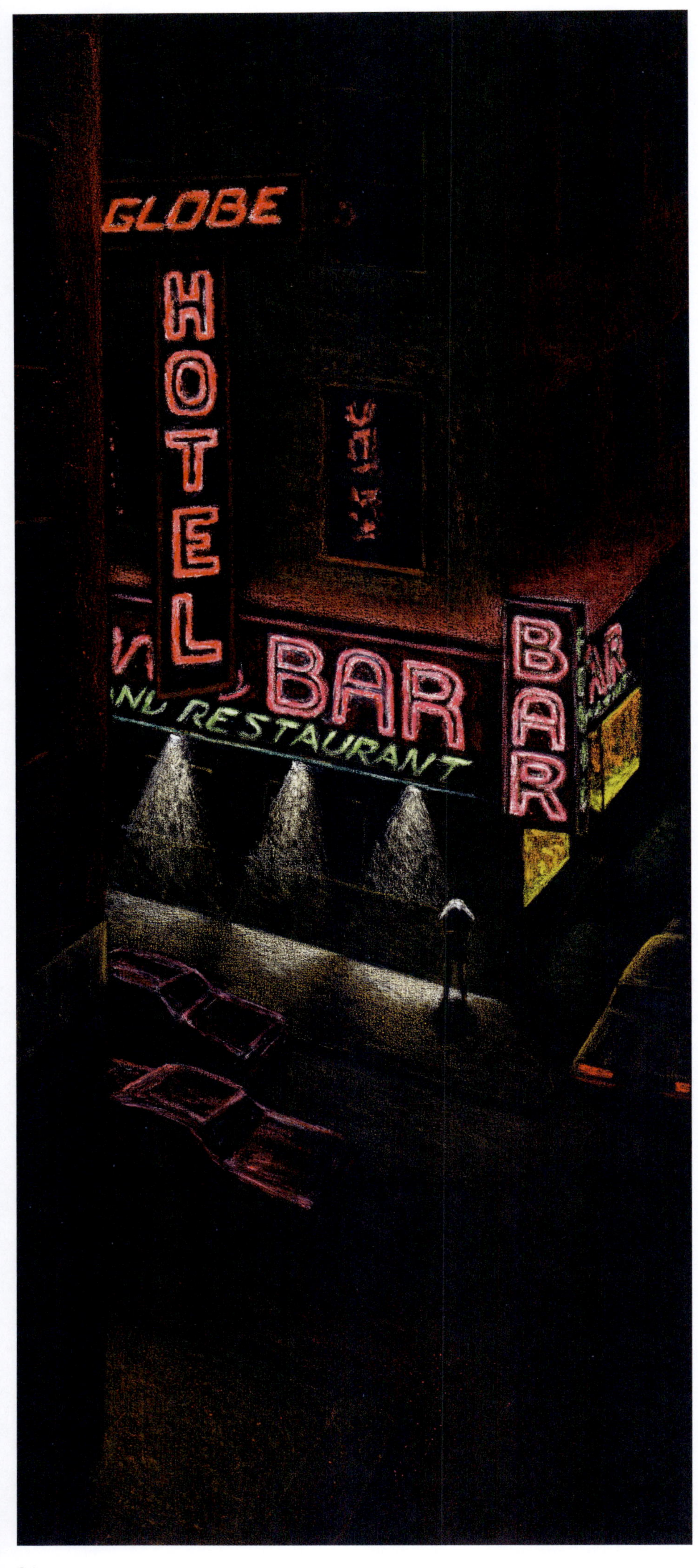

GLOBE
HOTEL
BAR
AND RESTAURANT
BAR
BAR

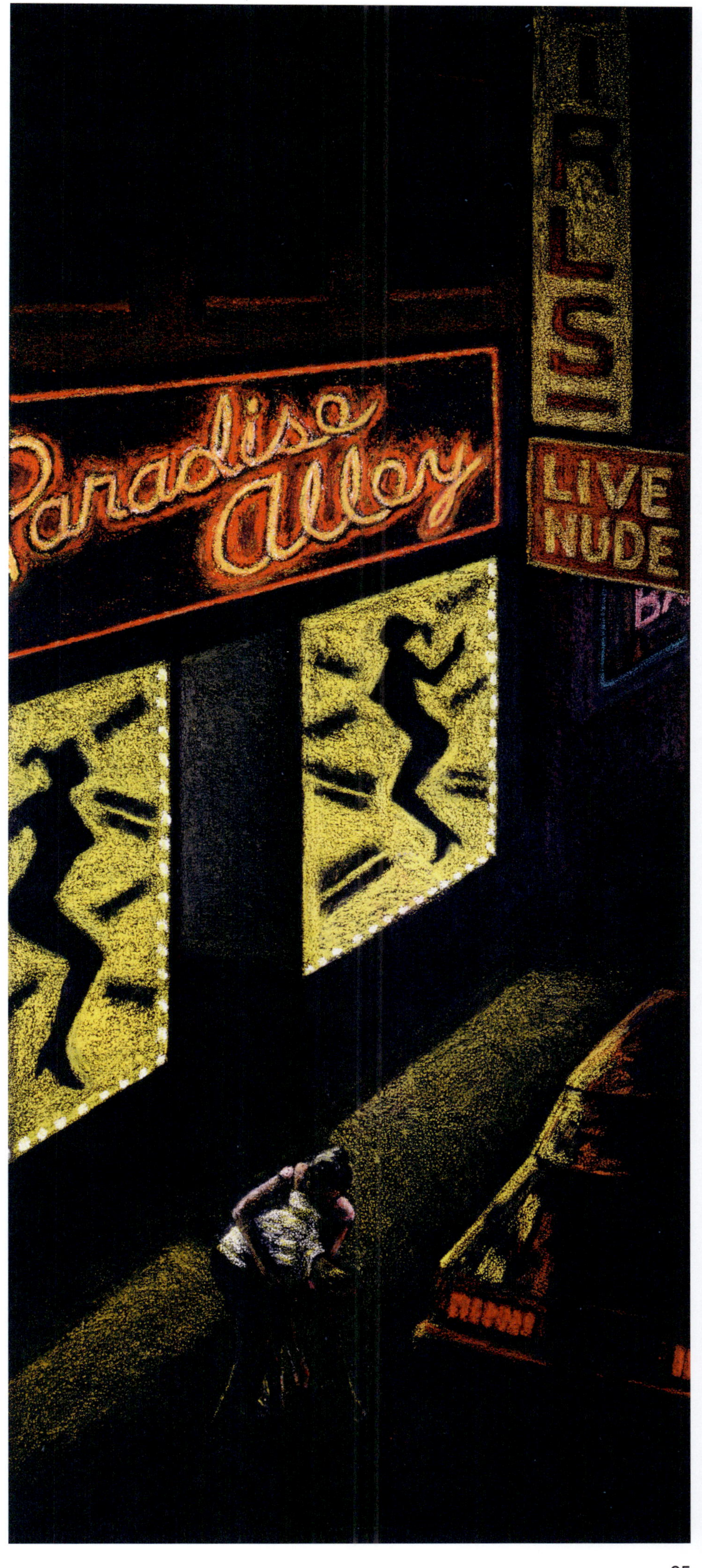
Paradise Alley
LIVE NUDE

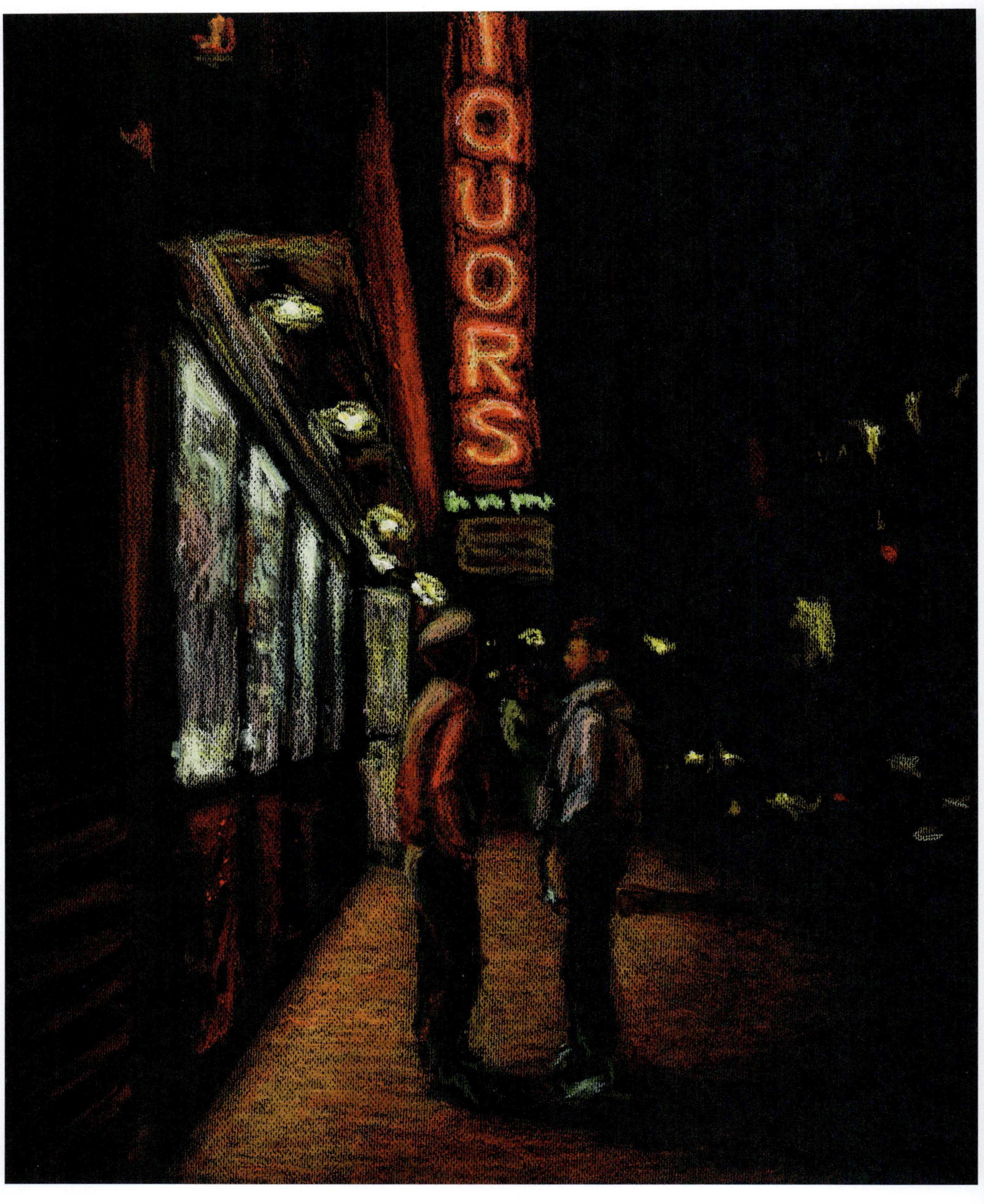
LIQUORS

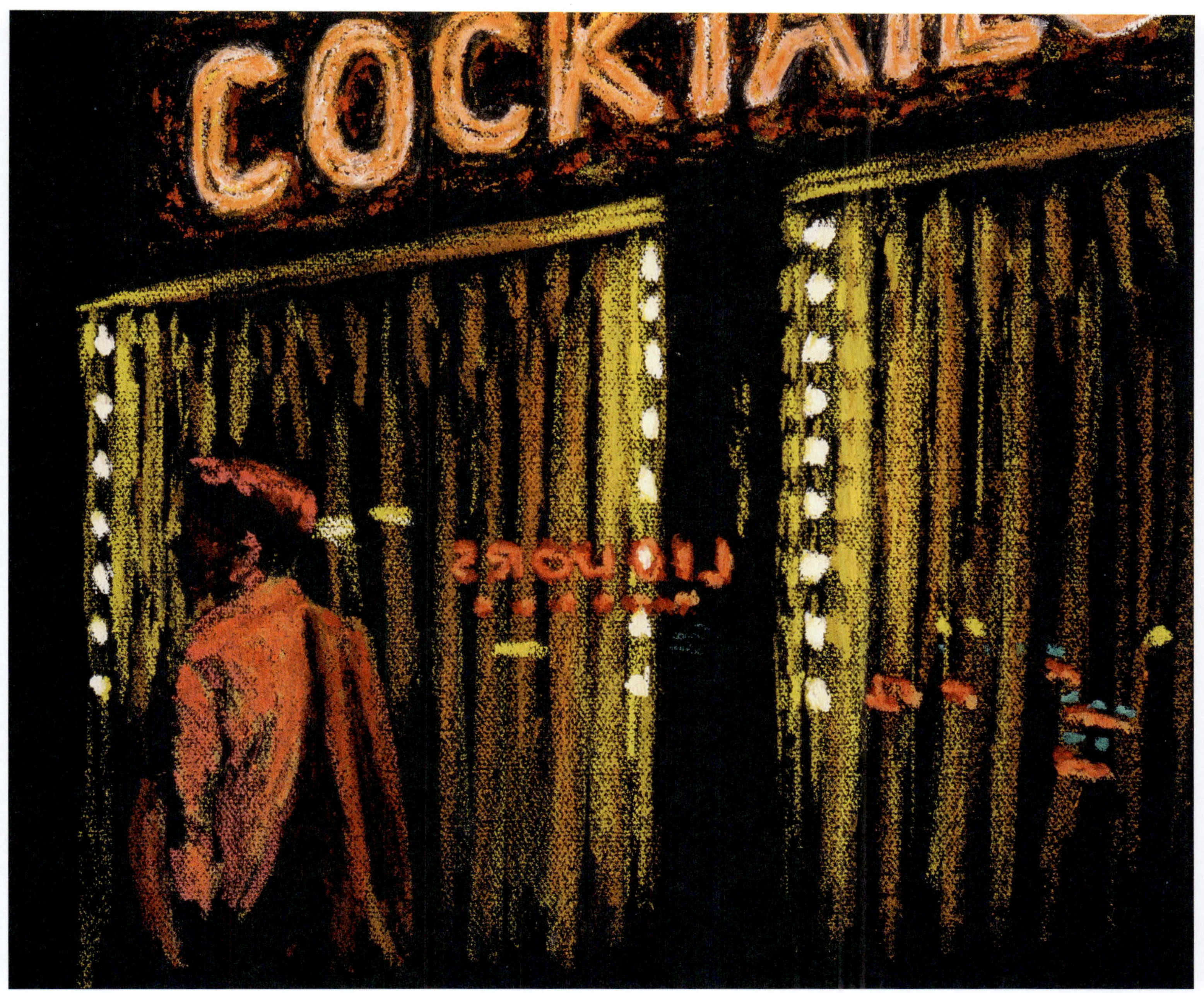

90   *Peepland Angel*. Gouache on Tyvek, 17 ½ x 23 in. 2017.
92   *Cheese Times Square*. Oil stick on paper, 22 x 29 ¾ in. 2010.
93   *Patti A*. Oil stick on paper, 11 ½ x 14 ½ in. 1980.
94   *White Haired Girl*. Oil stick on canvas, 90 x 40 in. 1983.
95   *Paradise Alley*. Oil stick on canvas, 90 x 40 in. 1983.
96   *Liquors Conversation*. Oil stick on black paper, 23 ½ x 19 ½ in. 1984.
97   Study for *Cocktails*. Oil stick on black paper, 9 ½ x 16 in. 1984.

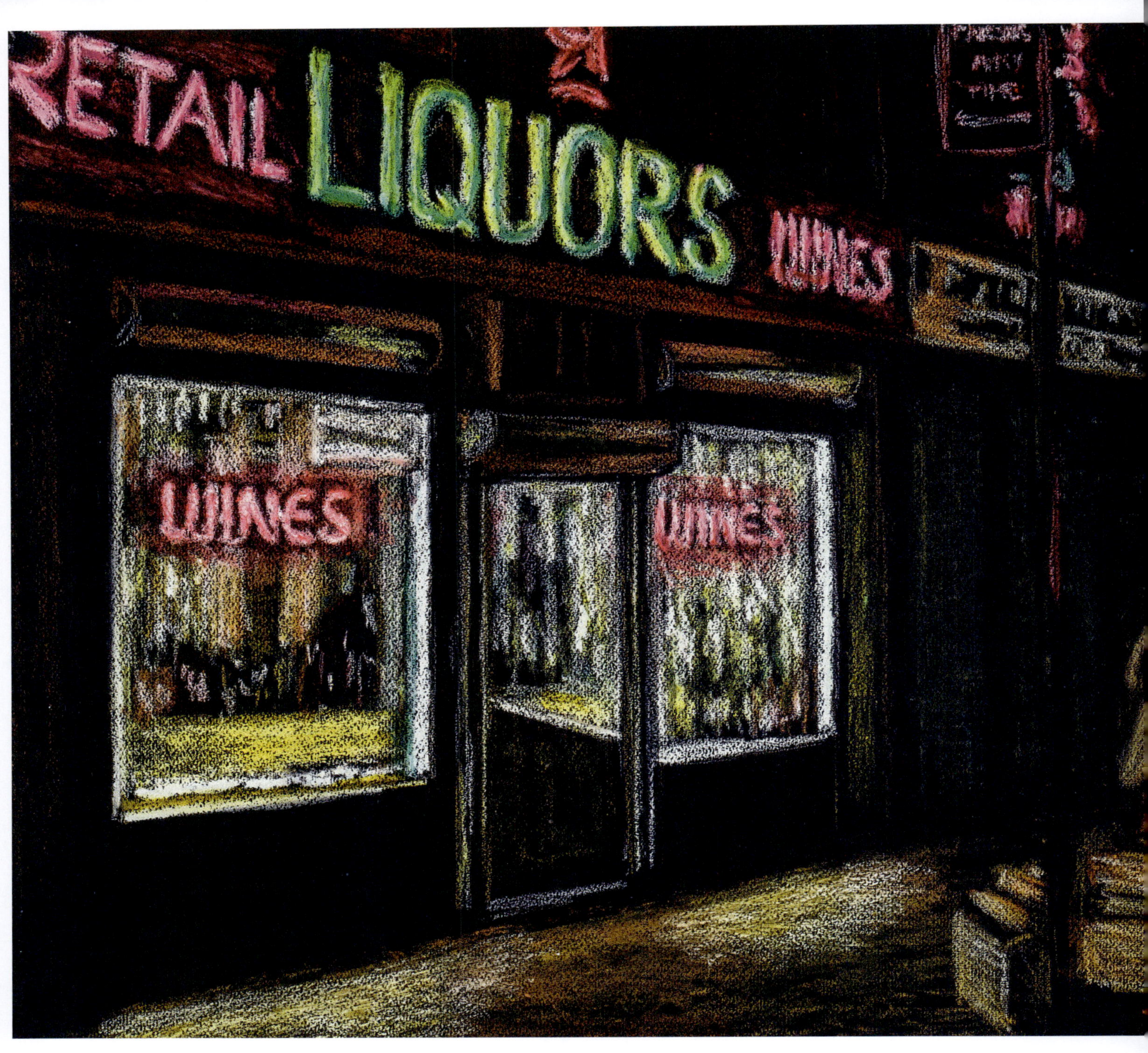

RETAIL LIQUORS WINES
WINES
WINES

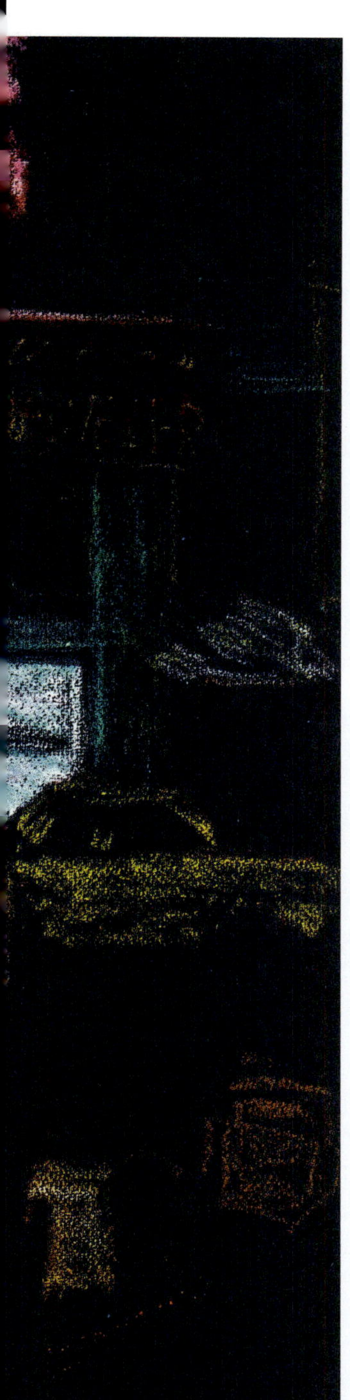

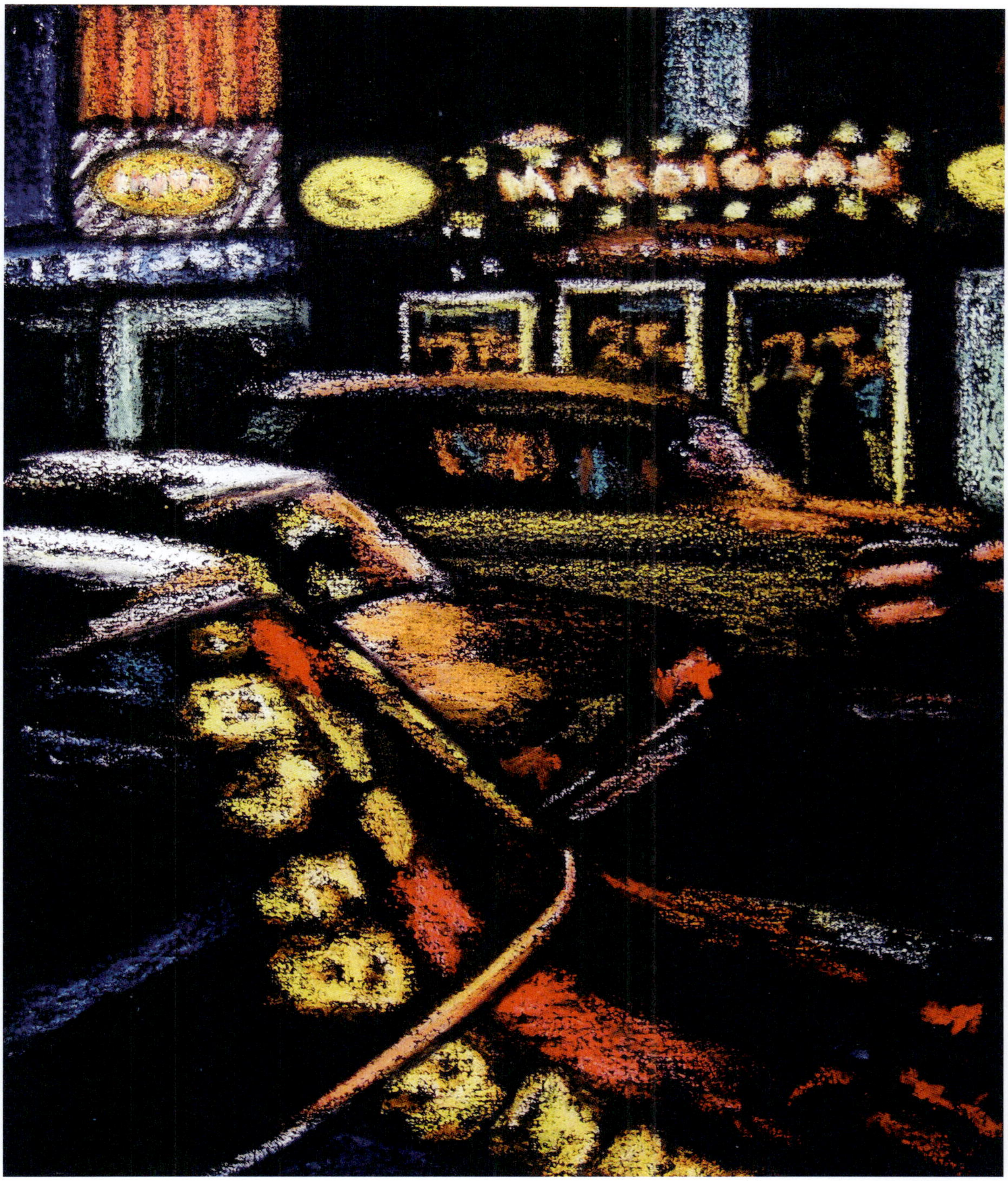

MARKTHALLEN

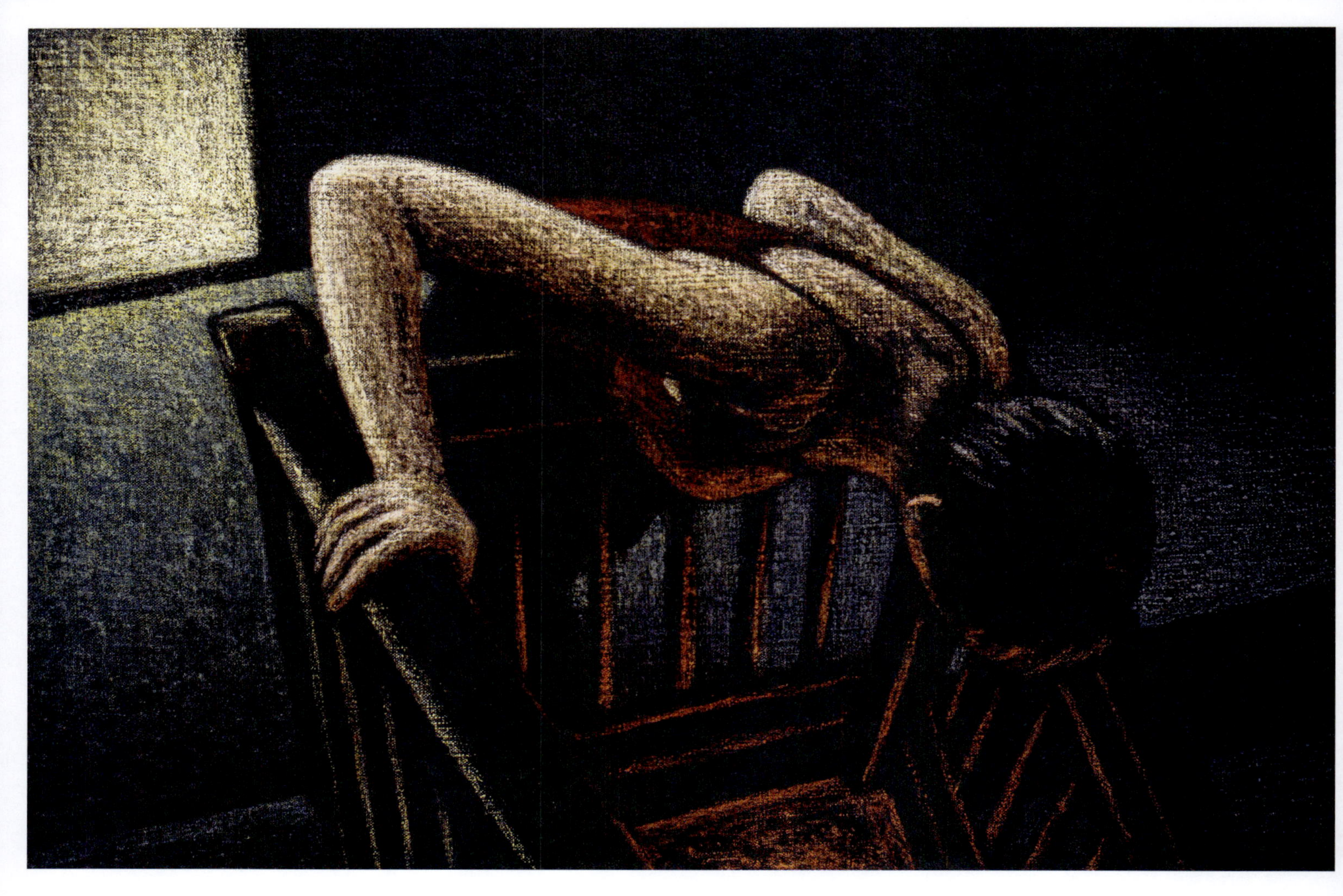

98   *Retail Liquors 43rd Street*. Oil stick on paper, 19 ½ x 27 ¾ in. 1983.
99   *Mardi Gras 8th Ave*. Oil stick on canvas, 18 x 16 in. 1983.
100   *Woman on Stairs Orange Face*. Oil stick on canvas, 32 x 50 in. 1985.
101   *Camille on the Stairs*. Oil stick on canvas, 64 x 34 in. 1985.

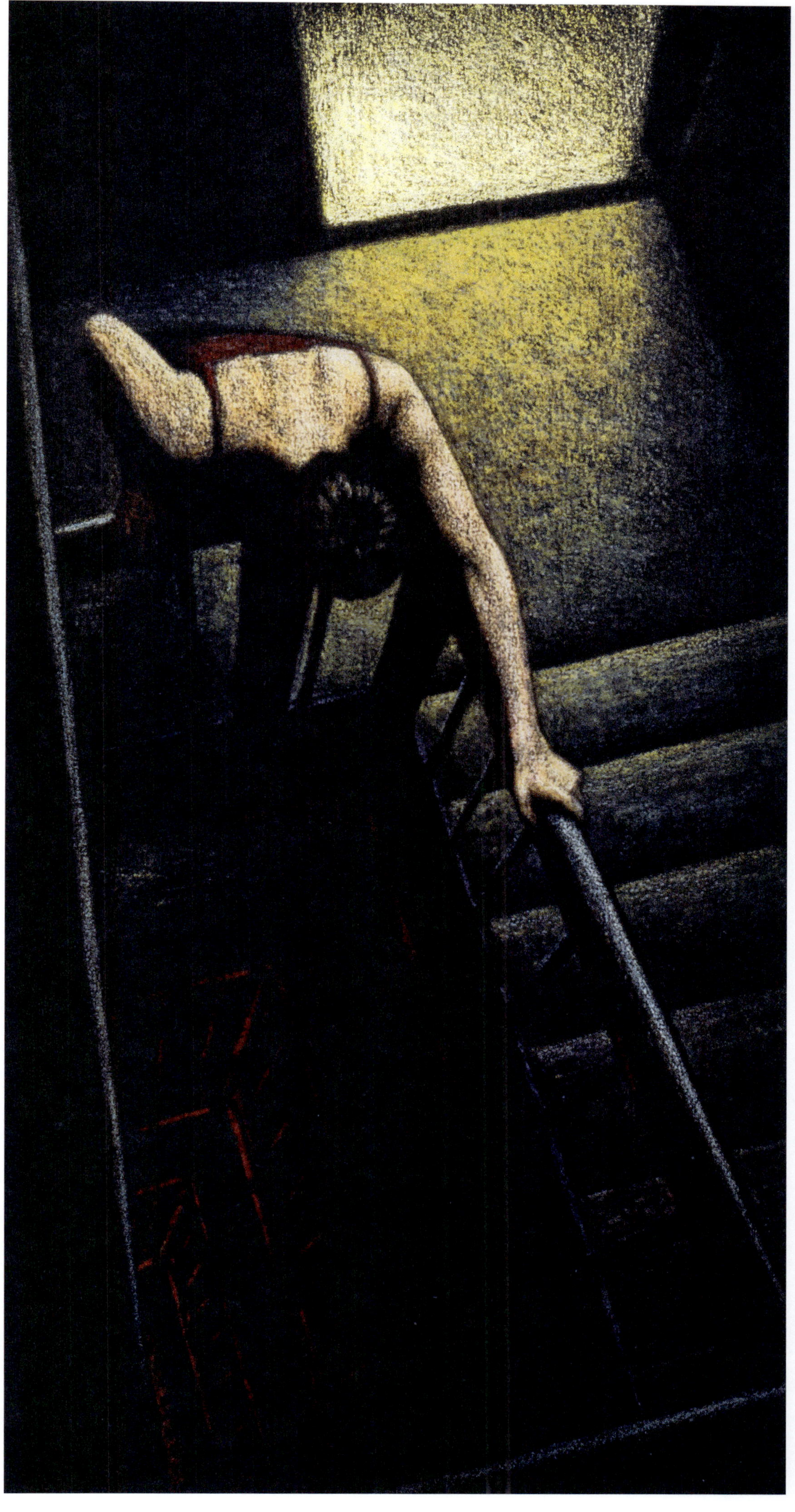

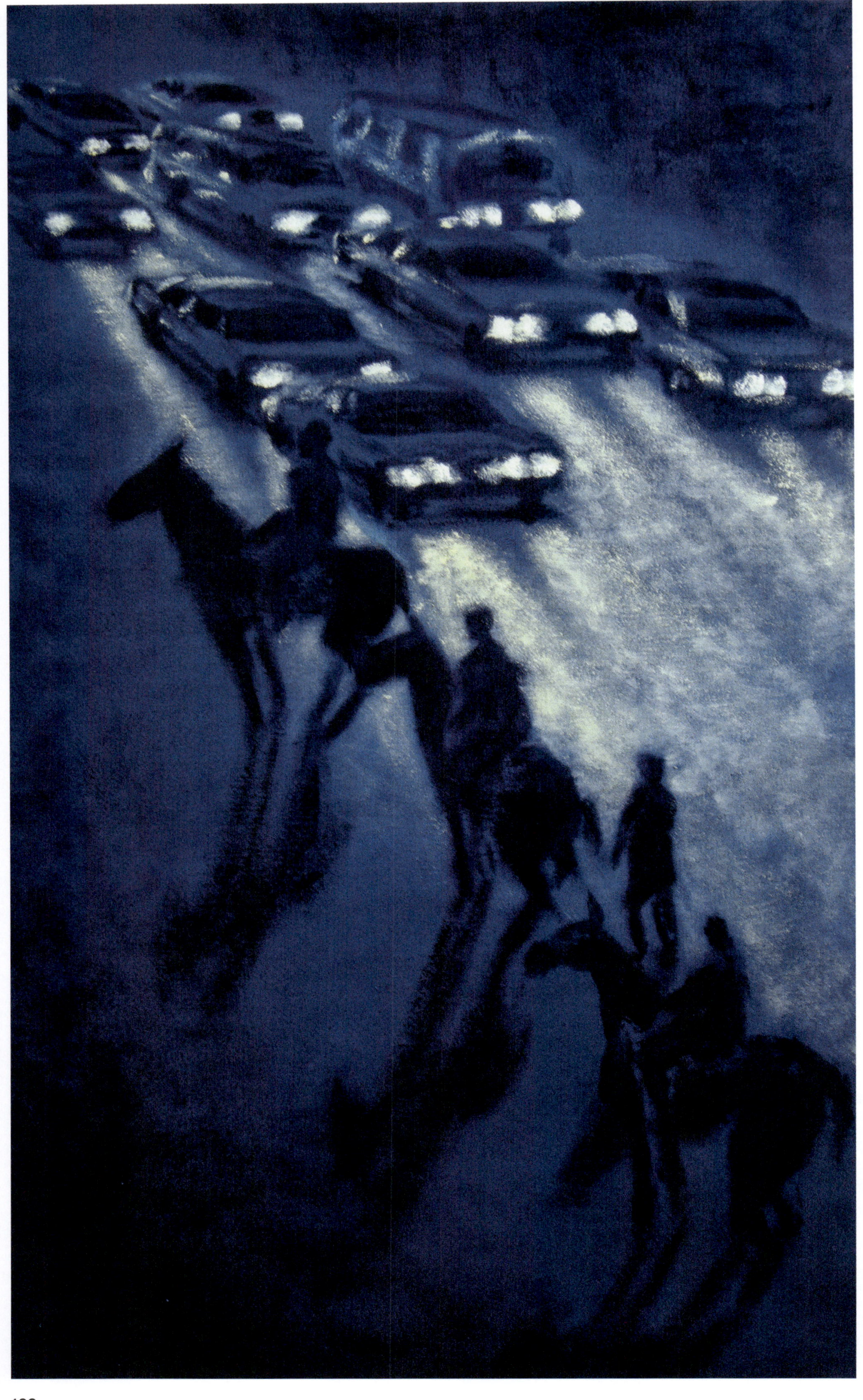

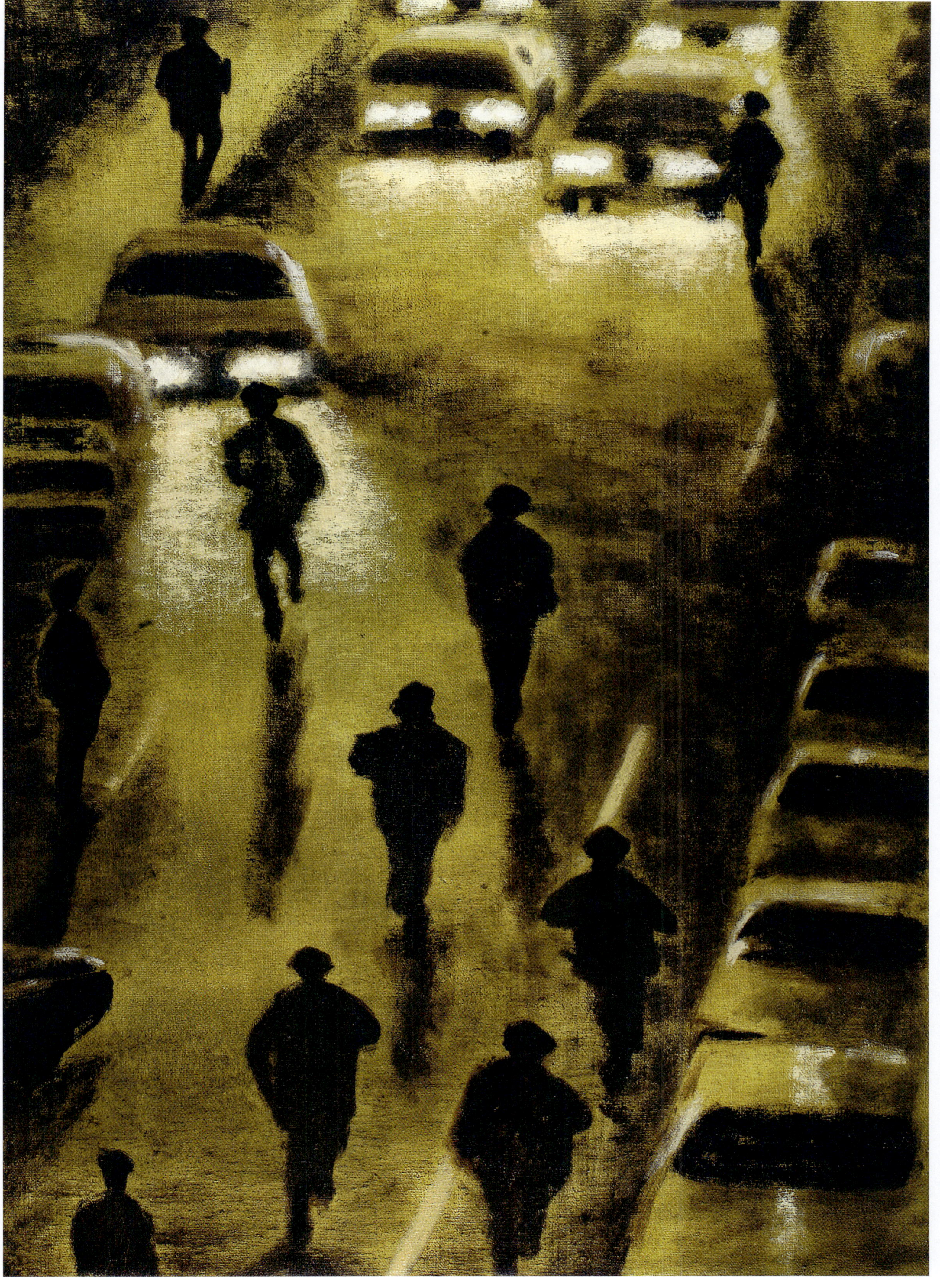

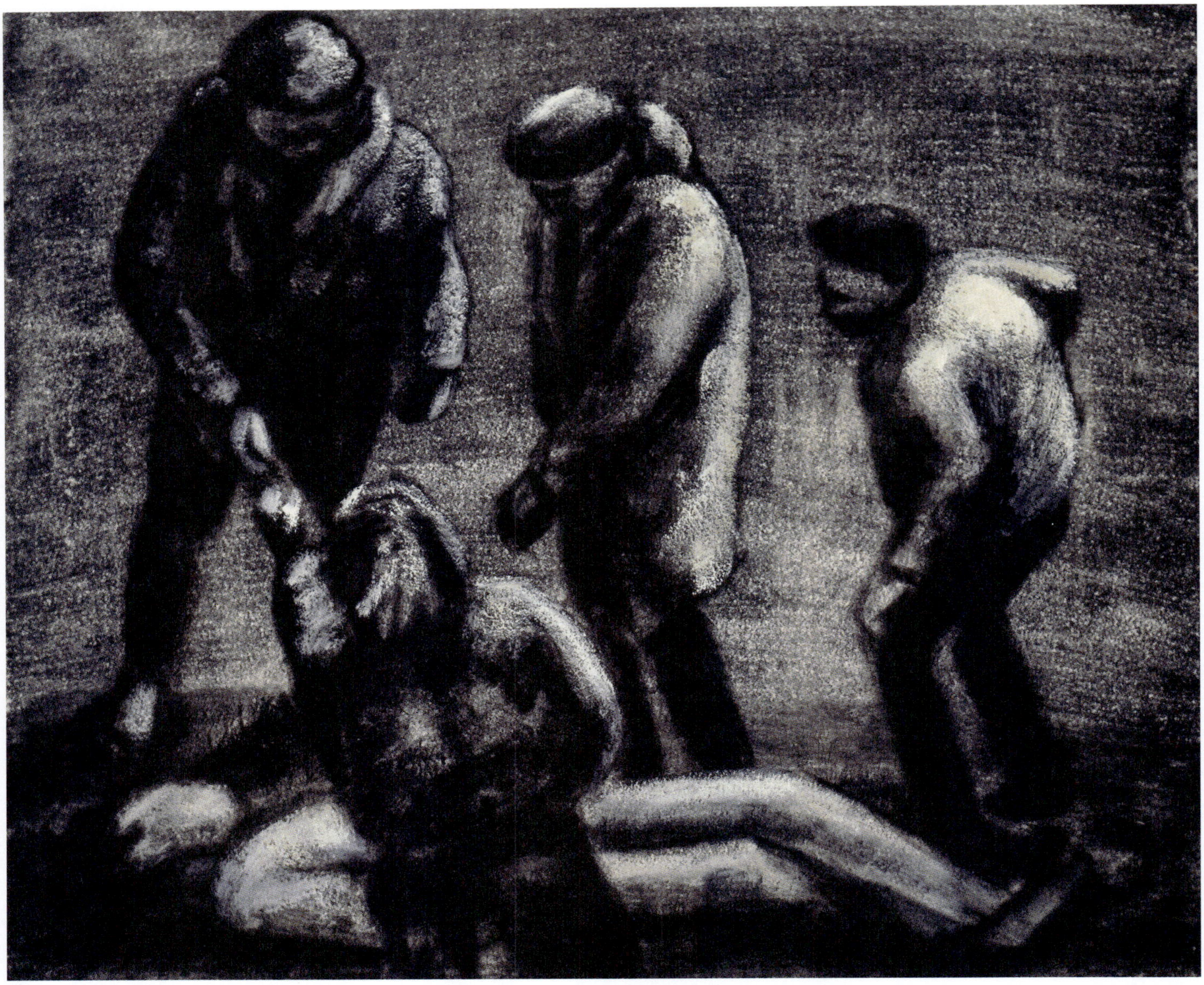

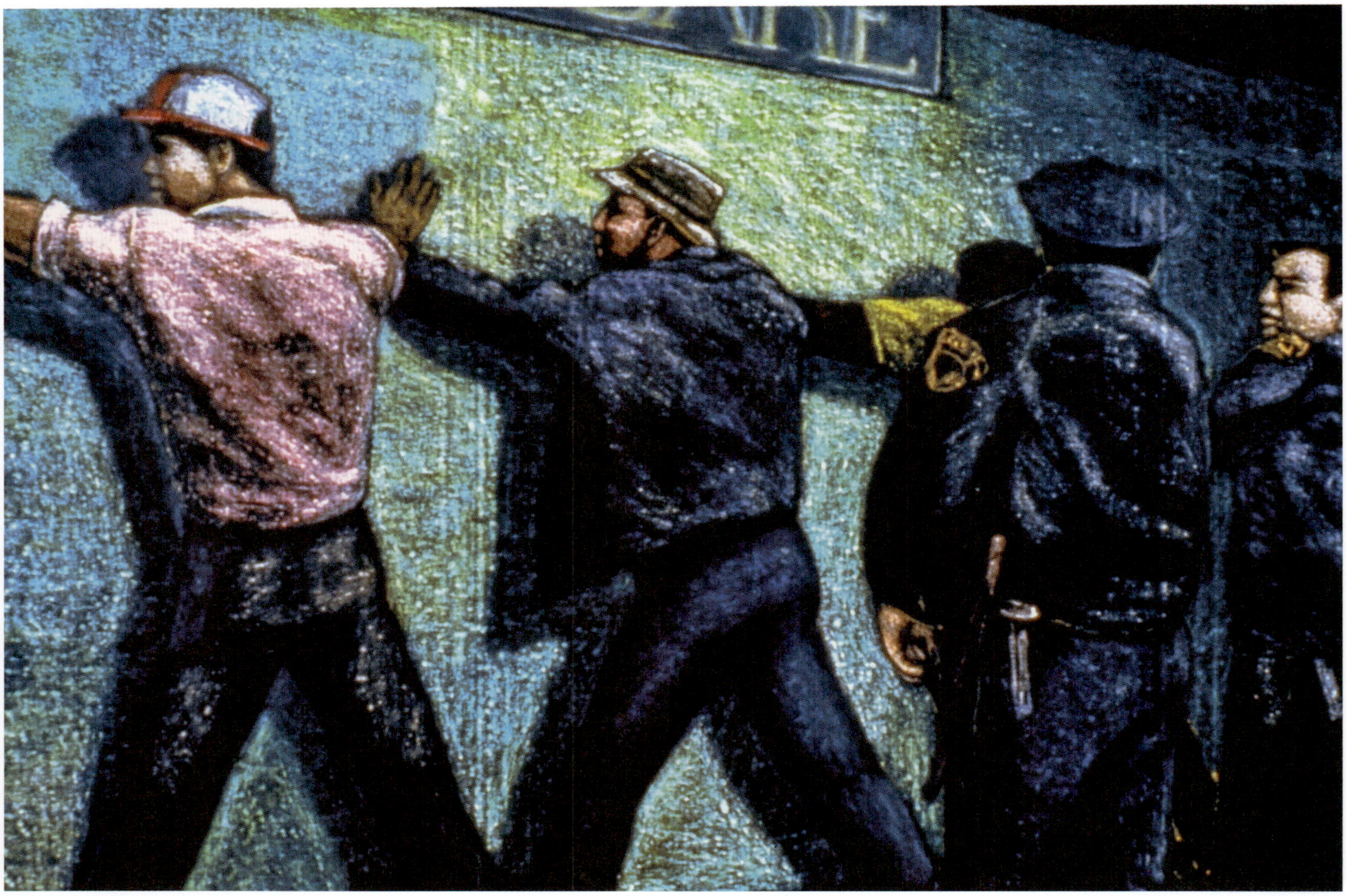

POLICE

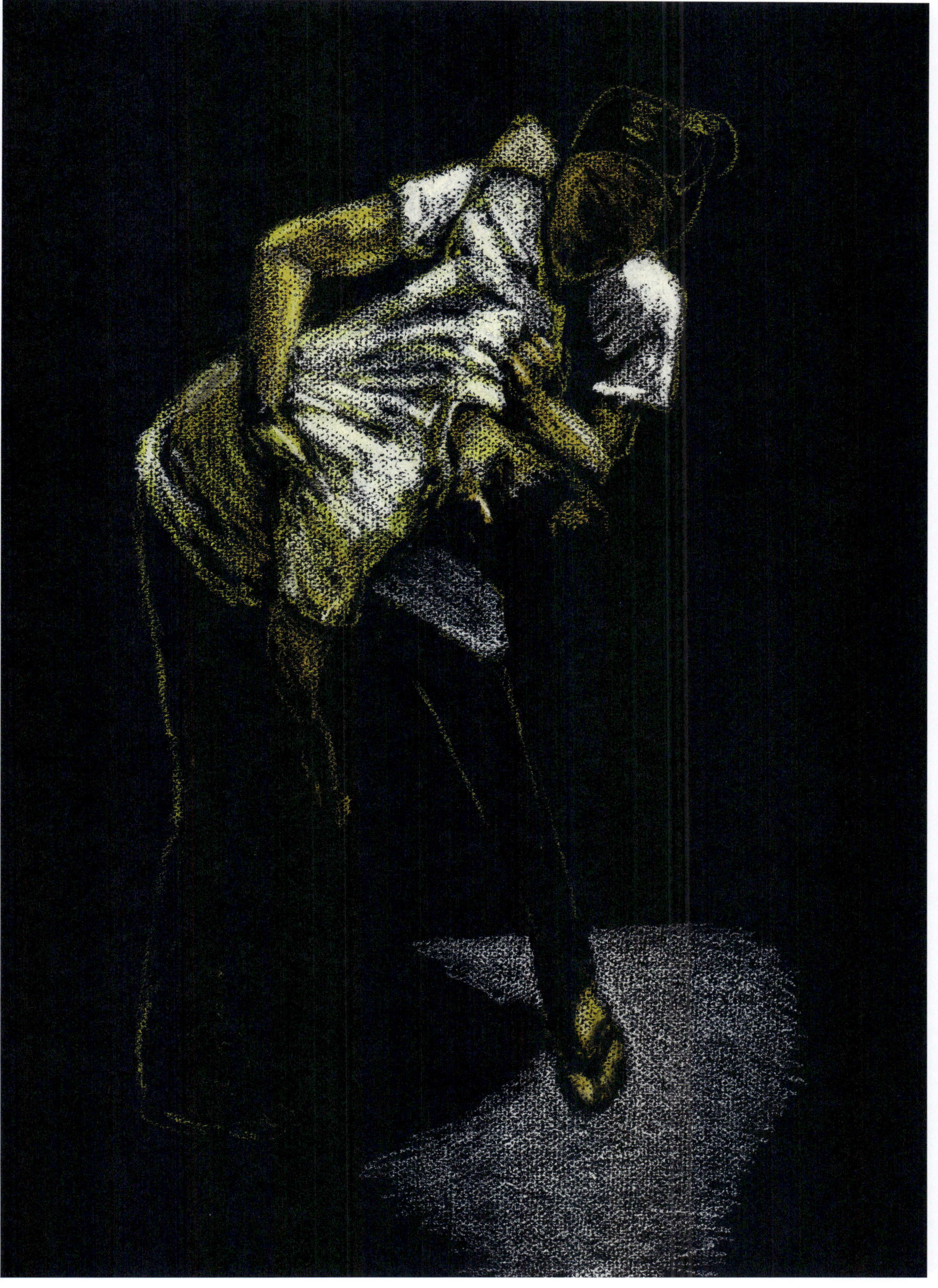

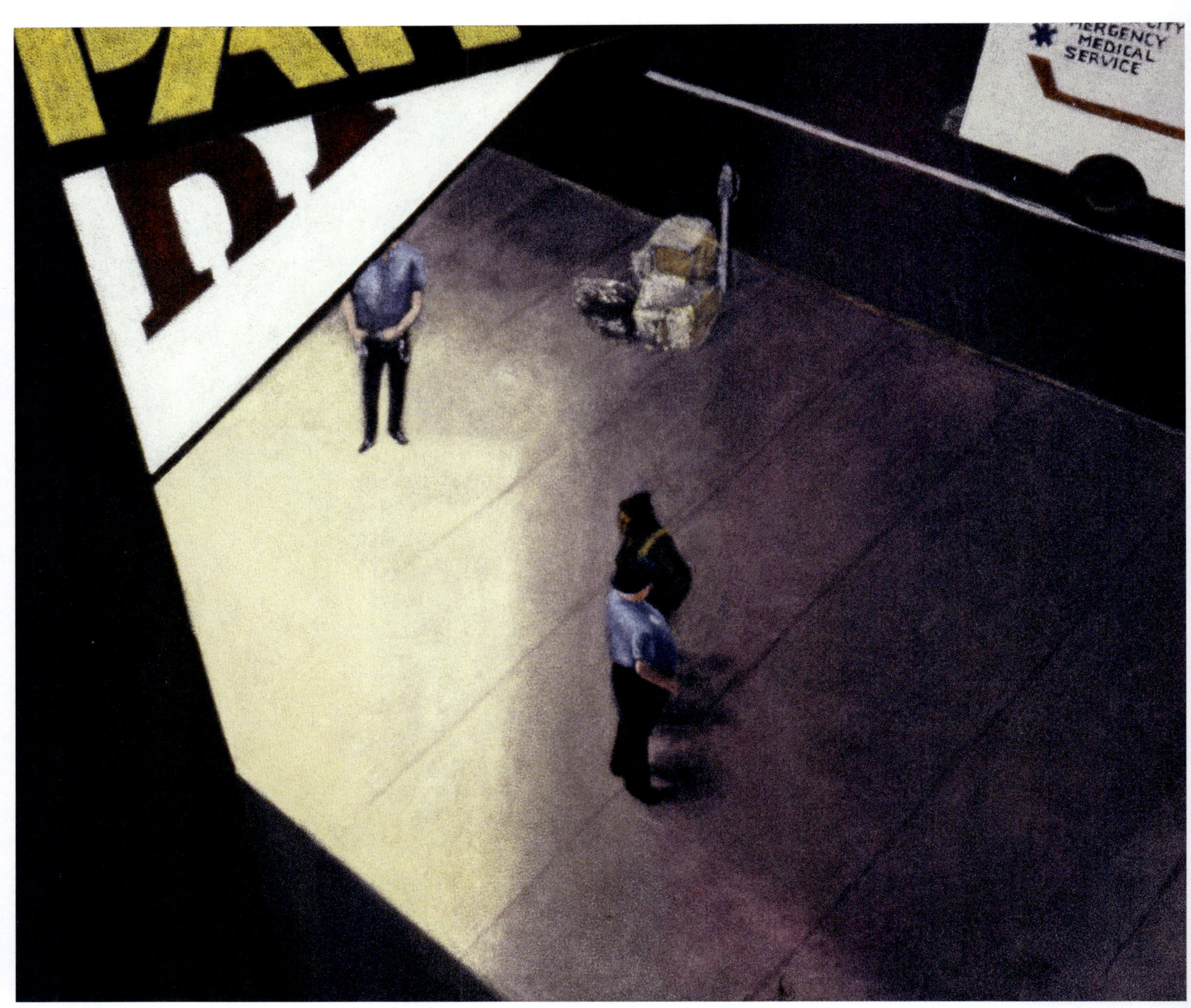

CITY
EMERGENCY
MEDICAL
SERVICE

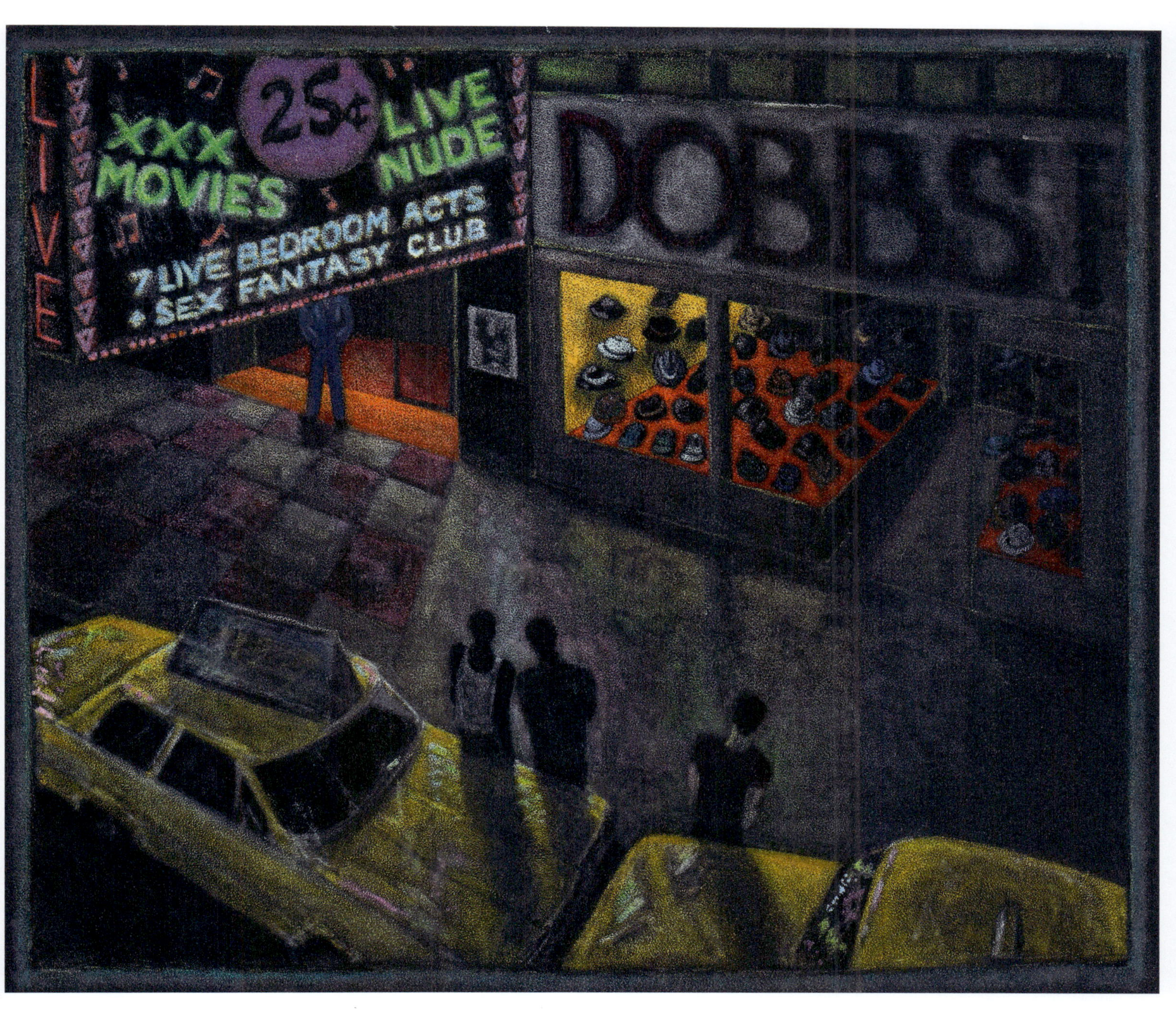
LIVE
XXX MOVIES
25¢
LIVE NUDE
7 LIVE BEDROOM ACTS
SEX FANTASY CLUB
DOBBS

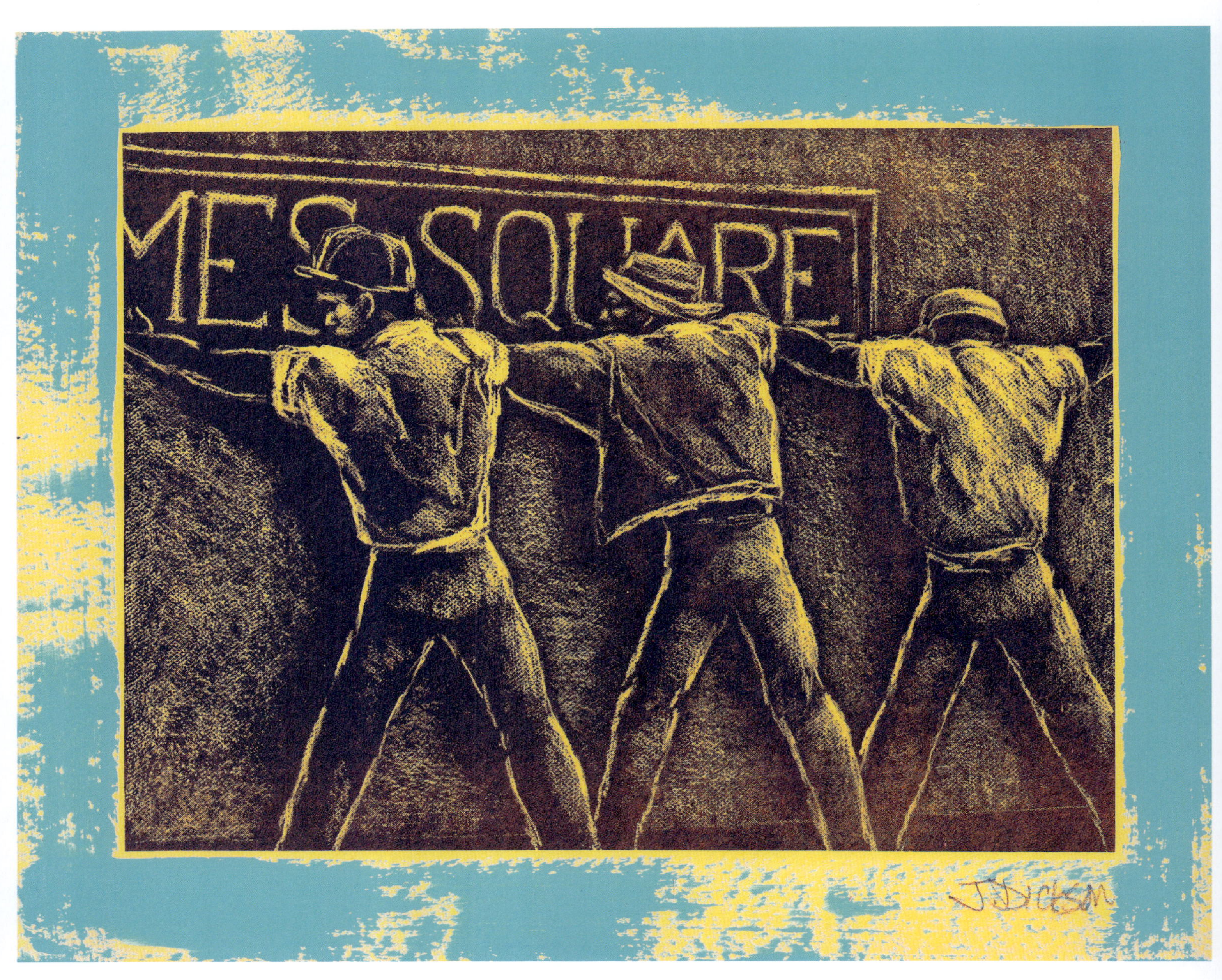
MES SQUARE
J Dickson

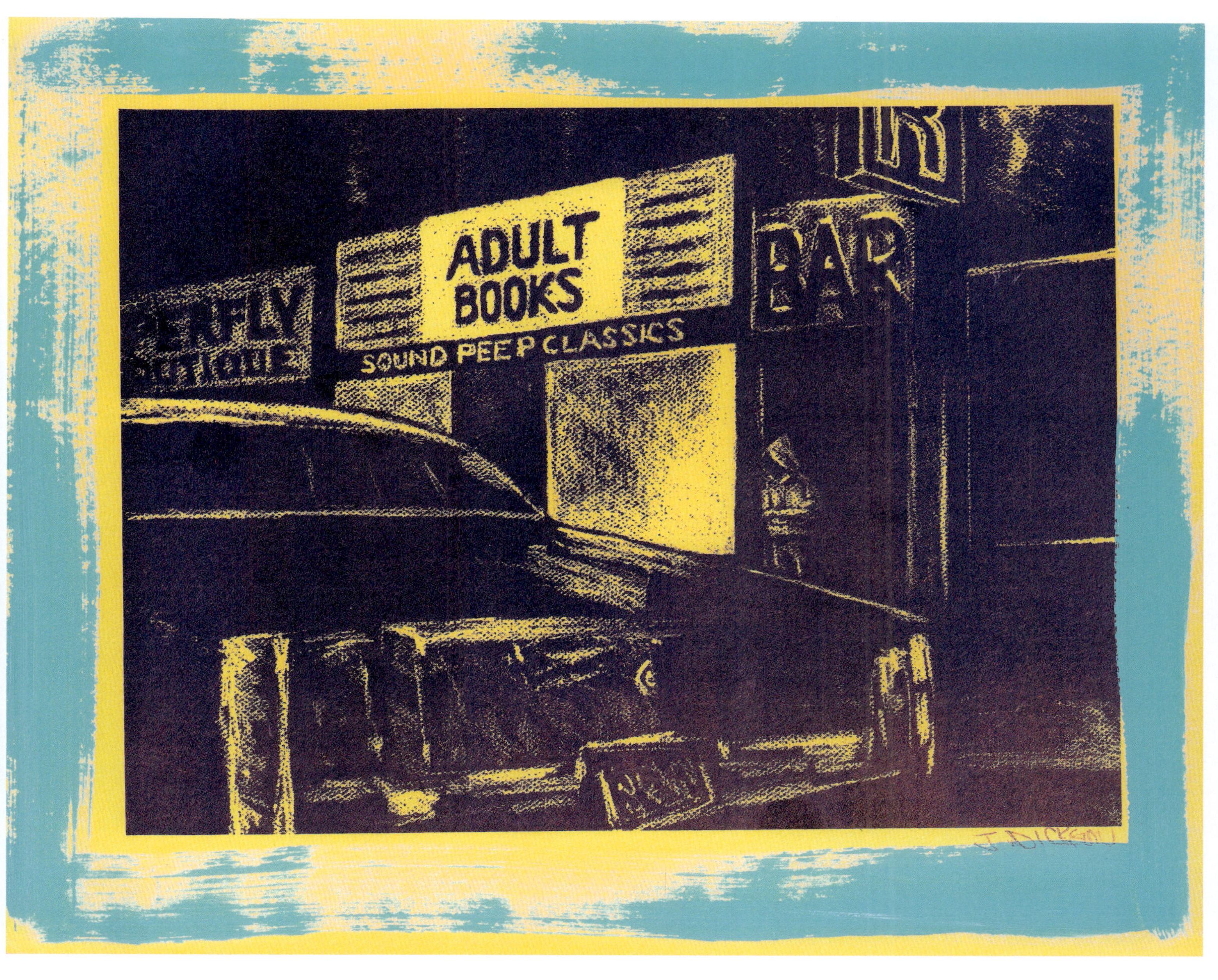
ADULT
BOOKS
SOUND PEEP CLASSICS
BAR

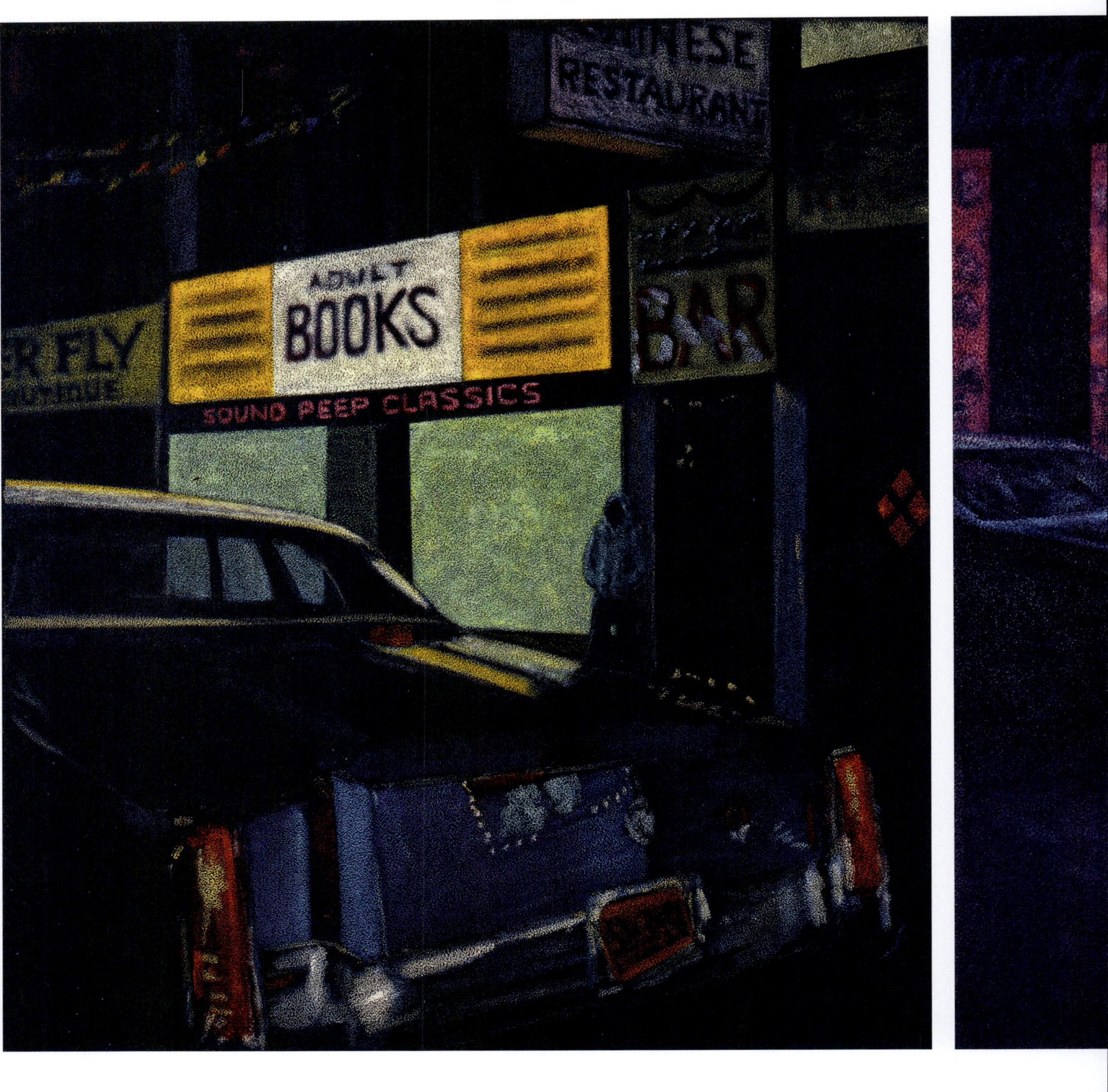
CHINESE
RESTAURANT
ADULT
BOOKS
SOUND PEEP CLASSICS
ER FLY
BAR

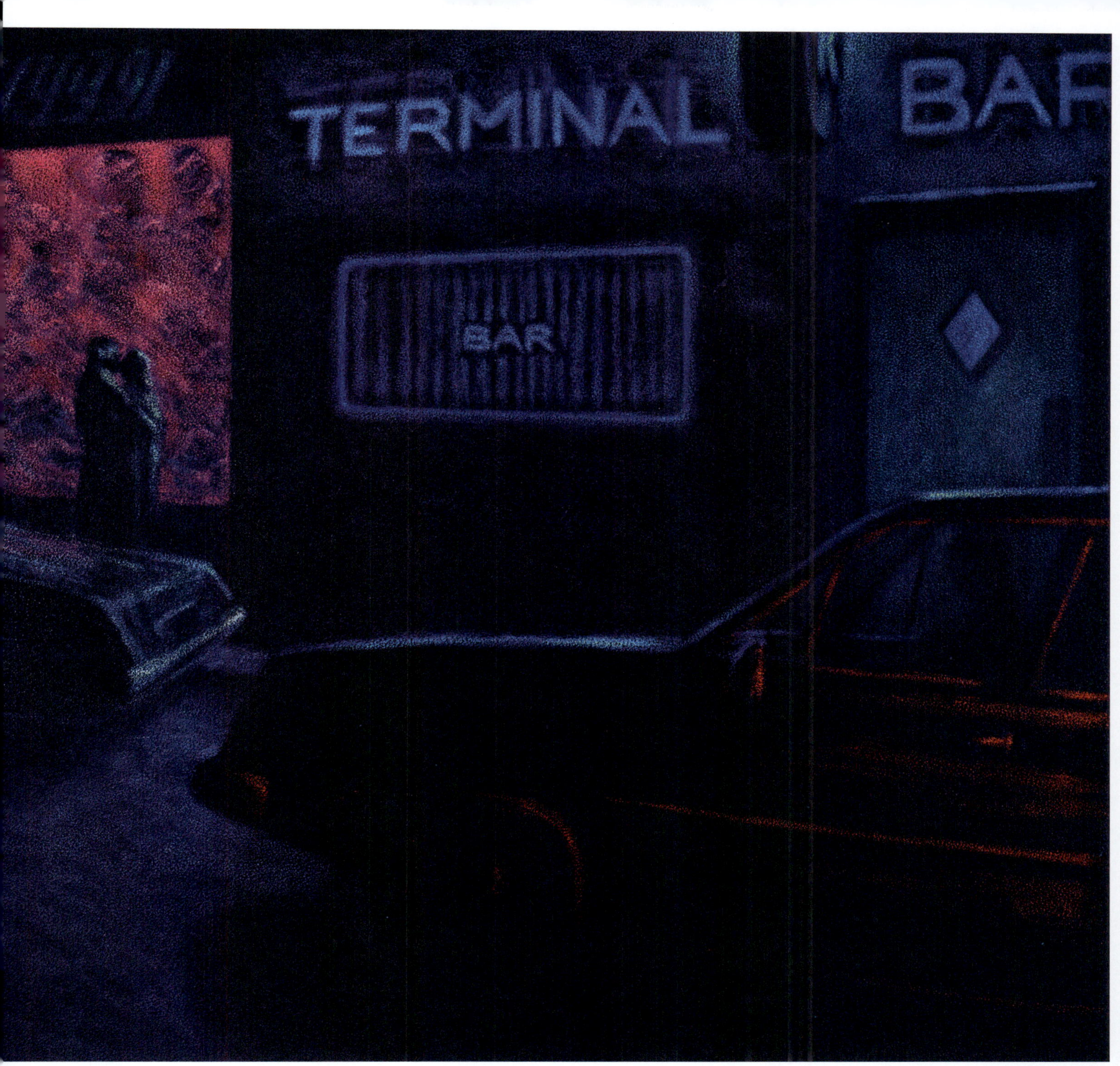
TERMINAL BAR
BAR

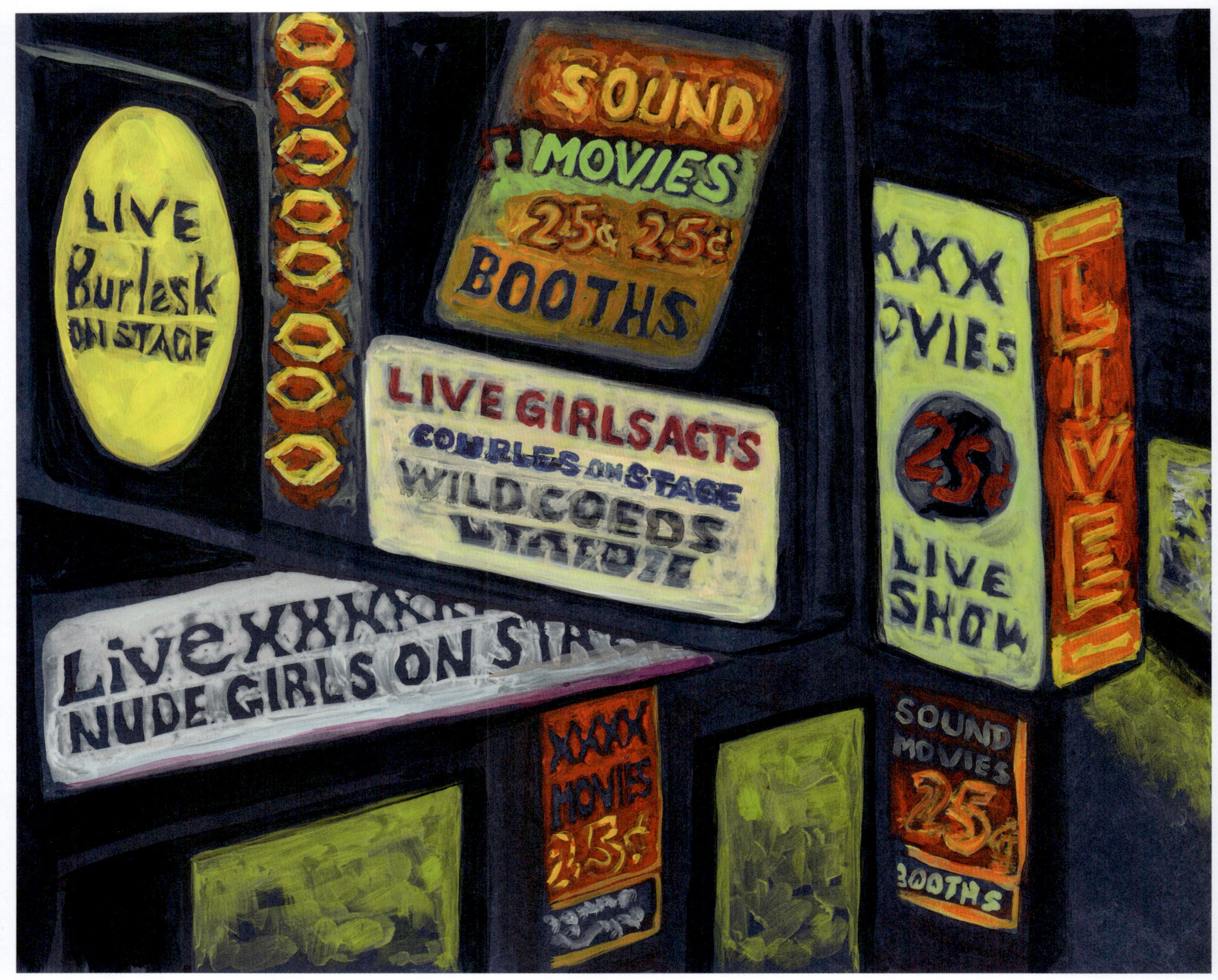

102   *Horses in Headlights II*. Oil on canvas, 48 x 30 in. 1991.
103   *Cops in Headlights I*. Oil on linen, 50 ½ x 36 in. 1991.
104   TOP: *K.O.* Oil and Rolotex on canvas, 24 x 30 in. 1989.
       BOTTOM: *Men Against the Wall*. Oil stick on canvas, 50 x 100 in. 1983.
105   Study for *Support*. Oil stick on paper, 20 x 16 in. 1983.
106   *Emergency Service*. Acrylic on vinyl, 44 x 60 in. 1982.
107   *Dobbs Hats*. Acrylic on vinyl, 48 x 52 in. 1981. Collection of the Whitney Museum of American Art.
108   *Times Square Offset (Up Against the Wall)*. Acrylic and offset, 8 ½ x 11 in. 1980.
109   *Adult Books*. Acrylic and xerox (offset with hand-coloring), 8 ½ x 11 in. 1980.
110   *El Dorado*. Acrylic on vinyl, 59 x 36 in. 1983.
111   *Terminal Bar*. Acrylic on vinyl, 34 x 48 in. 1981.
112   *Burlesque #1*. Gouache on Tyvek, 19 x 24 in. 2017.
113   *Dreams*. Oil stick on red paper, 27 ½ x 19 ¾ in. 1982.

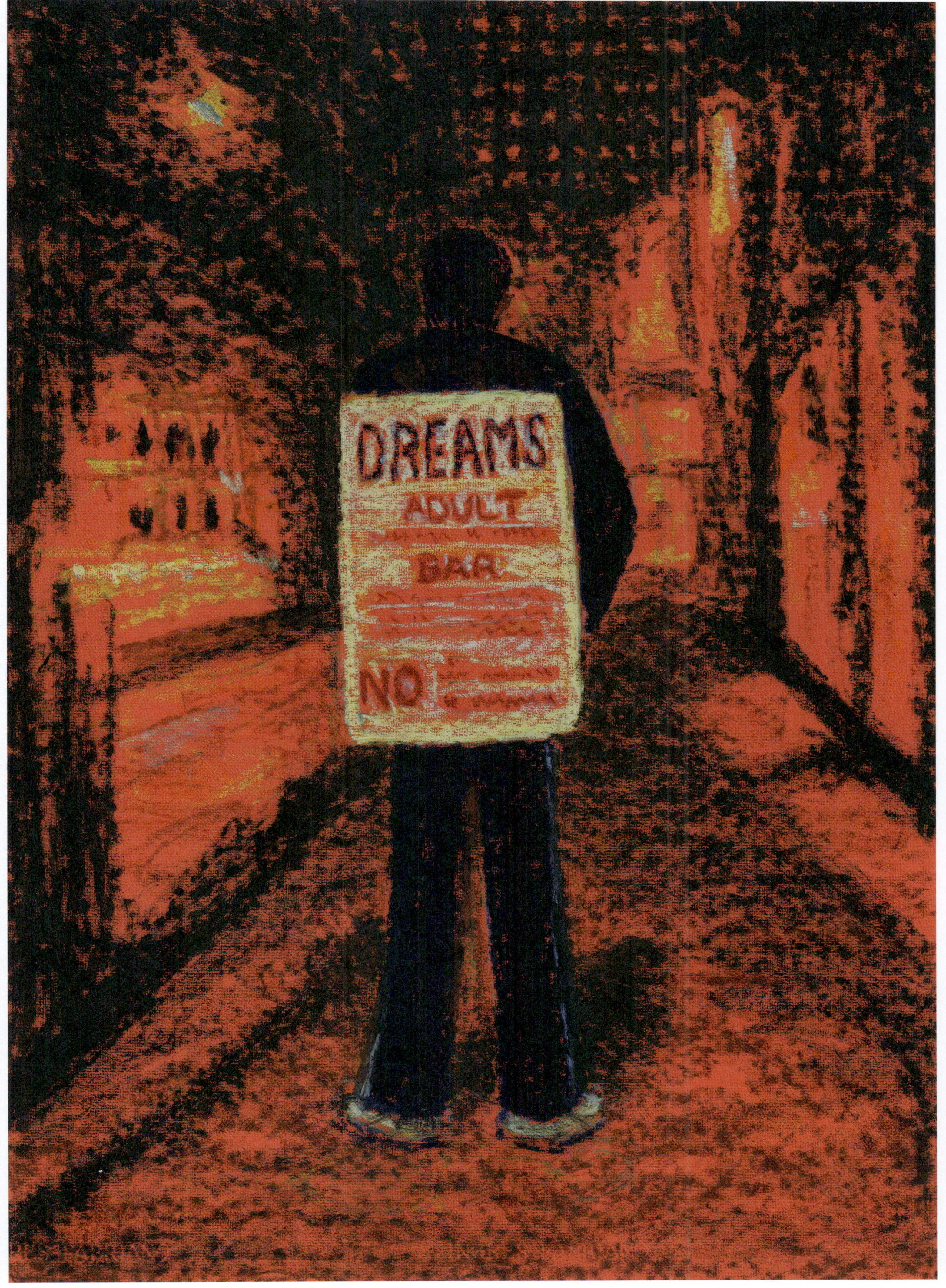
DREAMS
ADULT
BAR
NO

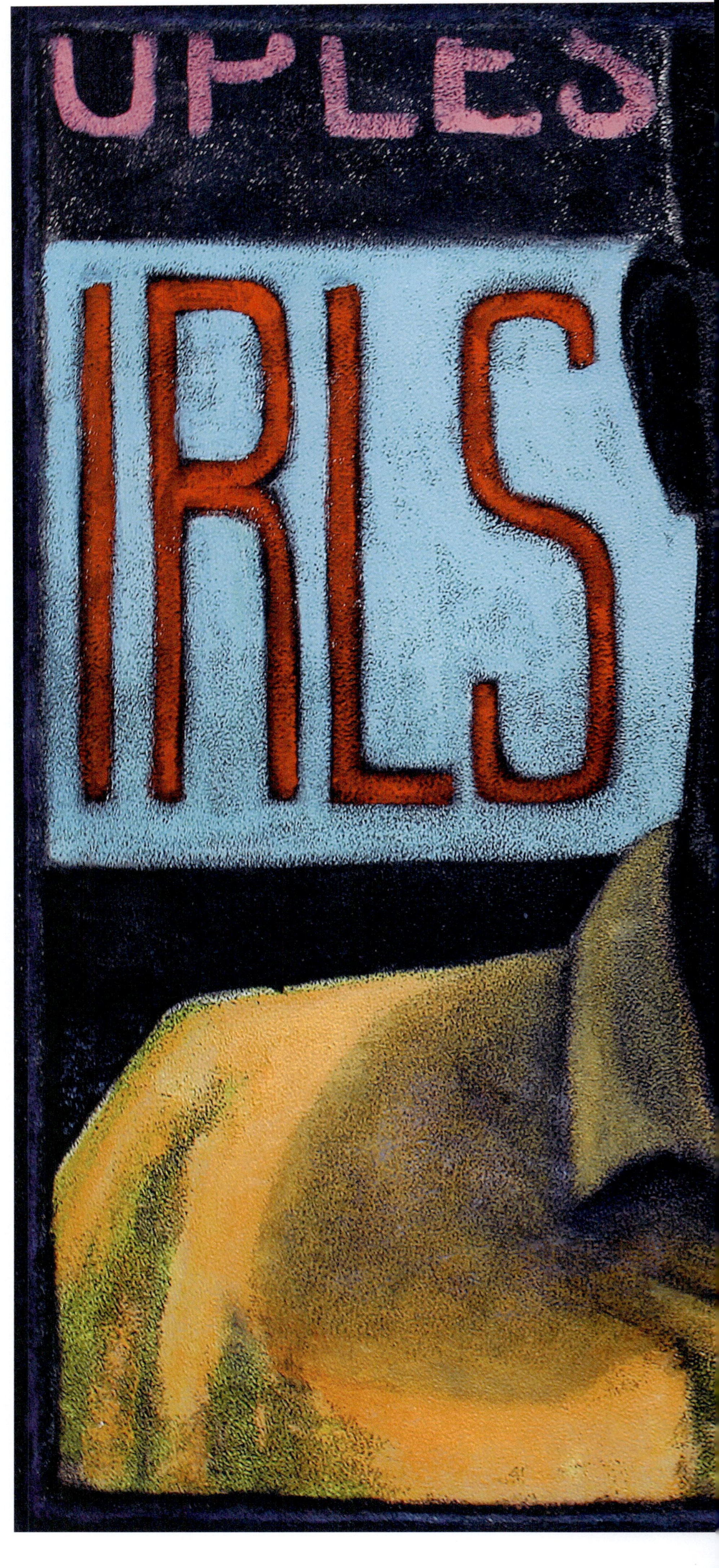
UPLES
IRLS

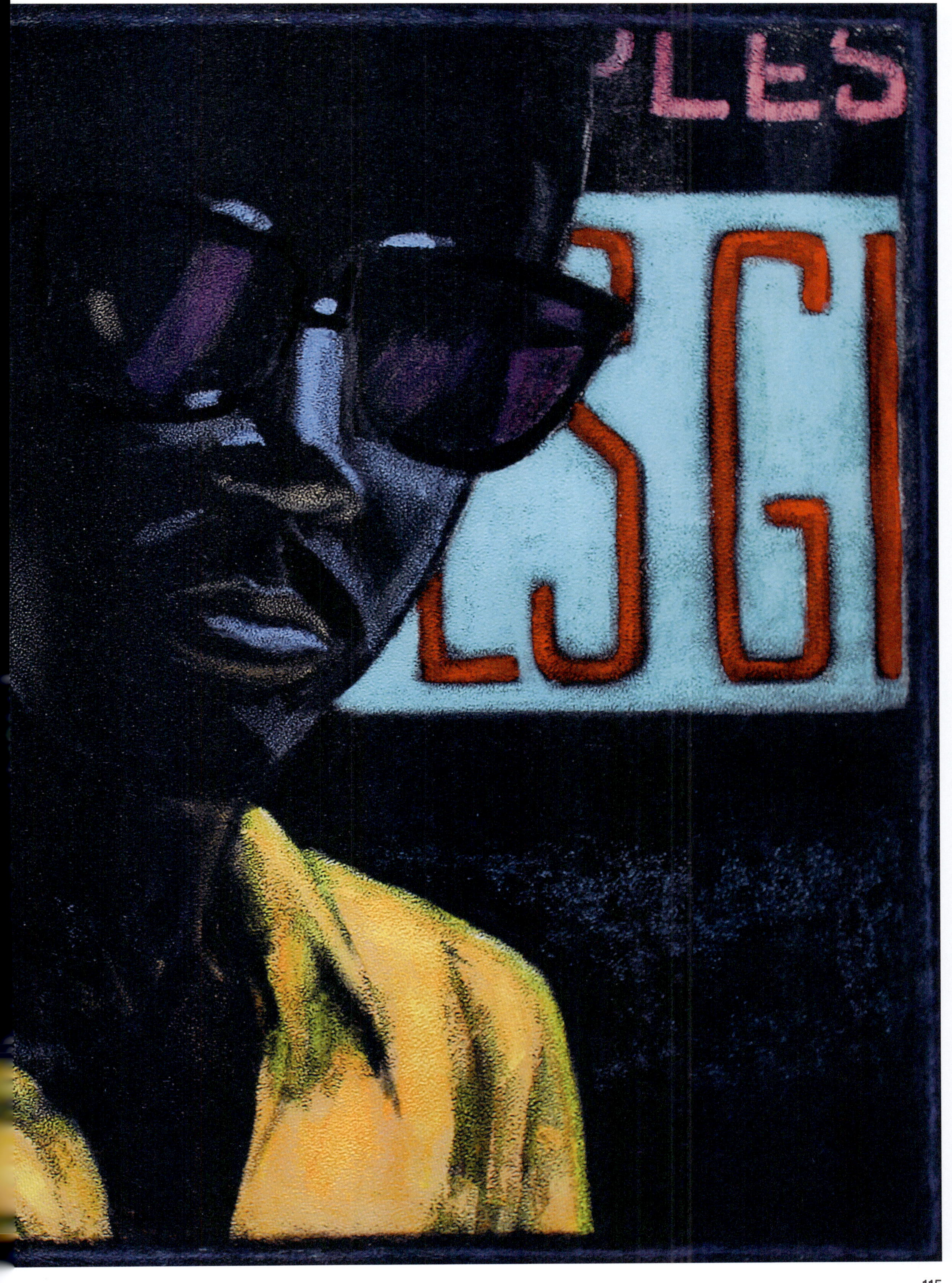

PLES
3GI

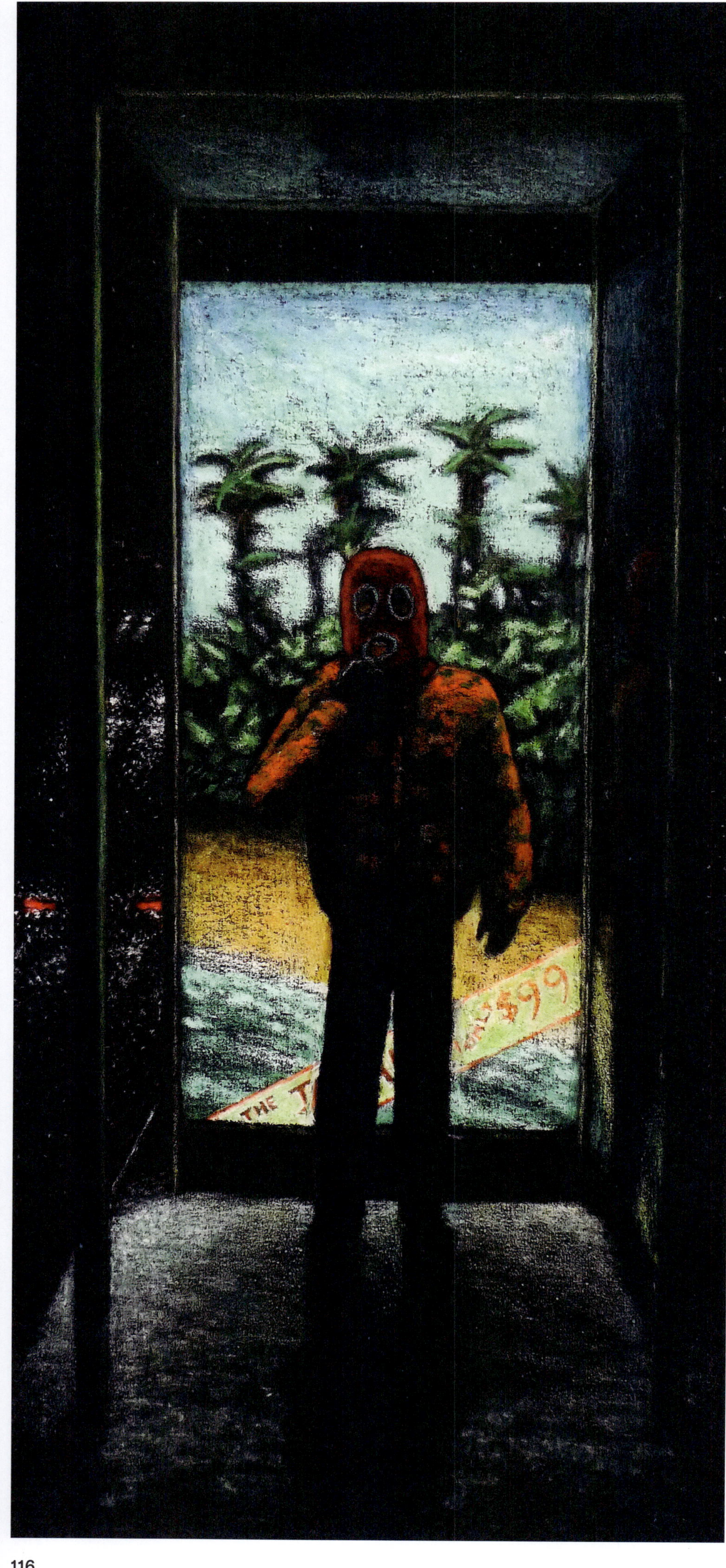
THE T
$99

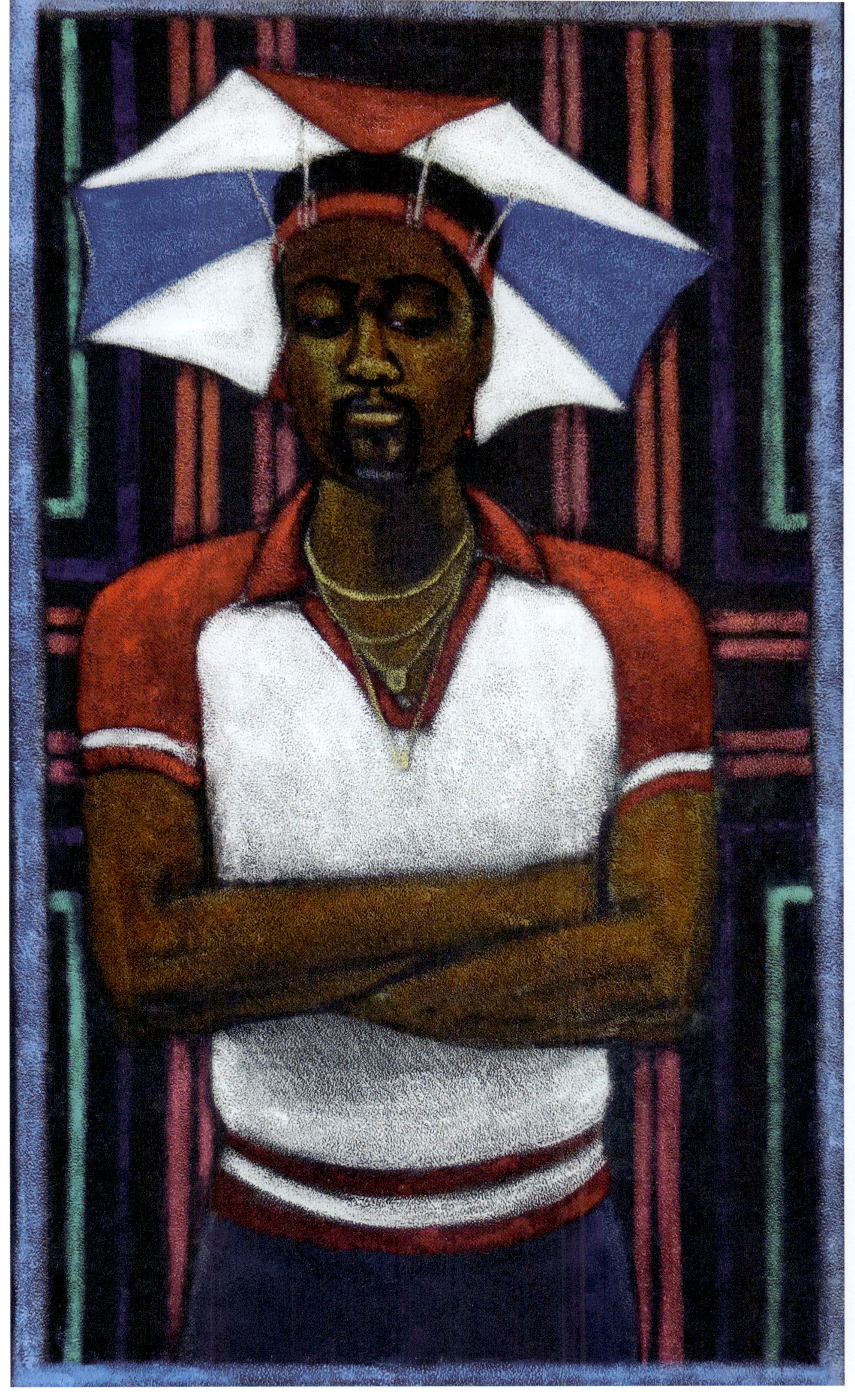

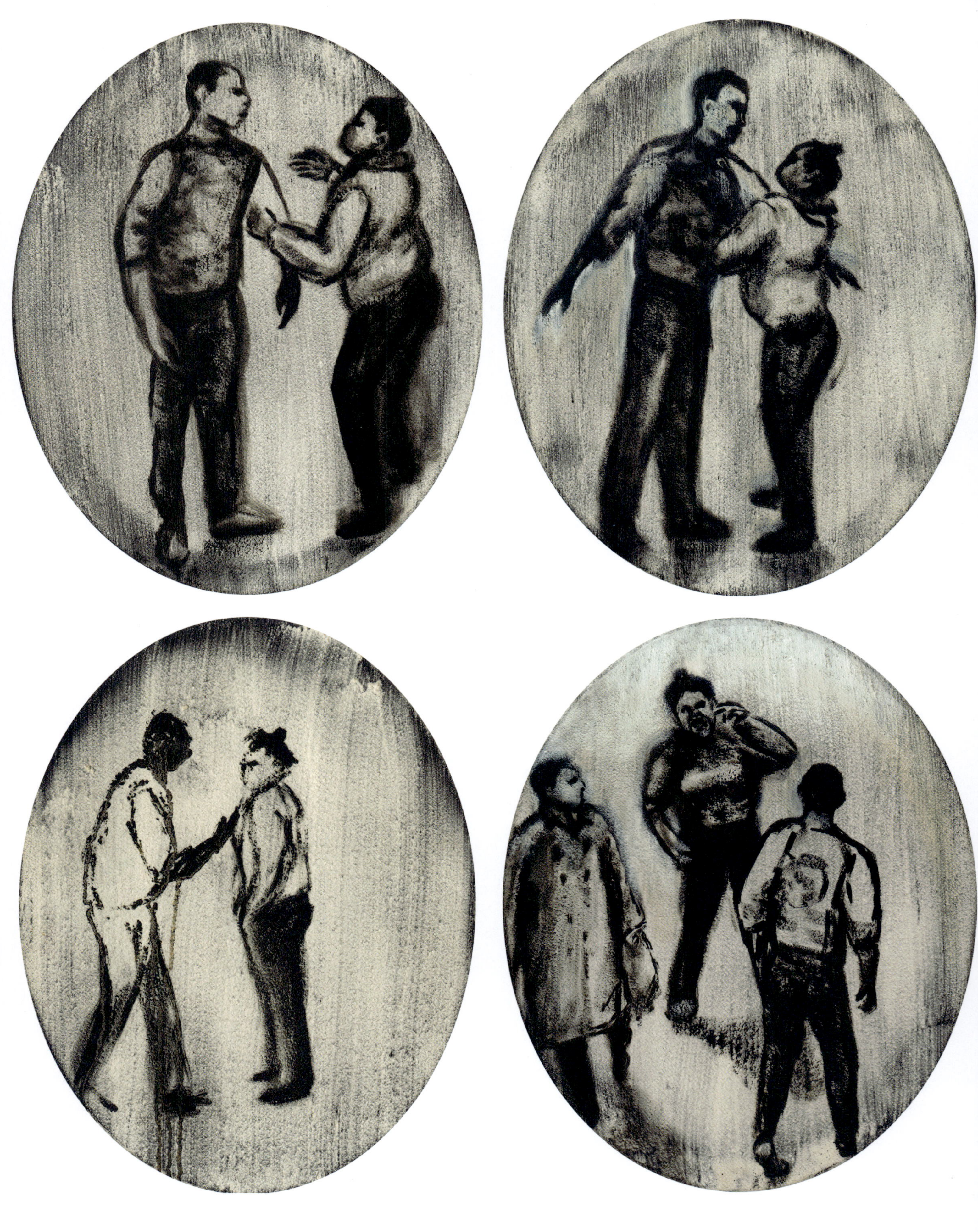

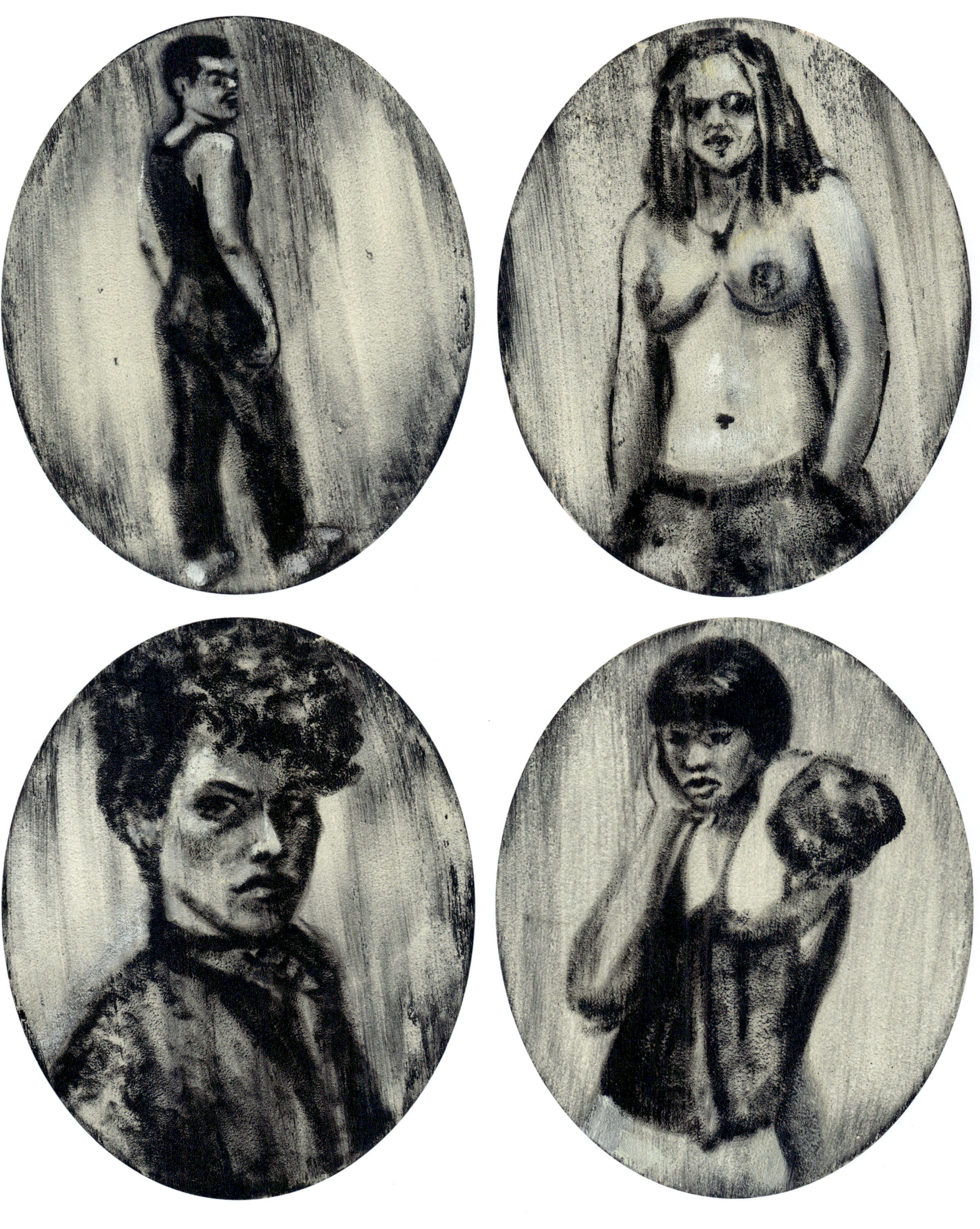

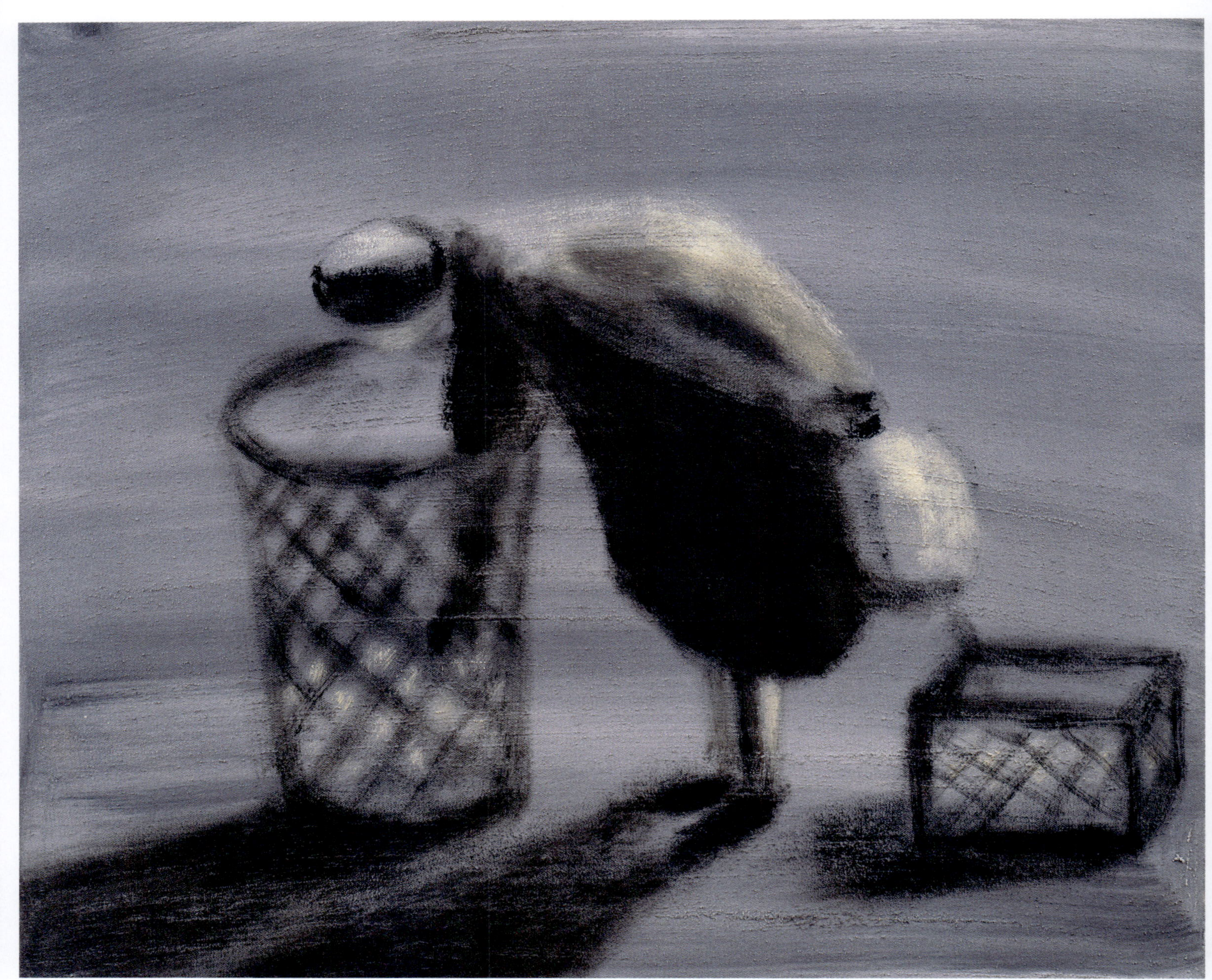

115   *Fred*. Acrylic on vinyl, 40 x 50 in. 1983. Collection of the Smithsonian Institution National Portrait Gallery.

116   *Bus Stop Boy II*. Oil stick on canvas, 70 x 34 in. 1984.

117   *Umbrella Hat Man*. Acrylic on vinyl, 50 x 30 in. 1981.

118   TOP LEFT: *Domestic Disturbance Take 2 #2*. Oil and Rolotex on canvas, 24 x 20 in. 1992.

        TOP RIGHT: *Domestic Disturbance Take 2 #3*. Oil and Rolotex on canvas, 24 x 20 in. 1992.

        BOTTOM LEFT: *Domestic Disturbance 1*. Oil and Rolotex on canvas, 20 x 16 in. 1991.

        BOTTOM RIGHT: *Domestic Disturbance Take 2 #4*. Oil and Rolotex on canvas, 24 x 20 in. 1992.

119   TOP LEFT: *Chico Looking Over His Shoulder*. Oil and Rolotex on canvas, 24 x 20 in. 1992.

        TOP RIGHT: *Yas Topless*. Oil and Rolotex on canvas, 24 x 20 in. 1992.

        BOTTOM LEFT: *Trust Me* (New Yorker *Self Portrait*). Oil and Celotex on canvas, 24 x 20 in. 1992.

        BOTTOM RIGHT: *Black Beauty*. Oil and Rolotex on canvas, 24 x 20 in. 1992.

120   *Old Lady With Crate 1*. Oil on canvas, 24 x 30 in. 1990.

121   *Authentic Military*. Oil and Rolotex on canvas, 30 x 23 in. 1995.

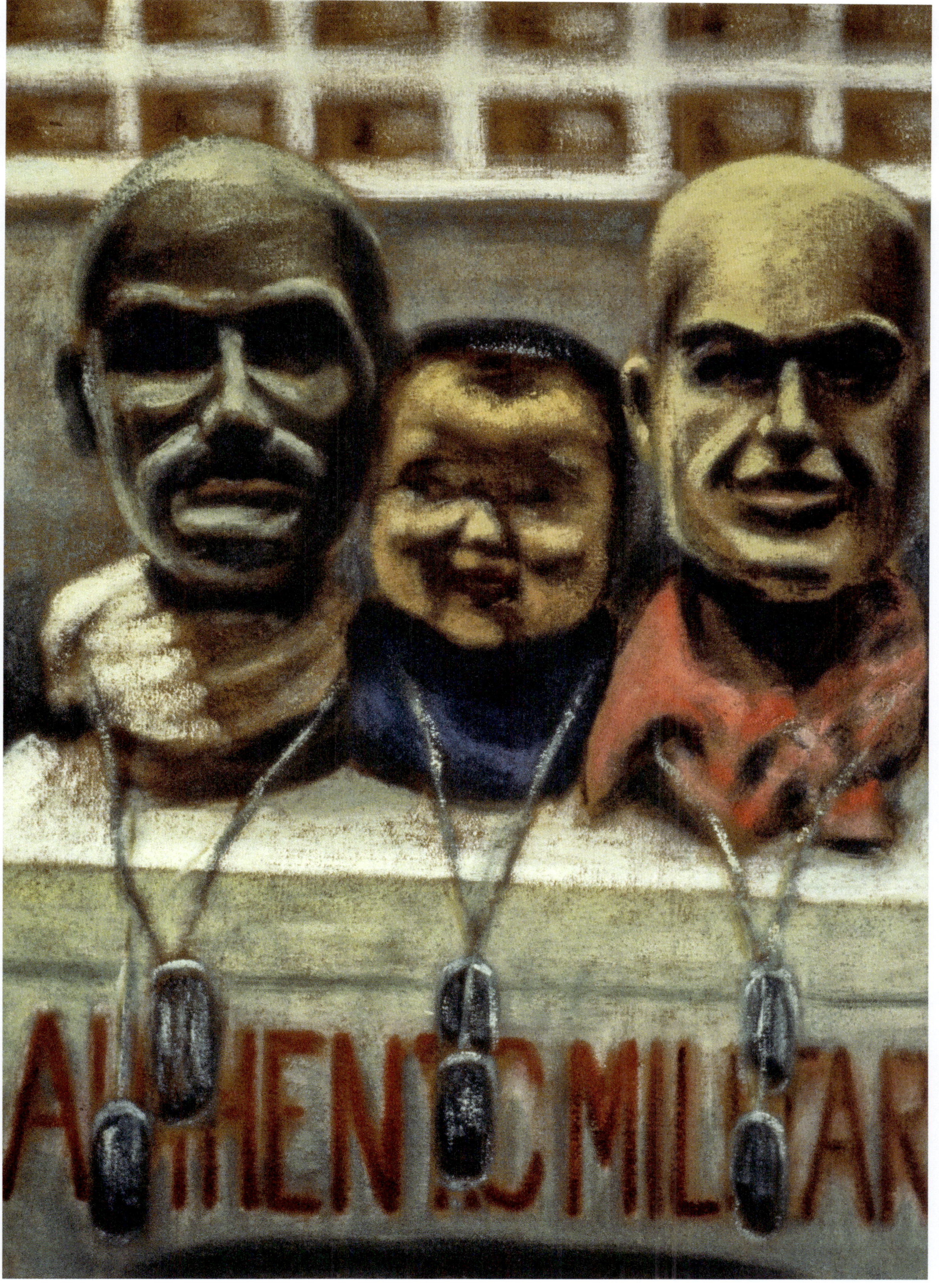
AUTHENTIC MILITAR

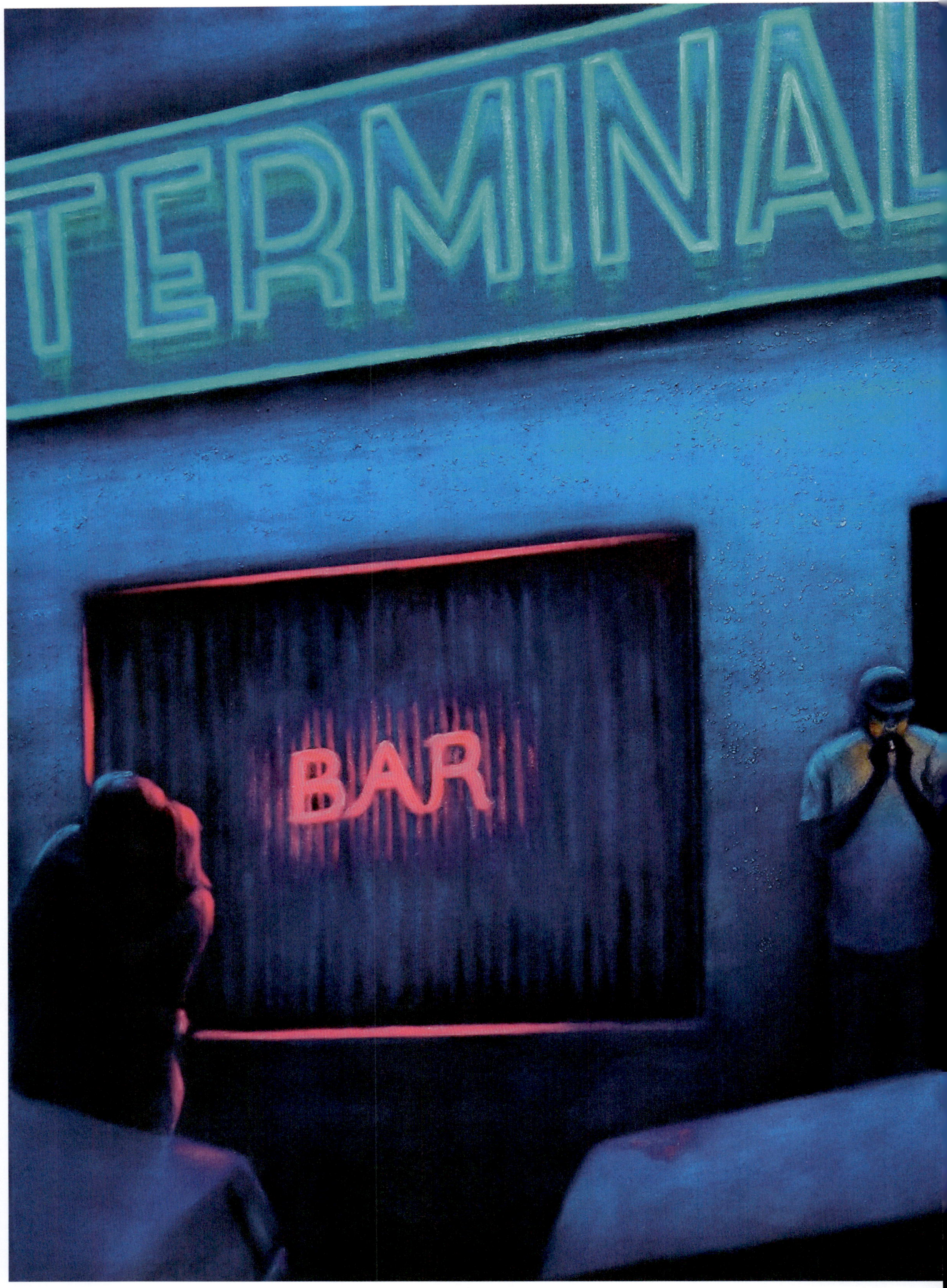

TERMINAL
BAR

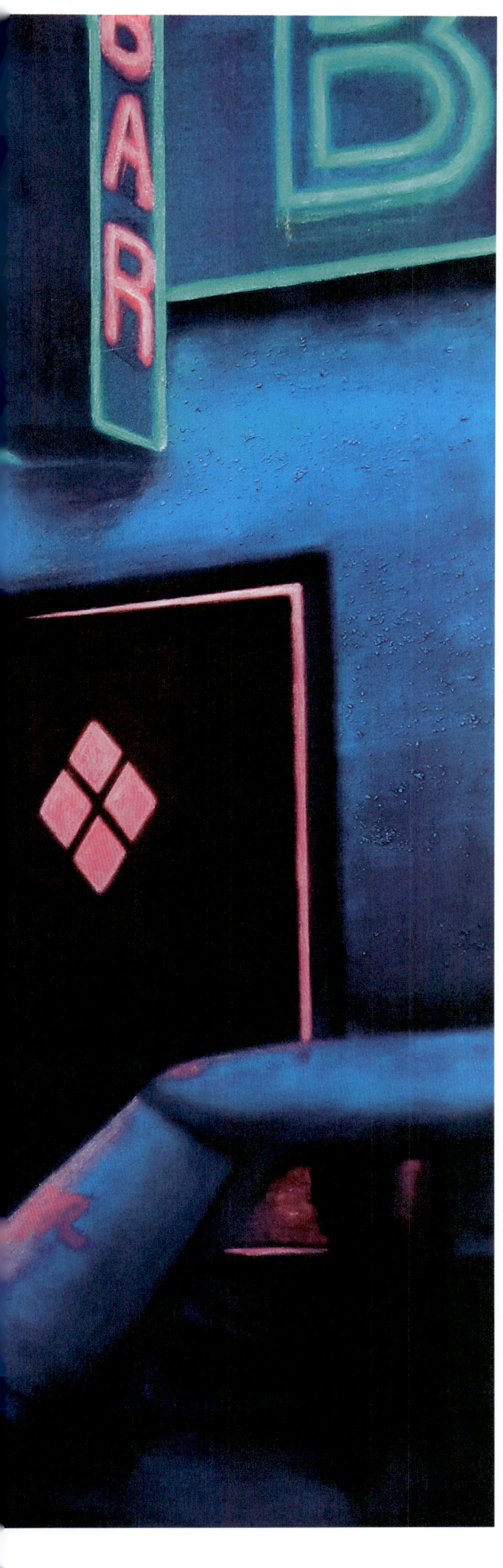

BAR
B

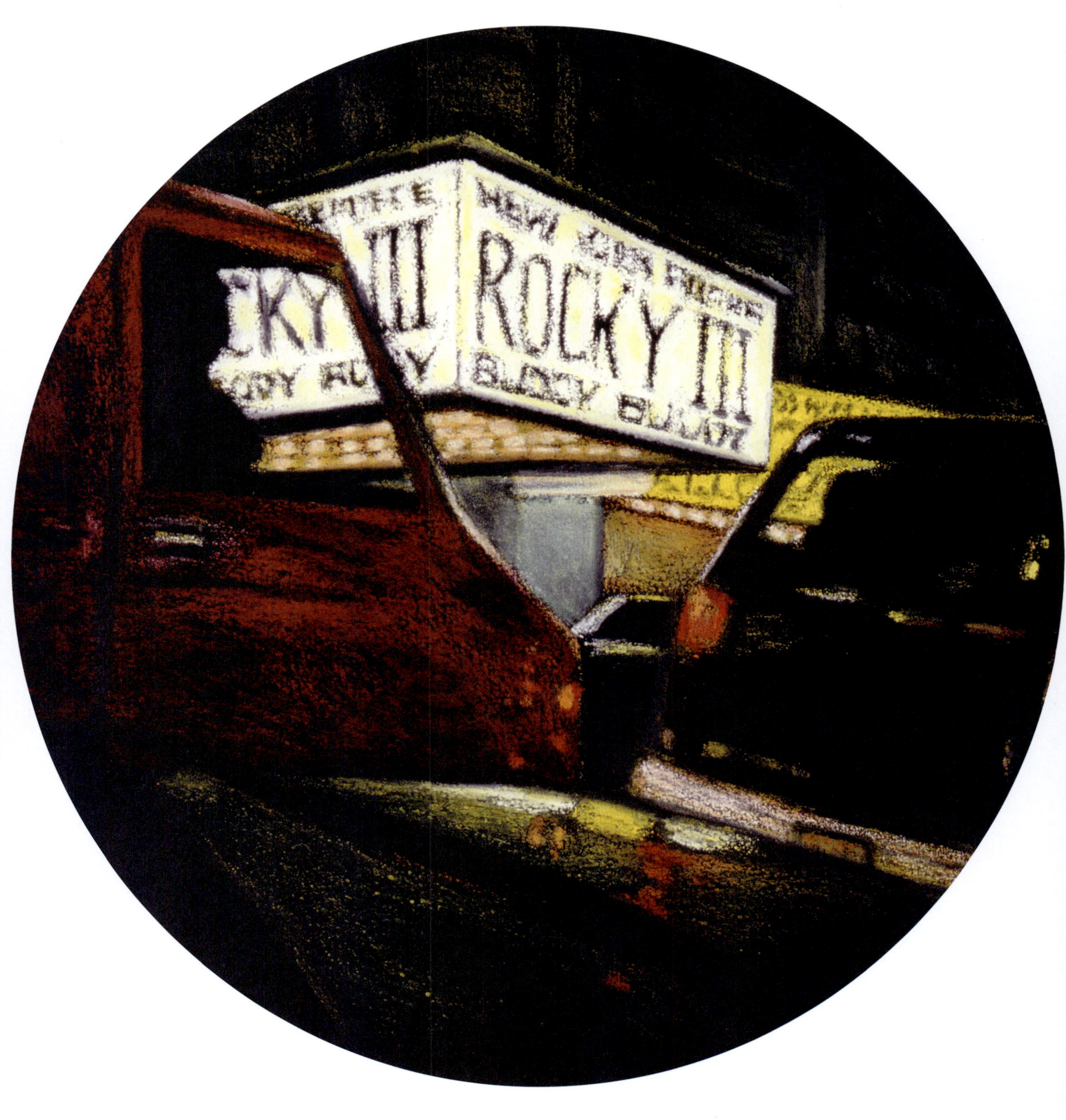

ROCKY III

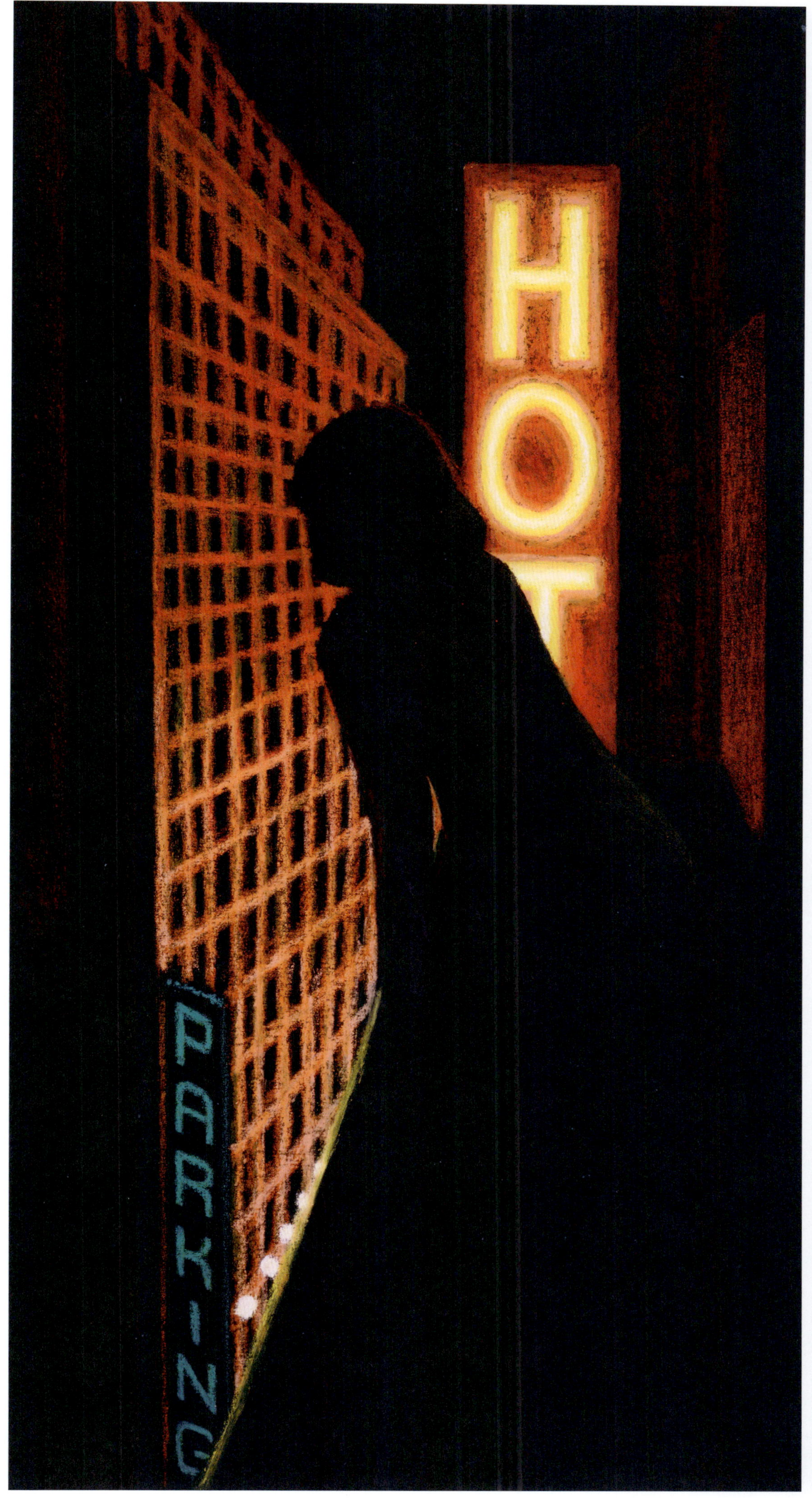

HOT
PARKING

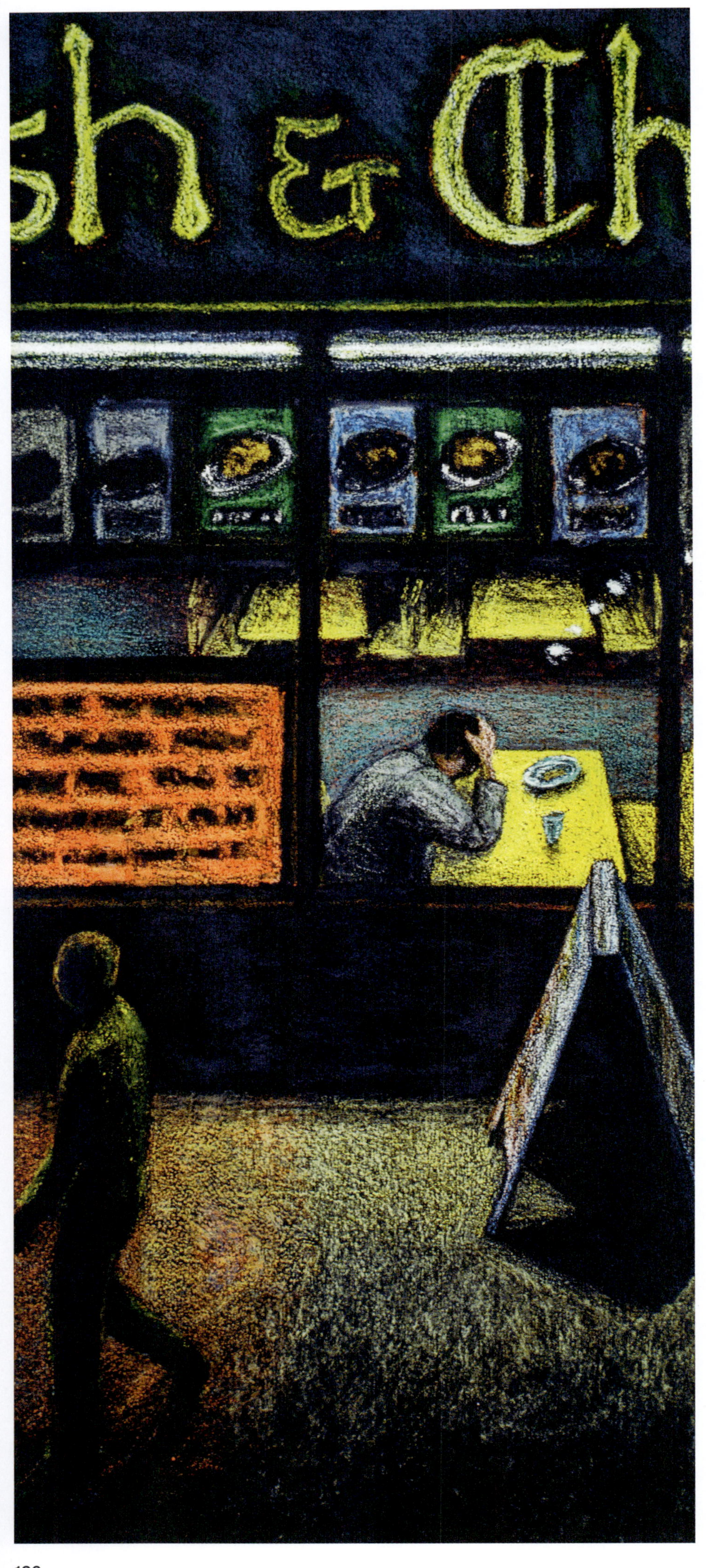
sh & Ch

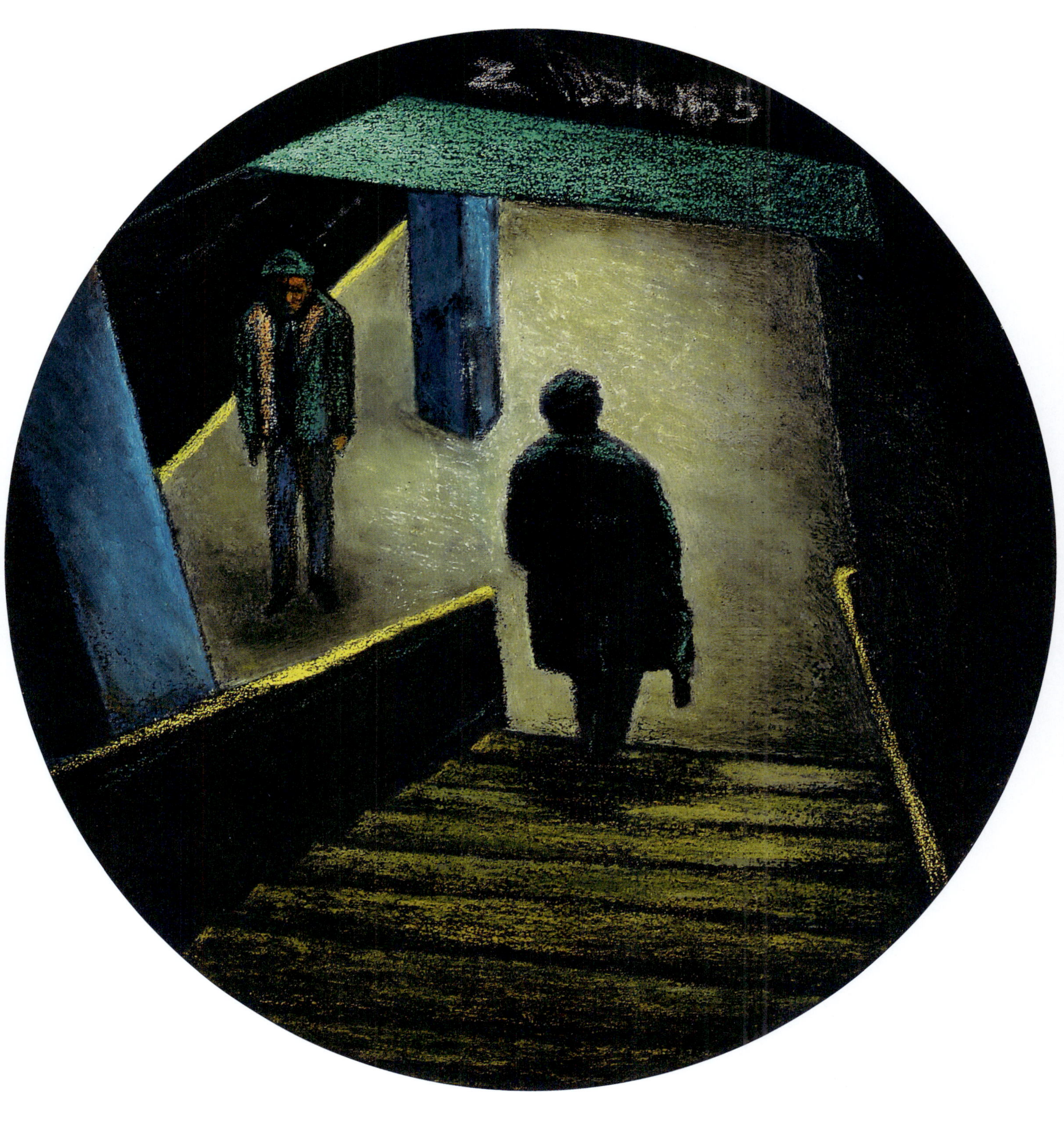

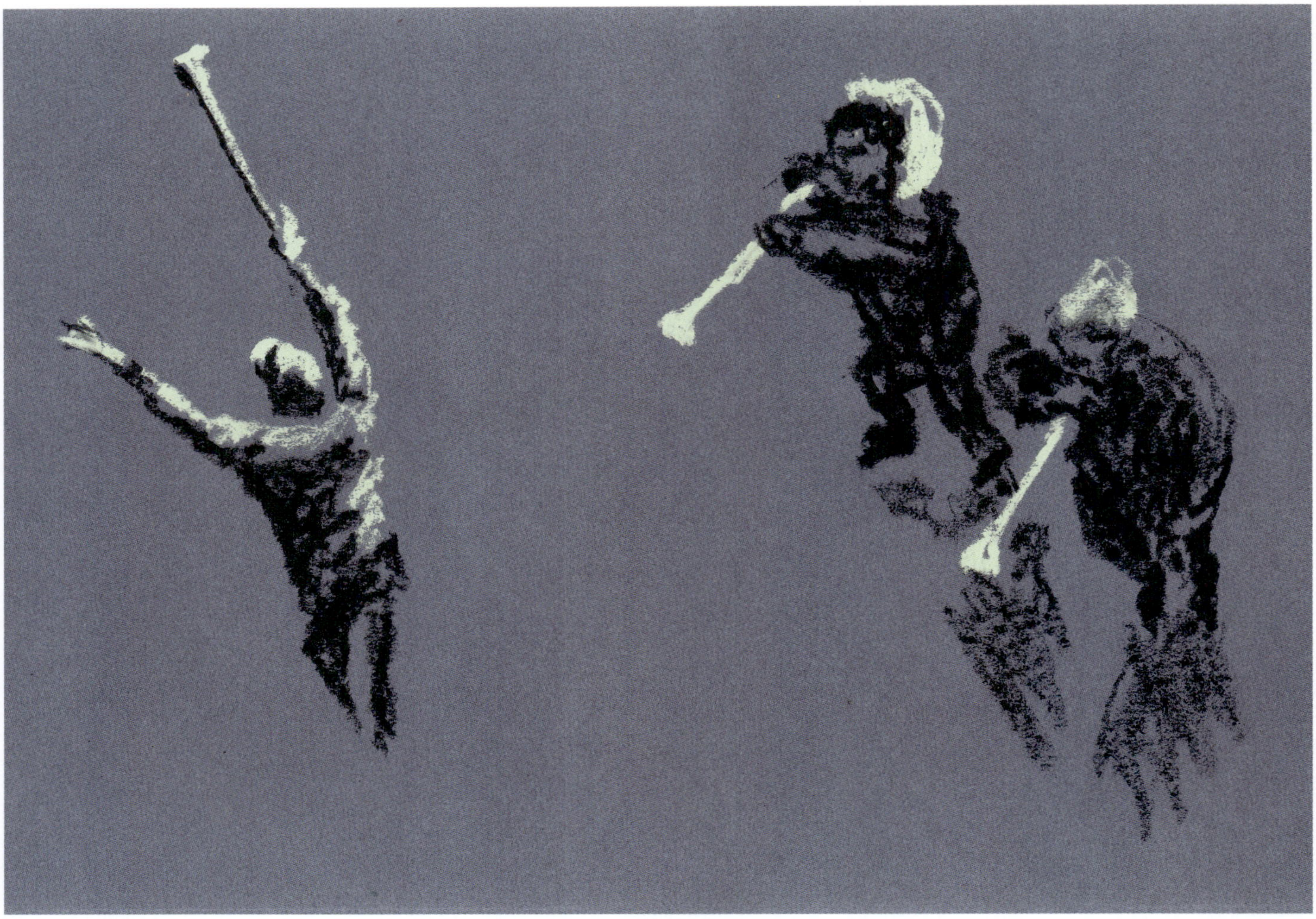

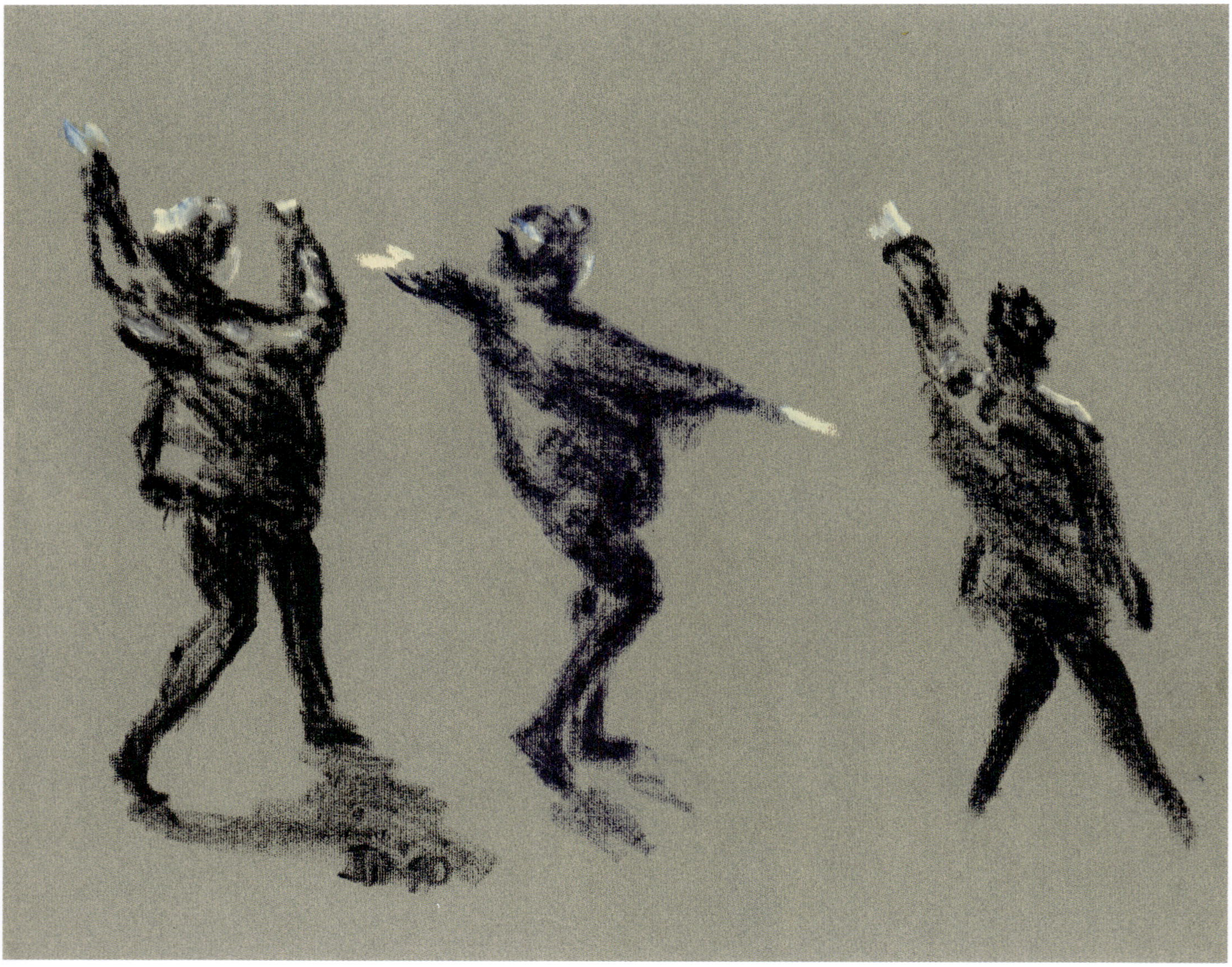

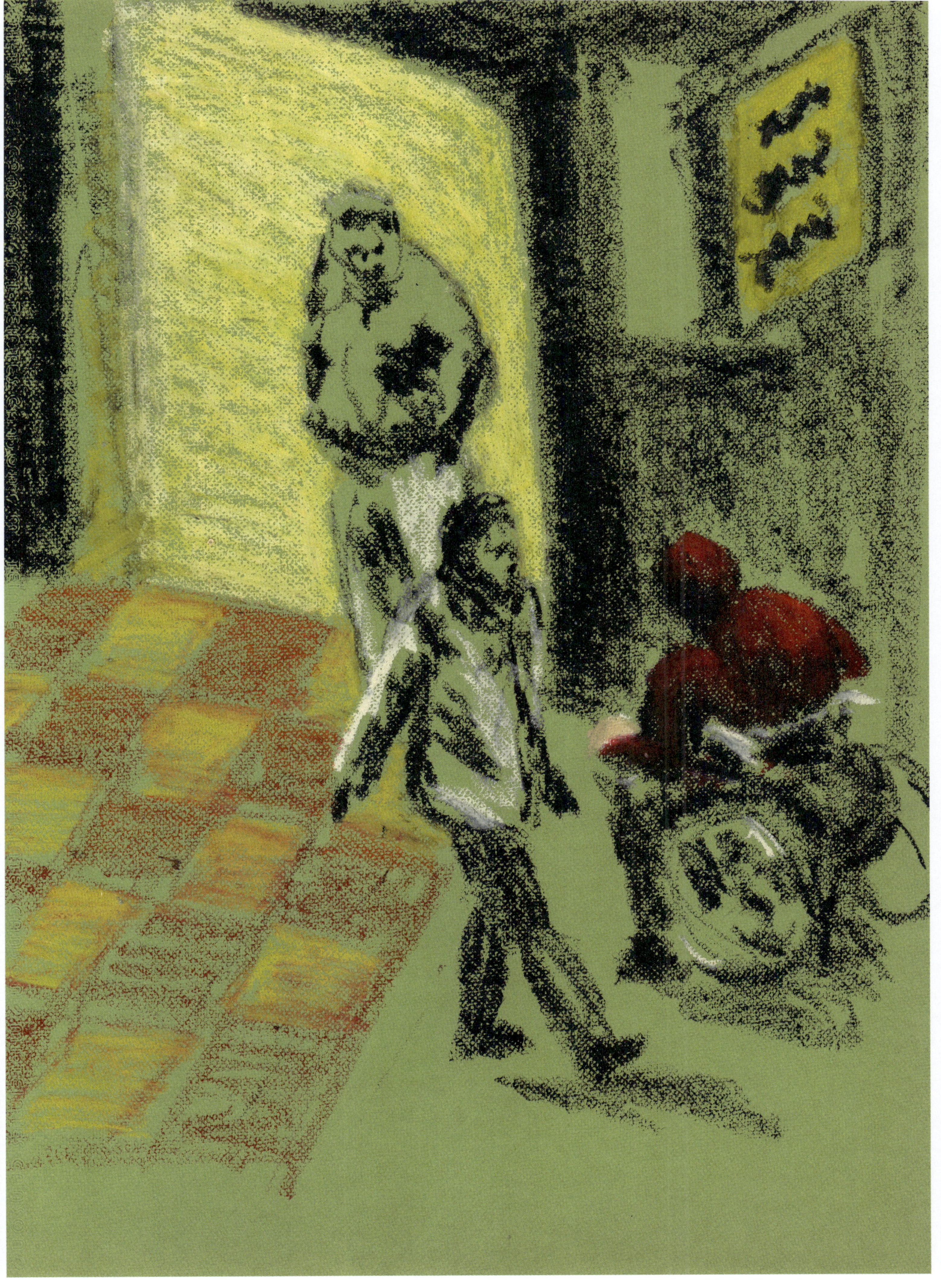

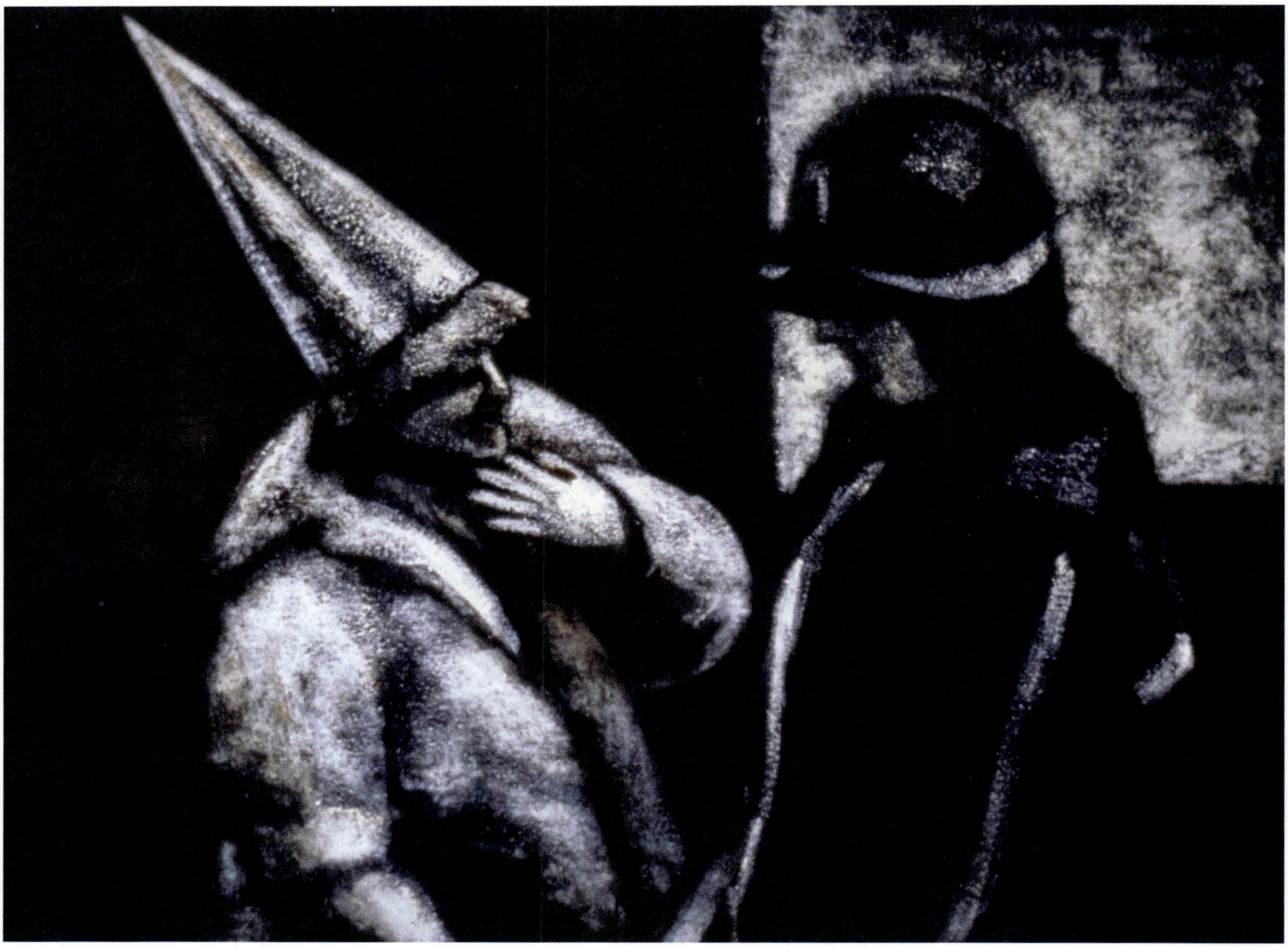

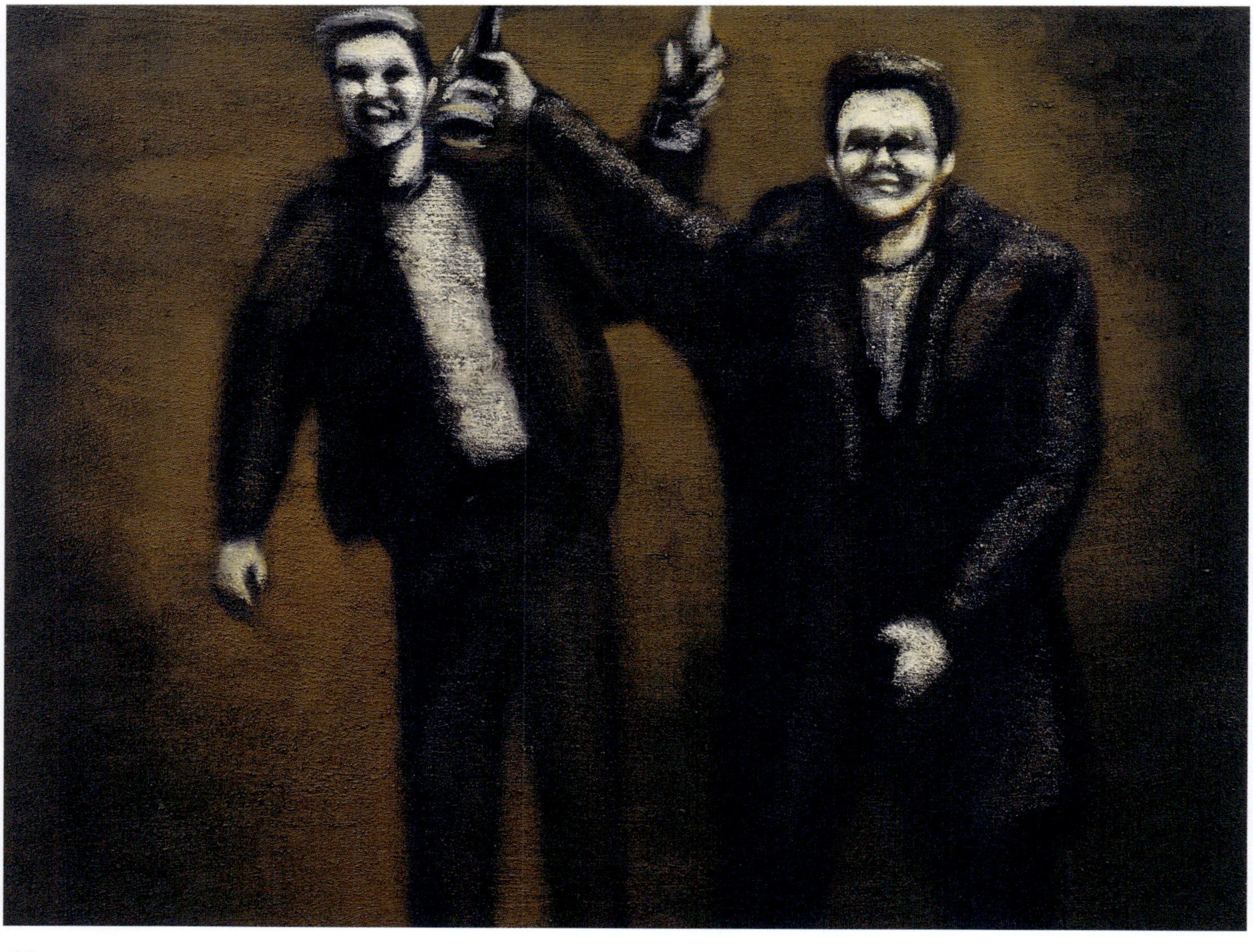

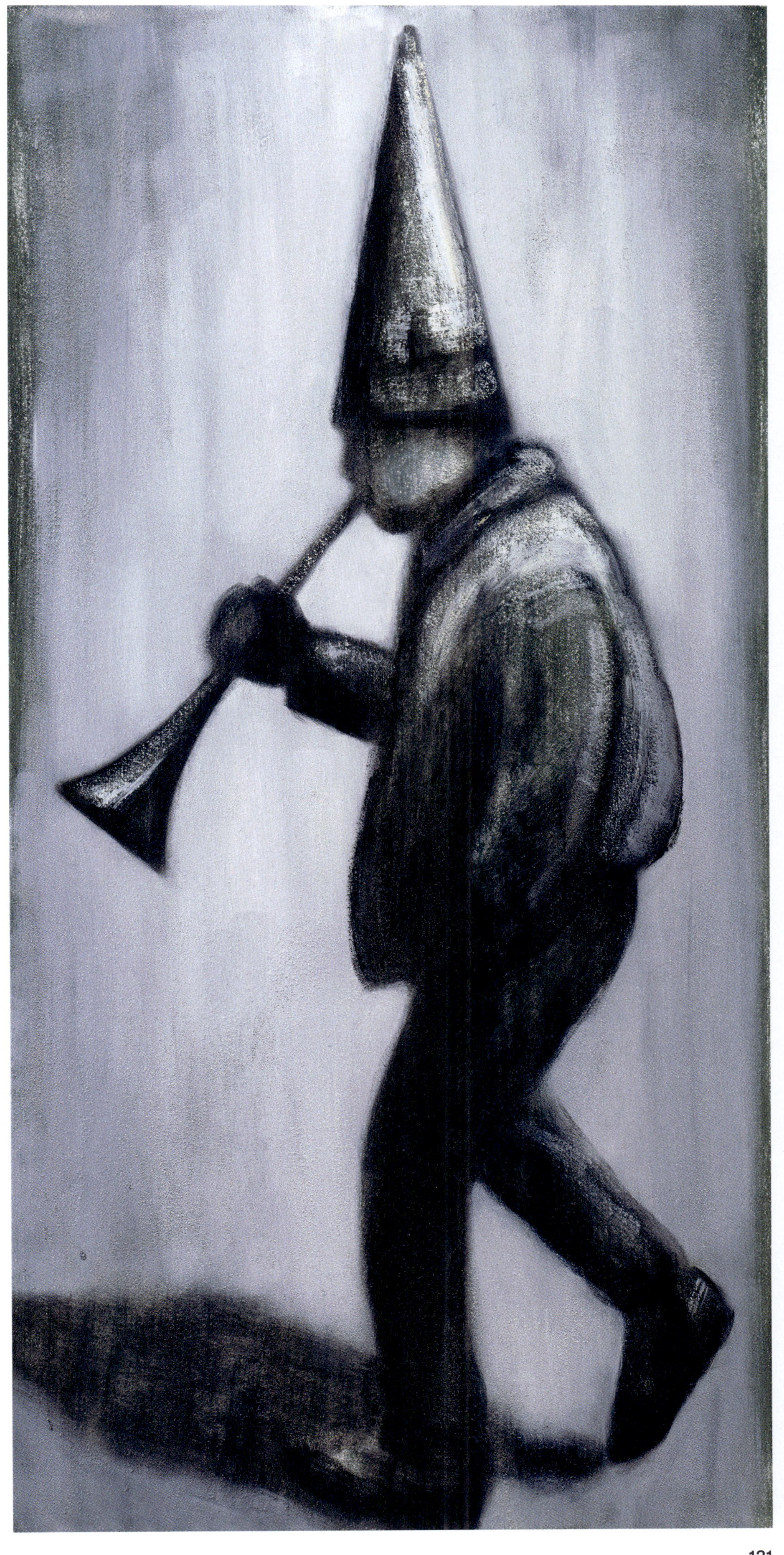

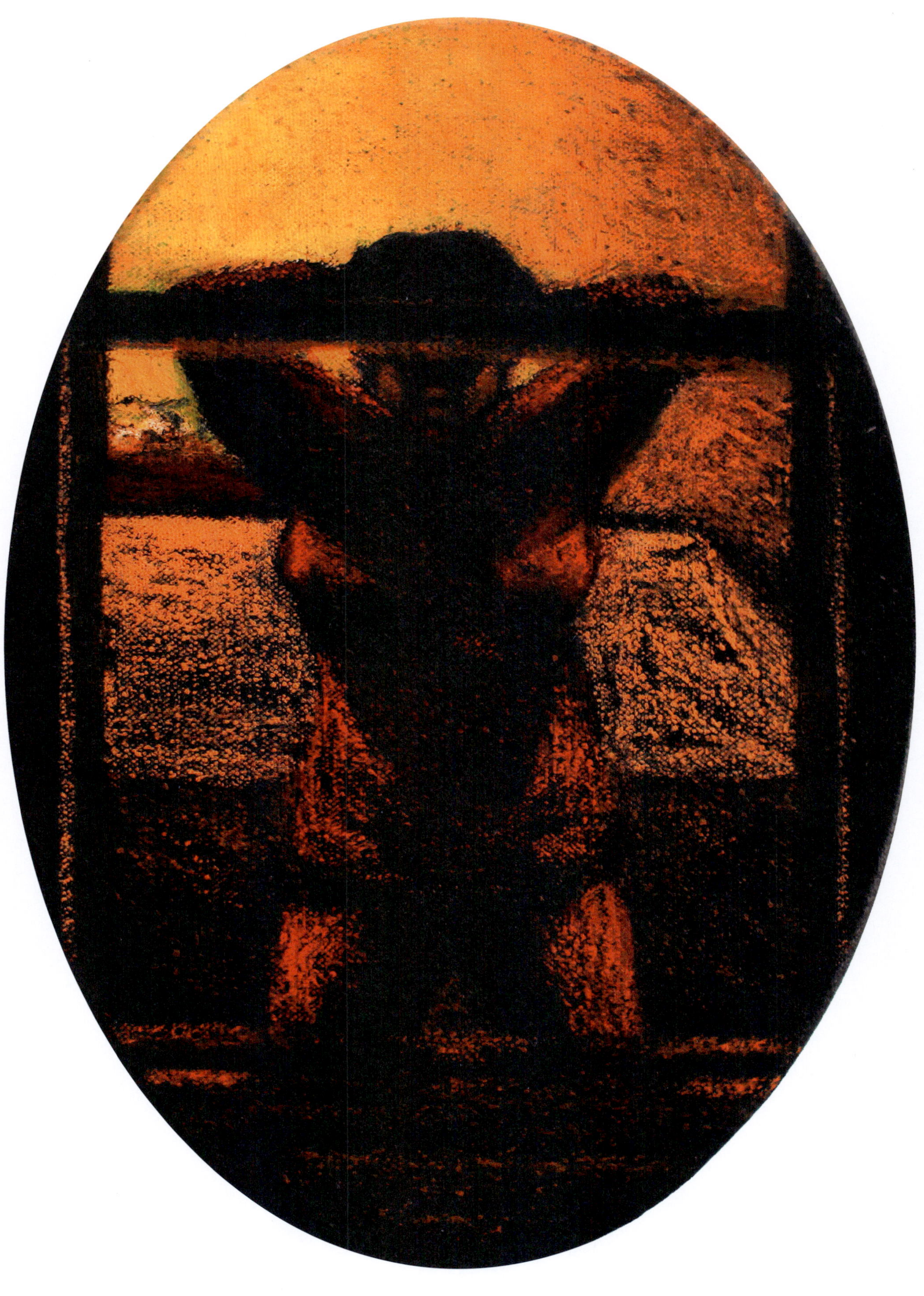

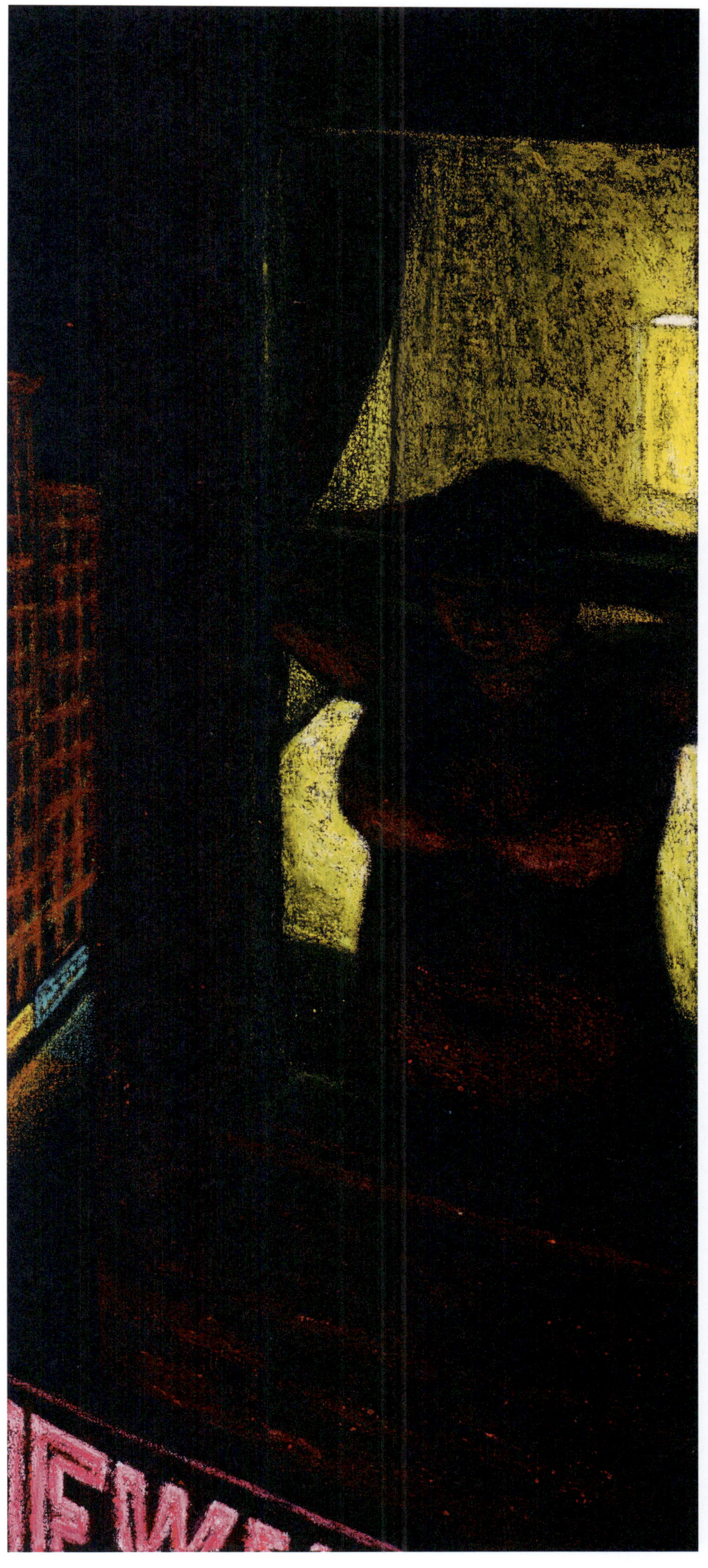

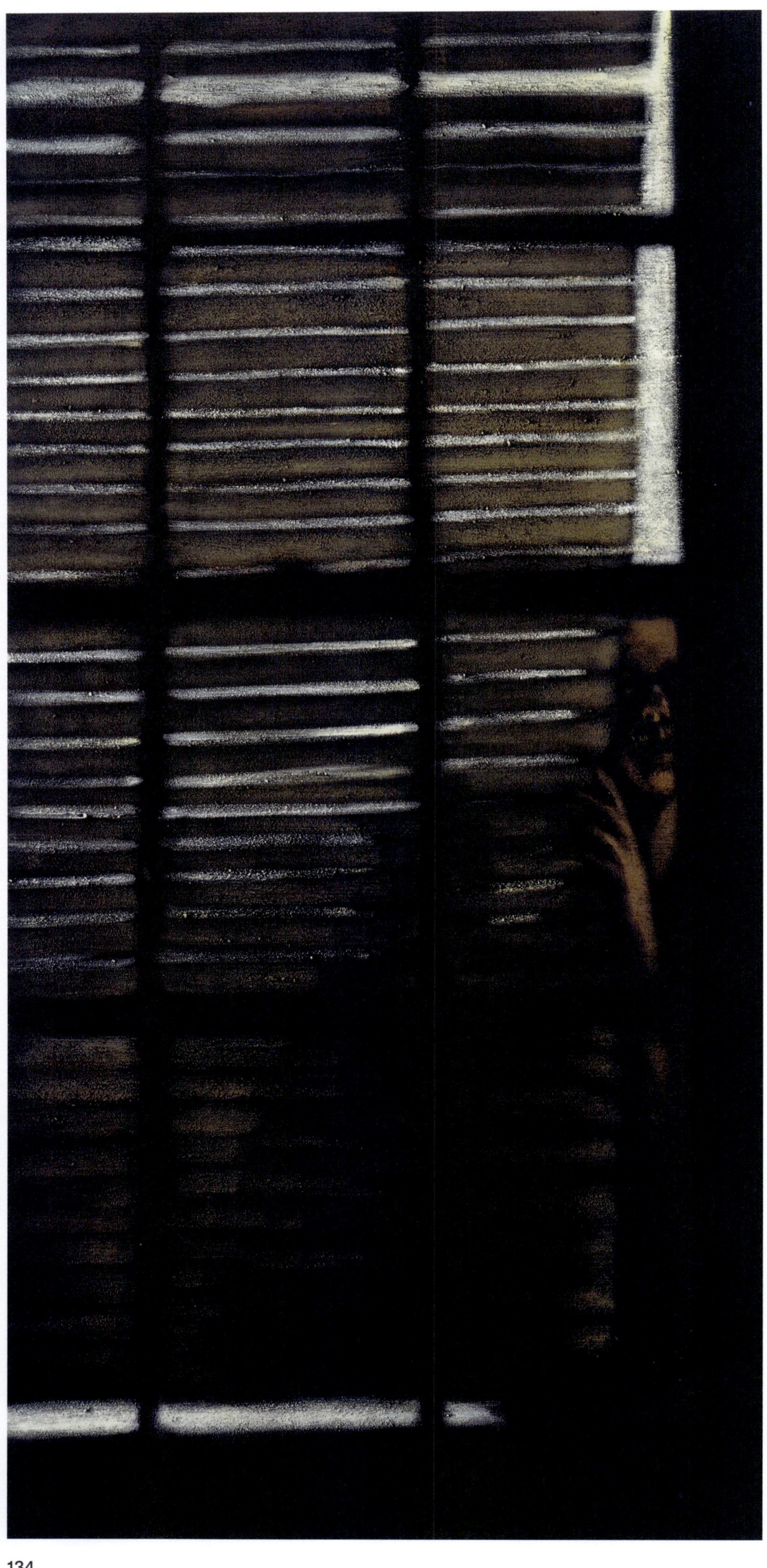

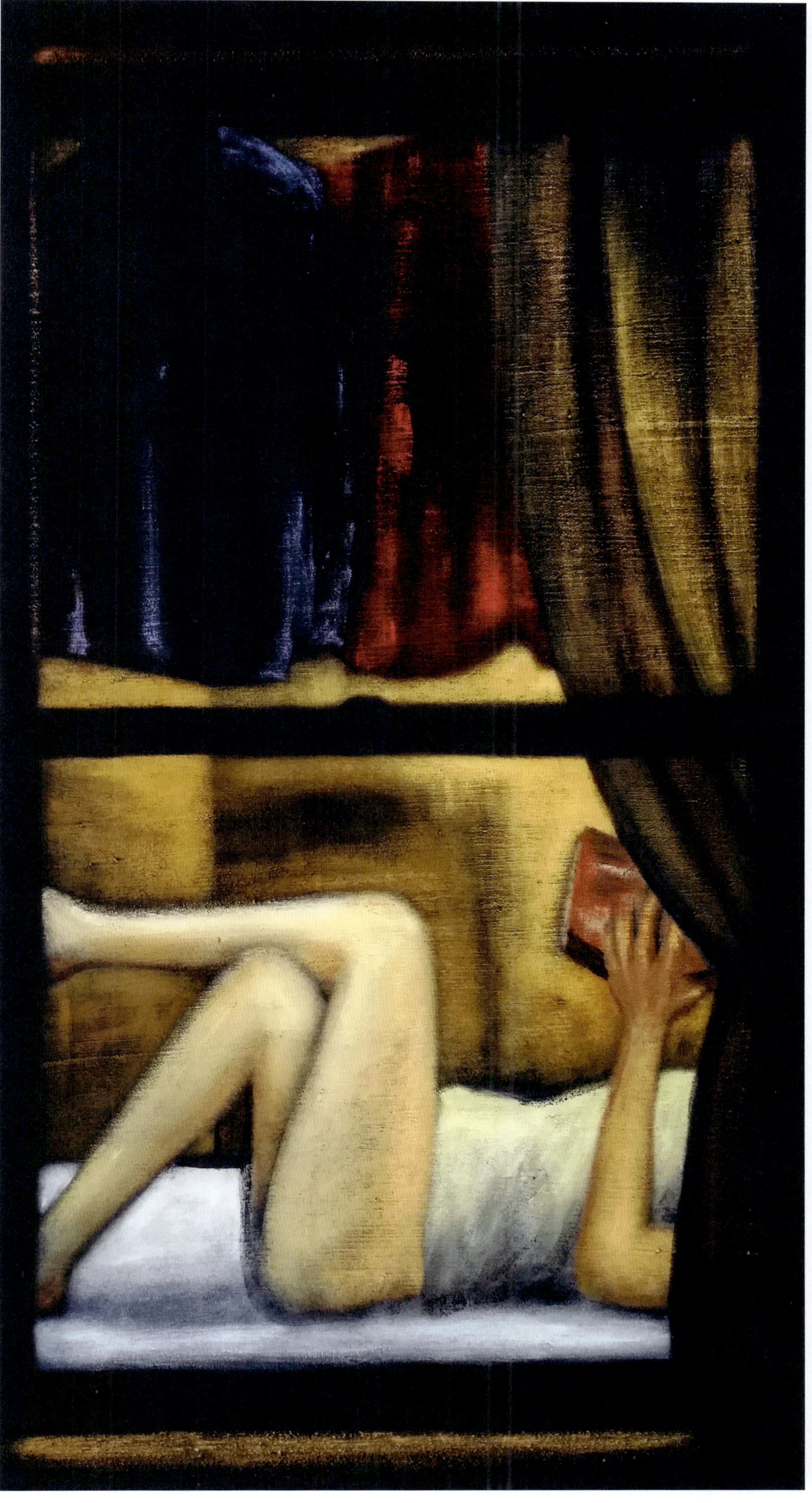

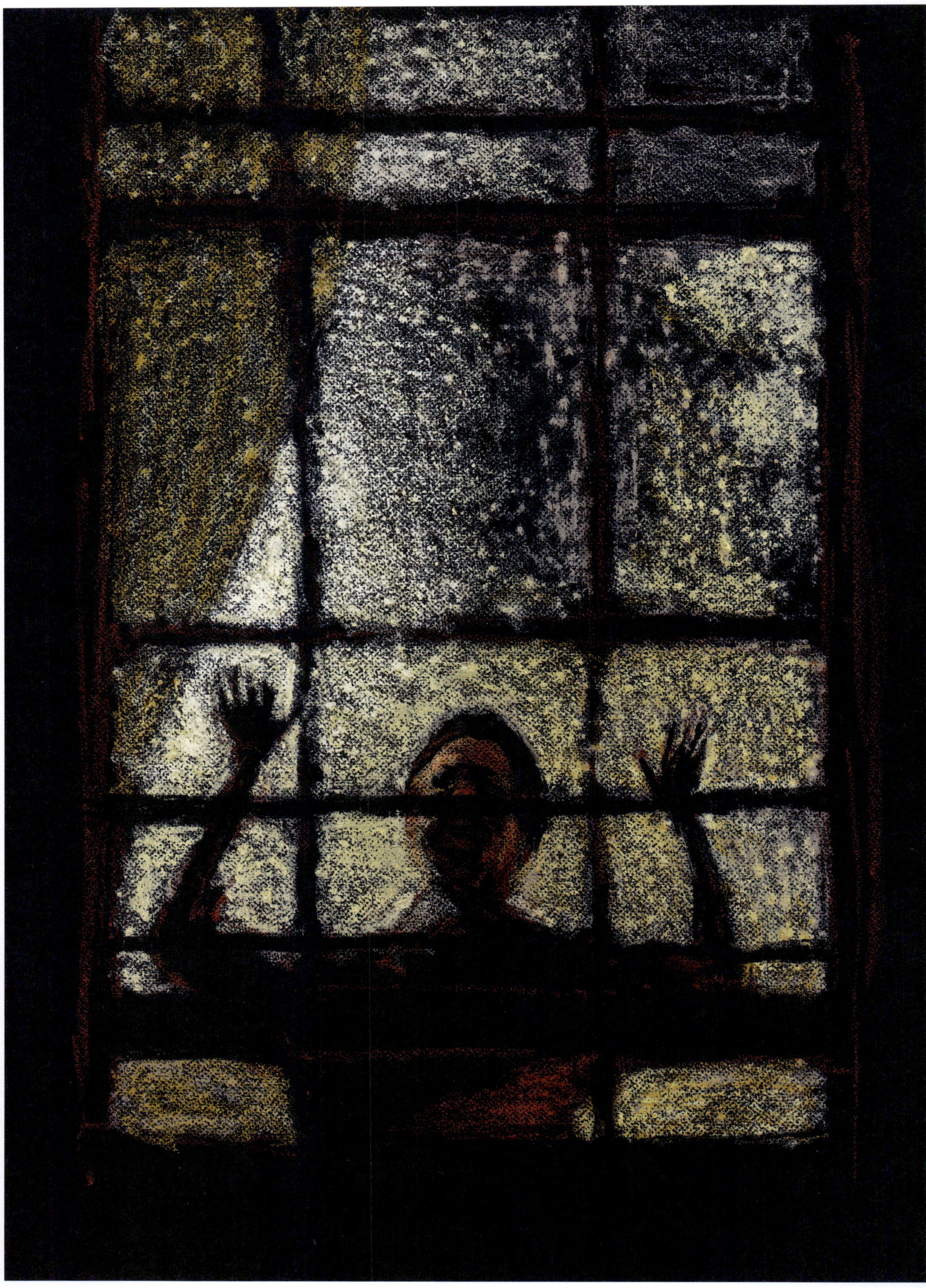

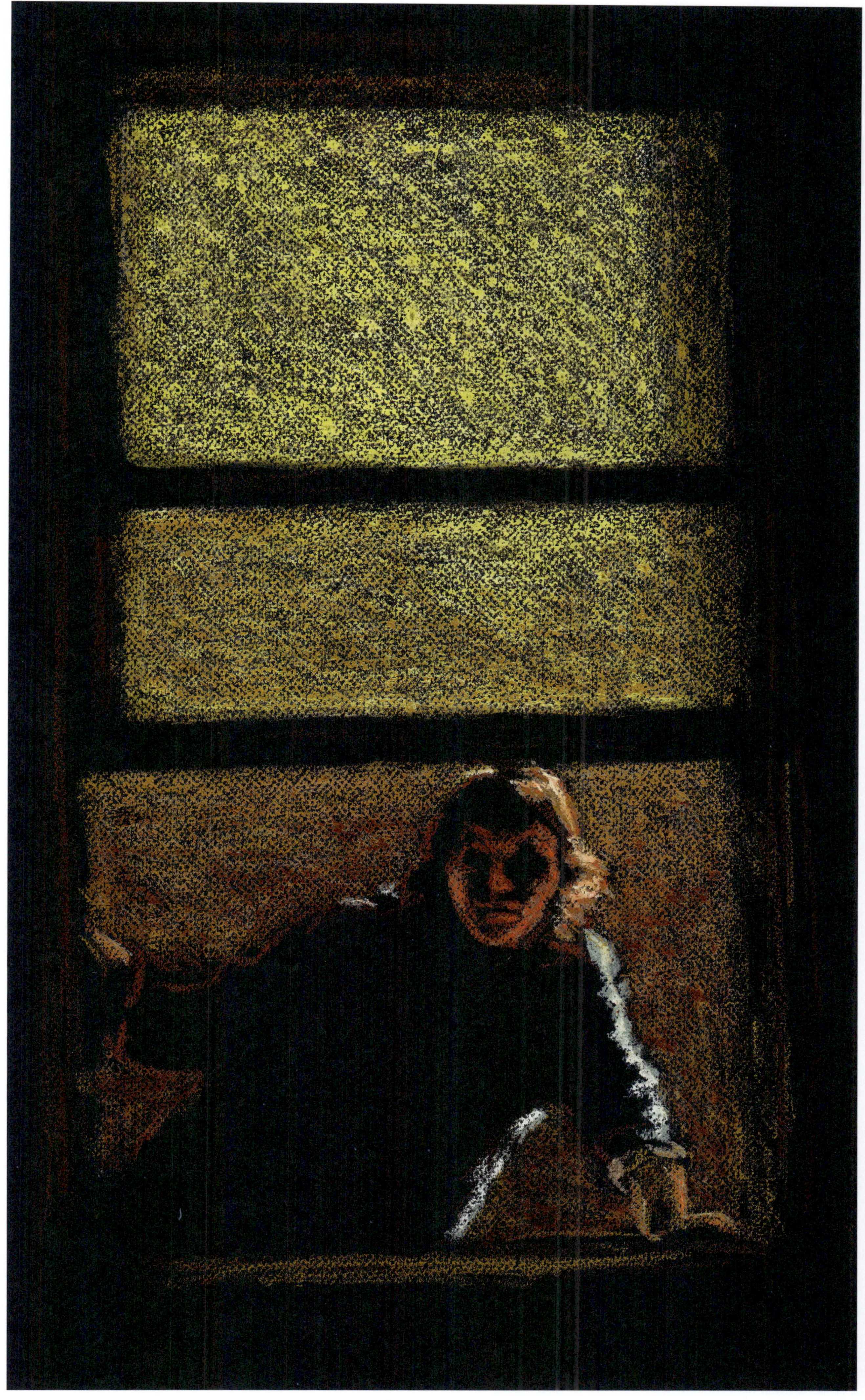

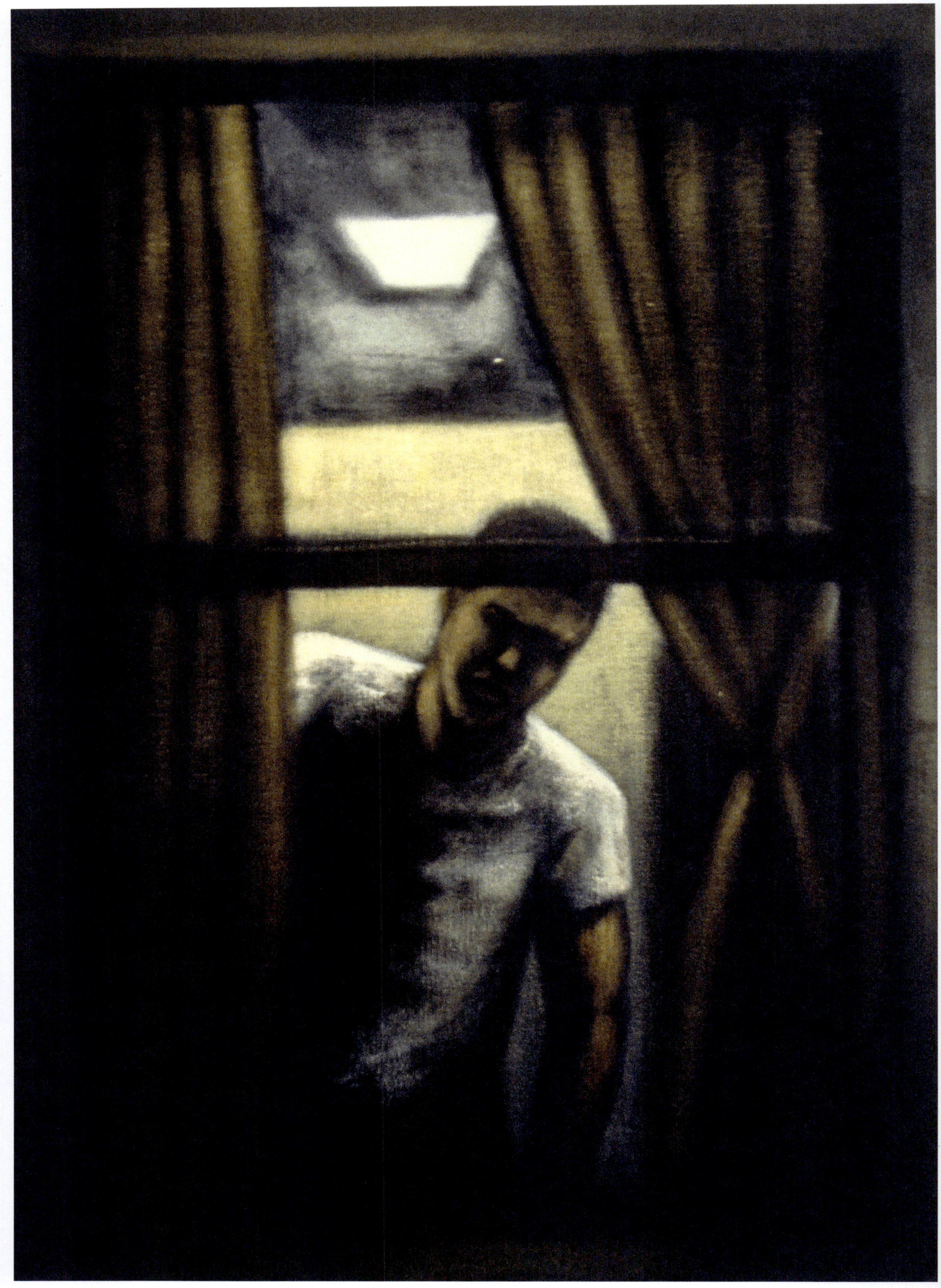

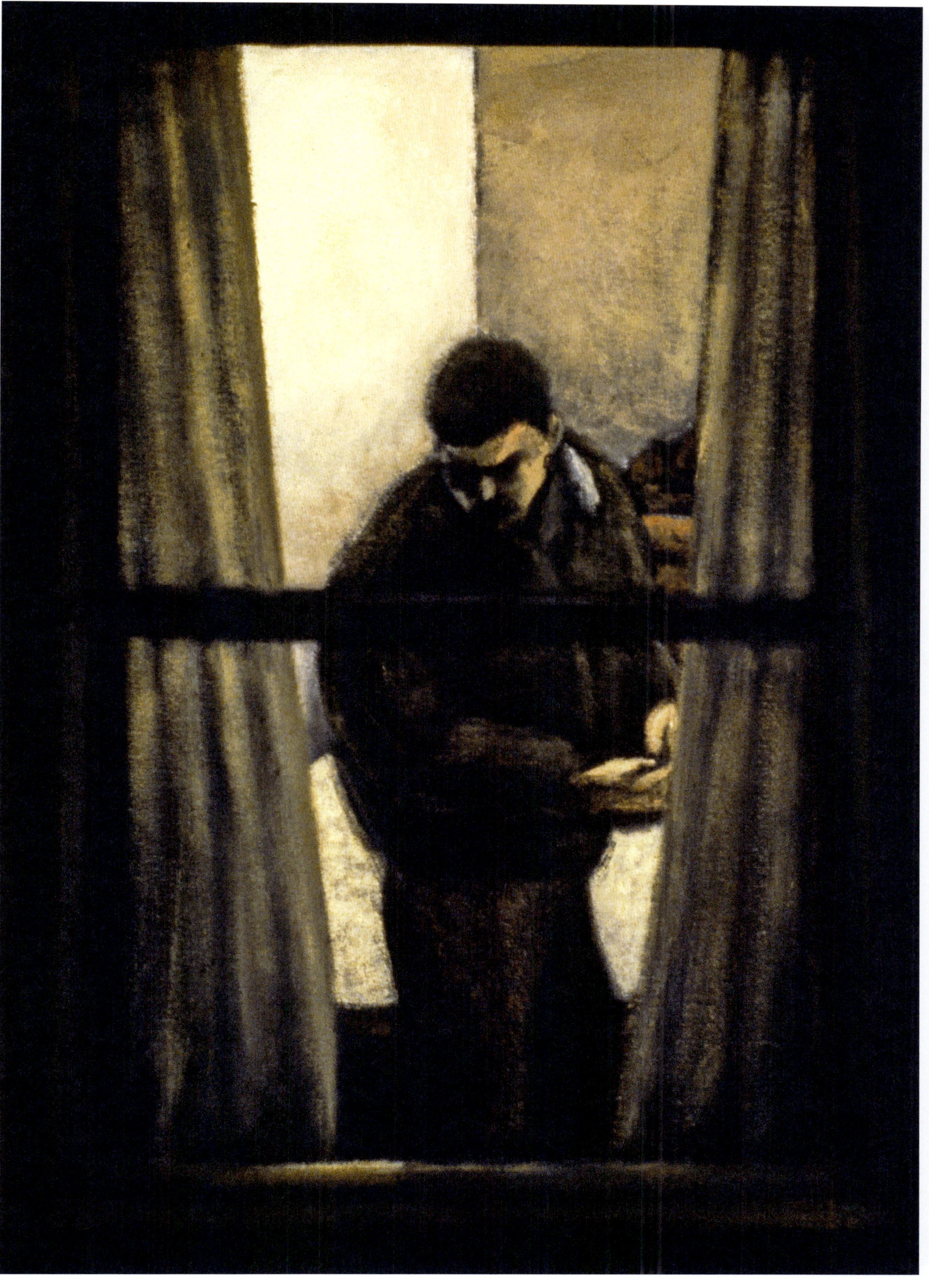

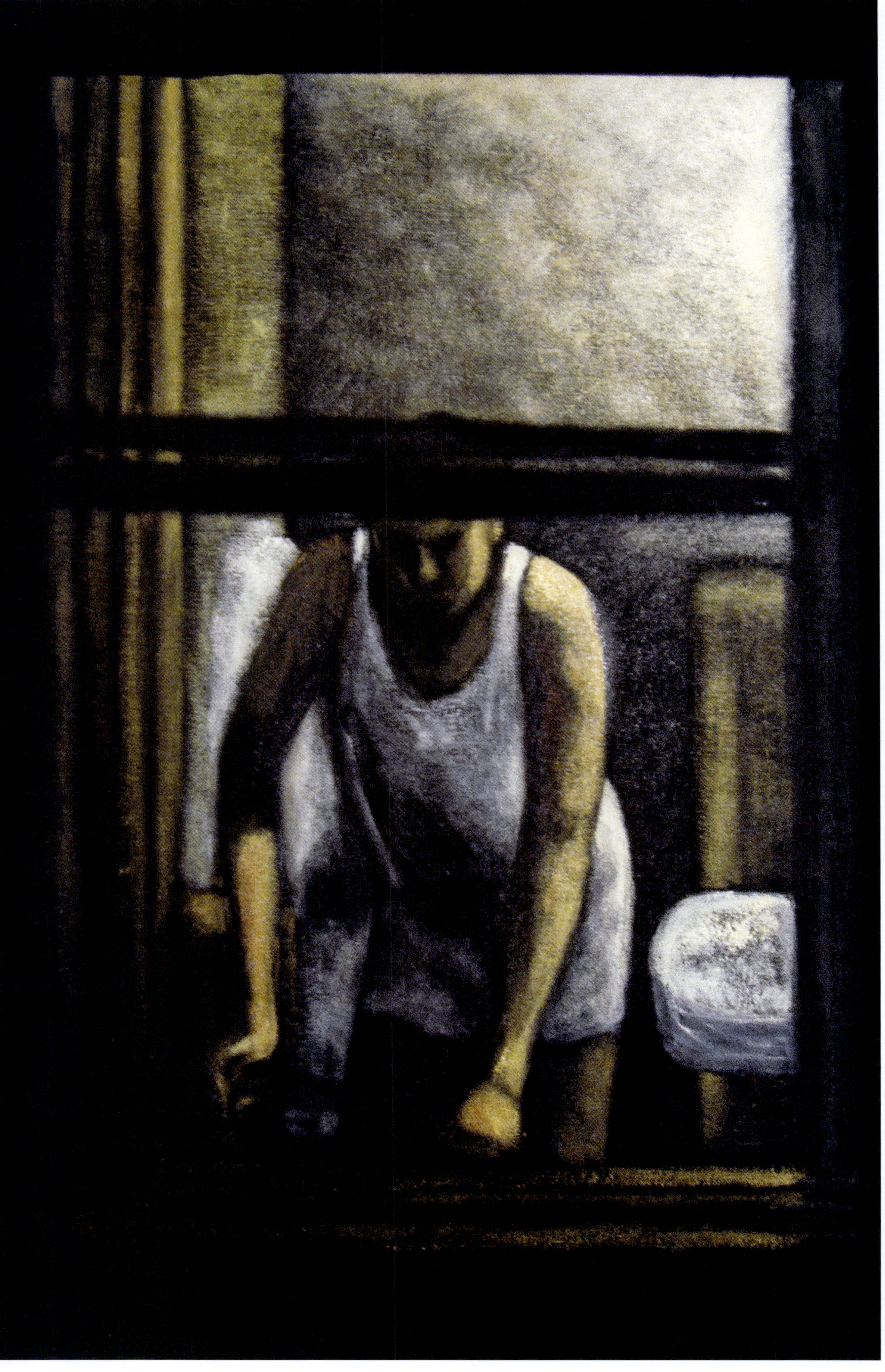

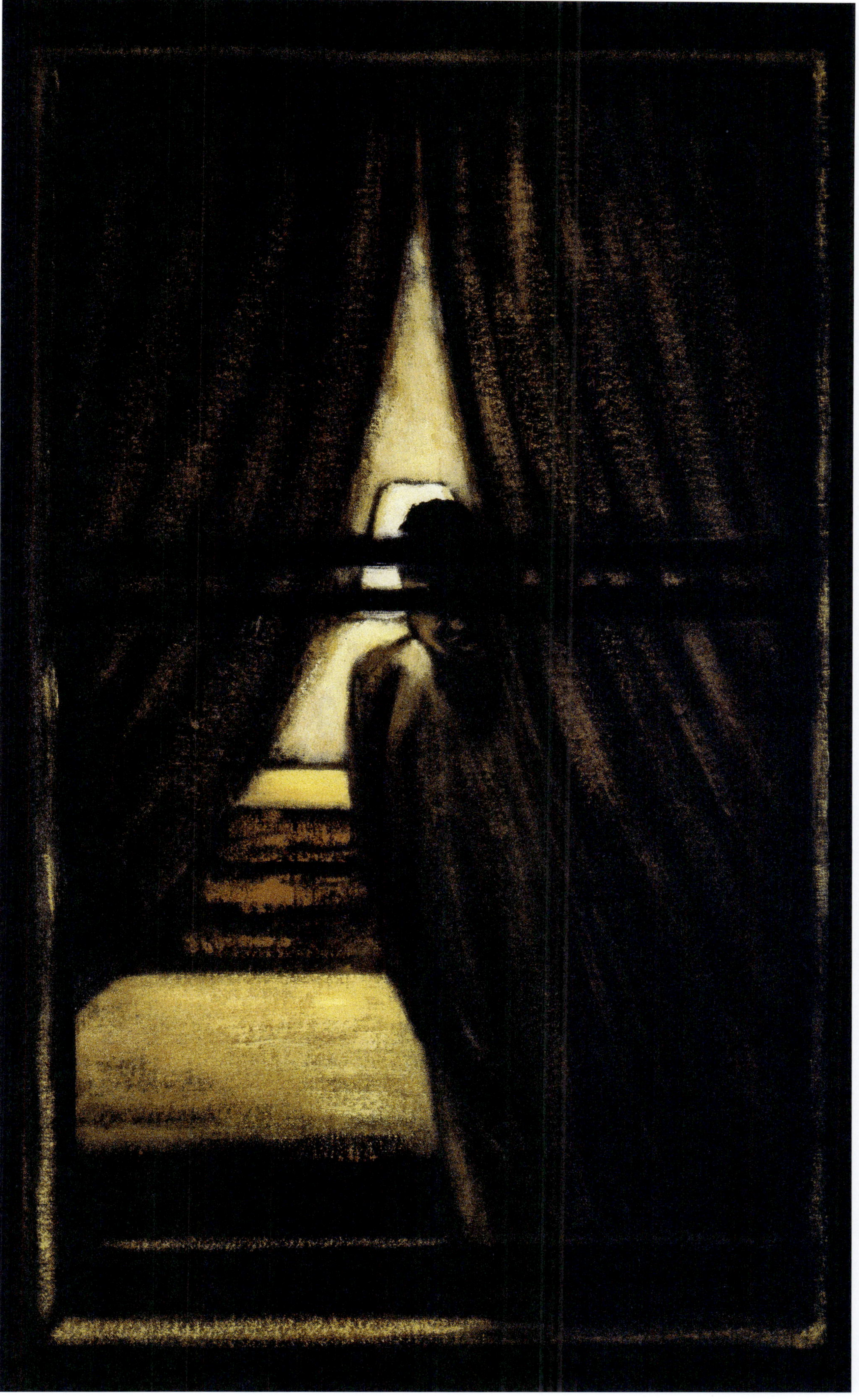

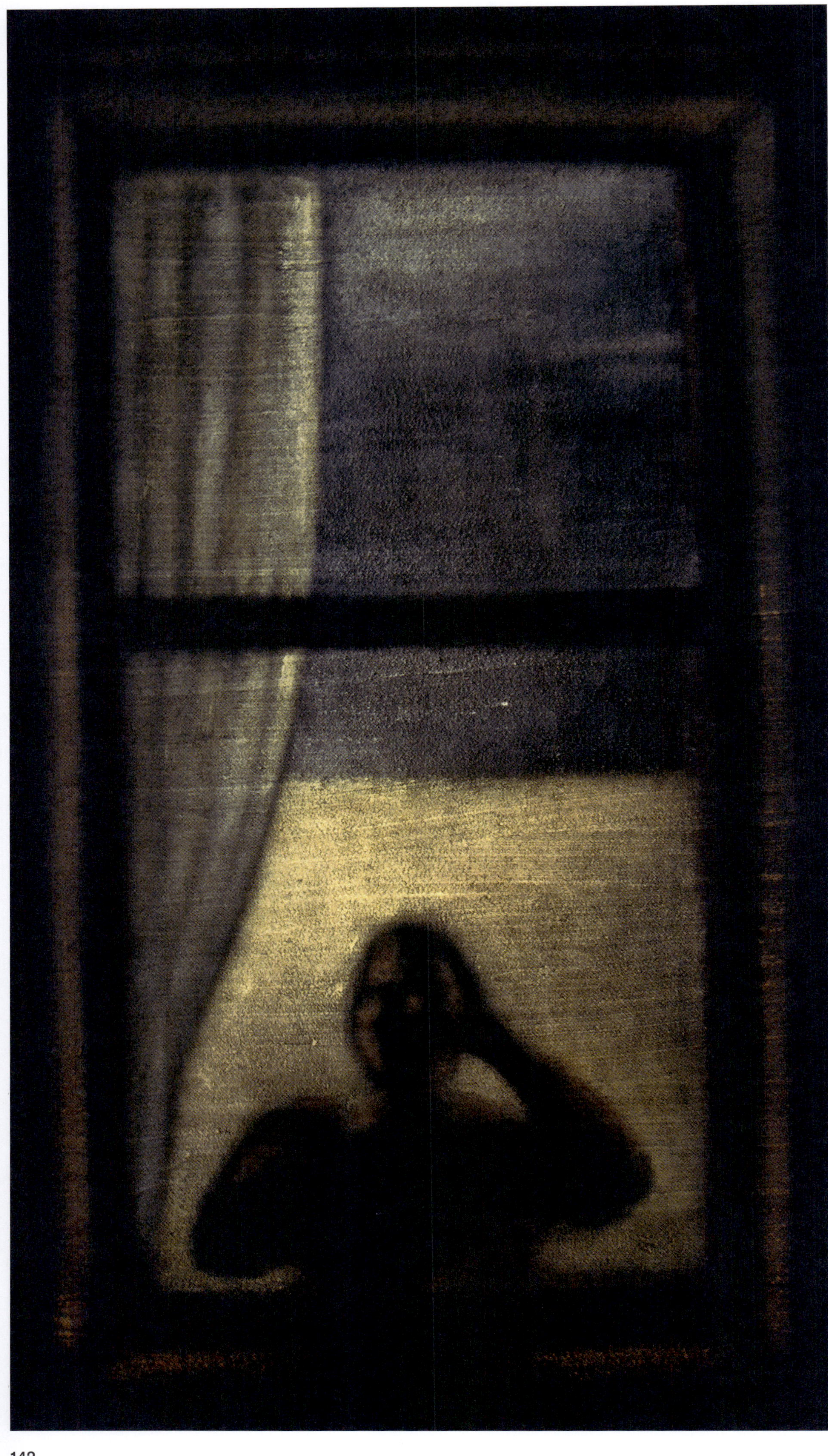

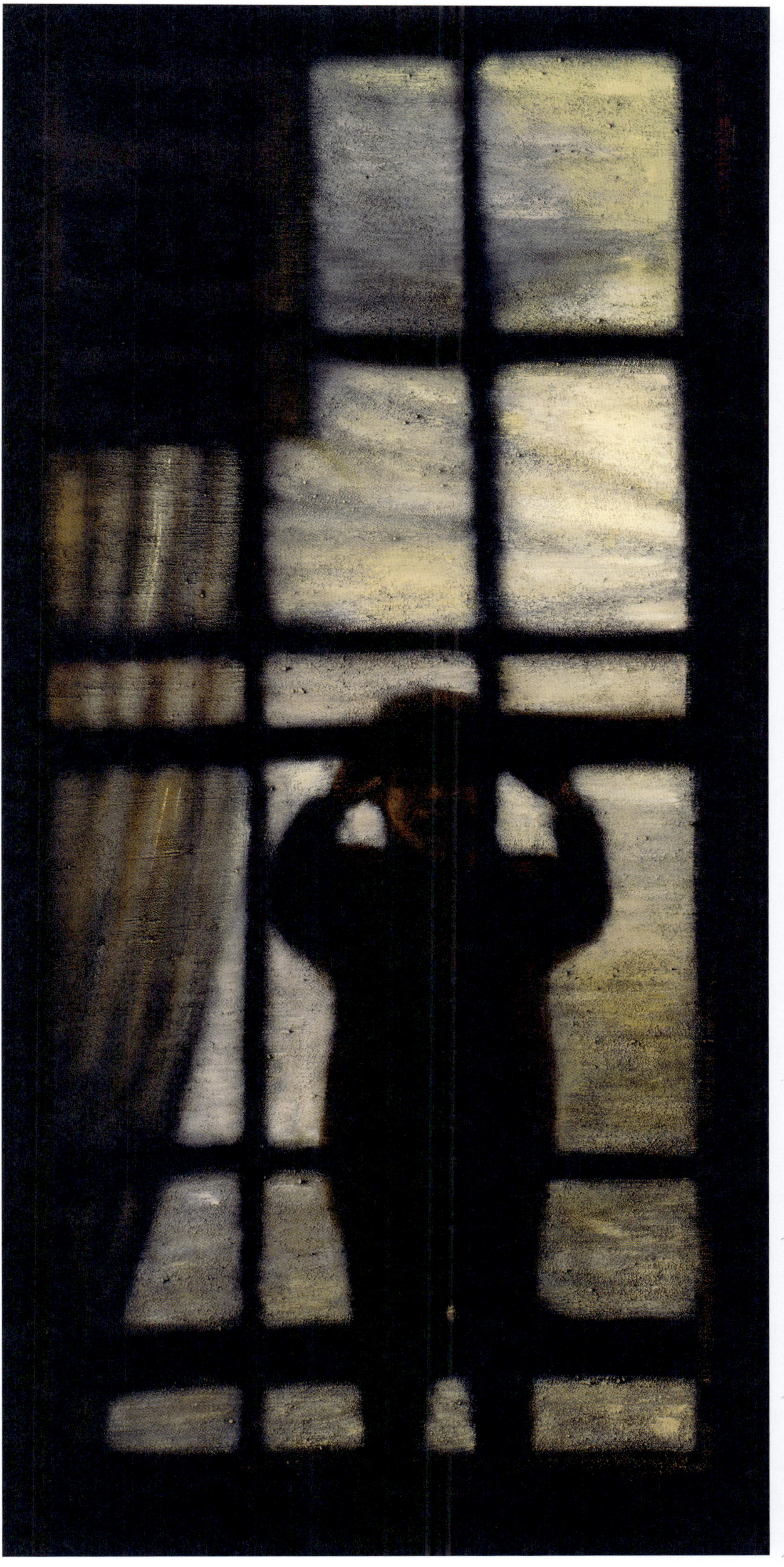

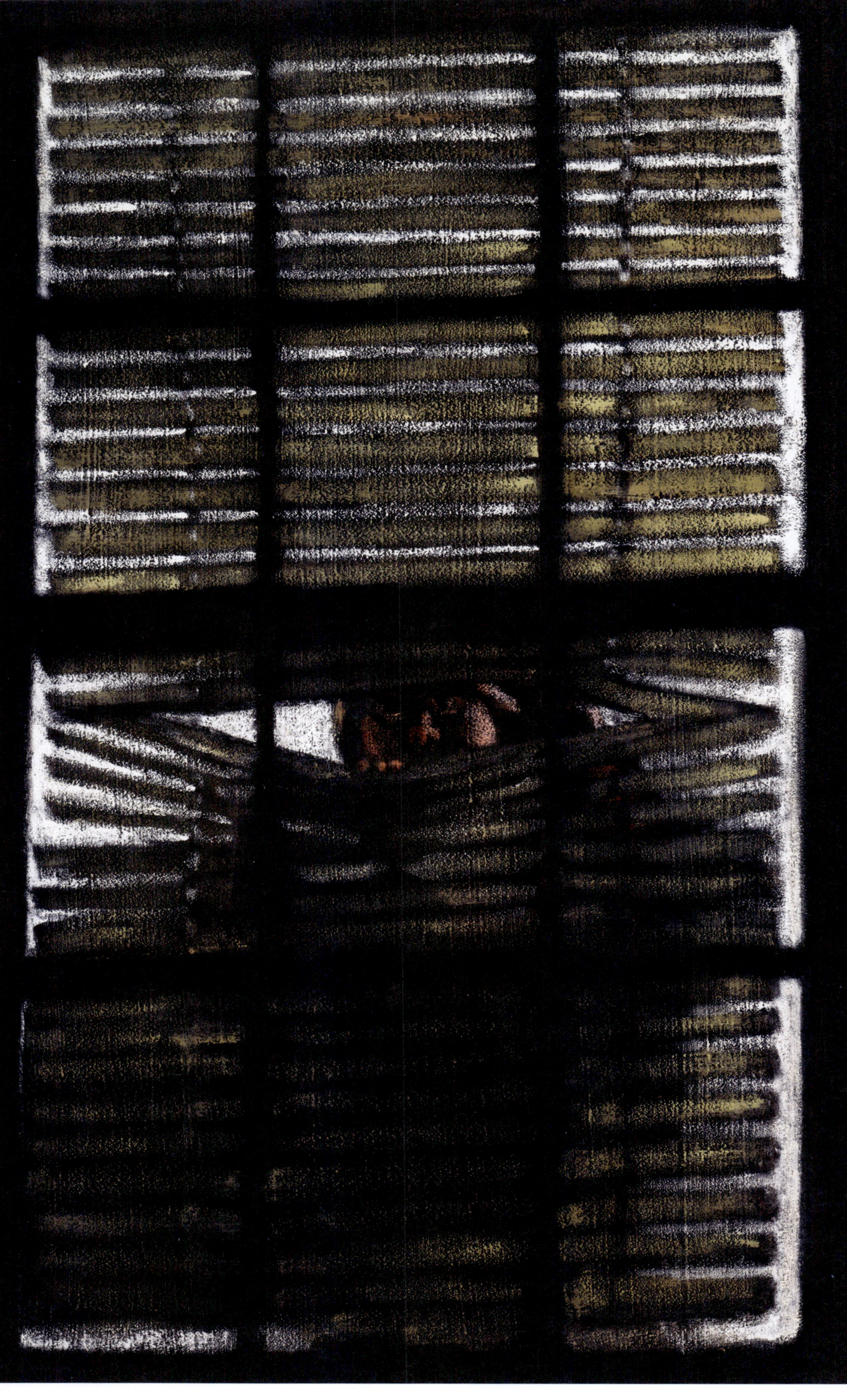

122   *Terminal Bar 2*. Oil on linen, 66 x 73 in. 2017.
124   *Rocky 3*. Oil stick on canvas, 24 in. diameter. 1983.
125   *Hotel Girl*. Oil stick on canvas, 86 x 44 in. 1983.
126   *Fish and Chips*. Oil stick on linen, 66 x 30 in. 1995.
127   *Subway Stairs 1*. Oil stick on canvas, 24 in. diameter. 1983.
128   TOP: Study for *Revelers with Horns*. Oil stick on blue paper, 15 ½ x 26 in. 1990.
       BOTTOM: Study for *Revelers*. Oil stick on gray paper, 20 x 26 in. 1990.
129   *Reveler in Wheelchair*, Oil stick on green paper, 25 ½ x 19 ½ in. 1991.
130   TOP: *Reveler – White Fairy*. Oil and Rolotex on canvas, 30 x 40 in. 1990.
       BOTTOM: *Reveler – Big Bottles*. Oil on canvas, 30 x 40 in. 1990.
131   *Reveler*. Oil on canvas, 60 x 30 in. 1990.
132   *Woman at the Window 3*. Oil stick on canvas, 12 x 9 in. 1983.
133   *Woman at the Window*. Oil stick on canvas, 42 x 19 in. 1983.
134   *Witness (BE)*. Oil and Rolotex on canvas, 70 x 35 in. 1991.
135   *Witness Reading in Bed*. Oil on canvas, 48 x 24 in. 1991.
136   Study for *Witness*. Oil stick on paper, 30 x 23 in. 1990.
137   Study for *Witness CF 2*. Oil stick, 25 ½ x 15 ¼ in. 1990.
138   Study for *Witness II*. Oil on canvas, 30 x 23 in. 1990.
139   Study for *Witness IV*. Oil on canvas, 30 x 23 in. 1990.
140   Study for *Witness III*. Oil on canvas, 30 x 23 in. 1990.
141   Study for *Witness*. Oil on canvas, 30 x 23 in. 1990.
142   *Witness (JA)*. Oil and pumice on canvas, 70 x 35 in. 1991.
143   *Witness (JP)*. Oil and Rolotex on canvas, 70 x 35 in. 1991.
144   *Witness 2 (BE)*. Oil and Rolotex on canvas, 48 x 30 in. 1991–1997.

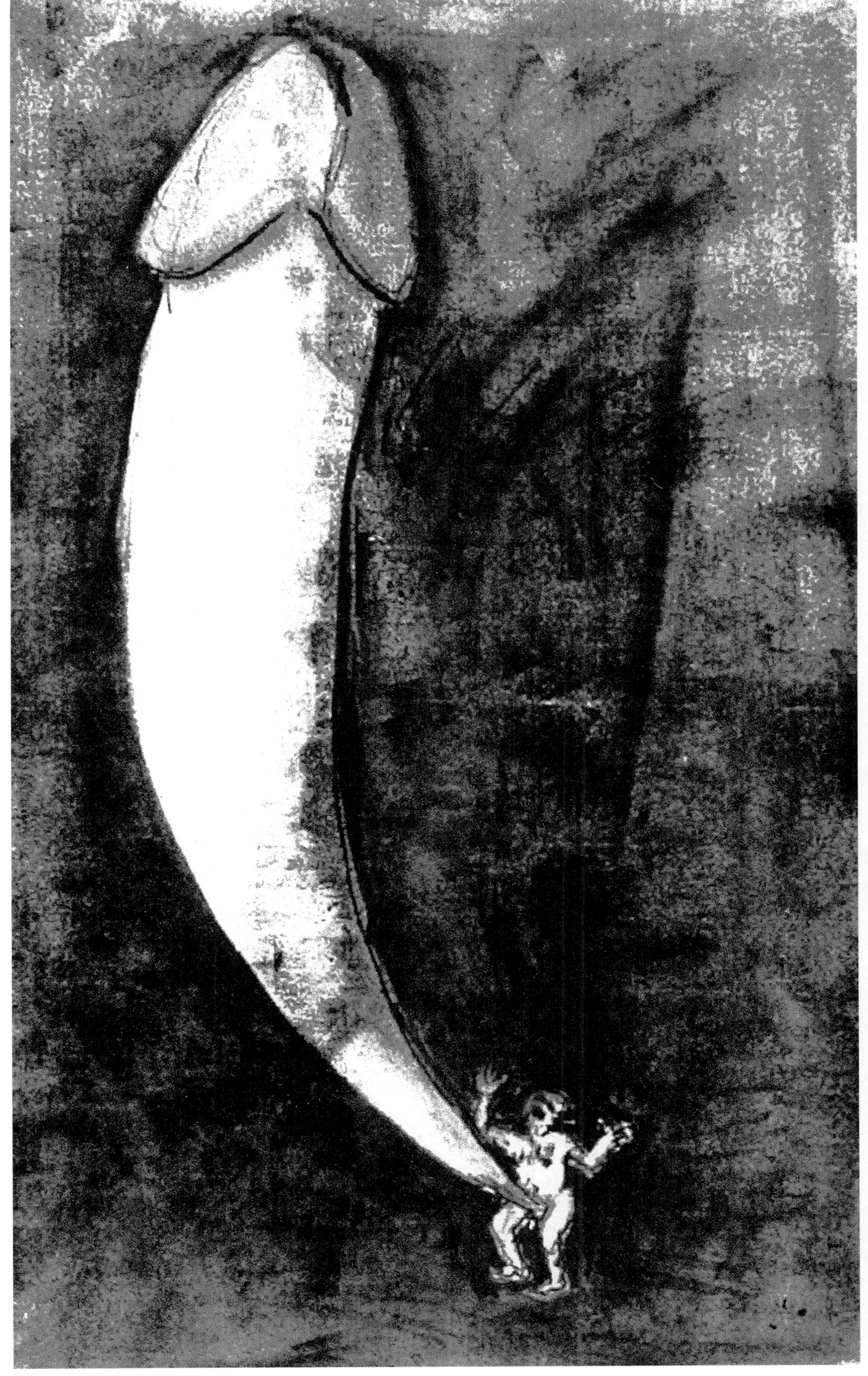

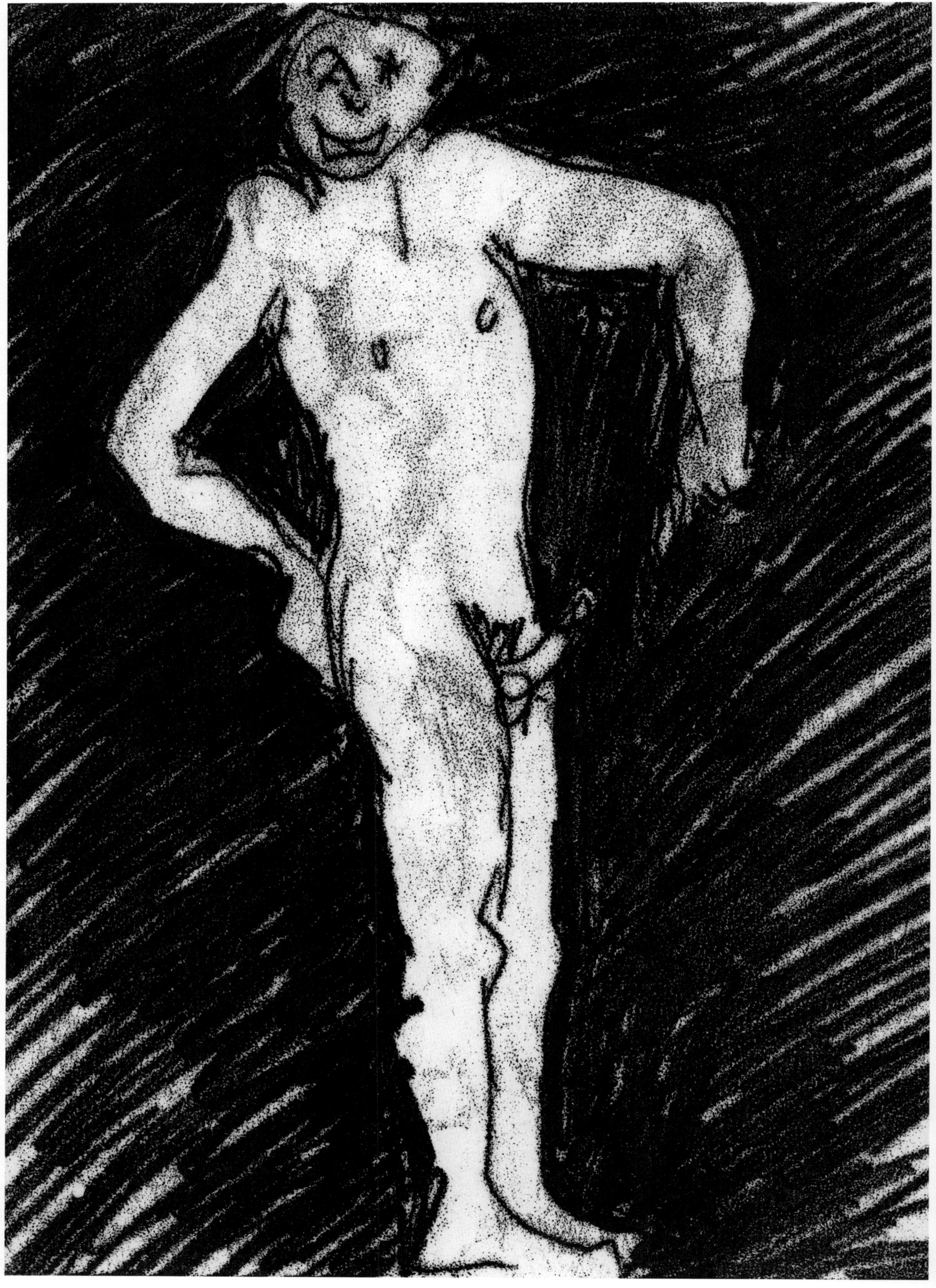

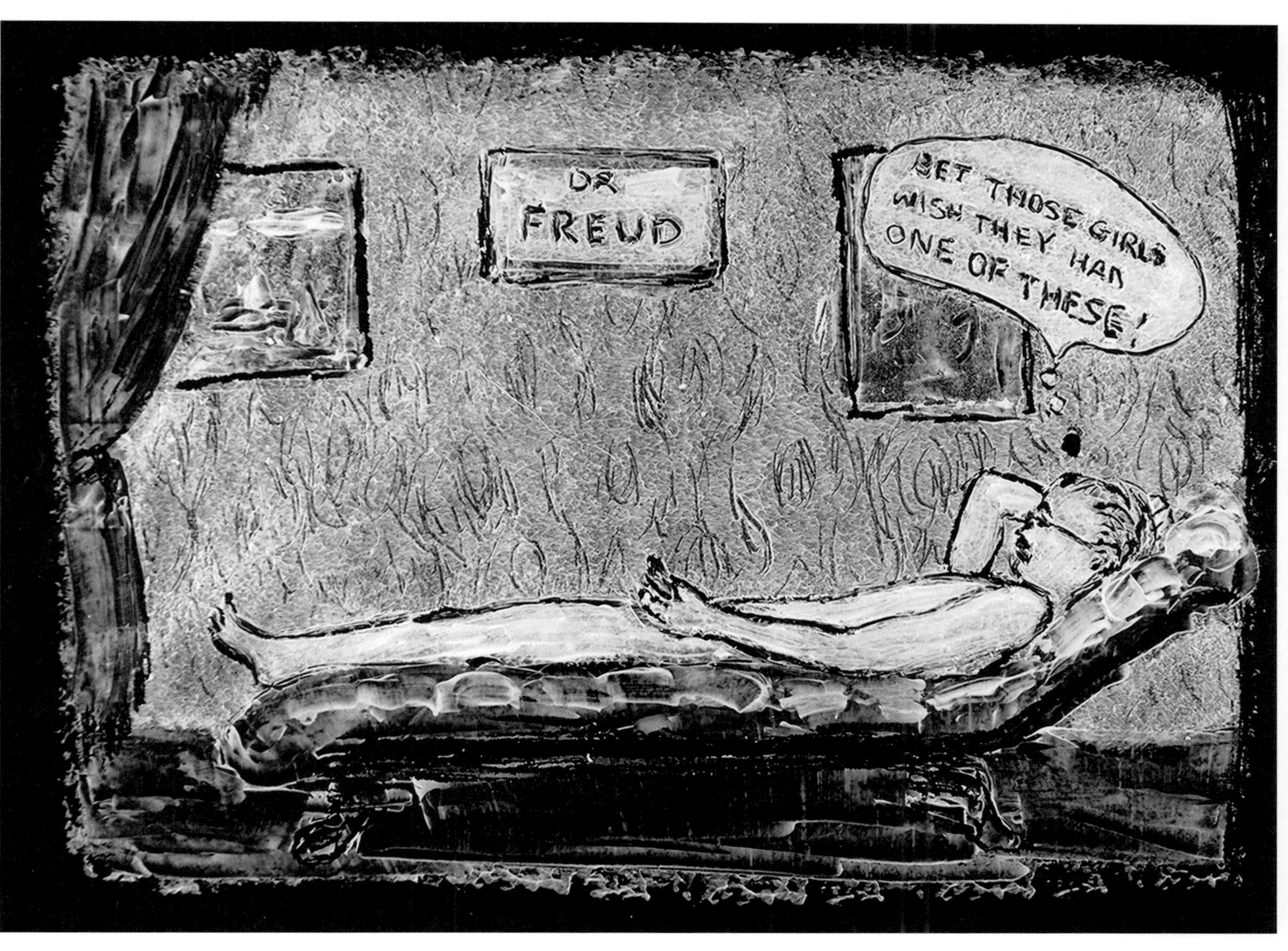

DR FREUD
BET THOSE GIRLS WISH THEY HAD ONE OF THESE!

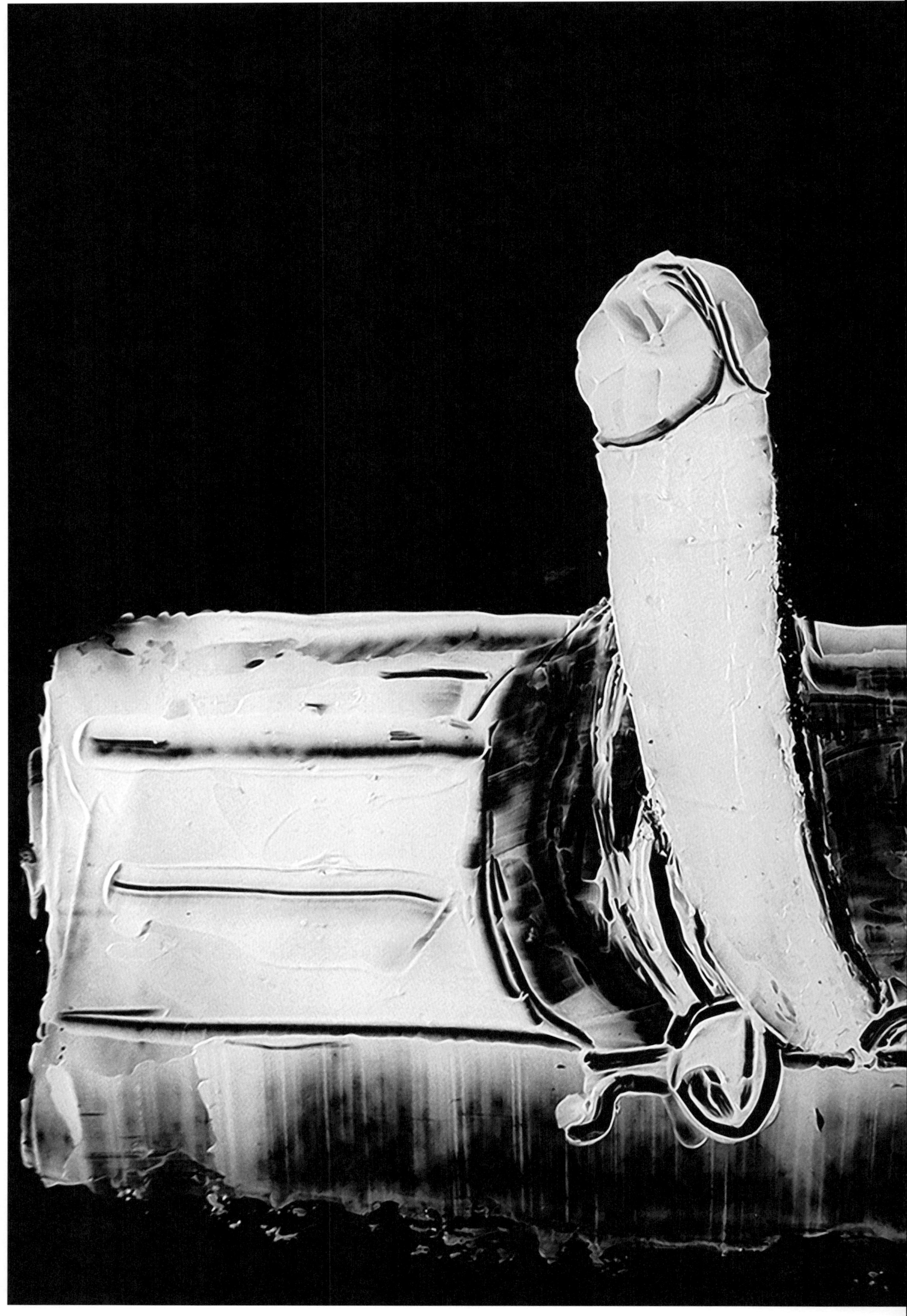

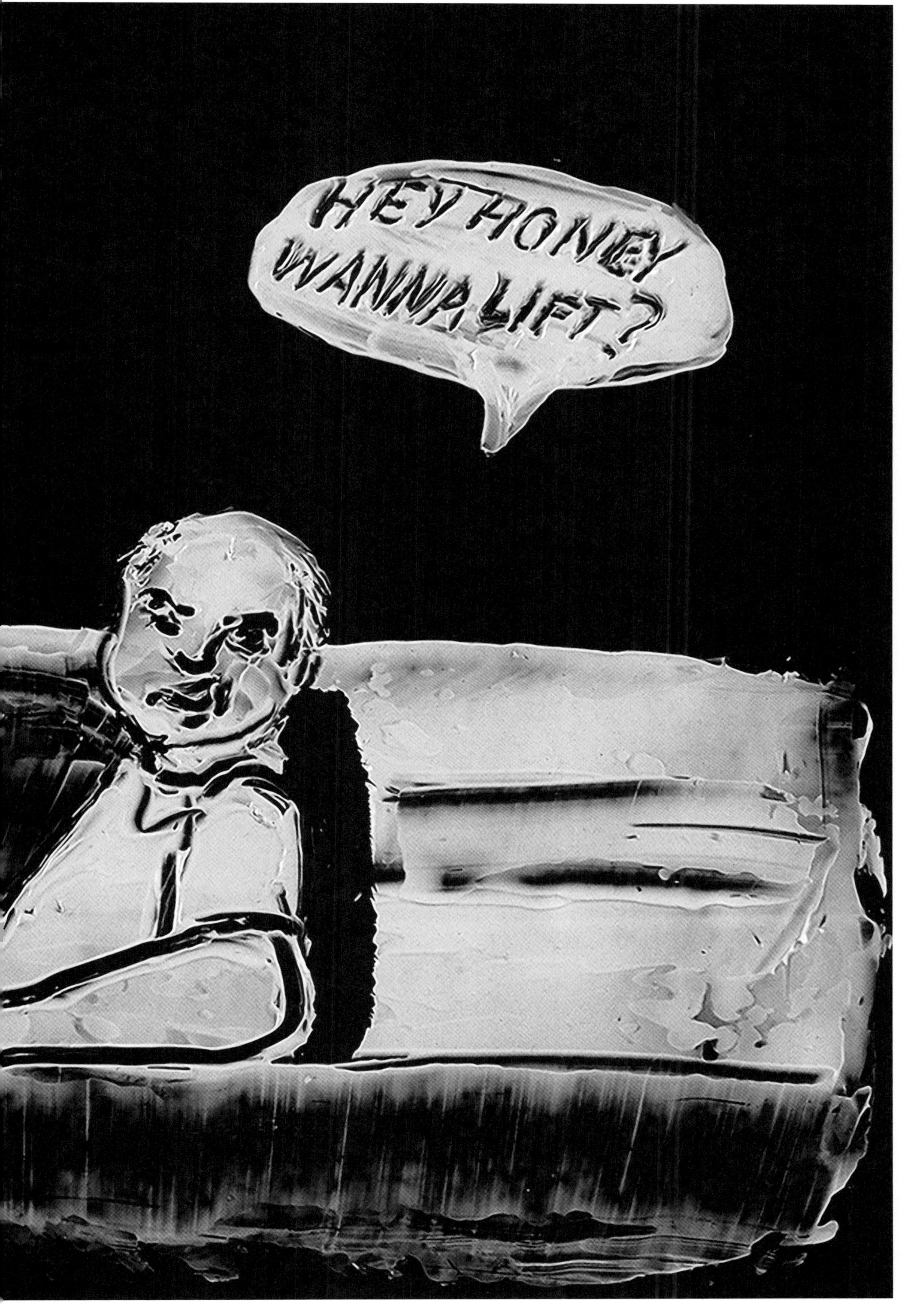

HEY HONEY
WANNA LIFT?

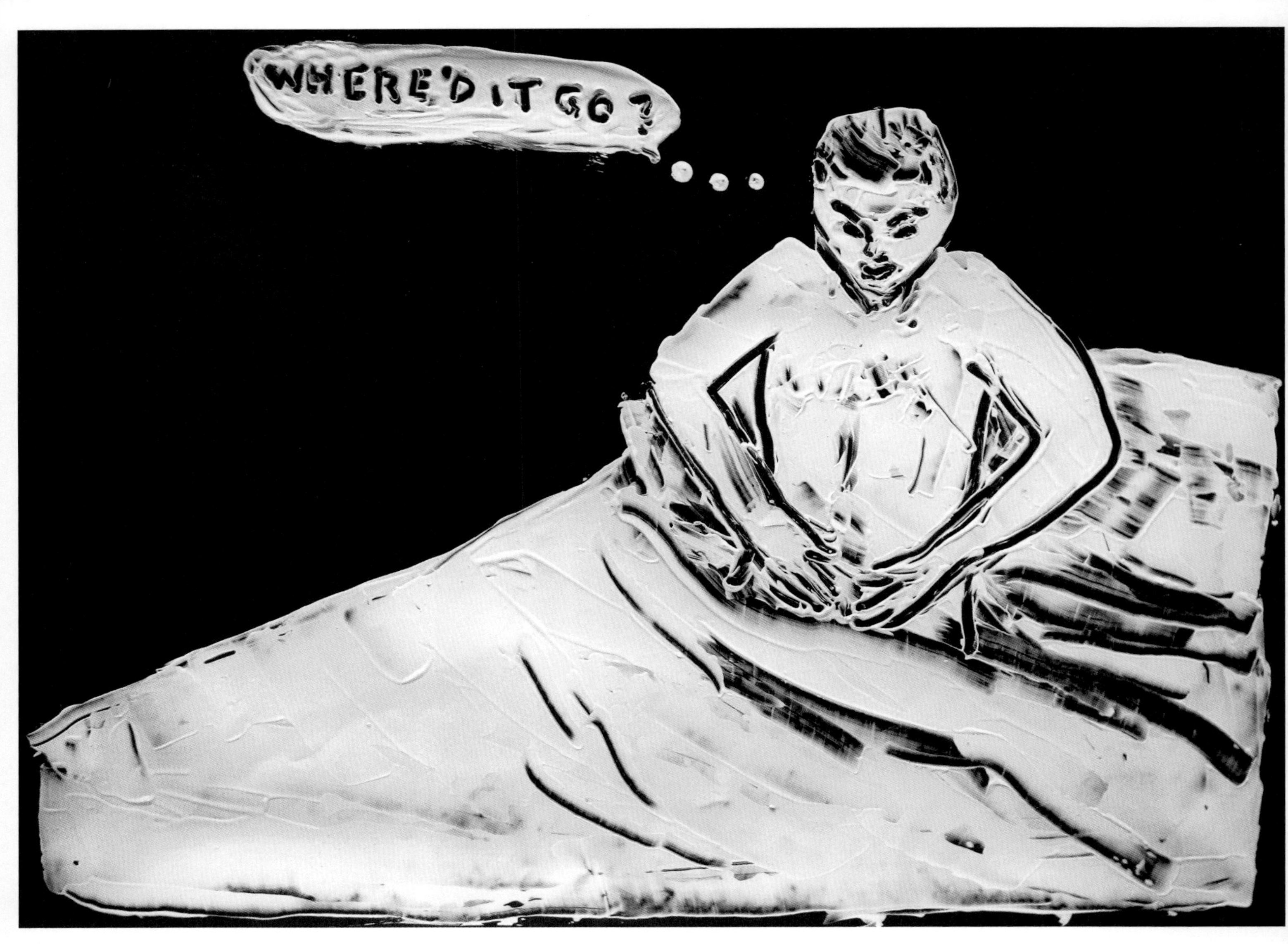

147   *World's Biggest* (from *Hey Honey Wanna Lift?*). Monoprint, oil on rice paper, 23 x 14 ½ in. 1980.
148   *Look!* (from *Hey Honey Wanna Lift?*). Hand-colored Xerox of monoprint, watercolor on Xerox. 1980.
149   *Dr. Freud* (from *Hey Honey Redux*). Acrylic on black plastic, 14 ½ x 20 ½ in. 2016.
150   *Hey Honey...* (from *Hey Honey Redux*). Acrylic on black plastic, 12 x 15 in. 2016.
152   *Where'd It Go?* (from *Hey Honey Redux*). Acrylic on black plastic, 14 ½ x 20 ½ in. 2016.
153   *Wow!* (from *Hey Honey Redux*). Acrylic on black plastic, 61 x 31 in. 2016.

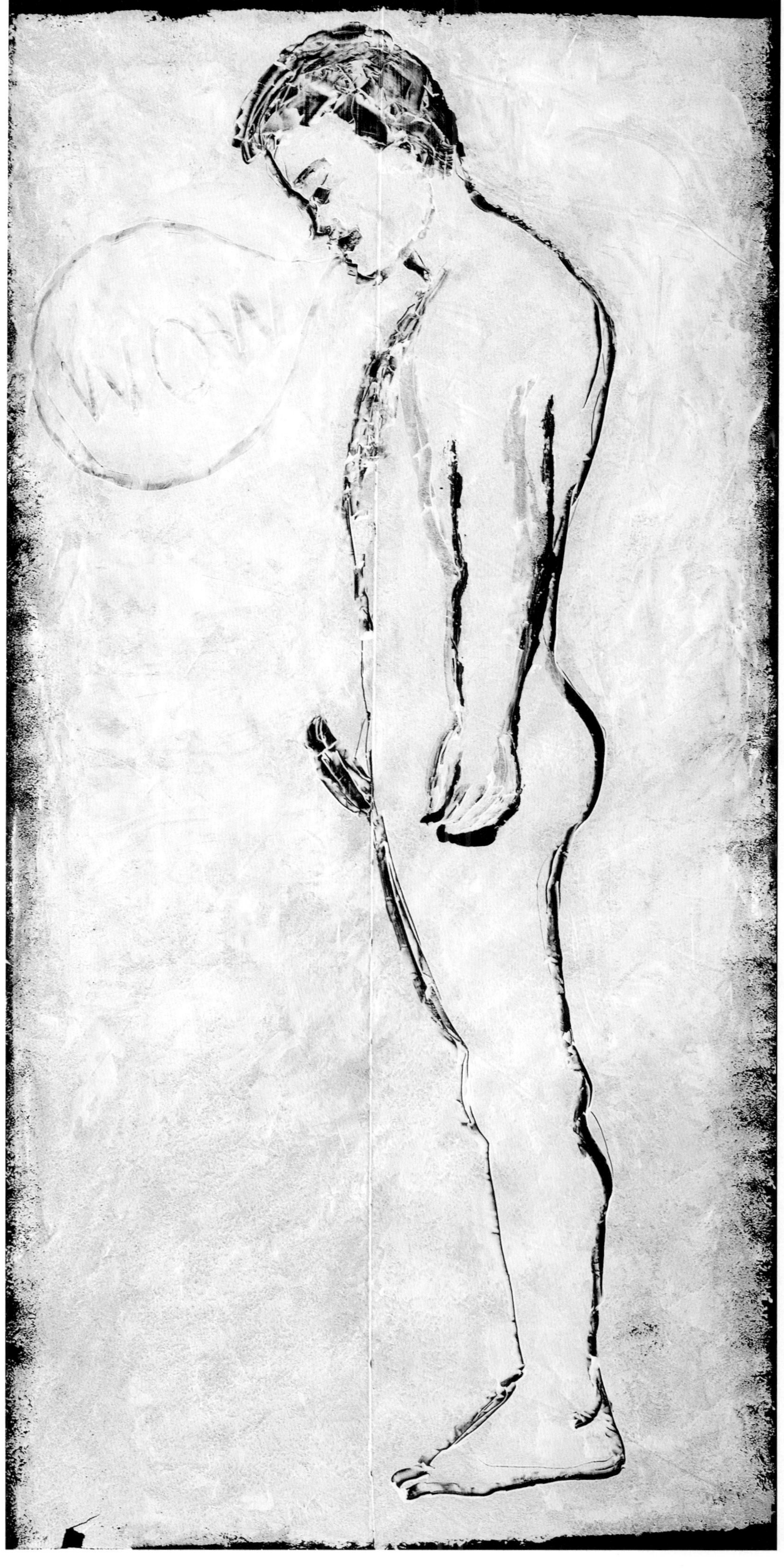
WOW

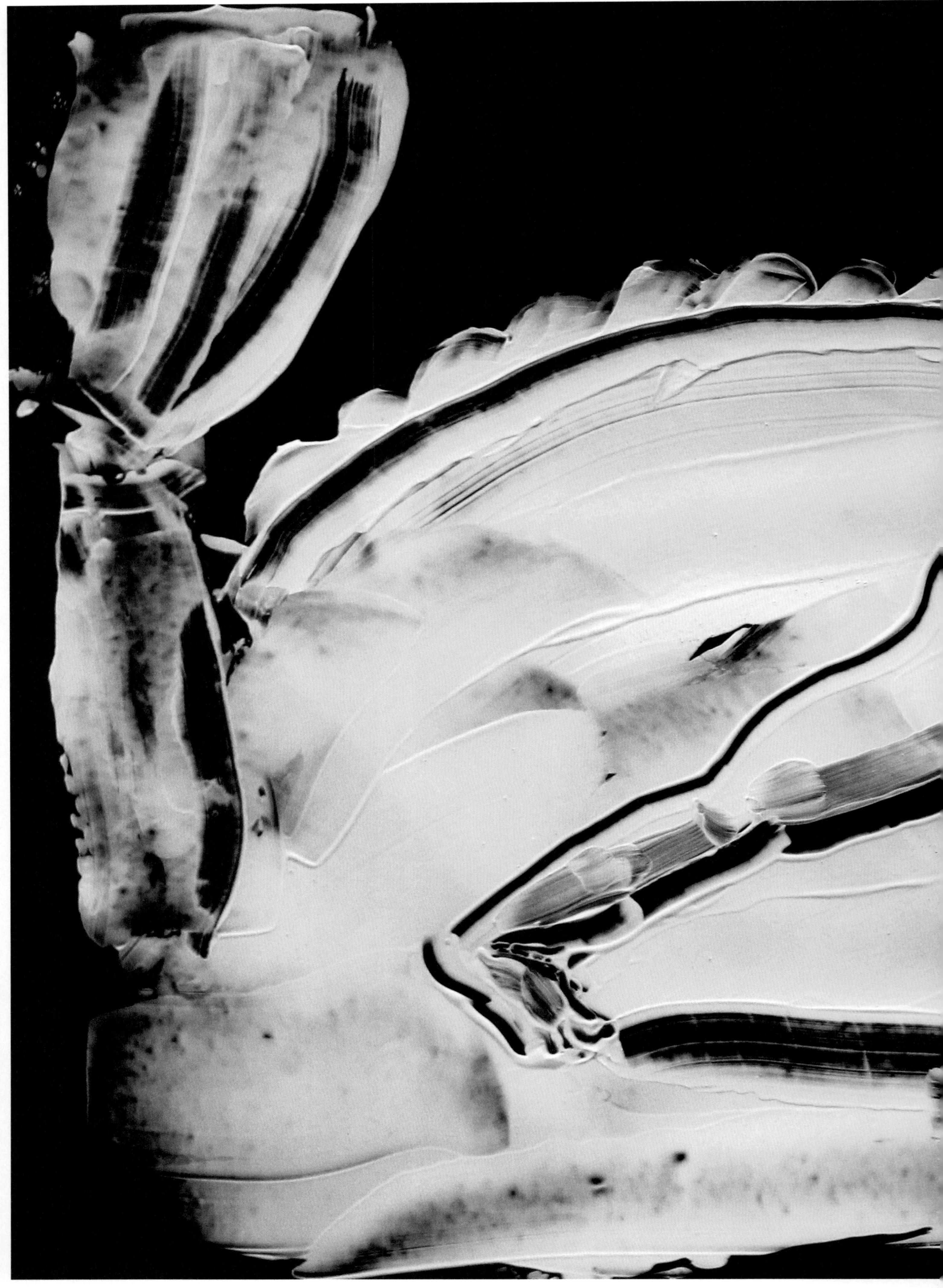

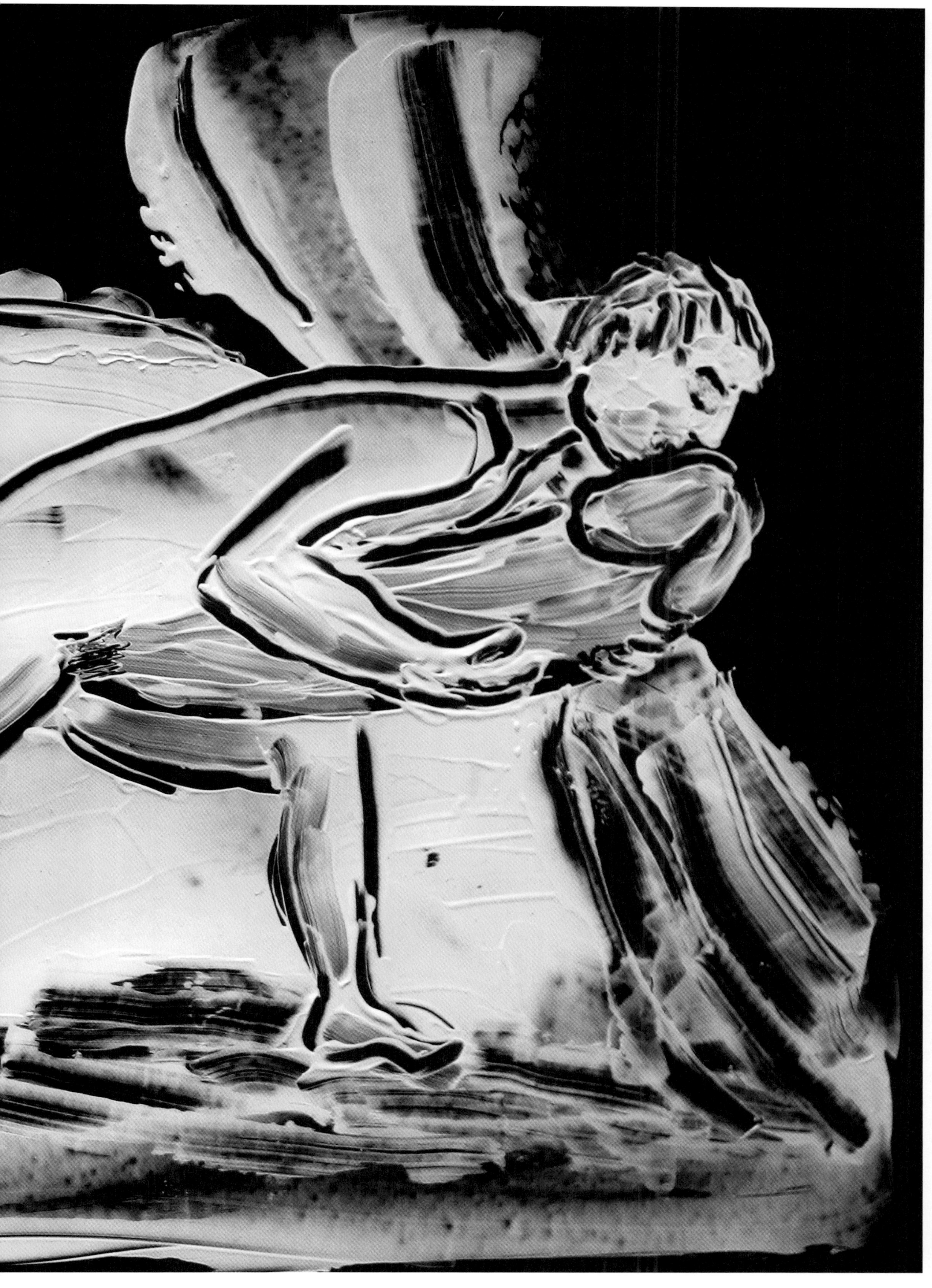

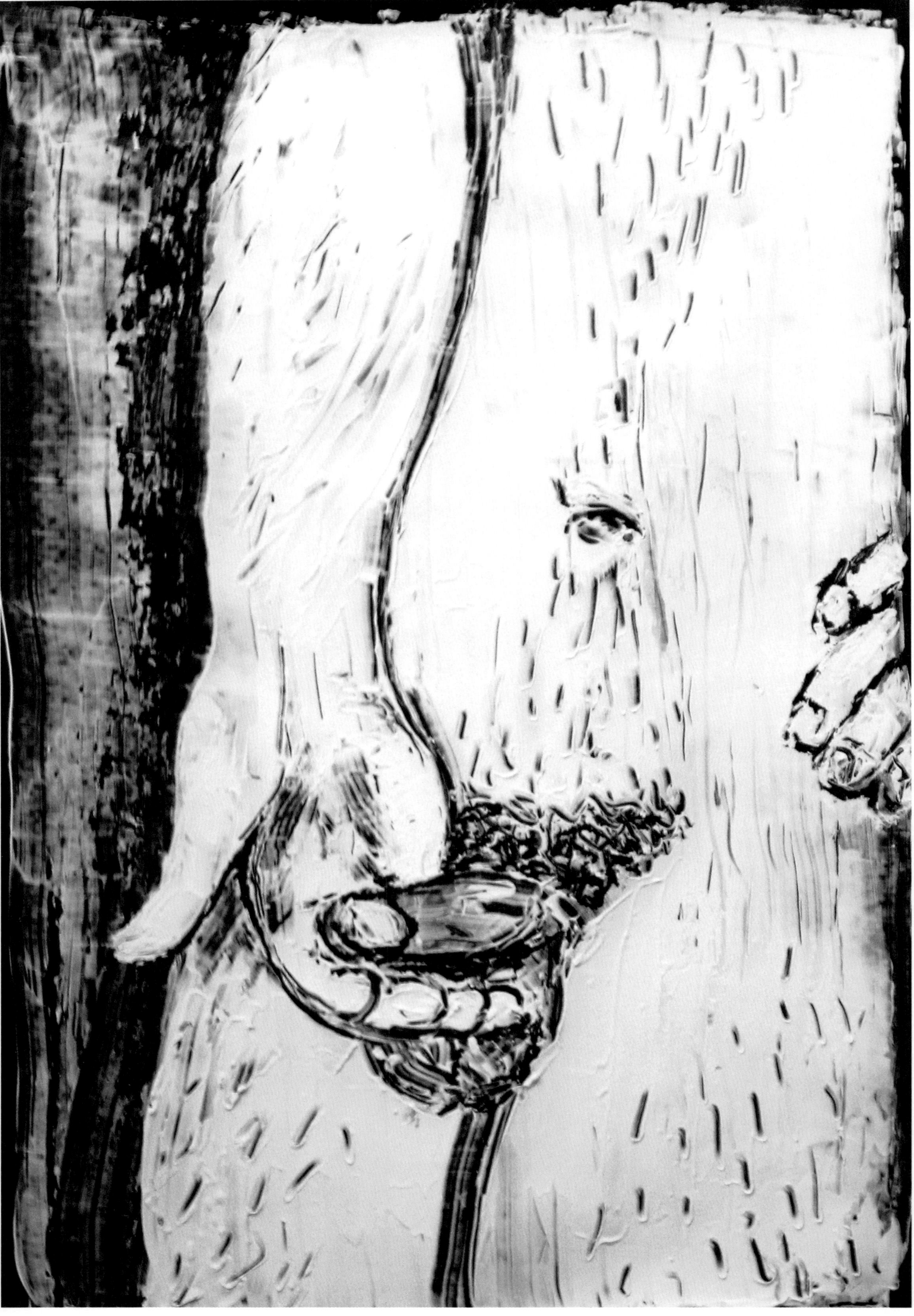

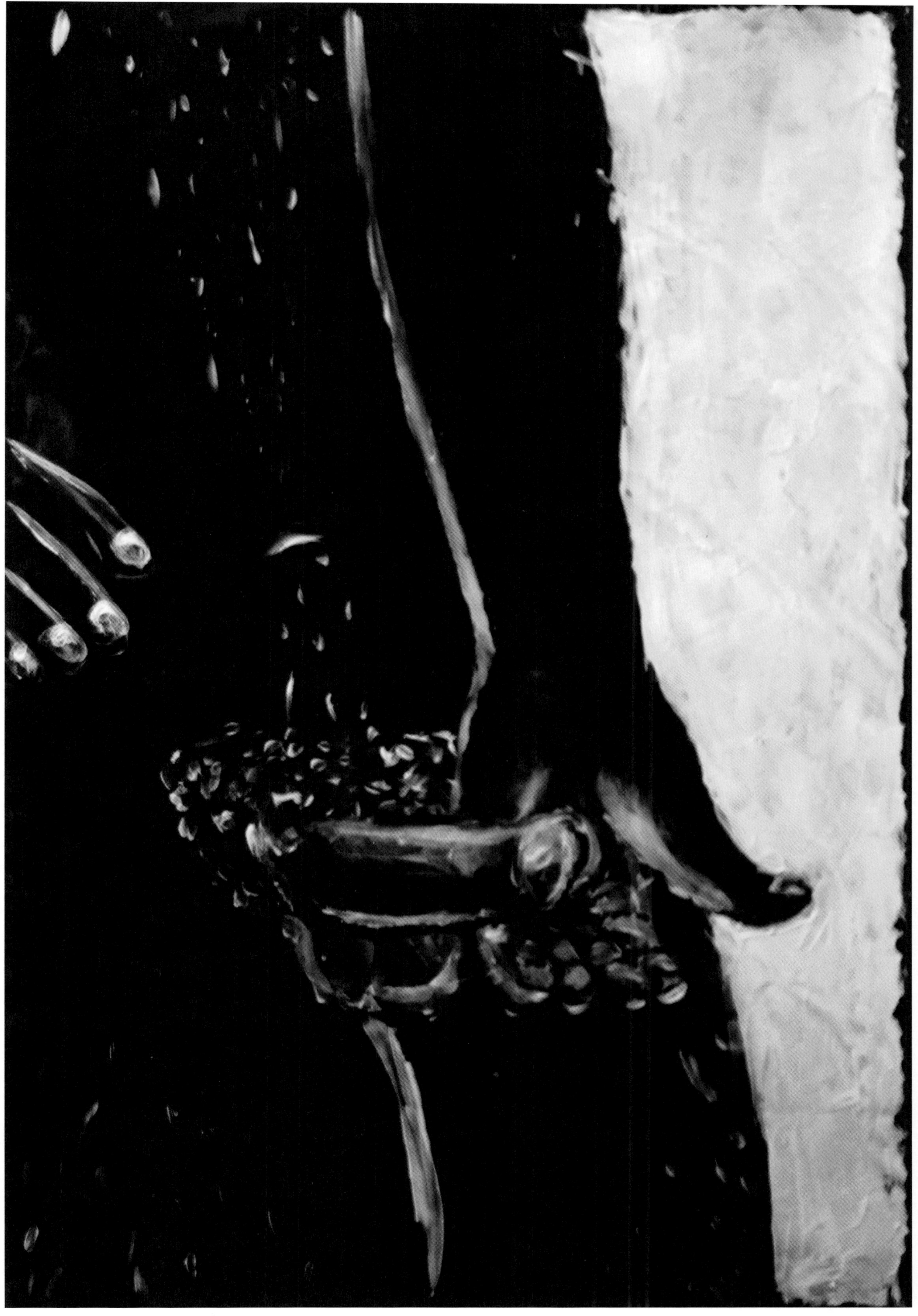

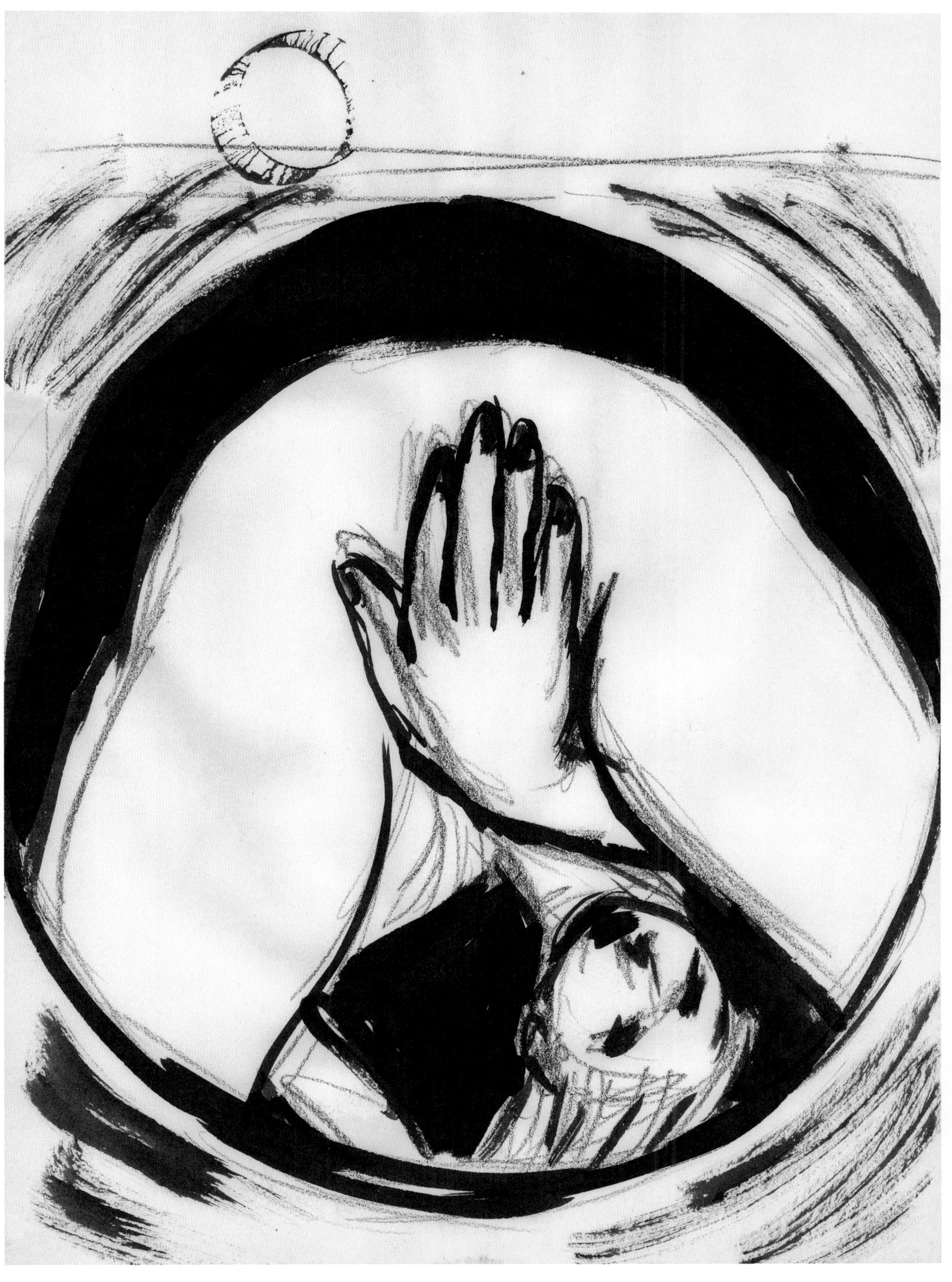

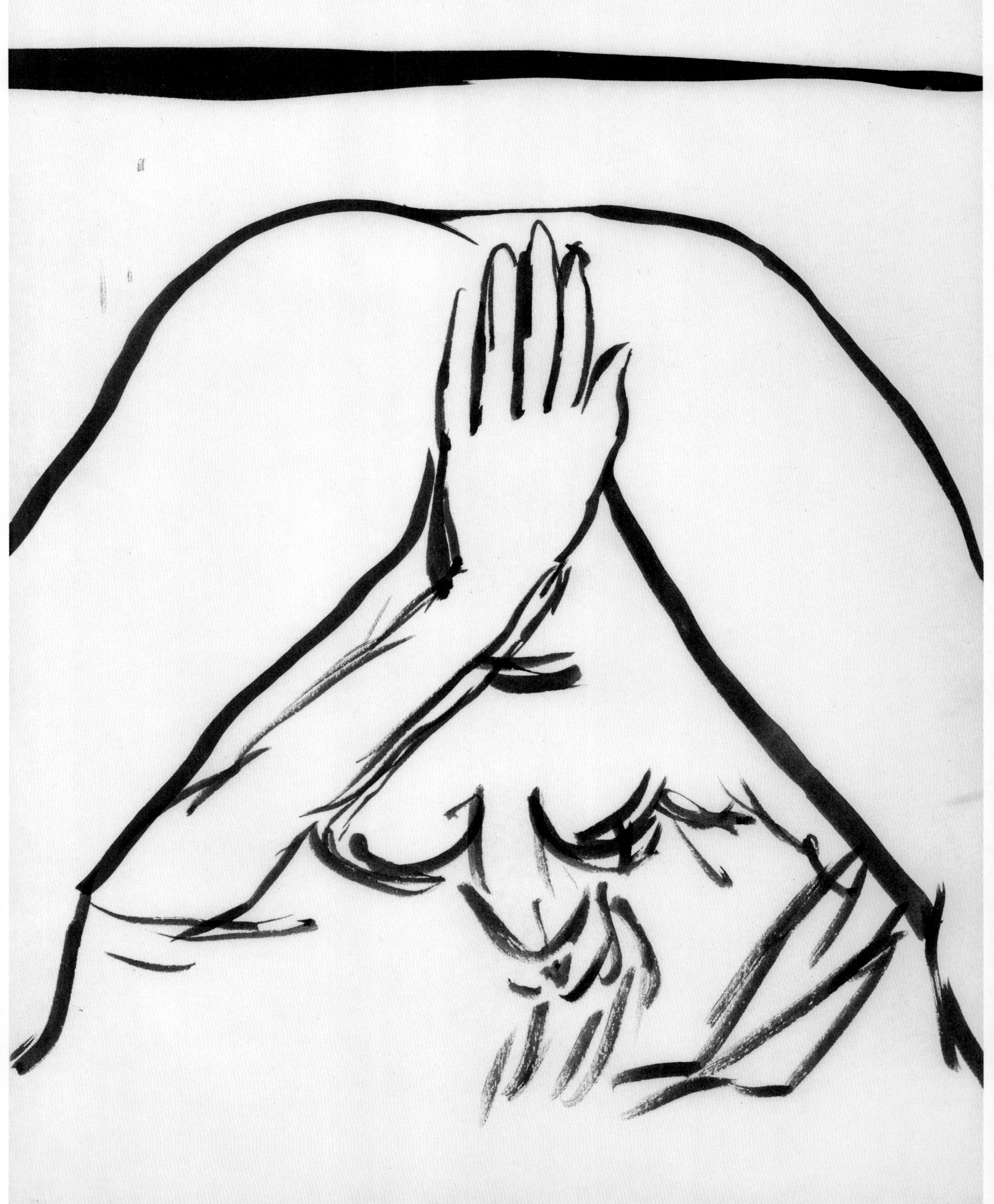

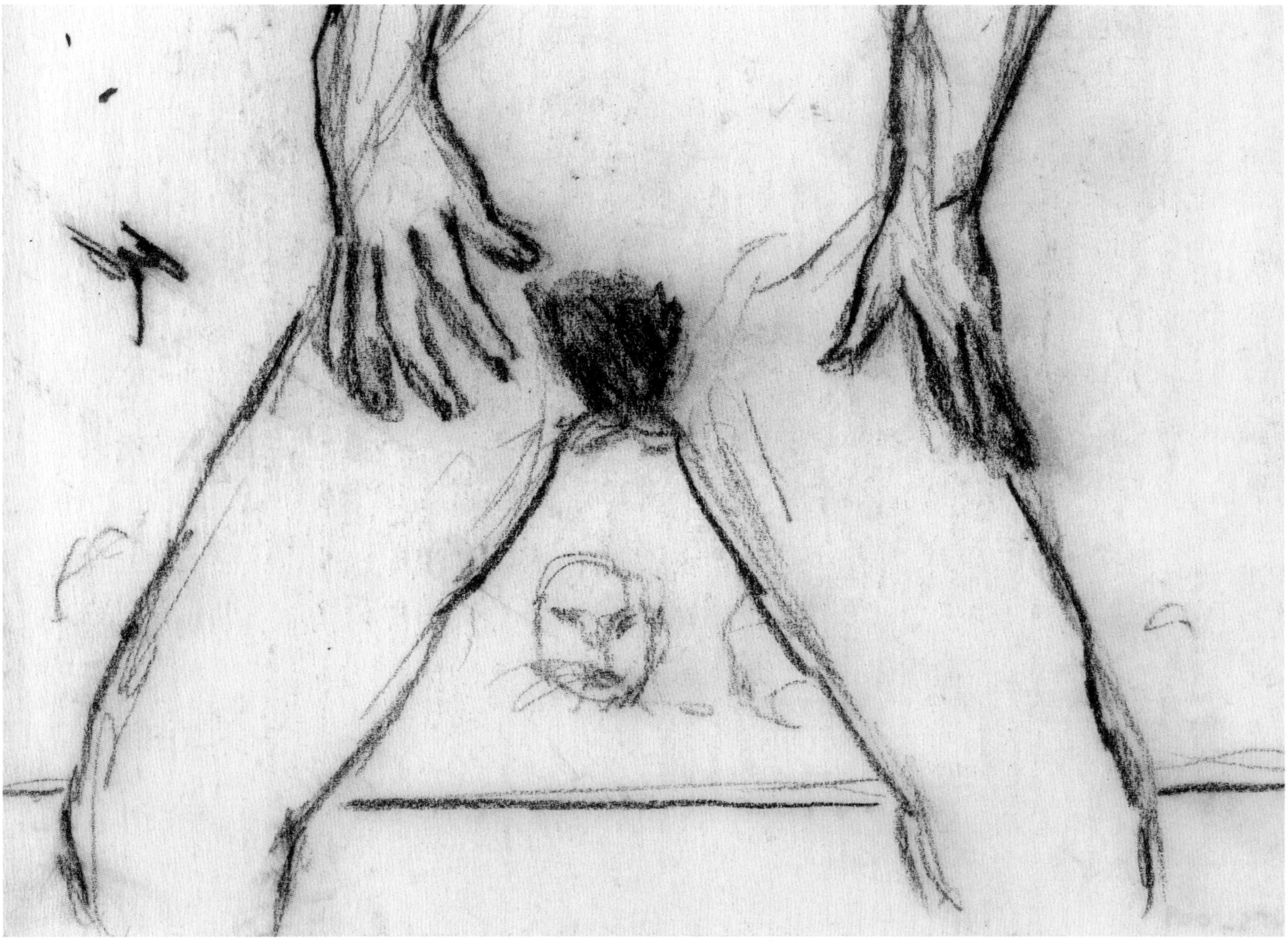

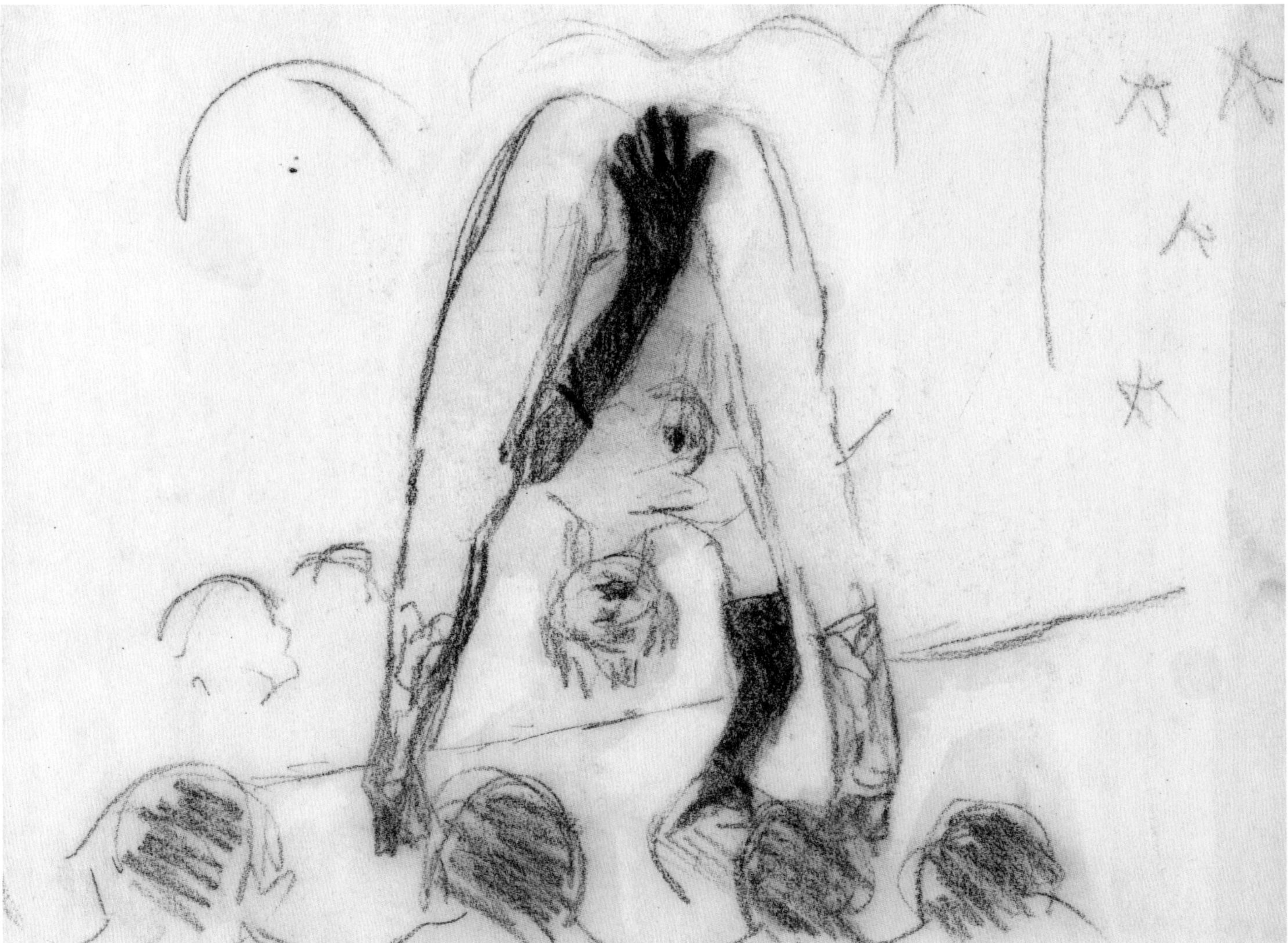

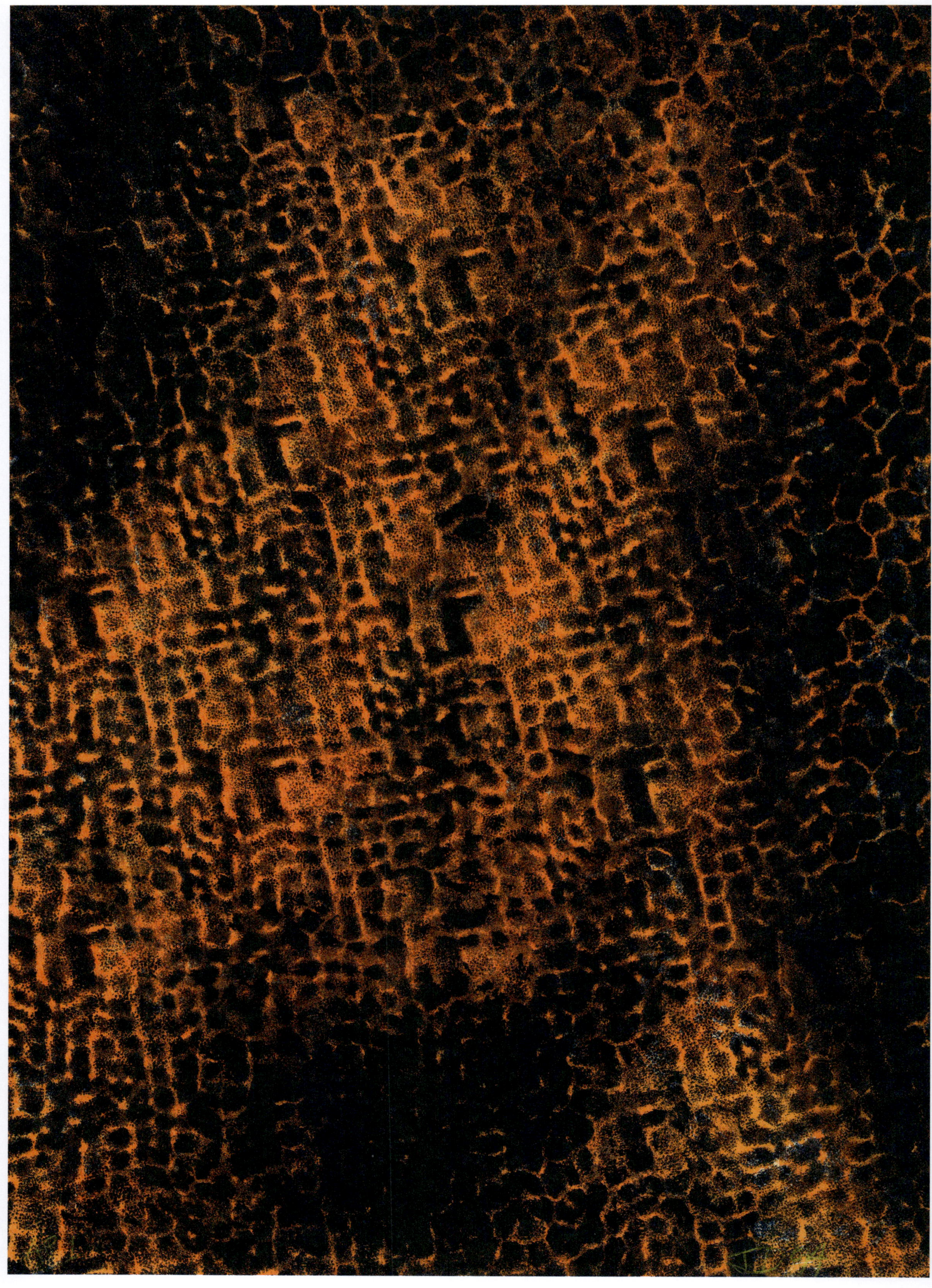

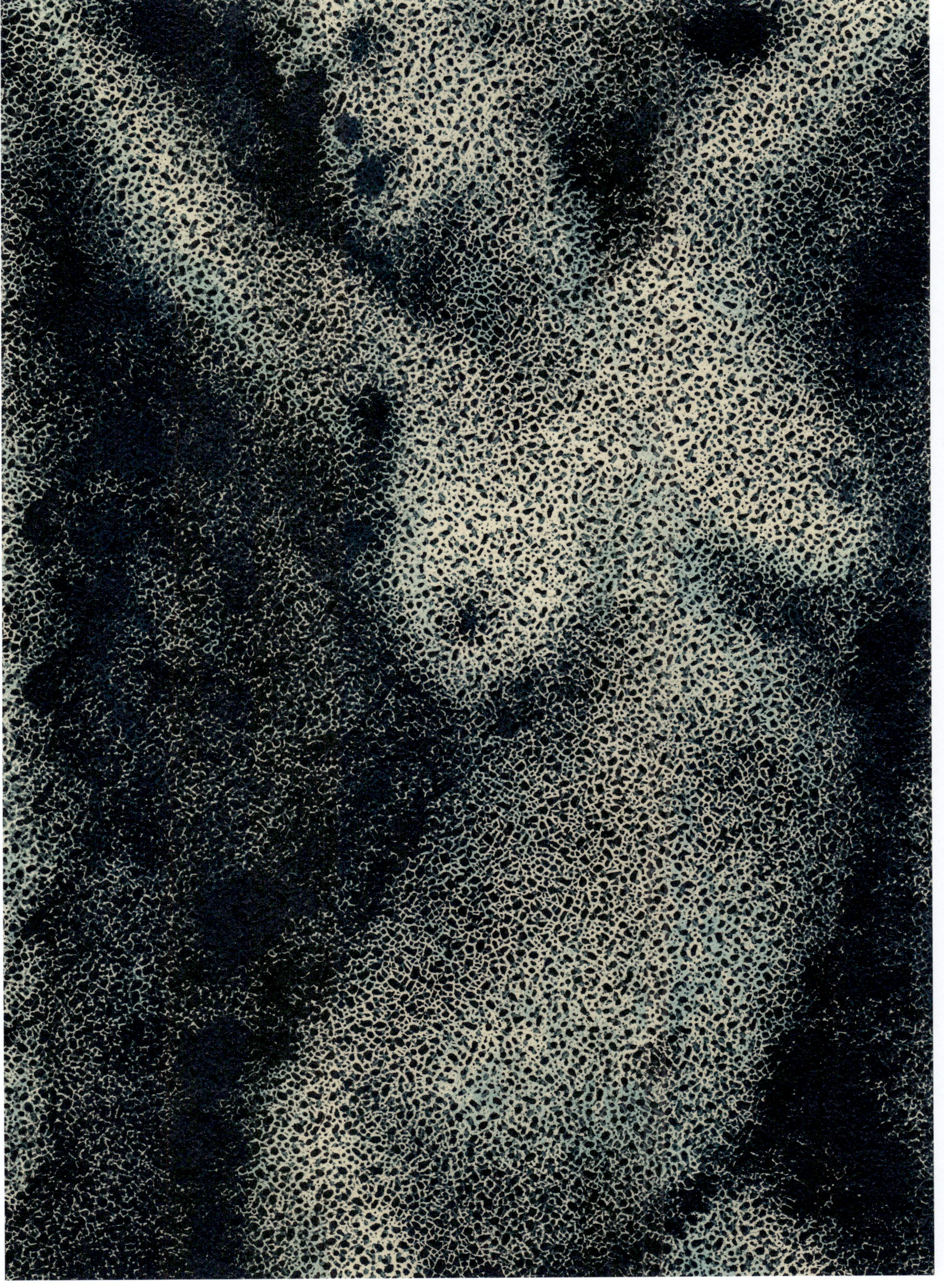

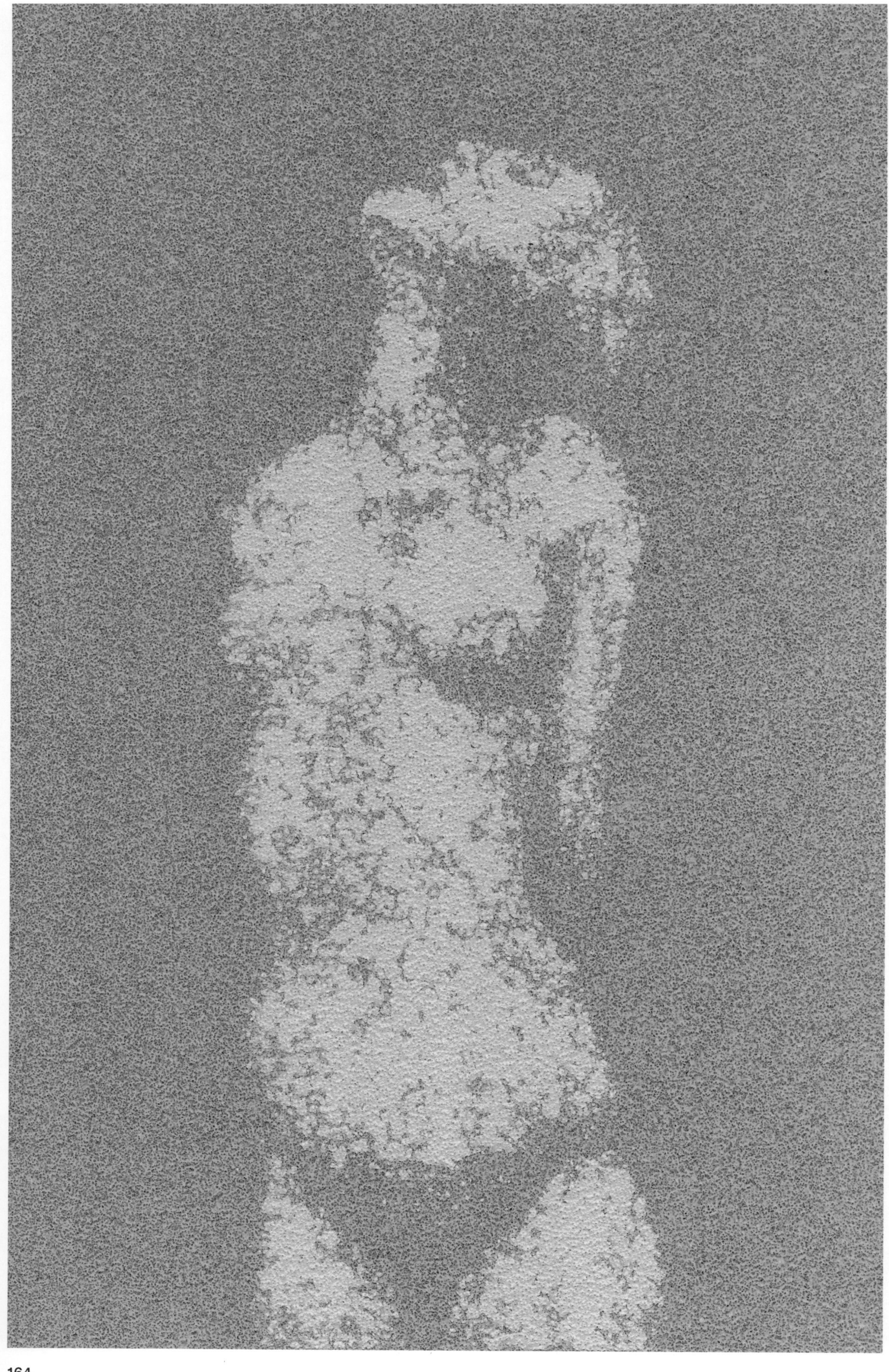

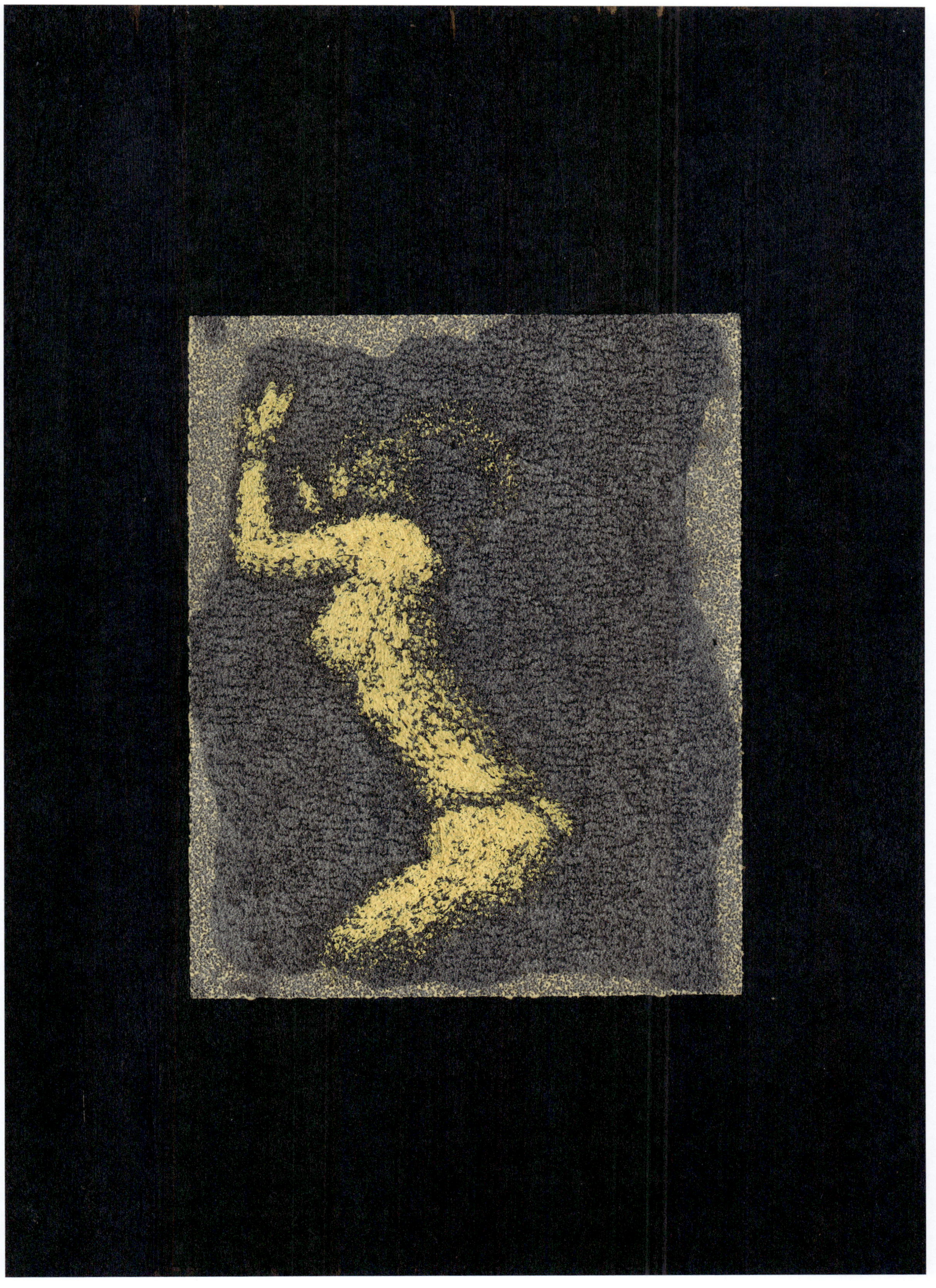

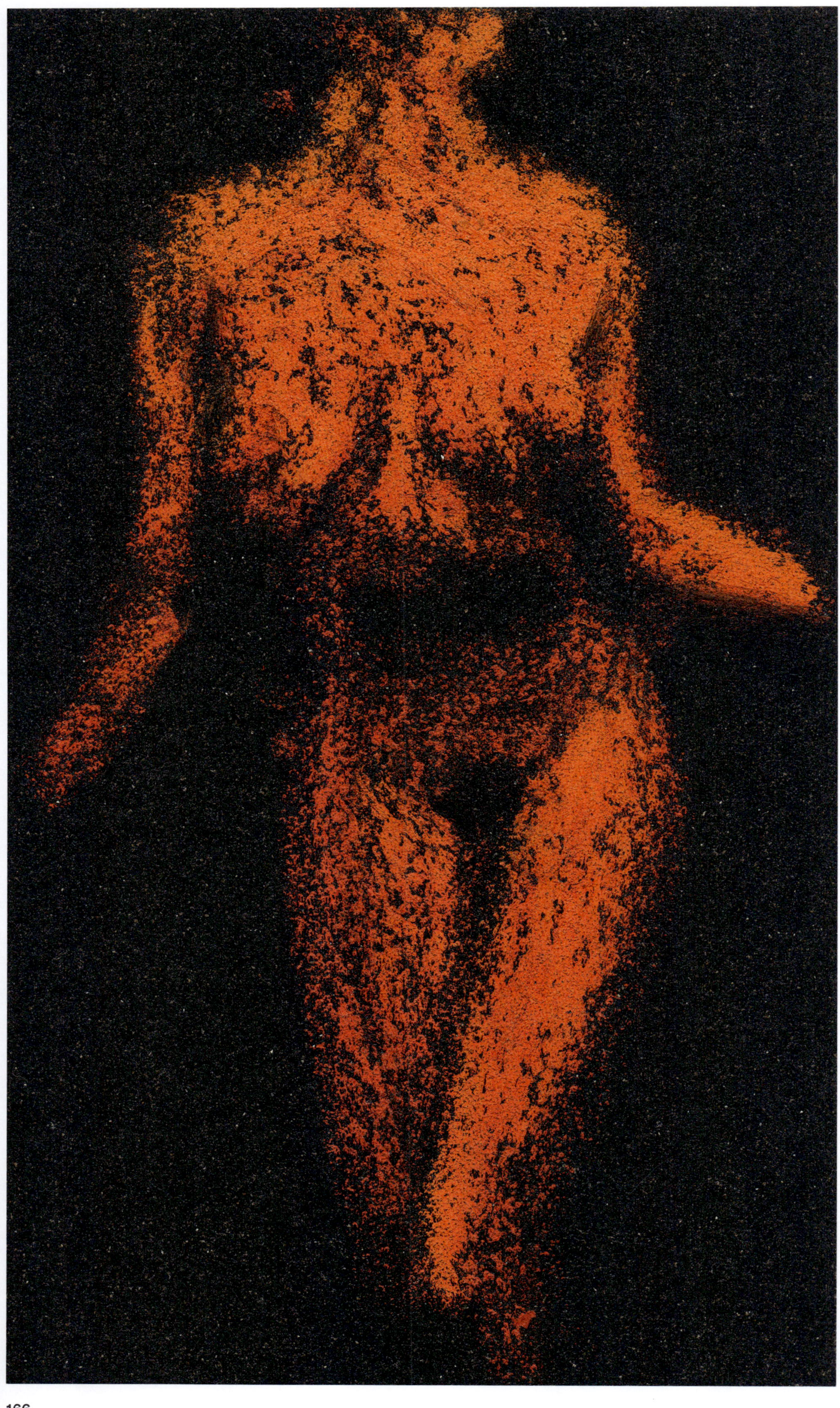

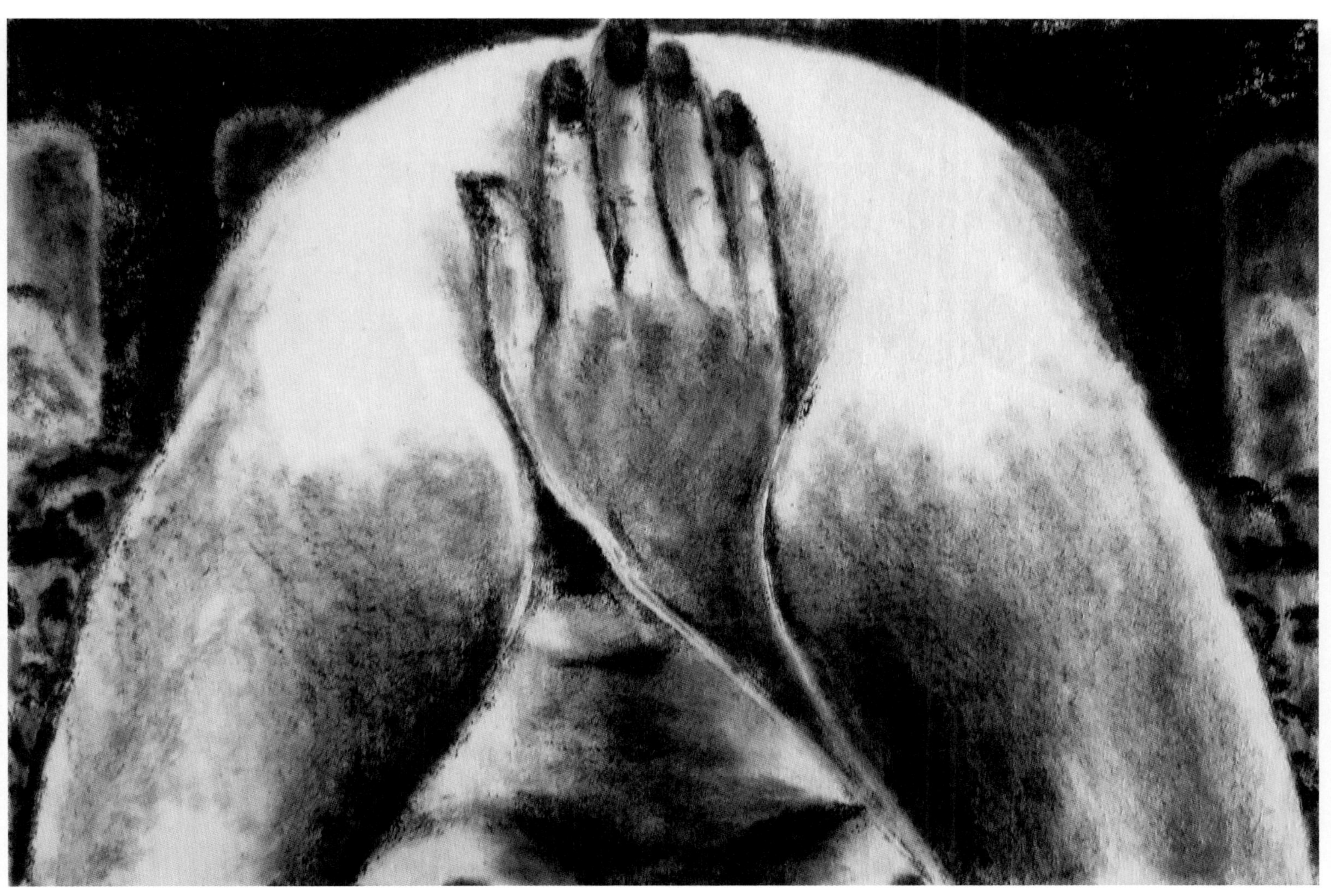

154   *A Kiss* (from *Hey Honey Redux*). Acrylic on black plastic, 14 ½ x 21 in. 2016.
156   *Little Friend White* (from *Hey Honey Redux*). Acrylic on black plastic, 21 x 15 in. 2016.
157   *Little Friend Black* (from *Hey Honey Redux*). Acrylic on black plastic, 21 x 15 in. 2016.
159   Study for *Money Shot #1*. Ink on paper, 14 x 10 ½ in. 1986.
160   Study for *Money Shot #2*. Ink on paper, 14 x 10 ½ in. 1986.
161   TOP: Untitled. Charcoal on paper, 8 ½ x 12 in. 1982.
      BOTTOM: Study for *Peep Voice Centerfold*. Charcoal on paper, 8 ½ x 12 in. 1982.
162   *Procuniar Print 3*. Monoprint, 15 x 20 ½ in. 1998.
163   *Procuniar Print 4 – Blue Stripper*. Monoprint with embossing, 29 ¾ x 16 ½ in. 1996.
164   *Live Girls Yellow*. Silkscreen on sandpaper, 11 x 9 in. 2001.
165   *Live Girls XXIII*. Oil and sandpaper on tar, 16 x 21 in. 1993.
166   *Live Girls 28*. Oil stick on emery cloth on wood, 11 x 9 in. 1992.
167   *East Village Eye Centerfold Stripper*. Monoprint, 9 x 23 in. 1982.

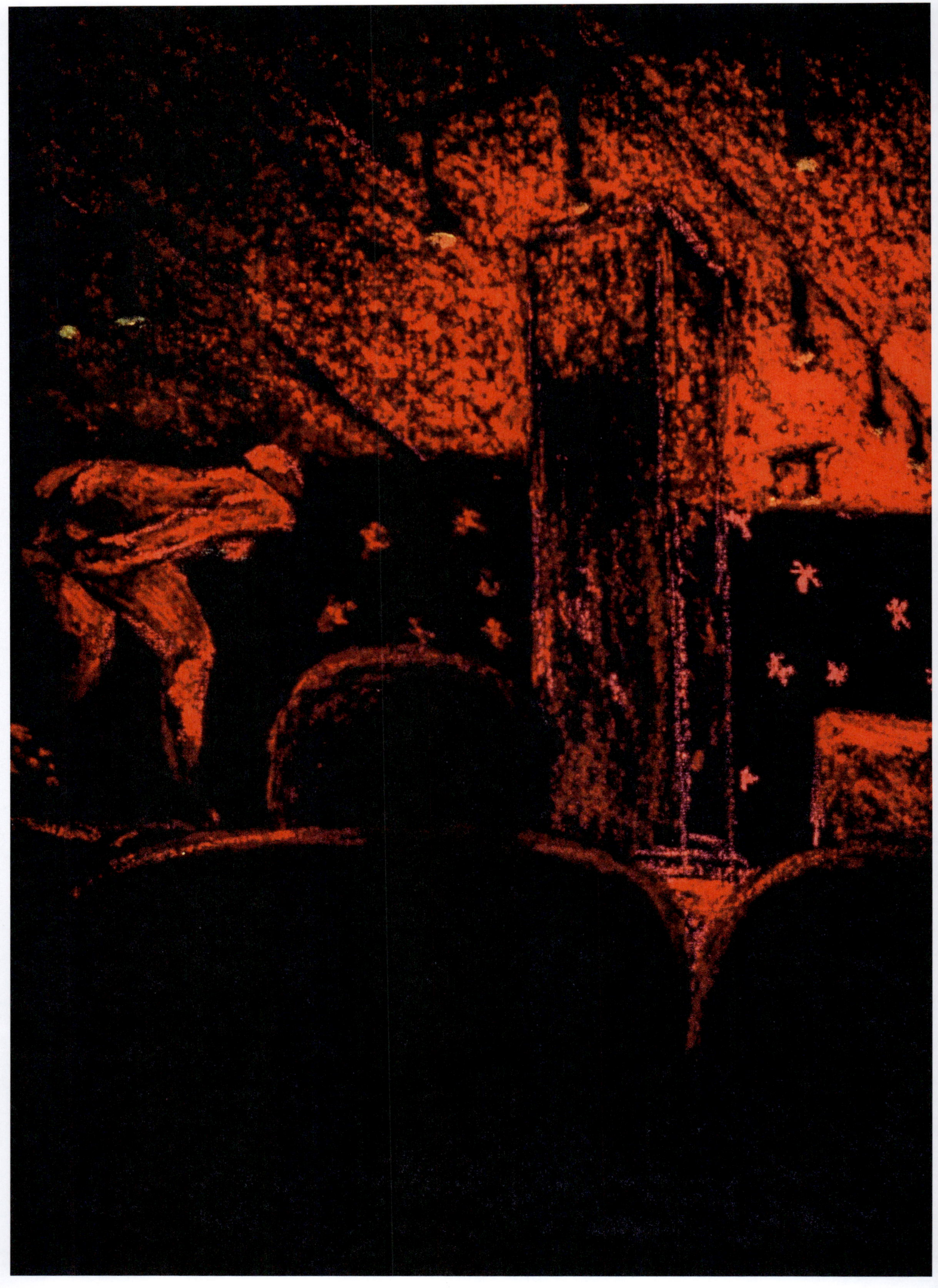

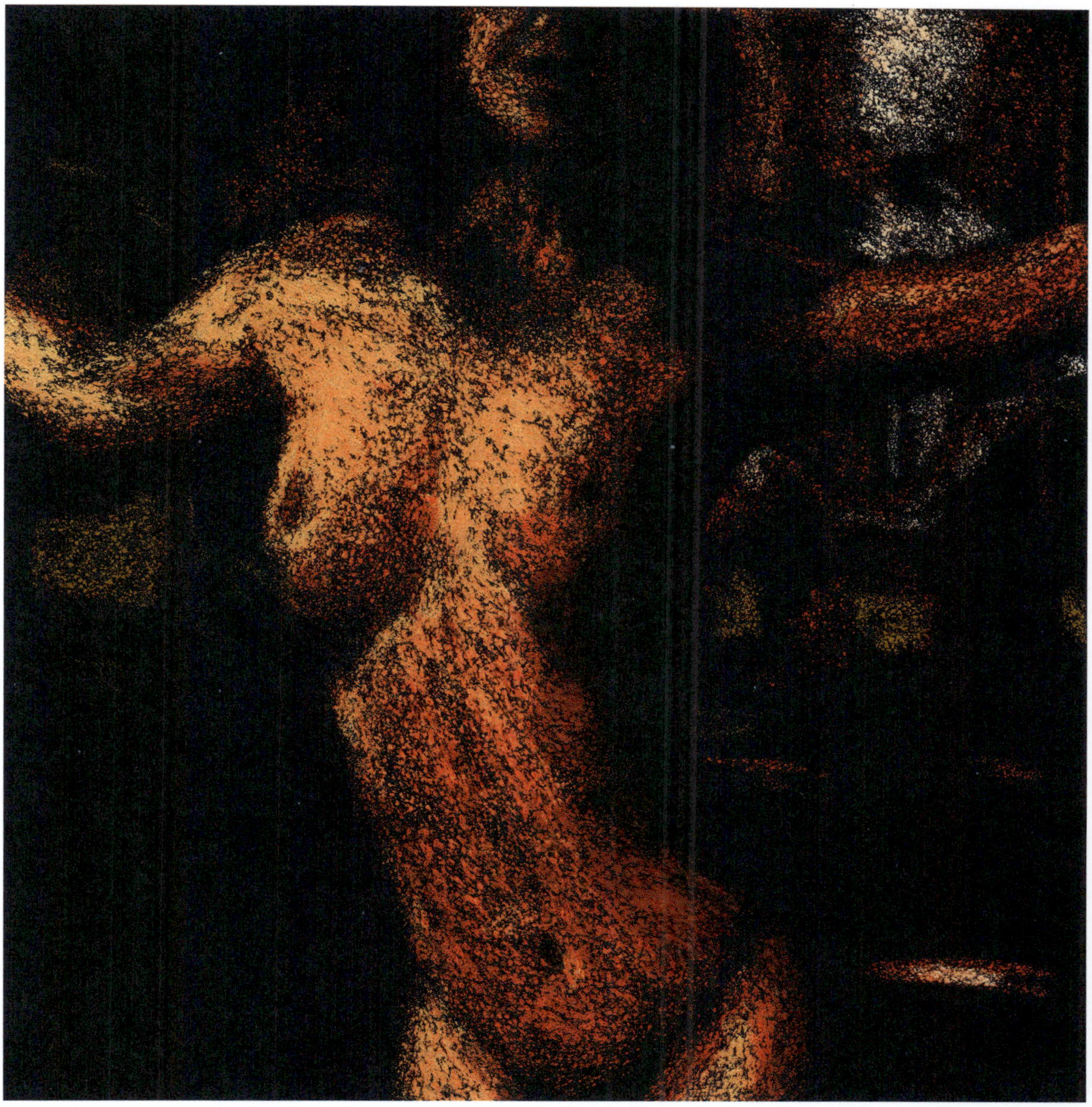

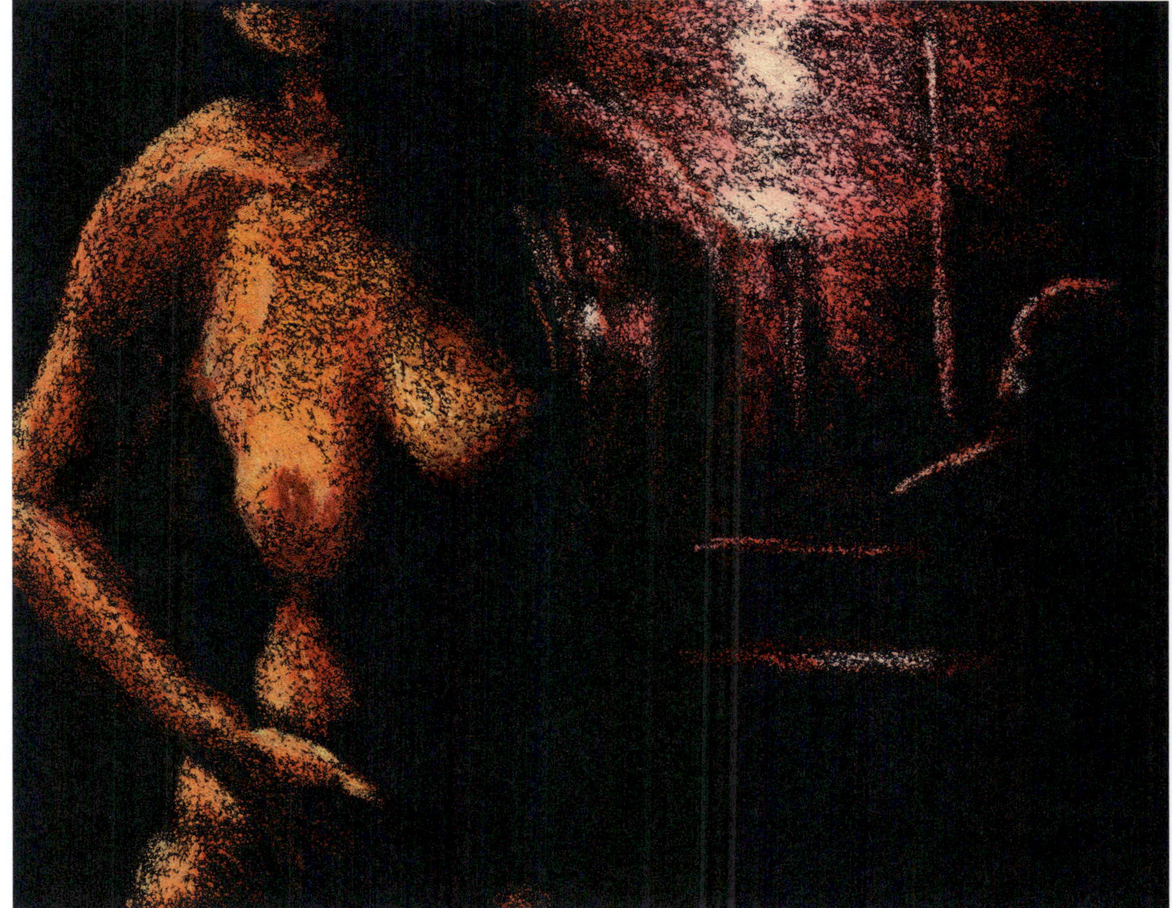

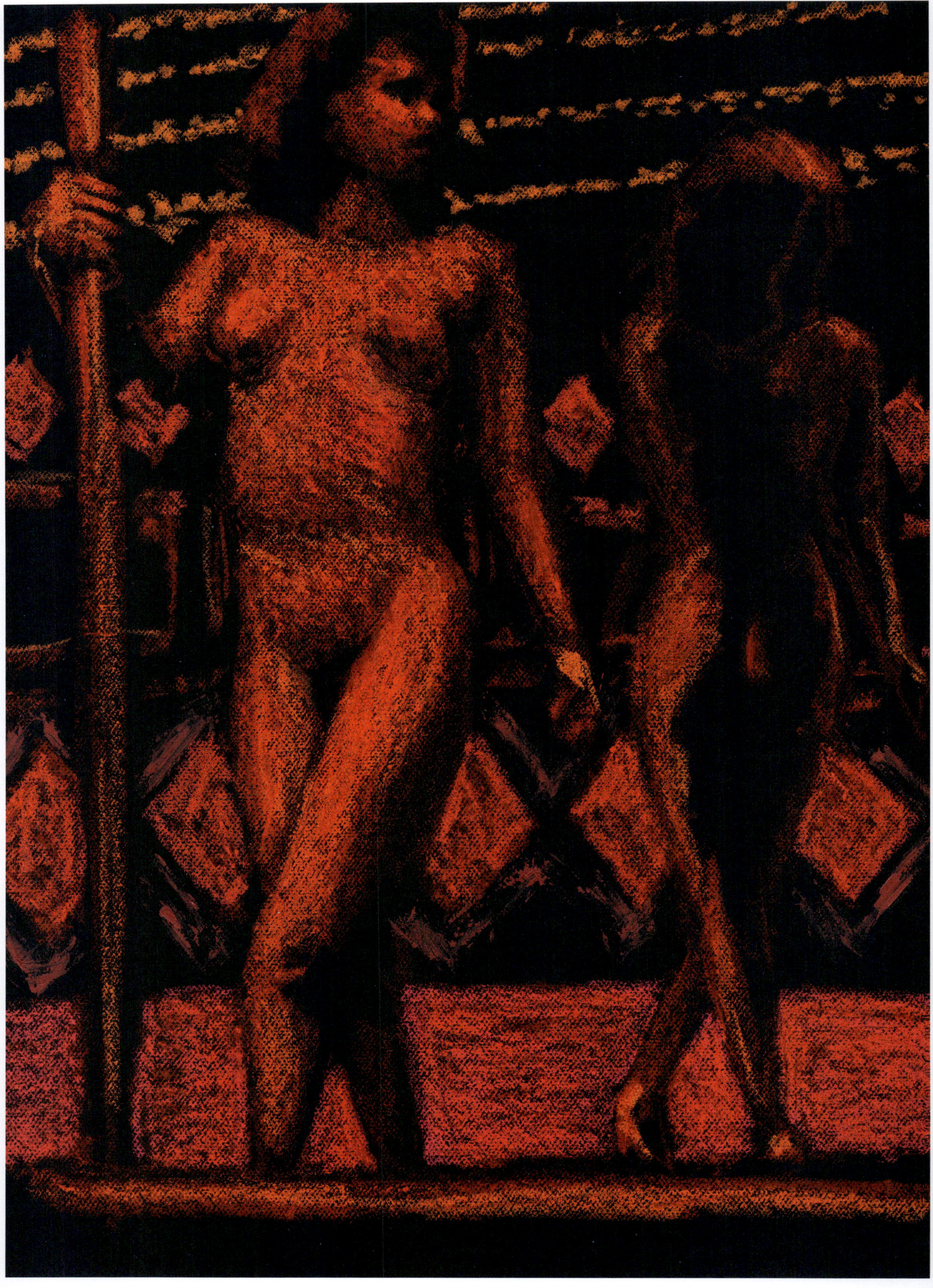

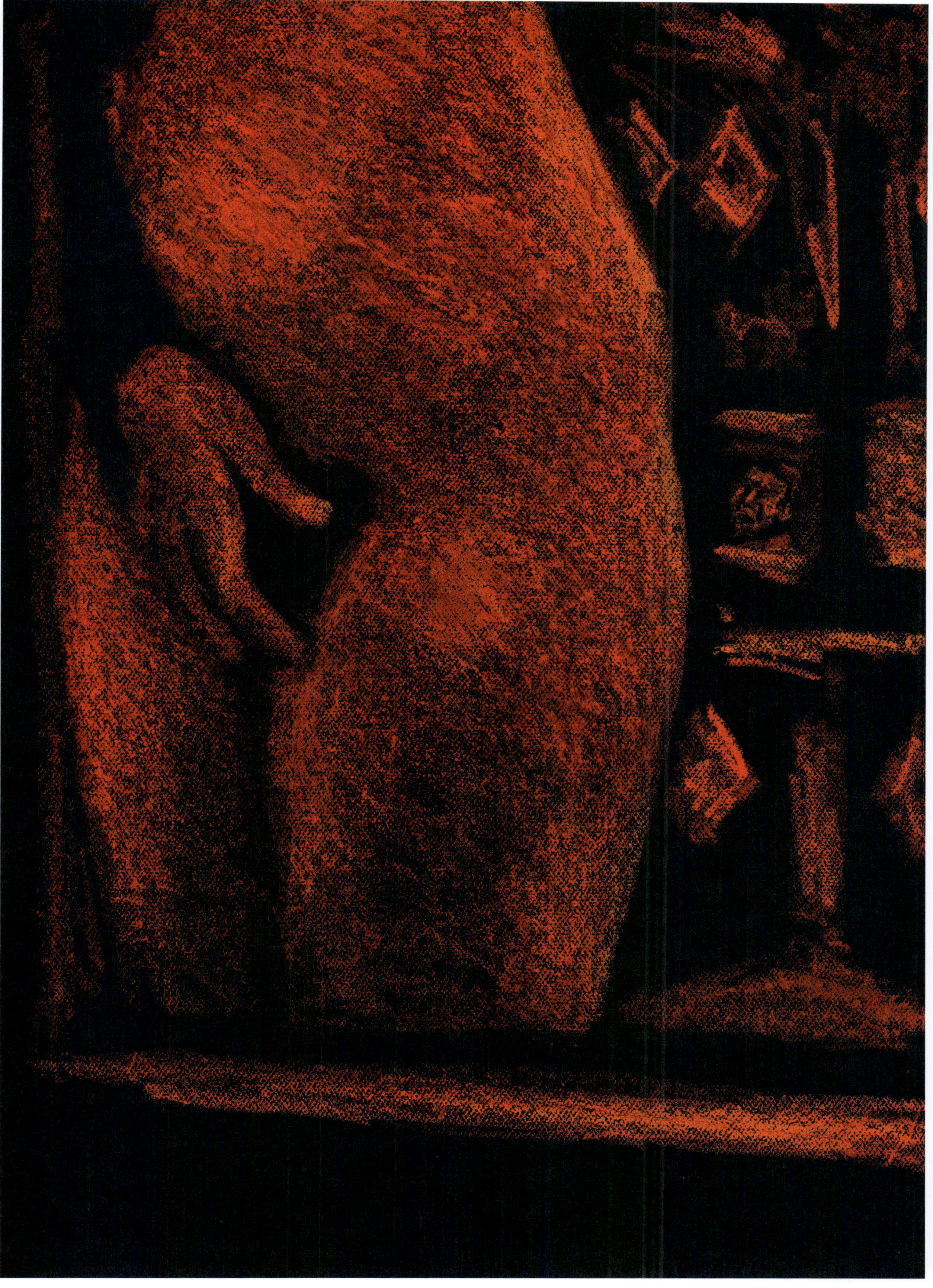

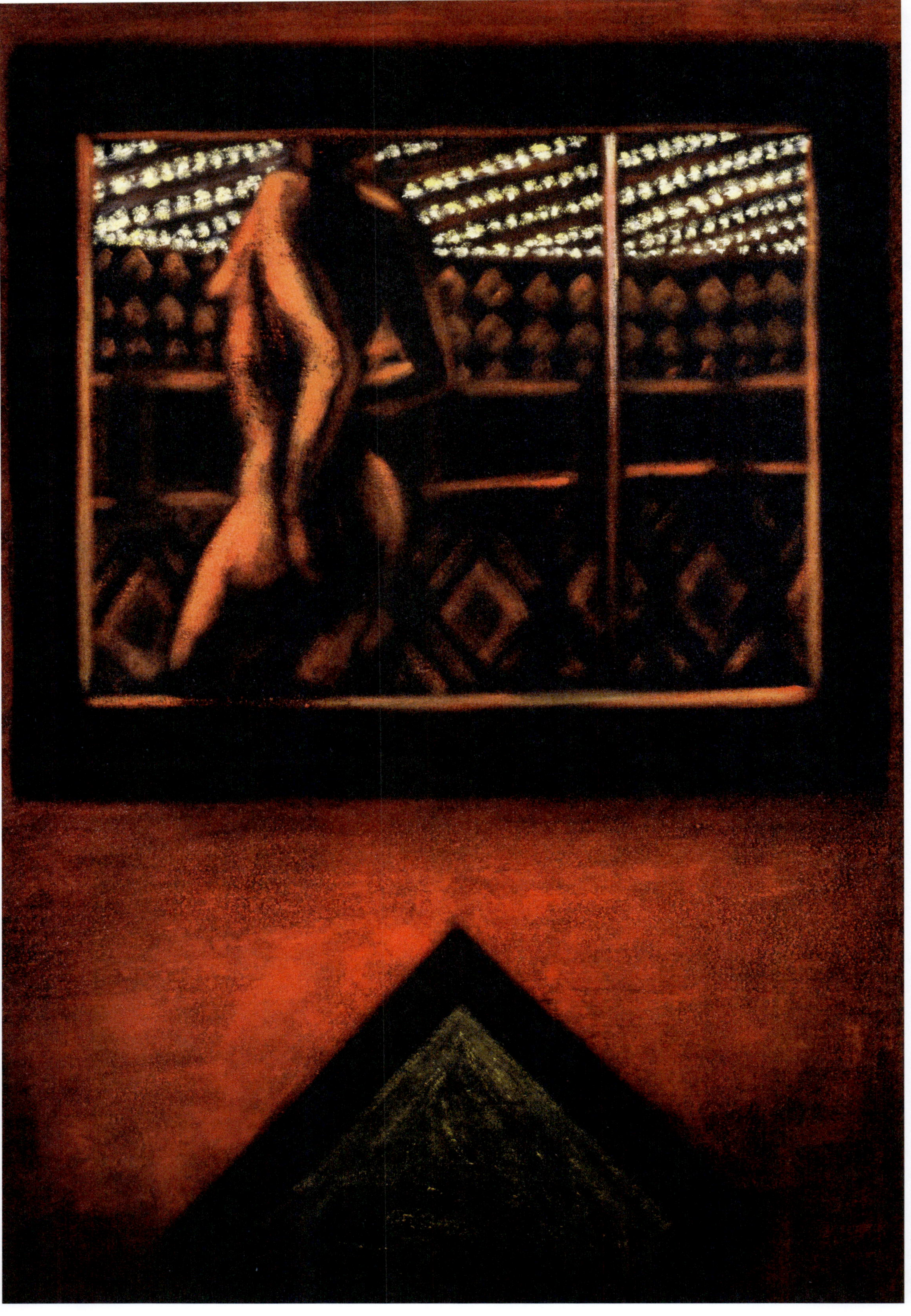

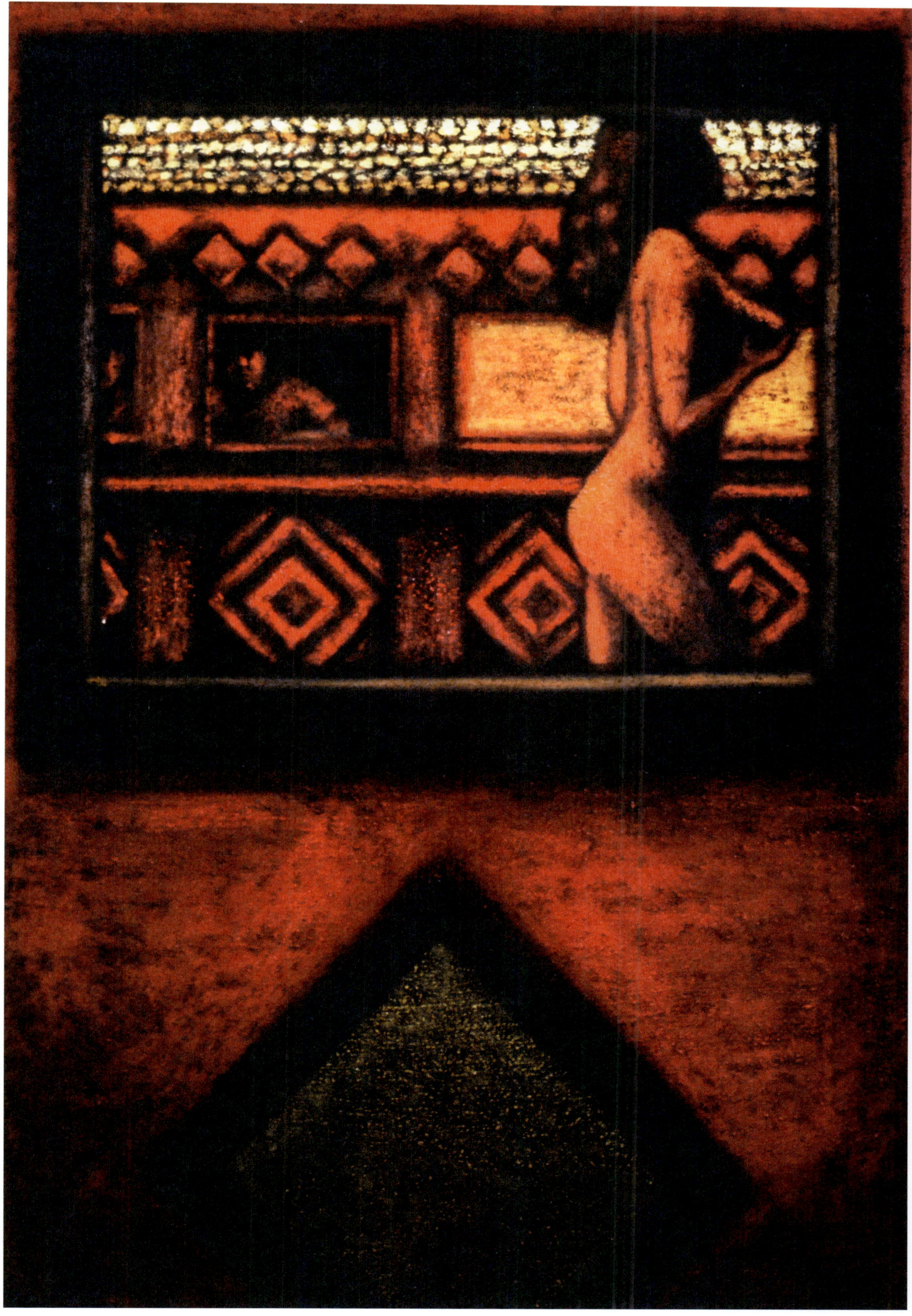

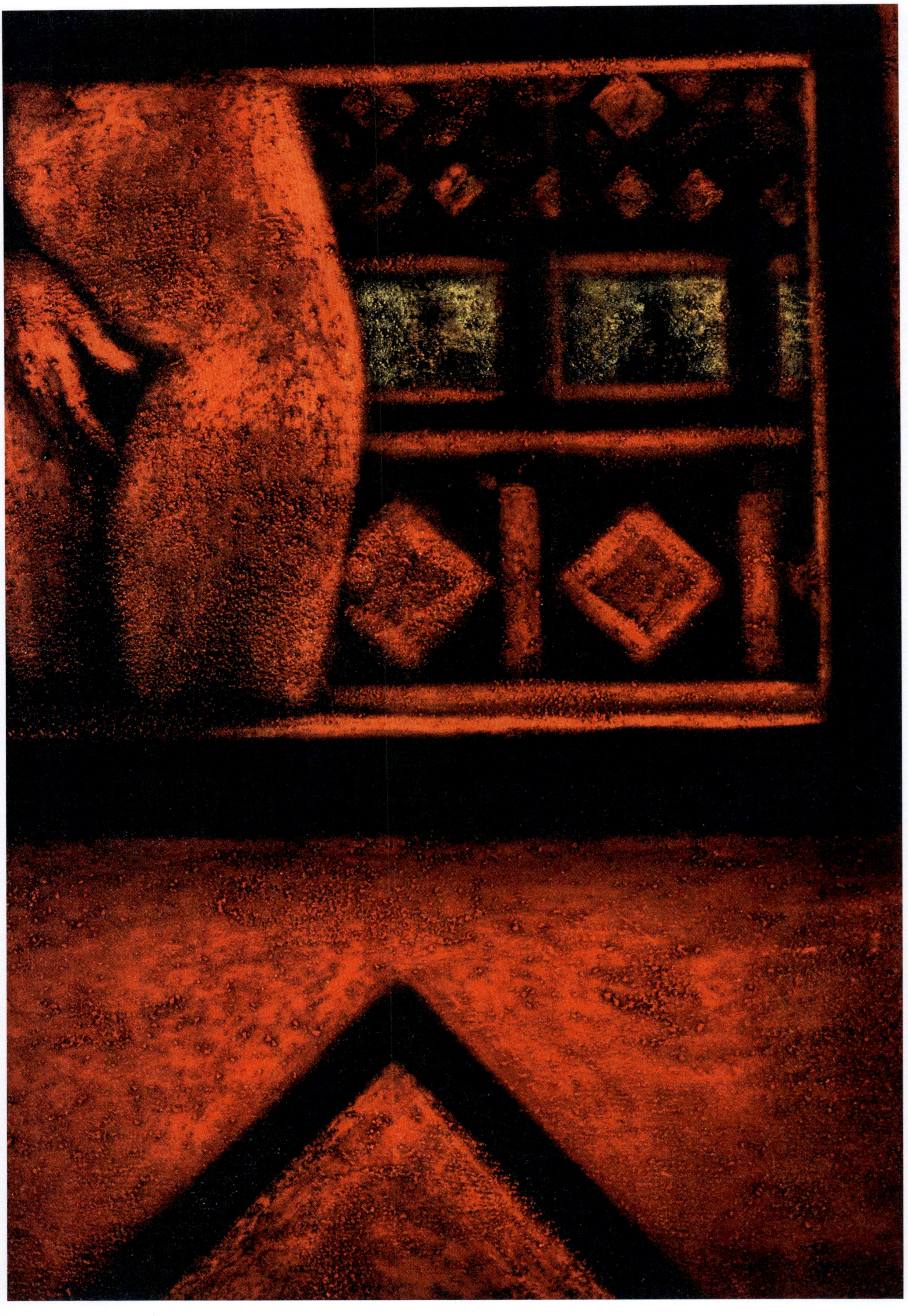

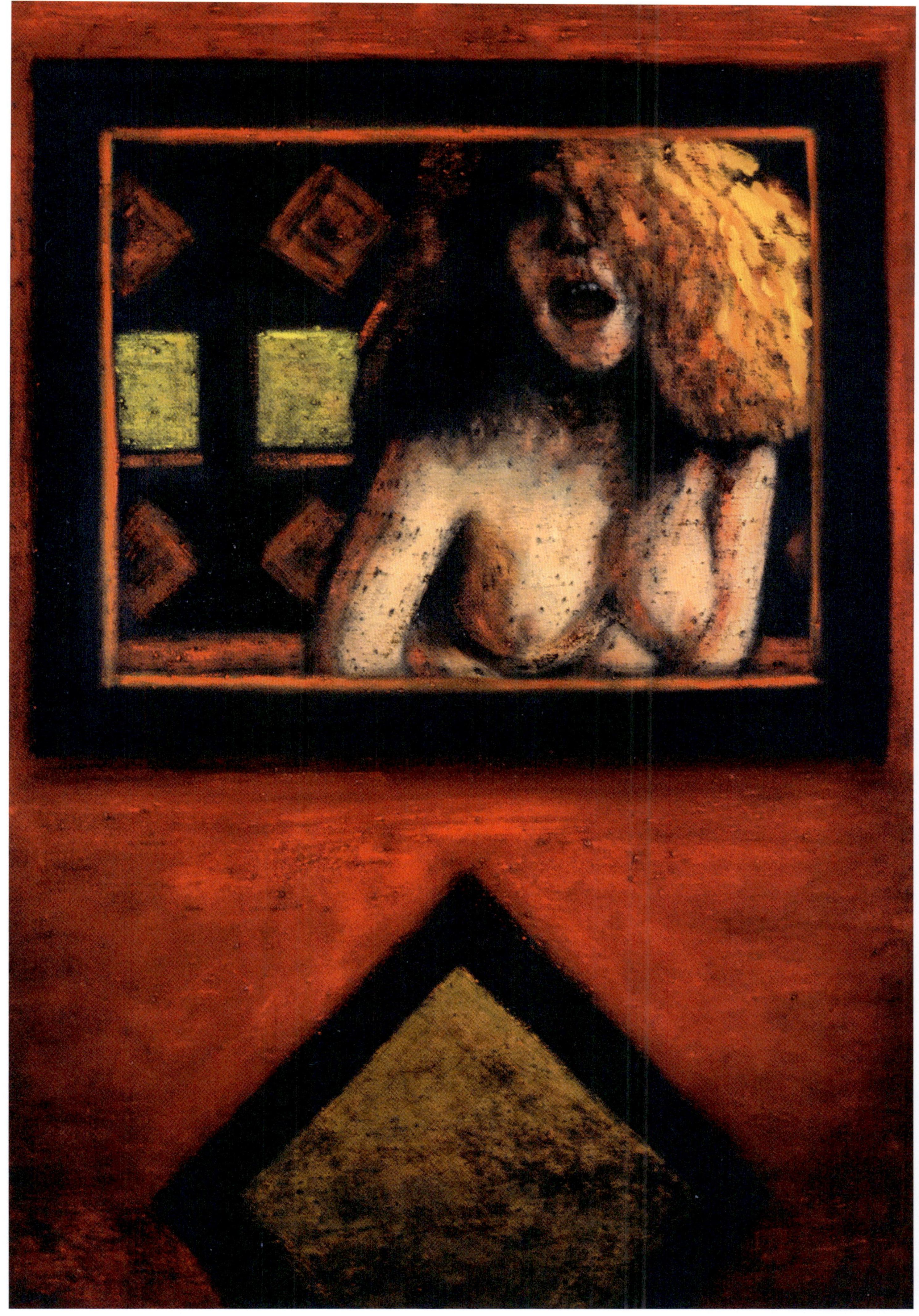

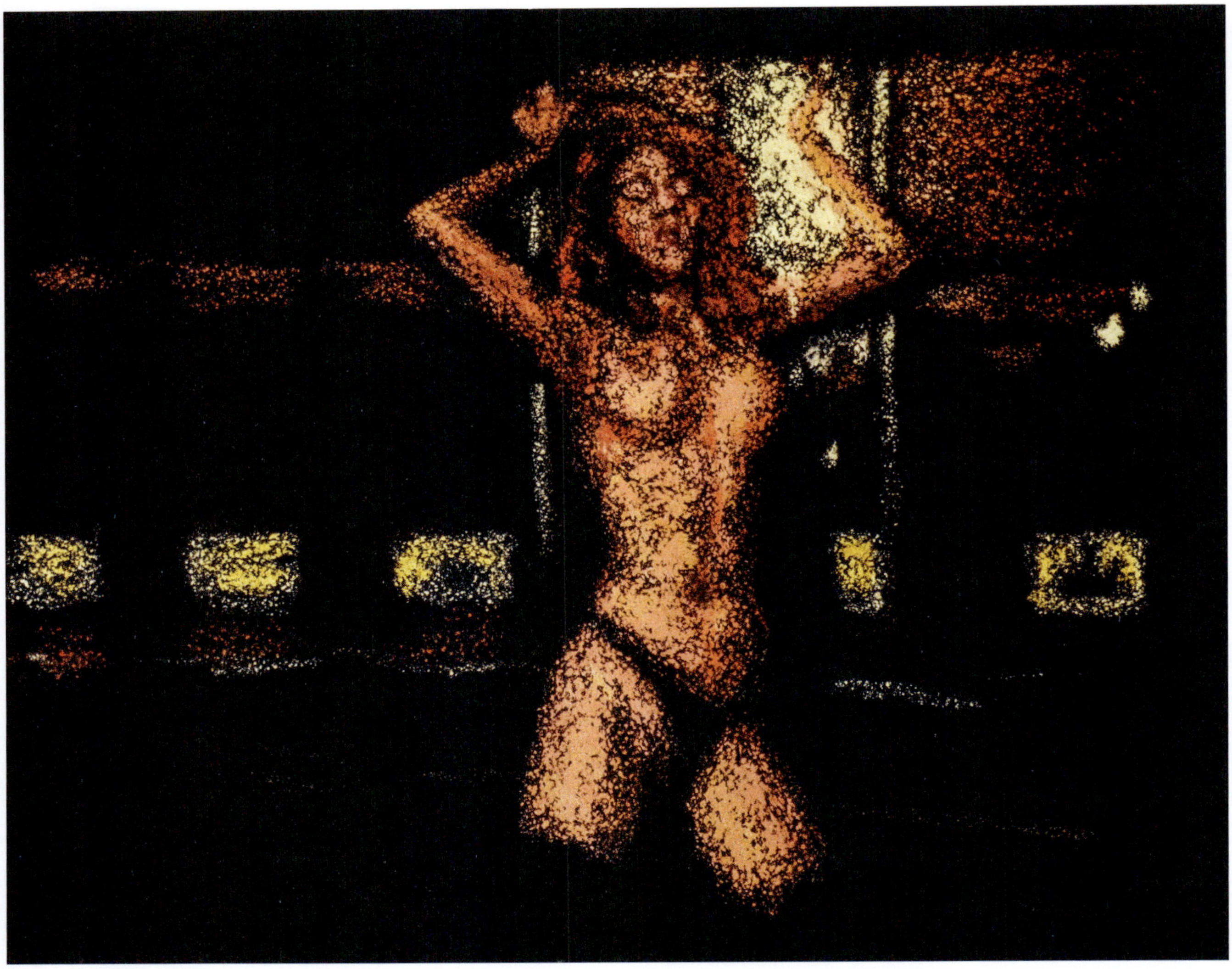

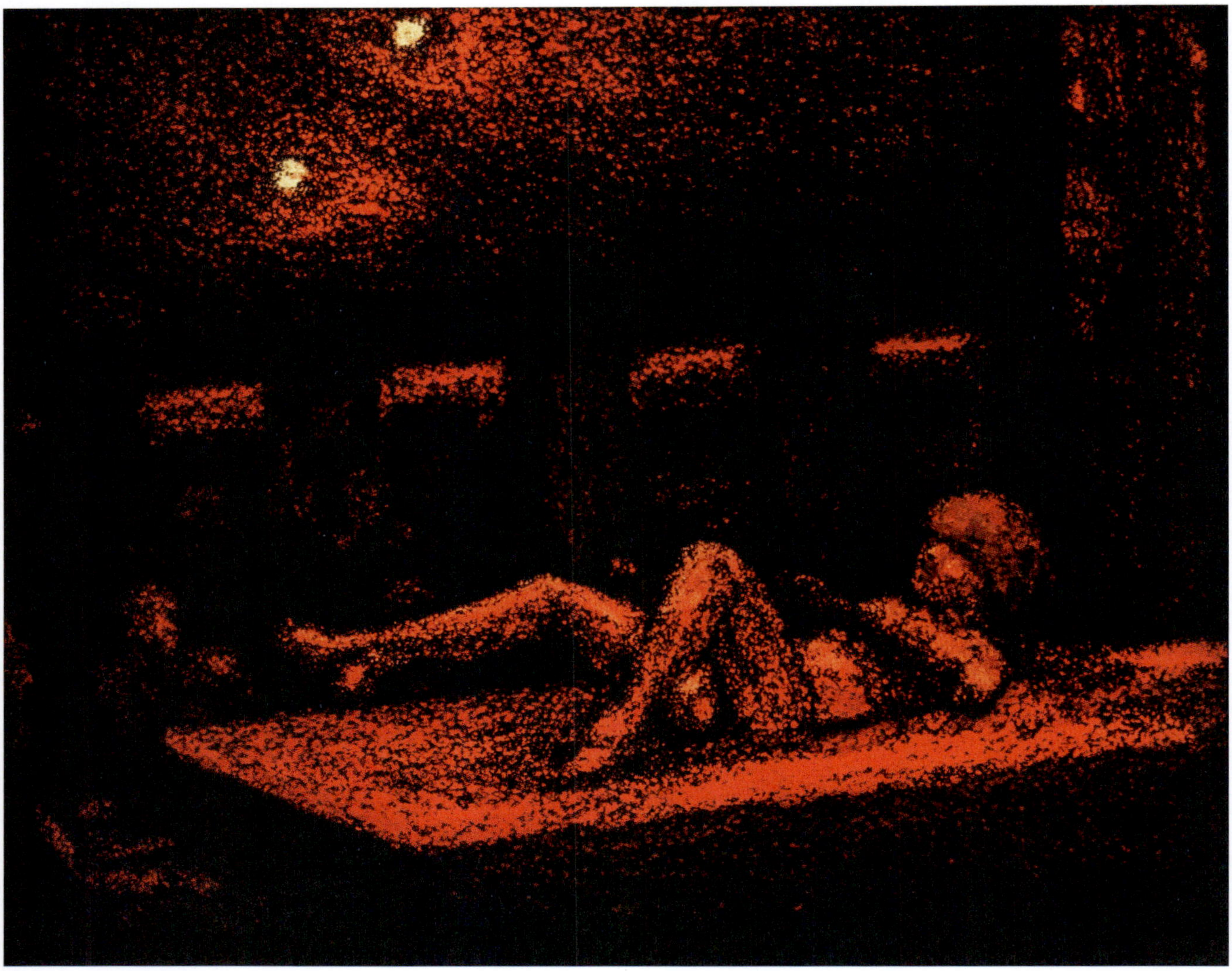

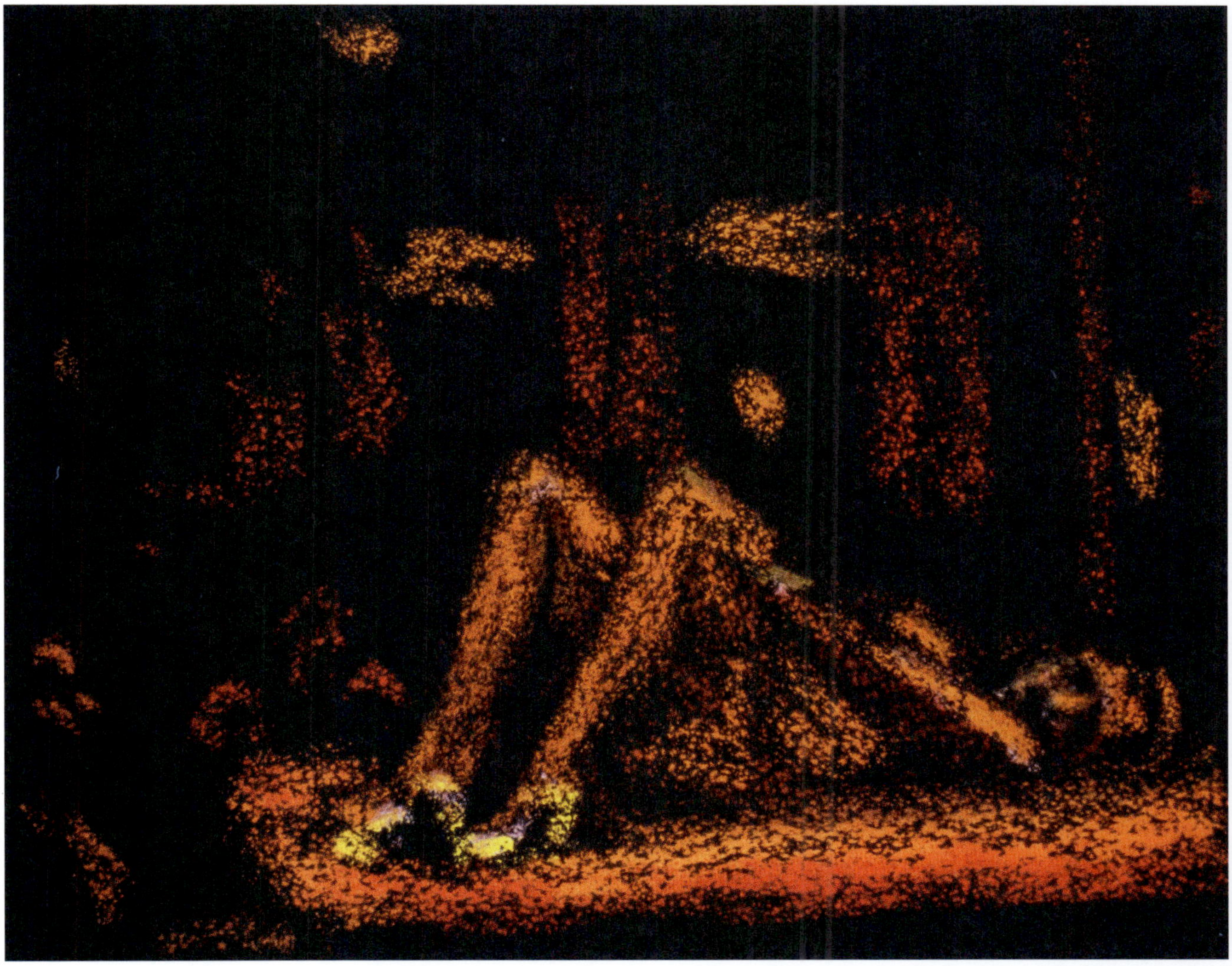

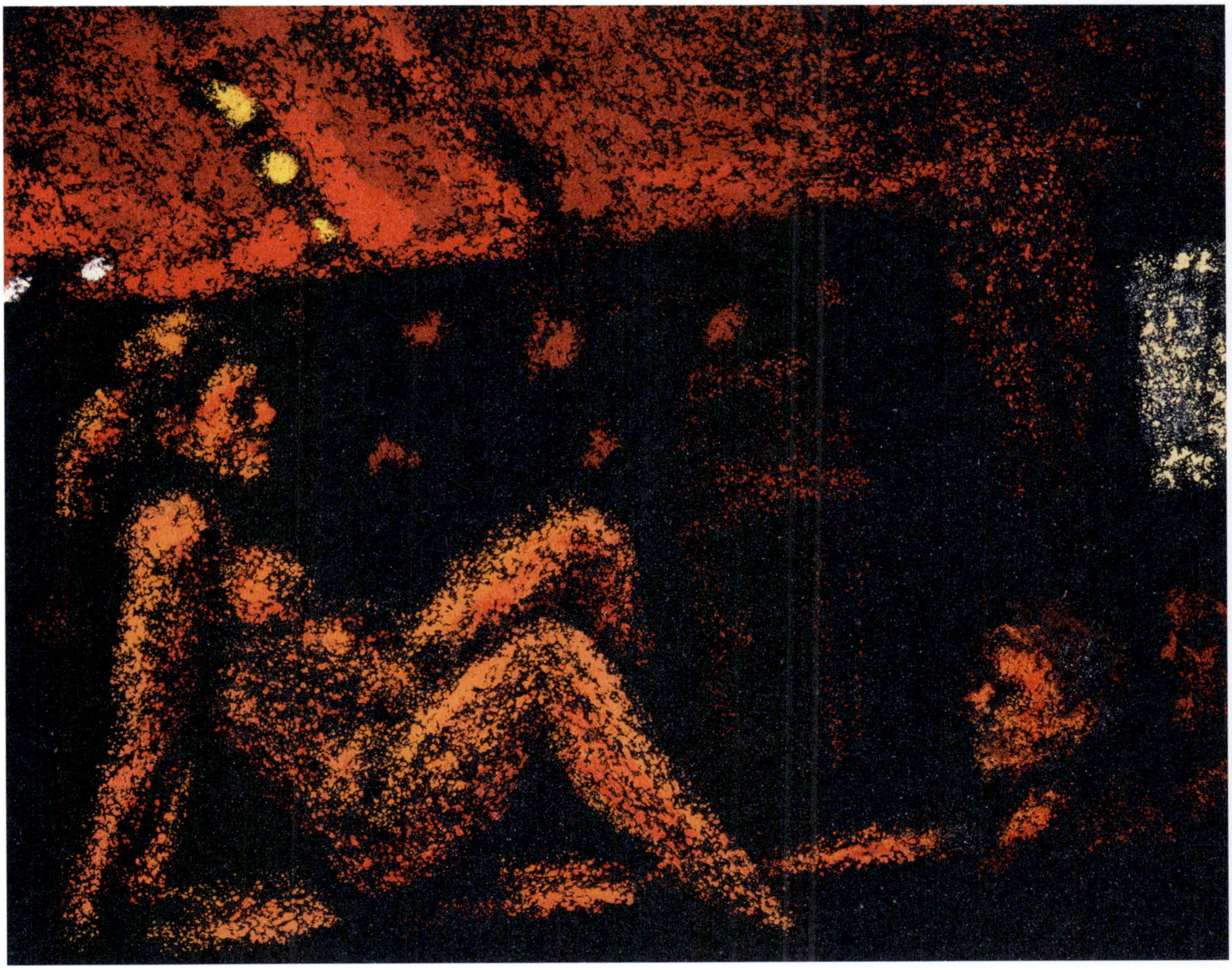

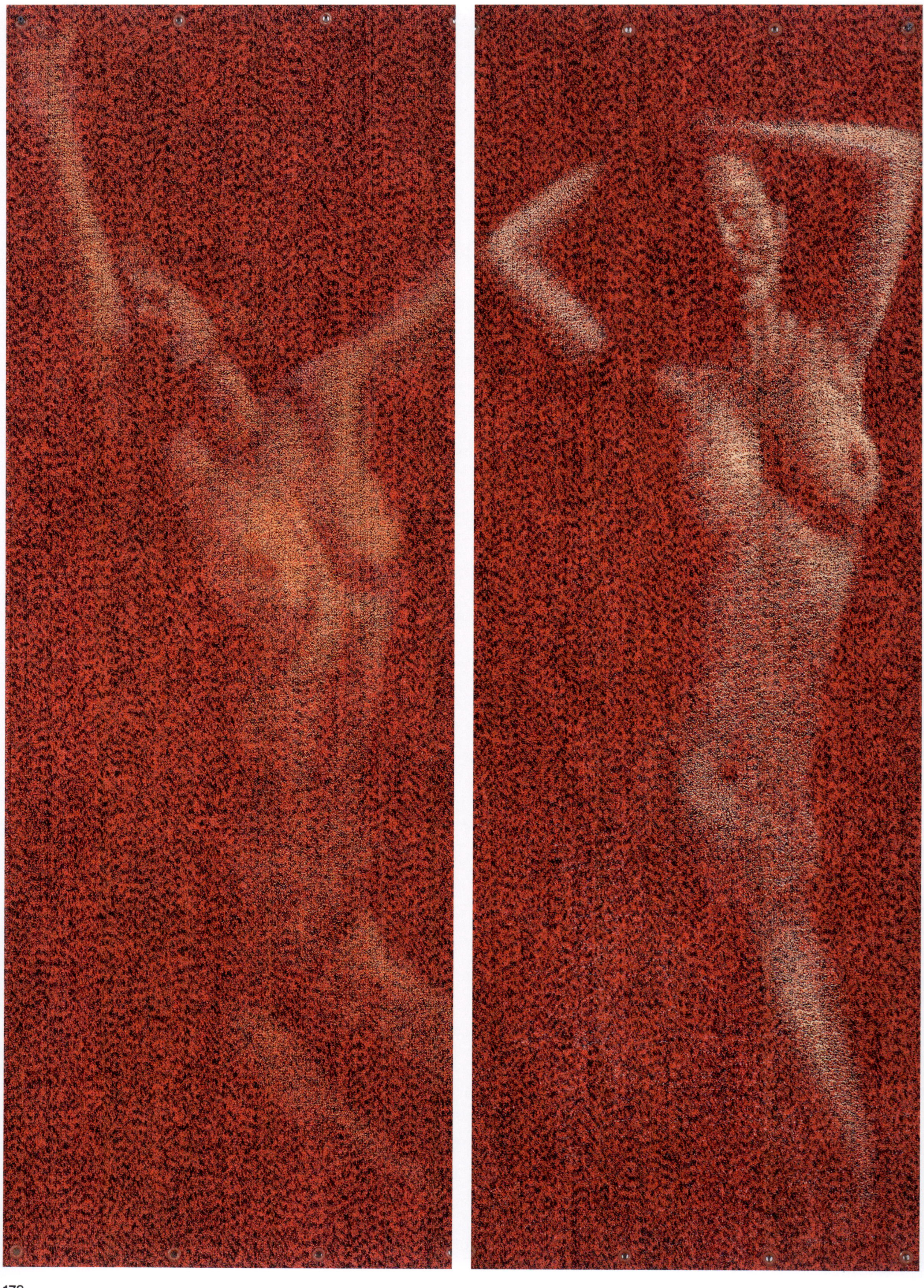

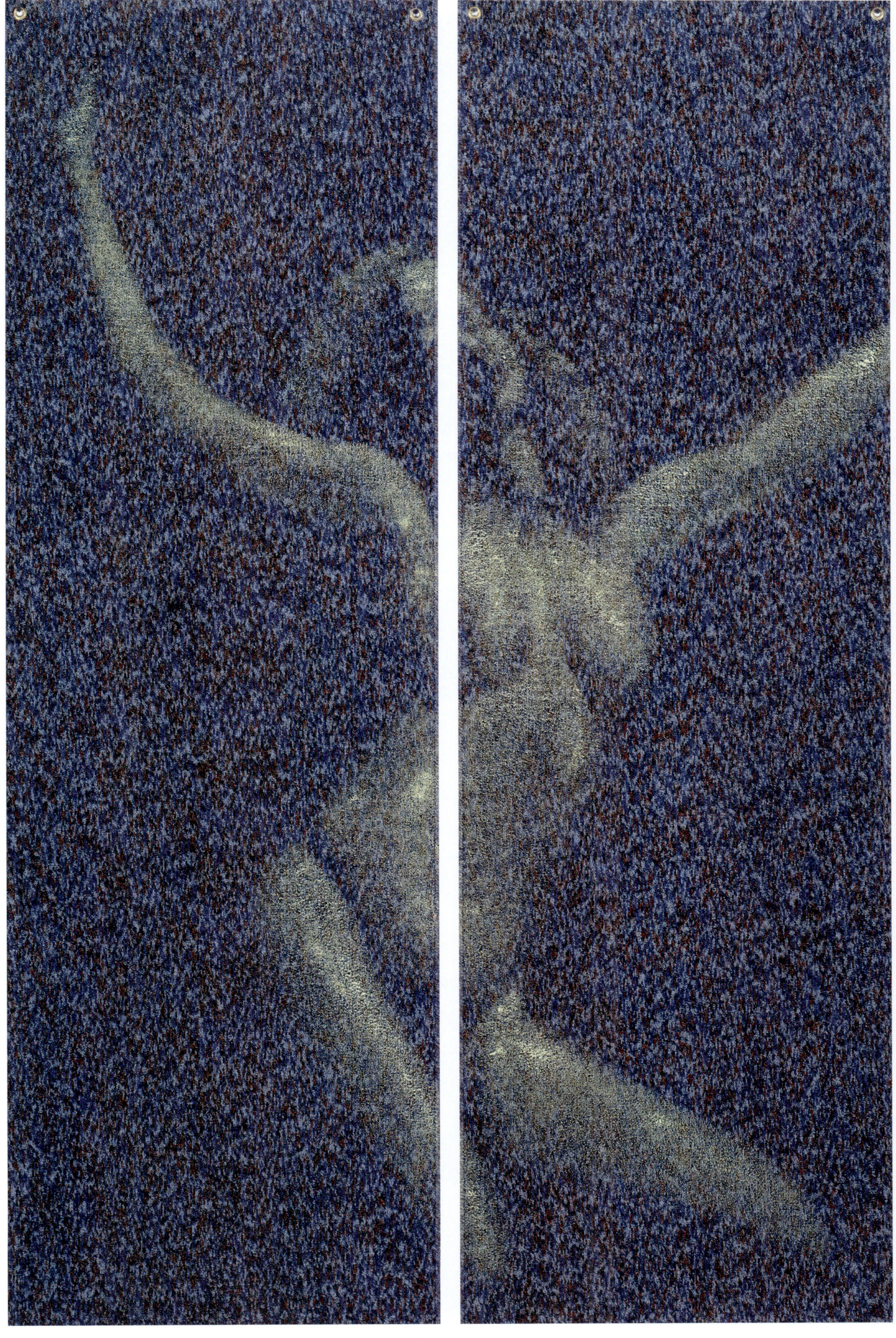

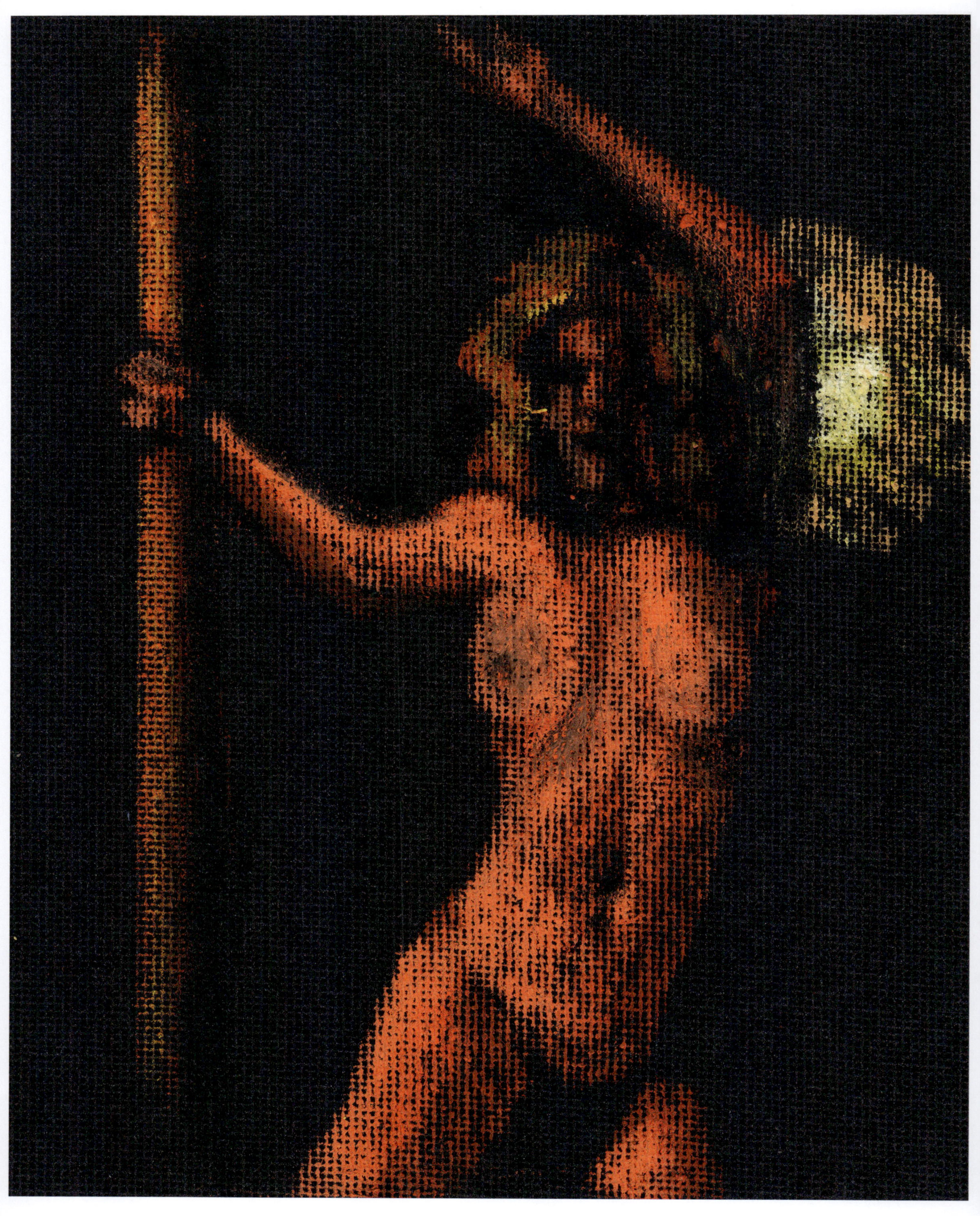

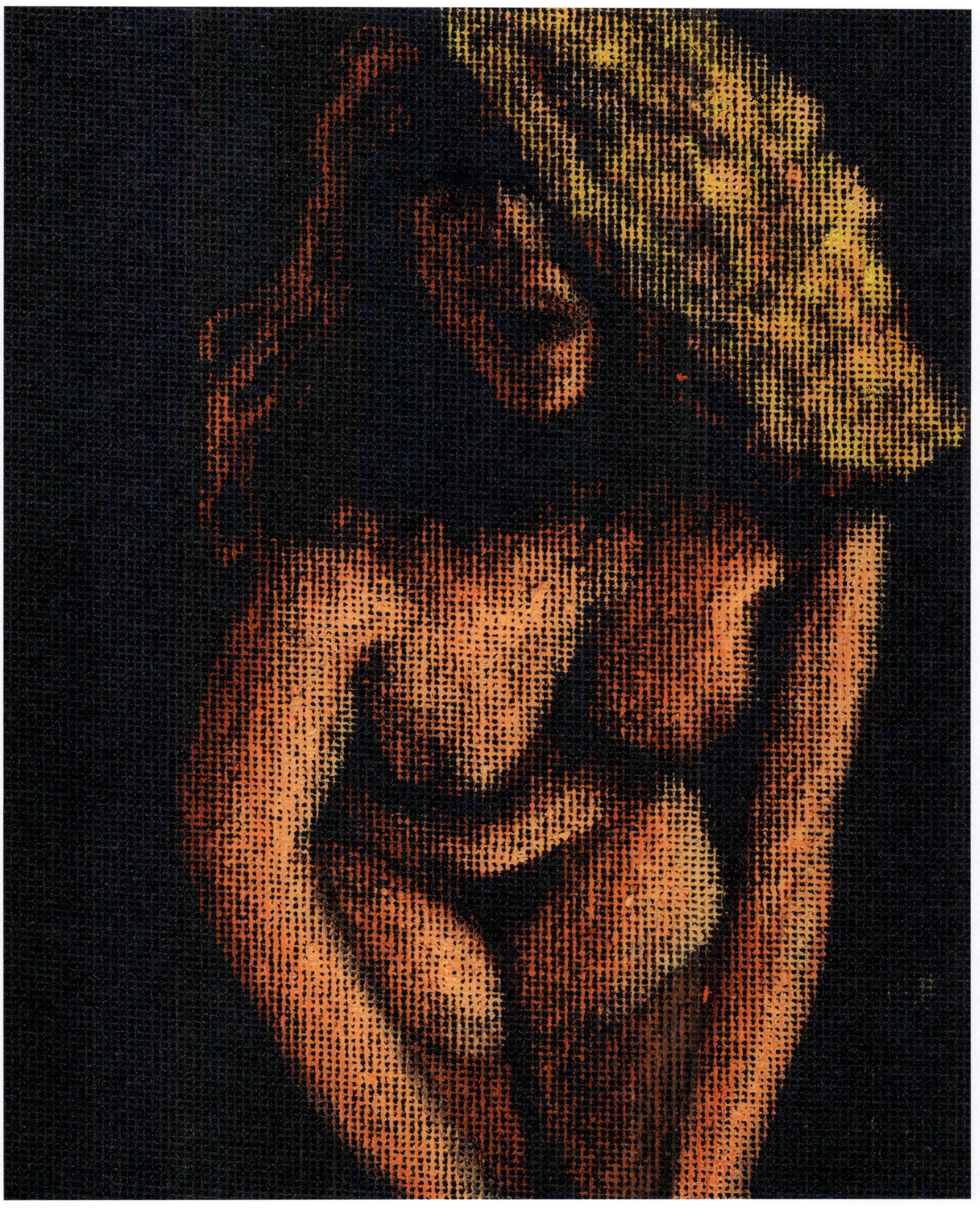

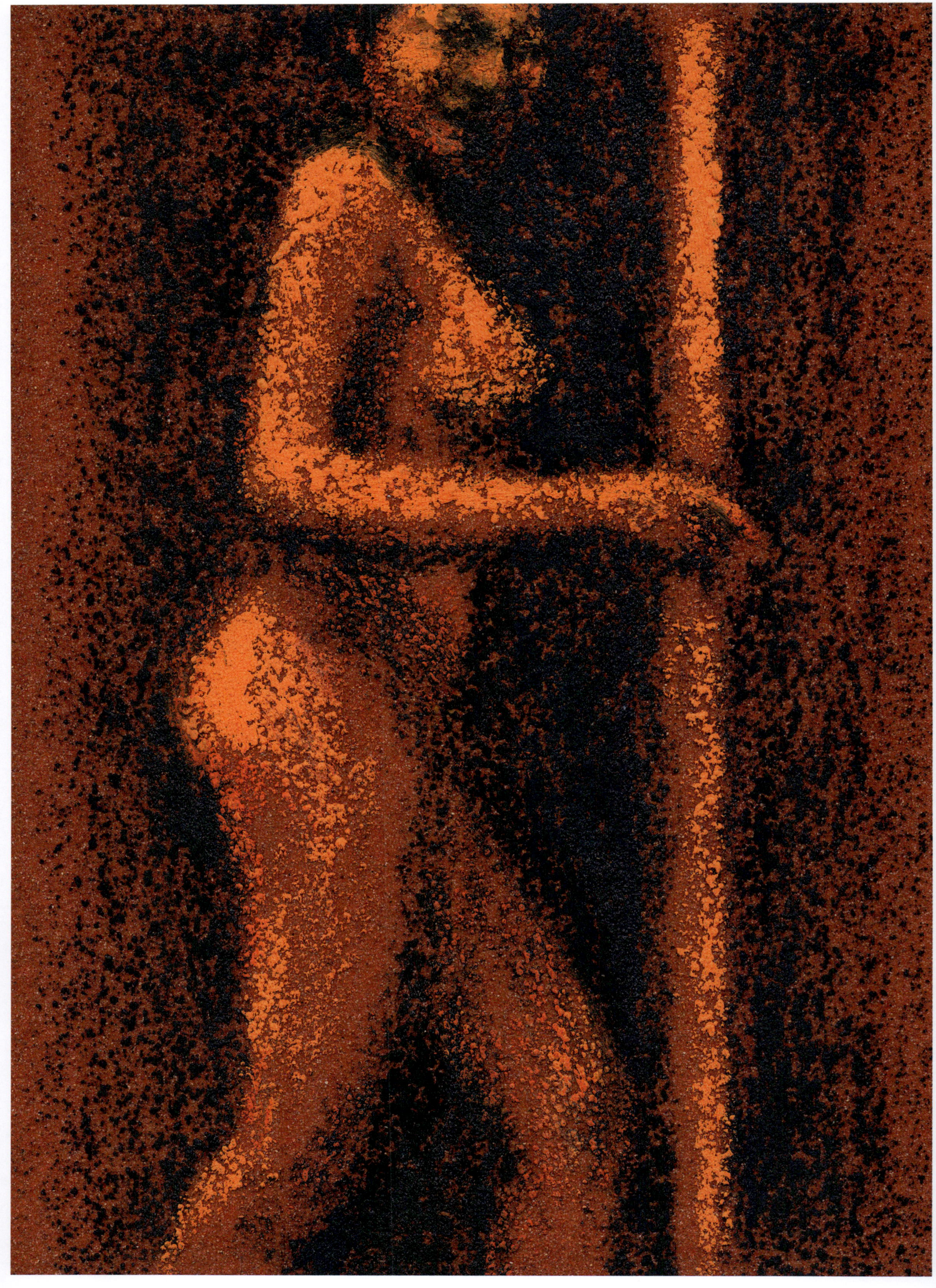

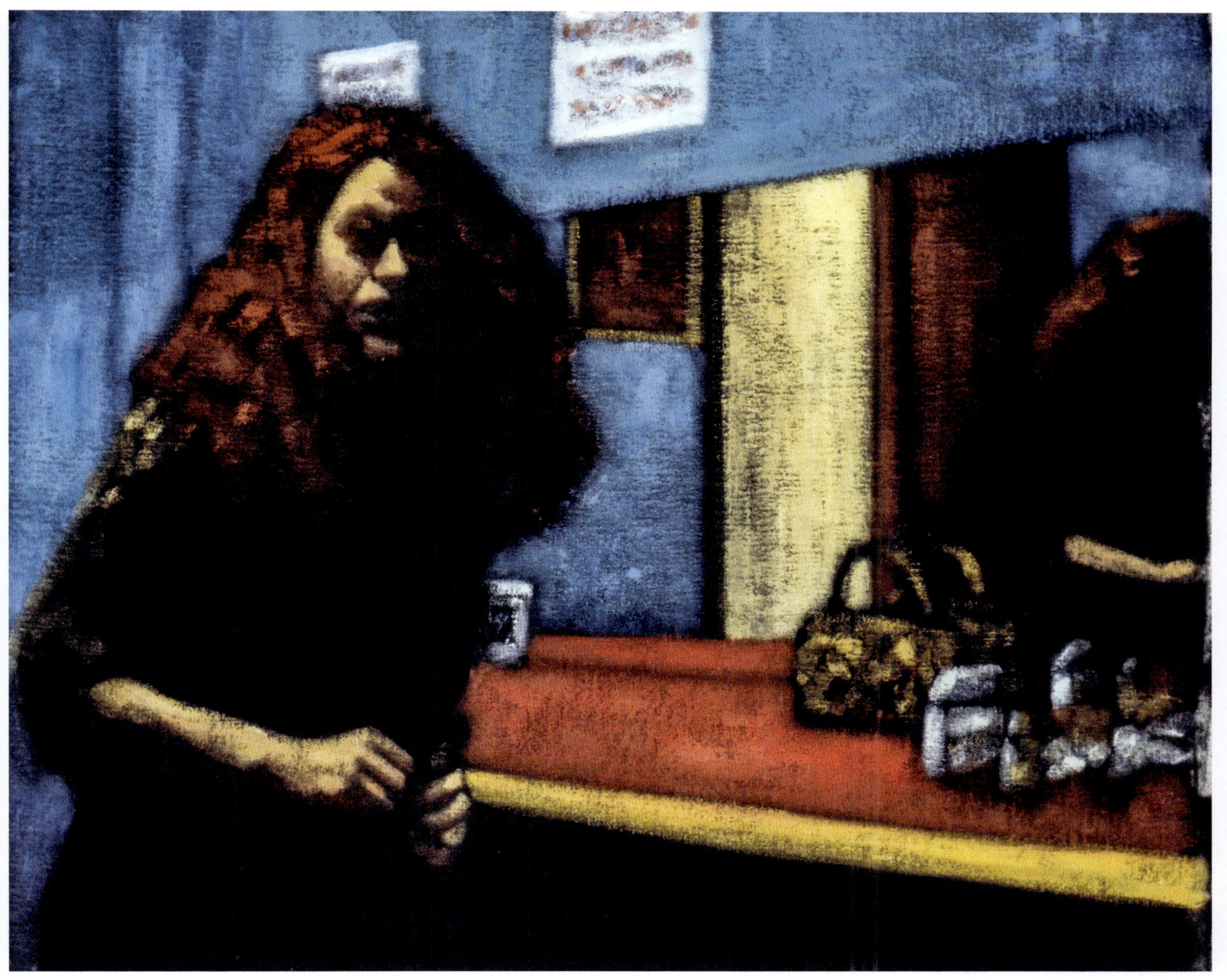

168   *Live Girl Bending Over*. Oil stick on black paper, 12 x 8 ½ in. 1993.
169   TOP: Study for *Live Girls* 2. Oil stick on emery cloth, 18 x 18 in. 1993.
       BOTTOM: Study for *Live Girls 1*. Oil stick on emery cloth, 14 x 18 in. 2001.
170   Study for *Live Girls 10*. Oil stick on black paper, 19 ½ x 25 ½ in. 1992.
171   Study for *Live Girls 9*. Oil stick on black paper, 25 ½ x 19 ¾ in. 1992.
172   *Peep III*. Oil and pumice on canvas, 57 x 40 in. 1993.
173   *Peep VII*. Oil and pumice on canvas, 57 x 40 in. 1992.
174   *Peep II*. Oil and pumice on canvas, 57 x 40 in. 1992–1996.
175   *Peep I*. Oil and pumice on canvas, 57 x 40 in. 1992.
176   TOP: *Melody Burlesque III*. Oil stick on emery cloth, 14 x 18 in. 1993.
       BOTTOM: *Melody Burlesque IV*. Oil stick on emery cloth, 14 ½ x 18 in. 1993.
177   TOP: *Live Girls V*. Oil stick on emery cloth, 9 x 11 in. 1992.
       BOTTOM: *Live Girls XI*. Oil stick on emery cloth, 11 x 9 in. 1992.
178   LEFT: *Red Shadow I*. Acrylic and oil on carpet, 72 x 27 in. 1993.
       RIGHT: *Red Shadow II*. Acrylic and oil on carpet, 72 x 27 in. 1993.
179   *Blue Shadow (Diptych)*. Acrylic medium and oil on carpet, 84 x 27 in. 1993.
180   *Live Girls Mesh 2*. Oil stick on mesh sandpaper, 11 x 9 in. 2017.
181   *Live Girls Mesh 3*. Oil stick on mesh sandpaper, 11 x 9 in. 2017.
182   *Live Girls VI*. Oil stick on emery cloth, 11 x 9 in. 1992.
183   *Jennifer in the Dressing Room*. Oil on canvas, 24 x 30 in. 1994.

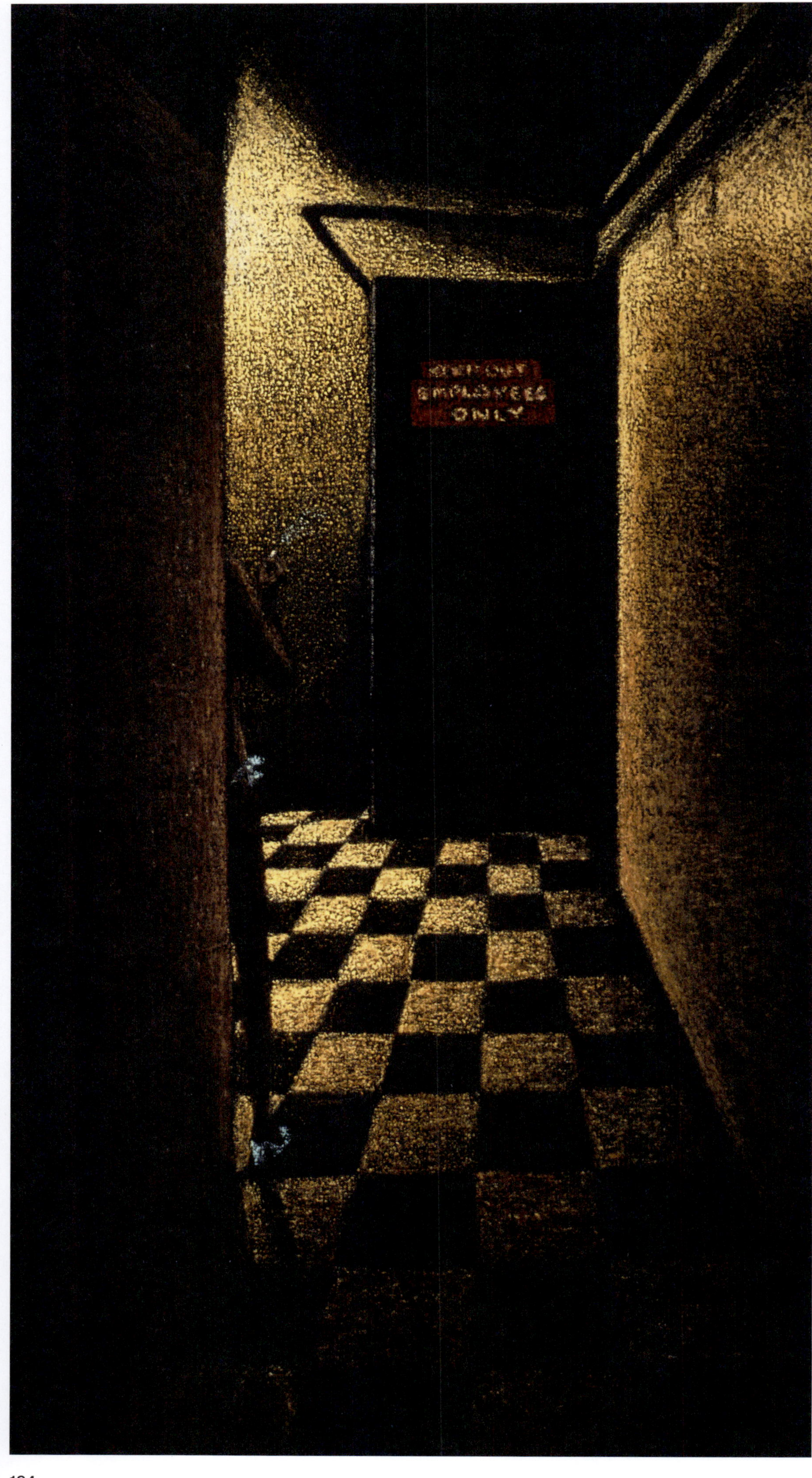
EMPLOYEES
ONLY

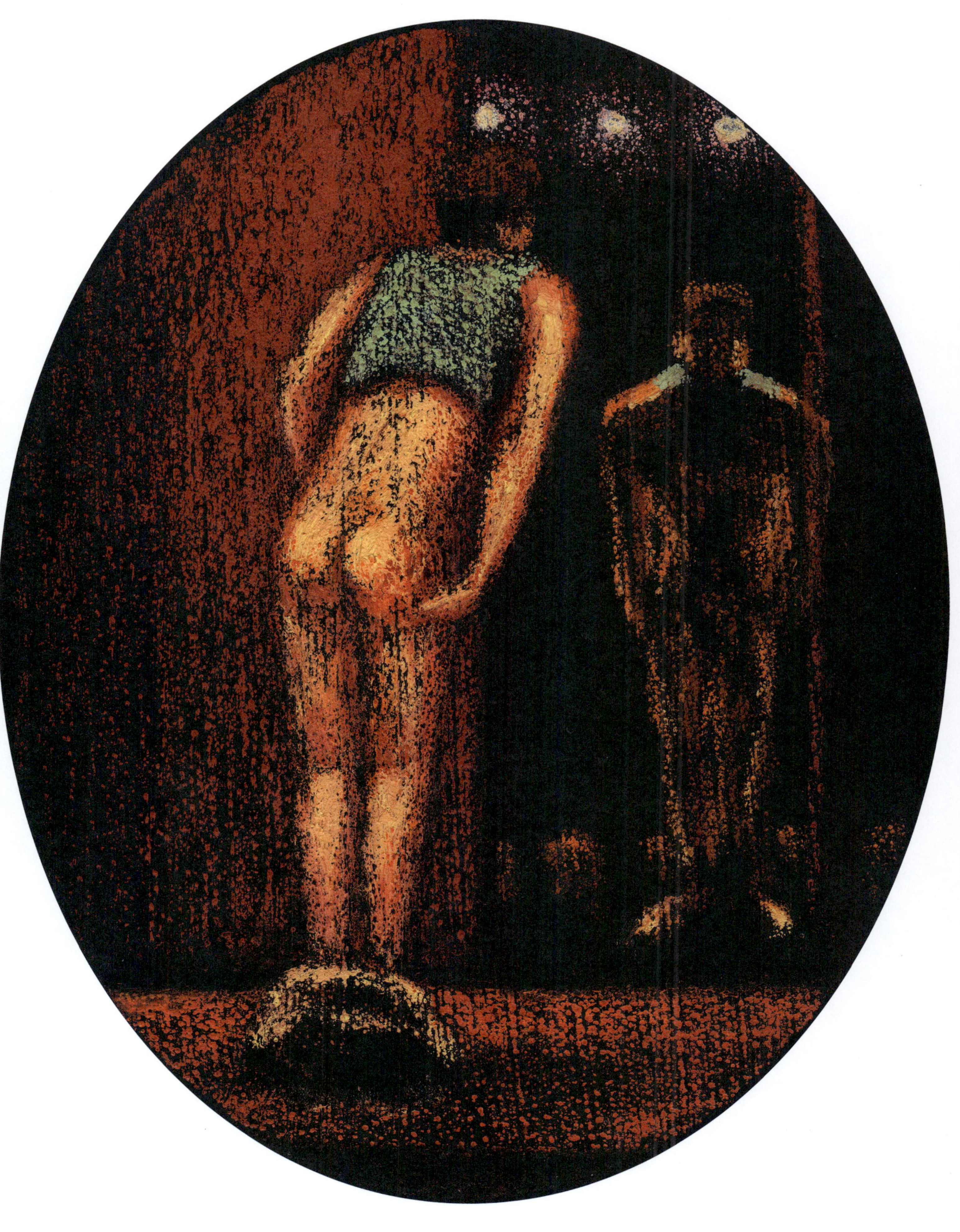

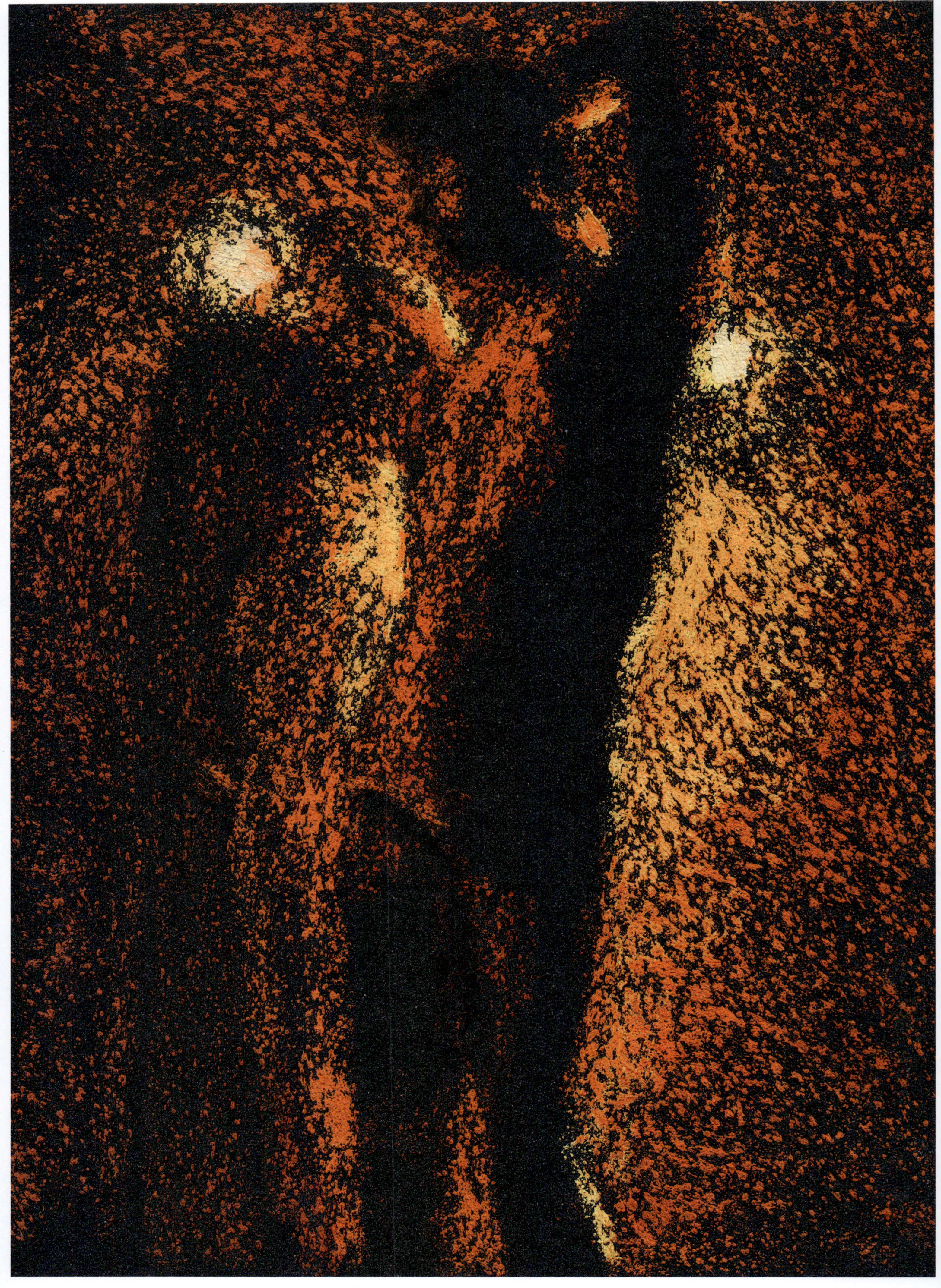

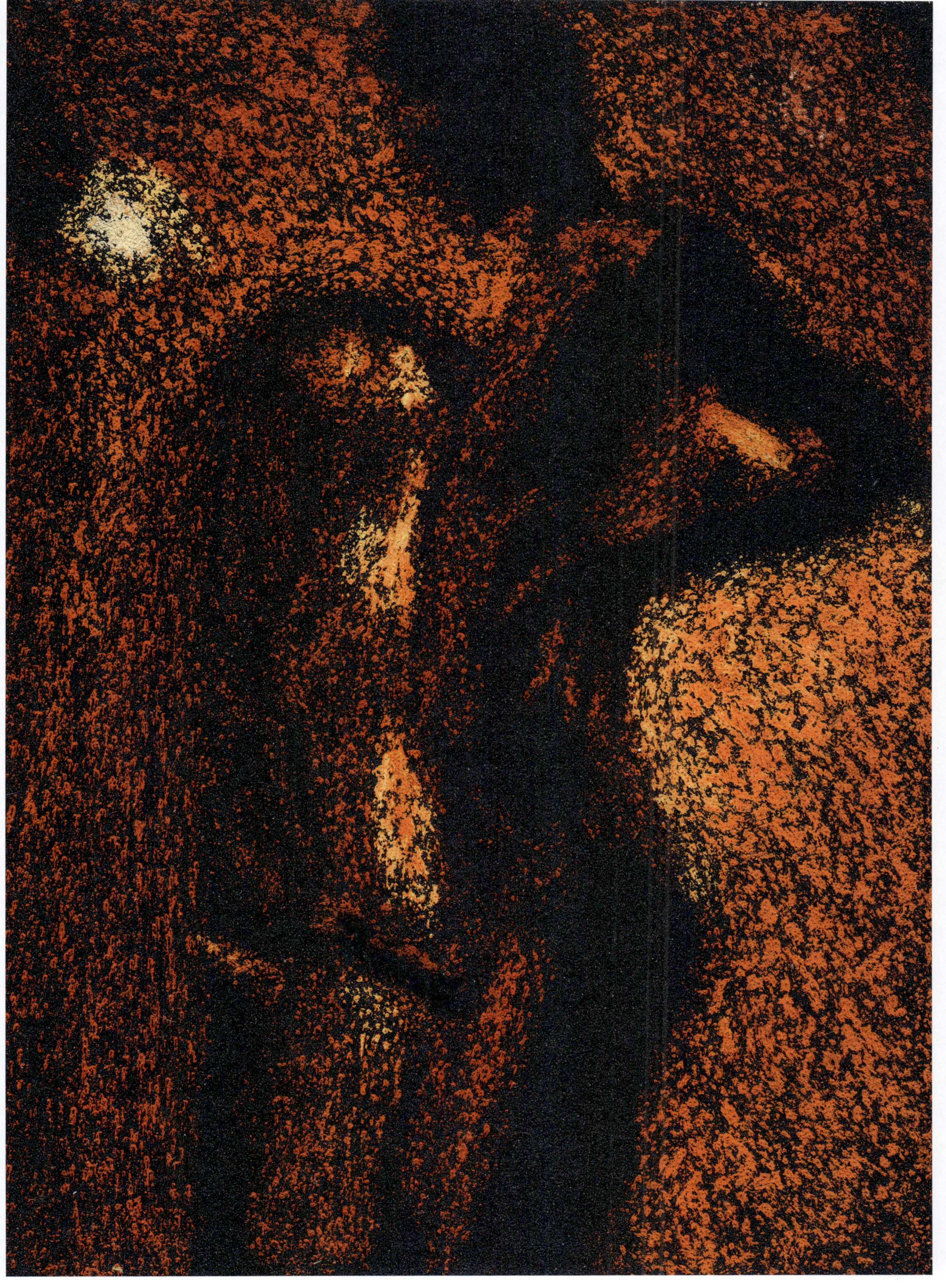

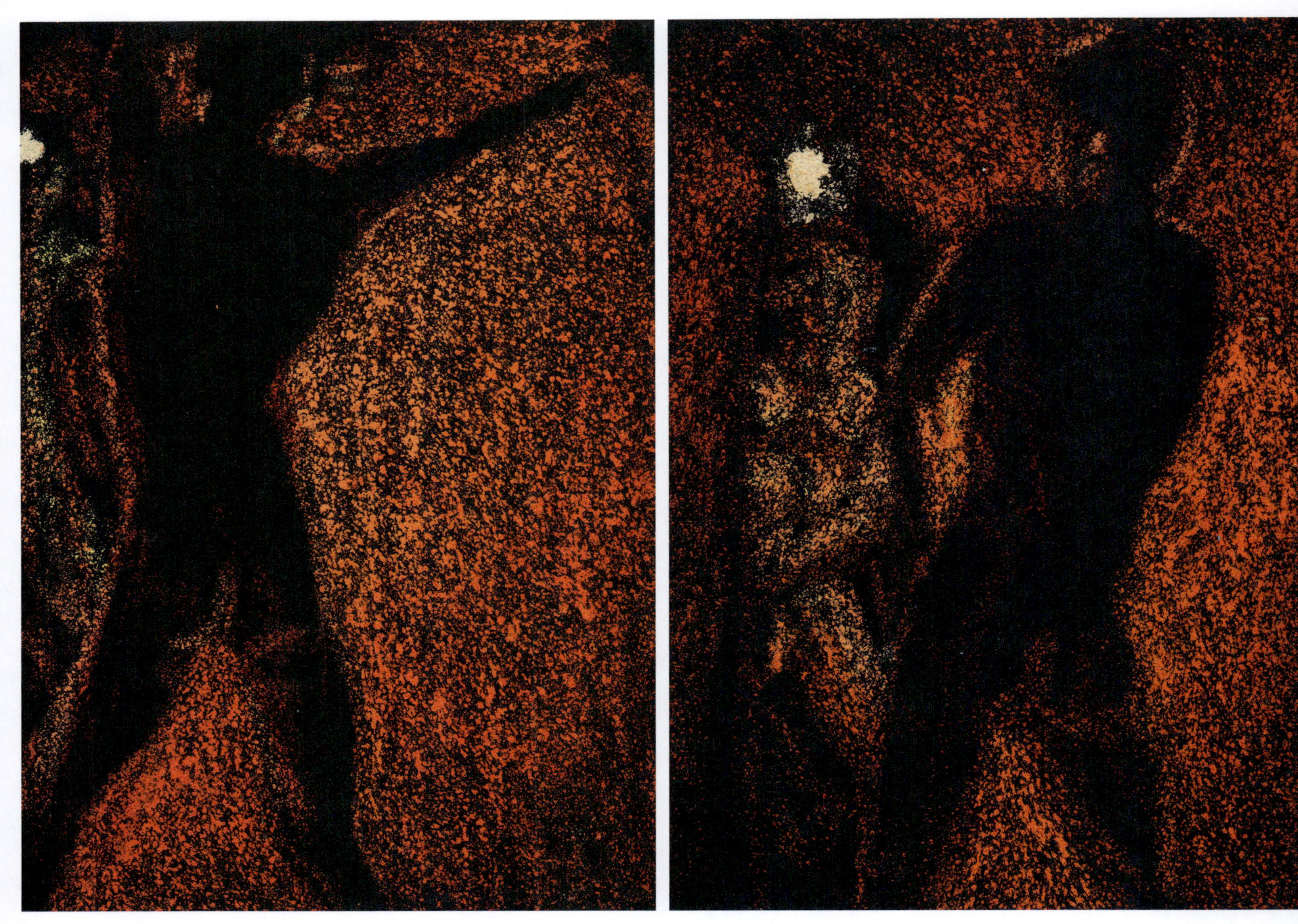

184   *Employees Only 2*. Oil stick on linen, 53 x 30 in. 2000.
185   *Chippendales (Oval)*. Oil and Rolotex on canvas, 24 x 20 in. 1993.
186   *Gaiety 7*. Oil stick on paper, 11 x 9 in. 1994.
187   *Gaiety 1*. Oil stick on emery cloth on wood, 11 x 9 in. 1994.
188   LEFT: *Gaiety 6*. Oil stick on emery cloth on wood, 11 x 8 in. 1994.
       RIGHT: *Gaiety 3*. Oil stick on emery cloth on wood, 12 x 8 in. 1994.
189   LEFT: *Gaiety 5*. Oil stick on sandpaper mounted on wood, 11 x 9 in. 1994.
       RIGHT: *Gaiety 8*. Oil stick on sandpaper, 11 x 9 in. 1994.

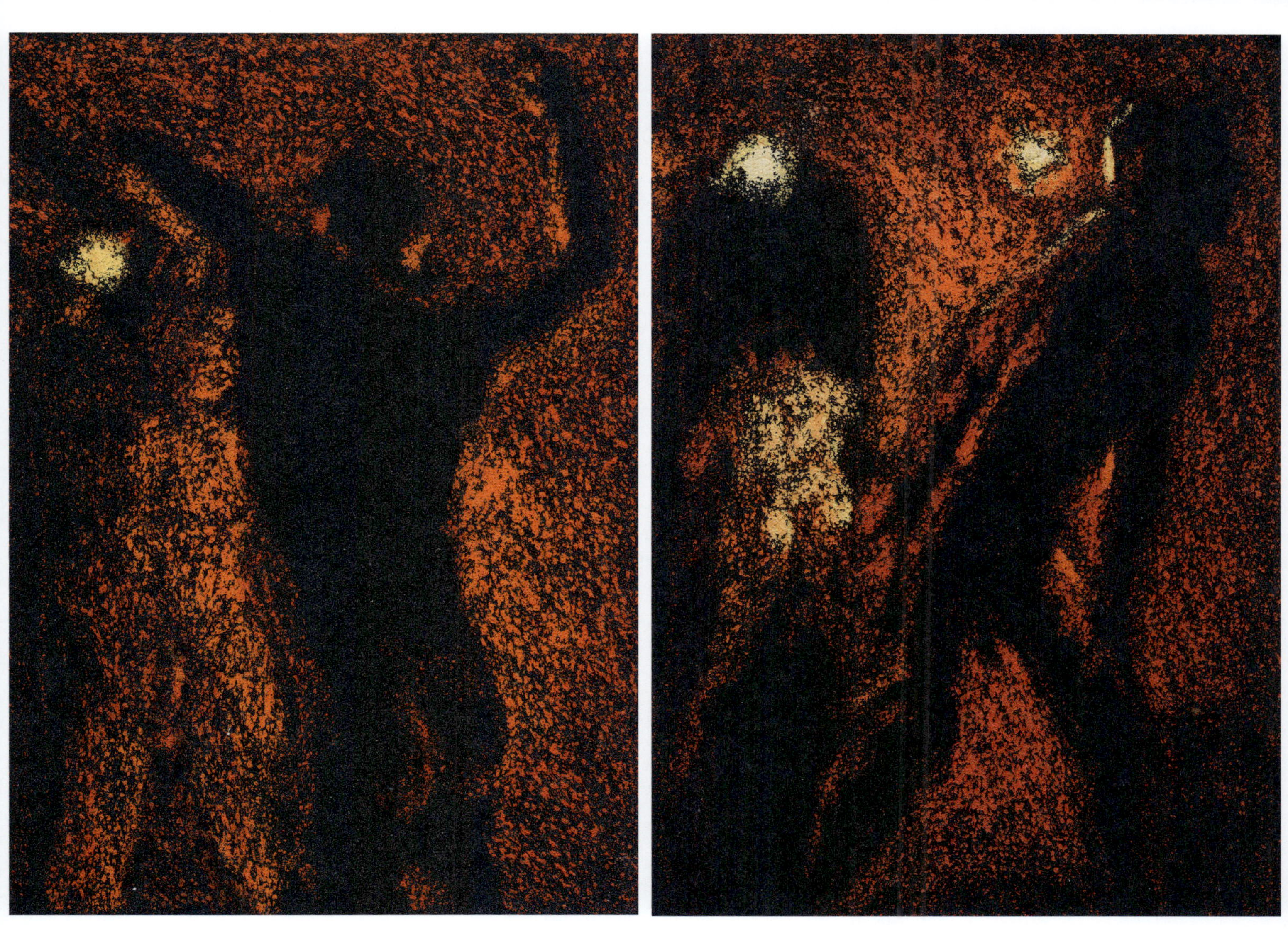

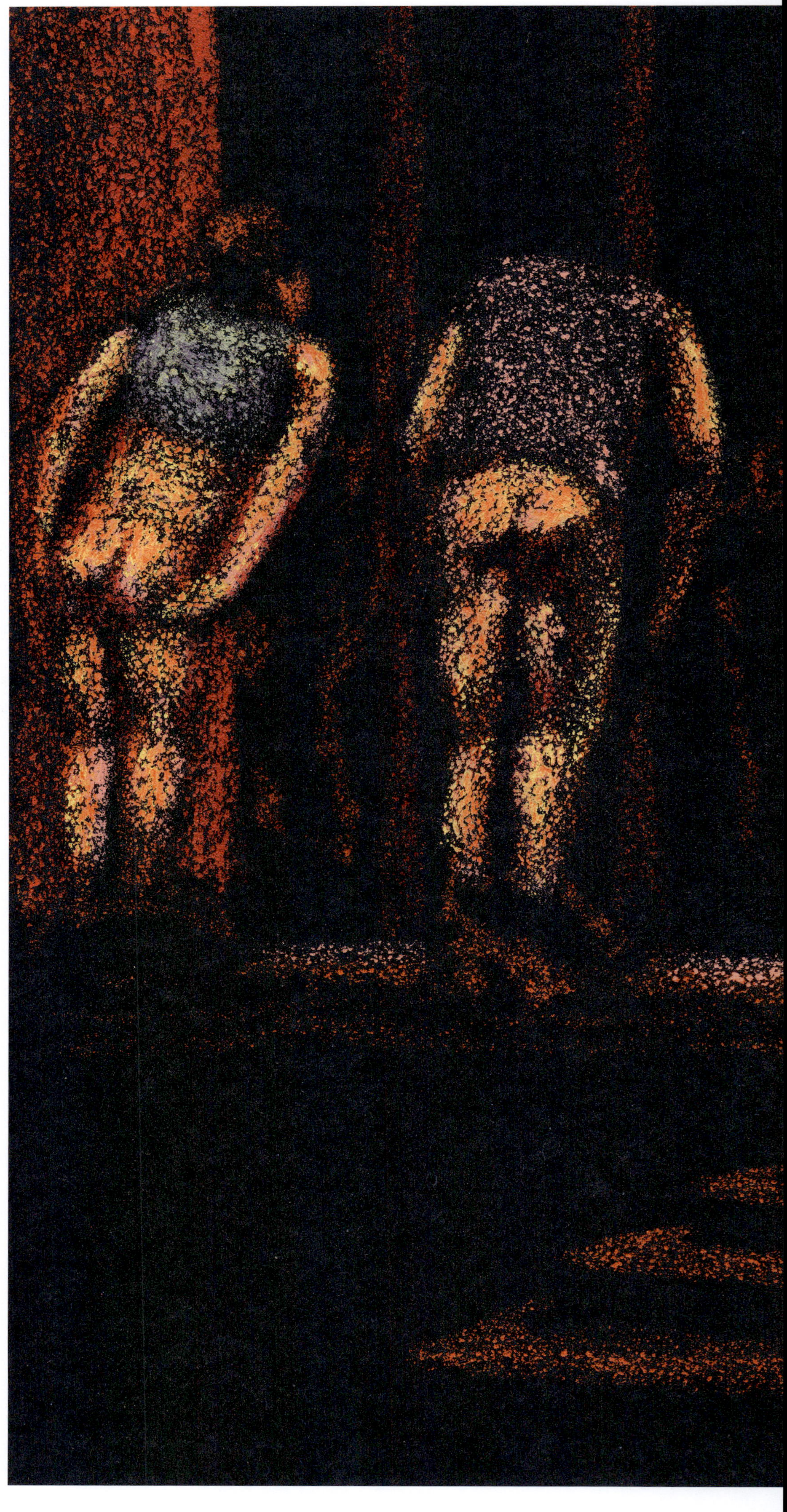

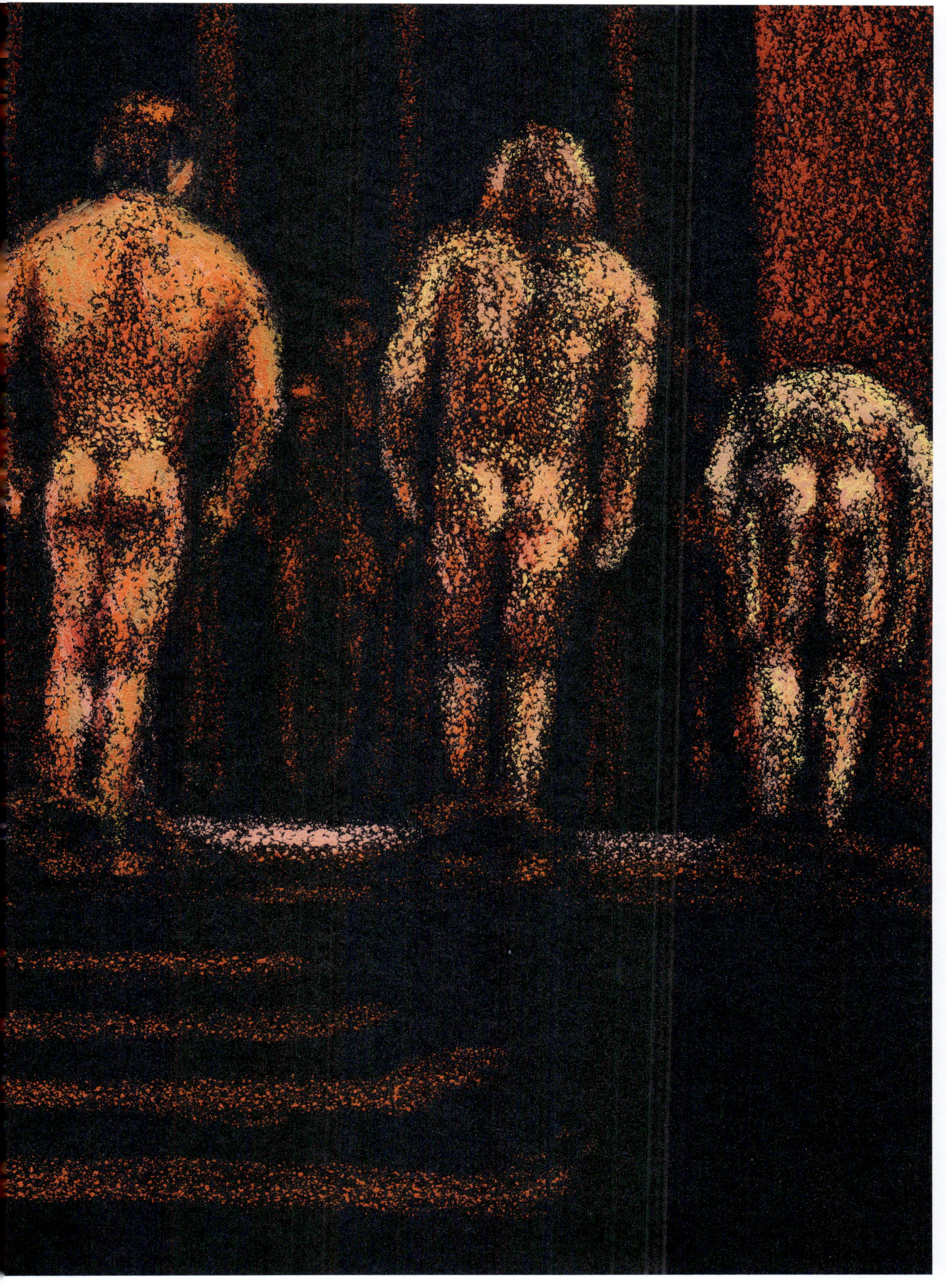

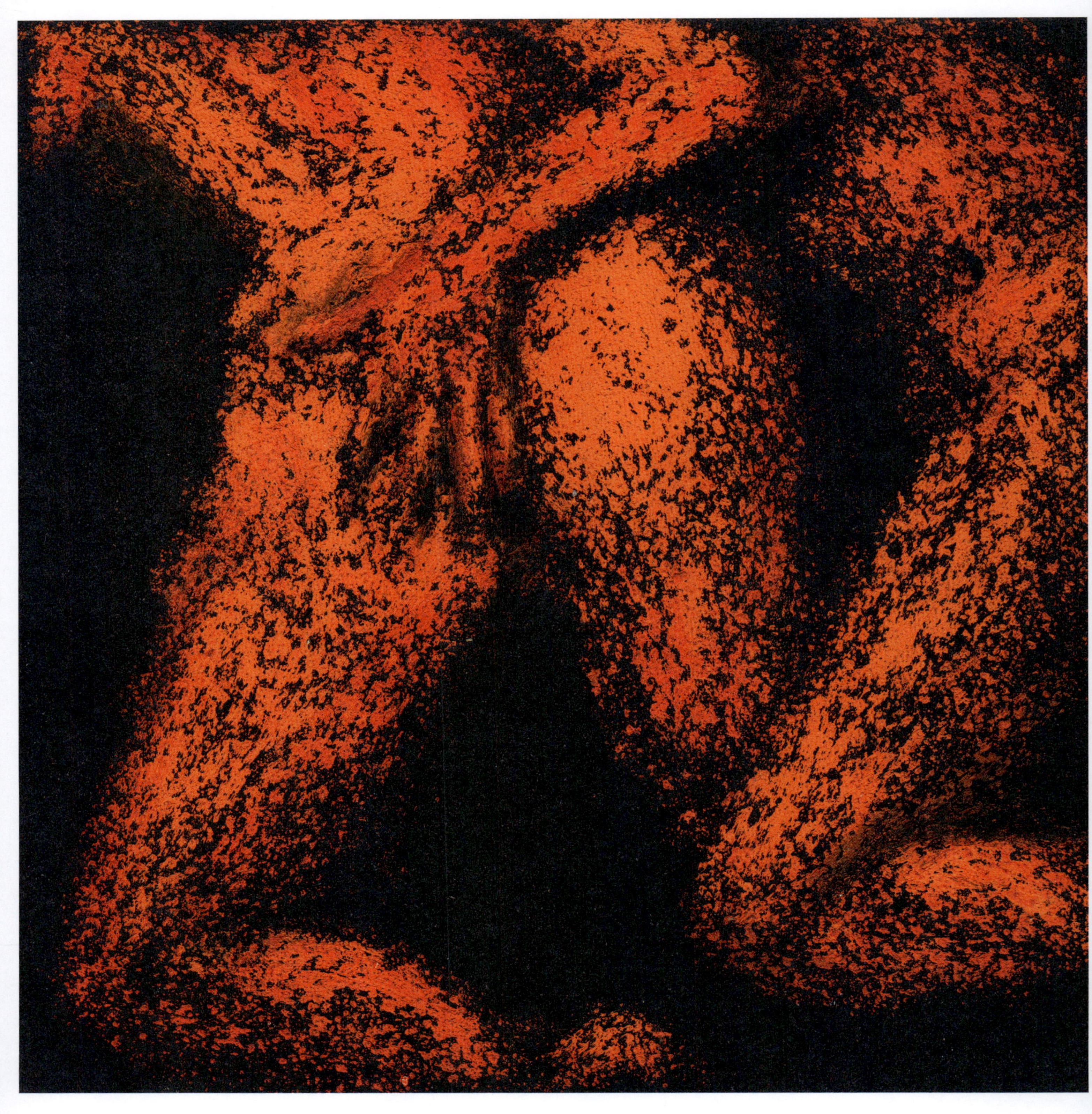

191   Study for *Chippendales*. Oil stick on emery cloth, 16 ¾ x 23 ⅛ in. 1993.
192   *Peep Couple*. Oil stick on emery cloth, 8 x 8 in. 1994.

EVERYONE DOWNTOWN LOVED TO VISIT OUR NEIGHBORHOOD AND BRING THEIR OUT-OF-TOWN FRIENDS BECAUSE IT WAS SO CRAZY. AND ALL THE HIP HOP PEOPLE CAME THROUGH TIMES SQUARE. IT'S SO CENTRAL. SO EVERYONE, UPTOWN OR DOWNTOWN, CAME TO US. AND THEN, IF IT WAS QUIET, WE'D GO TO TIN PAN ALLEY, OUR LOCAL HAUNT: NO TOURISTS, NO COMMUTERS, JUST HUSTLERS AND ART-ISTS. MY CLOSE FRIENDS ALL WORKED AND PERFORMED THERE. IT WAS A PLACE WHERE WE WOULD BOUNCE AROUND BIG IDEAS AND PROJECTS THAT THEN ACTUALLY HAPPENED.

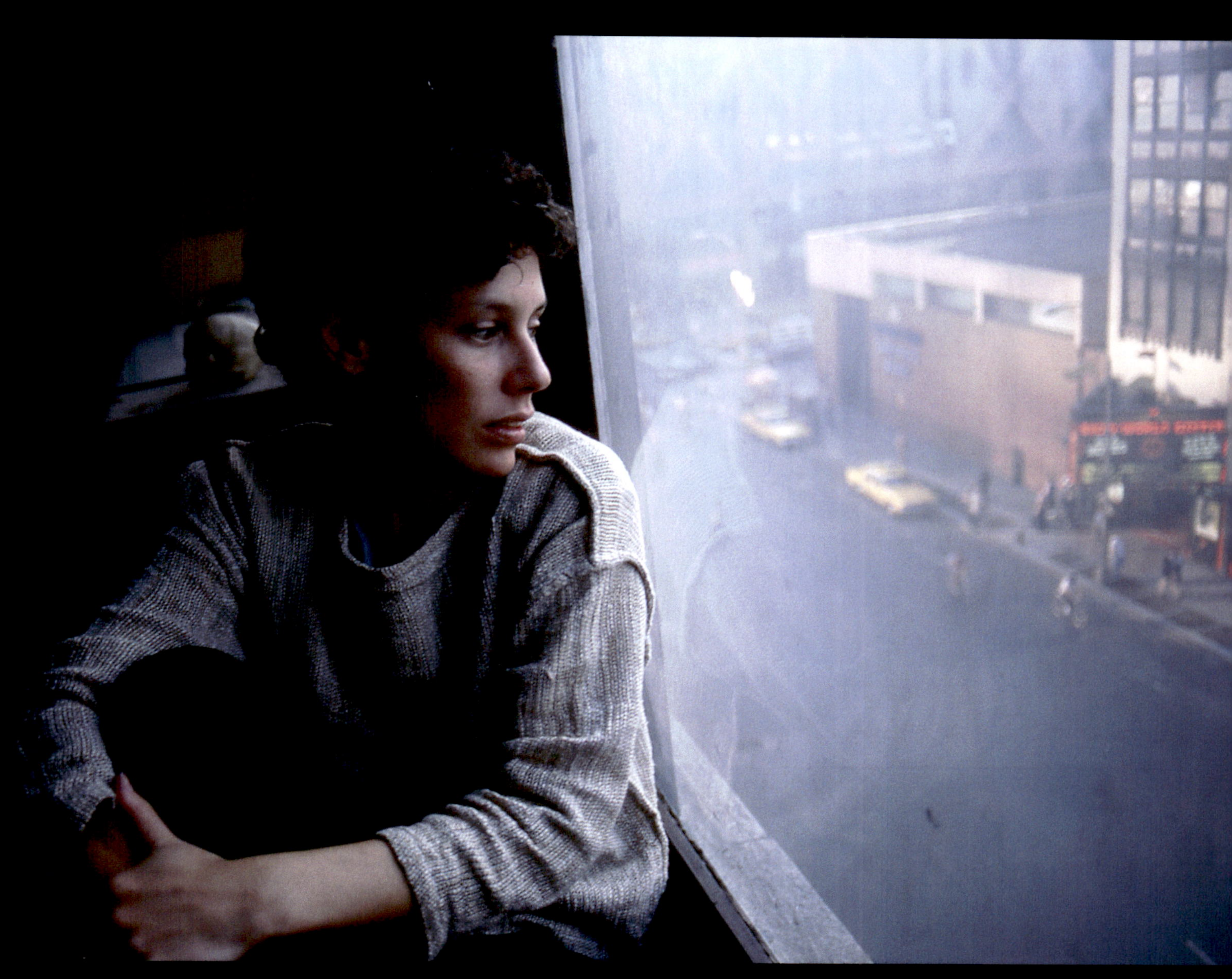

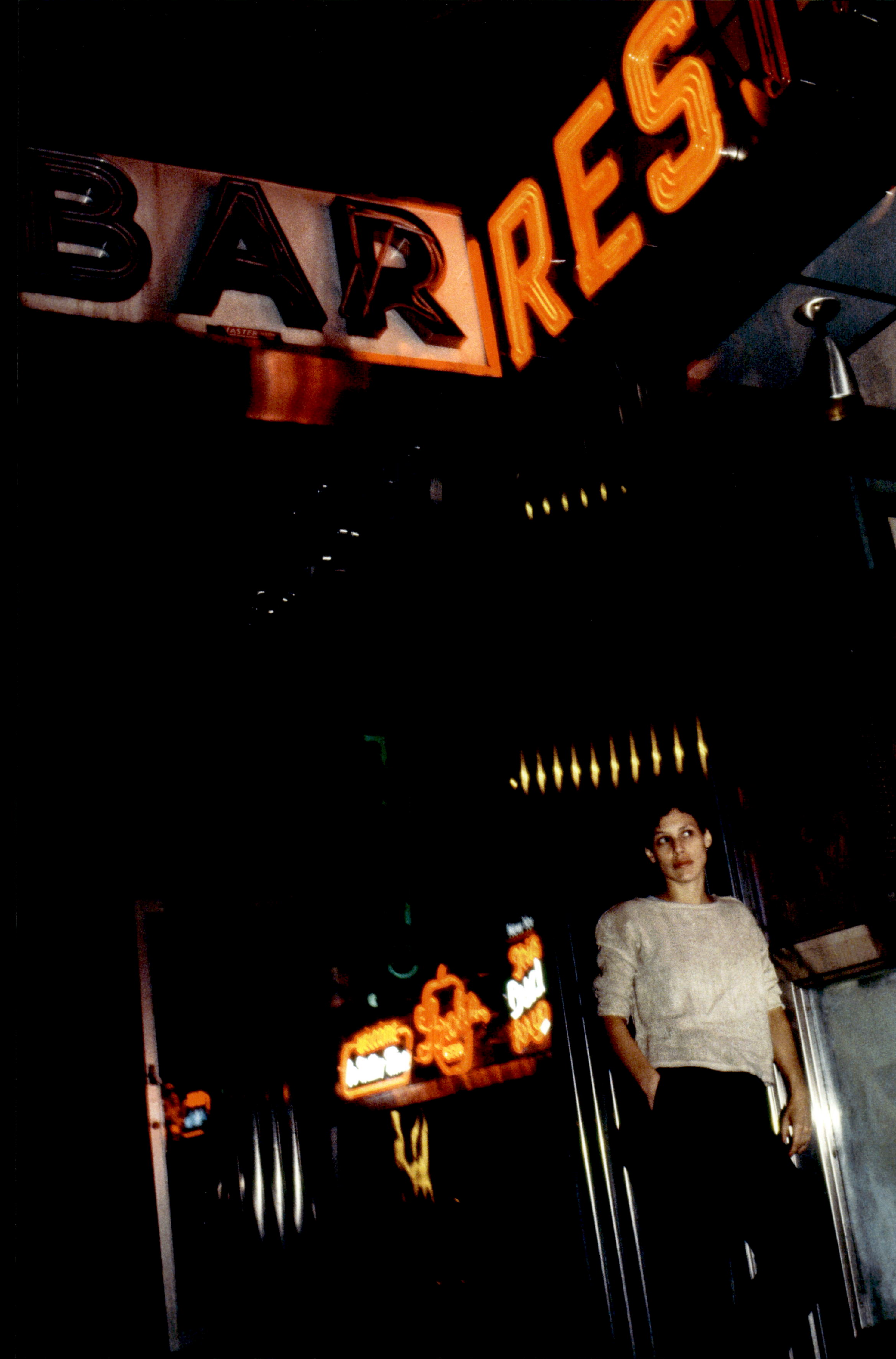

BAR
RES

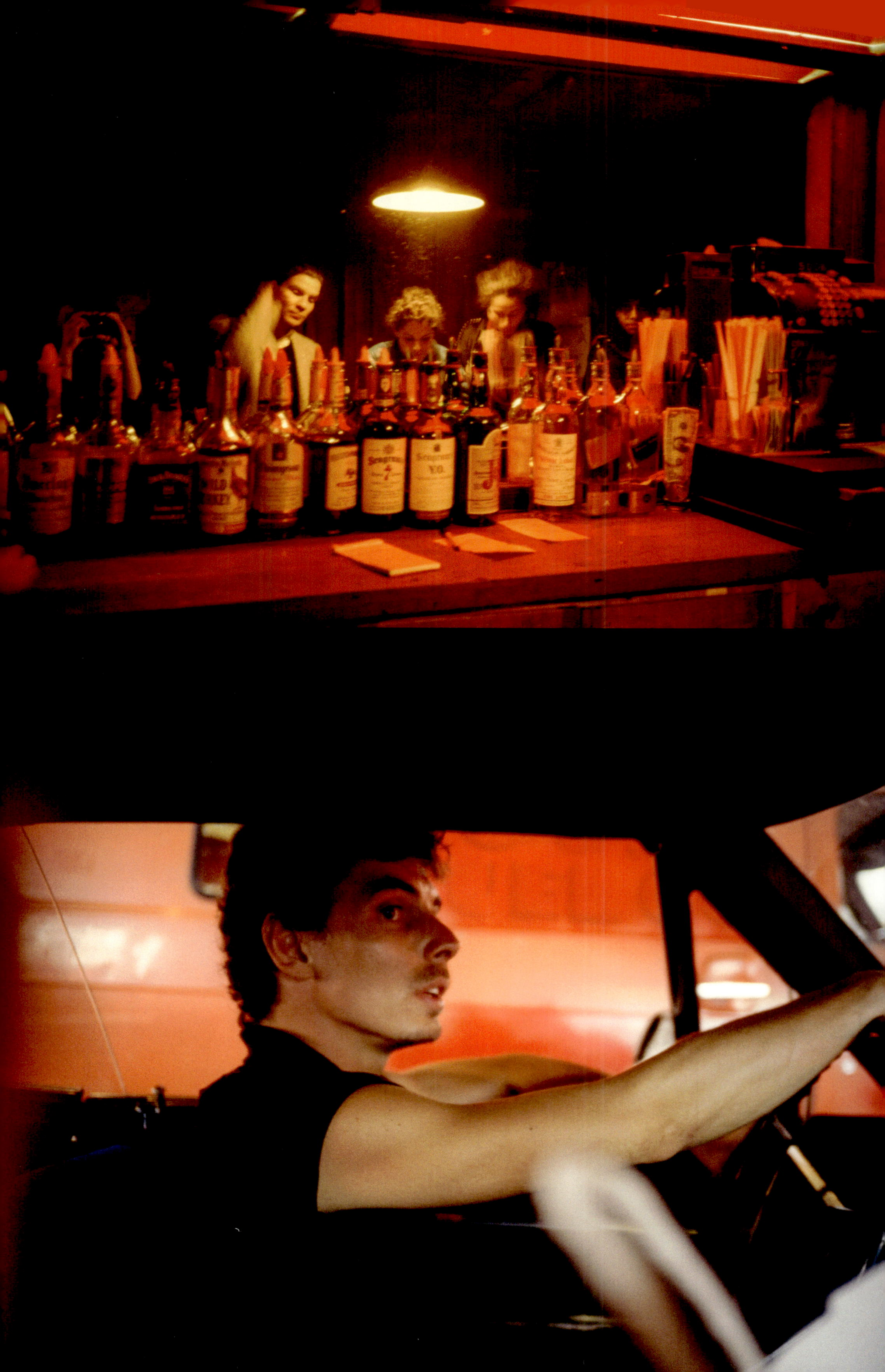

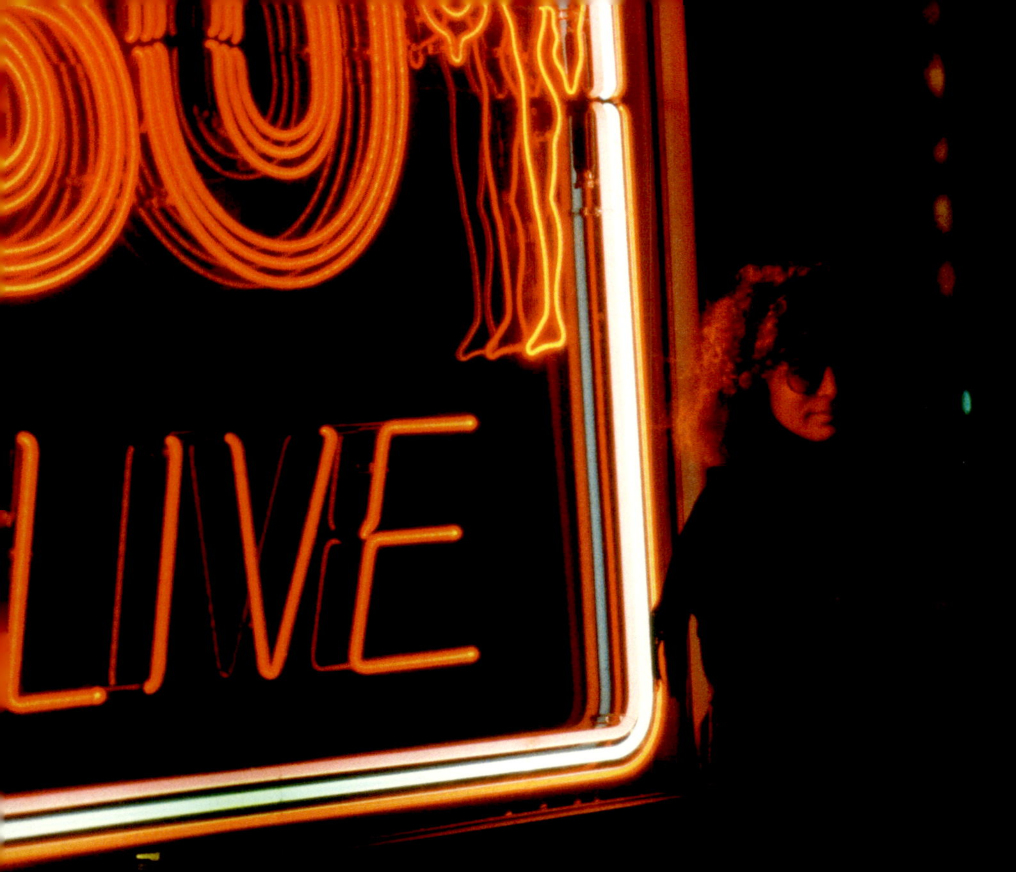

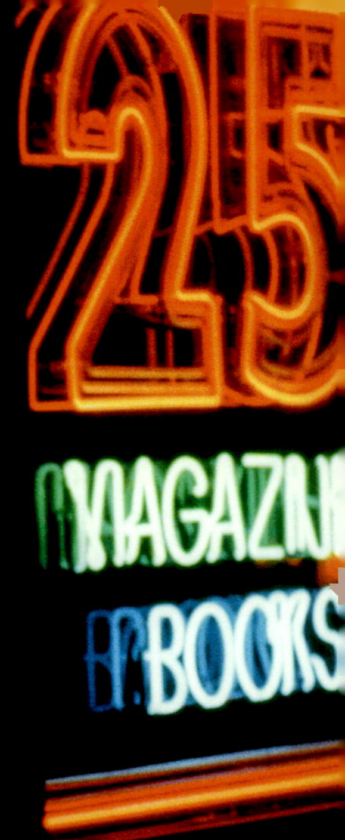

195   Photo by Nan Goldin for *ARTNews*, 1984.
196   Outside of 43rd Street Seafood. Photo by Nan Goldin for *ARTNews*, 1984.
197   TOP: Jody Harris, Cara Pearlman and Kiki Smith at Tin Pan Alley, early 1980s.
       BOTTOM: Jimmy De Sana driving, 1981.
198   Nan Goldin outside a sex shop, 1984.
199   Mimi Gross filming for an art project, 1979.

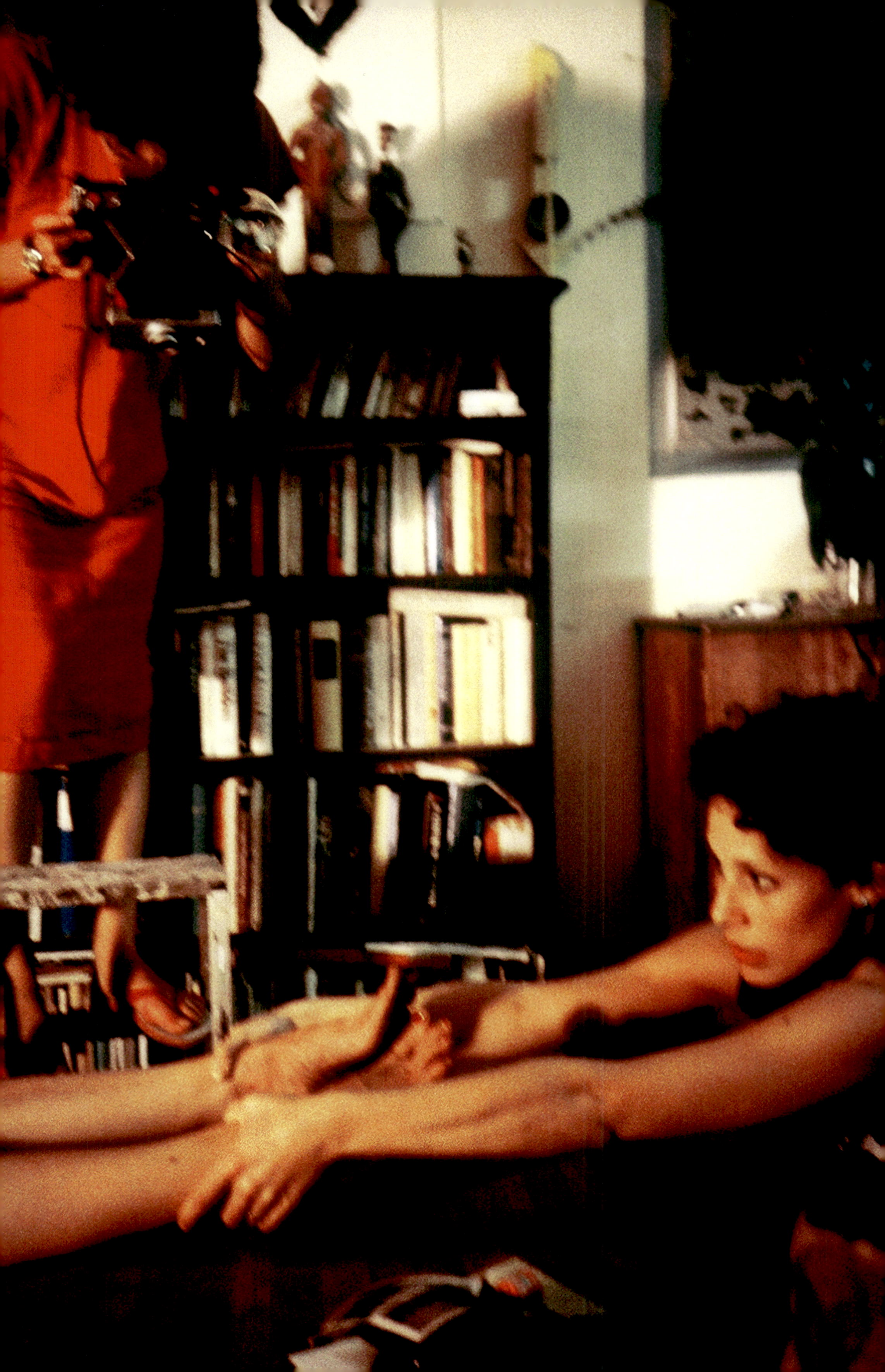

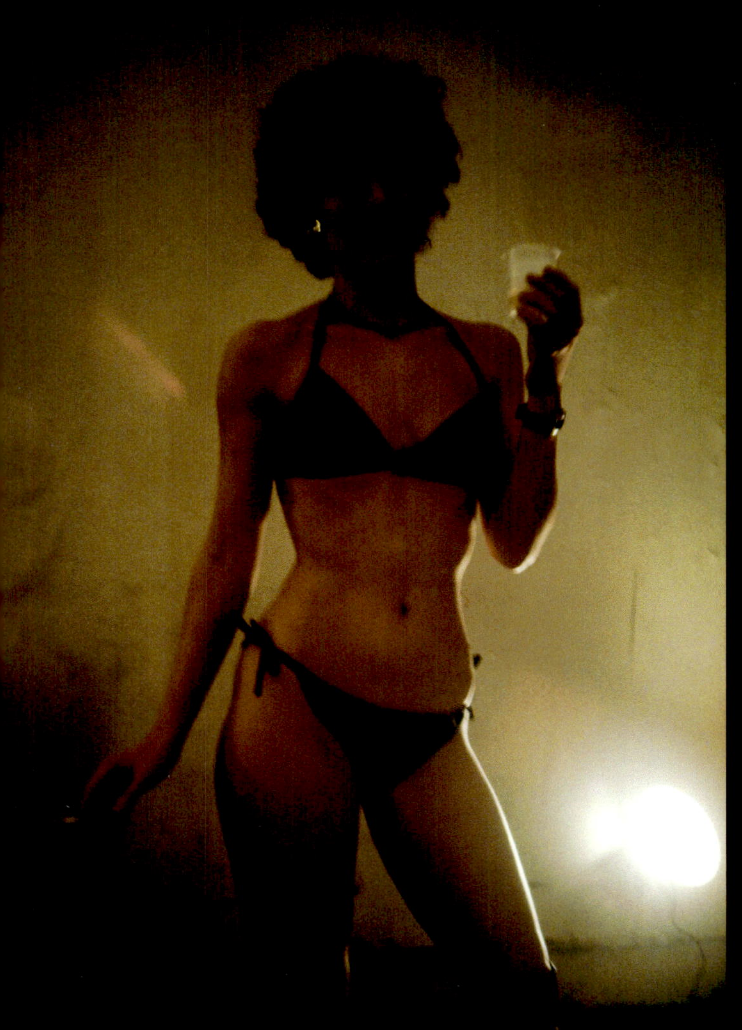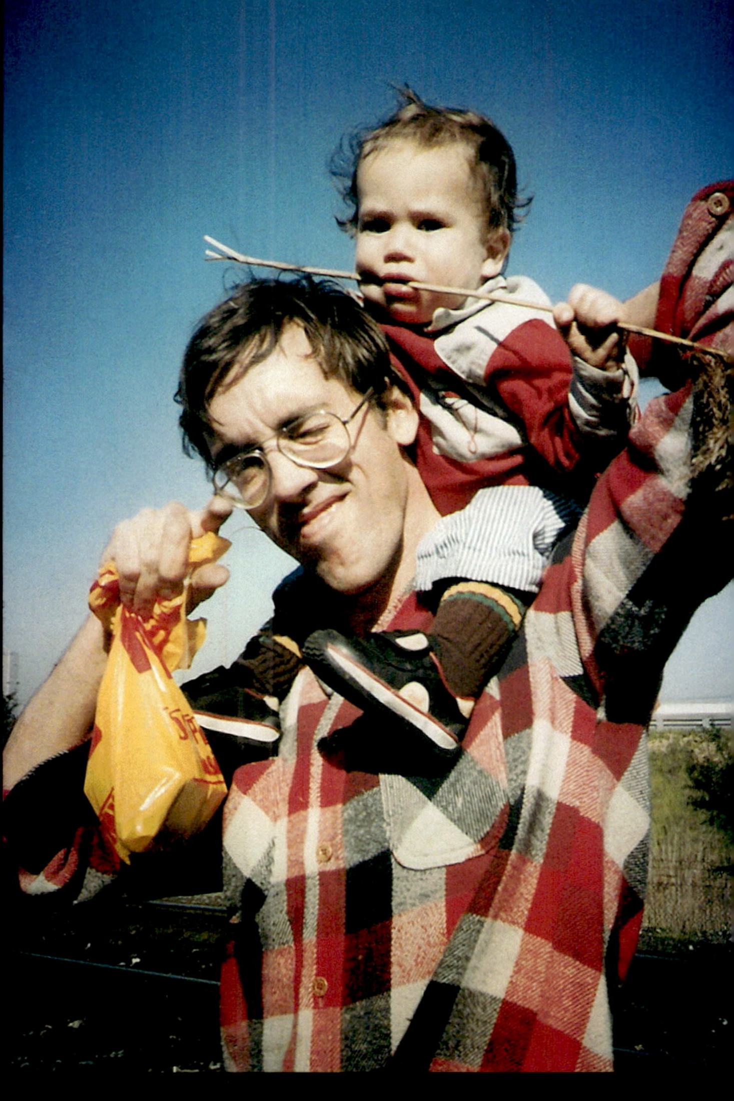

200   The crew of FUN Gallery, from Jimmy De Sana's photoshoot for a 1982 Rene Ricard
       article in *Artforum*. From left to right: Arch Connelly, Kenny Scharf, me, Futura,
       Fab 5 Freddy, Dondi White, Kiely Jenkins, and Patti Astor.
201   LEFT: Me in a Joe Lewis performance at ABC No Rio in 1981, wearing a bikini designed
       by Cookie Mueller.
       RIGHT: David Wojnarowicz holding an infant Joe Ahearn during a junkyard tour of
       New Jersey, 1986.

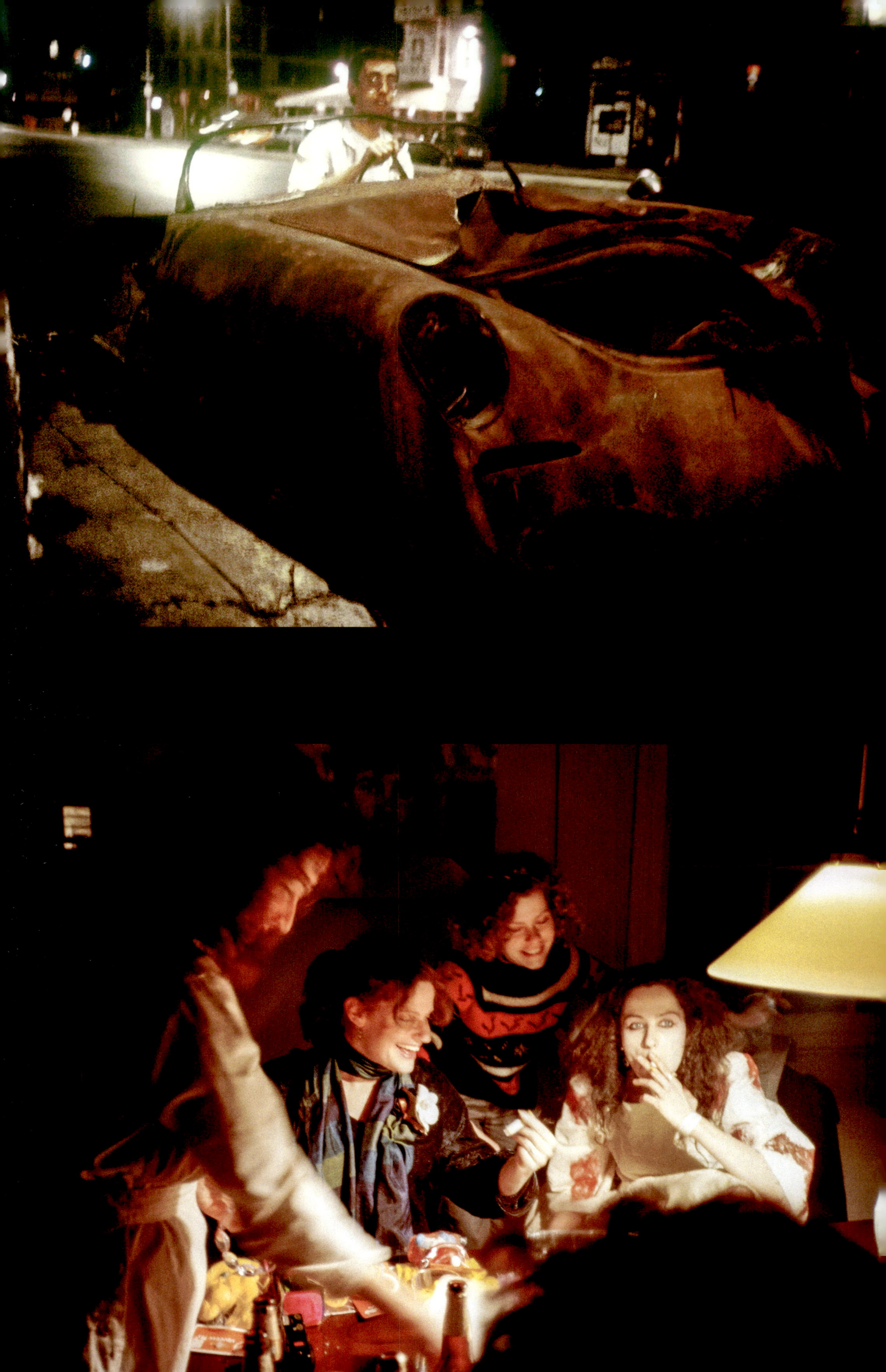

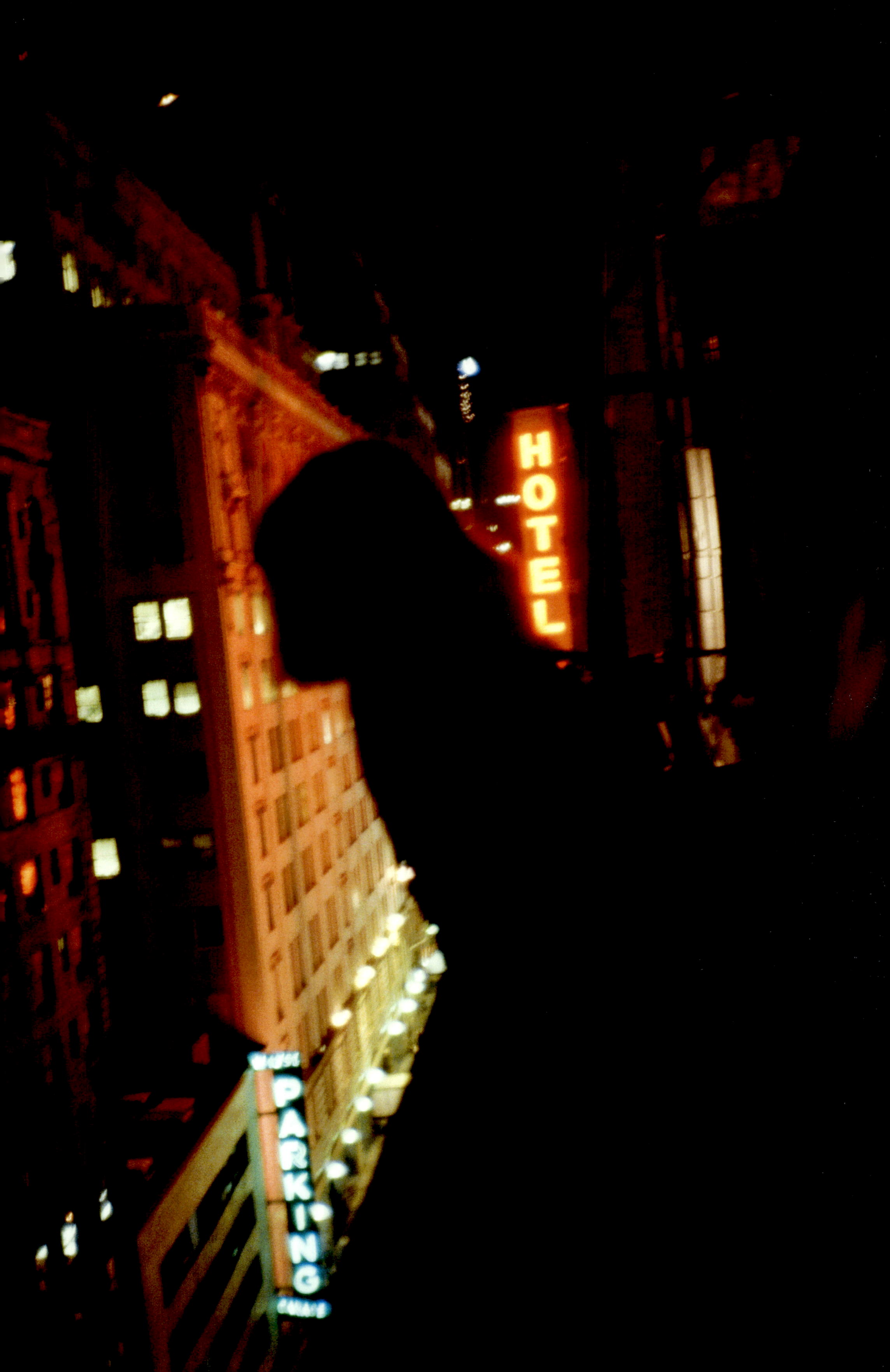
HOTEL
PARKING

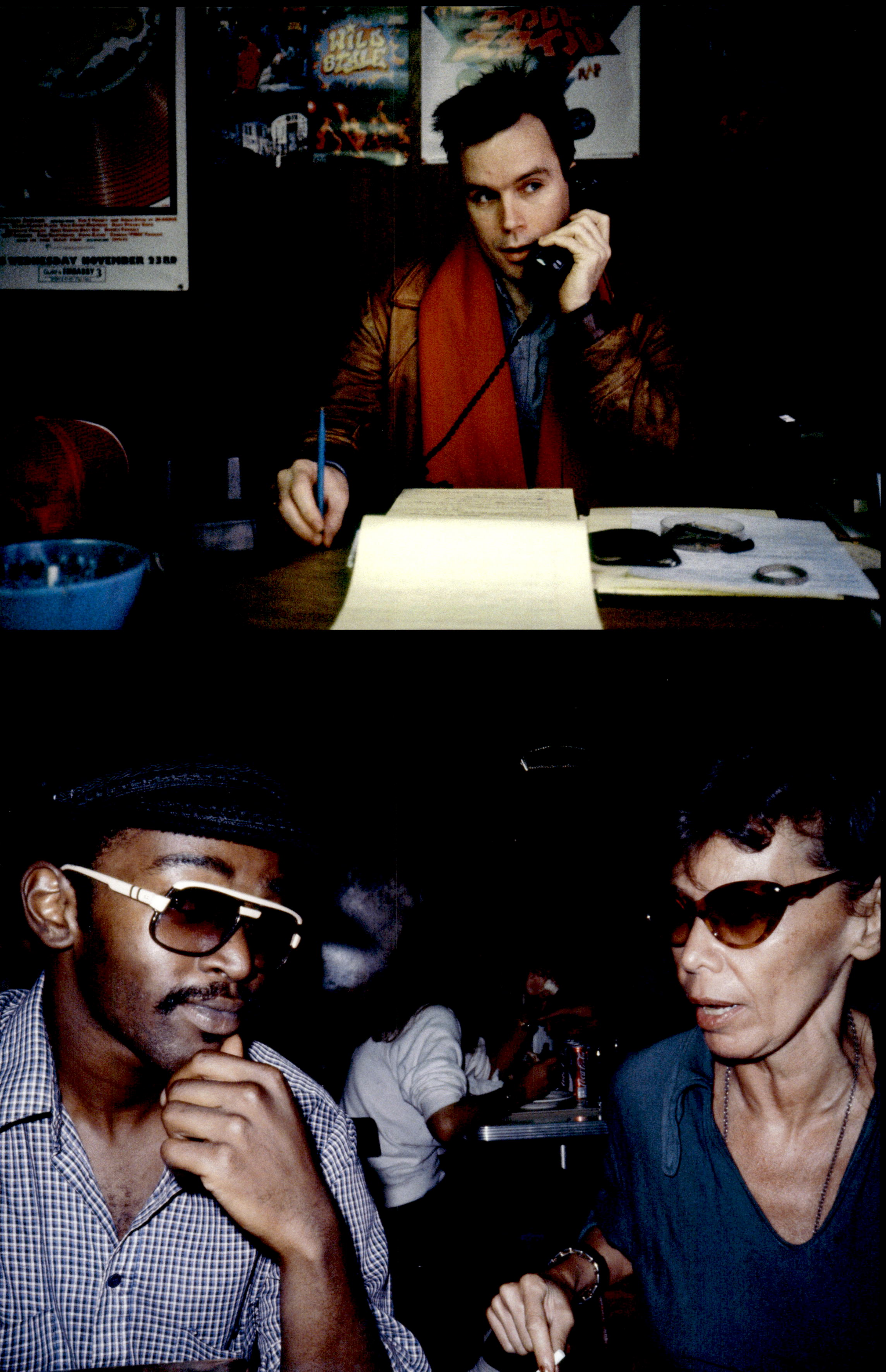

WILD STYLE
WEDNESDAY NOVEMBER 23RD

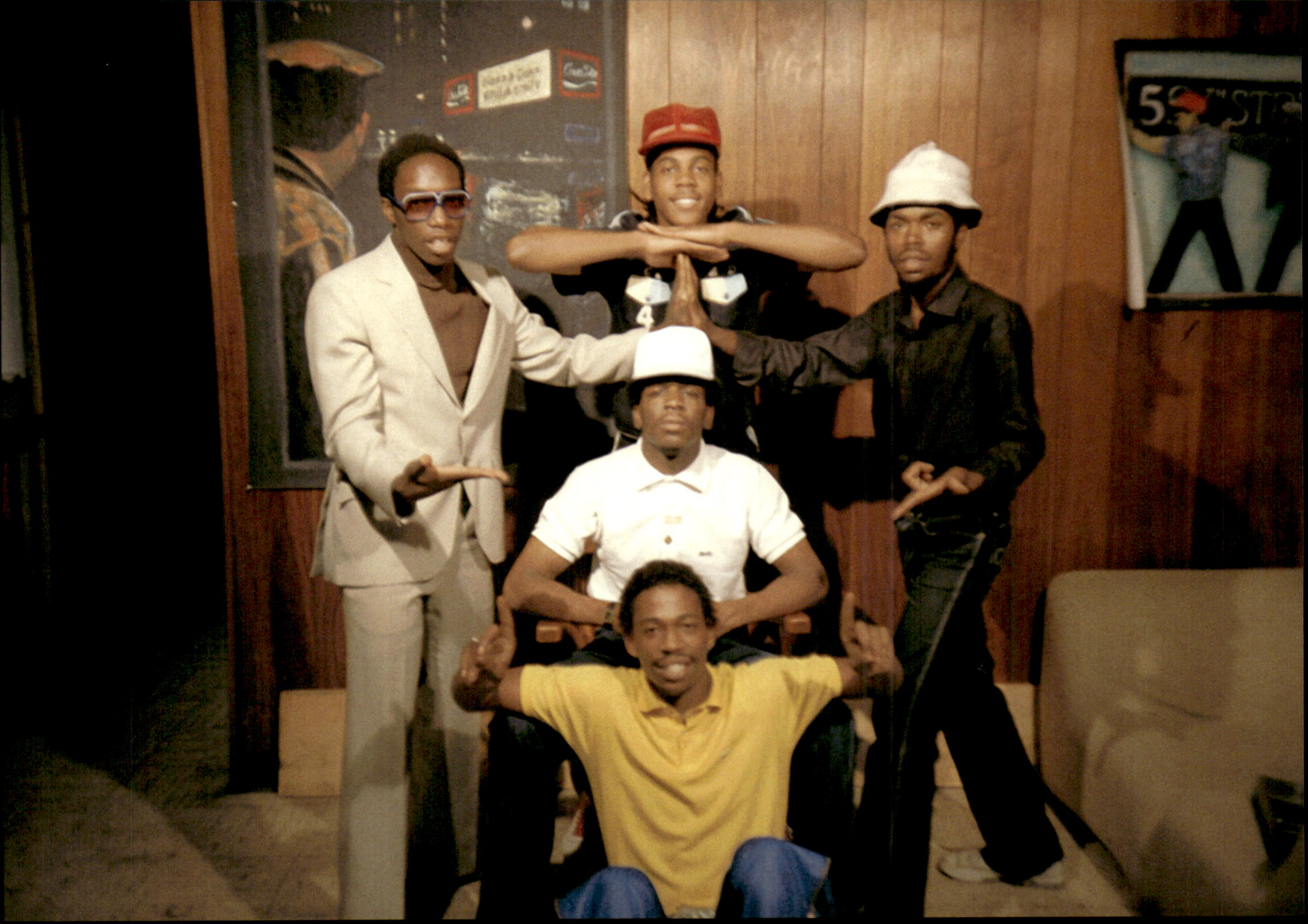

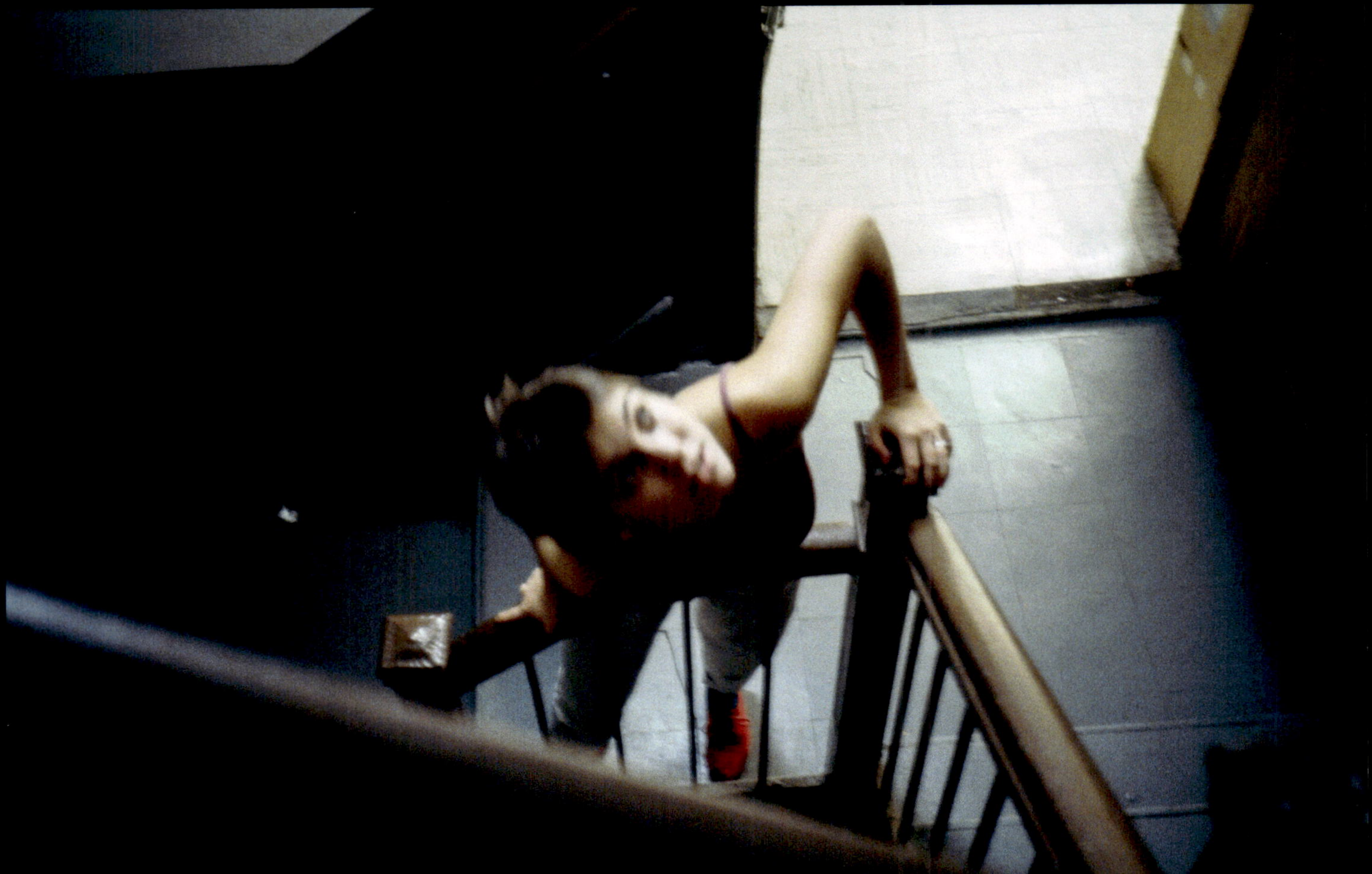

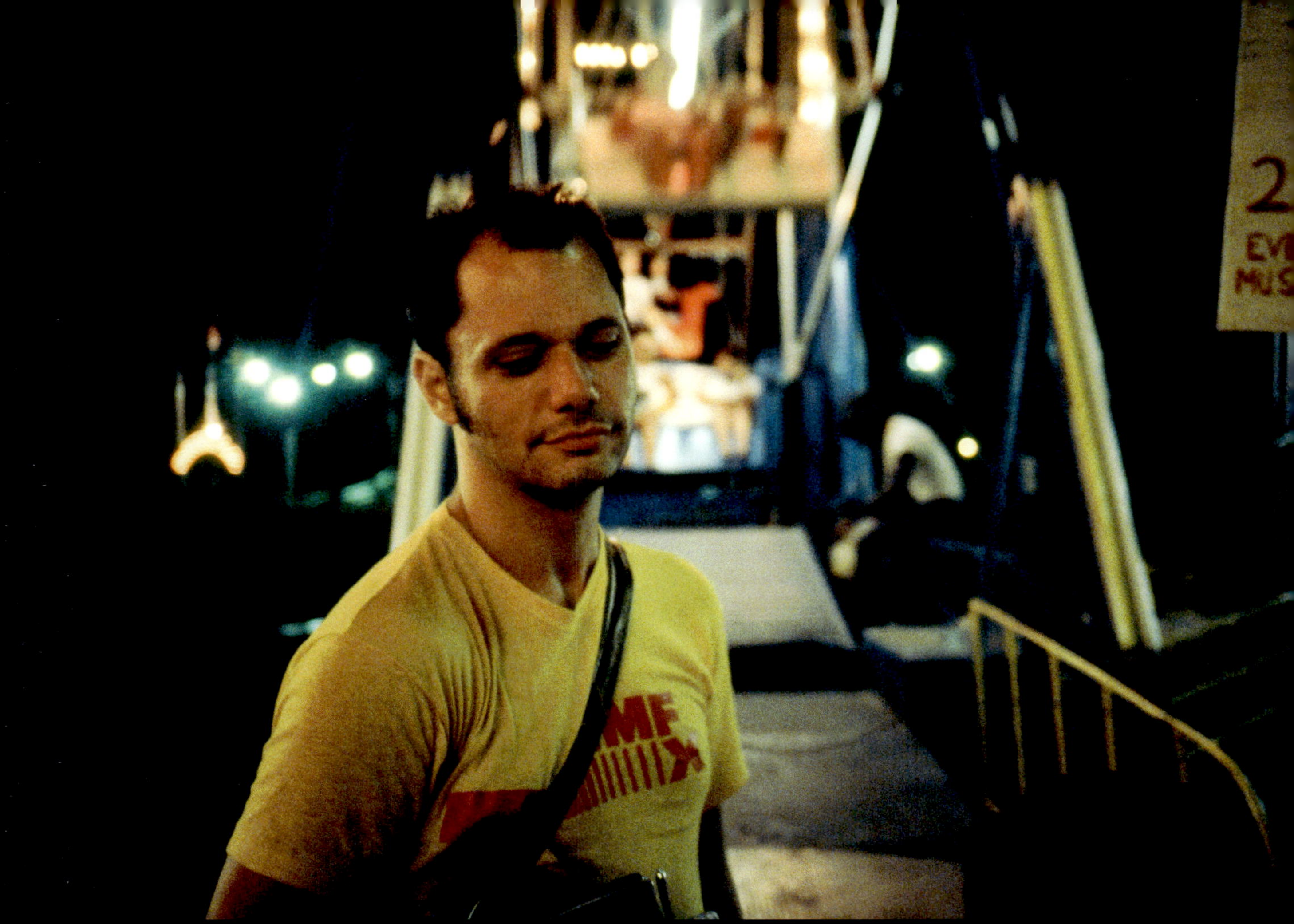

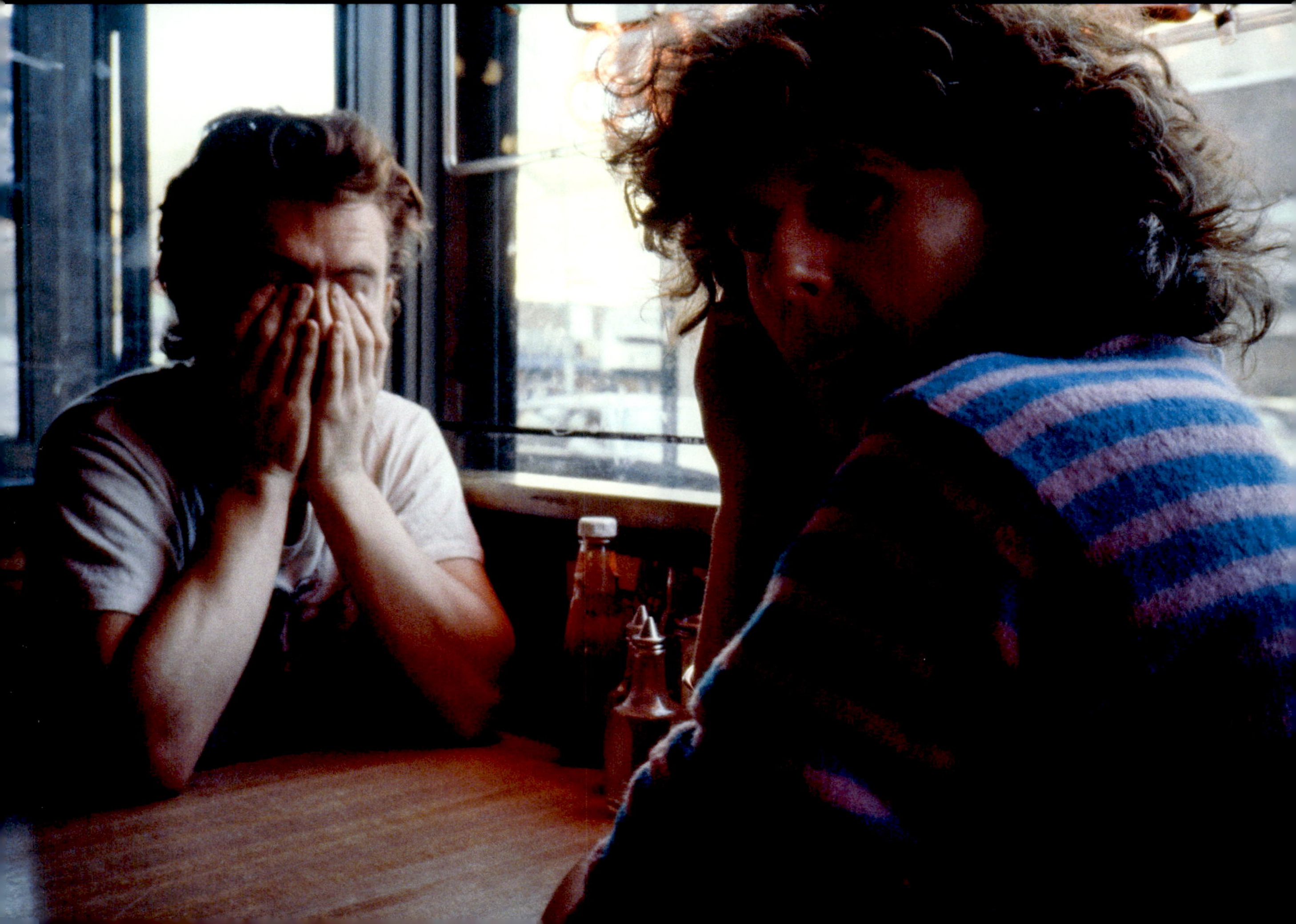

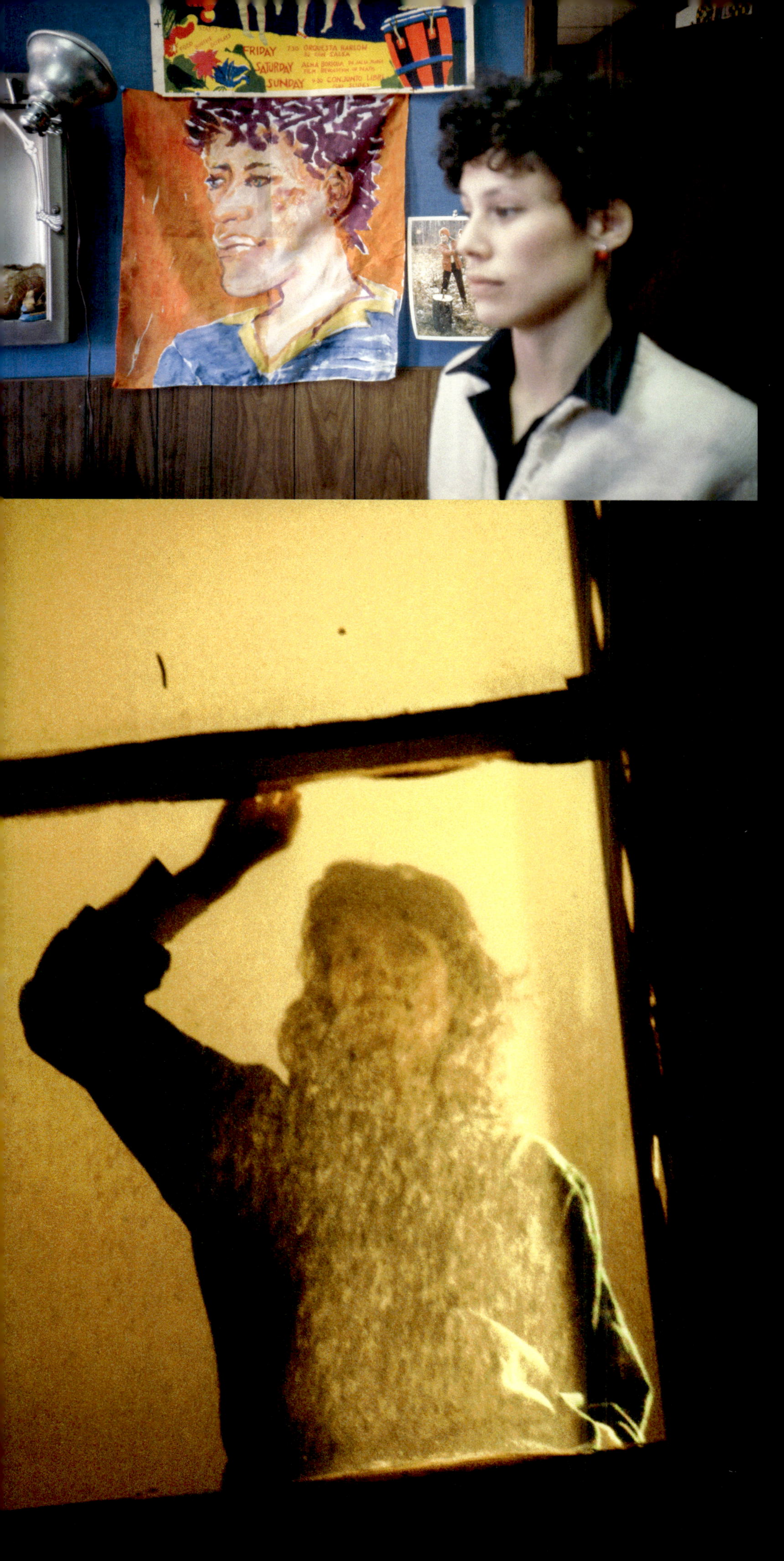

FRIDAY 7:30 ORQUESTA HARLOW
SATURDAY
SUNDAY 9:30 CONJUNTO LIBRE

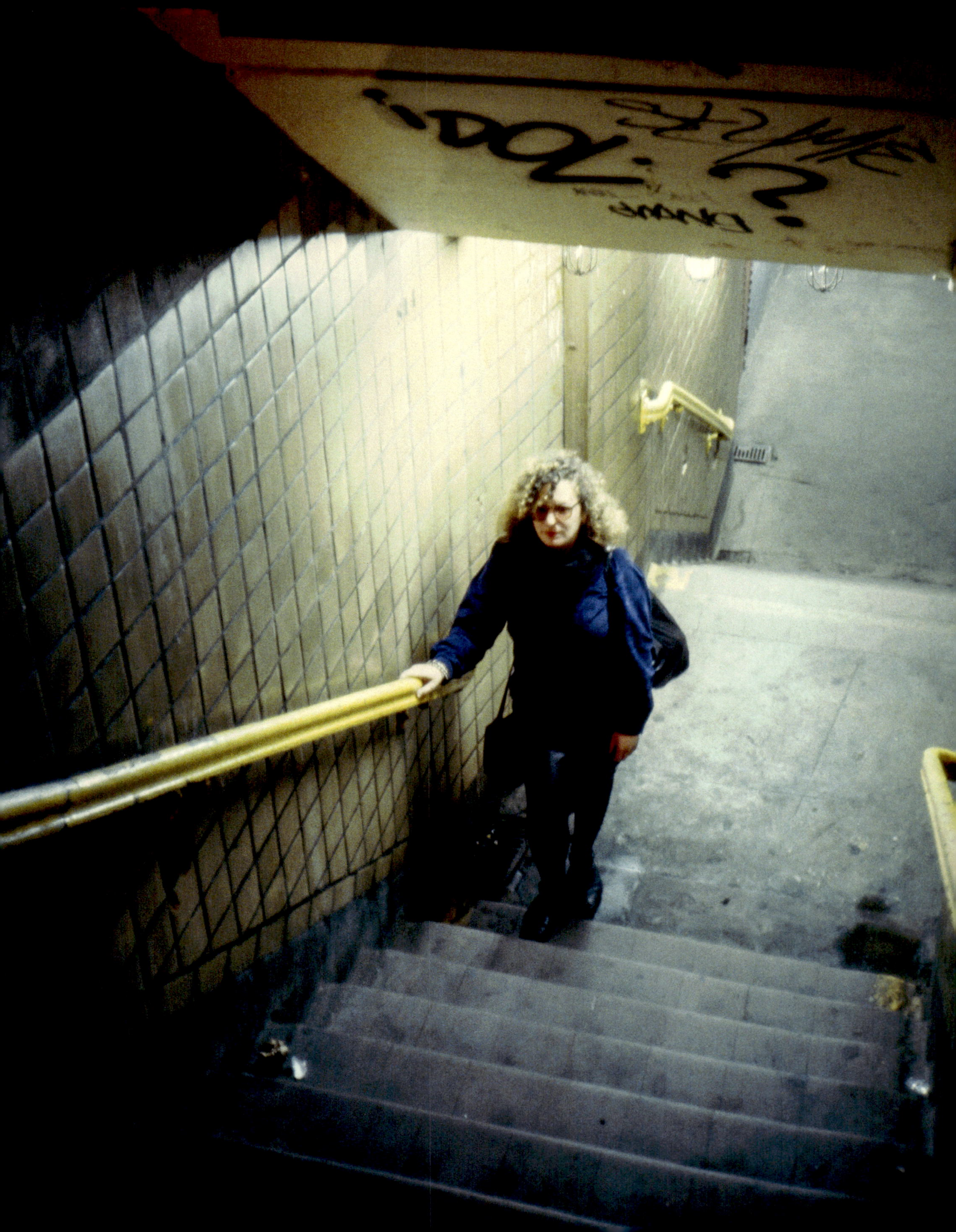

Change booth open 4:40pm-12mid
Mon to Sat & Hol
Token required at other times or
use 42nd St entrance

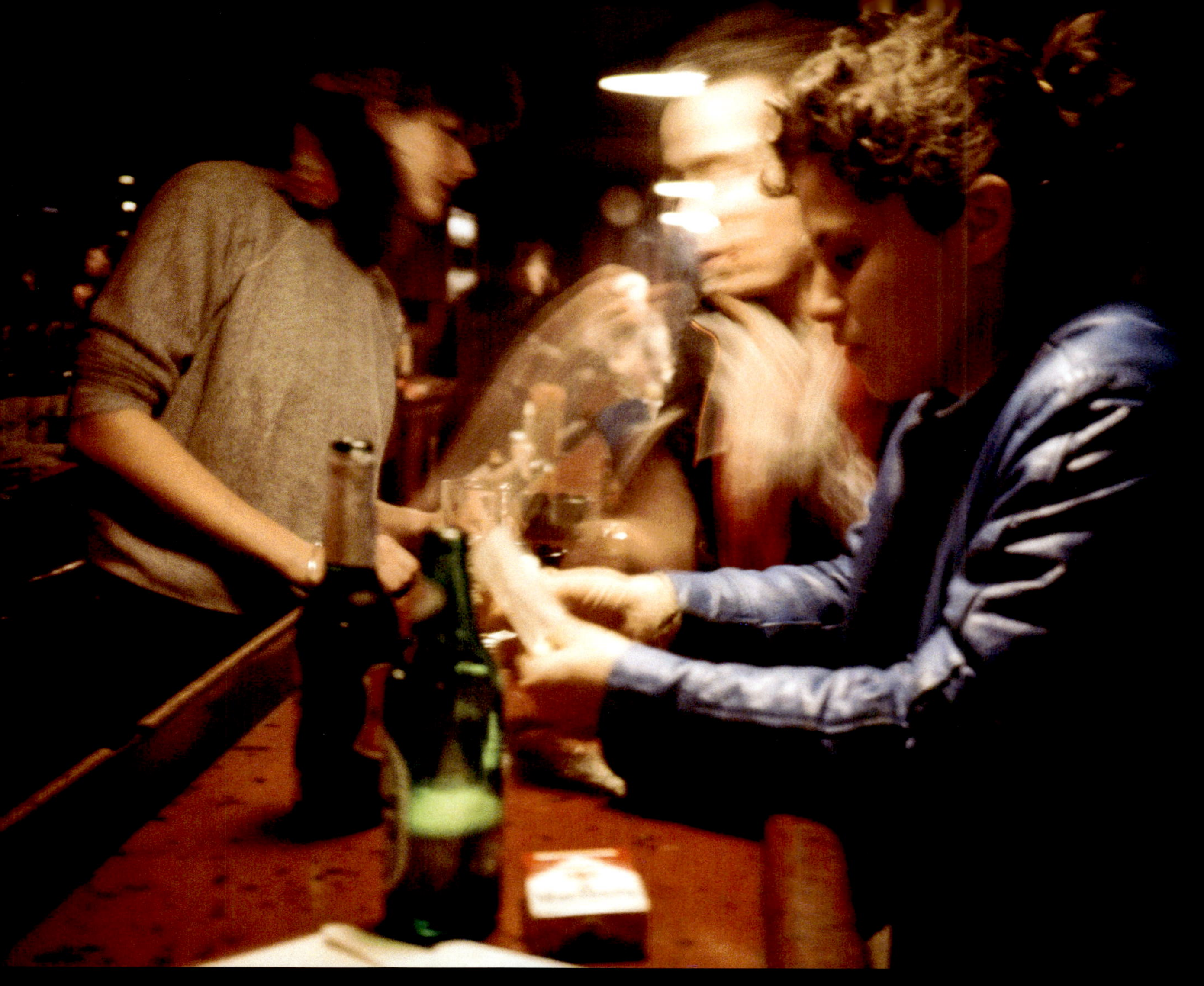

202   TOP: David Wojnarowicz on Second Avenue during Peter Hujar's 50th birthday party, 1984.
       BOTTOM: A Colab meeting: Ellen Cooper with Bebe, Seton, and Kiki Smith.
203   Filmmaker and artist Vivienne Dick on the roof of 276 W. 43 Street, performing in Scott and Beth B's 1980 film *The Offenders*. I made Spectacolor titles for the film and ran them after hours.
204   TOP: Charlie at 276 W. 43rd Street, 1983.
       BOTTOM: Fab Five Freddy and friend, ca. 1983.
205   TOP: The seminal hip hop group Cold Crush posing in front of two of my paintings, 1981.
       BOTTOM: Camille Pascal at 276 W. 43rd Street.
206   TOP: Artist Steve Brown at a state fair, late 1980s.
       BOTTOM: Robert Cooney and Ulli Rimkus at El Castillo de Jagua on the Lower East Side, early 1980s.
207   TOP: On 43rd Street, standing in front of Mimi Smith's portrait and Robert Cooney's poster, early 1980s.
       BOTTOM: Coleen Fitzgibbon modeling for a painting in the "Witness" series, 1990.
208   Nan Goldin in an entrance to the 42nd Street Subway, 1984.
209   Ulli Rimkus (behind the bar) and Cara Perlman at Tin Pan Alley, early 1980s.

PEOPLE HAD BEEN SAYING WE SHOULD DO A SHOW IN TIMES
SQUARE. CHRISTY RUPP AND I WENT TO AL LOVING'S STUDIO, ON
42ND STREET BETWEEN SIXTH AND SEVENTH AVENUE, TO SEE IF
THERE WAS A SPACE IN HIS BUILDING, WHICH THERE WASN'T. TOM
OTTERNESS AND JOHN AHEARN GOT TO THE DURST ORGANIZATION
AND GOT THE SPACE. THE BUILDING WAS BIG AND BROKEN UP
INTO MANY SPACES, SO DIFFERENT AREAS WERE ORGANIZED
BY DIFFERENT PEOPLE, AND WHOEVER HAD EACH AREA PICKED
A THEME. THEN ANYBODY STUCK IN WHATEVER THEY WANTED
WHEREVER, AND WE'D ARGUE UNTIL THE MOST STUBBORN OR
PERSUASIVE PERSON WON.

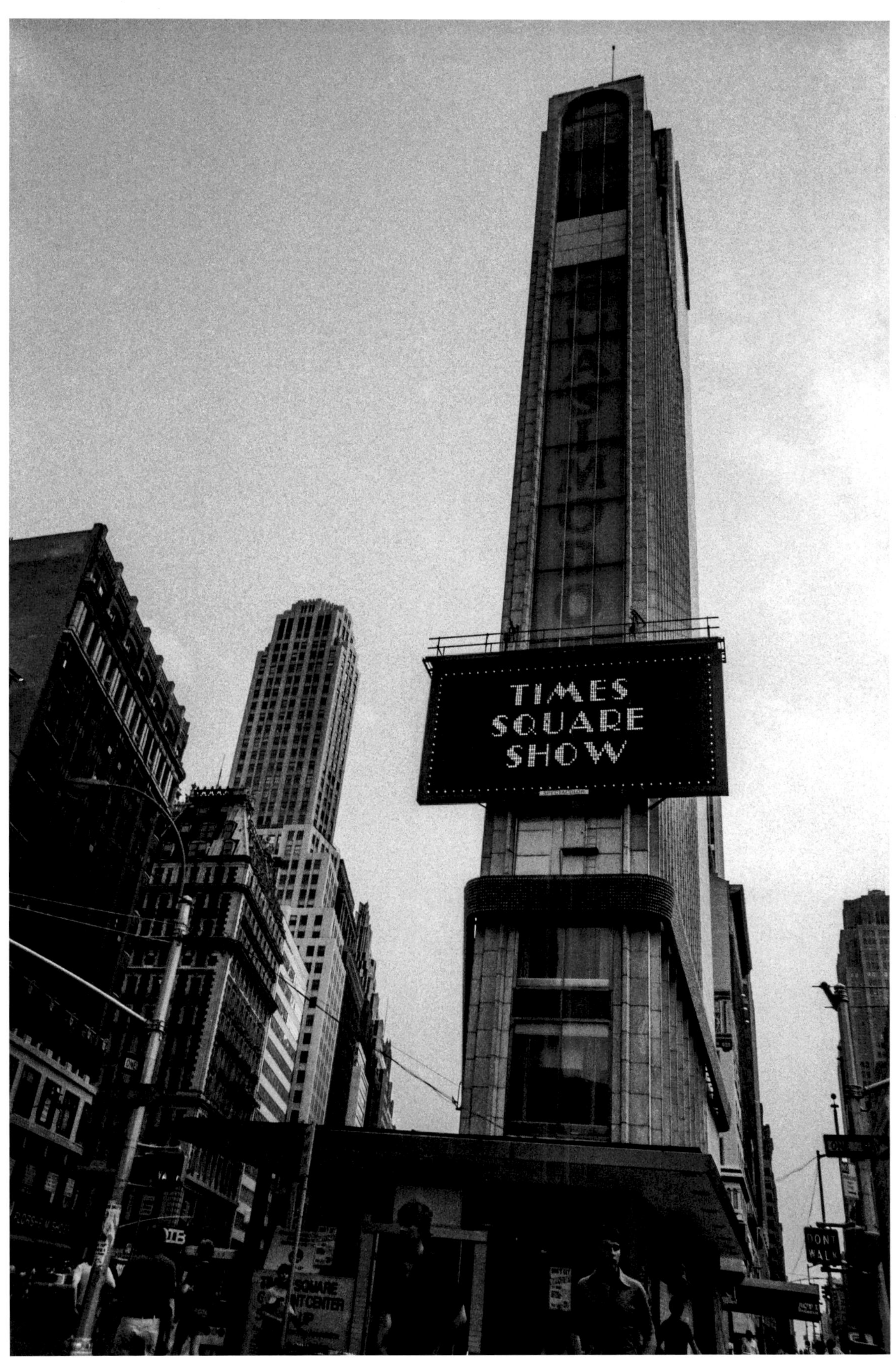

TIMES
SQUARE
SHOW

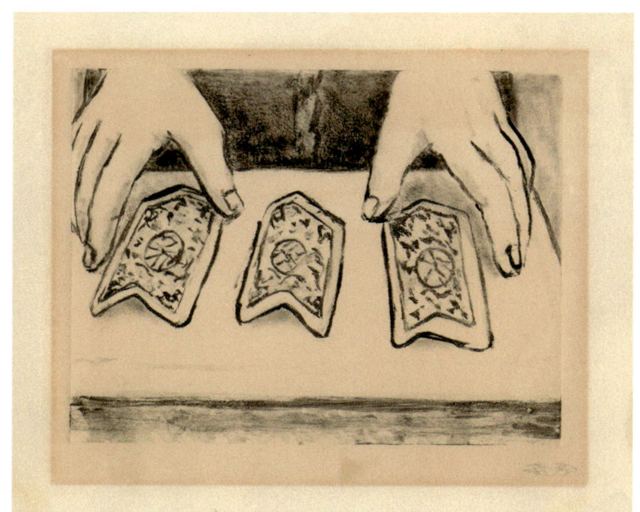
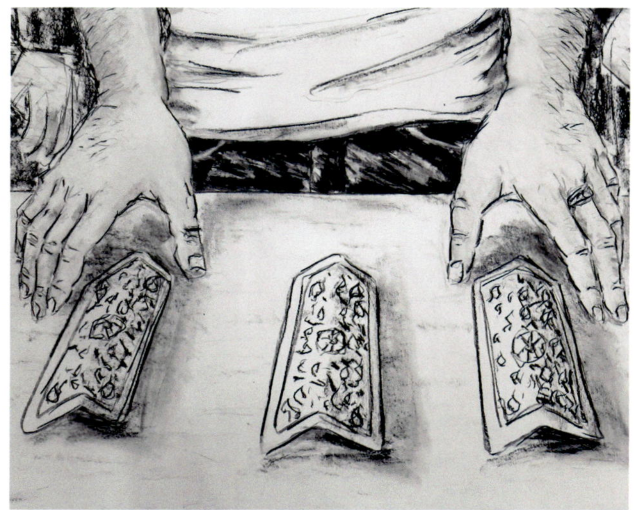
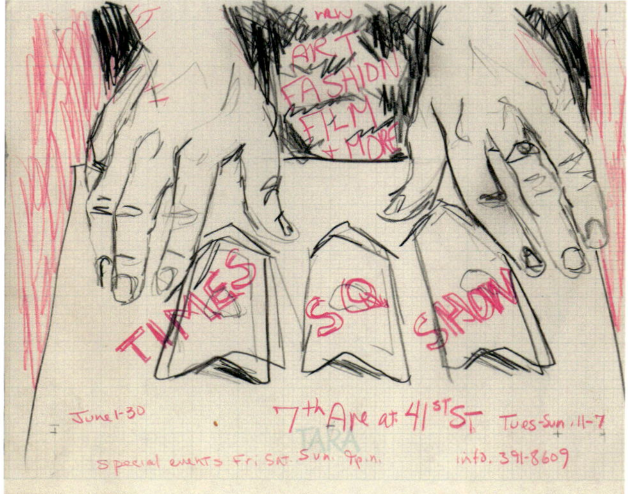

NEW
ART
FASHION
FILM
+ MORE
TIMES
SQ
SHOW
June 1-30
7th Ave at 41st St
Tues-Sun 11-7
special events Fri. Sat. Sun. 9p.m.
info. 391-8609

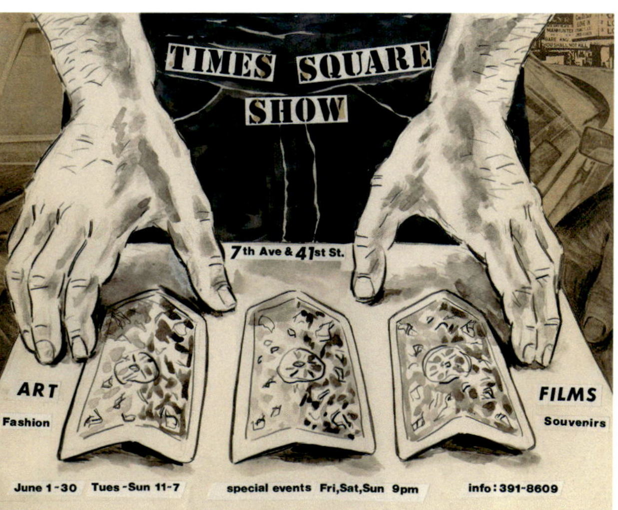

TIMES SQUARE
SHOW
7th Ave & 41st St.
ART
Fashion
FILMS
Souvenirs
June 1-30
Tues-Sun 11-7
special events
Fri,Sat,Sun 9pm
info: 391-8609

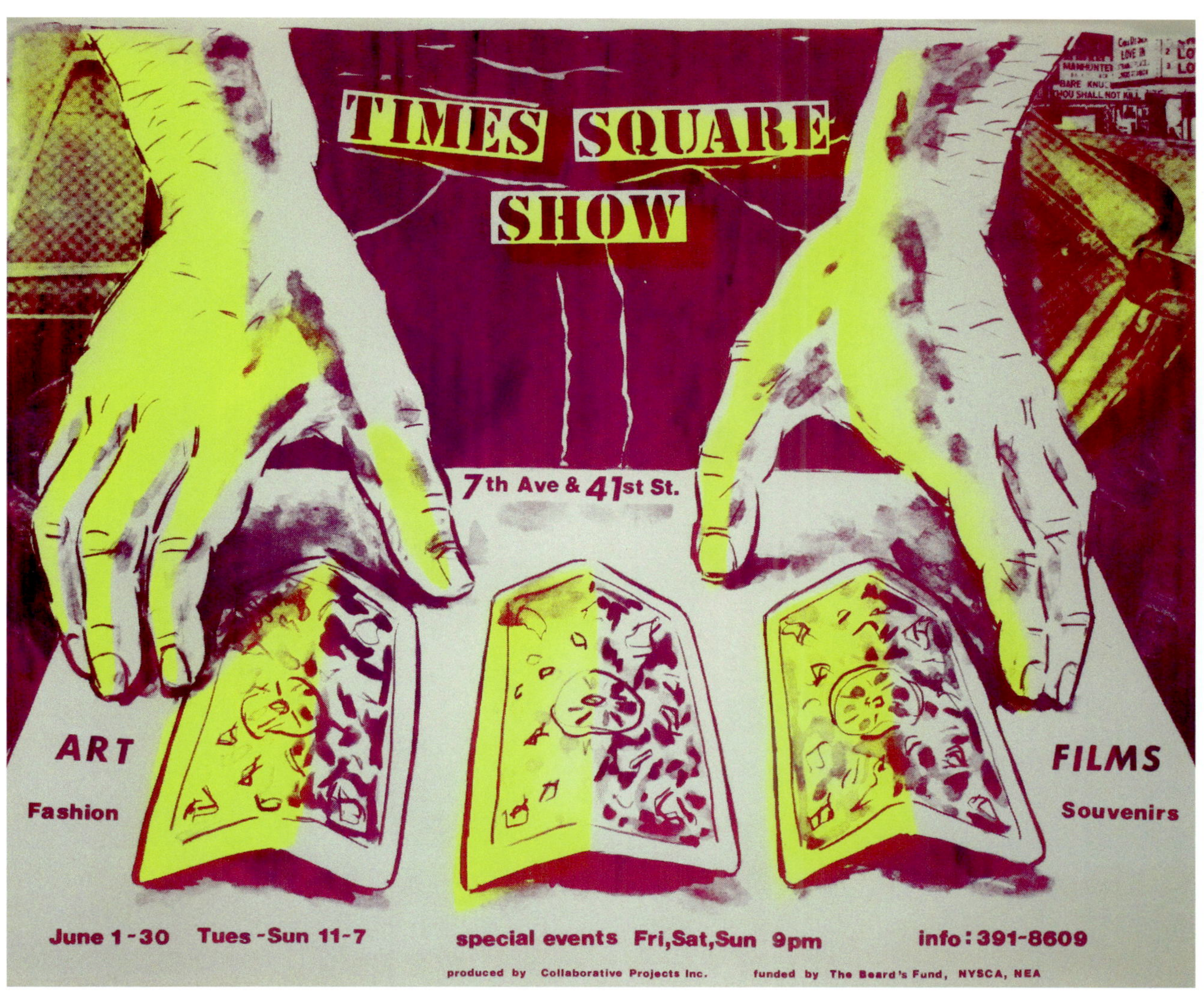

TIMES SQUARE
SHOW
7th Ave & 41st St.
ART
Fashion
FILMS
Souvenirs
June 1-30   Tues-Sun 11-7   special events   Fri,Sat,Sun 9pm   info: 391-8609
produced by   Collaborative Projects Inc.   funded by The Beard's Fund, NYSCA, NEA

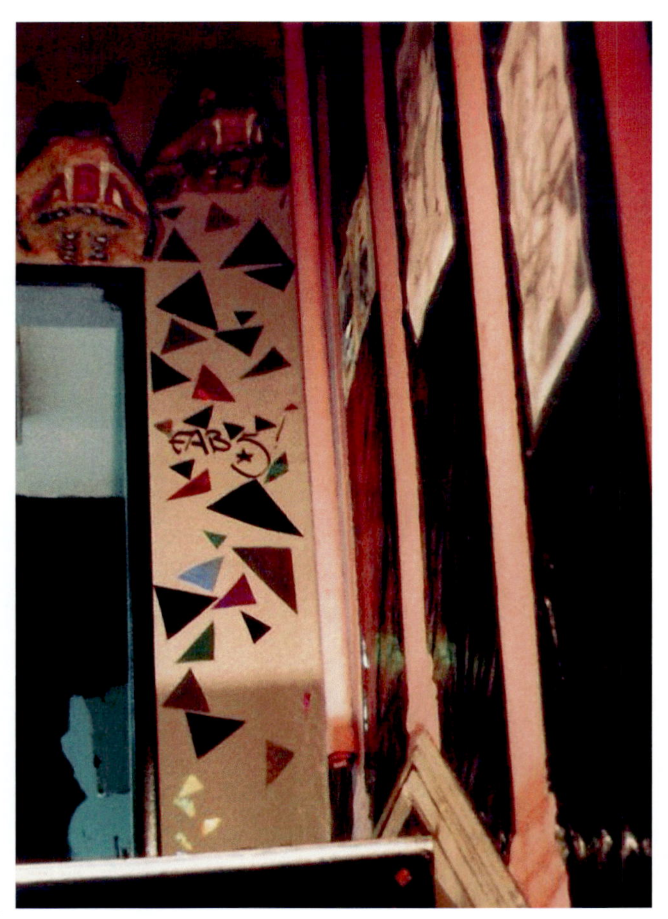
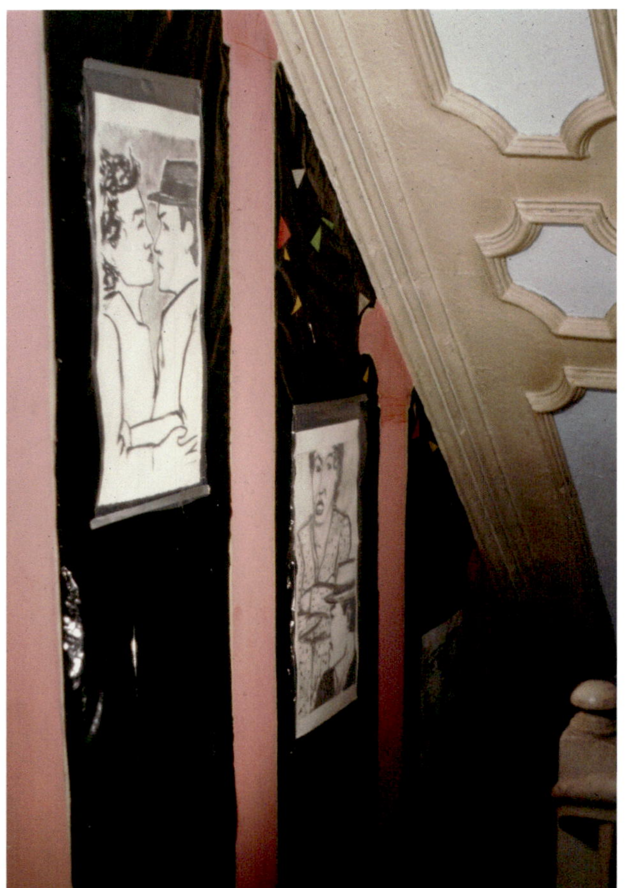
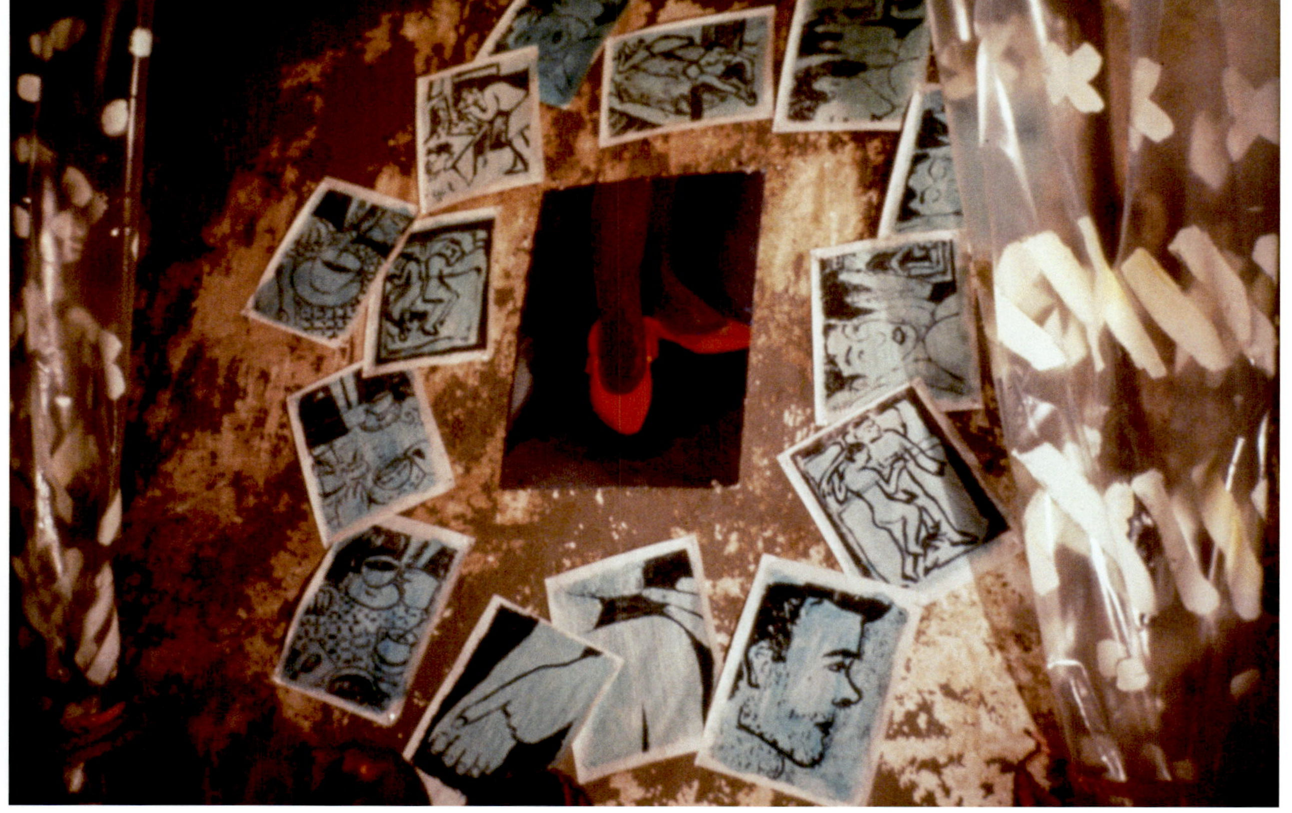

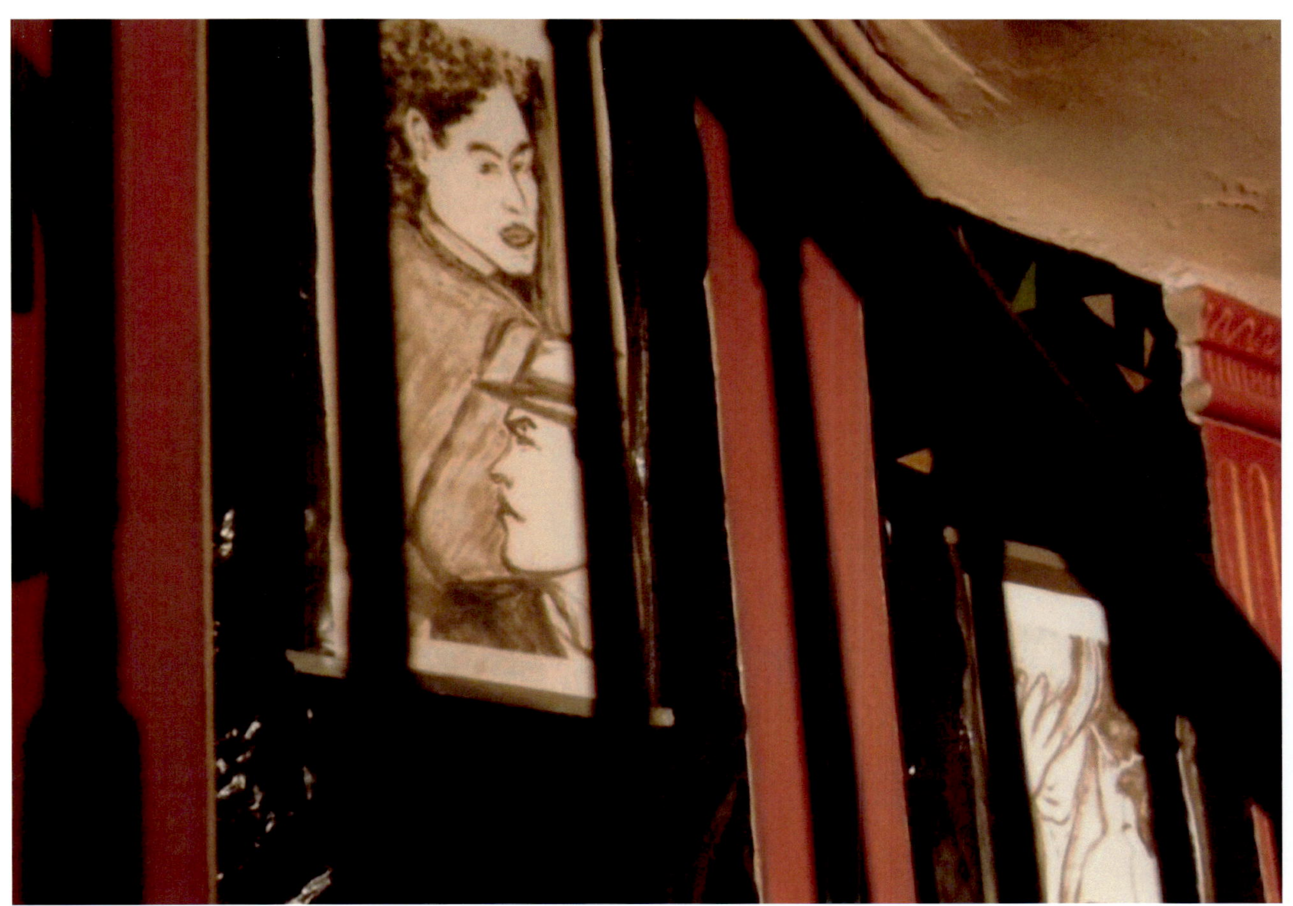

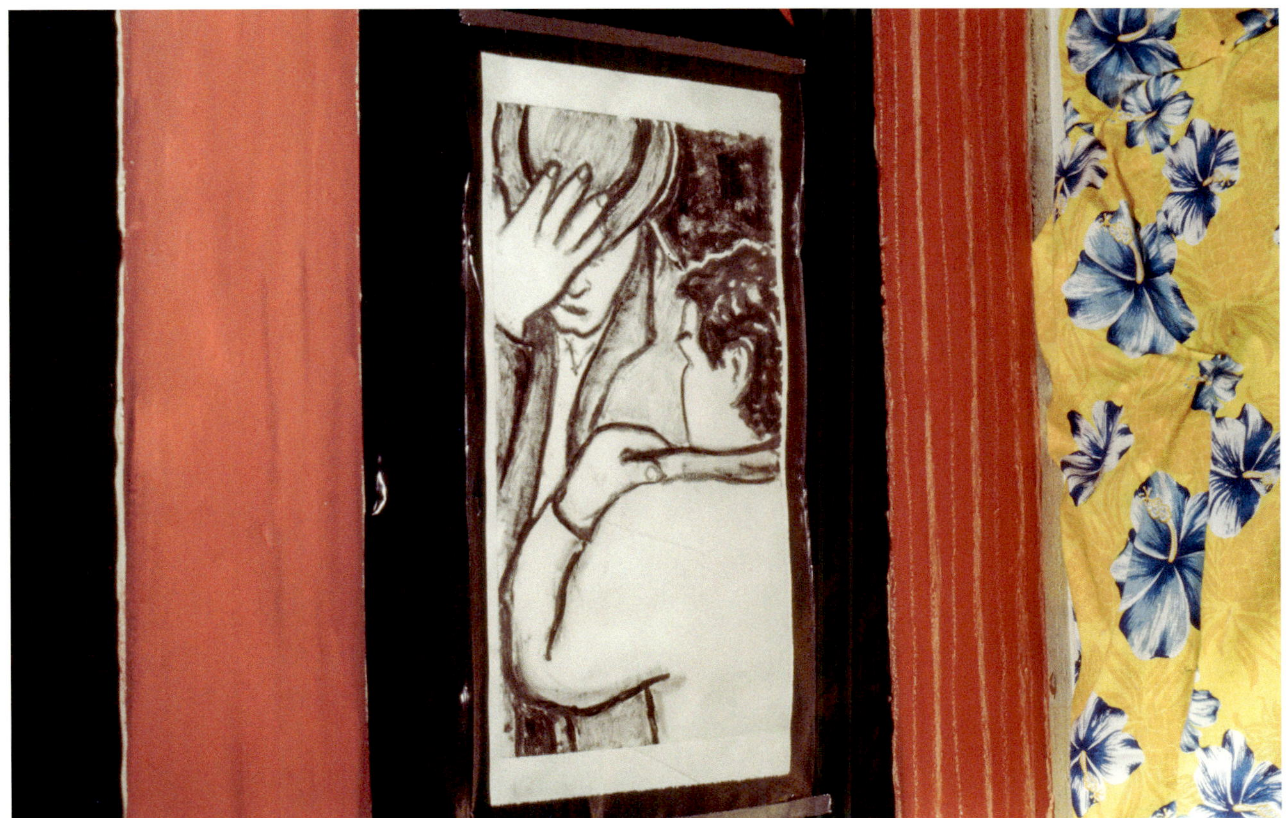

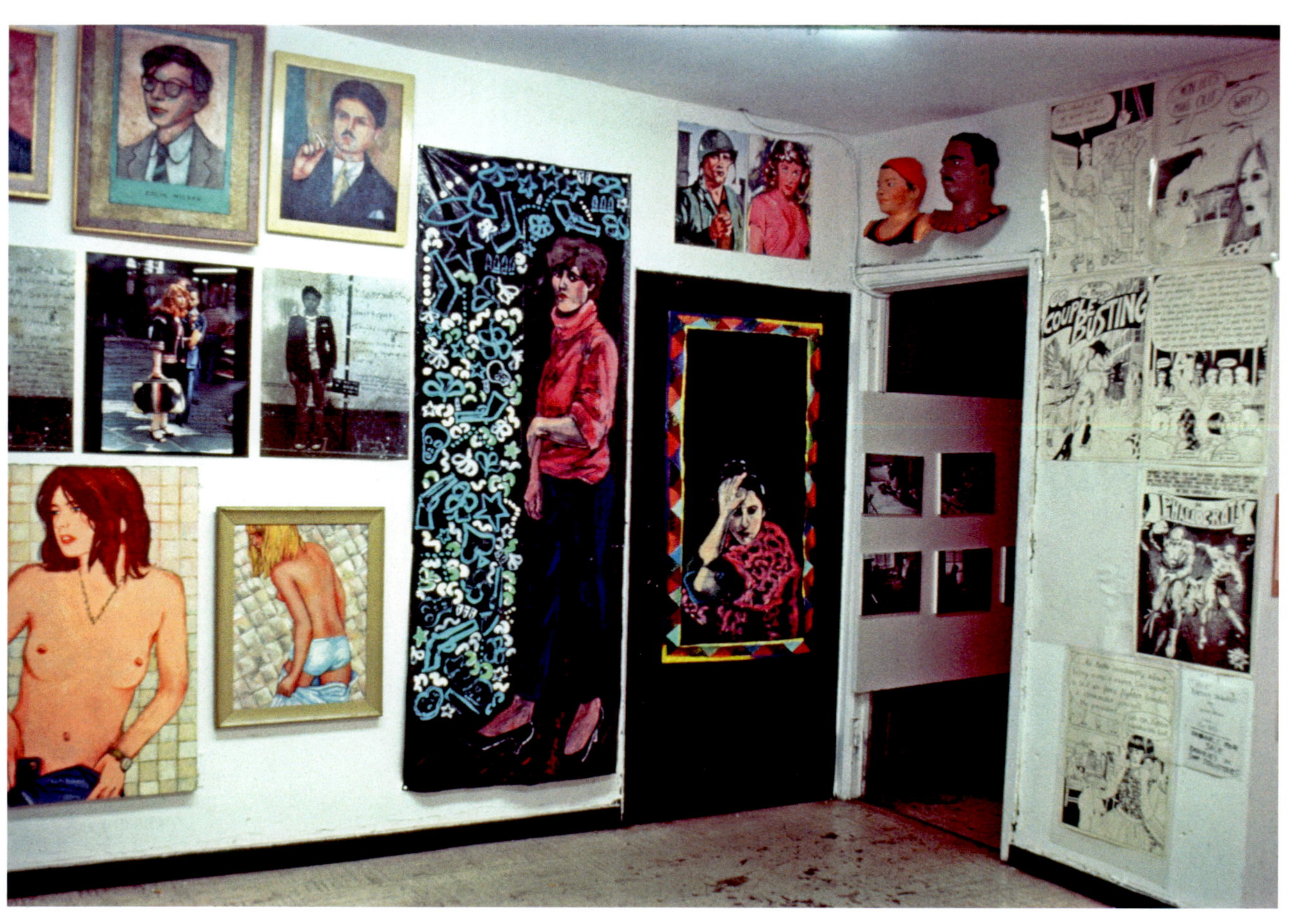

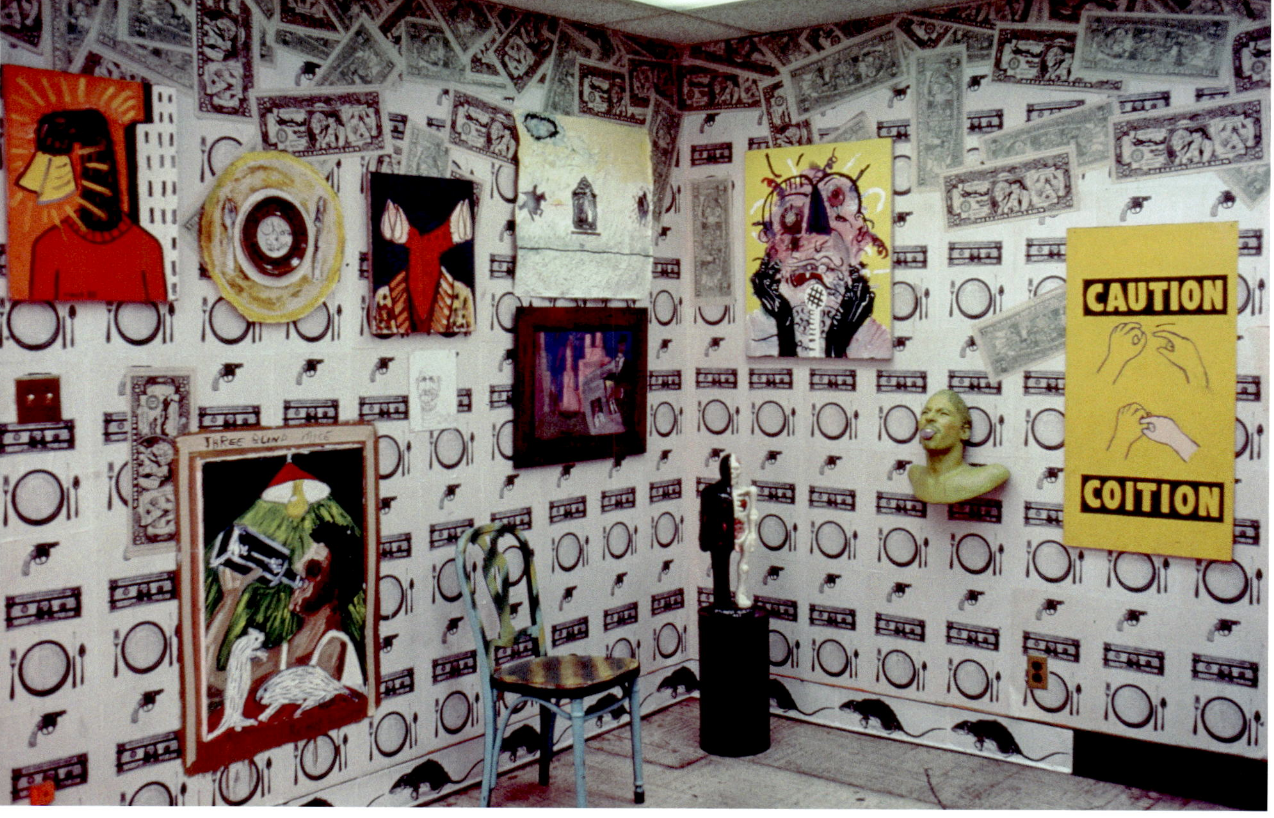

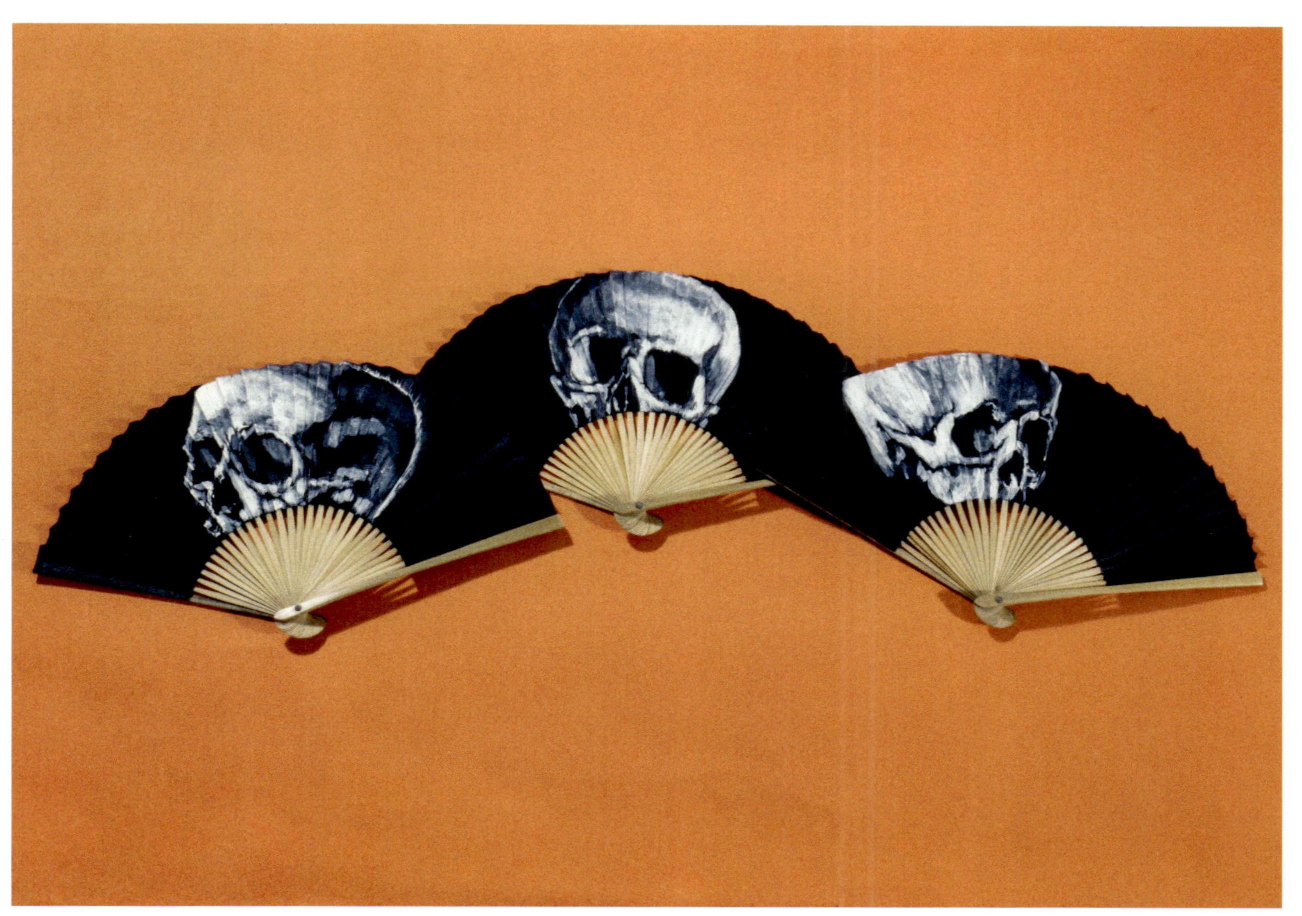

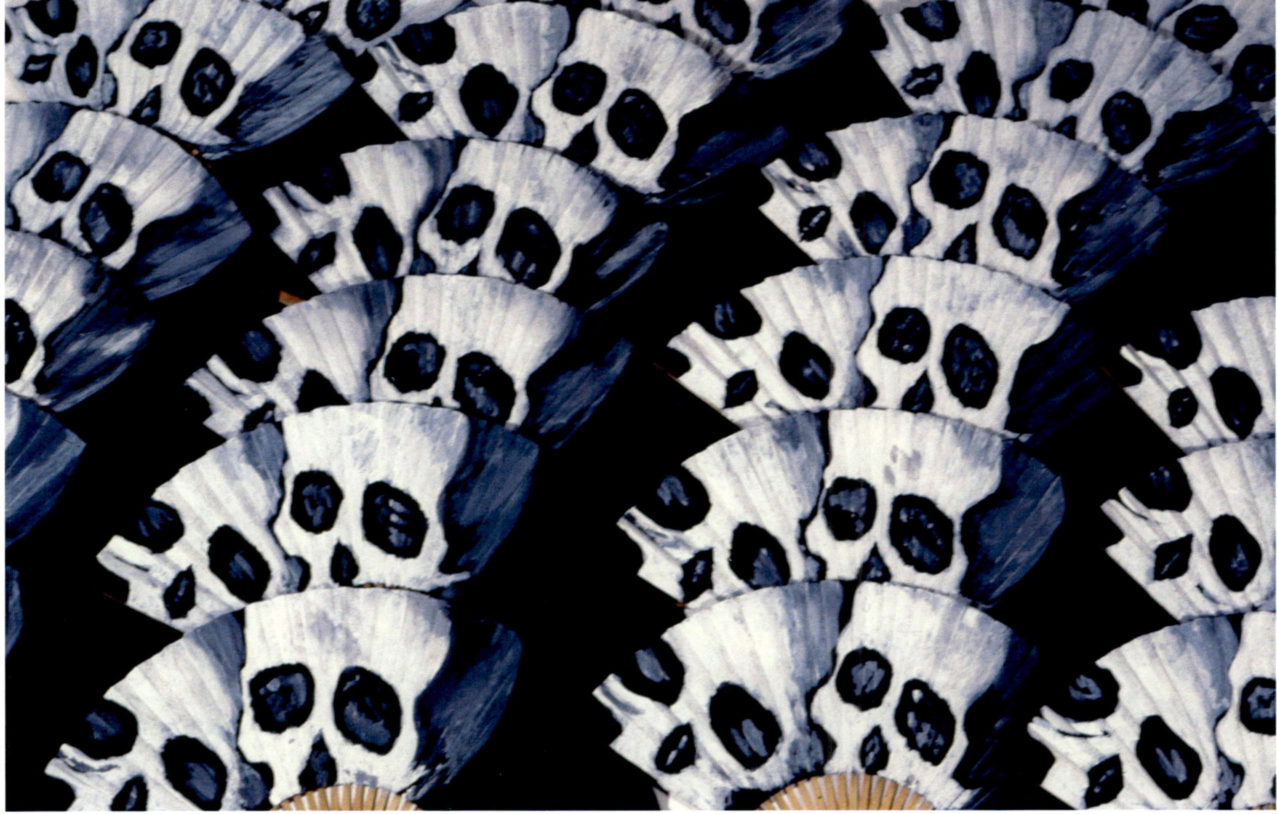

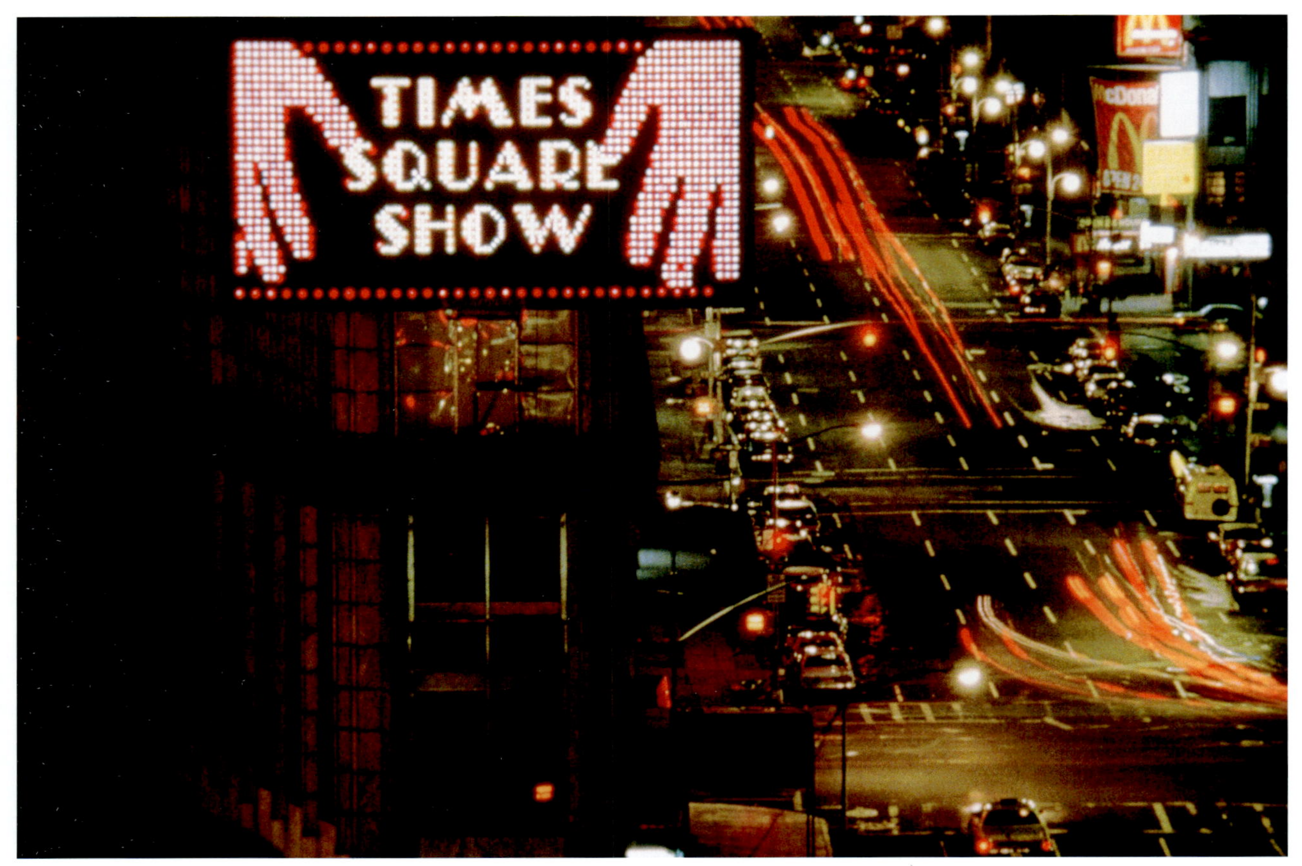

211   Spectacolor ad for the Times Square Show, 1980. Photograph by Wolfgang Staehle.
212   Designs for the iconic Times Square Show "Three-Card Monte" poster.
213   Monoprint of the original Times Square Show poster, 1979.
214   TOP LEFT: Installation shot of the Times Square Show.
       TOP RIGHT: Prints in the second-to-third floor stairwell of the Times Square Show. This work would later appear in *Living with Contradictions*.
       BOTTOM: The entryway to the Times Square Show on the venue's 4th floor landing. At the top of the stairwell, the viewer was greeted by my prints and painting surrounded by Jody Culkin's painted shower curtains.
215   TOP and BOTTOM: More prints in the Times Square Show, later published in *Living with Contradictions*.
216   TOP: Section of the Times Square Show curated by Andrea Callard. Photograph © Andrea Callard 2018.
       BOTTOM: Section of the Times Square Show curated by Tom Otterness.
217   TOP and BOTTOM: Painted fans from the Colab A. More Store.
218   Detail of the animated Spectacolor ad for the Times Square Show, featuring the poster's three-card monte hands. Photograph by John Marchael.

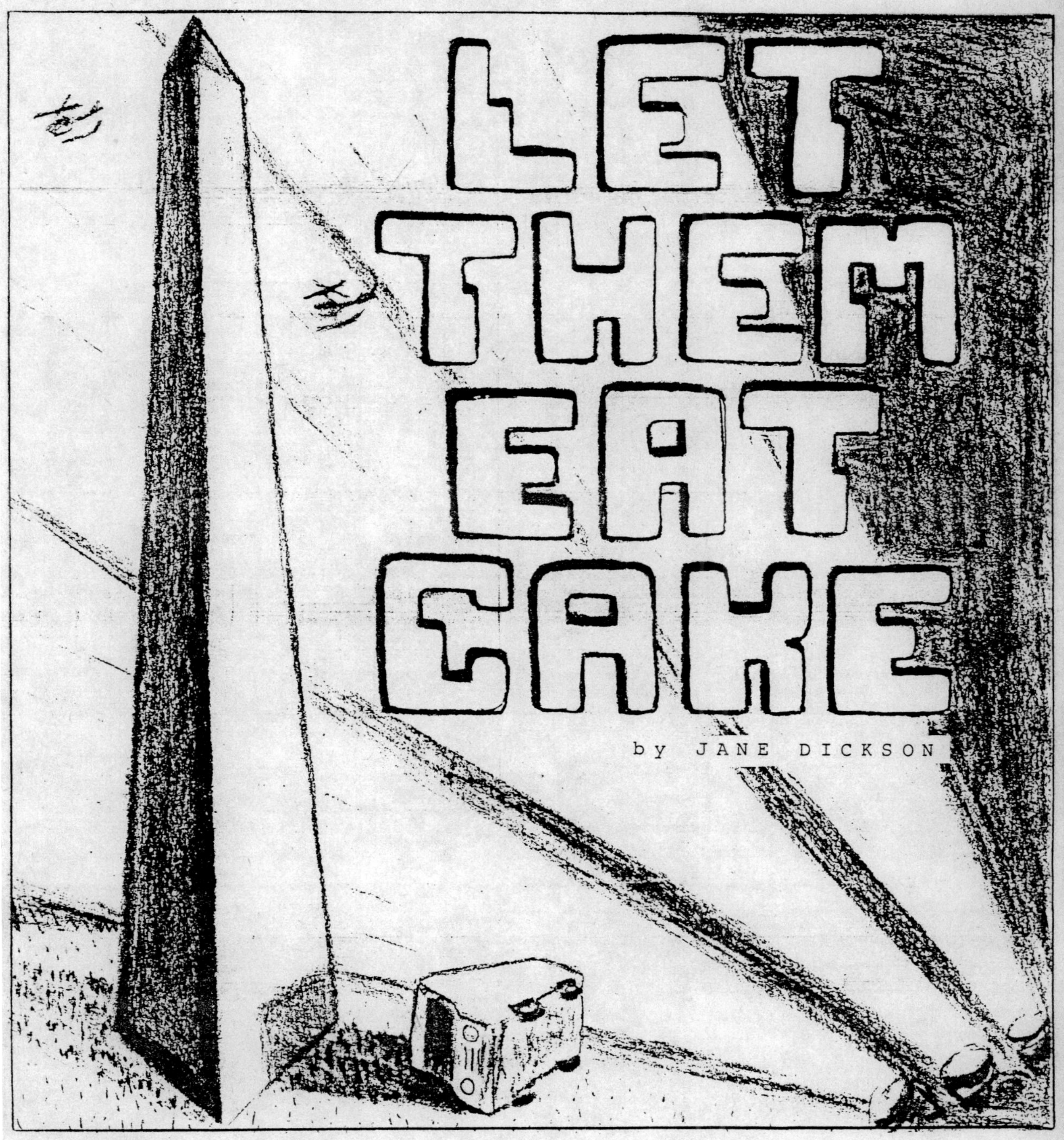

running every 20 minutes   Dec. 15 - 30
on the SPECTACOLOR computer lightboard at # 1 Times Square

Grand Finale: all "Messages To The Public"will run at midnight Dec. 31,1982

P A R T Y : Thurs. Dec. 16   9 - 11 p.m. at Tin Pan Alley 220 West 49 th St.

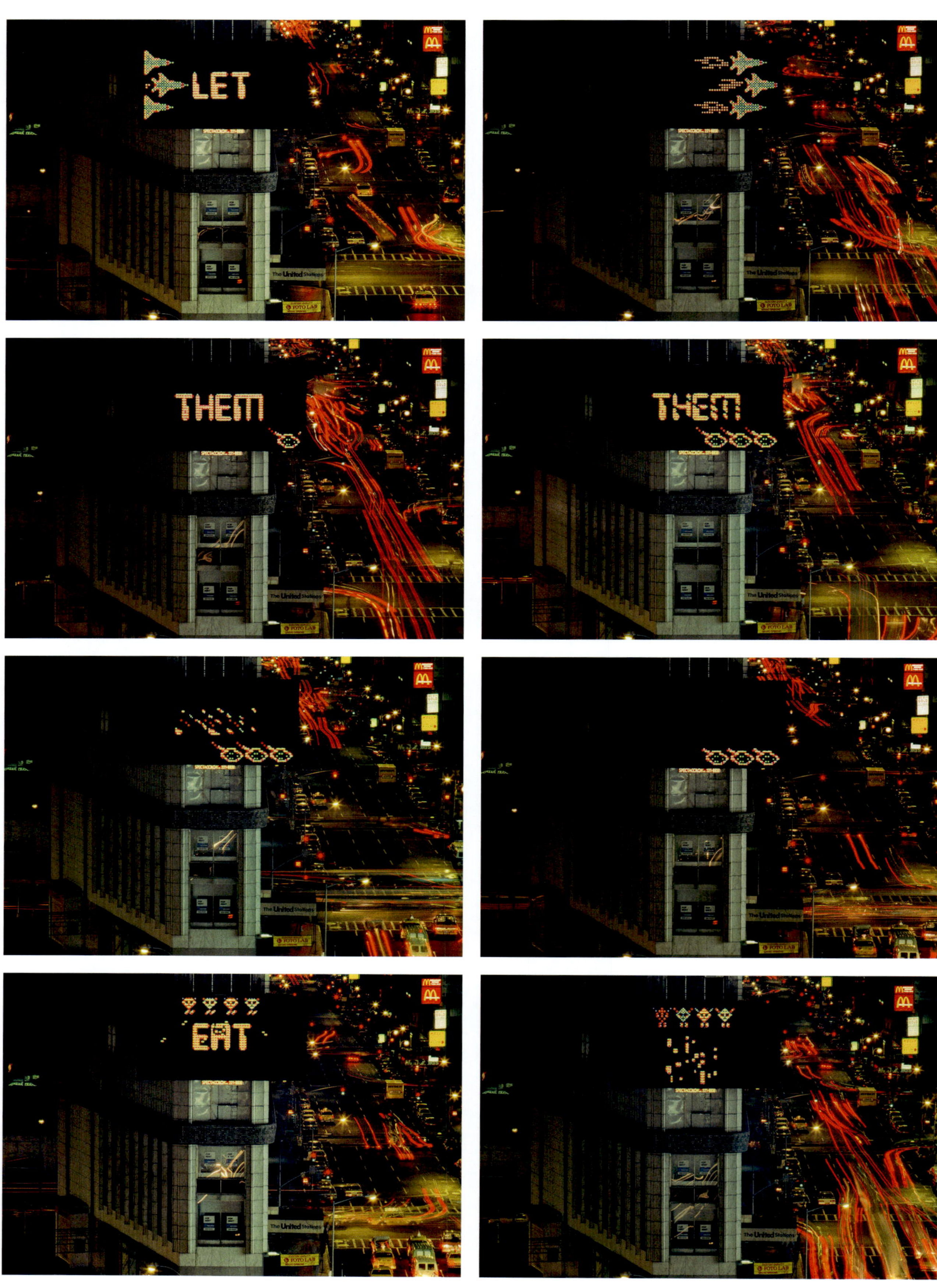
LET
THEM
THEM
EAT

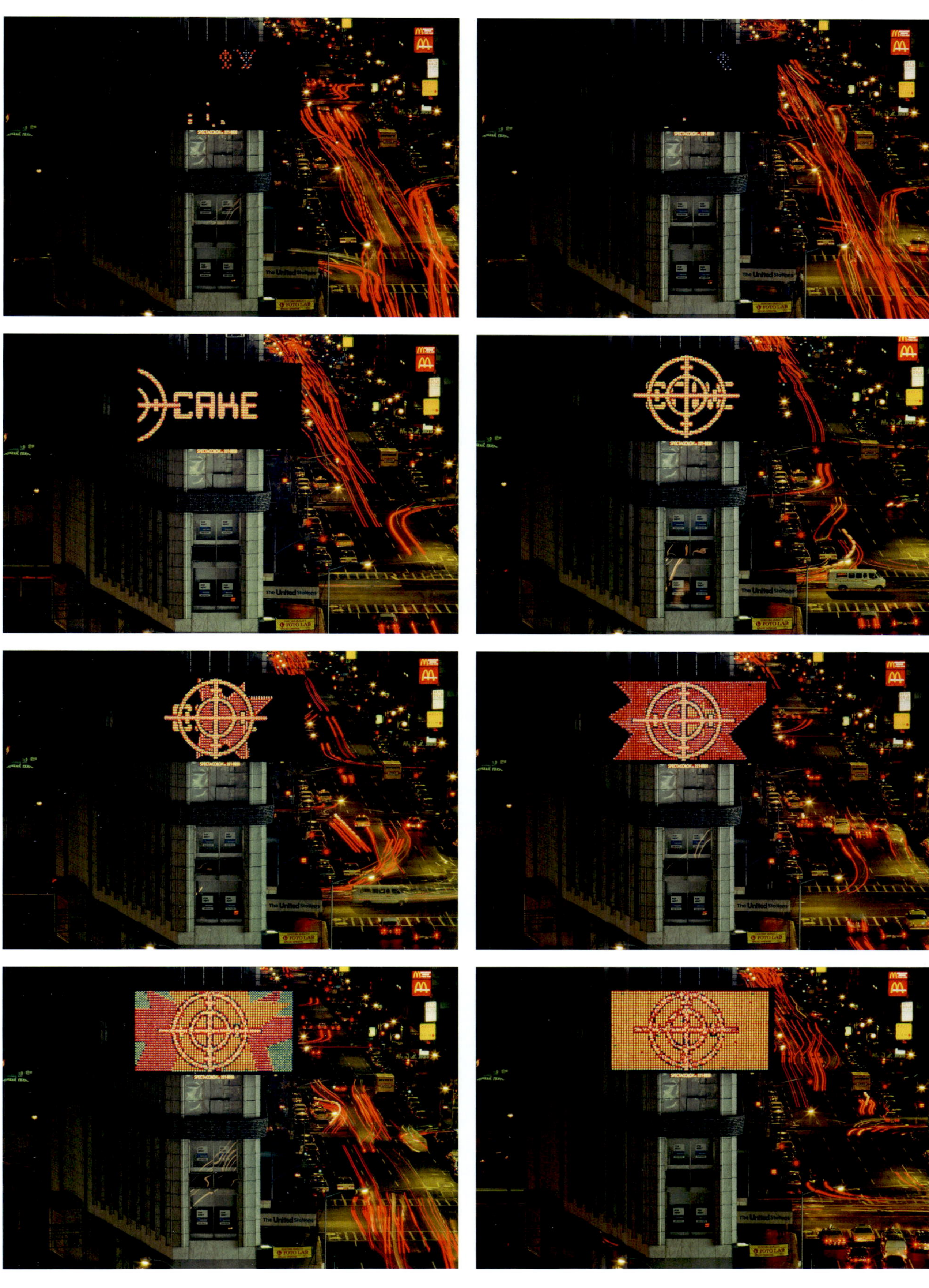
CAKE

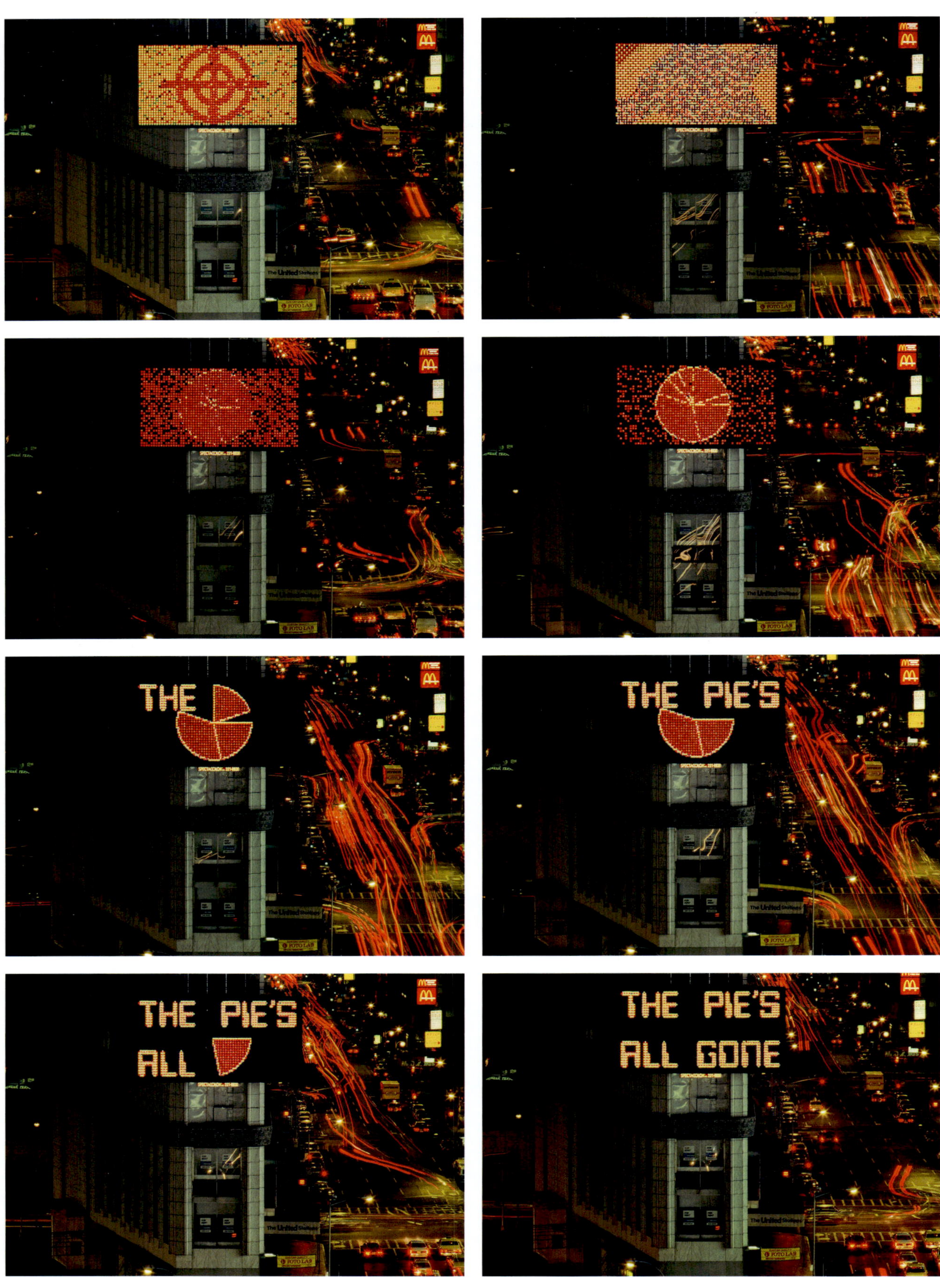
THE
THE PIE'S
THE PIE'S
ALL
THE PIE'S
ALL GONE

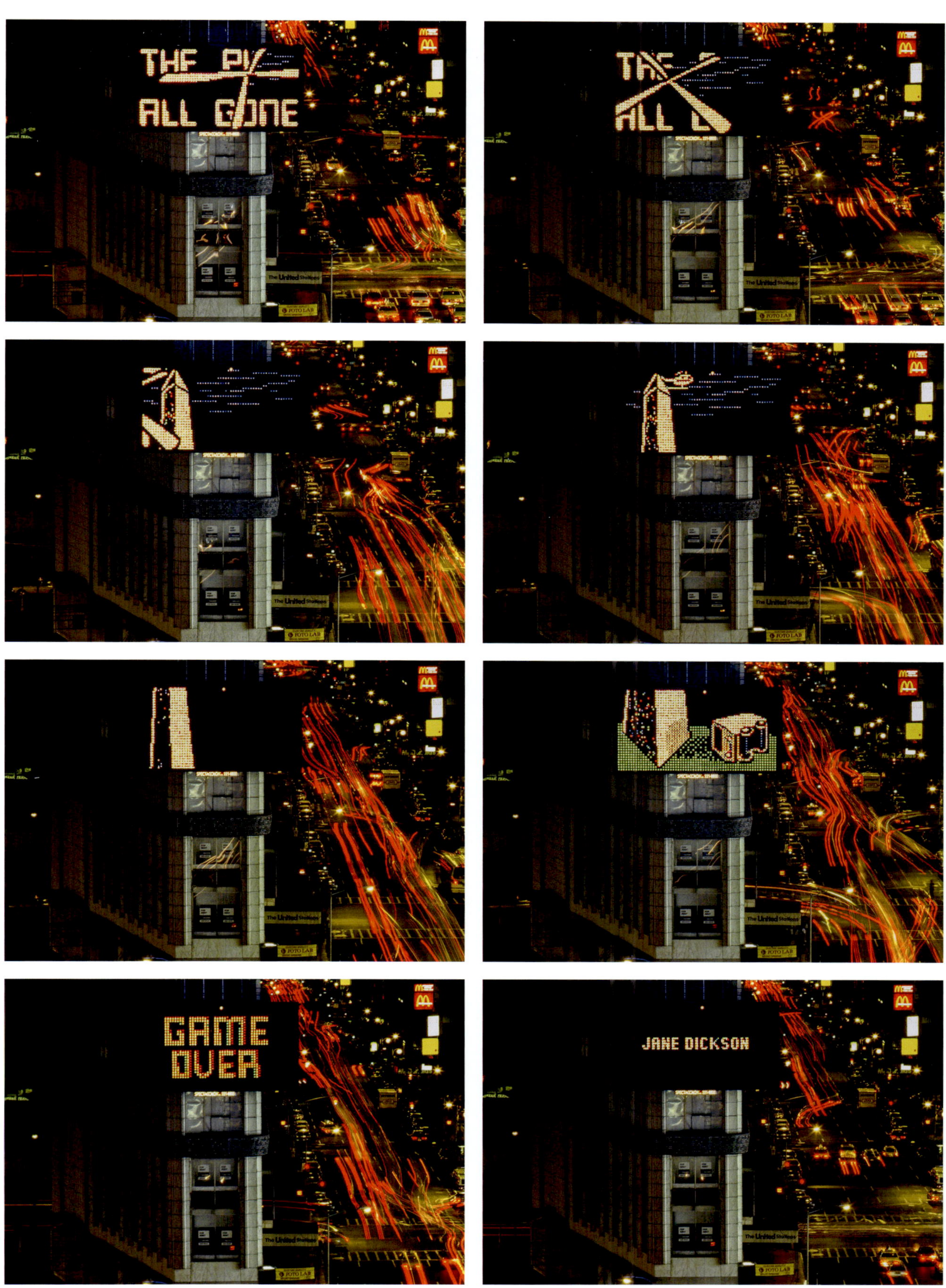

219   Poster for my piece *Let Them Eat Cake*, part of Messages to the Public, my 1982 series with the
        Public Art Fund.
220–3   Stills depicting the *Let Them Eat Cake* animation.

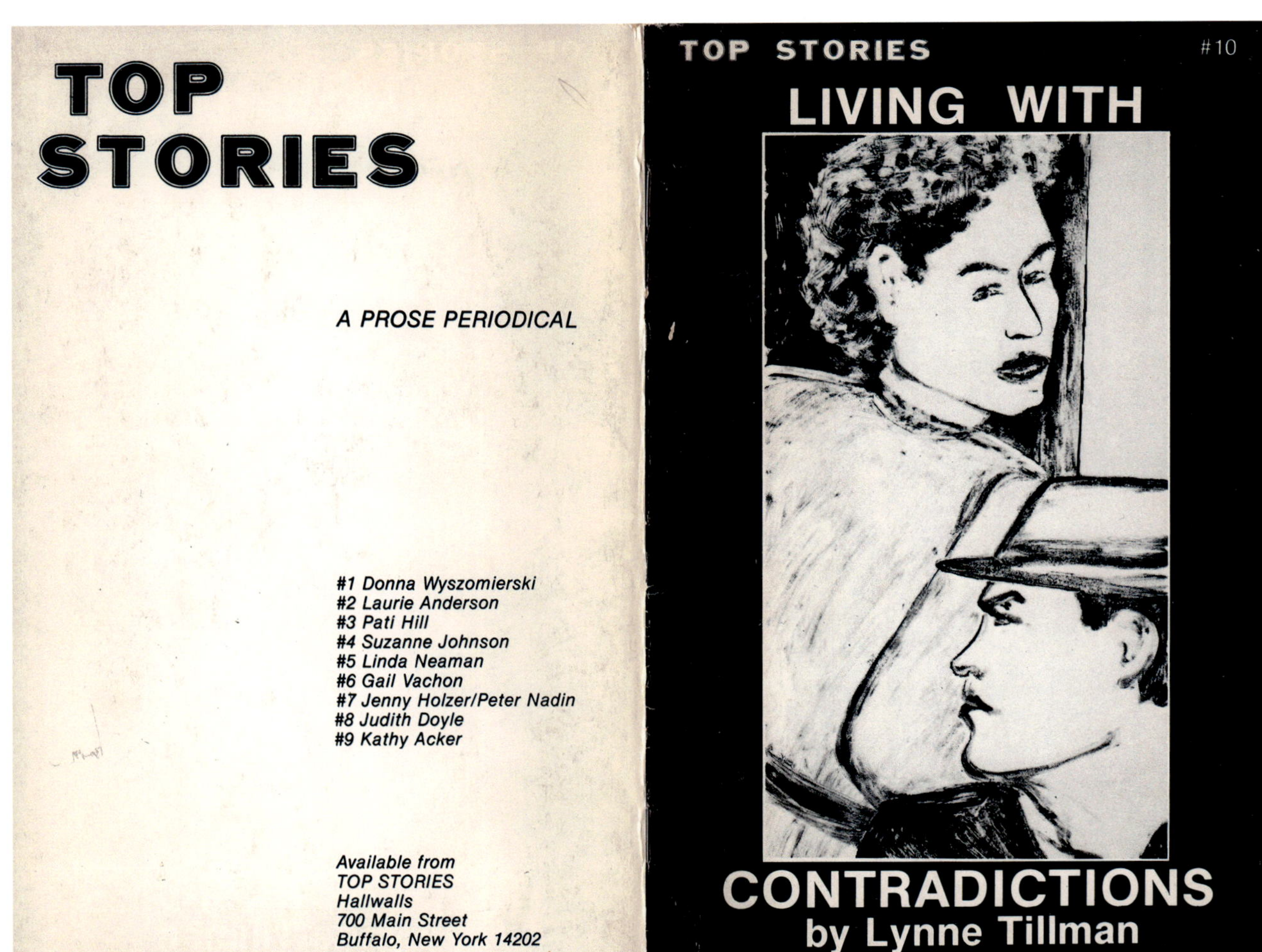

224   *Living with Contradictions* in its final publication form, with text by Lynne Tillman, from the *Top Stories*
      magazine series published by Anne Turyn.
225   Pieces from *Living with Contradictions*.

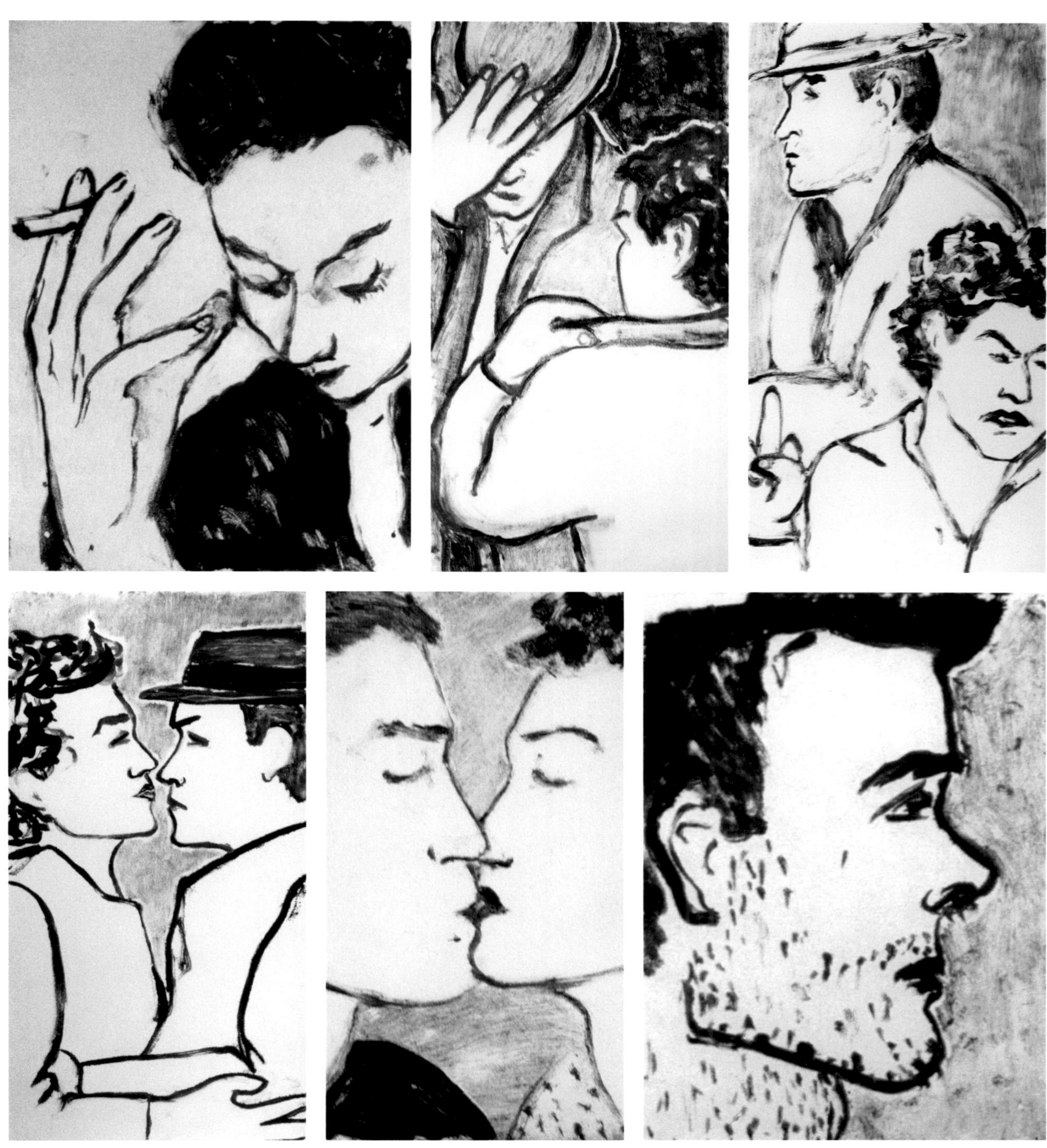

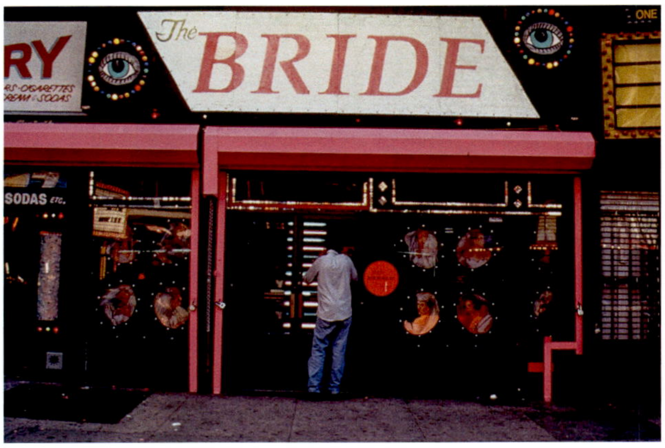

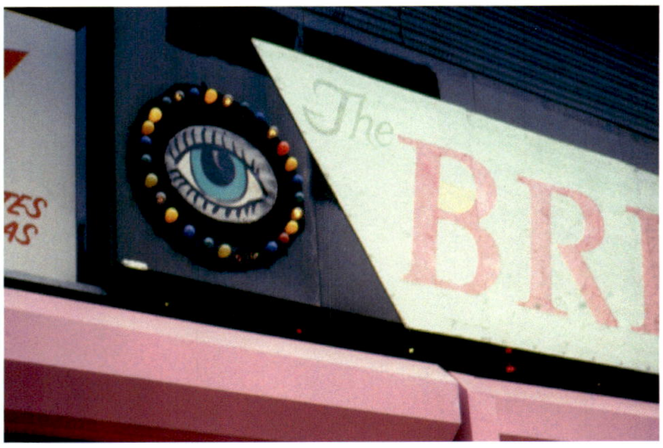

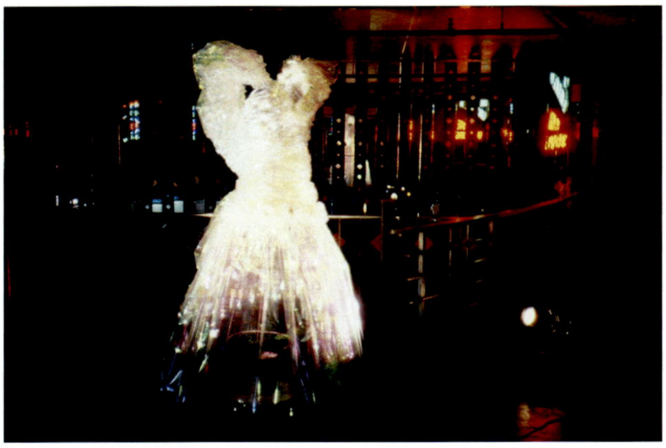

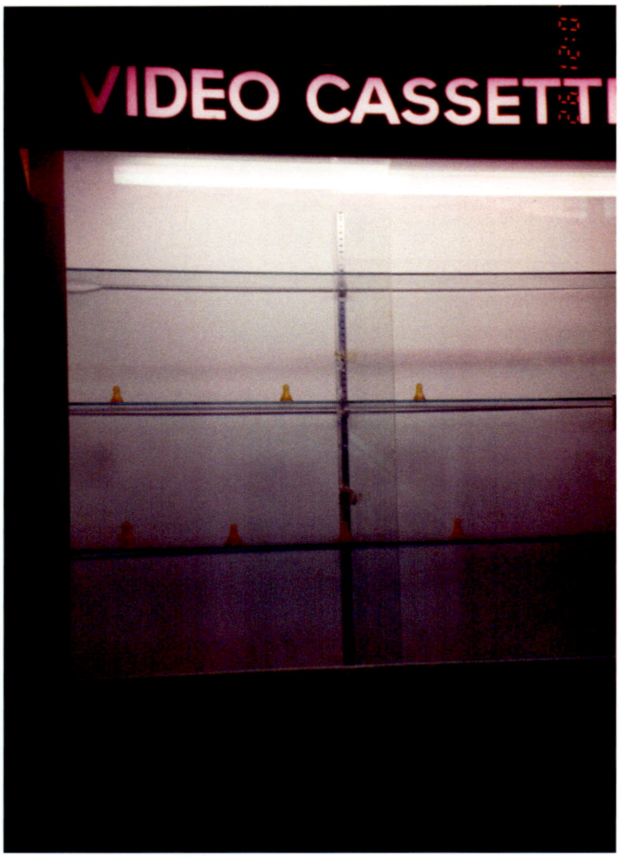

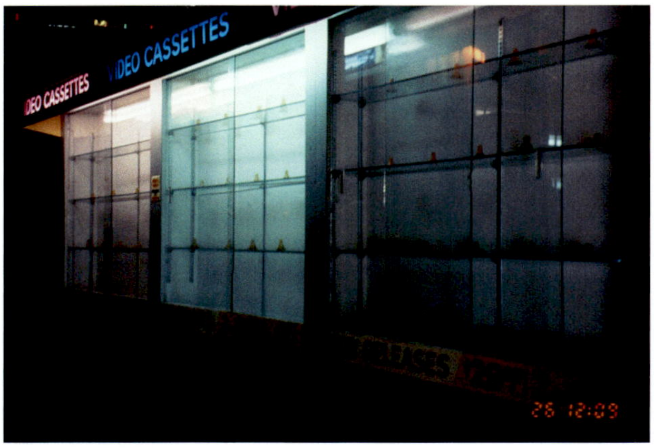

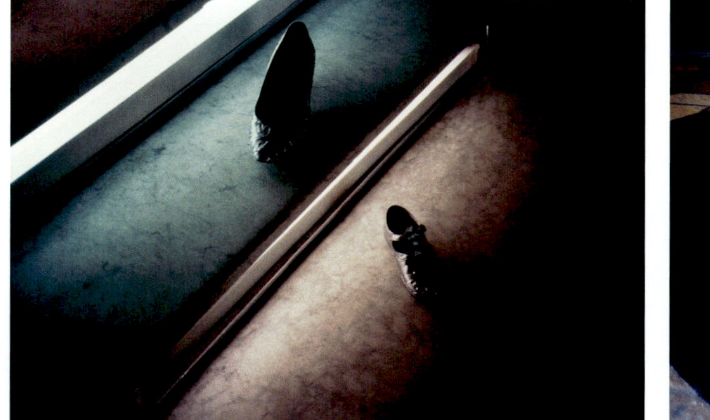
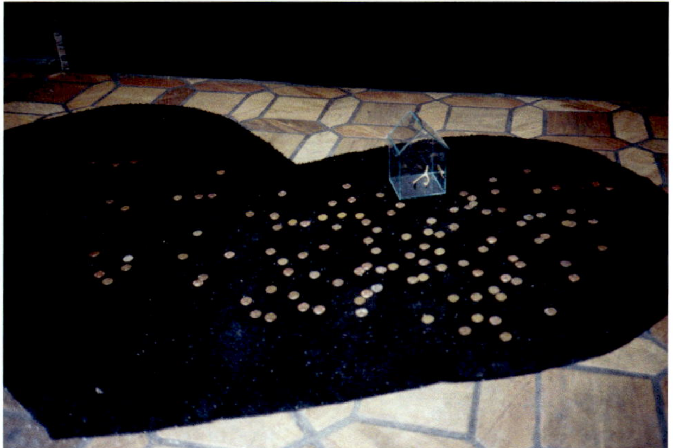

226–7   *The Bride*, a 1993 installation sponsored by Times Square Arts' Creative Time program that featured a bridal shop installed in the shuttered storefront of a porn video palace.

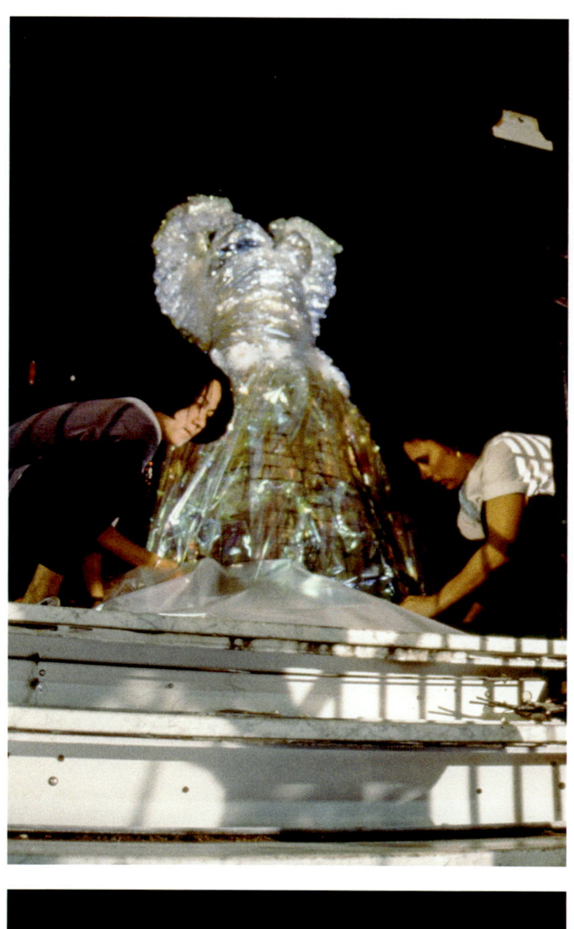

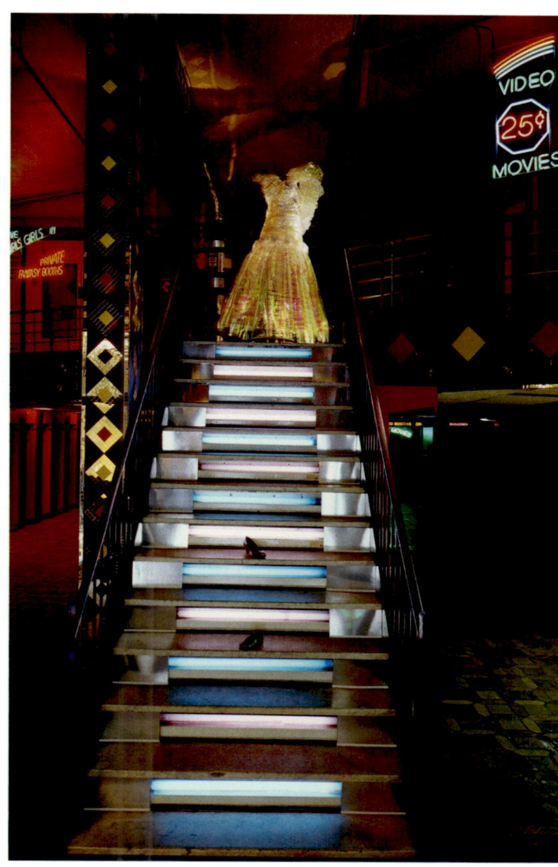
VIDEO
25¢
MOVIES
PRIVATE

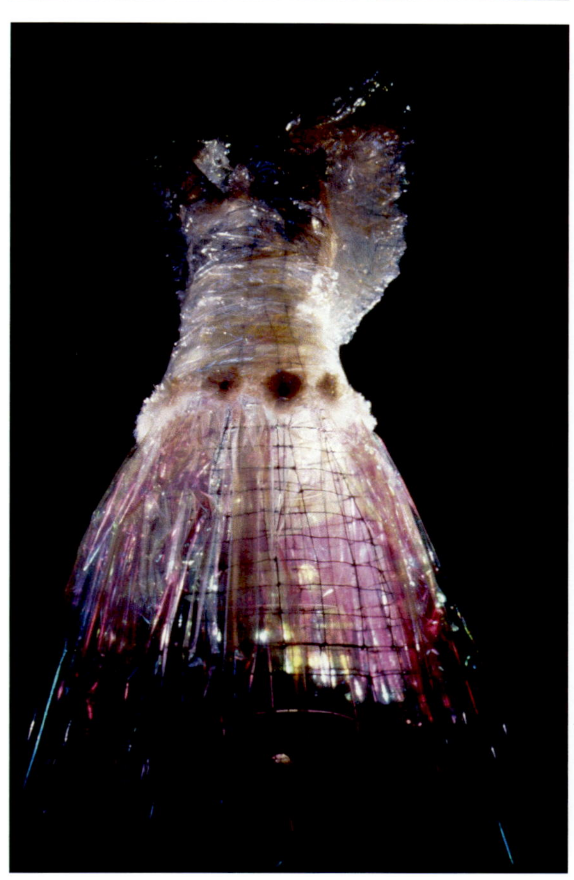

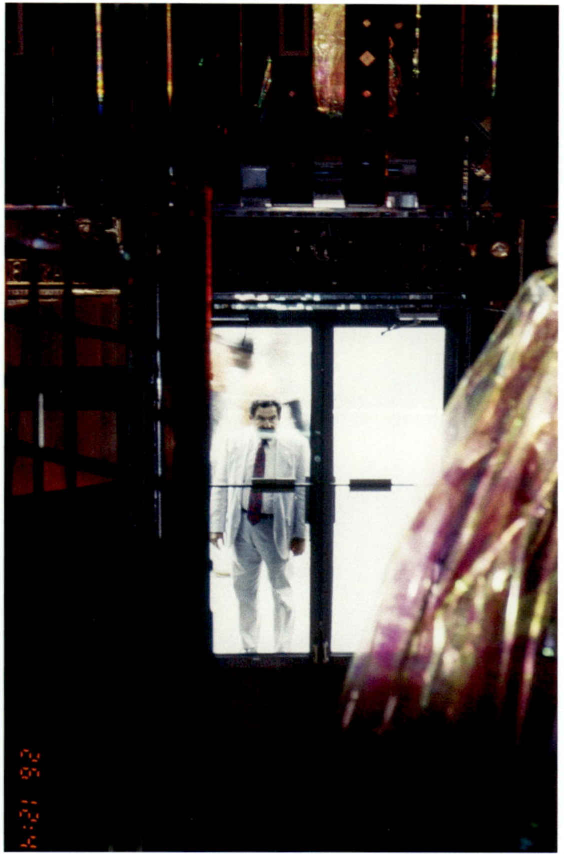

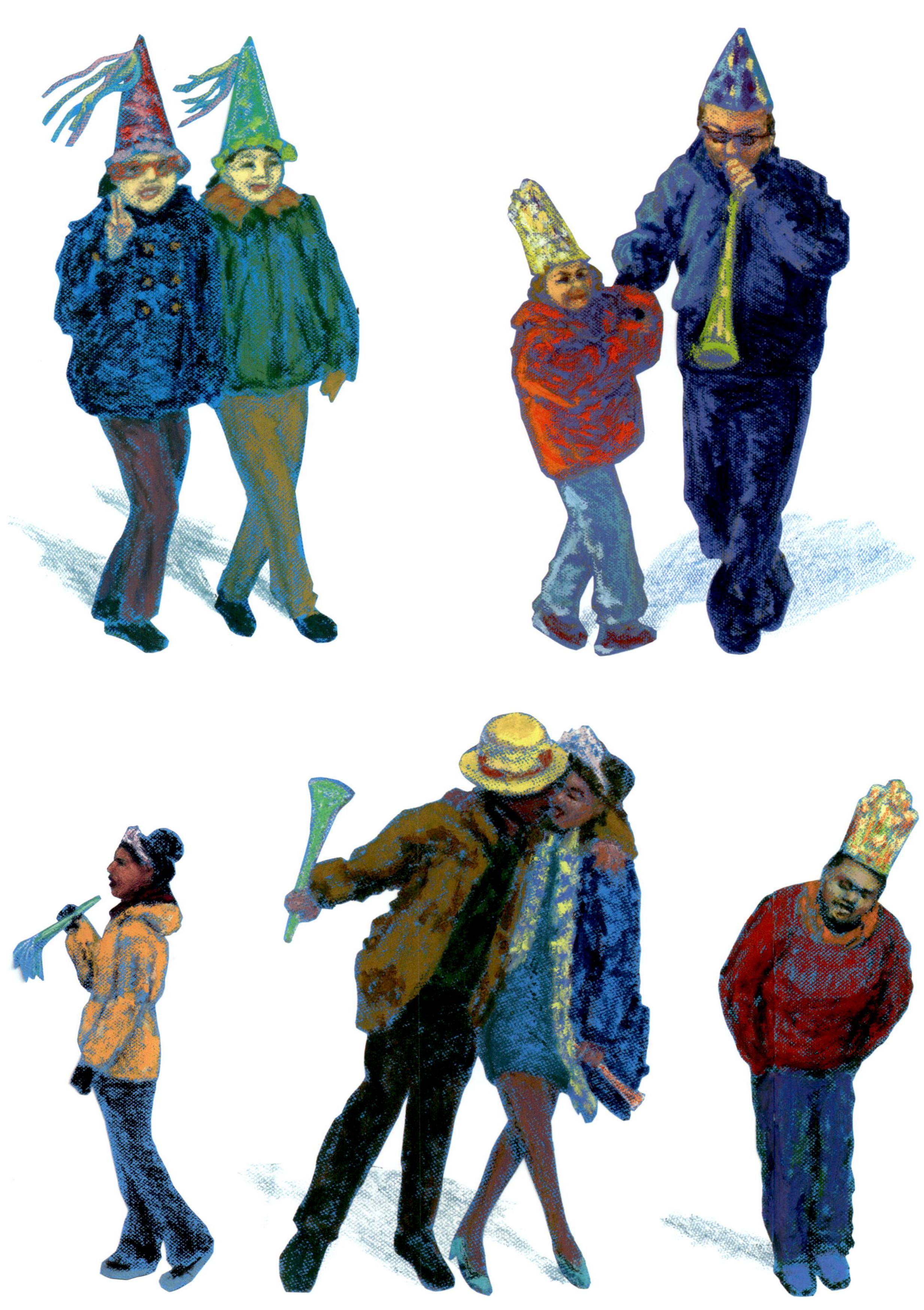

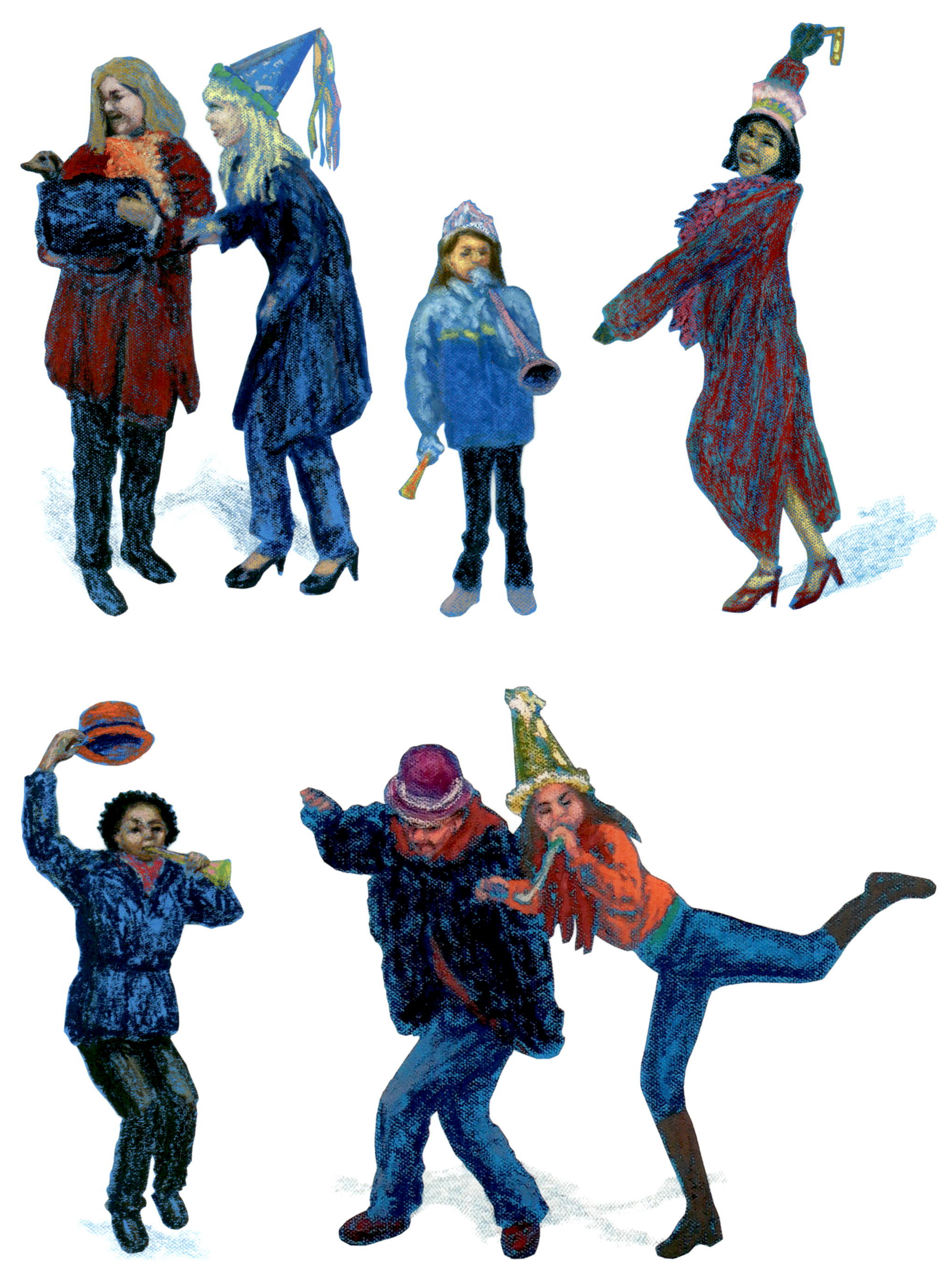

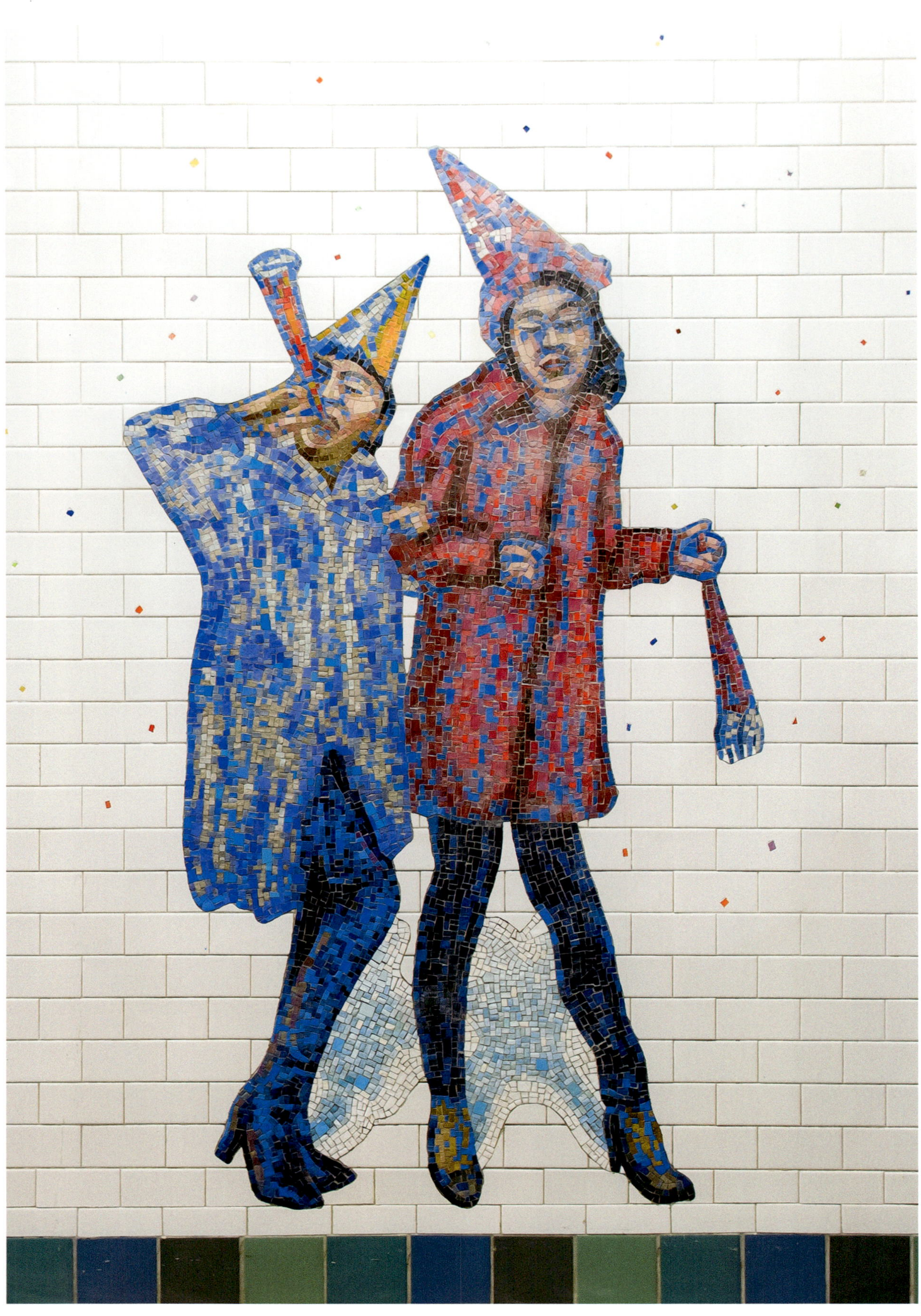

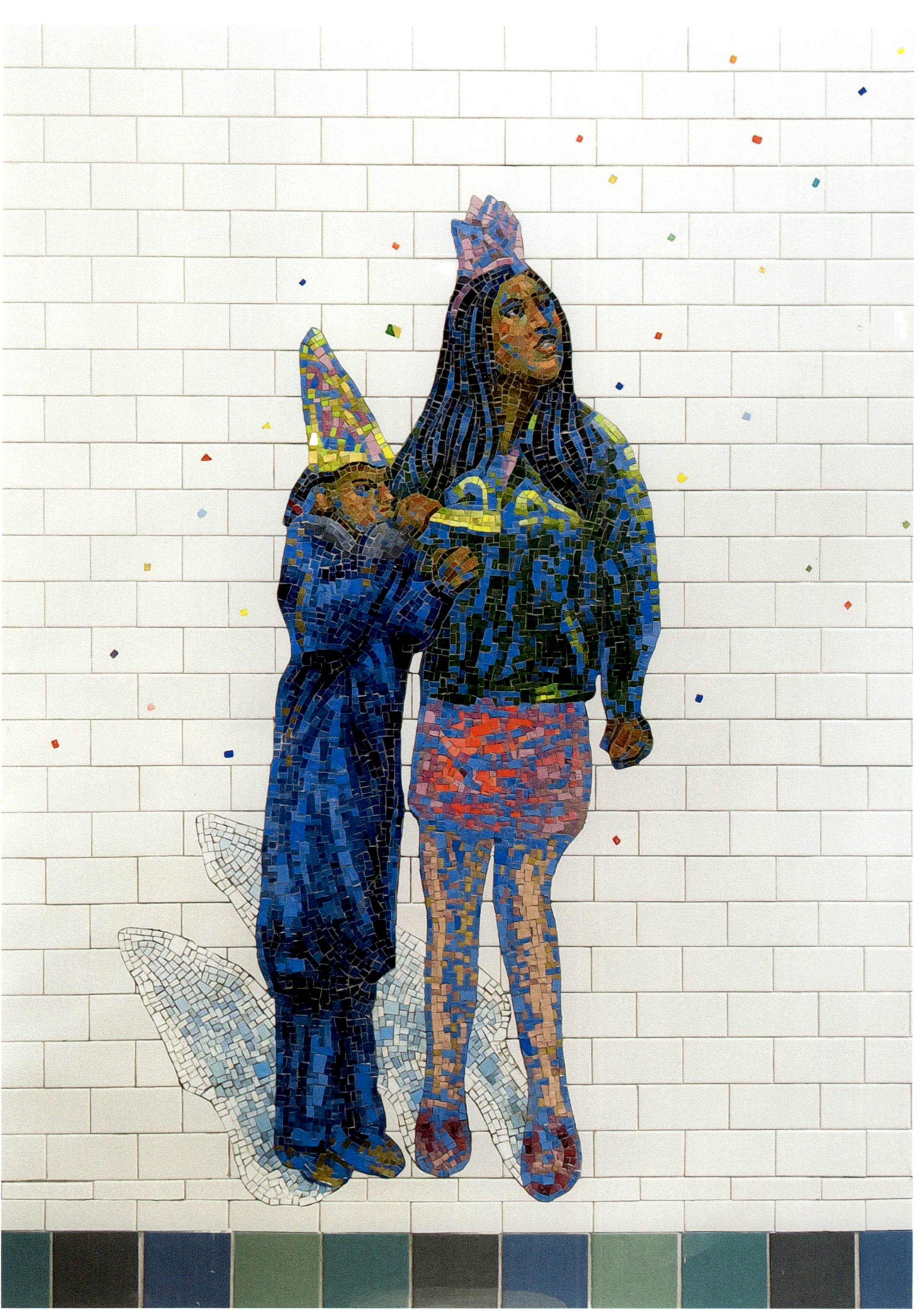

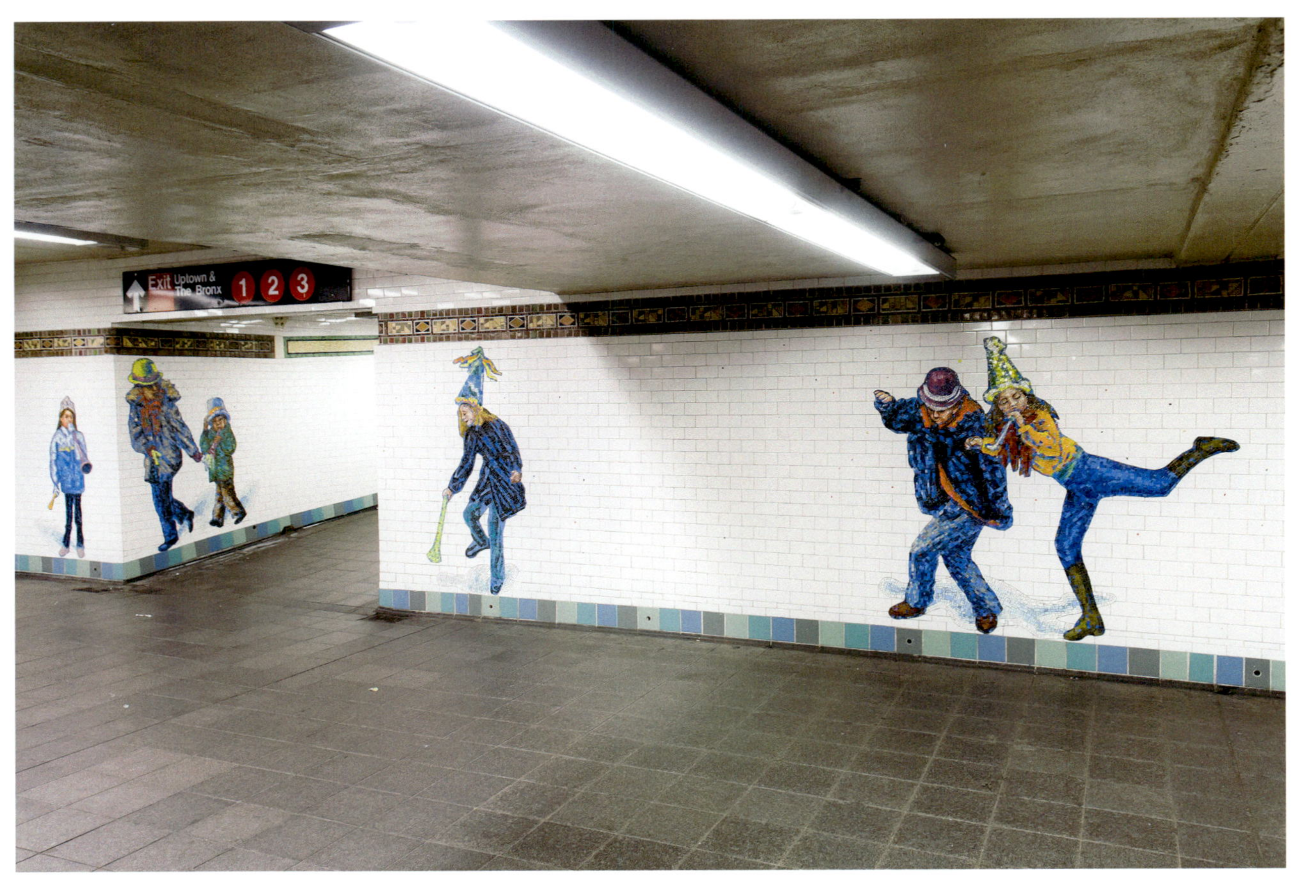

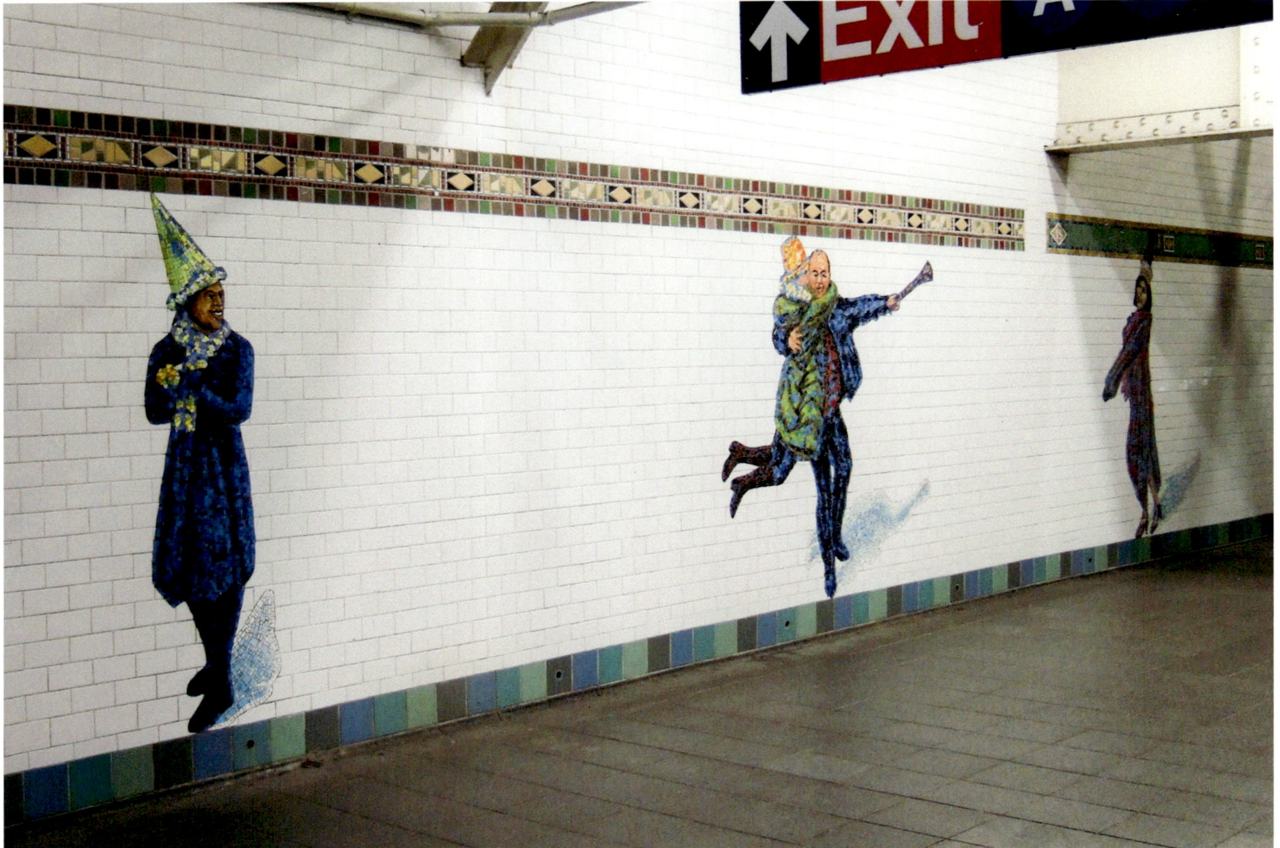

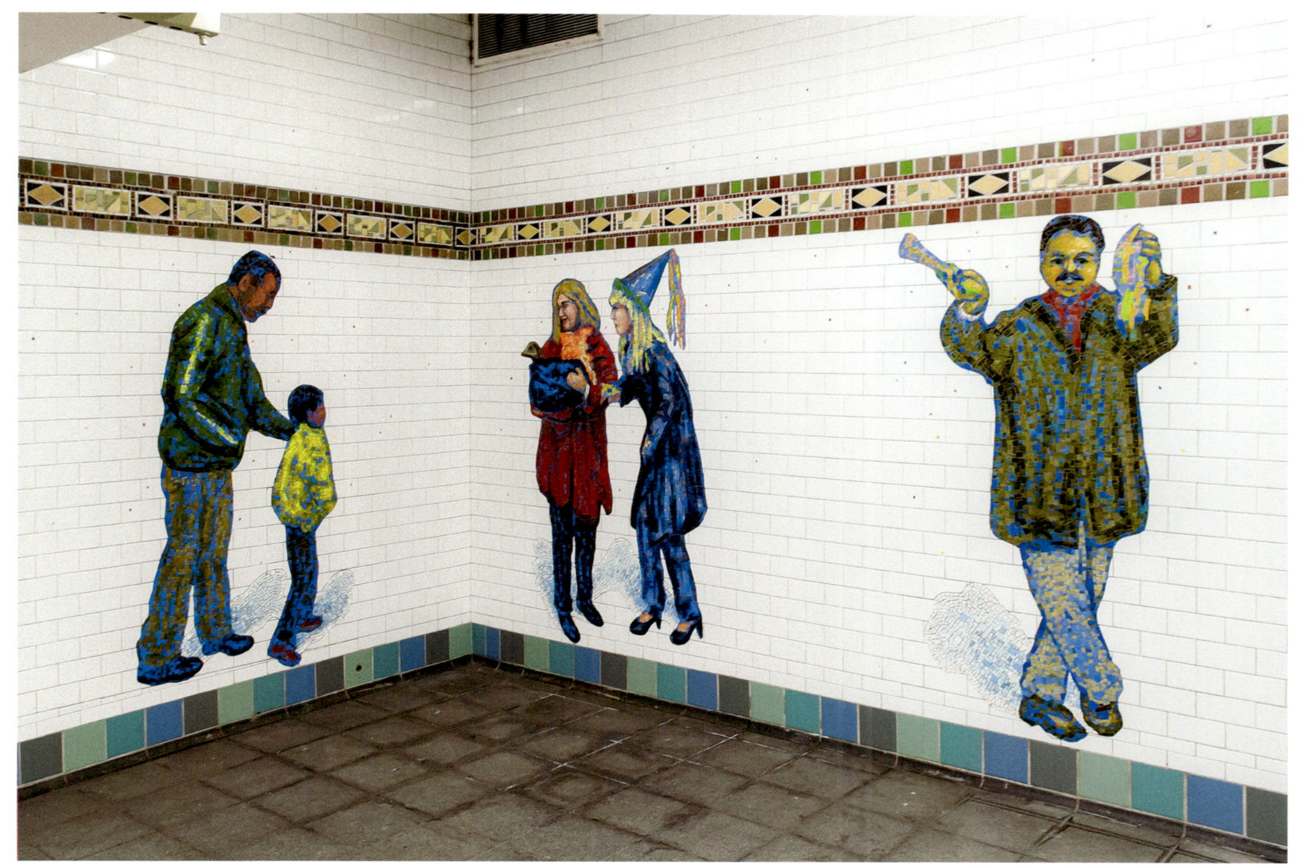

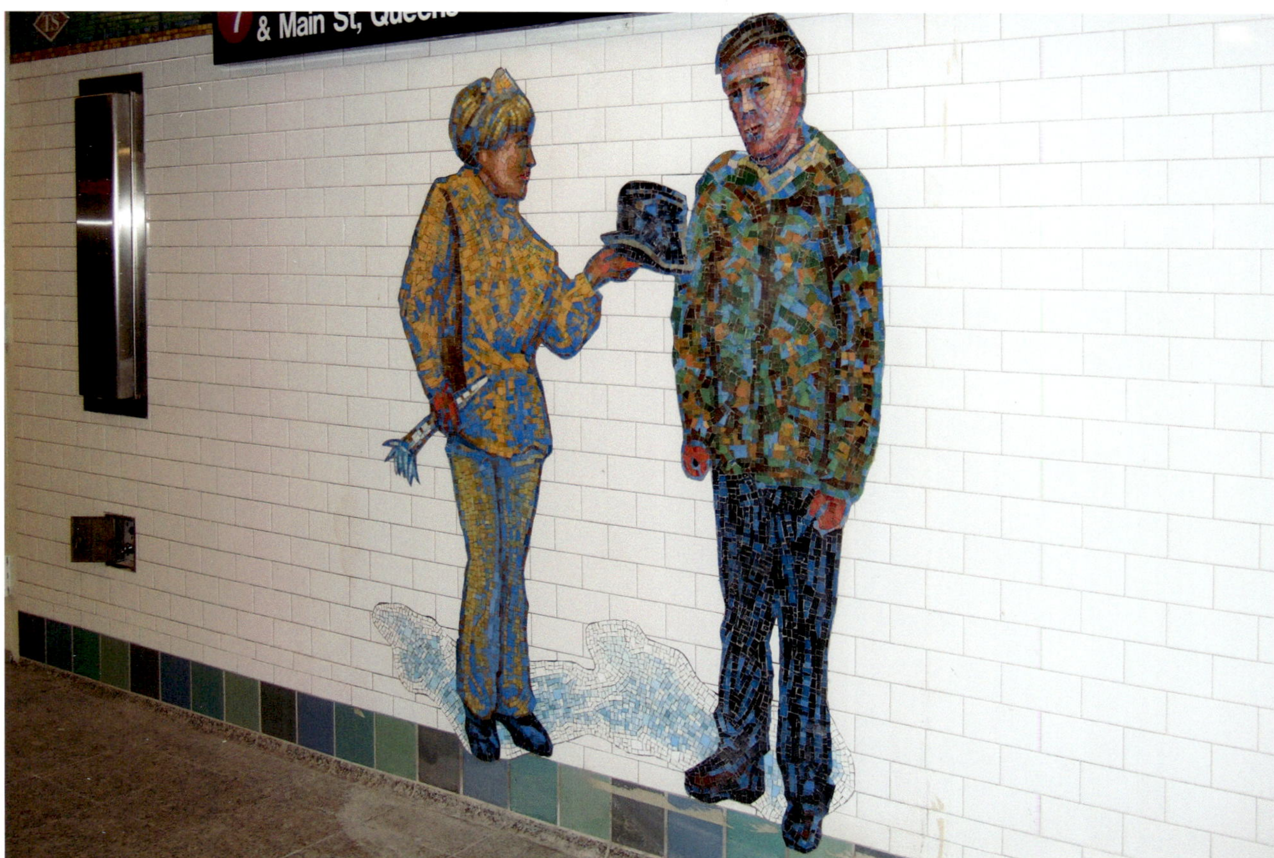
& Main St, Queens

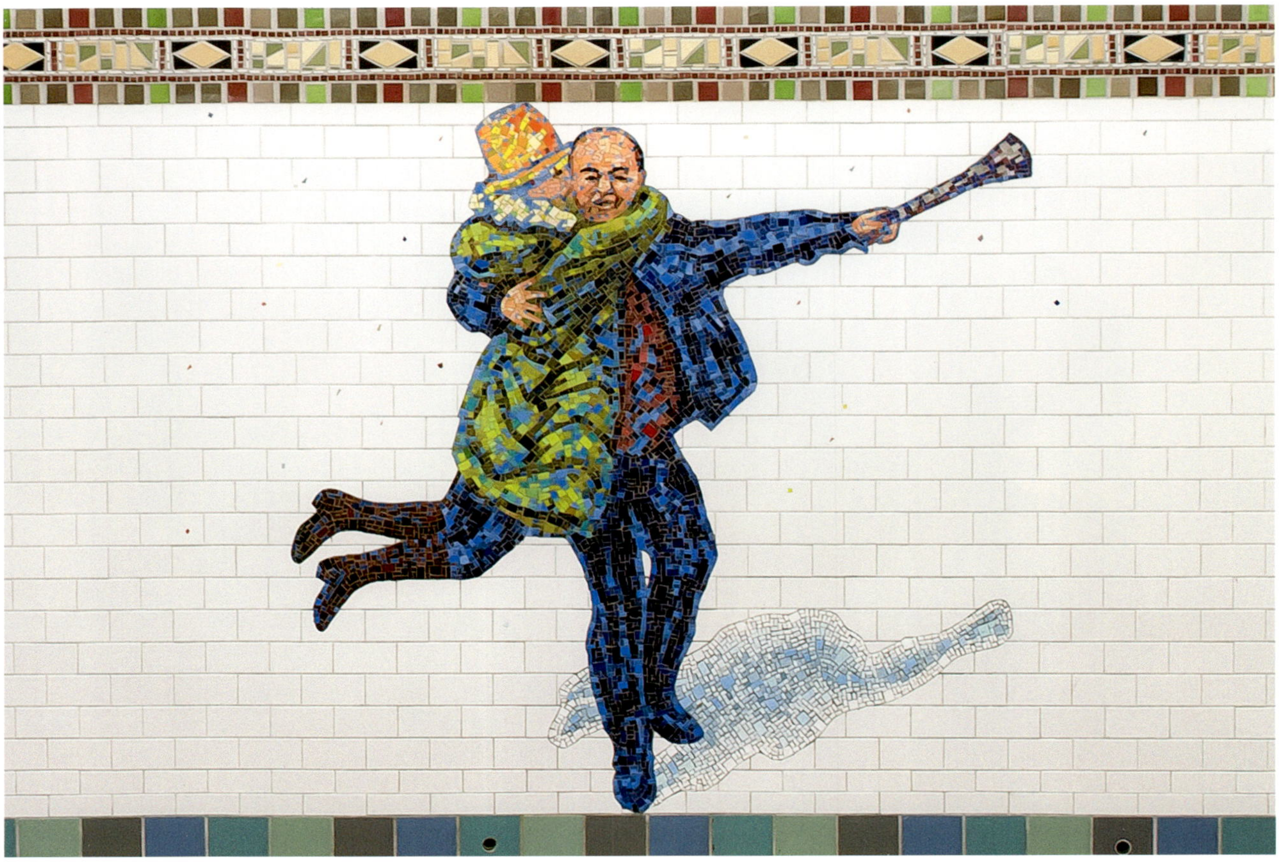

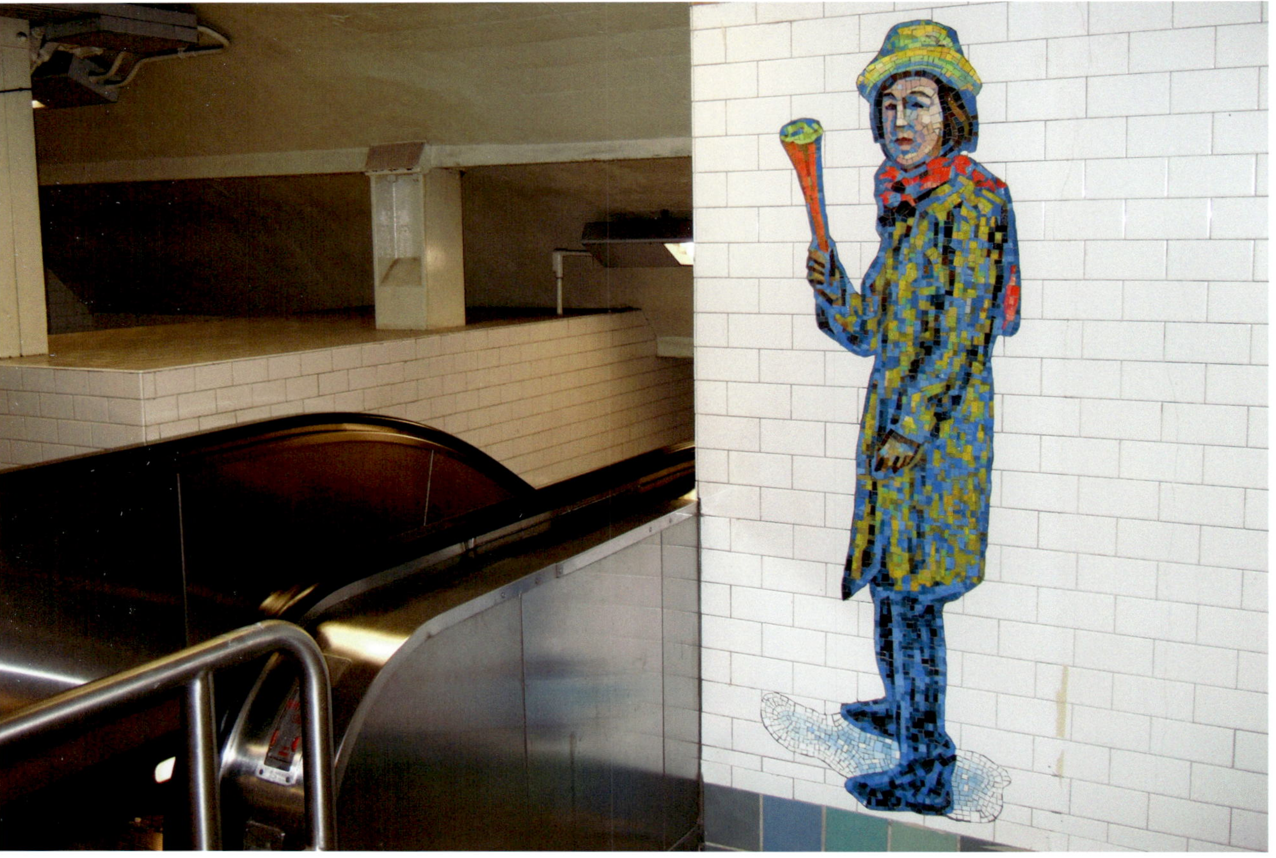

228–9   Studies for the "Revelers" subway mosaics, commissioned by the MTA in 2005.
230–5   Mosaics from the "Revelers" series after installation in the 42nd Street subway station.
        Photographs by Thierry Gourjon, 2008.

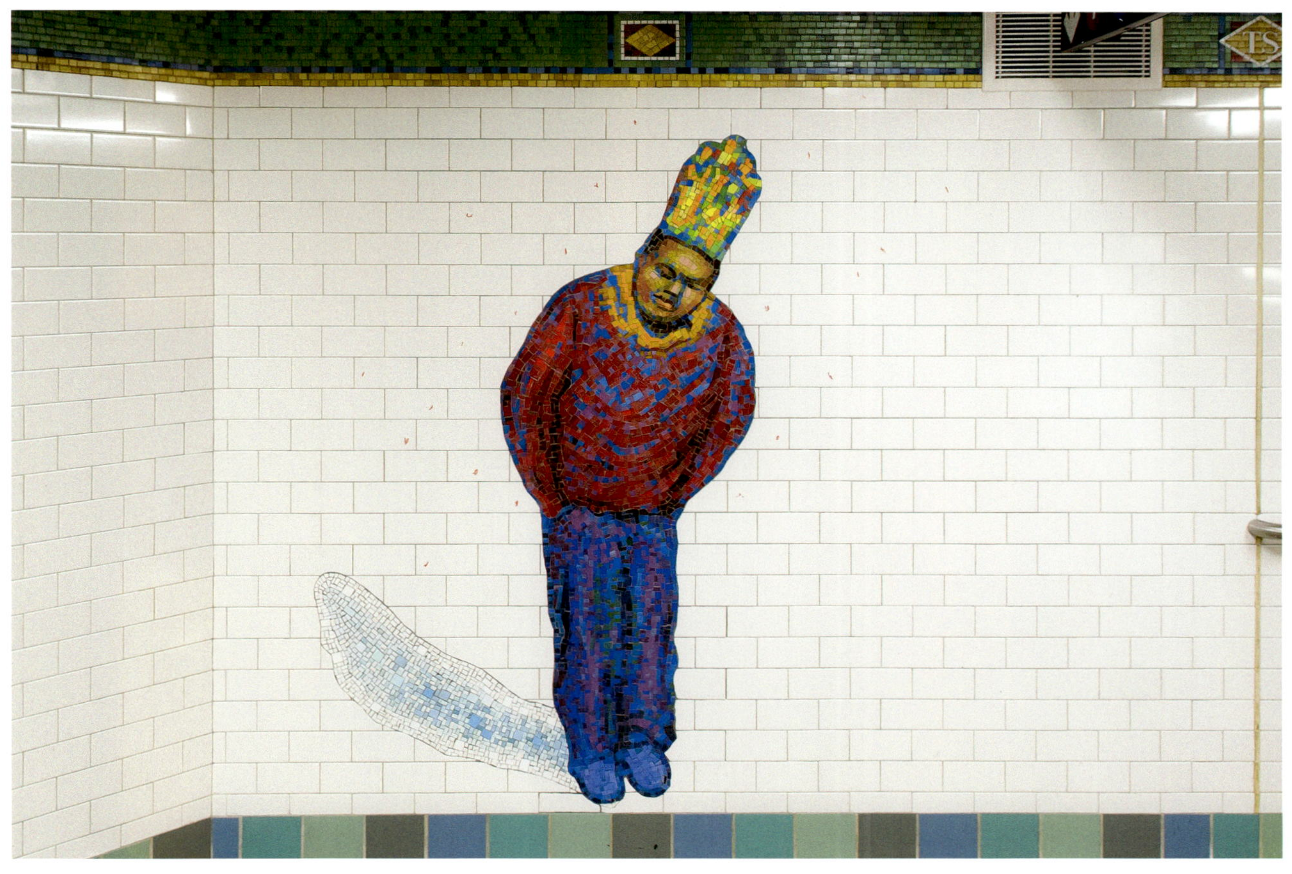

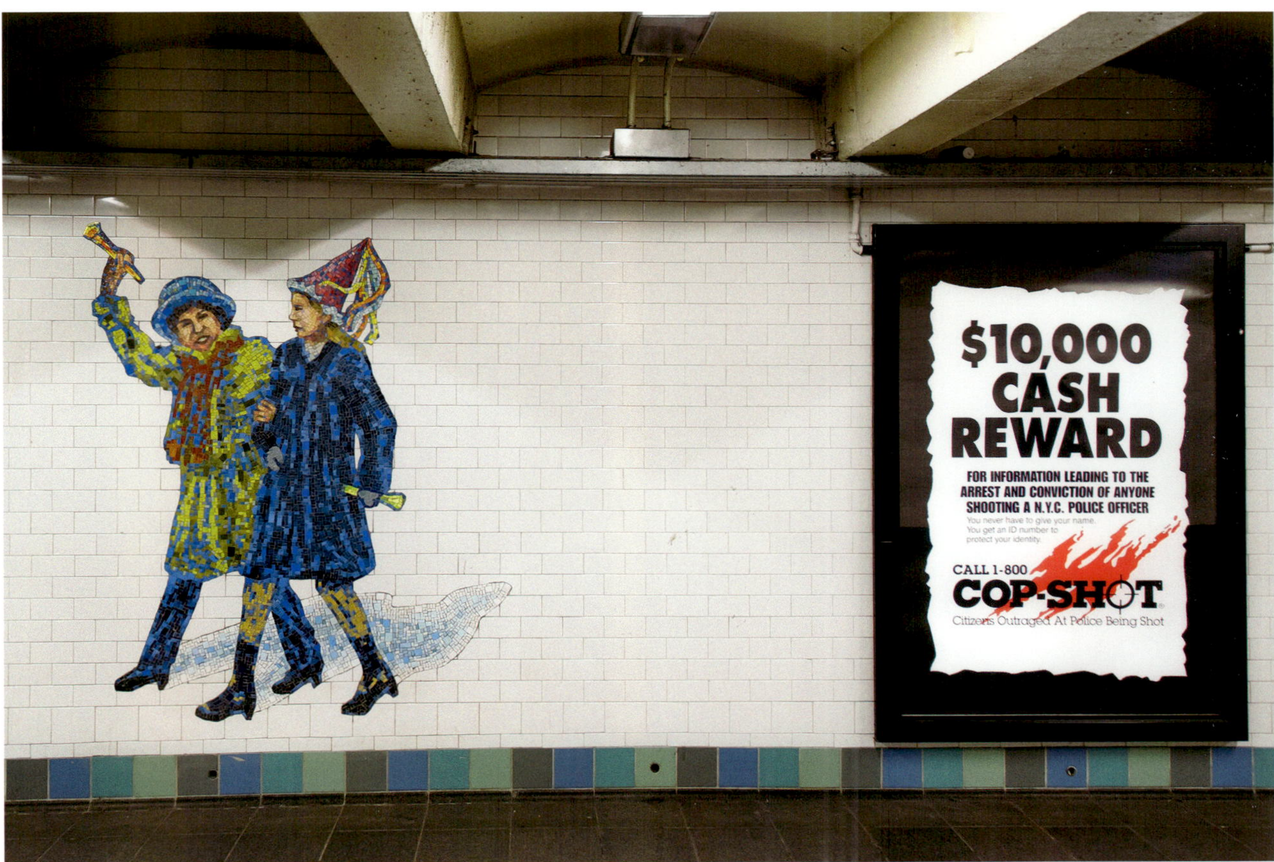
$10,000
CASH
REWARD
FOR INFORMATION LEADING TO THE
ARREST AND CONVICTION OF ANYONE
SHOOTING A N.Y.C. POLICE OFFICER
You never have to give your name.
You get an ID number to
protect your identity.
CALL 1-800
COP-SHOT
Citizens Outraged At Police Being Shot

Jane Dickson in conversation with Carlo McCormick

SODOM ON THE HUDSON

CM Jane, you know what this work reminded me of—beyond location—is the night. Most of your Times Square work has that nocturnal feel, and if you look at the history of photography of Times Square, part of it is always based off of the light. How was this site of illumination at night? It was seductive, but perilous. How do you remember the night at that time, and is it not kind of a muse in here as well?

JD Absolutely. Times Square has been celebrated for its illuminations since electricity was first invented. I became a small part of that history in 1978, when I got a job on the Spectacolor sign—the first digital animated light board in Times Square—by answering an ad in the *New York Times*: "Artist wanted, willing to learn computers." I had worked as a cel painter on Suzan Pitt's indie animated film *Asparagus*, so I had some animation experience. When the billboard hired me they said, "We've found that we can't teach art to a computer programmer, so we need to teach computer programming to an artist." There were no schools yet for digital art.

I chose to work nights and weekends, because I'm a night owl. I worked Friday and Sunday, like 3:00pm to midnight. It was a perfect time to finish there and go out to clubs, and since I didn't start till 3:00pm, I could sleep in when I needed.

I ran the New Year's Eve countdown for a couple years. Our sign was right under the ball drop, so that was intense. I thought, *This won't disrupt my studio practice much*. I didn't realize that Times Square would become my subject.

I worked there until 1983, when they tried to promote me to art director, after I had begun selling paintings. I knew that job would kill my painting, so I quit.

CM   In 1978, the whole city was rough, but especially Times Square. It was like "Sodom
        on the Hudson," is what the expression was.

JD   Yeah, it was scary, but I grew up in the insulated suburbs of Chicago, though in the
        careless parenting style of the 1960s. I remember taking the train into the city by
        myself by the time I was 10. Today that seems so crazy that it's hard to believe, but
        my parents had a lot of kids and didn't pay much attention. I felt like, "Let me at
        whatever I'm not supposed to see, whatever I'm not supposed to get into, let me at
        it." All of my work is a way to approach things I'm afraid of, to get a handle on them.

CM   The night, though, in its unpredictability, was an amazing thing: that it could
        be deserted, which could be really nice, or it could be deserted and really scary.
        It just required a different kind of navigation.

JD   I think as a little sister, I always needed to prove that I was tough, that I could keep
        up with the boys, even though I was a pipsqueak. I tried to project, "Don't mess
        with me. I can handle it. Whatever it is, I can handle it." I didn't want to hide or to
        be sheltered. I was scared, but that didn't stop me.

SEX AND PORNOGRAPHY

CM   One thing I've never really talked about much, and it wasn't really discussed
        that much then, but maybe it's a more timely subject now—is that so many of our
        friends were in the sex industry in one way or another. I mean, we knew girls that
        were stripping downtown at like, Billy's Topless and Baby Doll.

JD   Yeah. I never stripped, but a lot of our friends did.

CM   We had friends who did phone sex, we had friends who did the sets for porn
        movies, you know, not all of it was shaking your booty. But it was an industry that
        could support the artists. I mean, I knew guys in punk bands who were junkies and
        would go up to Rounds or Cowboys and Indians and turn tricks, you know? It ran all
        through our culture. And it was kind of normal, even though a lot of those experi-
        ences can be really scarring in the end.

JD   As people turned away from the overtly political, our generation took sexual libera-
tion to the max, trying to explore boundary-breaking by pushing the personal to the
limit, groping to find the edge. Gay culture was coming out in high gear then, and
all taboos were meant to be broken. I remember the *Village Voice* every week really
pushing, right up until AIDS, editorializing that if you weren't some kind of sexual
pioneer, if you weren't on the edge of transgressive sexuality, you were a reaction-
ary. I was around that, but to me that just seemed too complicated and exhausting.

CM   Yeah, it was kind of a libertarian thing. I mean, I had a lot of artist friends who
were working for *Screw* magazine; they wouldn't pay much, but they'd pay artists
for their drawings. That overlap between art and sex work was really in the air, and
you're one of the artists who did the most kind of deep-down investigation of what
that world was like.

JD   Well, weirdly I had been to the Playboy Club in Chicago with my dad in high school,
but the first real strip club I went to was because Guy Trebay at the *Voice* assigned
it to me. He did a series of four articles on Times Square, in '81, and he asked me
to illustrate them. The fourth article was about the Gaiety, an old strip club with a
little stage in the middle. I was like, *Hmm, now I have to go to this strip club…* I was
a little nervous.

CM   I remember the Gaiety.

JD   Sandra Schulberg, who's a documentary producer and art collector, was over that
day, so I invited her to come along for backup. So Sandra and Charlie came with
me to the Gaiety, and some of these images are from that night. I just snapped pictures from my lap with my little black Contax camera. It was insane that they didn't
bounce us, because no clubs allowed photos, and they'd watch women like a hawk,
afraid you were there to turn tricks, because if so, they'd want a cut. But this time
they didn't notice, or just let me do it somehow. Beginner's luck. Small cameras
were rare then, so maybe they really didn't notice.

This was before breast implants or online porn, and the girls just looked so normal.
It was still a thrill then for men to see a real naked woman of any shape. After that,
when I got to know Jennifer Kabat…

CM   But Jennifer wasn't around then, was she?

JD   No, this is later. I met Jennifer at David Wojnarowicz's memorial, in 1992. She was
      stripping her way through grad school. I'd been painting the outside of Times Square
      for almost a decade by then, and I knew that before we moved (which we had
      been trying to do since our kids were born), I would have to deal with the heart—
      Peepland, the inside of the sex clubs—and that I'd have to do it in paint, building
      on the studies I'd begun at the Gaiety.

      Before I knew much about stripping, I thought that it seemed purely degrading.
      But as I got to know friends who were stripping, they insisted, "Actually, shaking
      it can be really empowering." If you've got a great body, getting paid to show it off
      can be a thrill… till it's not. So I was interested in the complication of shifting sex-
      ual power dynamics that we're still wading through today.

CM   Right, there was that sex positivity, but there was also the idea that "Pornography
      is rape," you remember? Because there's a huge puritanical streak in America as
      well. So, those politics could play out through other parts of feminism, with guilt
      and shaming and stuff like that, right?

JD   What's more visceral and complicated than sex? No easy answers here. I'm not
      making images that tell you what to think. I see painting as a space where you
      can sift through your own ideas: *Is this pornography? Is that bad or good? Sexy
      or gross? From your viewpoint or mine?*

CM   There's also this notion of the female gaze. There wasn't a lot of awareness of it
      then, but what's different about you looking at these girls dancing, or the peep
      show? Is your gaze… more languid? You capture things at points of dissolve, not
      when they're really blinding; it's not like erotica where you smear the Vaseline on
      the lens so everything goes soft-focus. You're doing something else, which is more
      disembodying, and more about atmosphere and mood.

JD   There *was* a lot of awareness then, among women. We knew our viewpoint was not
      being seriously presented on any major platforms. It was marginalized to maga-
      zines like *HERESIES* and *Ms.* and to various women's collectives. One of my main

goals is to leave a record of how the world looked and felt, in this place, at this time, to this woman. The female gaze is not disembodied—it is very much embodied and grounded within the female form and experience, here in my experience.

What's "different" when I portray a female subject is that I know what it feels like to be in her spot. I'm not ogling the hot babe or critiquing the not-so-hot babe. I know what it feels like to be judged by hungry gazes, and this is not about playing to the male fantasy. I'm focusing on the vulnerability of real experience.

I remember being in a show in 1987, The Viewer as Voyeur, that a young man in the Whitney program was curating at the Whitney Phillip Morris. He told me he'd proposed including Joan Semmel's male nudes… he said Whitney higher-ups vetoed her from the show.

CM   They couldn't put dicks in a corporate lobby where the whole corporation's filled with dicks.

JD   As a '70s feminist artist, Semmel was consciously turning the tables by putting a reclining naked man in the passive role, and that seemed unacceptable. Male dominance was just totally the unquestioned, endorsed viewpoint then, and women's issues were deemed tangential.

CM   And regarding Times Square: I mean, obviously, we were all young, and when you're young, your mind's pretty much on sex anyway. But it did seem that, with the Times Square Show and with Tin Pan Alley, sex was much more of the foreground of the conversation.

JD   No question.

CM   Downtown, you'd come down and you might talk about housing, or you might talk about poverty, or you might talk about drugs. These were part of the conditions of the Lower East Side, but up there, sex was in your face.

JD   *Dirty Book Store. King Dick. The Male Box.* You really could not escape it. I began drawing the scenes I encountered when I was out on the street, and the action I saw out of the Spectacolor office windows on breaks, as soon as I began working in Times Square. I was in my 20s and I was still trying to figure out who I was as an artist. For work, I was making images with lightbulbs against a black background, and that investigation of light out of darkness really became a foundation of my art.

During the Times Square Show, I began a series of drawings: cartoons of pickup lines that I was receiving as a good-looking young woman going about my life in the city. I thought, *Well, I'm being offered these insights daily—instead of getting angry, let me mark those in drawings and laugh.*

So my series *Hey Honey Wanna Lift?* is clearly from a woman's viewpoint, of men presenting their hard-ons, and maybe the woman recipient of their attention is, like... not totally wowed. In the male fantasy, a guy pulls out his dick and the woman's like, "Yes! Let me follow! The godhead!"

CM   That's what we're finding out with all these sexual harassment cases. It's sort of like, damn man, that's the *last* thing they're interested in!

JD   Sometimes we're interested but... you know, sometimes not. I remember when I showed this work, some men got angry, and some thought any woman who drew dicks must want to see theirs, too. That got tiring. One strange guy lectured me on why I shouldn't burden the public with my neuroses, how I should keep them to myself! I'm thinking, *Really? A woman's view is neurosis unless it's worshipful?* And a man can do any kind of really aggressive, really sexual, really creepy art or slasher film, and everyone's like, "Oh, that's so profound." A woman making a film or TV show where women go around stalking and killing men? There have been a couple, and they were shocking and unpopular. But rape, torture and kill women? That's entertainment.

A woman's point of view is much more visible now, but still, it's the minority voice.

CM   And when you showed the work from *Hey Honey Wanna Lift?* was there a kind of "Me Too" moment that you felt then? Did a lot of girls you knew get it?

JD   Women always got it. Even to this day, it resonates. Steven Harvey sold the book at the last book fair, and he said, "Every single book I sold was to a woman who was with a bunch of her women friends, all laughing uproariously, and then she was like, 'I *have* to get this.'"

<u>THE TIMES SQUARE SHOW AND POLITICAL ART</u>

CM   How did the conversation go when you guys were trying to organize this big sprawling thing that became known as the Times Square Show, in 1980, when you guys were first dealing with it? Was it like someone said, "It should be about drugs," and someone said, "No, it should be about rock," and someone said, "No, it should be about sex," and all of a sudden it's like, "Oh, let's put them all together"? Because it did have a thematic.

JD   People had been saying we should do a show in Times Square. Christy Rupp and I went to Al Loving's studio, on 42nd Street between Sixth and Seventh Avenue, to see if there was a space in his building, which there wasn't. Tom Otterness and John Ahearn got to the Durst Organization and got the space.

CM   The Durst Organization had it? (*Laughs*) I love that. Which brother?

JD   Not sure, but I don't think the murderer was doing real estate—I only met a secretary. At the end of the show, Walter Robinson and I collected some Xeroxes to give them as a thank-you. The Xeroxes were unimpressive, and the building was a mess, so they were grouchy.

       I don't remember much territorial conversation during the planning, though there were plenty of skirmishes during installation.

CM   It was more like who got what space?

JD   The building was big and broken up into many spaces, so different areas were organized by different people, and whoever had each area picked a theme. Then anybody stuck in whatever they wanted wherever, and we'd argue until the most stubborn or persuasive person won.

       I'd already made the drawing of the three-card monte hands, you know, the betting scam that was very common in Times Square then. We used it for the show's

poster, and that poster is now the historical referent for every show about the
'80s. I also made an animated ad of the Times Square Show poster, of hands
shuffling the cards to reveal different info, which I talked my boss into running on
the Spectacolor light board around the corner every twenty minutes for the whole
month of the show.

I showed portraits of Kiki Smith and Ulli Rimkus on garbage bags in the portrait
room—garbage bags because I was exploring black backgrounds and I was thinking
about the disposability of our generation.

CM   Oh right, what is it with you and all these weird materials?

JD   There's something about touch, about the texture and referents of humble materials that often triggers my work. Garbage bags, sandpaper, carpet, AstroTurf all
became new platforms to launch on. A particular material adds resonance to that
subject. Garbage bags for skyscrapers and punks, AstroTurf for highway-scapes,
carpet samples for the home paintings, black sandpaper for the stripper series, etc.
But it all started with garbage bags in the late '70s.

CM   Did you show other work besides the garbage bags in the Times Square Show?

JD   Yeah. On the stairs, Jody Culkin and I did an installation including our work and work
by Mike Glier, David Hammons, Kiki Smith, and a little Fab 5 Freddy tag. I showed
the original prints I had made for *Living with Contradictions* there, which I invited
Lynne Tillman to write a text for later. The result of that collaboration became a book
published by *Top Stories*, the women's chapbook series, the next year.

Those drawings and prints for *Living with Contradictions* were really my profes-
sional beginning. That was the point when I decided, *From now on I'm only going to
make work about things that I actually know something about that's worth sharing.*
I started asking myself: *What do I really know?* Well, at that point, I was trying to
figure out how to live with a guy, and my friends and I were talking about the weird-
ness of guys a lot, so that's where I began.

CM   These were monoprints?

JD	Yeah. When I first got to New York, I'd met Mimi Gross and mentioned that I was into printmaking, and she said, "My upstairs neighbor's away and she's got an etching press if you want to use it." Mimi was still living in her and Red Grooms' old loft on Mulberry Street. Mimi gave me the key, and that was my first studio. It was like a dream. I'd walk through SoHo, Little Italy, Grand Street, and Broome Street and think, *I can't believe I'm here.* I started doing monoprints there. I brought Kiki over to make prints with me, and Philippe Bordaz, who was in that band with Jim Jarmusch, the Del-Byzanteens.

Later, Mimi and I made hand-painted silk scarves for an early Colab A. More Store, a holiday pop-up shop. She painted my portrait on one. I made images of the eco-disaster of mines on fire in Centralia, Pennsylvania, which have burned for forty-plus years; smoke comes up in the houses and they collapse. In those days someone would get an idea and we'd just do it, and then find a place to show it somewhere. It was fantastic.

CM	When you think of Melissa Rachleff's show Inventing Downtown, and you look at Mimi's drawings from that time and what Red Grooms was doing with Ruckus Manhattan, it was work that came out of the Ashcan Schools, from "The Eight" in Philly beforehand—this kind of "city as muse" approach had existed. How much were you aware of this kind of lineage, of doing a kind of plein air painting, but you know, in a collapsed urban structure?

JD	I was interested in that history of American painting, growing up in Chicago and going to school in Boston, both with museums that are deep in that era. My father was from Glasgow, an immigrant; my grandparents lived outside London. My mother was a German Jew who moved to Paris when I was 15, so I spent time in Europe growing up, and that made me hyper-conscious of being an American, for better or worse. So I decided I needed to examine what that "American-ness" was, exactly.

I studied anthropology in college for a while. With anthropological research, you find specific examples that reflect the issues of the whole: you know, this is the typical family structure, these are the typical rituals, and here are specific examples. I brought that approach into my artwork. I'm not so interested in the quirky, the personal, the unique. What I'm fascinated by is the way my life and interests reflect issues of the larger culture.

CM   Typical without being stereotypical.

JD   As for plein air, that's too much of a hassle for a young woman on the street. Anyway, I was interested in fleeting views or dangerous situations that I couldn't really stop and sketch, so I bought a little high-end camera and took it everywhere with me. I was a flâneur documenting this crazy scene: a painter, using the camera to take notes, trying to get some grip on what the hell was going on.

I didn't think of myself as a photographer—the technical aspects made me too impatient, and I never expected to show these photos. As a nearsighted person I'm used to blur, so I didn't worry much about focus. This was before autofocus existed. I think I learned to see and compose images as much from photographers and cinematographers as from painters: Weegee, Diane Arbus, Rudy Burckhardt, Nan Goldin, and Jamel Shabazz. And because I have to really know what I'm painting, have to have been there, I don't use other people's photos, except some of Charlie's pictures of situations that I experienced too.

CM   Those are also really vernacular views. If you look at the photographers who've done Times Square, if you look at the Ashcan School paintings, the work also had that thorny aspect, because it was about real life, and real life's not so pretty.

I don't know how your art history education worked, but for me, I was aware of all the stuff like the Ashcan School, or the WPA muralists, or the Mexican muralists, and all of this stuff which had content. And then all of a sudden, the idea was, "No, now we're only going to study abstract art." You can kind of see how that worked so well, because abstraction became the great metaphor for individuality in America, for this kind of great freedom. *Look at that guy Jackson, he just fucking pees on his canvases!*

JD   Yeah, it became so anti-collective and so *übermenschy*... the whole political, conservative M.O. is to go, "Hey! Look over there!" distracting us with some made-up outrage while they pick our pockets again. That was another way to redirect the leftist political energy of the 1930s, '40s, and '50s. The message was "Don't think about major political and social issues. Just think about freedom and individuality and self-expression and you can be famous. All that other stuff, that's communism." And that's a dirty word. Just because—why? Because we spit it like that: "Communism!"

CM   The same way they tell you, "That's just big government!" now.

JD   "Fake news!" Whatever it is. If you spit it enough, people don't really know why they're against it, but it's just a poison word.

CM   So when you guys were starting Colab, were you looking at other forms of collectivity and collaboration? Were you looking at the art world? Were you looking at '60s radicals?

JD   I didn't start Colab. I joined after the first show. The collective energy of Colab was thrilling, a welcome antidote to the "every man for himself" (emphasis on *man*) competitive ethos of the "serious" art world. The broad difference between Colab and the Pictures Generation people—though of course there was some crossover—was that generally, Pictures Generation artists understood and wanted to get into the existing art world system. They fit right in. But Colab members were oddballs, contrarians, utopians; questioning all the rules and experimenting with ways to reformulate that world to include diversity, and for artists not to give away all control to the cultural gatekeepers. That's why we made our own shows outside of designated art spaces: to have a say over the conversation, what view could be presented and who could present them. It was an outsider, adversarial stance.

It was a mess, but a fertile one. I also participated in many Group Material shows. It seemed that Group Material watched Colab and thought, *There are some good ideas here, but it's out of control. Let's keep it a small group with a clear plan and we can have more impact.* And that was true.

CM   When I think of you engaging so deeply and personally with Times Square, I think of it in contrast to the earlier version, which was the Art Workers' Coalition, Artists against the War—ego-driven artists that are only cooperating with each other; no one's really *collaborating*, right? And politically, you'd hear this kind of discourse about American imperialism and all the problems it had, and in the meantime, we were stepping over a junkie in the doorway who was passed out, and we were supposed to ignore that. There was something really different about that Colab generation because it wasn't about all these other global issues, which is where the '60s Left had moved onto. It was really about saying, "No, the city's fucking broken." You know, the Real Estate Show, the Times Square Show... these were real *actions*, in that way.

JD   I chose to come to New York to participate in the cultural upheaval that was going on here. I believe in global politics, but I can't stand sitting in meetings. I want to do things here and now that can make real changes, however small. I didn't want to live in some elite enclave, tsk-tsking from a safe remove. I came to the city to live in the urban chaos and to be forced to deal with the problems here that have now spread to every city and suburb.

When I got here, I thought, *How do I get a grip on this bombed-out crazy scary place?* I began to document whatever crossed my path. In hindsight, it's clear that what I notice out in the world is whatever I'm pondering in my own life. I look around to see how others are handling that issue, and I study them coping, and I paint that.

WE LIVE HERE

CM   Your work is much more psychological than even its political and social aspects. I'm thinking of the people looking out windows or from behind curtains or down staircases—it's like you have this contradiction within New York: a lot of people kind of piled in, but also an incredible amount of loneliness and a little bit of fear, even with something as seemingly joyful as "The Revelers." It was really loaded psychologically that way, right?

JD   Exactly. Everything I do is a psychological self-portrait on one level. So, yes, my early work? I was single (*laughs*), and the city was scary. And yes, there was a lot about loneliness and anticipation, waiting for something to happen, for my life to begin. And then when I did the early "Revelers" paintings, they're about many things—the savings and loan collapse, the market crash of 1989 and the gloom it spread—but on another level, I had one kid and another on the way. So suddenly, I'm noticing these chains of people pulling each other, pushing each other. My world and the "Revelers" pieces are not about loneliness. They might not be all happy, you know? The mother pulling her little girl... but they're about families and friends physically connecting, staggering but holding each other up. And in that particular series, you know, coming from a family of serious drinkers, on another level they're about that too: people who look happy but also, they're shitfaced.

CM   (*Laughs*) "What's it like when Dad's shitfaced?" Exactly.

JD   You know, it's scary.

CM   Especially for kids.

JD   Yeah. And also, like, what the fuck are people doing bringing four-year-olds to Times Square on New Year's Eve? I mean, we know what they're doing: they can't afford a babysitter. But perhaps that's not the optimal environment for your small fry.

CM   And then, of course, to raise a family there, and to be—

JD   (*Laughs*) Right, I'm like, "What the fuck are you doing, bringing them on New Year's Eve?" When I have mine here all the time! We *live* here. But I had to look at them to *see* it.

It took us years to find a place we could afford and move to, but when I became pregnant, I suddenly couldn't bear the smell of Times Square. It made me throw up, literally, so I began to paint demolition derbies to get myself out of town—Miami, Chicago, upstate. Fresh air, sort of. The cars crashing into each other felt like the impossibly conflicting parts of my life, and a visual equivalent to the death metal mentality that keeps us in endless wars. Lots to dig into there, too.

CM   Charlie did an amazing portrait, the movie *Doin' Time in Times Square*, which included footage of your kids' birthday parties interspersed with, you know, "What's that crazy sound out the window?" And I mean—it's brutal (*laughs*). The city was brutal and unforgiving at that time.

JD   You've gotta see *Jane in Peepland* too. Both movies evolved organically from our home movies. *Doin' Time* skews more toward our family and parenting, and *Jane in Peepland* is more about me as an artist, and includes some of the work that is in this book. Charlie bought a video camera when Joe was born in '86. So he started shooting, you know, Joe's first smile, whatever, and then, on the same tape, he'd videotape somebody getting busted… then it'd be me singing a lullaby, and then transvestites fighting beneath our window.

CM   I remember one scene from that movie where this guy just gets cold-cocked, knocked out, and Charlie just keeps the camera on him. And slowly, people come and they take off the guy's shoes, they take out his wallet… That was New York, man!

JD   And then more people keep coming and feel for his wallet, but they're like, "Oh, damn, somebody beat me to it." They're pretending that they're helping him, but really they're robbing him.

CM   I mean, as scary as it was living downtown, I always got terrified by your neighborhood. It was just—it was too unpredictable. Downtown, you could kind of see shit coming—it was much more abandoned—and you could step out of the way. I remember one time… I think it was a party for you, in a bowling alley in Times Square. I think it was a birthday party.

JD   That was the afterparty for my opening at Delahunty Gallery at Bowlmor Lanes in Port Authority. The bowling shoes there were pretty crusty.

CM   As we were all going there, I kind of got separated from everyone, and all of a sudden, I was surrounded by a bunch of kids who were trying to mug me. And Kiki Smith turned around and yelled, "Hey, leave that kid alone!" (*Laughs*) Jeez, I felt like I had just stepped off the bus from Ohio or something. I was just out of my element.

JD   I'm guessing your baby face and long red ponytail made you look like a mark.

CM   Yeah, maybe. But back to "The Revelers": how did those MTA mosaics come about? They feel very different—celebratory rather than bleak.

JD   Well, I'd been involved with the Public Art Fund, creating and organizing the Messages to the Public artists' animation series on Spectacolor with Jenny Dixon since 1980. I was on their advisory panel for a few years, where I met Sandra Bloodworth, director of the MTA Arts and Design program. I'd done an MTA poster for the Times Square station in the early '90s, and I'd been a finalist for mosaics for a couple of stations I didn't get, and they invited me to propose for Times Square. At this point we lived downtown, but I still had a studio on 39th Street near Eighth Avenue which was then still totally ungentrified, so I used that 42nd Street subway station every day.

As a younger artist, I wanted my work to bring attention to the undersides of America that we, as a nation, were mostly pretending didn't exist. But by the time I was commissioned to make these mosaics in 2005, we'd all been through 9/11, the big London subway bombing had recently happened, and I was recovering from a long struggle with colon cancer. Everyone was nervous going into the subways, so I didn't want to emphasize challenges we already knew too well. The world's an increasingly terrifying place, but positive collective energy is still real. It's the only thing that can save us. And New Year's Eve in Times Square is one expression of human optimism. I tried to capture that, to contribute a smile to the hassle of a commute. And it works: so many people reach out to me about it from all over the world, to say that it makes them happy when they pass it.

THIS *IS* WORK

CM   What I'm happy about with the Club 57 show at MoMA, which focused on the ephemera, films, and performances, was that it showed how, for this generation of artists, nightlife was integral to the art itself. It was about the kind of hybrid, mutant sounds coming out of the DJs in all these clubs at the time, where all these cultures were mixing. You know, you'd be listening to punk, and then to salsa, and then to some really great gay dance anthem.

JD   Yeah, nightlife was crucial for me early on. I just read Richard Boch's Mudd Club book, and it's very entertaining, but it's a parallel universe. I didn't know Richard, though we had so many people in common. The divide was that I never really got involved in drugs. His was this after-hours world that was all about drugs. I wasn't part of that. I could never stay up that late.

CM   The joke I always make is that at Club 57 everyone was taking mushrooms, and at Mudd Club they were all on heroin.

JD   I tried everything once and fortunately nothing stuck.

      Early on at the Spectacolor billboard, my boss said, "We just did a deal to do advertising for this club. Here, you kids can have the passes they gave us." So on an early date I said, "Charlie, pick me up at the sign at midnight. I have tickets to this place called... Studio 54."

CM   Studio 54, I had a feeling that was coming.

JD   It wasn't my speed—too society glam. We went to a lot of clubs: punk bars, discos, hip hop clubs, Tier 3, Mudd Club, Danceteria, the Tunnel, and the Roxy. I showed work in lots of them, starting with the first show Keith Haring curated at the Mudd Club in late 1980. I also just came across a flyer for a show I did there with Kiki Smith and Barbara Ess' band Y Pants. We were so cute! I showed a short animation I'd made, called "A Nice Hot Bath," of naked dancing women made of sand.

      Clubs were a great way to test out new ideas and get some feedback. They were a challenging context: in clubs, you really had to go huge to be noticed at all. Before social media, you had to go out to connect, to bounce ideas around and get projects going together. Music seemed much more dynamic and current than art at that moment. We were trying to figure out how to get that kind of energy into visual art too.

      I remember one night when I had just moved in with Charlie on Fulton Street, I'd been hanging out all day thinking, *I'm about to get to work in my studio.* Around 10:00pm, Charlie says, "Jane! Get dressed up. We're going to the Mudd Club." And I was like, "Oh no, I have to work in my studio tonight." I was saying that partially because I was a bit intimidated by the Mudd Club. Charlie replied, "Jane, this *is* work."

CM   It was. Going out was really very much part of the thing. I mean, I felt like I was wasting my life, but I never felt I was wasting any particular night!

JD   When I got to the Mudd that night, I ran into Joe Lewis, and he said, "Hey, I'm start-
       ing a press. Do you have a book you want to do?" and I said, "Yeah, I just did these
       images of pick-up lines, *Hey Honey Wanna Lift?*"

CM   Did Joe publish that? That's great.

JD   Yeah. That was Appearances Press. He did four books: me, Keith Haring, Tom
       Otterness, and Cara Perlman. We sat around Keith's loft and each stapled all
       our books together, then swapped 'em.

       Punk clubs—like strip clubs, and then hip hop places—were a little intimidating at
       first, but going into places where you're an outsider…

CM   They all turn into family at a certain point.

JD   Yeah. If I took a deep breath and plowed in, I could find a place and feel that I
       belonged there as much as I did anywhere.

       My nightlife ended abruptly, in May 1982. Charlie went to Cannes for the debut of
       Wild Style. I had my first show at Brooke Alexander the same week. It was crazy.
       I was in a lot of pain, but I was really busy and in denial. I walked 25 blocks from
       the gallery to the doctor's office, and the doctor said, "We're going to the hos-
       pital right now." I needed major abdominal surgery to stop hemorrhaging from
       a ruptured cyst. I protested—"But, I'm going to Cannes tomorrow." The doctor
       said, "You're not going anywhere." They put me in the maternity ward for a week,
       where everyone else seemed to have a baby and a baby daddy. Charlie called from
       Cannes and asked what he could do. I blurted "Marry me." Nothing like serious
       pain to make you reconsider priorities.

       So when he got back, we went to Our Lady of Port Authority and got married.
       Maggie Smith from Tin Pan Alley catered our wedding party in the Ramble in Central
       Park. I was so weak I could barely stand up. As soon as I recovered from that, I
       had an ectopic pregnancy and was back in the hospital for emergency surgery and
       another long recovery, followed by two challenging pregnancies, and then cancer.
       I kept painting and working day jobs, but didn't have much extra energy for clubbing.

JD   When I first arrived in NYC in 1977, I rented half of a loft on Duane Street in Tribeca, which was really desolate then. A year or so later, I moved in with Charlie on Fulton Street, into this tiny sliver of a loft with a toilet that we shared with Nancy Dwyer and Cindy Sherman, who lived across the hall.

Charlie began developing *Wild Style* mid-1980, and that mini loft was really too small to add a film office. I remember Charlie picking me up at my billboard job in Times Square one day and saying, "Wouldn't it be cool to have an office up here?" The film business was still centered around Times Square then, and all the old Deuce theaters were still showing movies. I said, "There's a cool-looking old building with huge windows down the block with a 'Lofts for Rent' sign," so we walked down 43rd Street and rang the bell. The building was zoned for theater companies, pending demolition for the New York State Times Square Redevelopment Project. We said we were a film company.

The super began at the top; most of the floors were empty. The twelfth floor and eleventh floor had great views, but I could see that the roof leaked a lot. We chose the sixth floor, because the elevator was shaky; I could do five, six flights, but I didn't want to hike further than that. Our floor had been some kind of medical clinic, with lots of fake wood paneling and little examining rooms. No one else lived there. It was just offices at first. After us, other artists and a gypsy family moved in.

We had a hot plate and a tiny doctor's sink with those long faucet handles, so you could turn them off with your elbows to be sterile, and a place to look at X-rays. We slept on a hide-a-bed couch for a long time. I took the corner with great windows for my studio and knocked down a few walls to open it up. I'd stare out the window and there'd be this whole world to paint.

The film office was at the other end by the elevator. But once real production began on *Wild Style*, there were too many people around, and I realized I couldn't paint there anymore. Through the door, I'd hear them, and I'd be like, "Is that Jean-Michel?," or, "Uh oh, everyone's screaming, I'd better go see what's up now." So I got a studio around the corner on 42nd. I needed to empty my mind of distractions to paint. It was that or quit painting and become a film wife, and that looked like a thankless task.

CM   But you were the only ones up there, practically, right? I mean, who else was living up there?

JD   Jimmy De Sana lived on 40th by Bryant Park, a much nicer nabe. For a while Keith and Kenny Scharf sublet Jimmy's loft, and some people had studios on 42nd.

CM   Mike Bidlo had a studio on 42nd, I remember.

JD   His studio was down Eighth Avenue, but on 42nd between Seventh and Eighth, where a lot of these photos were taken—the ones of the movie marquees— Arch Connelly and Brett De Palma were there. And there was a horror movie prosthetics studio making severed limbs down the hall from me.

CM   And the elevator wouldn't work on weekends, and there'd be no heat on weekends, it'd be locked... it was brutal.

JD   Yeah, the landlord was renting out the offices, but it was also condemned; they were just warehousing it till the city knocked it down. The landlord was renting to us, but the super was renting the halls and lobby to the drug dealers. So every time you entered or exited, there were these guys with dead eyes going, "Coke, speed, Valium, coke, speed, Valium..." And I'd go in and out five times a day, because I lived around the corner, and every single time, I'd be like, "No thanks." When I was pregnant, I remember thinking indignantly, *What, do you think I'm gonna do drugs when I'm pregnant?* Then I'd think, *Oh right, doesn't matter to them.* They were out of their minds—they'd just as soon knife you as blink. There were people shooting up in the hallways. That was really scary. My studio had been a blood lab—a place where you could sell your blood.

CM   Whoa! Talk about some tainted merchandise.

JD   Yeah, "conveniently located only steps from Port Authority." There were blood spatters on the walls when I got it. This was the beginning of AIDS, so the city had just closed all the blood-for-sale labs. I had that studio on 42nd from probably late '81 until '86. It had huge windows on the third floor, just above the movie marquees on the Deuce. I liked that it was close to the street. I took a lot of photos and painted out those windows, but the first time I wheeled baby Joe in the stroller past the drug dealers chanting, "Coke, speed, Valium, " I thought, *I can't do this with a baby. This is too creepy.* Right at that point, there was a flood in our home loft on 43rd, with water pouring through the ceiling. A theater company had moved out of the ninth floor, and junkies had broken the pipes while breaking in. I went up to see where all this water was coming from, and it was this beautiful open space. I rented it immediately and moved my studio back to 43rd Street.

So I had a studio upstairs on the ninth floor on 43rd Street from '86 to '93, and we lived on the sixth floor, which was perfect. Because when the elevator was out, I could go to my place, and then it was only three more flights, no big deal. But also, it was totally separate, so my kids didn't know where I was... you know, once the elevator shut, I was gone, but I could be home in a minute.

CM What did you think about the cultural landscape there? Downtown's is so rich, but Times Square was different.

JD Yeah, it was anonymous transients, but everyone downtown loved to visit and bring their out-of-town friends because it was so crazy. And all the hip hop people came through Times Square. It's so central. So everyone, uptown or downtown, came to us. And then, if it was quiet, we'd go to Tin Pan Alley.

CM Tin Pan Alley was your local haunt?

JD Totally.

CM With some places—like Max Fish, where there's a lot more cultural memory for whatever reason—it's like, people care about that history, the way they care about Club 57 and the Mudd Club. But other clubs get forgotten. Tin Pan Alley was really a radical place. It was started by Maggie Smith, right? And it's got a real political agenda, and an amazing cast of workers, right?

JD   Well, Max Fish is still open, and the Lower East Side culture still exists in pockets. But the Times Square of the 1980s was completely eradicated by New York's huge 1990s redevelopment plan.

CM   But Tin Pan was kind of a remarkable thing. Everyone was trying to work some level of social practice, social engagement into it. Back then, we didn't have the terms for it. But that place, to me, was the real laboratory, because that was an artists' bar filled with pimps and hookers and drug dealers and drug addicts.

JD   And the animators' union met there weekly. There were a lot of film people, and then all these British punks… it was such a mishmash. It was trying to be, and I think really succeeded in being, this great mixing.

CM   It was also a place where you had to behave yourself to some degree, right? Like, they didn't have some weedy kid with green hair doing security; they had people who would put you in your fucking place before you even saw it coming.

JD   Muscle, yeah. Because they were mob.

CM   Yeah. It was amazing that they had bands there, and poets, and all that crazy stuff, in Times Square, in the '80s. I mean… it's quite unbelievable, really. And it's amazing that people don't know that story. Did you show work there?

JD   I did: Maggie bought my *Up Against the Wall* painting, of young guys of color getting frisked. An early classic, painfully still relevant. She hung it near the entrance for years until the bar closed.

      It was my local bar—no tourists, no commuters, just hustlers and artists. My close friends, Kiki Smith, Ulli Rimkus, and Nan Goldin all worked and performed there. Kiki made hats, T-shirts, and scarves that she'd sell there. It was a place where we would bounce around big ideas and projects that then actually happened. After the Club 57 show, for God's sake, there needs to be an exhibition on Tin Pan Alley. Anyone? Whitney?

It was Steve d'Agrosa—Maggie's boyfriend, Steve—who started Tin Pan Alley. Maggie made it a cultural mecca, but Steve started and backed it.. I remember him at the bar—he seemed tough and old. We were in our 20s, and Steve was probably 40: Maggie's old man, who we knew was mob. He'd drop by briefly to get the money, and let Maggie do whatever she wanted.

CM   As broken-down as New York was then, I still remember a texture of neighborhoods. Downtown, we had a Dominican and Puerto Rican community, but Times Square always seemed to have had that part of its social fabric ripped. There were just too many transient people in and out of there. But what was it as a "neighborhood," in Jane Jacobs terms? Or was it just people who ran sleazy venues and the people who worked there and the patrons?

JD   We were on the corner of 43rd and Eighth. Eighth Avenue, from like 40th Street maybe to 49th, and then Broadway and Seventh—that was Times Square. And that was totally transients, commuters, theatergoers and welfare hotels. But I knew Benjamin, the vet shoeshine guy on the corner, who was probably an undercover cop. He seemed so smart, polite and curious to figure out what the hell I was doing there. There were my friends—the opera couple who ran the wonderfully old-fashioned Alps pharmacy on 42nd and Ninth. Our babysitter was part of a Polish enclave a few blocks over. That's what I loved: that community reforming in the ruins.

And of course we were surrounded by S.R.O.s, single room occupancy housing. Right across the street from us was the Times Square Motor Hotel S.R.O. I made the *Witness* painting series from the urban peek-a-boo there. I'd notice some guy across the way with his pants down, or even if he was doing nothing, if I stared he'd feel it and close his curtains, and vice versa. Sometimes I'd look up and realize someone across the way was staring at me. I began to consider the act of watching explicitly, because my work was being discussed frequently in terms of voyeurism. I wanted to think about what was intrusive, what was documentary, the predator/prey dynamic that makes it so scary to be watched unawares.

I tried to take photos of my neighbors, but they were hard to shoot, because they were running scams—alone, alert, and paranoid. I got bullets through my window twice, so I started to be more careful and took photos of my friends downtown looking out their windows, where it was less tense.

The Carter Hotel, next to us, was a welfare hotel too. There were hundreds of little children living in these hotels.

CM   We had a lot of those downtown, the Bowery and places like that.

JD   The Bowery was soul-crushed drunks who had given up. In Times Square, people were all hustling something. The women's shelter was near us, and they never had enough beds, so there were always homeless women roaming at night, all pretty crazy. It was quite challenging for me there as a young woman. Men just assumed I was available meat, and it was dangerous. There were muggings and gunfire on the street, and creeps breaking in from the stairwell. Charlie was mugged in our elevator once and choked until he passed out. He had purple fingerprint bruises around his neck for a week.

The other side of Eighth Avenue, going towards Ninth, was Hell's Kitchen. Our super, Whitey, was from the Westies gang.

CM   Right, that's the old gang from there.

JD   Yeah. He was Irish gang. Big, fat, and toothless, like an old white egg, like Humpty Dumpty.

CM   But to live in a neighborhood which isn't a neighborhood anymore, it's totally transient... this becomes a whole other kind of zone.

JD   I didn't see it as alienating. It was energizing to be in this indescribable soup of misfits, where the subtle alienation I had always felt growing up was explicit. The "lonely in the crowd" feeling of my work, that's part of my personal core, since I come from a very large dysfunctional family. I was always in a crowd, but not one that was communicating with each other, or really noticing each other in any helpful ways. That's part of why I gravitated to Times Square.

And on some really profound psychological level, I feel like I do the work I do to go, "Hey, look! This is what's *really* happening." I don't know if it ever actually worked with the people that I've wanted to make notice, but I found that there was this whole world of other people who I don't know who were like, "Yeah I see that! I get that! I'm right there."

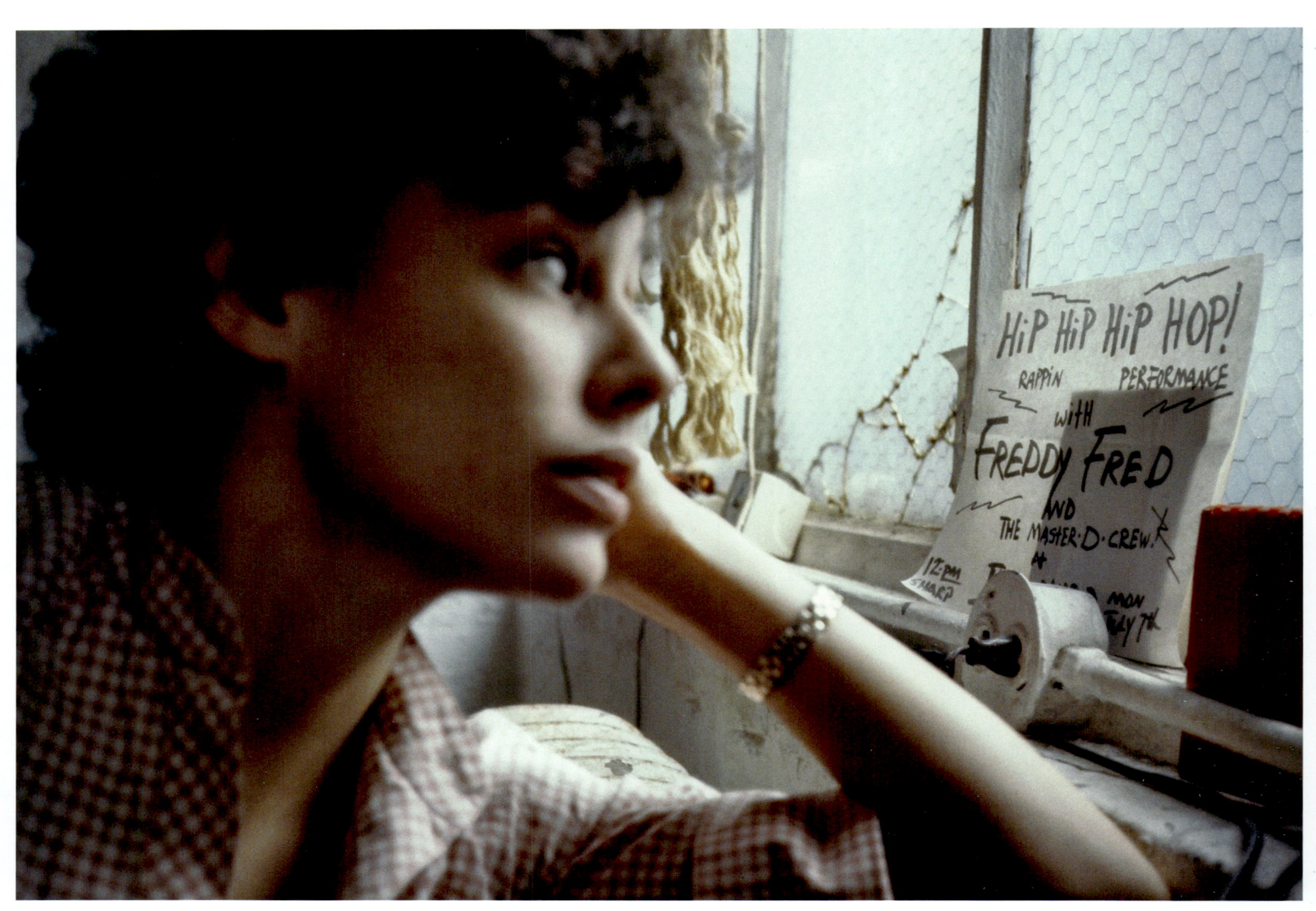
HiP HiP HiP HOP!
RAPPIN   PERFORMANCE
with
FREDDY FreD
AND
THE MASTER·D·CREW.
AT
12 PM
SHARP
MON
Jay 7th

Fab 5 Freddy

In 1982, Charlie Ahearn and I were deep in post-production on *Wild Style*, an idea I'd proposed to him in 1980 when we met at a seminal art exhibit called the Times Square Show. *Wild Style*—which I starred in, created original music for, and co-produced—would become the first feature film on hip hop culture. Around the time pre-production began on the film, Charlie decided to move with his wife, artist Jane Dickson, into the old office building where our *Wild Style* production was run, on 43rd Street at the corner of Eighth Avenue. Our modest dream at the time was to make a film we knew would appeal to our artsy-underground downtown creative friends, and to the Black and Latino folks from ghetto areas around the city that flocked to Times Square for a good time. This was not a residential building, but Charlie and Jane broke the rules and set up a living- and workspace for the film, complete with an old school Steenbeck flatbed editing machine. Jane had a painting studio in the corner, looking down on Eighth Avenue and across 43rd Street. As we were making the film, Jane was making art.

One day, while I was at the production office working on *Wild Style*, Jane asked me to come back to her studio and have a look at a piece she just finished. Wow, there it was: a portrait of me, made from a photo snapped a few weeks before, outside a closed strip club on the way to dinner at a nearby Chinese restaurant with Jane and Charlie. I was familiar with Jane's work—particularly some humorous drawings of men with gigantic phalluses—but this piece was different. It was painted on a gray material that made it unmistakably nighttime, and behind my image you could see portions of the glowing neon words "TOPLESS GIRLS." The reflection in my sunglasses was tinted by their rose-colored lenses.

I was struck at how this portrait captured a lot of what Times Square was about back then: sex. This was the Times Square I grew up knowing and loving, unlike the sterile, scrubbed-too-clean situation it is now. Back then, it was where inner-city folks came to see the newest kung fu, action, and horror films, and to play pinball and the earliest video games in huge arcades. Thousands of locals from all over New York City mixed with tourists from the world over, flooding the area around the clock to see Broadway plays and bask in the millions of flashing lights. And, of course, there was the seedy sex side—pimps and hookers walking the streets selling their services, drug dealers selling fake loose joints and drugs of all kinds, the numerous "massage parlors" that were really brothels, and the dozens of theaters and peep show shops that showed porn films and sold sex toys and X-rated magazines.

For the next few decades, Jane's art would follow the breakthrough of that portrait she made of me, with an impressive array of work depicting engaging images on those dark backgrounds: an entire world happening in the night, illuminated by her rich palette of colors that reach out and pull you in.

Last April, I visited the National Portrait Gallery in Washington, D.C., which had recently acquired Jane's portrait of me for their permanent collection. Along with a Michael Jackson portrait by my friend and inspiration Andy Warhol, a John Updike portrait by Alex Katz, and other American subjects painted by renowned artists, Jane's portrait hangs on a wall in the center of the gallery. A Nigerian security guard who led me to the gallery recognized the resemblance as I looked at the painting, smiled, and asked if it was actually me. When I replied that it was, he exploded with delight. I shared some of the story about how this portrait came to be, and a bit about my background exposing the beginnings of hip hop culture. Realizing I was the subject of the portrait, others in the gallery, including the security guard, asked to take cell phone photos with me. I chuckled at the stir I had created and told the security guard I was thinking of bringing a desk and a chair to set up my office in front of Jane's brilliant portrait of me, to bask in the honor of being on display, in such a prominent way, in one of America's most important museums.

ACKNOWLEDGMENTS

I gratefully acknowledge the critical dialogue which has challenged and buoyed my work over the years with Rocío Aranda-Alvarado, Doug Ashford, Patti Astor, Julie Ault, Janette Beckman, Barry Blinderman, Sandra Bloodworth, Holly Block, Andrea Blum, Krissie Bowden, Alan Breus, Rob Brinker, Steve Brown, Judith Bruce, Taína Caragol, Suzanne Dance, Susan Davis, Jeffrey Deitch, David Dickson, Henrietta Dickson, Jim Dickson, Jenny Dixon, Sara Driver, Stefan Eins, Chris Daze Ellis, Brigitte Engler, Leon Golub, Coleen Fitzgibbon, Brandon Fraad, Joe Fawbush, Deb Frizzell, Mike Glier, Elyse Goldberg, Thelma Golden, Nan Goldin, Bette Gordon, Claudia Gould, Francis Greenberger, David Hammons, Keith Haring, Steven Harvey, Annie Herron, Tara Hirschberg, David Hershkovitz, Susan Hodara, Jenny Holzer, Gary Indiana, Patricia Jones, Pam Joseph, Jennifer Kabat, Gerry Kagan, Jerry Kearns, Alitash Kebede, David Kiehl, Carole Ann Klonarides, Chris Kraus, Johan Kugelberg, Fran Kuzui, Liz Larner, Tom Lawson, Joe Lewis, Gary Lichtenstein, Michelle Loh, Sylvère Lotringer, John Crash Matos, Maripol, Carlo McCormick, John Miller, Mary-Ann Monforton, Susan Morgan, Ramsey Naito, Gina Nanni, Robert Norman, Glenn O'Brien, Tom Otterness, Jane Panetta, Suzan Pitt, Lee Quiñones, Yasmin Ramirez, Melissa Rachleff, Lorissa Rinehart, Kristen Rey, Dr. Revolt, Walter Robinson, Tim Rollins, Lisa Rosen, Aura Rosenberg, Katia Santibañez, James Siena, Sandra Schulberg, Kiki Smith, Maggie Smith, Mike Smith, Joanne Soja, Nancy Spero, Bill Stelling, Lynne Tillman, Simone Ver Eecke, Lily Wei, David Wojnarowicz, Lila Wolfe, Martin Wong, Linda Yablonsky, Nora York, and so many others.

My deepest thanks to my assistants for all their efforts in wrestling this material into a book: Cass Ballado, Christian Gomez, Dana Greenidge, Callie Janoff, Sarah Kavage, Mariah Kitner, Danielle Mysliwiec, Bailey Nolan, Maya Shah, Hanna Sheehan, Dondre Stuetley, Mikela Wesson, and Meghan Wilcox.

And finally, thanks to Pace University's Dyson College Keenan Summer Research grants for their support in helping put this together.

Jane Dickson, June 2018

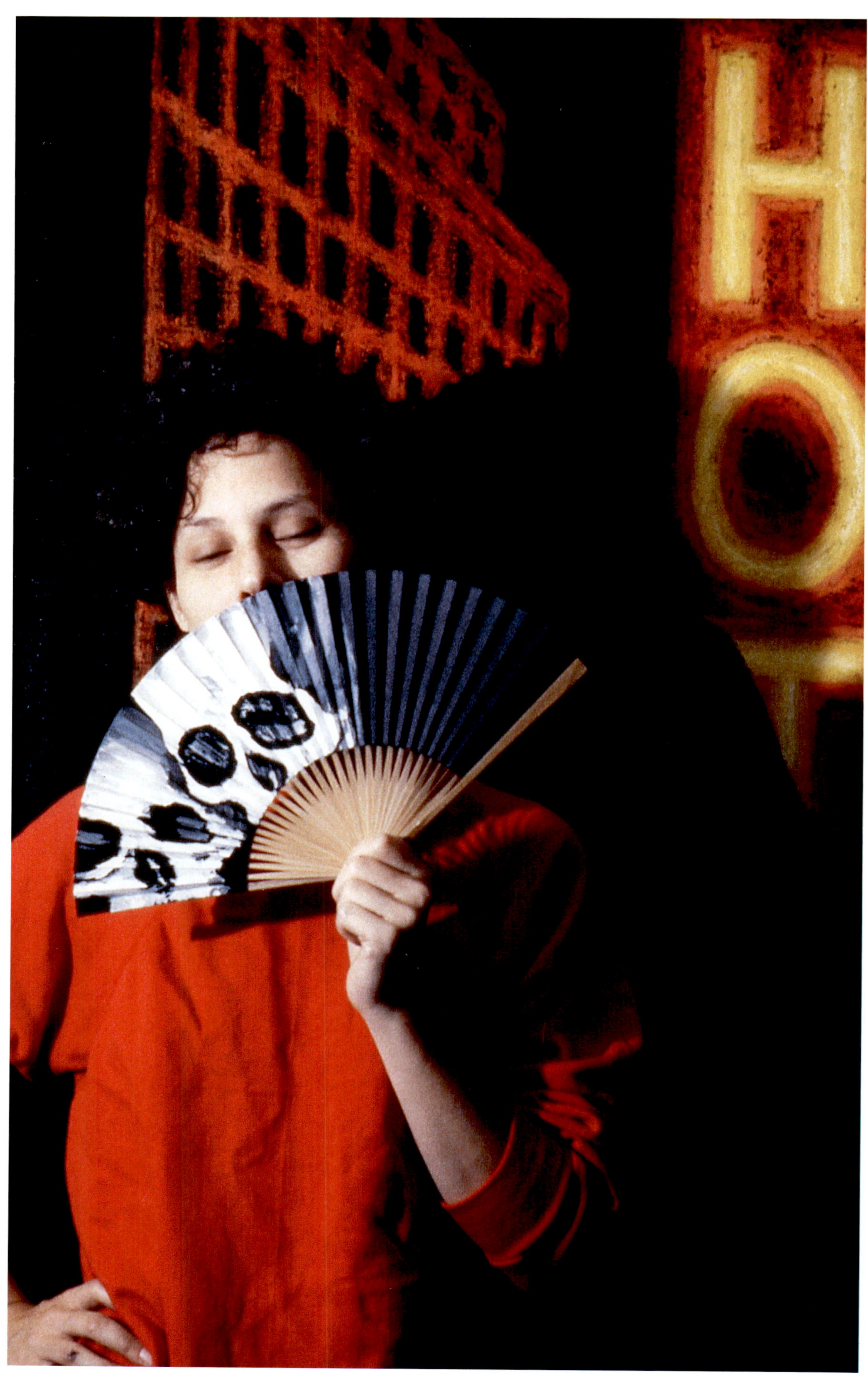